Official
SWiSHmax Bible

Official
SWiSHmax Bible

Donna L. Baker

WILEY

Wiley Publishing, Inc.

Official SWiSHmax Bible

Published by
Wiley Publishing, Inc.
111 River Street
Hoboken, N.J. 07030-5774
www.wiley.com

Copyright © 2005 by Wiley Publishing, Inc., Indianapolis, Indiana

Published simultaneously in Canada

Library of Congress Control Number is available from the publisher.

ISBN: 0-7645-7563-5

Manufactured in the United States of America

10 9 8 7 6 5 4 3 2

1B/QY/RR/QU/IN

WILEY

About the Author

Donna L. Baker is an author, graphic designer, and instructor who has trained Macromedia Flash users in both conference and classroom settings. She has been a writer and contributing editor for an online magazine since 1998, writing 10 to 11 graphics articles per year. Her articles have included three Flash series, covering V 3 through MX, as well as pieces on other animation software such as Adobe Live Motion.

She is the author of *CourseBuilder for Dreamweaver f/x and Design* (The Coriolis Group, 2001), *Acrobat 5: The Professional User's Guide* (Apress, 2002), *How to Use After Effects 5.5* (Que, 2002), *Acrobat 6: The Professional User's Guide* (Apress, 2003), *The 100 Best Acrobat 6 Tips & Tricks* (Peachpit, 2003), *Premiere 6.5 Complete Course* (Wiley, 2003), *Premiere Pro Complete Course* (Wiley, 2003), and *HTML Complete Course* (Wiley, 2003). She is the coauthor of Jan Kabili's *Photoshop cs Complete Course* (Wiley, 2004).

She has been working on the Internet since its very early days, building her first Web site in 1993. More information about and demos of motion graphics and video are available on her Web site at www.donnabaker.ca.

About the Tech Editor

Brian Ayers has been using SWiSH since early 2000. He founded the largest online SWiSH community, swish-tutorials.com, in 2002, which currently boasts more than 64,000 members. In late 2003, he started working for SWiSHzone as a technical writer and has contributed to several of its software packages including SWiSH2, SWiSHmax, SWiSHstudio, and SWiSHvideo. He has also published tutorials for various Web sites including Sonify.org and FontsForFlash.com. He is a musician and works as a freelance Web designer in his spare time.

Credits

Acquisitions Editor
Michael Roney

Project Editor
Cricket Krengel

Technical Editor
Brian Ayers

Copy Editor
Kim Heusel

Editorial Manager
Robyn Siesky

Vice President & Group Executive Publisher
Richard Swadley

Director of Publishing
Barry Pruett

Project Coordinator
Maridee Ennis

Graphics and Production Specialists
Beth Brooks, Carrie A. Foster,
Lauren Goddard, Joyce Haughey,
Jennifer Heleine, Heather Ryan,
Ron Terry

Quality Control Technician
John Greenough, Joe Niesen,
Dwight Ramsey

Proofreading and Indexing
TECHBOOKS Production Services

Cover Design
Anthony Bunyan

Special Help
Sarah Hellert, Maureen Spears,
Scott Tullis

To the enthusiastic and creative people who make up the SWiSH community

Foreword

In 1999, a group of developers and engineers in Sydney, Australia, started a company called SWiSHzone.com. Their goal was to develop a piece of software using the SWF format that could be readily used, was easy to learn, and was affordable.

Well, they accomplished that, and so much more!

Since those memorable early days, SWiSH has evolved into a range of software solutions, all surrounding the use of SWF movies. In the last few years, the core SWiSH product has evolved dramatically, and a collection of complementary programs is now available as well.

The first product developed by SWiSHzone.com, named SWiSH, was released in April 2000. It was designed to build text effects and was the first text effect tool available to Macromedia Flash users. The following July, the next version of the program was released. SWiSH version 1.5 (currently available as SWiSHlite) uses sounds and images in the animations along with text. In addition to allowing for sound and image file imports, the program provides more effects and controls for adjusting text kerning and leading. There were also improvements to object control, such as positioning and selecting. For the first time, a user could build a preloader, which is an animation that plays while the main animation is loading in a browser window.

The next product in the SWiSH evolution is SWiSH2, released in 2001. Its interface is similar to that used in SWiSHmax. Along with a more complete user interface and more than 150 effects, SWiSH2 added numerous tools and ways to add media and text using the Insert menu commands.

SWiSHmax was released in September 2003. The biggest advancement over previous versions is the inclusion of SWiSHscript programming language. SWiSHmax includes over 230 built-in effects for producing animations ranging from explosions to typewriter text. It also includes a suite of drawing and transformation tools. You can now use SWiSHmax to export SWF files that can play in a Flash player, or within Web pages. You can use exported SWiSHmax movies in other programs including Microsoft Word and PowerPoint.

While all this was happening, our user community mushroomed. SWiSHzone.com now has more than 200,000 customers in 120 countries. More than 95 percent of its customers are outside Australia, with 50 percent residing in the United States. The SWiSHzone.com Web site receives 500,000 unique visitors each month, and SWiSH products have been downloaded more than 3 million times — not bad for a company that is only five years old!

And now we have the book to go with the software! I'm thrilled to tell you that author Donna L. Baker has packed the *Official SWiSHMax* Bible with tips, techniques, and expert guidance that will help you take our powerful tools to their limits! The coolest features of the book include:

✦ Literally hundreds of sample projects and materials

✦ An appendix of effects describing the hundreds of visual effects included with the program

- ✦ Programming chapters that teach the user how to work with SWiSHscript

- ✦ A collection of contributors' chapters that shows how to use SWiSHmax to build real-life projects (from contributors who are among the most advanced SWiSHmax users in the world)

- ✦ A collection of Web appendixes that provides more information on working with PHP, XML, and other technologies that complement SWiSHmax

What's more, this entire book has been tech edited by Brian Ayers, owner of swish-tutorials.com, the world's preeminent SWiSH site!

So sit back, start creating, and enjoy. You're in good hands!

David Michie

Founder and CEO, SWiSHzone.com

Acknowledgments

What an interesting experience! It's not often that a writer has an opportunity to investigate and describe a piece of software that is just becoming a "big thing." I used SWiSH in its first incarnation; it was intriguing. I knew it had the potential to grow into something much more. Kudos to the SWiSHzone people for bringing this software such a long way in such a short time.

I have enjoyed this experience tremendously, thanks in no small part to the huge and active SWiSHmax community. It seems that no matter what my question, there is someone, somewhere who has the answer. The dedication and enthusiasm of those involved with the program is amazing.

Thanks to Brian Ayers for his masterful tech editing. He is an icon in the SWiSHmax community, and it has been my pleasure to learn from his wealth of experience and creativity. Speaking of icons, a huge thanks to the "special guest stars" appearing in Part VII of the book and in the Web site appendixes. Your efforts are very much appreciated, and it has been an honor to work with all of you.

My thanks to the Wiley publishing team — it has been a super experience. Thanks to Mike Roney for responding to my enthusiasm about SWiSHmax with this book opportunity. Most special thanks to my incomparable editor, Cricket Krengel, who has not only led me by the hand through the Bible-building process, but has also proven that 1,800 miles isn't too far to travel to have coffee.

Of course, thanks to my agent at Waterside Productions, Matt Wagner, for keeping track of my affairs. Thanks to my husband Terry for his overwhelming patience. It is possible to work and remodel a house at the same time. Thanks to my daughter Erin for being the interesting little person she is. And thanks to my family, who accept my obsessive work habits as normal behavior, especially Bev. And where would I be without Deena's contributions on a regular basis?

This book is brought to you in part by: my muse and constant musical companion, Tom Waits; lots and lots of freshly ground coffee; and two big dogs snoring under my desk.

Contents at a Glance

Contents

Part III: Animating Your Movie   251

Chapter 14: Customizing Core Effects 301

Part IV: Exploring SWiSHmax Objects   321

Chapter 15: Creating Sprite and Instance Objects 323

Part VIII: Appendixes 589

Note: There are also four bonus appendixes covering SWiSHstudio, PHP scripting, XML menus, and MovieClip properties that can be found on the companion Web site at www.wiley.com/go/swishmax.

Introduction

SWiSHmax is a Macromedia Flash creation tool that can be used for a range of projects from animation to interactive Flash presentations and Web site interfaces. The program allows you to control both the appearance of objects in a movie as well as the timing of objects. It is relatively simple to create animations in SWiSHmax using one or more of its hundreds of effects. There is so much more to the program, such as using actions to control movies and add interactive elements, which you learn about in this book.

Official SWiSHmax Bible is the comprehensive reference for easily creating Flash-formatted Web content using SWiSHmax. The book offers a companion Web site that includes dozens of examples and projects from the book. Also on the Web site you will find additional material, such as information on PHP and XML.

Web designers, both professional and amateur, are using the program to create compelling Flash material. Small-business owners and site developers interested in producing their own animations and interactive movies for the Web are using SWiSHmax. Flash MX users wanting similar tools that are as powerful but simpler to use are moving to SWiSHmax. With one program, this book, some experimentation, and some time, you can create compelling material to use on your Web site; you can even build an entire Web site using SWiSHmax.

Understanding the icons used in this book

There are several icons throughout this book that are used to draw you to areas providing specific types of information. The icons' images are simple to understand, and each is labeled. Here's what they mean:

Tip   A tip adds practical information to the topic being discussed, such as advice on when to use a technique.

Note   A note provides a bit more background information that isn't required to understand the topic at hand.

Caution   When you see the Caution icon, it means there are circumstances in which you should take care using the process or technique under discussion.

The cross-references point you to in-depth information about a topic in other chapters.

Most chapters have related files and sample projects. This icon identifies available material and where it is located on the book's Web site.

How the book is organized

This book is divided into parts, each pertaining to a particular phase of working with SWiSHmax. Part I is the place to start if you are new to SWiSHmax. Parts II through IV give you what you need to know to create and animate a movie. If you are familiar with building movies and adding effects in SWiSHmax or have worked with SWiSH2, you may want to jump into Part V, which shows you how to work with SWiSHscript to make your movies interactive. If you plan to use your SWiSHmax-created Flash movies in other programs, you can learn about these and other export issues in Part VI. Everyone, regardless of level of experience, will find information, tips, and expert advice in Part VII, which is a selection of projects contributed by SWiSHmax users worldwide.

Part I: Getting Started with SWiSHmax

Get a taste of working with SWiSHmax by completing a QuickStart project (Chapter 1). Learn about the program's interface and commands, and how you can customize the interface to suit the way you work (Chapter 2). Project planning is discussed and demonstrated in Chapter 3, as are the methods for starting and saving a new project.

Part II: The Basic SWiSHmax Building Blocks

Learn about managing content for your project in this section. You learn how to coordinate the content of your movie in several panels in Chapter 4. In Chapter 5, you learn how to use the SWiSHmax drawing tools to create a range of material for your projects. Once a shape is drawn, learn to modify and manipulate those shapes in Chapter 6. Add and work with color and fills using the information you learn in Chapter 7. Of course, you use material imported into the program as well as that you create in SWiSHmax; learn about importing images in Chapter 8. You can also use animations in your SWiSHmax projects, and you learn about working with imported animations in Chapter 9. Learn to add and manipulate text using the information in Chapter 10, and learn to work with sound files in Chapter 11.

Part III: Animating Your Movie

Part III is all about effects. Learn the basics of applying and working with effects (Chapter 12). Discover how to use a collection of effects in Chapter 13, and round out your effects knowledge with information about customizing core effects (Chapter 14).

Part IV: Exploring SWiSHmax Objects

Throughout the book you read about different movie elements, both imported and created internally. In Chapter 15, you learn all about sprites and instances, which are specific types of objects. Learn to work with button objects in Chapter 16.

Part V: Adding Interactivity to a Movie

In Part V, you learn how to program elements of your movies to make them interactive. Learn how to write SWiSHscript using two methods and how to evaluate your scripts in Chapter 17. In Chapter 18, you learn how events trigger actions and the types of events used in SWiSHmax. The outcome of an event is an action, which is covered in Chapter 19.

Part VI: Distributing SWiSHmax Movies

You certainly want to share your masterpieces with the world. Learn how to test and prepare a movie for export in Chapter 20, and learn about different methods of exporting movies in Chapter 21. Using SWiSHmax movies in other programs, such as Dreamweaver and PowerPoint, is discussed in Chapter 22.

Part VII: Sample Projects

The final part of the book takes your learning to the next level. A number of expert users have generously contributed projects to the book to show you SWiSHmax in action. Learn about numerous ways to construct menus in Chapter 23. In Chapter 24, learn different ways to build a movie preloader. Learn how to plan and construct a Web site interface in Chapter 25. In Chapter 26, learn about working with PHP scripting as you build a shopping cart movie. You learn to construct a photo gallery in Chapter 27. Learn more complex scripting by building the horoscope of the day project in Chapter 28.

Part VIII: Appendixes

Information about the very special guest contributors to this book is included in Appendix A. Great resources that are available on the Internet make up Appendix B. A list of menus, toolbars, and keyboard accelerators is included as Appendix C. In Appendix D, you'll find an outline of the hundreds of effects contained in SWiSHmax.

A Note about Installation Requirements and Process

You can use SWiSHmax on Windows-based computers only. Following are minimum requirements in order to run SWiSHmax:

- ✦ Windows 95/98/Me/NT4/2000/XP
- ✦ Pentium II processor
- ✦ 64MB of RAM
- ✦ 800x600 pixels by 256-color display

You do not need to have the Macromedia Flash program installed on your computer. SWiSHmax is a separate program, not a plug-in for any other product. Macromedia Flash MX 2004 (and earlier versions) is an application used for developing animations, interactive content, and Web applications.

SWiSHmax is available as an online download. You use the same download as a free trial, or convert it to a licensed copy by purchasing a license key. The trial period allows you to use the program for 14 days or a prescribed number of sessions. If you haven't already, go to www.swishzone.com to download a free trial or to purchase your own copy.

Web materials

The book's companion Web site at www.wiley.com/comp-books/swishmax contains all the practice files and projects referenced in the book. Most chapters include one or more practice or sample projects; some include six or more. The files are named according to their chapter and sample numbers, and referenced in the text for ease of understanding.

Several additional appendixes are available from the book's companion Web site. Appendix E explains how to use SWiSHstudio, a companion product to SWiSHmax that is used for creating various forms of output. Appendix F shows you how to extend your movie's capabilities using the PHP scripting language. In Appendix G Ian Hinkley explains XML issues and how to use XML in SWiSHmax. And finally, Appendix H lists MovieClip properties and supported SWF versions.

Other SWiSHzone products

There are a number of additional products that you may want to investigate as your skill and interest in movie creation develops. For the most part, they are stand-alone products with one exception — a plug-in for Macromedia Flash MX 2004. Any of the products described, such as Web site interfaces or photo albums, can also be built using SWiSHmax, as you learn throughout the book.

SWiSHpowerFX plug-in for Flash MX 2004. SWiSHpowerFX is a Macromedia Flash MX 2004 extension used to create text effects. The plug-in includes more than 50 customizable effects.

SWiSHpix. SWiSHpix is a program designed to create Flash photo albums that you can use in a number of ways such as screensavers, on a Web site, or burned onto a CD.

SWiSHstudio. SWiSHstudio is another program used to convert output from SWiSHmax to a number of formats including projector executables, screensavers, or copied directly to a CD-ROM in a few steps. Learn about SWiSHstudio in Appendix E.

SWiSHsites. Creating an entire Web site template from scratch is time consuming. If you prefer, you can use SWiSHsites, which are royalty-free SWiSH2/SWiSHmax templates.

Welcome to the book

You are about to embark on an interesting adventure. Throughout the chapters in this book, you will learn about a very interesting piece of software. Whether you want to build SWF movies for your Web site, create content for CDs, or build scripted forms, there is something for you in these pages.

The book contains many illustrations to guide you as you learn the SWiSHmax program's features. For the most part, any images you see in the book are taken from the hundreds of sample files, movies, and source material available from the book's Web site.

Enjoy the experience!

Getting Started with SWiSHmax

SWiSHmax QuickStart

What if you want to have an animated logo to add some punch to your Web site? Or show your customers your products in an interactive and attractive way? Or create a photo gallery showing your vacation pictures? Or build a way for your customers to talk to you directly online?

You can use one program to build all of these objects and many more. For everyone from beginners to seasoned Web design veterans, SWiSHmax has something to offer. With SWiSHmax, your imagination, and some know-how, you can create a wide range of material to use on your Web site — or even create an entire Web site. You can also create material to use in a range of other programs from Dreamweaver to PowerPoint.

Creating simple animations is one of SWiSHmax's strong features, yet it is only the tip of the SWiSHmax iceberg. Throughout this book, you learn much more about working with different types of files and effects, using actions to control a movie, and working with SWiSHmax output in other programs.

First, I am going to take you on a quick stroll through the different aspects of the program so you can gain an understanding of what can be accomplished with this remarkable piece of software.

What Does SWiSHmax Do?

Anyone who has spent any time on the Internet has seen Flash movies of varying degrees of complexity, interactivity, and skill. Historically, the movies you saw online were built using Macromedia Flash. In recent years, a number of other products have been developed that can produce much of the same output or subsets of the output as the Flash program does. Most notably among these other programs is SWiSHmax.

SWiSHmax is a Flash creation tool that can be used for a range of projects from animation to interactive Flash presentations and Web site interfaces. The program allows you to control both the appearance of objects in a movie as well as the timing of objects. Movies are controlled in one of three ways:

✦ **The content of a movie changes based on time.** You work with the SWiSHmax Timeline to control the appearance and location of objects.

✦ **The content of a movie changes based on user interaction.** You add controls that initiate reactions to user actions such as clicking a button or moving the mouse cursor.

✦ **The content of a movie changes based both on time and action.** A user's interaction with an object, such as clicking a button or typing text, can cause an event to happen over time such as running another movie.

A SWiSHmax movie is made up of one or more scenes. Each scene has a separate Timeline sequence. The project you create in this QuickStart chapter uses one scene.

The scene or scenes in a SWiSHmax movie hold a number of components, including:

✦ **Objects.** SWiSHmax differentiates objects on the basis of their complexity. Simple shapes, such as a square or circle, are a single indivisible shape; complex shapes, are collections of shapes or text. There are also other types of objects such as sprites, which are collections of objects and effects, and instances, which are copies of sprites. These are covered in detail in Chapters 15 and 16.

✦ **Effects.** Effects are animations that change the appearance of an object over time. Detailed explanations can be found in Chapters 12 through 14.

✦ **Events.** These are actions that occur when a movie reaches a specific frame on the Timeline or as a result of a mouse or keyboard action. You learn more about events in Chapter 18.

✦ **Actions.** Actions are operations that are triggered by events. There is a wide range of actions with which you can work, ranging from movie controls to sounds to mouse actions, all of which are covered in Chapter 19.

This chapter describes the basic workflow you use to create a SWiSHmax movie. In this chapter, you get a head start on your adventures with SWiSHmax by completing a simple QuickStart project. At the end of the project, not only do you have a sense of how the program works, but you also have a logo in SWF (Shockwave Flash) format that you can use on a Web site.

Note   SWF is a standard file format used for exporting your SWiSHmax movies.

You'll learn how to start a project and how to add or create elements of your logo, including graphics, text, sound, and images. When you have assembled the parts, you add some animation. Finally, you'll export the logo both as a SWF file and a Web page.

The processes used in creating the movie are broken down into a series of discussions and steps. The steps contain both generic instructions if you are following along with your own files, as well as instructions for using the files available from the book's Web site.

Working with an Animation Program

As you see shortly when you get into SWiSHmax, there are two major components of the program—the Timeline and the Layout panel, shown in Figure 1-1.

Outline panel   Layout panel   Timeline

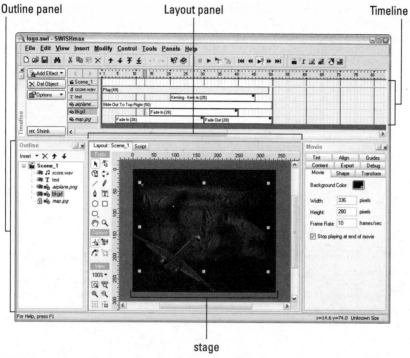

Figure 1-1: Your movie takes place in both the Timeline and the Layout panels.

In the Layout panel, you construct, assemble, and draw the elements that go into your SWiSHmax creation. The Timeline is used to determine WHEN you see your graphics or text. Not only must you draw or compose something to use in your project, but you must also define when the objects are seen.

In addition to assembling visual components like images, text, and sound, such as a background score, you also work extensively with different actions. Actions are assigned and controlled in the Timeline as well and are based on time.

Your First SWiSHmax Movie

The next sections take you through building a simple SWF (Shockwave Flash) movie in SWiSHmax. As you work through the steps, you learn how to add different types of elements to your project over time, how to draw a simple shape and add text, and then how to animate the components of your movie. Finally, you learn how to save both the SWF movie and a Web page used for displaying the movie.

Cross-Reference SWF (Shockwave Flash) is the standard export format for SWiSHmax movies. You learn about exporting and export file formats in Chapter 21.

You can use the files provided for the sample project or work with your own files. The sample project builds a simple animated logo complete with music for your company, Up and Away Travel. Figure 1-2 shows several frames of the animation. The material required to create the logo is available from the book's Web site in the folder named chapter01. The logo starts with an airplane moving across the screen. As it moves, a map of the world slowly appears, and then starts to fade as the airplane moves out of the screen. The company name and a background rectangle slowly appear and overlay the fading map.

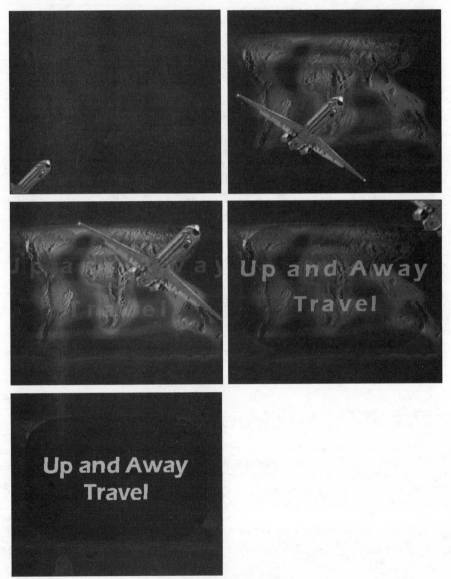

Figure 1-2: The sample project's logo changes over time.

Starting a SWiSHmax project

A SWiSHmax project contains all the objects used in the final movie, as well as actions, scripts, effects, and other elements that together make up what you see in the final product. To start, you create a new project using one of the SWiSHmax templates, define how it is going to look, and set the speed at which the movie plays. To create a new project, follow these steps:

1. **Open SWiSHmax.** Double-click the program icon in the Programs listing; the program opens, and you are given a set of options for starting. You can choose from:

   - Start a new empty movie

   - Start a new movie from a template

   - Work on an existing movie

   - Reopen the last movie you worked on

2. **Choose a start option.** To work with the project files, choose the option Start a new movie from a template. The list of templates opens.

3. **Choose a template and click Open.** For the project, choose Large Rectangle (336 x 280) .swi and click Open. The dialog box closes, and you are in the program. You see a large white rectangle (the stage) on the Layout panel's workspace. The rectangle is the viewable area of your movie. If you look at the Layout panel tab, the first horizontal row in the Timeline, and the first heading in the Outline panel, you can see all three areas now have a listing called Scene_1.

Note   When SWiSHmax is installed on your computer a set of templates for common forms of movies is installed automatically.

4. **Save the movie.** Click File ➪ Save to open the Save dialog box and name your movie. If you have been following along with the sample project, type **logo** in the Save dialog box.

Tip   By default, the program saves your movies in a numbered sequence; you see the file is named movie1.swi if you don't choose a name for it.

5. **Click the Save in dropdown arrow at the top of the dialog box and browse to the location where you want to store your project files.** Select your storage folder, and click Save. The dialog box closes and you return to the program. The movie name appears at the top of the program window.

On The Web Site   A copy of the finished SWiSHmax file in this example is available from the book's Web site. It is in the chapter01 folder and named logo.swi.

To the right of the Layer panel, the Movie tab is displayed when you start a new project. You can change the movie's properties, such as its background color and frame rate, in the Movie panel. To change a movie's properties, follow these steps:

1. **Change the Background Color on the Movie panel (Figure 1-3).** Click the Background Color swatch (it appears in white initially) to open the Color Selector.

Figure 1-3: Make changes to the background color and speed of the movie.

2. **Select an alternate color for the background.** To create the sample project, click the dark blue color that is fifth from the top of the second row. The Color Selector closes, and the Background Color swatch appears with the blue color you selected.

Tip   Basic primary colors are shown in the left-most column of the Color Selector; the blue color you use is to the right of the bright yellow sample.

3. **Change the frame rate of the movie.** Try clicking the 30 frames/sec field on the Movie panel to activate the text. Type **10** to change the frame rate to 10 fps (frames per second).

4. **Choose File ➪ Save and save the file with the modified settings.**

Tip   It is a good habit to save every few minutes and after you have spent some time configuring settings.

Importing elements

There are a variety of program formats you can use in your projects. Table 1-1 lists the file formats that SWiSHmax supports.

Table 1-1: File Formats Supported by SWiSHmax

Media	File Formats
Text	Plain text
Raster Images	Windows bitmaps, GIF, JPEG, and PNG images
Vector Graphics	Windows Metafile, Enhanced Metafile, Flash Graphics
Animation	Animated GIF, Flash Animation, Flash Projector, SWiSH movie
Sound	Wave and MP3 formats

Cross-Reference   You can learn about importing images in Chapter 8 and about importing and working with sound in Chapter 11.

The sample project has four visual elements and one sound used as a soundtrack. Two of the objects are imported images, one is a shape you draw in the program, and the fourth is text you add in SWiSHmax.

> **Note** You can work with your own images and sound file if you prefer. You need one full-size image in any allowed format for the background, one GIF or PNG image with a transparent background to apply motion effects to, and some music you can use as a soundtrack.

The steps include general instructions, as well as how to use the images and sound files from the book's Web site. The three files are in the Chapter01 folder. To import the files you need for the project, follow these steps:

1. **Choose File ⇨ Import, and browse to the location of the folder where you are storing the artwork for your SWiSHmax projects.**

2. **Press the Ctrl key, and select the files you want to use.** If you are working with the sample project files, click the two image files and the sound file to select them: airplane.png, map.jpg, and score.wav.

3. **Click Open.** The dialog box closes, and the files are imported into the program. When a sound file is imported, the program asks if you want to use the sound as a soundtrack. Click Yes. The clips are added to the project.

> **Note** When you add a graphic object, it is placed at the center of the movie automatically.

Take a look around the program and see what is happening before starting the drawing and animating processes.

First, view the list in the Outline panel displayed by default to the left of the Layout panel. In the listing you see the two images you imported as well as the soundtrack music file. Each file is listed under the Scene_1 heading and has an eye icon indicating the layer is visible (or audible in the case of the sound file). Each file also has an icon identifying the layer as a graphic or music file. When you look at the list displayed in the Timeline, you see the files listed in the same order.

The music file can be placed anywhere in the sequence, but you must use a particular order for both the imported images and the layers you create. If you are working with your own files, the GIF image with the transparent background must be placed higher in the list than the solid image used for the background.

The higher the element appears in the list, the higher it is in the stacking order. For example, if the airplane image is above the map image in the list, then it appears on top of the map; if the map image is above the airplane in the list, then you wouldn't be able to see the airplane because the map covers it. Check your list, and make sure the order is correct. If it isn't, click one of the file names in either the Outline list or the Timeline list and drag it up or down.

> **Note** When you move an image in one area (Outline panel or Timeline) it is also moved in the other area.

Tip   You can select the elements for your movie in the Open dialog box in the order you want them to appear in the scene, or simply select them sequentially and then shuffle the order in the Outline panel.

Look at the music file you imported. The sample project's music file is named score.wav. As mentioned earlier, the order in the layer listing of files isn't important. The score.wav row stretches from 1 to 49 frames on the Timeline, as shown in Figure 1-4. A pale blue rectangle with the label Play (49) fills the music's row, meaning the music will play for 49 of the 50 frames of your logo. To listen to the soundtrack, follow these steps:

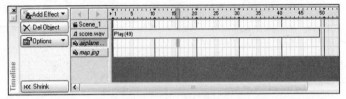

Figure 1-4: The sound file displays on the Timeline for the length of the movie.

1. **Click the music file's name in either the Outline panel or the Timeline to select it.** The Sound panel at the right of the screen is active, as shown in Figure 1-5. The music file's name is shown in the dialog box.

2. **Click Properties on the Sound panel (next to the music file's label).** The Properties for Sound dialog box opens, also shown in Figure 1-5. The dialog box also includes the name of your music file in quotations; the sample project's file is named "score.wav."

3. **Click Play.** When you finish listening to the music, click Stop.

4. **Click OK to close the Properties for Sound dialog box.**

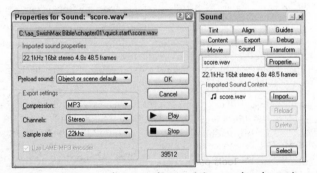

Figure 1-5: You can listen to the movie's soundtrack music.

Caution   When you add files to a project an .sbk file is added to the project's storage folder. Don't delete this file — it is a backup for your movie.

Creating objects

The SWiSHmax Toolbox contains a number of drawing tools that you can use to create graphical elements for your movie. You can draw a variety of shapes by hand or use preconfigured AutoShapes, explained later in this section.

Cross-Reference See Chapter 5 to learn more about drawing, Chapter 6 to learn how to modify drawings, and Chapter 7 to learn how to work with color.

Tip You can hide and/or lock layers in the Layout window to make it easier to work. Select a layer, and click the eye icon to the left of the label's name in the Outline panel to change the visibility status. Click once to display an *x* drawn through the eye icon, indicating the associated layer is hidden. Click the eye icon twice and the associated layer is locked, indicated by a gold lock to the left of the object's label in the Outline panel.

Note You leave the background layer locked for the remainder of the movie construction process. When you use stationary layers, locking them is a good idea. When you select other objects on the stage, you can be sure the locked object(s) isn't moved by mistake.

SWiSHmax has a set of tools for drawing different shapes. Follow these steps to select an AutoShape tool and draw a shape:

1. **Click the visible AutoShape tool in the Tools panel, and hold the mouse button down until the submenu opens, as shown in Figure 1-6.**

Autoshape tool

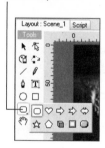

Figure 1-6: Select an AutoShape from the submenu.

2. **Click a tool from the submenu.** If you are working on the sample project, click the rounded rectangle tool. The submenu closes, and the selected tool is active.

Note The AutoShape displayed in the Tools panel continues to show the most recently selected tool until you select a different one.

3. **Click the stage on the Layout panel with the tool and drag to construct the AutoShape.** To complete the shape used in the sample project, click the stage at about the position of Alaska on the map layer and drag to draw a rounded rectangle that covers most of the continents shown on the map. The Shape panel becomes active in the panels at the right of the program window.

4. **In the Shape panel, click the Name field to make it active and type a name to identify the shape.** The rectangle used in the sample project is named **bkdg**. The name changes in both the Outline panel and the Timeline.

Note   If you don't name the objects you add or create in the program, the default names are used. That isn't a problem when there are only a few objects, but when you are working with a large number of objects it can be quite confusing. Naming objects as you add them is a good habit to develop.

By default, any shapes you draw in SWiSHmax are filled with a bright red color. Here's how to change to a custom color:

1. **In the Shapes panel, click the solid red sample to open the Color Selector (Figure 1-7).**

Click here to open the Color Selector

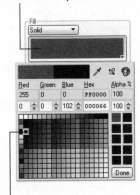

Click on a color swatch to select a color

Figure 1-7: Select a color for the shape.

2. **Click a color swatch to select an alternate color.** If you are creating the sample project, click the dark blue color third from the top in the second row from the left (next to the bright blue); or click in the field below the Hex label and type **000066.** A dark blue is applied to the shape.

Cross-Reference   There are a number of ways to choose a color. See Chapter 7, to learn more.

Tip   If you click a color swatch, the Color Selector closes automatically; if you type a color number, click Done to close the Color Selector. The color is applied after the Color Selector closes.

Cross-Reference

Hex refers to Hexadecimal, which is a color system. You learn more about this method of naming color in Chapter 7.

In addition to selecting a color for your shapes, you can also modify the level of transparency, referred to as an Alpha value. Learn about Alpha values in Chapter 7.

When you draw a shape on the stage, you can estimate its size and position, or you can use the Transform tab to set a precise size and location. To precisely set the location and size, follow these steps:

1. **Click the shape on the stage to make it active.**

2. **Click the Transform tab to display the current size and position settings for the shape.**

3. **Click the Resize checkbox to make it active in the Modes section of the panel.**

4. **Click a field to make it active and then type an alternate value.** To re-create the size and location of the sample project's **bkgd** shape, type these values: X: **22**, Y: **36**, W: **290**, and H: **190**.

Cross-Reference

The X and Y location references refer to the anchor point position. See Chapter 6 to learn about anchor points and other transforming processes.

5. **Click File ⇨ Save to save the movie with the completed shape.**

Before moving on, check the location of the Autoshape layer in the Outline panel and move the layer, if necessary. It should be second to last in the listing (if you are creating the sample project, only the background layer should be below it). Autoshapes can be used for a wide range of purposes, including as a background for the text, which is explained in the next section.

Tip

If you move anything around in a file, make sure to click Save before closing or the rearranged version will be lost.

Adding text to a movie

One of the most common elements used in a movie is text. In SWiSHmax, you can animate any basic text you add to the movie. A special command called Break Apart allows you to animate the individual letters and apply effects, such as explosions. Follow these steps to add text to a movie:

1. **Click the Text tool in the Tools panel as shown in Figure 1-8, and then move the tool over the movie.** A cross-hair icon appears.

2. **Click the stage on the Layout panel.** A default block of text named Text is added to the movie. The Text panel at the right of the program window is active.

3. **In the Text panel, click the default name (Text) in the text area of the panel to select it.** Type replacement text. For the sample logo project, type **Up and Away Travel**. Press Enter after Away to force the last word to its own line.

Text tool

Text panel

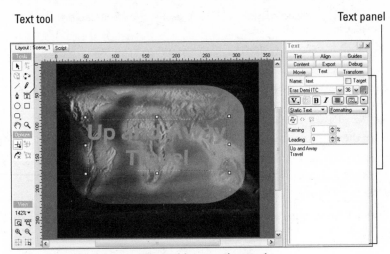

Figure 1-8: Use the Text tool to add text to the movie.

SWiSHmax allows you to customize the text you add to a movie. You can change the font, color, and other characteristics such as the spacing between letters. To customize text, follow these steps:

1. **Click the dropdown arrow to the right of the Font Name field at the top of the Text panel to select an alternate font.** Select a font such as Eras Demi ITC or a similar font from the list for the sample project (Figure 1-9).

Font

Font size

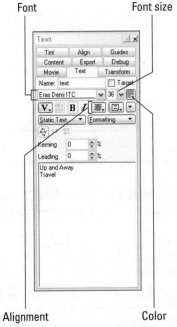

Alignment

Color

Figure 1-9: Customize the text in the Text panel.

Note There are a number of common fonts you can use if you don't have the suggested font in your system. Arial, Bank Gothic, and Century Gothic are similar to Eras Demi.

2. **Click the dropdown arrow to the right of the Font Size field and select an alternate font size.** The text size of the sample project is 36.

3. **Click the color swatch to open the Color Selector to select a custom color.** Click on a color swatch in the panel to select it. You can also enter a Hex number in the Hex field. For the sample project, type **CC6699** in the Hex field, which is a dark pink.

4. **Click the Text Justification icon and choose an alternate alignment for the text, if desired.** For the sample project, click Center Justify to center the text on the stage.

5. **Click the Text type button and choose Static Text from the dropdown list.** The Static Text label appears on the button.

Tip If you don't know the name of the buttons, move your mouse cursor over a button to display a tooltip.

When you are finished editing your text, check its location in the Outline panel or the Timeline, and move the layer, if necessary. For the sample project, make sure the text layer is third from the bottom, above the bkdg shape and the map.jpg layers.

Aligning objects with one another

There is one thing you should check before you start animating. Look at the stage, and make sure the objects are placed on the stage where you want them to appear. The location of a drawn object or text depends on where you click the stage with the tool when you start constructing the object.

Before you begin to animate the objects in a movie, make sure the text and the text background Autoshape are aligned to your liking.

Note For the sample logo project, the center of both the text and the background should be the same.

When you set the position for an object, you can move the object and eyeball the location or use menu commands and make sure its location is exact.

1. **Select the text layer, and then press the Ctrl key and select the Autoshape layer.** Make sure you select the layers in this order.

2. **Click the Align relative to button to display the dropdown list and choose Relative to Stage.**

3. **Click Modify ➪ Align ➪ Center (Horizontally).** This aligns both elements horizontally.

4. **Click Modify ➪ Align ➪ Center (Vertically).** The text position shifts to the center of the Autoshape layer. Save the file.

Applying Effects to the Movie Layers

Now the fun starts! One of SWiSHmax's strongest features is quick and effective animation. A word of caution before you start — there are dozens (if not hundreds!) of pre-built animations from which you can choose. With such a banquet of effects, it can be difficult to find the right animations to use and to restrain yourself from choosing one of everything.

There are numerous variations to use with the pre-built animations. Animations involve changing an object visually over time. The most common animation you may think of is movement, but you can also animate size, color, and transparency for the layers of a movie.

Using a flying effect

Animation can be used to make images appear to fly across the screen. Whether you use the airplane in the sample project or a picture of a flowerpot, the background of the image must be transparent in order to make the effect realistic. Otherwise, you see a flying flowerpot and its white background move across the screen. Somehow that doesn't have the same impact!

When you add motion to an object, you see a dotted red line on the workspace that identifies how the object moves over time. The dotted line is called a *motion path* and is a useful tool for evaluating how an effect will look.

To create the effect that an image is flying across the screen, follow these steps:

1. **Click the name of the object you want to animate in the Outline panel to select the image on the Layout panel.**

2. **Choose View ➪ Preview Frame.** You can see the status of the animation at any specific frame using this viewing option.

Caution

There are different ways to preview your work. As you are constructing and animating, make sure the option described in Step 2 is selected. This allows you to see where an object is at any frame of the movie. Otherwise, you see only the starting location for the image or graphic.

3. **Click the Zoom factor dropdown list in the Tools panel and select 75%.** The stage is shown in the Layout panel with workspace surrounding it as shown in Figure 1-10.

4. **Click and drag the image down and left until just the upper-right tip of the image is within the margins of the stage, also shown in Figure 1-10.** The animation you apply will move the object up and diagonally across the screen.

Zoom control

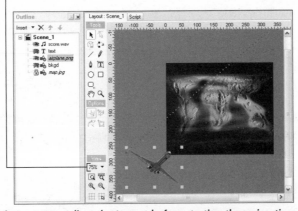

Figure 1-10: Adjust the Layout before starting the animation.

5. **In the Timeline, click the Frame on the time ruler where you want to start the effect.** The play head moves to the selected frame. For the sample project, click Frame 1 as shown in Figure 1-11.

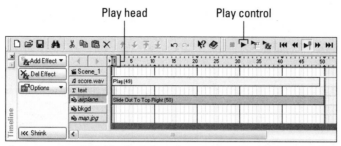

Play head   Play control

Figure 1-11: Add and adjust the effect on the Timeline.

6. **Click the Add Effect button at the left of the Timeline to open the main effects listings and choose an effect.** For the sample project, click Slide ⇨ Out to Top Right. The menu closes and the effect is added to the image's row in the Timeline.

Effects are always added to the Timeline at their default frame lengths.

7. **Extend the end frame for the effect in the Timeline by clicking and dragging the right edge of the effect's rectangle to the desired length.** For the sample project, the effect ends at Frame 50. When you see the cursor change to ││, click and drag the edge right to Frame 50 on the Timeline. Remember to save the project.

For the sample project, the effect's rectangle should extend across the entire animation's Timeline. That is, it should start at Frame 1 and end at Frame 50.

Look closely at the screen and see if you understand what happens when you perform different actions. Don't worry if you don't. Starting in Chapter 12 you learn to work with effects in depth.

To view the effect you've just added, click the Play button on the Control toolbar and watch. In the sample project, you see the airplane start at the bottom left and move across the stage, finally disappearing at the top right. Click the Stop button when you are finished viewing.

Fading the background

Although a static background is attractive, you can easily add effects to enhance a movie project. One of the most common and useful effects is to fade in the background, often followed by a fade-out toward the end of the animation. To add a fade effect, follow these steps:

If you are using the sample project, you are working with the map layer.

1. **Click the background image's layer in the Timeline to select it.** For the sample project, click the map.jpg label.

Note The name of an object on the Timeline is referred to as a label. The layer is the object on the stage.

Tip You can also select the layer in the Outline panel or on the Layout panel.

2. **Click the Add Effect button on the Timeline, and then click Fade ➪ Fade In (see Figure 1-12).** The effect places a 10-frame rectangle on the image's row in the Timeline.

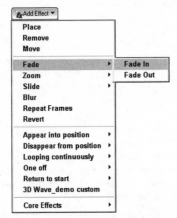

Figure 1-12: Select the Fade In effect from the Effects menu.

3. **Move your cursor over the effect, and then click and drag left or right to position the effect at the frame where you want it to start.** For the sample map.jpg layer, drag the effect until the first frame is at Frame 5.

4. **Move your cursor over the right margin of the effect, and click and drag to increase the effect to the desired length.** For the sample project, drag to increase the length of the effect to 26 frames, ending at Frame 30.

Note When you change the length of an effect on the Timeline, the number in brackets after the effect's name also changes.

Click Play on the Control toolbar to play the movie and watch the effect. With SWiSHmax, you can easily reuse an effect you've already added to a movie. Instead of selecting the same effects through the Effects menu, here's a quick way to add another effect:

1. **Click the Fade In effect on the background image's row on the Timeline to select it.** You added the effect in the previous set of steps. If you are working with the sample project, the effect is applied to the map.jpg image.

2. **Right-click the effect on the Timeline to open the shortcut menu.** Click Copy Effect from the shortcut menu.

3. **Click the frame on the image's row on the Timeline where you want the new effect to be placed.** For the sample project, click Frame 31 on the map.jpg image's row on the Timeline to identify the location to place the new effect.

4. **Right-click to open the shortcut menu again, and click Paste Effect.** A copy of the Fade In effect is added to the Timeline at the frame you selected in Step 3. For the sample project, the copied effect is pasted to the Timeline starting at Frame 31 and ending at Frame 56.

5. **Adjust the length of the pasted effect, if desired.** For the sample project, move the mouse cursor over the right margin of the effect at Frame 56, and click drag left until the effect reaches Frame 50, making the effect the length of the movie.

Tip   In addition to copying and pasting an effect for one object, you can paste the same effect to other objects. In the sample project, a copy of the Fade In effect was added to the bkgd Autoshape layer to make the animation smoother.

You may think this is quick, but the effect isn't the right one because the idea is for the background image to fade in and then fade out again. Quite right. Follow these steps to modify the copy of the effect:

1. **Right-click the copy of the Fade In effect on the Timeline to open the context menu.** For the sample project, the second copy starts at Frame 31 and ends at Frame 50.

2. **Click Properties in the shortcut menu to open the Fade In Settings dialog box.**

Note   Each time you open the Properties dialog box, the tab that was used when you last opened the dialog box appears. For example, if you have been following along with the steps, earlier you modified the Motion settings for the animation. This time, when you open the dialog box, the Motion tab is displayed.

Tip   To quickly open the properties for an effect, you can double-click the effect's rectangle on the Timeline rather than using the shortcut menu.

3. **Click the Fade tab and click Fade out.** There are two directions for a fade. When you select Fade out, the name of the dialog box changes to Fade Out Settings.

4. **Click Close to close the dialog box.** On the Timeline, shown in Figure 1-13, you see the name of the effect has changed to Fade Out, which is what the background image is supposed to do.

5. **Click Play on the Control toolbar to preview the movie and see the effects you've added.** Don't forget to save your project.

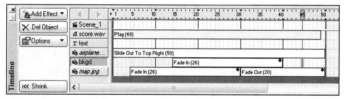

Figure 1-13: Read the name and length of the effects on the Timeline.

Adding text animation

Text can be boring; text can be interesting. I vote for interesting. In this QuickStart, you have seen how to add both text and an Autoshape. SWiSHmax offers many text effects from which you can select that can add interest to a movie.

Having text appear into its position gives the text an interesting way to enter the movie. The Appear into Position effect is one used specifically for text. Follow these steps to add the effect to text:

1. **Click a text object in the Outline panel or the label in the Timeline to select it.**

2. **Click the Add Effect button in the Timeline and then click Appear into position ⇨ Kerning - Kern In. from the effects list.** The effect is added to the Timeline at its default length of 20 frames.

3. **Reposition the effect by clicking and dragging it right or left on the Timeline to start at the desired frame.** For the sample project, drag the effect to start at Frame 20.

4. **Click and drag an edge of the effect right or left with the mouse to increase or decrease its length.** If you are working on the sample project, increase the effect's length to 25 frames, ending at Frame 45.

> **Tip**
>
> The Appear into Position effect used in the steps is one of dozens. The Kerning effect is about halfway down the second column of effects.

5. **Click Play on the Controller to preview the movie.** You see the text letters gradually move closer to one another until they are in their final positions.

You can also change the way the text looks by changing its color. If you are working with the sample project, you see that the text color is very similar to that of the background rectangle, making it difficult to see the letters clearly. Follow these steps to change the text color as the effect plays:

1. **Right-click the Kerning - Kern In effect on the text object's row on the Timeline to open the shortcut menu.**

2. **Click Properties to open the Kerning - Kern In Settings dialog box.** Click the Motion tab as shown in Figure 1-14.

3. **Click the Color button and select the Fade to Color option.** Change the default value from 100% to a lower value if you want to partially fade the color. For the sample project, leave the default value of 100% in the Fade to Color value.

4. **Click the color swatch to open the Color Selector, and select a custom color for the Fade to Color effect.** For the sample project, click the dark gold color as shown in Figure 1-14, or type **FF9900** in the field below the Hex column to select the color.

5. **Click Done to accept the color and close the Color Selector.** Click OK to close the Kerning - Kern In Settings dialog box.

6. **Preview your movie.** The elements of your movie experience multiple changes in animation over its duration and ends with a change in the text color.

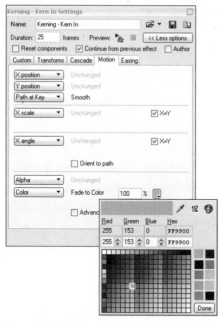

Figure 1-14: Choose a custom color to use for the text animation.

Previewing and Exporting a Movie

Once your movie is complete, you need to preview it to see how it will appear on a Web site. And, it's a good idea to test the movie before you export it. That way, you can see how the movie looks in a player, not surrounded by the rest of the SWiSHmax program. It's simpler to see any errors when you aren't distracted by the program's interface.

Click File ⇨ Test ⇨ In Player. The Macromedia Flash Player opens and you see the movie running as shown in Figure 1-15. It stops when it has played through. To view it again in the Flash player, either click Control ⇨ Play in the Flash Player menu, or press Ctrl+Enter on the keyboard.

Figure 1-15: Preview your movie in the Flash Player before exporting.

Note

If the stand-alone Flash Player is not detected on your system, SWiSHmax uses a projector installed with the program.

Cross-Reference

Read more about testing movies in Chapter 22.

SWiSHmax offers you several ways to export a movie. The options include:

✦ SWF (Shockwave Flash)

✦ SWF and HTML

✦ EXE file (a stand-alone executable file that doesn't require a player to run)

✦ AVI (video format)

In this section, you learn how to export the Web page as well as the Flash movie. To export the movie and its Web page, follow these steps:

1. **Click File ➪ Export ➪ HTML + SWF.** The Publish SWiSHmax Movie dialog box appears.

Cross-Reference

You learn how to create other forms of exports in Chapter 22.

2. **Browse to the location where you want to store the file, and change the name if desired.** By default, both the sample movie and Web page use the project name.

3. **Click Save to save the files.** The Publish SWiSHmax Movie dialog box closes.

Note

By default, the files are named using the .swi file name and stored in the main SWiSHmax folder on your hard drive.

4. **A dialog box opens asking if you want to edit the HTML file.** Click No to close the dialog box.

5. **Open your Web browser.**

6. **Click File ➪ Open and click Browse.**

7. **Navigate to the folder where you saved your project file and select it from the list.** Click OK. The page loads, and your movie plays.

On The Web Site

Copies of the logo.swf and logo.html files are available on the book's Web site in the chapter01 folder.

Cross-Reference

Chapter 23 describes how to use your movie and an exported Web page in a number of different programs.

Summary

This chapter described some basics of creating movies in SWiSHmax and gave you an opportunity to try out the program by creating an animated movie. You learned how to:

✦ Open the program and create a new movie using a template

✦ Import and arrange graphic elements

✦ Draw and color a simple shape

✦ Add text to a movie

✦ Add a soundtrack to a movie

✦ Animate objects over time

✦ Animate color and opacity of elements

✦ Preview a movie

✦ Export a Flash movie and a Web page

✦   ✦   ✦

Welcome to SWiSHmax

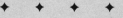
In this chapter, you take a tour of SWiSHmax. You learn how to make your way around the program, and then look at the different parts of the SWiSHmax interface. You also learn how to set user preferences and make some changes to the program layout. Finally, you take a look at the Help files and what they can do for you.

Most computer programs, SWiSHmax among them, are designed to give you an opportunity to customize the layout of the program. In SWiSHmax, not only can you use a number of default toolbars; you can customize the toolbars with additional commands and remove items from the existing toolbars.

There are also many default keystroke command combinations in SWiSHmax, and you can customize the commands.

As you learn in this chapter, you can reconfigure the arrangement, size, and grouping of the panels in SWiSHmax. In the Timeline, you can choose optional methods of displaying the frames in your movie.

Menus

The top section of the program window contains the menu items and toolbars. Menus in SWiSHmax work just as menus work in other Windows-based programs. To use the menu bar, move the mouse over a menu title and click to display the menu items in a list. Move your mouse over the list, and click when the pointer highlights the item you want to choose. The menu closes, applying the menu item's effect.

Tip   If you look at the Status bar (the horizontal border at the bottom of the program window), you see a small description of the command your mouse pointer is highlighting.

If there is an arrow to the right of the menu item's name, when you pause the pointer over the item another menu appears. Move your mouse over the list and click the item you want to choose. In some cases, items in the submenu have arrows to the right of their names, indicating another submenu. If a menu item is grayed-out it means that item is inactive. Not all commands can be applied to all objects. In many cases, you must select an object to activate menu commands.

Cross-Reference See Appendix C for a detailed description of the commands used in SWiSHmax.

The File menu

Use the commands in the File menu, shown in Figure 2-1, for managing the files you work with in SWiSHmax. Use the menu's commands for creating new movies, managing existing movies, and importing and exporting objects and movies.

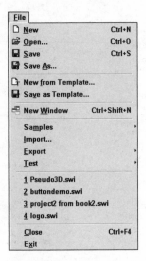

Figure 2-1: Choose commands from the File menu for creating, managing, and exporting objects and movies.

There are several ways to begin a new movie. You can choose commands to start with a blank movie, or you can create a new one based on a preconfigured template. To help you on your way, the File menu contains a list of sample movies you can load into the program to see how different features of the program work. You can also use a New Window command to open two or more copies of the SWiSHmax program window, which is handy if you want to copy material from one movie into another.

You can save a file in a number of ways as well. For example, you can save the file in a specific location on your hard drive and then save it with another name or in another location. You can also save a file you created as a template that can be reused.

Also in the File menu are several commands for testing your movie. You can view a report describing the movie's contents or test the movie in a Web browser or Flash player. Once you are satisfied with how your movie works, there are a number of ways you can export your finished movie, ranging from a SWF (Shockwave Flash) movie to a Web page, to a video, or as an executable, stand-alone player file.

The File menu also contains commands for closing the currently displayed movie and for closing the program itself.

You may see a list of file names prefaced by numbers (1, 2, 3, and so on) if you have opened files in SWiSHmax previously. These files are the last files you worked with in the program; click a name to reopen the SWI file without having to locate it on your computer.

Caution   If you move a file after saving it and try to open it by clicking it from the list at the bottom of the File menu, the program will not be able to find it. You will have to open it using the File ⇨ Open command.

The Edit menu

The Edit menu contains commands for making changes to a movie and its components. As you can see in Figure 2-2, the commands range from ways to view objects in your movie to viewing object properties. You will notice in the figure that some of the commands are grayed-out. This occurs for three reasons:

✦ **Some commands are not active unless an object is selected in your movie.** For example, you can't click any of the Hide or Lock commands unless an object in a scene is selected.

✦ **Sometimes a specific type of object must be selected.** For example, you can't click the Expand Object command unless the selected object is a grouped object.

✦ **Some commands aren't active until another command is applied.** For example, unless you have copied an object or effect, the Paste commands aren't available for use.

Figure 2-2: The Edit commands are used to make changes to a movie and its components.

The Edit menu contains a number of common Windows program commands such as Cut, Copy, Paste, Select, and Find although there are some variations in the commands particular to the scenes and objects you use in SWiSHmax. You also find in the Edit menu two handy commands — Redo and Undo.

The Track as Menu command is used to define how a button added to your movie behaves; the Make Instance command is used to create a duplicate of a nested Timeline known as a sprite.

A collection of commands is available for hiding, showing, and locking objects in the movie. There is also a group of commands used for viewing the contents of a variety of objects. You can even choose a command that displays an object's properties and a command that opens the program's Preferences.

The View menu

The View menu includes commands for changing how you see the movie and its components. You can choose commands for showing and hiding items and tools used for working with objects' locations on the Layout window's stage, as shown in Figure 2-3.

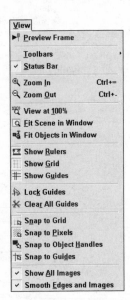

Figure 2-3: You can choose from a range of commands for viewing your movie and its components.

You can select from the set of five toolbars included with SWiSHmax, or you can use the choices in the View menu to create your own. There are many commands that toggle or turn on and off. The state of the command remains based on your previous selection. For example, if you click View ➪ Toolbars ➪ Grouping and the check mark appears to the left of the Grouping toolbar's label on the menu, the toolbar is visible in the program. In order to turn the toolbar off, click View ➪ Toolbars ➪ Grouping again. This time, the check mark to the left of the toolbar's name disappears, and the toolbar is no longer visible in the program.

From the View menu, you can select from numerous commands to display the contents of your movie at different magnifications and using different display settings. Also in the View menu, you can choose from several commands that assist you in the layout of a movie's elements such as rulers and guides. Snapping is another layout assistance method that automatically moves, or snaps, an object to a specified object or location. There are four snapping options in the View menu.

Two default commands for viewing a movie's content are found in the View menu. These include a command to show or hide images and one to smooth the edges of drawn objects and images.

The Insert menu

The Insert menu includes commands used to add a variety of objects to your movie project, as shown in Figure 2-4. You can choose from eight commands used for inserting new elements into your movie ranging from scenes to images to sounds.

Figure 2-4: Add different types of objects, effects, and scripts to your movie using the Insert menu commands.

The largest collections of commands in SWiSHmax are the effects. You can choose an effect from the Insert ➪ Effect menu command. The commands are divided into categories and appear in a cascading menu arrangement.

The key to an interactive movie is the use of scripts. The SWiSHmax Insert menu contains a number of categories of scripts used in your movies, as well as a set of commands used to insert and remove blocks of time, either frames or seconds, from the Timeline.

The Modify menu

The Modify menu includes commands used to change the properties of different types of objects in your movie, such as text, images, and groups of objects. As shown in Figure 2-5, the Modify menu is divided into several groups of commands based on their functions.

Figure 2-5: Use Modify menu commands to change properties of objects in your movie.

The four grouping commands are used to combine a number of objects into a single object that is then used for a variety of purposes; click Ungroup to reverse any grouping command. The Modify menu allows you to change selected objects into interactive buttons or sprites. You can choose from one of three Break Apart commands that break text and other objects into a variety of segments.

When you are using multiple objects in your movie you can control the visibility of each object in reference to the other objects using the Order commands.

The Modify menu also offers Transform commands that enable you to rotate or flip objects in your movie in a number of ways, Align commands to align objects vertically and horizontally on the stage, the Distribute commands to space objects on the stage in a number of ways, and the Make Same command to create consistently sized objects.

The Modify commands also include a number of commands applicable to text: six commands to align blocks of text in different ways, commands to make text bold or italic, and four commands that determine how the text in a text box flows. The final group of text commands applies different font types to the selected text in your movie.

The Control menu

The Control menu lists commands that you can use to play and preview the movie's Timeline, as shown in Figure 2-6.

Figure 2-6: You can view your movie using Control commands.

The Control menu commands (as well as the Control toolbar buttons) are analogous to a device controller like that on your CD player or VCR. Along with the usual commands such as Play, Stop, Rewind, and Fast Forward (called Cue to End in SWiSHmax), you can choose commands that apply to specific components of your movie. For example, you can play an entire movie, a single Timeline, an effect, or a single frame.

Note On the Control toolbar, the Cue to End command is referred to as the Go to End command.

The Tools menu

The Tools menu has only three selections, as you can see in Figure 2-7. Use these commands to customize the way the program appears and to customize the commands on the menus and toolbars. You can also assign Accelerator (shortcut) keys.

Figure 2-7: Use the commands in the Tools menu to change how you interact with SWiSHmax.

The Panels menu

The Panels menu includes a complete list of the panels used in SWiSHmax. The default display of panels includes the Timeline, which shows your movie's content over time; the Outline panel, which lists the components of the movie; the Layout panel, which shows you the movie's stage; and the Scripts panel, which is used to add interactivity to your movie. The remaining panels are combined in a group at the right-lower side of the program window.

All the panels are toggled; that is, when a panel is visible on the screen, you see a check mark next to the name in the menu. In Figure 2-8, all the panels are toggled to On. To close a panel, select the Panels menu item from the menu list and then click the panel name on the menu to deselect it. By default, all the program's panels are displayed in the program window.

Figure 2-8: The program's panels are toggled on and off in the Panels menu.

The Help menu

In the Help menu, you find a collection of commands that you can use to learn to use SWiSHmax, find online information and updates, and learn about program components (see Figure 2-9).

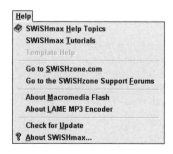

Figure 2-9: You can learn about the program using the Help menu's commands.

Two key commands in the Help menu are the SWiSHmax Help Topics command, which opens the Help files, and the SWiSHmax Tutorials command, which opens a set of tutorials. Other commands in the Help menu provide information on some of the program's component technology, such as its MP3 encoder and Flash player. There are also a number of commands you can choose to find information online at SWiSHzone.com and its support network. You learn more about finding Help later in the chapter.

Different Ways to Access Commands

One thing you notice as you look through the menus is that some of the commands appear with icons next to the command name. In Figure 2-10, the Insert menu is displayed as an example. Each of the top six commands includes an icon to the left of the command name. If you look to the right of the menu in the figure, you see the same icons on a toolbar. As you learn in the section, Working with Toolbars, SWiSHmax contains a number of toolbars you can use instead of menu items to apply commands to your movie.

Figure 2-10: Some of the menu commands are also available on toolbars.

Look again at Figure 2-10. You can see some commands, such as Insert Frame(s), are followed by a keystroke combination. You can apply the command by using keystrokes rather than by opening the menu and clicking the command.

Tip   Pay attention to the keystroke shortcuts for different commands and try them out. As your skill develops, so does the speed at which you can create your masterpieces by using keystrokes instead of clicking menus or toolbar buttons.

Look one more time at Figure 2-10. Notice that a letter is underlined in the menu heading "Insert" and also the commands listed under the menu have an underlined letter. Instead of using the programmed or default Accelerator keys, you can work with other keystrokes to access nearly all the commands in the program. The key is the Alt key on your keyboard. Press Alt+I, for example, and the Insert menu appears. Then press Alt+T and a new text item is added to your movie.

Cross-Reference   Appendix C includes the default list of SWiSHmax keyboard shortcuts.

Working with Toolbars

If you remember things visually and respond to visual cues, using toolbars may be a good option for you. Figure 2-11 shows the five toolbars available in SWiSHmax. They are arranged in the same order as that listed in the View ➪ Toolbars command. The toolbars are separated slightly on the program window so you can see the contents of each more clearly.

Figure 2-11: Use the toolbars to apply many common commands in the program.

To open a toolbar, click View ➪ Toolbars and select the toolbar. Toolbars that are already displayed have a check mark next to their names in the menu. To close a toolbar, click View ➪ Toolbars and deselect the toolbar by clicking its check mark. You can also drag the toolbar from the toolbar docking area into the program window, and it will float there. Click the vertical pair of lines at the left of a toolbar to drag it — otherwise you activate a command. When the toolbar floats, an X appears in the upper-right corner; click the X to close the toolbar.

To use a toolbar icon, move your mouse over the icon and click. In Figure 2-12, the Break into Letters icon is under the mouse pointer, as indicated by the visible tooltip. The status bar at the bottom of the program window displays a longer explanation of the tool. In the example, the tooltip reads Break into Letters. At the bottom of the window, the status bar message reads, "Breaks each selected text object to separate letters."

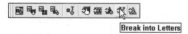

Figure 2-12: You can find the name and function of icons on the toolbars.

SWiSHmax contains five toolbars. They are Standard, Insert, Control, Grouping, and Export.

The Standard toolbar. This toolbar contains common commands you work with when building a movie project such as creating, opening, and saving movies. Use the Find icon to search for text, and delete or copy and paste selected content. The toolbar includes the Undo and Redo commands as well as the four commands used to move an object's position in the stacking order of a scene.

The Insert toolbar. You can quickly add different objects to your movie using commands from the Insert toolbar. The options include adding a scene, text, image, button, sprite, or content.

The Control toolbar. The Control toolbar contains commands for controlling playback of the Timeline and includes commands for playback. It also includes specific commands for playing an effect or a selected frame as well as the entire movie.

The Grouping toolbar. The Grouping toolbar contains items from the Modify menu. You can choose from four different Grouping commands, change selected objects to buttons or sprites using Convert icons, or click a Break Apart icon to separate groups of objects or text or break a single object into segments.

The Export toolbar. Use the commands on the Export toolbar to test your movie in a player, a Web browser, or read its report. You can choose from five export options by clicking one of the export icons.

Understanding the Timeline

The Timeline represents your movie over time. Each division or frame of the Timeline represents a portion of a second of your movie based on the *frame rate*. The frame rate is how many frames of a movie play per second. The higher the frame rate, the smaller the divisions on the Timeline and the faster the animation plays. For example, if you use a frame rate of 30 fps (frames per second) each second is divided into 30 frames, each of which is $\frac{1}{30}$ of a second long. If you use a frame rate of 10 fps, one second is divided into 10 frames, each of which is $\frac{1}{10}$ of a second long.

Time is shown from left to right. The first frame on the Timeline corresponds with what is first seen in your movie. Each scene in a movie has its own Timeline. Each *sprite* in a movie also has its own Timeline. A sprite is a movie used within a larger scene or a larger movie. Each sprite has its own objects and effects.

Until you add an effect or action to the Timeline, its length is zero frames. Figure 2-13 shows the Timeline for a sample project. The Scene label is active; different features of the Timeline are identified on the figure.

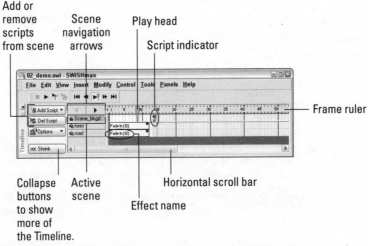

Figure 2-13: Use the Timeline to control your movie over time.

✦ **Scene navigation arrows.** Click these arrows to move between scenes. Scenes are assigned a location on the Timeline according to their order in the Outline panel. In the example, **Scene_bkgd** is the first scene added to the movie. Clicking the right arrow moves to the Timeline for **Scene_cars**, the second scene added to the movie.

Note

If your movie has only one scene, the navigation arrows are inactive.

✦ **Active scene.** The name of the scene currently active in the Timeline, **Scene_bkgd** in the figure, is indicated by the label's gray background in the Object panel. The scene is placed at the top row of the Timeline, and its objects are listed in subsequent rows. The Scene's row shows frame events and actions applied to the scene.

Tip

To activate an object or effect listed in the active scene on the Timeline, simply click the object or effect.

✦ **Add Script/Del Script buttons.** These buttons are used for adding to or removing scripts from a scene. When the scene's label is selected in the Timeline, the Script buttons are active.

Note

You don't add effects to a scene; only frame events and actions can be added to a scene.

✦ **Effect name.** Each effect added to an object is labeled; in addition, its duration is shown in brackets. In the example, the Fade In effect lasts for 12 frames.

✦ **Script indicator.** A script added to a scene displays an icon at the frame where it is placed. The script icons differ slightly according to their actions. The script indicator in the figure indicates that when the Timeline play head reaches frame 14, the movie jumps to another scene, as indicated by the arrow.

✦ **Play head.** The frame currently active in the movie is indicated by the red play head. The play head moves automatically when you play or move the controls.

✦ **Frame ruler.** The frame ruler is shown across the top of the Timeline and shows the frame numbers. If the option is selected, the ruler also shows markers for each second.

✦ **Shrink button.** Click the Shrink button to collapse and expand the buttons by displaying or hiding the buttons' labels. In the figure, the buttons are shown expanded; in the next figure they are collapsed.

✦ **Horizontal scrollbar.** Drag the scrollbar left and right to view the length of the Timeline when your movie is longer than the number of frames displayed in the Timeline panel.

Depending on the height of the Timeline panel and the number of objects in a scene, you may have a vertical scrollbar as well. It can be inconvenient to scroll up and down the rows of the Timeline. Instead, move your mouse cursor over the horizontal edge at the bottom of the Timeline and click and drag down to increase the amount of program space given to the Timeline. Of course, click and drag up to decrease the amount of space.

You can customize the appearance of the Timeline, as shown in Figure 2-14.

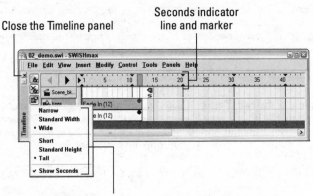

Close the Timeline panel

Seconds indicator line and marker

Options menu allows you to determine how the Timeline looks

Figure 2-14: You can modify the appearance of the Timeline.

✦ **Close Panel.** Click the small X in the upper-left of the Timeline to close the Timeline panel. To reopen it, click Panels ➪ Timeline.

✦ **Options.** Click the Options button to display the menu shown in Figure 2-15. You can choose several options:

- Choose a width for the Timeline frames; the figure shows the Wide option.

- Choose a height for the Timeline frames; the figure shows the Tall option.

- The Show Seconds option is selected.

✦ **Second divisions.** The second divisions are identified by a dark vertical stroke through the frames and arrows marking each second on the Frame ruler. They only appear when Show Seconds is selected as an option.

Figure 2-15: The Outline panel appears to the left of the program window by default.

Viewing and Managing your Movie's Elements

SWiSHmax uses default arrangements for the program's panels. The Outline panel is placed at the left of the program window, the Layout and Script panels are tabbed in the central part of the window, and the panels used to configure and modify the objects in your movie are tabbed as a group at the right side of the window.

The Outline panel

The Outline panel is at the left of the screen by default. You can expand and contract the width of the panel. Move your cursor over the right margin of the Outline panel. When the cursor changes to | |, click and drag it left to decrease the width of the Outline panel or to the right to increase the width.

The active scene in the movie is shown in bold text in the Outline view; the active element is highlighted. Other scenes are grayed out. As shown in Figure 2-15, **Scene_cars** is the active scene; the text element named **rock and roll** is the active element.

Each element in the Outline panel includes icons that indicate their visibility status as well as what type of element they are. In the figure, an eye icon appears to the left of some of the elements. This means the element is visible in the Layout panel. Those showing an eye with an X drawn through them are hidden from view in the Layout panel. The elements showing a yellow lock are visible, but locked into their current position in the Layout panel; you can apply some effects but you can't move the element. You can change from one visibility option to the next by clicking the icon. All elements are initially visible. Click once and the element is hidden. You can click again to lock the element and then click again to unlock it.

To the immediate right of the elements' visibility indicator are icons that identify the type of element. In the figure, the rock and roll element is text, indicated by the T icon. The remaining elements are graphic elements.

Some of the command icons are located at the top of the Outline panel. Click Insert to open a list of insertion options ranging from text to a soundtrack. The list is the same as that found in the Insert menu. If you click the red X to the right of the Insert drop-down menu label, the selected item is deleted from the project. In the figure, the rock and roll object is selected, so clicking the red X deletes the object.

The Outline panel displays the contents of a scene in a hierarchy. In the example, the red circle, called **Shape** in **Scene_cars**, is higher on the list than the other objects. The higher up the list (or stacking order) an element is placed, the closer the object is to the front of what you see in the Layout panel. You can move an element closer up or further down in the stacking order in several ways. You can select an element and drag it up or down on the list; or you can click the upward or downward arrows to move it.

Note   The Outline panel and Timeline show the same elements arranged in the same order. Moving an object in one area moves it in the other as well.

The Layout panel

The Layout and Script panels are tabbed together at the center of the screen with the Layout panel and Toolbox active by default. The name of the active scene is shown at the top of the panel. In Figure 2-16, the **Scene_cars** scene is active.

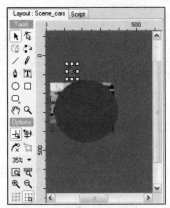

Figure 2-16: The Layout panel is tabbed with the Script panel.

Cross-Reference   Chapter 17 describes working with the Script panel.

The area that comprises your movie is called the stage. The entire space of the Layout panel (aside from the tools) is called the workspace. Rulers are shown around the stage horizontally and vertically. The rulers are hidden by default. You can display the rulers by clicking View ➪ Show Rulers.

The Toolbox, shown in Figure 2-16, is a part of the Layout panel; you can't separate it from the rest of the panel. Click to select a tool. The active tool is indicated by a gray rectangular button shape framing the tool's icon. The Select tool in the upper-left corner of the Toolbox is the active tool.

Move your mouse over the tools and a tooltip naming the tool appears. A short description of the tool also appears on the Status bar at the bottom of the program window. Not all tools are active at all times. Some tools are active only when a specific type of object is selected on the stage or a particular command is selected from the menus. For example, if you have a button object selected on the stage, you can't use some of the fill or transform tools. The tools in the Toolbox allow you to create motion paths, lines, curves, text, ellipses, rectangles, and preconfigured shapes (see Figure 2-17). You can also reshape, pan, zoom, scale objects, resize, rotate and skew, and more.

   Figure 2-17: You can choose from a variety of preconfigured AutoShapes.

Cross-Reference   You use the drawing tools and rulers in Chapter 5 when you learn to draw in SWiSHmax.

Depending on the size of the program window and the magnification of the stage, you may or may not see horizontal and vertical scrollbars on the Layout panel.

The grouped panels

The default program arrangement groups all the remaining panels at the right side of the program window. As shown in Figure 2-18, the tabs are distributed so you see the name of each panel. The active panel is shown with a gold bar above its name (the Text panel is active in the figure) and is also shown at the top of the panel grouping.

Figure 2-18: A number of panels are grouped together by default.

Continued

✦ Click the X to close a single docked panel (such as the Outline panel) or the group of panels on the right of the program window.

✦ You can tab the panels together. Double-click a docked panel to float it, and then drag it over the upper portion of the panel you want to dock it with. To switch from one of the tabbed panels to the other, click the panel's tab to display its contents.

✦ You can dock two panels vertically at the edge of the program window as shown in the figure. Double-click a docked panel to float it and drag it over the lower portion of the panel you want to dock it with. To switch from one of the docked panels to the other, click the Expand/Contract button.

As your skill working with SWiSHmax develops, notice how and where you move the mouse to perform different activities. You may find it easier to use some of these tips to speed up your work.

When you select an object in your movie, its associated panel is activated and displayed. The program panels that make up the default group are:

✦ **Align.** The Align panel lists options for aligning, distributing, and spacing selected elements on the stage.

✦ **Content.** The objects available in your project are sorted by type and listed in the Content panel.

✦ **Debug.** Use the Debug panel to evaluate and test your movie's scripts.

✦ **Export.** The Export panel displays options for testing and exporting your movies.

✦ **Guides.** The Guides panel is used to configure the guides, grids, snap to grid, and rulers used in the Layout panel.

✦ **Movie.** Define basic properties for the entire movie, such as the background color and frame rate in the Movie panel.

✦ **Scene.** The Scene panel shows options for the selected scene including color, events, and links.

✦ **Tint.** On the Tint panel, you can adjust the color and alpha settings for a selected object that includes color transformation.

✦ **Transform.** The Transform panel displays ways a selected object can be modified, such as the position, height and width, rotation, or skew.

Customizing the Toolbars

Sometimes it is convenient to make changes to the layout of the program according to how you work. In SWiSHmax you can customize the program interface to tailor it to your liking. The most common change is adding or removing icons from the toolbars. For example, if you work with Accelerator keys a lot, you don't need some of the icons on the Standard toolbar. Here's how to change the contents of a toolbar:

1. **Click View ⇨ Toolbars, and select the toolbar you want to modify.**

2. **Click Tools ⇨ Customize to open the Customize dialog box.** Click Toolbars to display the Toolbars tab. The visible toolbars in the program window are checked in the Toolbars list.

3. **Click the name of the toolbar you want to change in the Toolbars list to select it.**

4. **Click an icon on the toolbar that you want to remove and drag it off the toolbar.** Release the mouse and the icon is gone.

5. **Continue removing icons, and then click Close to close the Customize dialog box.** Your custom toolbar is complete.

Note

To restore a single toolbar to its original configuration, click Reset in the Customize dialog box. To reset all toolbars, click Reset All in the Customize dialog box.

You can combine content from different toolbars as well. Follow these steps.

1. **Click View ⇨ Toolbars, and select the toolbar you want to modify.**

2. **Click Tools ⇨ Customize to open the Customize dialog box.** Click Toolbars to display the Toolbars tab. The visible toolbars in the program window are checked in the Toolbars list.

3. **Click the name of the toolbar you want to change in the Toolbars list to select it.**

4. **Click the Commands tab in the Customize dialog box, and then click the Category containing the command you want to add.**

5. **Click the item you want to add to the toolbar, and drag it to the toolbar.**

6. **When a vertical I-beam appears, drag your mouse pointer left or right until the I-beam is in the position where you want the icon added.**

7. **Release the mouse and the icon is added.**

Customizing Accelerator Keys

SWiSHmax refers to a shortcut key as an Accelerator. You can add custom Accelerator keyboard shortcuts to match the way you like to work. The program contains more than 30 preconfigured Accelerator keys that you can modify as well. For example, the SWiSHmax Accelerator key for Ungroup is Ctrl+U. If you are accustomed to working in illustration programs, you may be more comfortable changing the Accelerator key to Ctrl+Shift+G.

Cross-Reference   Appendix C contains a list of the default SWiSHmax Accelerator keys.

Follow these steps to customize an Accelerator key.

1. **Click Tools ➪ Customize to open the Customize dialog box.**

2. **Click Keyboard to display the options for creating Accelerator keys.**

3. **Click to select the command you want to receive the new Accelerator key.**

4. **Press the new Accelerator keys.**

5. **Click the Assign button, and the keystroke combination is assigned to the command.**

In Figure 2-19, the Lock command is selected in the Edit menu. The Current Keys field is blank, indicating there is no Accelerator (shortcut) key for the command. The new Accelerator key assigned to the command, Ctrl+L, is shown in the figure.

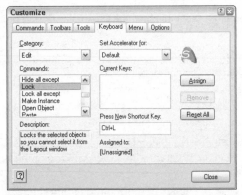

Figure 2-19: Create custom Accelerators in the Customize dialog box.

Use the Help Keyboard to keep track of the Accelerators. Click Tools ➪ Keyboard Map to open the Help Keyboard dialog box. Click the Category drop-down menu to display the list of menu items. The Edit category is shown in Figure 2-20. The menu item's commands are listed, as are keyboard accelerators and an explanation of the command. A custom command for the Lock command is selected in the figure.

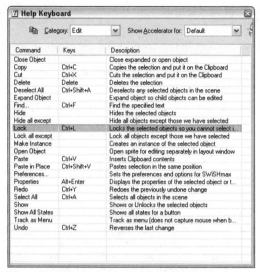

Figure 2-20: Check the Accelerator keys in the program from the Help Keyboard dialog box.

Customizing Menus

Click the Menu tab in the Customize dialog box. SWiSHmax includes both a default menu and a movie menu. To move or add commands to the menus, click the Commands tab in the Customize dialog box, and drag commands to the menus or drag them off the menus.

You can also customize context menus, such as the menu named My Menu shown in Figure 2-21. Choose a context menu from the list (the defaults are —— or none, and My Menu). Click the Commands tab in the Customize dialog box, and drag commands to the menus or drag them off the menus. Like other customizations, click Reset to remove the changes you have made.

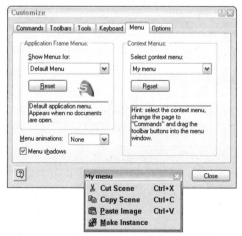

Figure 2-21: Reconfigure menus according to how you like to work.

The Help Files

You can access the Help files in several ways. Click the Help button on the Standard toolbar, click Help ➪ SWiSHmax Help Topics, or press F1 on the keyboard. The SWiSHmax Help files are arranged under several tabs. Figure 2-22 shows the Contents tab of the Help menu as well as a file. There are a number of features shown in the figure.

The Help files' contents are arranged in a set of books. Click a closed book to display a selection of subheadings, click a subheading to display further headings or topics, and so on. In the figure, the User Interface book is clicked in the Contents tab; the contents appear in the right pane of the Help window.

Tip   Text that is in blue and underlined provides links to other material in the Help files; links that you have already visited are shown in maroon.

You can navigate through the contents of the Help files using the links at the top of the Contents window. Click Top to return to the first level of the section you are reading, Next to go to the next item in the Help files, and Previous to return to the item you viewed previously. You can also navigate through the Help files using the menu at the top of the SWiSHmax Help window. The icons are self-explanatory. Click Hide to collapse the Contents listing. The buttons are listed again in the Options drop-down menu.

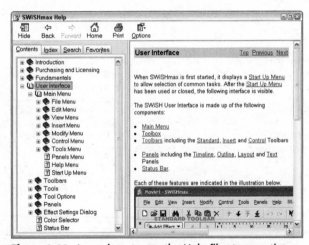

Figure 2-22: Learn how to use the Help files to save time.

If you don't understand how the contents of the Help files are arranged in the Contents menu or you are unsure which book contains the topic you are looking for, you can use other options to find the information you need.

Click Index and type the term to find information based on keywords indexed from the Help files. If you aren't sure of the keywords used in the program, click the Search tab, type some search words, and then click List Topics to list the closest matches to your query.

Once you find information you can save its location. With the topic you want to refer to in the Contents window, click the Favorites tab, and then click Add at the bottom of the dialog box. Next time you need to refer to a page, you can select it from your Favorites list rather than searching through the other tabs.

SWiSHmax has a number of very valuable tutorials included in the Help files. If you already have the Help files open, scroll down the Contents menu and click Tutorials to open the list. If you are working in the program, click Help ➪ SWiSHmax Tutorials to open the Help files and display the Tutorial listing in the Contents pane automatically.

There are several types of tutorials. For example, you can learn how to use the program's basic functions in a series of tutorials called Creating Your First SWiSH Movie. Learn how to make animated buttons, how to work with different types of scripts in the Scripting Tutorials, or learn to use SWiSHmax with other programs.

Summary

This chapter took you on a guided tour through SWiSHmax and showed you how to work with the program's interface. You learned the following:

✦ How the SWiSHmax program window is organized.

✦ What goes into the toolbars and menus.

✦ How to work in the Timeline and how to configure its layout.

✦ How to use and modify the default panel layout.

✦ How to modify the interface using custom toolbar and menu arrangements.

✦ How to use the different Help features.

✦   ✦   ✦

Starting a New Movie Project

"**I**f you build it, they will come." There is some truth to this old quote in some cases, but it doesn't cut it when it comes to designing Flash movies and interfaces. You need to know what *it* is and who *they* are. Learning to use a program like SWiSHmax that creates effects at the click of a button isn't that difficult. However, using the tools to produce creative output designed appropriately requires skill and knowledge.

This chapter briefly takes you through some design and planning issues. You will learn how to define what you will include in a movie, based on the audience you are working with. You see how to choose design elements.

You also learn how to transfer your ideas into an actual plan for the movie. Once you have a design idea in mind, you can start a new movie from scratch, or use one of the templates provided, as you will see. You can also use your own designs as templates you can reuse.

Why are you Building a Movie?

The first step in designing a movie is deciding why you are doing it at all. For those who are learning to use SWiSHmax for the first time, the obvious reason you are building a movie is to learn how to do it. But beyond the obvious are reasons that you should consider as you develop your expertise and build movies for both fun and profit.

Consider two general scenarios, both of which you are likely to experience. The first is an advertising movie; the second is a Web site interface. The stated purpose of any advertising piece should be short, direct, and to the point. If you put together a clear purpose, it can serve as a ready-made slogan in some instances, or at least a simple thought that guides you as you work on the rest of the design process.

Defining a purpose for your project

There are dozens of reasons to build a movie — anything from simply making a movie to jazz up your personal Web site to explaining services provided by a nonprofit organization to establishing a presence for you or your company.

Make sure you know what your purpose is when beginning to build a movie. Otherwise, it's difficult to make concrete decisions about what you are designing. Visitors to your Web site need to know what you are doing online — that is, are you selling something, providing information on some topic or area of interest, or are you a nonprofit organization?

Defining the purpose of a movie, regardless of its scope, identifies what you plan to accomplish. Here are a couple of examples.

Urbanize. This advertising example is for an online furniture company. The company specializes in funky, lower-priced items. The purpose of the ad is to announce a sale on chairs. A frame of the movie is shown in Figure 3-1.

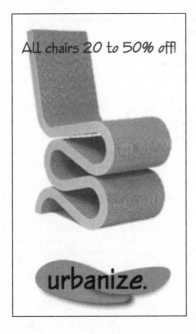

Figure 3-1: An ad for a furniture store catering to young people with a lot of style but not a lot of money needs a specific look.

Bluebell Workshop. This example Web site sells handmade high-end toys and gifts that appeal to young girls (Figure 3-2). The products include dolls and plush toys. The site's purpose is to describe its products and how they are crafted and to provide contact information for prospective clients.

On The Web Site

The *Urbanize.* project files are available from the book's Web site in the chapter03 folder, in the subfolder named ch03_sample01. The files include the images, SWI file, backup file, and the SWF movie. An image of the interface for the Bluebell Workshop movie is also available from the book's Web site in the chapter03 folder. The file is named ch03_bluebellworkshop.png.

Figure 3-2: A Web site interface for a specialty doll company also needs a specific look.

Defining an audience for your movie

The science of describing populations and groups is called *demographics*. There are many ways to categorize people demographically. Consider yourself for a moment. How could you be described? Some of the description is quite obvious, such as your age range, level of education, physical characteristics, career or field of study, where you live, and so on. That is just the tip of the demographic iceberg. Other ways to categorize an audience are based on lifestyle analysis, or *psychographics*, and consider how people live, what interests them, and what they like such as hobbies, sports, and other leisure activities.

You may have a sense that there are almost limitless ways to define an audience, and you would be right. You can define an audience in extremely general terms, which isn't very useful. For example, if you are selling men's clothing, you have about a 50 percent chance that everyone visiting your site is going to be male, but that certainly doesn't mean they are interested in your products. By defining the type of person who buys your product, your chance of success increases dramatically.

If your site sells clothing specifically for tall men and sells very high-end and expensive leisure and sports clothing products, your audience is much more clearly defined. Some types of information are irrelevant. Does it really matter if the man you are targeting has two children or none? Not really. In addition to his stature, what is relevant are his income and interests. He must be able to afford your products as well as have a need for some of your specialty products. It's difficult to sell a motorcycle jacket to someone without a motorcycle.

Of course, there are always exceptions to every rule and people who are attracted to a site and its message or product that don't strictly fall within the defined audience.

Note A part of defining an audience includes understanding the level of technology your viewers are likely to use, which is explained later in the chapter.

For both of the sample movies mentioned in the previous section, the audiences are very different. The Urbanize. furniture store sells funky, attractive, lower-priced home items online. Its audience most likely is composed of viewers who are young adults, both male and female; are people who have recently left college or are starting employment in their chosen careers; have limited disposable income; have a sense of style; and live in urban settings or are interested in an urban lifestyle.

The Bluebell Workshop, on the other hand, has a Web site designed to promote its range of handmade high-end toys designed for young girls. The site has two markets. The young girls who would enjoy their products are known as the *primary market*; the adults (parents and grandparents, for example) who purchase the products are known as the *secondary market*. The primary viewer is most likely a young girl in the 6- to 12-year age range who has an interest in toys such as plush unicorns and china dolls. The secondary viewer is most likely a married adult with a higher-than-average disposable income and a higher-than-average education. Can you see how the audiences are characterized? A furniture store that sells interesting, urban-oriented products is going to appeal to younger person with style sense, but who doesn't have the income to buy expensive designer products. On the other hand, a site that sells high-end children's toys is going to appeal to a group with much more disposable income.

Technical considerations

Another important planning element is determining how your movie fits in with the rest of a Web page or a Web site. There are a number of factors to consider ensuring the movie you build reaches your intended audience, including:

✦ How long a viewer waits to see your movie

✦ The screen resolution the average viewer will be using

✦ Whether the movie is intended only for a Web audience

✦ Whether it can be delivered on a CD or downloaded for playback offline

 Cross-Reference Chapter 20 discusses export planning issues; Chapter 22 covers exporting movies.

Making Design Choices

When you imagine the name of a product or an idea or the subject of a movie, what colors come to mind? How do you envision the movies are laid out and animated? How do their respective logos look? What about the text? You want to make design choices that enhance the message of your movie or site.

Design is based on elements and principles. This book isn't the place for a long, theoretical discussion, but here are some brief ideas. As you read through the list, consider how each concept can be applied to a movie.

✦ **Lines.** A line is a linear mark that varies in appearance.

✦ **Shapes.** A shape is a defined geometric or organic form.

✦ **Direction.** Elements in a composition use one of three directions — horizontal, vertical, or oblique. Vertical direction suggests balance, formality, and alertness; oblique suggests movement and action; horizontal direction suggests calmness, stability, and tranquility. The connotation of lines applies to animation as well as to a static element.

Common color associations

Here are some colors and commonly associated characteristics to think about:

✦ **Black.** Power, elegance, formality, death, evil, mystery

✦ **Blue.** Stability, trust, loyalty, wisdom, confidence, intelligence, truth

✦ **Brown.** Earthy, stability, reliability

✦ **Green.** Growth, harmony, freshness, fertility, safety; dark green—money

✦ **Orange.** Enthusiasm, happiness, creativity, determination, success, stimulation

✦ **Purple.** Power, nobility, wealth, wisdom, dignity, creativity, mystery, magic

✦ **Red.** Vibrancy, energy, danger, strength, power, determination, passion

✦ **White.** Light, goodness, innocence, purity, safety, cleanliness

✦ **Yellow.** Joy, happiness, intellect, energy

✦ **Size.** In a composition, size refers to the relationship of one shape to another based on the amount of space each occupies.

✦ **Texture.** Texture describes the surface quality of an object, either tactile or visual.

✦ **Color.** Hue refers to the actual color of an object; value refers to the lightness or darkness of a color. Different colors have different references. Color provokes feelings and reactions although color associations or interpretations are not global. Different cultures may interpret color in entirely different ways.

Tip   Remember that design elements apply to text as well as to other graphic objects.

Translating Your Designs

When you have decided on the type of movie you want to build, the audience you are building it for, and considered the design aspects of your movie, it's time to translate your design into a movie.

Planning a movie on paper takes far less time than plunging into a big design project and deciding partway through that you should have planned the process differently. Of course, regardless of your best intentions, a plan is only a plan and is subject to change as you are working. Just as having a purpose helps to define your audience and the elements of your movie, having a plan helps to focus your actual design and construction process.

Planning occurs on several levels. The complexity of your movie project determines how much planning is required. For example, a simple ad doesn't require an organizational chart, while a site interface may or may not need extensive storyboarding. The Bluebell Workshop example discussed earlier in the chapter would likely need an organizational chart and process flowchart during its creation process. There are four main ways you can plan your project: an organizational chart, a process flowchart, a content object description, and a storyboard.

Organizational chart

An organizational chart, also called a *site chart* or *navigation flowchart*, describes the overall structure of the project. Use an organizational chart when the movie uses more than one layout. If your movie has one single component, such as a simple ad running on a single Timeline, there isn't anything to organize! On the other hand, if you are constructing an entire site, you need to chart the relationship of the different elements to keep track of the structure. If you are creating a simple Web site movie interface, the organizational chart may look something like Figure 3-3.

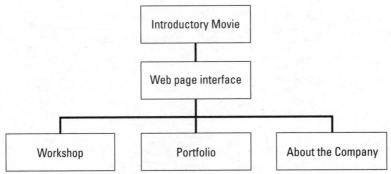

Figure 3-3: Construct an organizational chart for a Web site interface.

If you follow the hierarchy in the chart, you will see that there is an introductory movie that leads to the Web page interface. From that interface branch three subsections of the site where the viewer can learn about the company, its products, and how they are made.

Process flowchart

A process flowchart is an outline of the decision-making required of the viewer. Use it in any movie where the viewer has to make decisions, such as clicking a button or choosing an option. A Web site interface movie is interactive. That is, the movie's interface remains constant until the viewer interacts with it in some way by clicking a button, moving a mouse over an object, and so on. Chart how the viewer can interact with your movie and what happens as a result of an interaction in a process flow chart. Figure 3-4 shows a single decision-making process for a portion of the organizational chart shown in the previous figure.

Once viewers reach the Web site interface page, they are presented with three choices that lead to three subsequent pages, each having other options. The options available when viewers choose the Workshop link from the interface page are shown in the figure.

Content object description

A content object description is an information development term that refers to an outline of the components of the flowchart or organizational chart. Content objects are the building blocks of your movie. Each object can be described in terms of its format, purpose, and how it is used. There are many terms used to describe the same process depending on the industry or discipline. For example, the software industry describes the same process as a *functional specification* to explain how a piece of software works from the user's perspective.

If you are building a simple movie, the planning process is less complicated as there is no interaction between the movie and the viewer. Regardless of the complexity of a movie, you need a list of elements that are used to create the project. An example of a content object description is described in Table 3-1.

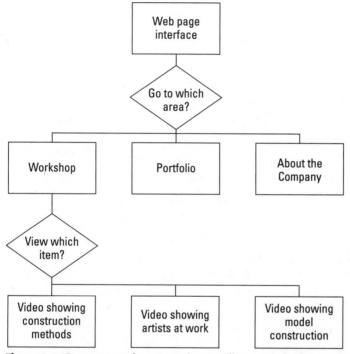

Figure 3-4: Demonstrate how your viewer will move through your site.

The description contains information about several aspects of the movie's content. These aspects, which correlate to the column headings in the table, are:

✦ **Name.** The name used for the object in your movie.

✦ **Type.** Define the type of object you are using in the movie. You can also specify where the object is created.

✦ **Description.** Describe what the object does in the movie.

✦ **Use.** Identify why you are including the object in the movie.

Note The content object description included in Table 3-1 is an example of one method you can use to define what makes up a movie.

Table 3-1: Sample Content Object Description

Name	Type	Description	Use*
bkgd	SWiSHmax graphic	Background for the animated furniture	Focus the viewer's attention
chair01	Imported PNG image	First animated chair in ad	Show viewer sample of sale items
chair02	Imported PNG image	Second animated chair in ad	Show viewer sample of sale items
chair03	Imported PNG image	Third animated chair in ad	Show viewer sample of sale items
slogan	SWiSHmax text	"Put your bum in our chairs" text animation	Caption for ad
msg01	SWiSHmax text	"All chairs 20-50% off" text animation	Sales info message
logo01	Imported PNG image	Urbanize. logo graphic and text for animating	Company branding

* It may seem like overkill to include a column stating the use of an object, but if you can't describe how it is used in the movie, do you need to use it at all?

Storyboarding

A storyboard is a series of illustrations that represent a process such as development of an animation. Use a storyboard to show how a movie looks over time. The term *storyboard* was originally used to describe a set of drawings representing the flow of a cartoon or movie; the term has made the transition to digital design of all types. While it isn't a requirement to storyboard a project, it is a good work habit to develop.

Sketches for a storyboard don't have to be elaborate, as you can see in Figure 3-5. The point is to identify how the elements of the movie appear on the stage and the time you need to develop the animation. It takes a few minutes to quickly scribble a simple plan; it can take hours trying to organize and animate a group of elements when you have no idea how the movie should look and progress.

Pre-Start Checklist

You may have considered how and why you want to build a movie. Before you start, take a few minutes and organize the content you want to use. Preplanning can save time and confusion. Here are some ideas to consider:

Reusing material

Use and reuse material when possible to save time. If you are repurposing material for a number of different types of media, such as a Web page, brochure, and a Flash movie, look at the common features. For example, you might find that images used on a Web site are perfect for your movie project, or you may be able to import a block of text from a brochure that saves time when you are working in SWiSHmax as you don't have to rekey the text. An example is shown in Figure 3-6; rather than rekeying an entire block of text, it is imported as a single text object.

Cross-Reference   You learn about text in Chapter 10.

Rough storyboard for Urbanize. skyscraper ad   @ 10 fps.

Figure 3-5: Use a storyboard to lay out the elements of the movie over time.

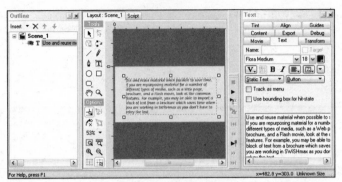

Figure 3-6: Consider whether you have objects such as text that can be reused in a movie to save time.

Assembling the content

Try to assemble all of the content in one location. This idea is especially important if you are reusing material. For the most part, files you work with in SWiSHmax are quite small, and because hard drive space is easy to come by, make copies of text, images, logos, and so on, and put them in the same source folder.

Renaming files

You should rename files to keep track of your media. In Table 3-1, a sample content object description was presented. Use a naming system such as the one in that example or another system that is meaningful to you. For a more complex project, consider using levels of naming. For example, if you have three scenes, each using two video files, you could use the scene number and the video number for each file, such as scene01_video01 and scene03_video02. If you plan to use scene names, consider naming the files something like work_video01 and work_video02.

Cross-
Reference   Learn more about organizing movie content and naming in Chapter 4.

The particular naming conventions you use aren't the important factor; it is much more important that the names are representative of your material and that you can identify the media by looking at the file name.

Configuring content for compliance

Always make sure to configure content to comply with SWiSHmax's allowable formats. It is often easier to work in batches than to perform one task at a time. While you are assembling and possibly renaming your project files, pay attention to the file formats. If necessary, open the files that aren't usable in SWiSHmax in their source programs and convert them to a suitable format. If you check the file formats in advance, your thoughts aren't disrupted when you are working in SWiSHmax and need to import another file, only to realize you have to convert its format first.

Cross-Reference You learn about importing graphic objects in Chapter 8, importing animations and Flash movies in Chapter 9, importing text objects in Chapter 10, and importing sound objects in Chapter 11.

Importing and building graphics

Decide when you should import graphics and when they can be built in SWiSHmax. Sometimes it is much more convenient to draw a simple graphic shape in SWiSHmax than to create it in another program, save a file, and then import it. Not only does it save time, but the SWiSHmax files that are created are smaller than art that is imported. Of course, if you are reusing material such as simple drawn shapes from other sources, it makes little sense to take the time to redraw them in SWiSHmax.

There are differences between shapes drawn in SWiSHmax and those you import. Look at the Flash movie shown in Figure 3-7. From left to right, the shapes are a GIF file, a JPG file, a PNG file, and a shape drawn in SWiSHmax. While both the GIF and PNG formats provide transparency (you don't see any background to the image like in the JPG image), only the shape drawn in SWiSHmax has smooth edges all around the shape. Imported images are raster images, while those you build within SWiSHmax are vector-based images.

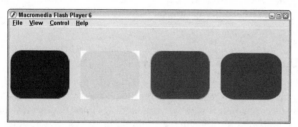

Figure 3-7: Drawing shapes in SWiSHmax may produce better quality images.

Sometimes it is necessary to experiment to determine whether to use an imported image or create one in SWiSHmax.

Cross-Reference Learn about working with shapes in Chapter 5.

Starting a SWiSHmax Movie

There are several ways to start a new SWiSHmax movie. From your desktop, click Start ➪ Programs ➪ SWiSHmax to open the program. The startup menu window shown in Figure 3-8 appears and asks you what you want to do. You can choose to:

✦ Start a new empty movie

✦ Start a new movie using a template

✦ Work on an existing movie

✦ Work on the last movie you opened

Note   When you install SWiSHmax, a shortcut icon is placed on your desktop. You can double-click the icon to open the program rather than selecting it from the Program menu.

Figure 3-8: Select one of four options for starting a new SWiSHmax movie.

Starting a new empty movie

The preconfigured templates provided with the program may not provide the movie characteristics you want to use or, you may not be sure of the size of movie you want to create. In these circumstances, select the new empty movie option. To start a new movie using the default program settings, click Start a new empty movie from the What do you want to do? dialog box. The dialog box closes, the previous settings used in the program appear, and the Movie panel is active.

Starting a new movie from a template

SWiSHmax contains a selection of preconfigured templates you can use to create a movie. SWiSHmax installs a set of templates with the rest of the program installation. The templates are located in the SWITemplates folder, which is within the main SWiSHmax folder on your hard drive. Follow these steps to start a new movie using a template:

1. **From your desktop, click Start ⇨ Programs ⇨ SWiSHmax to open the program.** The What do you want to do? dialog box appears.

2. **Click Start a new movie from a template.** The dialog box closes, and the Select Template dialog box opens (Figure 3-9).

3. **Click the name of the template you want to use in the list to select it.** The template names include a brief description, such as skyscraper or banner, as well as the movie's dimensions in pixels. The size is always written as the width x height, such as 468 x 60 for a full banner.

4. **Click the Show Preview option at the bottom of the dialog box to see a preview of the selected template.**

5. **Click Open.** The Show Preview dialog box closes, and the template loads into the program.

Note   You can cancel the template choice. Instead of selecting a template from the list, click Cancel on the Show Preview dialog box. The dialog box closes, and a new default movie is loaded into the program.

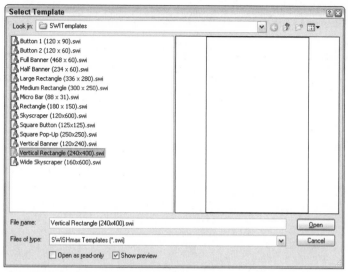

Figure 3-9: Select a template for your movie from the preinstalled list.

Work on an existing movie

You can select any of the SWiSHmax movies you have worked with previously. Follow these steps to locate existing movie files:

1. **From your desktop, click Start ⇨ Programs ⇨ SWiSHmax to open the program.** The What do you want to do? startup menu dialog box appears.

2. **Click Work on an existing movie.** The dialog box closes, and the Open dialog box opens, showing the last folder that was opened in SWiSHmax.

3. **Click the Look In drop-down arrow to display the contents of your hard drive as shown in Figure 3-10.** Browse to the folder containing the SWI file you want to work with and click it. The folder's contents appear in the Open dialog box.

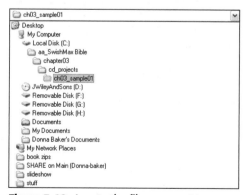

Figure 3-10: Locate the file you want to use on your hard drive.

Tip   The only files you see displayed in the dialog box are SWI files. All other file types are hidden.

4. **Click the SWI file you want to work with.**

5. **Click Preview at the bottom of the dialog box.** The preview of your movie runs in the dialog box as shown in Figure 3-11.

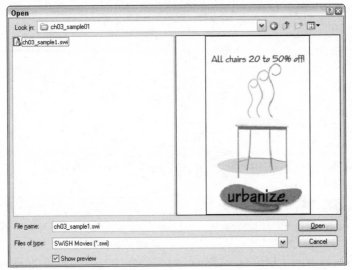

Figure 3-11: Preview your selected movie before opening it in the program.

6. **Click Open to open the file in SWiSHmax and close the Open dialog box.**

Work on the last movie you opened

You can resume working with the movie you used in your last SWiSHmax session. To open the most recent movie you worked on, simply click Work on the last movie you opened in the What do you want to do? dialog box. The dialog box closes, and the SWI movie file opens in SWiSHmax. The most recent settings used in the program appear.

Controlling how the program starts

Using the What do you want to do? startup menu dialog box is a quick and simple way to start working in SWiSHmax. You may prefer to hide the prompt dialog box from view — some people prefer to use menu items, toolbar buttons, or accelerator keys.

To hide the dialog box, click the Show this prompt at startup check box at the bottom of the dialog box to deselect it. The next time you open the program, the dialog box is hidden.

The menu items and toolbar buttons or accelerator keys you can use to start working in SWiSHmax are listed in Table 3-2. The toolbar buttons are all found on the Standard toolbar, which you can open by clicking View ➪ Toolbars ➪ Standard.

Table 3-2: Startup Options

Startup menu option	Menu choices	Toolbar button	Accelerator keys
Start a new empty movie	Click File ➪ New		Ctrl+N
Start a new movie from a template	Click File ➪ New from Template	No toolbar button available on default toolbar	No default shortcut
Work on an existing movie	Click File ➪ Open		Ctrl+O
Work on the last movie you opened	Choose from the listed previously opened files in the File menu*	No toolbar button available	No default shortcut

*If the file listed in the File menu has been moved to a different location on your hard drive since the last time you used it, the Open dialog box appears and you must locate the file again.

What if you change your mind and prefer to see the startup menu again? Follow these steps:

1. **Click Edit ➪ Preferences, or click Tools ➪ Preferences.** The Preferences dialog box opens.

2. **On the General tab, click Show startup menu in the Startup options area on the tab (shown in Figure 3-12).**

3. **Click OK to close the dialog box.** The next time you open the program the What do you want to do? dialog box opens.

Saving your Movie Project Files

You can save a movie at any time. Once you start a new movie, take a few seconds and save it. Also, as you continue working, save the file every few minutes and whenever you have made significant changes, such as adding effects or scripts to your movie.

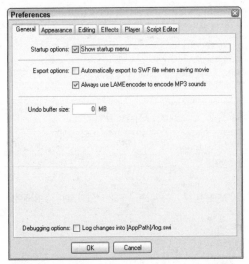

Figure 3-12: Reset the preference to display the startup menu again.

The method you use to save a file depends on its status. Follow these steps for saving a new file:

1. **Click File ⇨ Save to save a new file.** The Save As dialog box opens. The file is named Movie1.swi by default as shown in Figure 3-13. Although you click the File ⇨ Save command, the Save As dialog box opened because you haven't named the file previously.

Figure 3-13: New files are saved in the Save As dialog box.

2. **Click the Save in drop-down arrow.** Locate the folder you want to use to store the file.

3. **Click the folder's name to select it.** The folder opens in the Save As dialog box.

4. **Type the name of the file in the File name field.**

5. **Click Save to save the file.** The dialog box closes, and you return to the program. The name of the file appears at the top of the program window.

Alternatively, you can save a file by clicking the Save button on the Standard toolbar. As described in the previous steps, the Save As dialog box opens if the file is new. Once a movie has been saved, the next time you click File ➪ Save (or click the toolbar button) the movie is automatically saved, and no dialog box appears.

You can resave a movie using a new name or a different storage location on your hard drive at any time. To alter the name or location of a saved file, click File ➪ Save As to open the Save As dialog box. Locate the folder you want to use for storage and/or type a new name for the file in the File name field, and then click Save.

A good reason to save a file is for reuse as a template. You may find yourself working on a series of similar movies or configuring the layout of a movie to meet specific requirements. Instead of trying to remember or guessing (and guessing incorrectly!) what the settings were, save the movie file as a template.

The files you save as templates can be used like all other SWiSHmax templates. Follow these steps to save a file as a template:

1. **Click File ➪ Save As Template.** The Save Template dialog box opens and the contents of the SWITemplates folder appears, shown in Figure 3-14.

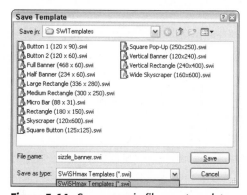

Figure 3-14: Save a movie file as a template.

> **Tip**   The default set of templates installed with SWiSHmax is stored in the SWITemplates folder, a subfolder of the main SWiSHmax program folder.

2. **Type a name for the template in the File Name dialog box.** The only file format available is the .swi file format, shown in the figure.

3. **Click Save to save the file as a template.** The dialog box closes, and you have a new template.

You can reuse any of your custom templates just as you use the program's pre-built templates. Your new template is listed with the other program templates, as shown in Figure 3-15. Once you have started your movie file and initially saved it, you can set the Movie options.

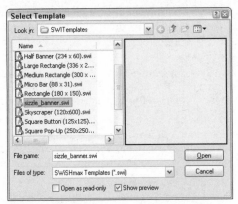

Figure 3-15: Select your custom templates from the program's templates list.

Choosing Movie Options

Whenever you open or create a movie, the rectangular shape of the movie is shown as the stage on the Layout panel, and the Movie panel at the right of the program window is active. The Movie panel contains settings that are common to the entire movie. That is, they are not specific to an individual element or part of the movie. You can:

✦ Change the background color

✦ Modify the dimensions of the movie

✦ Change the frame rate of the movie

✦ Add a command to automatically stop the movie once it plays

Background color

The default color for a movie's background is white. You can set the background color for the entire movie rather than drawing a rectangle shape the full size of your movie's stage and coloring it to serve as a background. The background color choices are solid colors only; you cannot modify the transparency, or alpha value, of a movie's background color, although you can modify both transparency and color for individual scenes within a movie. The background color you choose in SWiSHmax is also used as the background for the exported HTML page's background color. Follow these steps to change the background color:

1. **Click the tab for the Movie panel in the panel group. The Movie panel is now active.**

2. **Click the Background Color color swatch in the Movie panel.** The Color Selector opens, shown in Figure 3-16.

3. **Click a color from the palette.** The color is applied to the stage and the Color Selector closes automatically.

Cross-Reference

Learn more about methods for choosing color in Chapter 7.

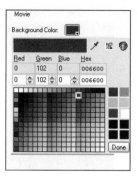

Figure 3-16: Select a color for the background of the movie.

The color you select for the movie's background is also used for the background color of any exported HTML pages. In Figure 3-17, a sample movie with a dark pink color as the movie's background uses the same color on the Web page. The figure shows both a portion of the Web page and its code in Dreamweaver MX 2004.

Figure 3-17: The movie's background color is automatically set as the Web page background color.

Movie size

In SWiSHmax, all sizes are expressed in pixels; monitors generally display 72 ppi, or pixels per inch. The default size of a movie stage is 400 x 300 pixels, which means the stage is 400 pixels wide and 300 pixels high. You can create a movie of up to 3277 x 3277 pixels, which is about 45½ inches square. When you create a new movie from a template, all the default templates include the size of the stage in the names, such as Wide Skyscraper (160 x 600).swi or Button 2 (120 x 60).swi.

In the program, the movie's dimensions are listed in the Movie panel shown in Figure 3-18. Follow these steps to change the movie's dimensions:

1. **In the Movie panel, click the Width field and type a new value to change the width of the movie.**

2. **Click the Height field and type a new value to change the height of the movie.**

3. **Press Enter on the keyboard to change the values for the dimensions and alter the appearance of the movie stage within the Layout panel.** You can also click the mouse anywhere on the program outside the Movie panel to apply the changes.

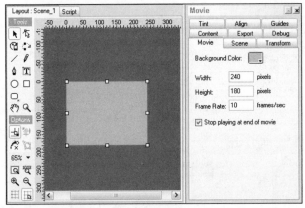

Figure 3-18: Change the size of the movie's stage in the Movie panel.

You can change the size of the movie at any time during the moviemaking process.

If you prefer, you can change the stage size visually in the Layout window. Follow these steps:

1. **Click the Select tool in the Layout panel's toolbox.**

2. **Click the stage in the Layout panel's workspace.** The stage displays eight resize handles around its edges.

3. **Click and drag the resize handles to change the dimensions of the stage:**

   • Click and drag a handle on the top or bottom edge to increase or decrease the height of the movie.

   • Click and drag a handle on the left or right edge to increase or decrease the width of the movie.

   • Click and drag a handle from one of the corners to resize the stage proportionally.

You can drag the resize handles beyond the edges of the visible Layout panel. To zoom in and out to see the boundaries of the stage more clearly, click the Fit to Window or Zoom 100% tools in the Toolbox.

When you have modified the stage's dimensions on the Layout panel, you see the values are changed in the Width and Height fields on the Movie panel. The stage's size is the dimensions for the movie for export unless you choose specific settings in the Export panel.

Learn more about export settings in Chapter 21.

Screen resolutions

Your computer monitor uses different screen resolutions expressed in pixels. A pixel is a distinct dot on the screen. At 800 x 600 pixels, which is a common screen resolution, the screen could display 800 distinct dots on each of 600 lines, or 480,000 pixels. In reality, some of the pixel space is taken up by the edges of the monitor, giving you only 760 x 420 pixels of visible area. SWF movies are generally played in a Web browser, which contains a number of toolbars at the top of the window as well as a status bar at the bottom of the window. Thus the available space to view a movie without scroll bars decreases even further.

Changing resolution changes the number of pixels seen on the screen. The content of the pixel doesn't change; only the size of the pixel changes. In Figure 3-19, the image at the left is shown at a low resolution; the same image at the right is shown at a high resolution.

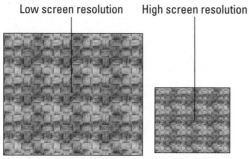

Low screen resolution   High screen resolution

Figure 3-19: The size of a pixel changes when you change the screen resolution.

You see the images use different amounts of screen space to display the same content. The resolution of the screen is not the same as the size of the monitor. A 15-inch monitor may use the same resolution as a 19-inch monitor.

If your screen is configured to use an 800 x 600-pixel resolution, a movie sized at 600 x 480 pixels fills most of the Web browser window, as shown in Figure 3-20. If the screen is set to 1600 x 1200 pixels, the same movie fills only a portion of the Web browser window, shown in Figure 3-21.

It's best to design a movie using the 800 x 600-pixel resolution. That way, you know that your viewers can see the content at 800 x 600 pixels as well as any higher-resolution settings they may be using. As you learn in Chapter 24, which discusses testing a movie for export, you can specify that the movie be resized to the Web browser window.

To change the resolution of your computer screen to see how a movie looks at different resolutions, follow these steps:

1. **Right-click any blank area of your desktop to display a shortcut menu.**

2. **Click Properties in the shortcut menu that appears.** The Display Properties dialog box opens.

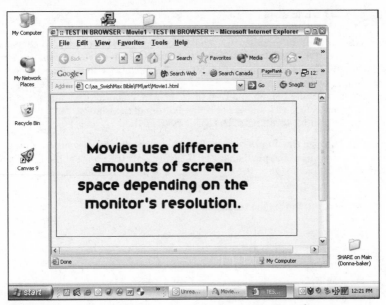

Figure 3-20: A movie takes up more screen space on a monitor set to 800 x 600 pixels.

Figure 3-21: A movie uses less screen space with a monitor setting of 1600 x 1200.

3. **Click the Settings tab to display color and resolution options as shown in Figure 3-22.**

Figure 3-22: Reset your screen's resolution in the Display Properties dialog box.

4. **Click and drag the Screen Resolution slider to reset the resolution.** Drag the slider to the left to decrease the resolution and to the right to increase the resolution.

5. **Click Apply to reset the monitor.** The screen goes black and then reappears using the modified resolution.

6. **Click OK to close the dialog box.**

Frame rate

In SWiSHmax, you assemble and animate a movie based on frame rate. The frame rate determines the speed at which the movie plays. The higher the number of frames per second, the faster the movie plays. For example, at the program's default frame rate of 12 fps (frames per second) you see the content of 12 frames in a second. If the frame rate is increased to 30 fps, you see the content of 30 frames in a second.

It's best to select the frame rate before starting your movie. While you can change the frame rate at any time, changing the rate after you have finished building a movie may require modifying some of the animations you have added so they run well at an alternate frame rate. To change the frame rate, click the Frame rate field on the Movie panel and type a new value. Press Enter or click the mouse somewhere outside the Movie panel to accept the change and modify the frame rate.

A frame rate that is too slow makes your movie's animation jerky, and sometimes it appears to start and stop. If the frame rate is too high, the animation can become blurry. In general terms, a frame rate of 12 fps produces a movie that looks good on a Web page, which is why it is the default rate.

Note   In contrast to delivery of a movie on the Web, motion pictures use a frame rate of 24 fps, and television uses a frame rate of 29.97 fps (in most of the world).

A faster movie produces a larger SWF movie file. Two sample movies that use the same source material, movie size, and effects are quite different in file size based on their respective frame rates as shown in Figure 3-23.

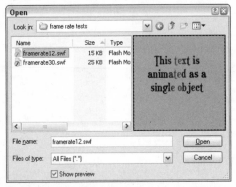

Figure 3-23: Different frame rates produce significantly different file sizes.

The first sample movie, framerate12.swf, has a file size of 15KB. The movie runs for four seconds, or a total of 48 frames. Contrast that with the second sample movie, framerate30.swf. This sample uses a frame rate of 30 fps, so creating a four-second movie requires 120 frames. The file size for the movie at this higher frame rate is 25KB, or 60 percent more than the same movie using a slower frame rate.

A faster frame rate doesn't necessarily produce a better movie. Other factors that can affect the movie's playback quality include the viewer's Internet connection and download speed, as well as the speed of viewer's computer.

Stopping movie playbackp

You can automatically make the movie play through once and stop without adding a script to the movie manually. On the Movie panel, click the Stop playing at end of movie check box. You don't see the action in the Timeline or written in the Scripts panel. You can see that a script is added to the movie in the Report, shown in Figure 3-24.

To view a movie's report, click File ➪ Test ➪ Report to display the contents of the movie in a Notepad window.

 Cross-Reference   Learn more about the Report window in Chapter 20.

Clicking the check box to add a script to stop the movie when it has played only once works for the main Timeline of the movie. If you have sprites playing in your movie, the sprites may continue to play, depending on how they are scripted and designed.

This line indicates the number
of scripts in a movie

```
Report                                                    _ □ ✕
Frame size: 200 x 200 pixels
Frame rate: 12.00 frames/sec
Total number of frames: 48 frames

- Entire Movie ----Tags---------------
+       Header:               20 bytes
+       Shapes:       17    1987 bytes
+       Script:        1       4 bytes
+     PlaceTags:     694   10331 bytes
+    RemoveTags:      33     132 bytes
+    ShowFrames:      48      96 bytes
+       BgColor:       1       5 bytes
+       PSPaths:       1       2 bytes
+        EndTag:       1       2 bytes
-----------------------------------------
         Total:     796   12579 bytes
```

Figure 3-24: A script is automatically added to stop the movie.

Summary

This chapter was all about preparation. You learned how to provide focus for your project by identifying characteristics of your audience and how to appeal to those specific characteristics. You also learned how to plan a movie, and then create a movie project. In this chapter you learned how to:

✦ Decide what your movie is for and who is going to view it.

✦ Apply elements of design so the movie you plan appeals to your intended audience.

✦ Build an organizational chart for a movie project.

✦ Create a process flowchart for a movie project.

✦ Describe the contents for a movie in such a way that you can quickly see what elements are in the movie as well as their purpose.

✦ Use a storyboard to chart the progress of your movie visually.

✦ Organize and name your project's files.

✦ Evaluate the objects you want to use based on how they work in SWiSHmax.

✦ Open a movie in SWiSHmax.

✦ Save a movie.

✦ Save a new template.

✦ Select different options for your movie such as size, color, and frame rate.

✦   ✦   ✦

The Basic SWiSHmax Building Blocks

Viewing a Movie's Content

Working efficiently in a program requires an understanding of how the different windows and panels interrelate with one another and how making a change in one panel produces effects in other panels and areas of the program.

In this chapter, you learn about the panels that make up the basic SWiSHmax interface. The three basic panels that make up the SWiSHmax interface all show the same information, but in different ways.

First up is the Outline panel, which organizes the content in your movie in a list. The content may be either created in SWiSHmax or imported. The Outline panel also displays the hierarchy, or organization of the content in your movie. You learn how to add, remove, and organize content in your movie using the Outline panel.

You learn to work with the Layout panel and visually organize the content in your movie. The Layout panel shows the content of your movie spatially, that is, where an object is in relation to other objects on the Layout panel's stage.

You also learn how to work with the Timeline panel, the third major working panel in SWiSHmax. The Timeline displays the contents of your movie numerically in frames placed on a time ruler. It shows when a certain object appears or disappears, has effects applied, when actions are applied, and so on. In this chapter, in addition to working with the basics of the Timeline, you also learn how to use two effects that either show or hide an object at a particular time.

The last panel you work with in this chapter is the Content panel, one of the panel group at the right of the program window. A movie project might include dozens of imported images and other objects. Using the Content panel, you can manage the imported content of your movie in a number of ways.

Understanding Time and Space

Although this title sounds like it should be discussed in some science fiction program, or at the very least a physics textbook, it is actually the basis of working with SWiSHmax. One of the most difficult ideas to understand when working with an animation program is that you must consider time (temporal factors) and space (spatial factors) at all times. What does this mean? Well, until you understand how to work with these dimensions, it means a lot of frustration and confusion. Once the ideas make sense — and they will — you find yourself thinking in entirely new ways. It's fun.

You construct, assemble, and draw the elements that go into your SWiSHmax creation in the Layout panel. The Timeline determines *when* you see your graphics or text. Not only must you draw or import visual elements or sound in your project, but you must also define when the objects are seen. As you learn later in the book, in addition to assembling visual components and sound, you also work extensively with different actions. Some actions are assigned and controlled in the Timeline as well, and are based on time.

Cross-Reference   Actions are covered in detail in Chapters 18 and 19.

Working with the Outline Panel

You'll refer frequently to the Outline panel as you are working. The panel is docked at the bottom left of the program window by default. The Outline panel shows the objects in your movie, the types of objects, and their relationships to one another. A sample movie is used in this chapter to illustrate the processes described and discussed.

On The Web Site   The chapter04 folder contains a SWI file, a SWF movie, and the source material used for the example project in this chapter. The program file is named ch04_sample01.swi. For your experimenting fun, there are some additional image and thumbnail image files you can use to expand the project.

The active scene in a movie is shown in bold text in the Outline view; the active element is highlighted. As shown in Figure 4-1, the Preload scene is the active scene and other scenes are grayed out.

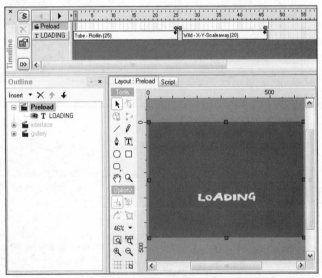

Figure 4-1: An object, such as a scene, selected in one panel is automatically selected in other panels.

When an object, such as a scene is selected in the Outline view, its Timeline is displayed, and the Scene object is also selected on the Layout panel, indicated by the handles surrounding the stage. Choosing an object on any one of the three panels automatically chooses the same object on the other two panels. Also, depending on the type of object selected, an additional panel displays on the panel group at the right side of the program window. For example, choosing a rectangle in the Timeline, Outline, or Layout panels automatically displays the Shape panel; similarly, choosing a Text object automatically displays the Text panel.

If you have several objects with similar names, it may be useful to see a bit more information than that provided by default. Follow these steps to modify a program preference to see a thumbnail in the Outline panel:

1. **Click Edit ⇨ Preferences or Tools ⇨ Preferences.** The Preferences dialog box opens.

2. **Click the Appearance tab to display some viewing options.**

3. **Click the Show Formatting check box shown in Figure 4-2.**

4. **Click OK to close the dialog box and change the program preferences.**

Figure 4-2: Modify a program preference to display thumbnails in the Outline panel.

The objects in the Outline panel will show the color of the text and the background color as well as the actual text characters (Figure 4-3). Changing the preference displays thumbnails and text color on the Outline and Content panels, as well as the Timeline. To revert to the program's default, reopen the Preferences dialog box and deselect the Show Formatting check box on the Appearances tab.

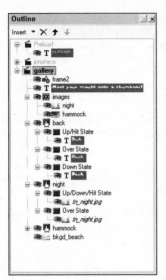

Figure 4-3: Thumbnails provide visual information about your project's objects.

Caution   Displaying thumbnails isn't always a good idea. If your project uses a lot of text, for example, it can be difficult to determine which text object is which when you see a thumbnail. The default program setting shows the objects' letters.

Be aware that displaying thumbnails requires more processing power. If you are using an older computer, or an operating system older than Windows 2000, you may find the program runs more slowly.

Using the Outline panel's hierarchy

A SWiSHmax movie can be complex, using numerous objects and multiple scenes. The Outline panel's contents are listed in a hierarchy.

The parent or most high-level object is a scene, represented by an icon that looks like a movie clapboard. A scene can contain any other types of elements such as individual drawings, text, images, and so on. There can be dozens of objects in one scene.

You can add a new scene to a movie by clicking the Insert ⇨ Scene command or clicking the Insert ⇨ Scene option in the Outline panel's Insert menu. A new blank scene is added. Icons to the left of the scenes' names indicate whether the scenes contain content or not.

 When a scene contains content, you see an expand (+) icon to the left of the scene's icon. This means that the view is collapsed and that the scene contains child or lower-level objects of the parent scene object. Click the (+) icon to expand the contents of the scene. When you open a scene, you may or may not see further (+) icons, indicating other levels of objects lower in the hierarchy than the child objects listed.

When an element or object is displaying all its content, you see a collapse (-) icon to the left of the object's icon, meaning the object's view is fully expanded. Clicking the icon collapses the view one level.

Visualizing a Hierarchy

Understanding the relationships between objects in a hierarchy can be difficult to visualize. In the figure you see four scenes. The scenes named **Preload** and **interface** are collapsed; these scenes are parent objects to some other objects. Clicking the expand icon to the left of the scene's icon opens a scene's hierarchy.

Scene_4 is at the bottom of the list. This scene is blank, has no child objects as there are no objects added to the scene, and there is no collapse or expand icon to the left of the scene's clapboard icon.

The scene named **gallery** is expanded. You see seven child objects of the scene object, including the graphics named **frame2** and **bkgd_beach**, text, a sprite called **images**, and three buttons.

If you look further, you see that the sprite named **images** is expanded. The **images** sprite is a parent object to two more objects; the images named **night** and **hammock**.

The point of this exploration is to understand how all these objects are nested within one another. In practical terms, this is important information. Which object you select in the hierarchy determines what you can do in the program, as well as determining the effect of applying different commands. If you click a scene such as the **gallery** scene selected in the figure, pressing the Delete key removes the scene completely from your movie. Clicking an object, such as the graphic named **frame2** in the figure allows you to work with the object in the Layout panel, apply effects in the Timeline, modify its properties in the panels, or delete the object from the **gallery** scene.

Cross-Reference

In the sidebar figure you can see an eye icon to the left of the icons indicating the type of object in a scene. Learn about controlling visibility of objects in Chapter 6.

Object order in the Outline panel

The way you organize material in the Outline panel does more than identify what objects are children of which other objects. The structure also identifies the stacking order of the objects in the scene. In some cases, the stacking order is important; in other cases it makes no difference.

Ordering scenes

The order in which the scenes in your movie are listed in the Outline panel doesn't make a difference as each is independent of the other — in other words, they are each high-level parent objects. For a movie with lots of scenes, however, a bit of advanced planning can save you time and frustration. It's best to arrange the scenes in a movie's outline according to how they appear in the movie where practical. For example, for a simple Web site interface the order of appearance might be:

✦ A preloader movie runs while the main movie is being loaded.

✦ The intro movie to the Web site plays.

✦ The Web site's interface displays, including a series of buttons that the user clicks to move to other areas of the site.

✦ Clicking one button opens a product listing on one side of the interface. As the viewer clicks items in the list, a product image and information appear at the other side of the interface.

✦ Clicking one button opens a page containing a list of topics about the company listed on one side of the interface. As the viewer clicks items in the list, information about the company, such as its history, philosophy, key personnel, and so on, display at the other side of the interface.

The scenes in the project's Outline panel might be listed in this order: preloader, movie, interface, products, and about us.

If you arrange a project's order based on the flow of the movie, it's simple until you get to the interface. At that point, look at your interface's organization. If you have a set of buttons from left to right across the top of the interface, list the scenes in the movie according to that same listing — the left-most button on the screen is first in the list. There certainly isn't any rule that says you must organize scenes in this way, but it helps you to correlate what part of the movie you are working on when you can associate the scene's location in the Outline panel with the location in the movie.

Ordering content in a scene

Just as there isn't a rule for organizing scenes, there sometimes isn't a rule for organizing content in a scene. Figure 4-4 shows a scene from a sample movie.

On The Web Site

The sample movie shown in Figure 4-4 is available on the book's Web site in the chapter04 folder, named ch04_sample01.swi.

Figure 4-4: Sometimes the content of a scene
can be listed in any order.

In the sample movie, there are four objects overlaying the background. These are background
picture, black frame, Gallery text, and E-mail text. None of the background objects overlaps
the other; they are each placed on a distinct location on the stage. As a result, you could use
any order in the scene's listing in the Outline panel without affecting their appearance.

On the other hand, the order of objects may be very important in some circumstances as
shown in Figure 4-5. In this example, four grouped objects (a shape and a text number) are
arranged on the stage. If you look at how the shapes overlap, you see the square is placed
below the circle, which is placed below the triangle, and the arrow overlays the triangle.

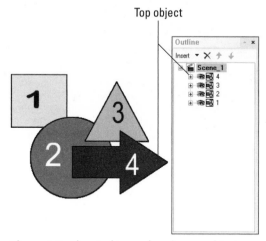

Figure 4-5: The stacking order of some objects
depends on their location in the Outline panel's list.

Cross-Reference Learn about drawing objects in Chapter 5 and grouping objects in Chapter 6.

There are a number of ways you can reorder the content in a movie's scene, all of which are quick. The Outline panel contains buttons you can click to reorder content in a movie. The buttons become active depending on the object selected and its location in the hierarchy. You can only reorder objects with the same ranking in the hierarchy. For example, if you have several scenes, you can move a selected scene upward in the Outline panel; if you have several objects in a single scene, clicking the up arrow moves the selected object higher in the list within the scene.

 Click the upward arrow button to move the selected object closer to the front of the stacking order, which is represented as a position higher on the list in the Outline panel. If the object selected is the first item in the list for a scene or the movie, the upward arrow button is inactive.

 Click the downward arrow button to move the selected object further from the front of the stacking order or farther down the list in the Outline panel. If the object selected is the last item on the list for a scene or the movie, the downward arrow button is inactive.

Tip   If you have the Standard toolbar open you can use the two arrow buttons on that toolbar instead of the buttons on the Outline panel.

Note   You can also move objects using your mouse or accelerator keys. Click the object in the list to select it, and then drag it up or down to place it in the correct position. To use accelerator keys, click the object in the list to select it, and then press Ctrl+Up Arrow to move the object up; press Ctrl+Down Arrow to move the object down the list. Repeat the accelerator keystrokes to move the object repeatedly until it reaches its final location.

Cross-Reference   Stacking order is also important when you are creating and assembling drawn objects on the stage. In Chapter 5, you learn more about object orders.

Working with the Timeline

The Timeline represents your project over time. Chapter 2 described the different components and tools that make up the Timeline. The content in your movie is arranged in scenes. You must have at least one scene in a movie; you can use dozens if you want — and if you can manage that many!

Cross-Reference   Chapter 2 explains ways to customize the Timeline view, such as changing the size of the frames.

Moving between scenes

The contents of one scene at a time are listed in rows in the Timeline.

 When your movie has several scenes, a pair of arrows on the Timeline ruler becomes active. These arrows are used to display different scenes in the Timeline. Follow these steps to switch among scenes in the Timeline:

1. **Click the left arrow on the Timeline ruler above the object labels to move to a previous scene.** The scene's name is listed in the first row of the Timeline. If the left arrow is grayed out, you are viewing the first scene listed in the Outline panel in the Timeline.

2. **Click the right arrow on the Timeline ruler above the object labels to move to scenes subsequent to the one you are viewing.** The scene's name is listed in the first row of the Timeline. If the right arrow is grayed out, you are viewing the final scene listed in the Outline panel in the Timeline.

3. **Confirm the Timeline is the one you want to work with by viewing it in the Outline panel.** The scene displayed in the Timeline is shown expanded in the Outline view and its name is selected, appearing in bold text.

Changing Timelines within a scene

One type of object you work with in SWiSHmax is called a sprite. A sprite is a single object that is composed of other objects and contains its own Timeline. For example, you may draw several objects and animate them, as shown in Figure 4-6. In this example, the two stars are animated and are listed on the Timeline as one object in the scene named **intro**. The sprite, named **stars**, is shown expanded in the Outline panel. To work with a sprite's Timeline in a scene's Timeline, follow these steps:

Figure 4-6: Sprites are used to contain objects and actions within a single named object.

1. **Double-click the label of the sprite in the Timeline.** The sprite's Timeline opens, shown in Figure 4-7. The Timeline is the same as that of the scene, except for one additional control. Where a scene displays forward and backward arrows to indicate that there are other scenes in your movie, a sprite's Timeline shows a button with an angled upward arrow overlaying a folder icon and the name of the parent scene, in the example, the parent scene is named **intro**.

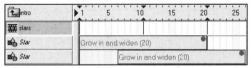

Figure 4-7: A Timeline placed within a scene's Timeline displays additional controls.

2. **To return to the parent scene that contains the sprite Timeline, click the upward arrow to the left of the parent scene's name.** The parent scene displays in the Timeline, and the direction icons return to left and right arrows.

Learn all about sprites in Chapter 15.

Defining when an object plays in a movie

When you add objects to a project, they are listed in the Outline panel and also on the Timeline. By default, objects are visible for the length of the movie, appearing at the first frame and ending at the last frame.

 A scene's objects are listed in the Timeline in a series of rows. Click an object's label, and the Add Effect button at the upper left of the Timeline is displayed and active. There are hundreds of effects available in SWiSHmax. When you choose an effect, it is applied to the selected object's row on the Timeline at the frame selected. All effects have a default length of time that is either a specific number of frames, such as 1 frame or 10 frames, or varies according to the type of effect — some typewriter effects, for example, vary in length according to the settings and the number of letters animated. You can modify the length of time for many effects.

By default, when you add an object to your movie, it appears at the first frame and stays as is. However, if you apply an effect, instead of showing up automatically at the first frame the object appears at the frame you specify for the start of the effect. The frame you specify can be the first frame, or any other frame in the movie. If you use several effects, the object first appears at the first frame you specified for the first effect.

You control when an object appears and disappears by using a combination of effects. For example, you can choose a fade effect to have an object fade in starting at the first frame of a movie, or use a Place effect and have it suddenly appear at a specific frame. Once an object is visible, it remains visible for the remainder of the movie's play back until you use another effect to remove it.

You learn about different uses and categories of effects in Chapters 12 through 14.

Determining when an object appears

In movies such as animations, for example, you probably don't want to see all the objects for the entire movie, but you may not want to apply effects to an object, either. You can specify when an object appears and when it disappears from the movie using specific effects.

1. **Select the desired scene, and click the object's label in the Timeline to make it active.** The Add Effect button becomes active.

You can select the object on the Layout panel or the Outline panel, but because you are working in the Timeline, save some mouse movement and click the object in the Timeline.

2. **Click the time ruler on the Timeline at the frame where you want the object to appear in your movie.** The red play head moves to the frame you selected as shown in Figure 4-8.

A gray background is shown down the column representing the selected frame. It can assist you in placing objects in your movie by serving as a guide.

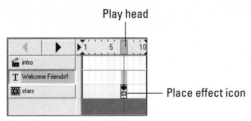

Figure 4-8: Select a frame by clicking
the time ruler to move the play head.

3. **Click the Add Effect button to open the list.** Click Place as shown in Figure 4-9. The menu list closes and the start frame for the object is defined.

Figure 4-9: Use the Place effect to control when an object appears in your movie.

The Place effect places an icon on the Timeline at the selected frame; you can see the icon in Figure 4-8. The length of this effect cannot be adjusted.

Removing an object from the stage

You use a different effect to remove an object from your movie at a specified frame.

Follow these steps to define the frame at which an object disappears from your movie's stage:

1. **Select the desired scene, and click the object's label in the Timeline to make it active.** The Add Effect button becomes active.

2. **Click the frame on the time ruler on the Timeline where you want to place the effect.** The red playback head moves to the selected frame, and a vertical shadow indicates the frame's column on the Timeline.

3. **Click the Add Effects button to display the menu shown in Figure 4-9.** Click Remove. The menu closes, and an icon is added to the Timeline at the frame defined in Step 2. The Remove effect's icon is shown in Figure 4-10. In the movie portrayed in the figure, the text object disappears at Frame 11.

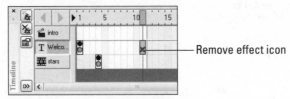

Remove effect icon

Figure 4-10: Use a Remove effect to define when an object is removed from your movie's stage.

Tip   You can use either the Place or Remove effect by itself. Define the starting frame for an object you want to play until the end of a movie; define the ending frame for an object you want to remove from the stage before the end of a movie.

Tip   Selecting an object to make it active in one panel also makes it active in other panels:

✦ The object is selected in the expanded scene in the Outline panel

✦ The scene containing the object is displayed on the Timeline and the object's label is selected

✦ The object is selected in the Layout panel

Working with the Content panel

The Outline panel shows the contents of your movie's scenes and the relationships among the elements of the movie. The Timeline shows your movie as it evolves over time, as well as actions and effects. The Layout panel displays how your movie looks on the stage. One additional panel contributes to keeping your project in order and can save you time coordinating your movie and its components.

The Contents panel is a listing of imported movie components and sprites constructed within your project organized by type. To view the Contents panel, click the Content tab in the panels grouped at the right of the SWiSHmax program window, or click Panels ➪ Content. The Content panel for the sample project provided for this chapter is shown in Figure 4-11.

On The Web Site   The sample project referenced through much of this chapter is available from the book's Web site. The project is ch04_sample01.swi and is located in the Chapter04 folder.

The Content panel arranges some of the contents of a movie alphabetically within a set of folders. The folders contain imported objects including images or sounds, as well as sprites that you create in SWiSHmax. Buttons, text, or any objects you create using the drawing tools in SWiSHmax aren't included in the Contents panel. Open and close folders by clicking the (-) and (+) indicators to the left of the folders' names. When viewing a movie in the Content panel, there is no indication of where the files are used within your movie's scenes, or even if they are used at all. The Sounds and Images folder merely list the names of the files you have imported into the project; the Sprites folder lists the sprites you have created in a project.

Figure 4-11: The contents of a movie are arranged by type in the Content panel.

You use the Content panel for two purposes. First, you view the imported content in your movie. Regardless of whether an image or sound is used, it is stored in the project file which can contribute to the file's size tremendously. Second, the Content panel lists the sprites constructed in the project. You can use the listing in the Content panel as an easy way to add a copy, or instance, of the sprite to the movie from the Content panel.

You can manage a project's files in the Content panel in a number of ways. These include:

✦ Import a variety of media files into your project

✦ Add objects to the selected scene

✦ Delete objects from the project

✦ Update media files used in a movie

✦ View an object's properties

One way to import material into a project is clicking File ➪ Import and then selecting files. Rather than using menu commands, you can import files into your project through the Content panel. Follow these steps:

1. **Click the Content panel in the panel group.** The Content panel appears.

2. **Click Import on the Content panel's menu options.** An Open dialog box appears.

3. **Browse to the location of the file you want to import.**

4. **Click the file in the dialog box listings.** To see a preview, click the Show Preview check box at the bottom of the Open dialog box as shown in Figure 4-12.

5. **Click Open to close the dialog box.** The object is imported into the project and added to the applicable folder.

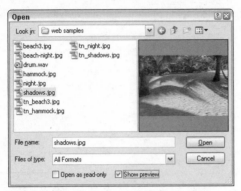

Figure 4-12: You can preview files before importing into the Content panel.

Importing objects through the Content panel doesn't add them to the movie's Timeline, it merely adds them to the project file. You can add objects directly to a scene from the Content panel.

A new project often contains a lot of different images and other types of media. Sometimes it is simpler to add the scenes in the Outline panel and then select each scene and add the objects from the Content panel. Once the imported objects are added to your scenes, you can start organizing the arrangement in the Outline panel.

Follow these steps to add objects to the project outline from the Content panel:

1. **In the Outline panel, click the scene you want to add objects into to make it active.** Make sure you have selected the correct scene because the selected objects in the Content panel are added to the active scene in the Outline panel.

2. **In the Content panel, click the file you want to add to the Outline panel to select it.**

Tip

You can select several files at once. Click the first file in a sequence of contiguous files and then press Shift and click the last file in the sequence to select the group of files.

To select a group of noncontiguous files, click the first file you want to transfer to select it and then press Ctrl as you click to select the other files you want to transfer.

3. **Click the Add to Scene button at the bottom of the Content panel.** The file is transferred to the Outline view and added to the scene as shown in Figure 4-13.

Note

Figure 4-13 shows the Outline and Content panels; the Layout panel was removed from the image to show you the relationships between the panels' contents more readily.

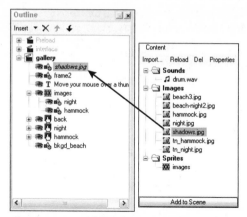

Figure 4-13: Add files from the list in the Content panel to the project's Outline panel.

If you prefer, you can work with the Layout panel instead of the Outline panel to add files from the Content panel. Simply select the scene you want to place the content into in the Outline panel or Timeline, click the file(s) in the Content panel that you want to add, then drag the file(s) to the stage on the Layout panel as shown in Figure 4-14.

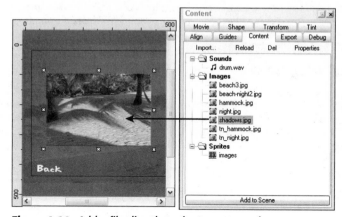

Figure 4-14: Add a file directly to the Layout panel.

The object is added to the stage, added to the scene's listing in the Outline panel, and its label appears in a new row on the Timeline.

Cleaning up a project

Sometimes you import a collection of images and other objects when you start a SWiSHmax project and then discover that you have too many images or you change your design ideas, and so on.

Periodically, take a few minutes and look through the Content panel for unused objects and delete them, particularly if you are working in a long session, or are making a lot of changes to your images as you are working. You may be the type of person who works in progressive stages, and likes to keep variations of image files in a project just in case. Regardless of your working style you can easily remove content during a session. Select the object in the Content panel folder listings and then click Delete on the Content panel's commands. A file that isn't used is deleted from the project.

Don't worry about deleting a file by mistake. If a file is used in your movie, SWiSHmax displays a dialog box like that shown in Figure 4-15. If you intend to delete the object, read the message and then proceed; otherwise, click Cancel to close the dialog box.

Figure 4-15: SWiSHmax won't let you delete files used in your movie by mistake.

Fortunately, SWiSHmax takes care of cleanup on a regular basis. If you have extra image or sound files that aren't used in the project, after the project is closed and reopened, only those files used in the project are displayed in the Content panel. SWiSHmax automatically clears unused files.

Showing object properties

The Content panel lists objects imported into your movie by type, as well as listing sprites created in the movie. You can view the basic properties of an image directly from the Content panel. Click the name of an object in the Content panel to select it, and then click Properties from the menu items at the top of the Content panel, or simply double-click the object to display an Image Properties information dialog box. Figure 4-16 shows the properties for an image.

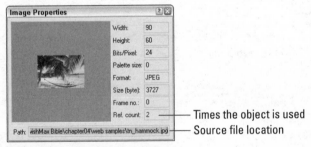

Figure 4-16: View properties of an object directly from the Content panel.

The information contained in the properties display varies by type of object, of course. One important feature on the image properties shown in Figure 4-16 is the Ref. count. In the figure, the Ref. count is 2, meaning there are two copies of the image used in the project.

Another nice feature of the Image Properties dialog box is the path. At the bottom of the Image Properties dialog box you see the location on the hard drive where the file is located. You can view properties for only one object at a time. Unless the dialog box used for viewing one object is closed, you can't view properties of another object.

Tip   Click X at the top right of the Properties information dialog box to close it.

Cross-Reference   Learn how to work with imported images in Chapter 8.

Replacing an object

The final feature of the Content panel is the Reload process, useful for multitasking. Suppose you have added an image to a project, and then decide you need to make a slight change using the source program in which you created the original image. Instead of closing SWiSHmax and opening your image program, leave your project and the program open, and then open your source program, make the changes, and save the file again. In SWiSHmax, you can simply reload the image, replacing the original with the amended version, and it is ready for use in your project again. Follow these steps to reload an image object:

1. **On the Content panel, click to select the object you want to reload.**

2. **Click Reload on the Content panel's menu.** A second listing for the object is added to the Content panel as shown in Figure 4-17.

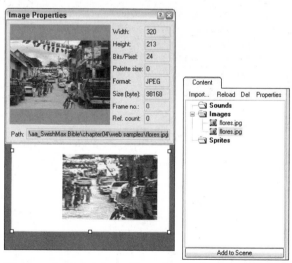

Figure 4-17: Reload an object after modifying it in its source program.

3. **Select the copy of the image you want to use in your movie, and add it to a scene.** If you aren't sure which image is which, double-click each name and read the properties.

4. **Manually delete the original listing in the Content panel.**

Alternatively, if you save, close, and reopen the project the unused version is deleted. If your project is complex, and you don't want to forget what you were working on, reload the image instead of closing and reopening the project.

Summary

This chapter was all about viewing. You learned how to view your movie's contents in a number of locations and how to add some specific effects to view your contents at specific points in the movie. You learned how to:

✦ Understand the hierarchy of a movie's elements.

✦ Show and hide information in the Outline panel.

✦ Reorder the arrangement of scenes in a project.

✦ Organize the objects in a scene.

✦ View Timelines within a scene on the Timeline.

✦ Define when an object appears and disappears on the stage.

✦ Manage a movie's media using the Content panel, including adding and replacing objects, and viewing an object's properties.

✦ ✦ ✦

Drawing in SWiSHmax

Some projects use a large number of objects. Instead of building each object in an illustration or image manipulation program and then importing it into SWiSHmax, you can create many types of objects from within the program.

In this chapter, you are introduced to the SWiSHmax drawing tools used for creating graphics. The Layout panel includes a Toolbox with a variety of drawing tools. You can choose from simple objects such as lines and rectangles, to more complex objects such as stars and button shapes. You can draw complex objects using a Bézier tool, adding segments to the object one by one based on points you add called Bézier points.

The tools may seem simple at first glance — the Line tool draws a line, after all, but there is considerably more to drawing than that.

To assist you in your designing process, SWiSHmax includes a number of tools that help with placement. You often use grid lines and guides to place an object on the stage; the grid lines and guides can be customized according to your design requirements. You can also use a number of visibility tools to clearly see your masterpiece develop on the stage.

The SWiSHmax Toolbox

The tools you use in SWiSHmax to draw shapes and objects are contained within the Toolbox. The Toolbox is a permanent part of the Layout panel and is docked at the left side of the panel. The layout of the Toolbox is static, meaning you don't add or remove items from the Toolbox. For the most part, the tools that are active on the Toolbox are those available for use; the exception is the AutoShape tool, which displays a submenu from which you choose a shape.

The majority of the drawing tools are identified on Figure 5-1. Those tools not identified on the figure are used for special purposes, such as creating a motion path or transforming an object, and are discussed in upcoming chapters.

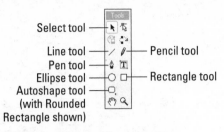

Select tool ——
Line tool ——
Pencil tool
Pen tool ——
Ellipse tool ——
Rectangle tool
Autoshape tool ——
(with Rounded
Rectangle shown)

Figure 5-1: The SWiSHmax Toolbox contains a number of drawing tools.

Understanding shapes

Paths connected by points are the basic elements of drawn objects. A path consists of at least two points, each connecting one or more line segments that can be either straight or curved, creating a shape. A shape is described as open or closed. Examples of the two types of shapes are shown in Figure 5-2:

✦ An open shape (on the left in Figure 5-2) is a path with unconnected endpoints; the path may be straight, curved, or wiggly. An open shape displays a line, or stroke.

✦ A closed shape has the same beginning and ending point, which creates a continuous path around the periphery of the shape (on the right in Figure 5-2). A closed shape can have both a line around its periphery, as well as a fill (color, patterns, or images that fill the shape).

Figure 5-2: Shapes are either open or closed.

You learn about strokes and fills in Chapter 7.

Shapes are also categorized as simple or complex. The drawing tools in SWiSHmax create simple shapes, which are shapes comprised of one object. A number of objects selected and grouped using one of several different methods is a complex shape. In Figure 5-3, the flower-shaped object is composed of several heart shapes; when grouped together, they make one complex shape.

A complex shape is not the same thing as a complex object. A complex object is a term used by SWiSHmax to define an object that can be broken into component sections for applying effects.

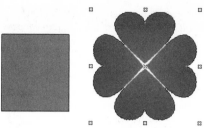

Figure 5-3: Shapes may be either simple, like the square, or complex, like the flower.

Cross-Reference   Learn more about grouping in Chapter 6.

Finally, shapes are identified as geometric or free-form. A geometric shape is easily recognizable and corresponds to the shapes available in the SWiSHmax Toolbox. Geometric shapes are symmetrical. A free-form shape, on the other hand, is just that—a shape drawn using individual points and path segments that can be anything from a spaceship to a dog. Geometric and free-form shape examples are shown in Figure 5-4. You learn more about working with points and path segments later in the chapter.

Figure 5-4: Shapes are either geometric (left) or free-form (right).

Drawing basic shapes

SWiSHmax provides a number of basic geometric drawing tools including the Line, Rectangle, Ellipse, and AutoShape tools. When you click a tool in the Toolbox and move the mouse over the stage, the cursor displays cross hairs and an image of the selected tool. After you click to select a tool in the Toolbox and then use it, it is deselected, and returns to the Select tool by default.

Tip   You can permanently select a tool in the Toolbox by double-clicking its icon. The tool is activated, and remains active until you select a different tool.

The default tool in the Toolbox is the Select tool. If you click an object on the Layout panel using the Select tool, you see a set of square handles around the margins of the shape, indicating it is selected. A selected shape can be moved, resized, deleted, or copied. Whenever you use a drawing tool it reverts to the Select tool once the specific tool has been used. The Shape tool selects an entire object as compared to the Reshape tool, which is used to select elements of a shape. You learn more about the Reshape tool later in this chapter.

Tip   If you are unsure of a tool's function, position your mouse over the tool in the Toolbox. A pop-up message names the tool. Look at the status bar at the bottom of the program window for a brief message on how to use the tool.

Line tool

The simplest tool to use is the Line tool. A line is composed of two endpoints and a drawn segment that connects the two endpoints. You can also construct lines using the Pencil and Bézier tools, which you learn about later in the chapter.

In Figure 5-5, two copies of the same line are shown on the stage. The upper line is selected. You can see the line is made up of two unconnected endpoints and a connecting path. To draw a straight line, follow these steps:

Figure 5-5: The most basic shape is a straight line.

1. **Click the Line tool in the Toolbox to select it.**

2. **Click the stage where you want the line to start and drag in the direction you want the line to extend.** To constrain the direction of the line to 15-degree increments, press the Shift key as you drag the mouse.

3. **Release the mouse when the line is the correct length.** The Shape panel becomes active in the panel group at the right side of the program window.

4. **Click the name field on the Shape panel to make it active.** Type a name for the shape.

Caution   SWiSHmax assigns the default name **Shape** to lines, rectangles, and ellipses. It isn't a problem if you are working with only a few shapes. However, if you are building an animation that uses a fair number of drawn objects, it is difficult to figure out which **Shape** is which.

Note   The Shape panel includes settings for assigning the shape as a target or setting its tracking to track as menu. A shape is used as a target when you want it used in scripted interactions; a shape is tracked as a menu if it is used as part of a button or link set. The default settings for both these features are deselected.

Ellipse and Rectangle tools

The Ellipse tool is used to construct ovals or circles, both of which are closed shapes, meaning the starting and end points are the same, and the finished shape has a continuous edge.

Use the Rectangle shape to draw a rectangle or a square, again a closed shape.

Follow these steps to draw an ellipse or rectangle:

1. **Click the tool from the Toolbox.**

2. **Click the stage where you want to start the drawing and drag diagonally or downward to construct the shape.** The position of the cursor indicates the upper left corner of the finished drawing. If you want to draw a perfect square or circle, press the Shift key as you drag. This constrains the shape to equal sizes horizontally and vertically.

Cross-Reference   To read more about transforming shapes, see Chapter 6.

3. **Release the mouse when the shape is the right size.** The Shape panel becomes active in the panel group at the right side of the program window as shown in Figure 5-6. The object is named Shape by default.

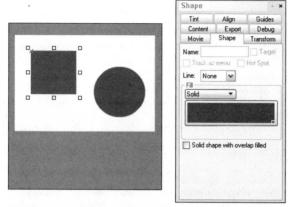

Figure 5-6: When you release the mouse, the shape is drawn and the Shape panel is displayed on the program window.

4. **Click in the name field on the Shape panel to make it active.** Type a name for the shape.

Using AutoShapes

You can choose from a number of common shapes to add to your movie. The shapes, called AutoShapes, are contained in a submenu of the Toolbox. The AutoShape displayed in the Toolbox continues to show the most recently selected tool until you select a different one.

Here's how to choose a tool and draw an AutoShape for your movie:

1. **Click the visible AutoShape tool in the Toolbox on the Layout panel and hold the mouse button down.** The submenu opens, as shown in Figure 5-7.

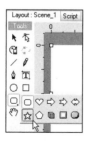

Figure 5-7: Choose an AutoShape from the Toolbox's submenu.

2. **Click a tool from the submenu.** The submenu closes, and the selected tool is active.

3. **Click the stage on the Layout panel with the tool where you want to place the upper-left edge of the drawing and drag downward and to the right to construct the AutoShape.** Press the Shift key while dragging if you want to constrain the object to an equal width and height.

Tip   You can also click from any corner and drag the mouse diagonally to draw the shape.

4. **Release the mouse when the shape is the correct size.** The Shape panel becomes active in the panels at the right of the program window.

5. **In the Shape panel, click the Name field to make it active, and type a name to identify the shape.** The name changes in both the Outline panel and the Timeline.

Note   The AutoShapes use the type of shape as the default name, unlike squares and circles and lines that are simply named **Shape**. For example, if you draw a star, its default name is **Star**; a 3D cube is named **3D Cube**, and so on.

Reshaping AutoShapes

The AutoShapes have a specific design advantage in that they are configured with special controls to allow you to modify the basic shape. For example, you can change the number of points on a star or each point's depth, or change the depth of a button. Each of the AutoShapes has its own particular adjustments. The adjustments are made by clicking and dragging a special anchor called an *AutoShape anchor*. As you move the anchor, you see a cursor (shown in the following figures) indicating the AutoShape anchor is active.

Rounded rectangle tool

The Rounded rectangle tool has one AutoShape anchor. Click and drag the AutoShape anchor up and toward a corner to decrease the roundness of the edges. Drag the AutoShape anchor toward the center of the object to increase the roundness. When your dragged AutoShape anchor reaches the object's anchor (the small x in the center of the image shown in Figure 5-8) the shape converts from a rectangle to an ellipse.

Autoshape anchor   Central anchor point

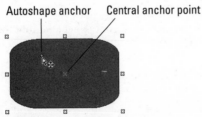

Figure 5-8: You can modify the roundness of a rounded rectangle.

Heart tool

The Heart tool is used for drawing triangles as well as hearts. You can use drawn hearts as is, or as part of a larger image, such as the flower shape shown back in Figure 5-3. The

Heart tool has one AutoShape anchor. Clicking and dragging the anchor downward increases the depth and curvature of the heart. Dragging the anchor upward flattens the sides of the heart and the final shape is a triangle as shown in Figure 5-9.

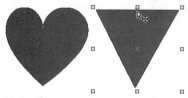

Figure 5-9: Use the Heart tool to draw hearts or triangles.

Arrow tool

The AutoShapes include three arrow tools: a simple arrow, a notched arrow, and a two-ended arrow. All arrow tools contain one AutoShape anchor. Click and drag the AutoShape anchor upward and downward to increase the depth of the arrowhead and the shaft of the arrow. You can make other shapes using the arrow tools as well, as you can see in Figure 5-10. Drag the AutoShape anchor left to make a triangle from the basic arrow or a chevron from the notched arrow. Drag the AutoShape anchor toward the middle of the double-ended arrow to create a diamond shape. In the figure, the modified AutoShape is shown below the standard AutoShape.

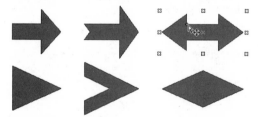

Figure 5-10: You can draw several types of arrows or create other AutoShapes using the Arrow tools.

Star tool

The Star tool is a very versatile AutoShape. You can use the tool to draw the default five-point star, but you can also construct several other shapes using the same tool as seen in Figure 5-11. The shape contains three AutoShape anchors:

✦ The AutoShape anchor at the tip of the point is used to rotate the star. Click and drag the shape to rotate it clockwise or counterclockwise.

✦ The AutoShape anchor between the points is used to determine the depth between the points of the star.

✦ The AutoShape anchor at the center of the star is used to add or remove more points from the star. Move the mouse over the central anchor and click the left mouse button to add more points; right-click to remove points from the star.

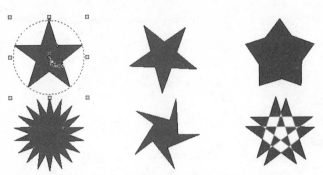

Figure 5-11: The Star tool can be configured to create numerous shapes.

You can modify the AutoShape anchors in combination. For example, create a swirl (like that shown in the bottom center of Figure 5-11) by both rotating the star and dragging the depth anchor downward. You can create a multitude of different shapes by moving the AutoShape anchor between the points and the central AutoShape anchor.

Polygon tool

Use the Polygon tool to draw a multisided figure. Click the central AutoShape anchor to add sides to the figure; right-click to remove sides from the figure. The default has five sides; you can add and remove sides to create shapes ranging from a triangle to a circle. Click and drag the AutoShape anchor on the outer edge to rotate the polygon (see Figure 5-12).

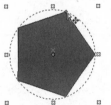

Figure 5-12: You can change the number of sides and the rotation of a basic polygon.

Cube tool

The Cube tool draws a three-dimensional shape and contains three AutoShape anchors. The Cube AutoShape uses three anchors:

✦ Click and drag the AutoShape anchor at the top center of the shape (selected in Figure 5-13) to change the appearance of light on the cube. Drag right to simulate a light over the right side of the cube, creating a dark shadow on the left of the cube. Drag left to simulate light closer to the left edge of the cube, creating lighter shadow on the left side of the cube. Move the AutoShape anchor downward to simulate the angle the light strikes the front of the cube.

✦ Drag the left corner anchor to increase or decrease the depth of the cube.

✦ Reposition the bottom-right AutoShape anchor to modify the perspective. Drag down and right to flatten the perspective; drag up and left to sharpen the perspective.

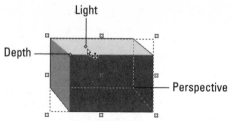

Figure 5-13: You can adjust the perspective and shadow of a 3D cube shape.

Beveled button tool

Use the Beveled button tool to draw a simulated three-dimensional button. The tool uses two AutoShape anchors. The outermost AutoShape anchor can be moved in any direction to simulate the position of a light source. In the right image in Figure 5-14, the light source is moved to the lower-right area of the shape. The innermost AutoShape anchor is used to adjust the depth of the bevel.

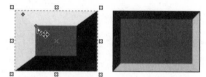

Figure 5-14: You can change the light source and depth of a beveled button.

Rounded button tool

The Rounded button tool combines some of the features of the Rounded rectangle tool with those of the Beveled button tool. In Figure 5-15, the image at the left shows the default Rounded button AutoShape. The right image shows the shape after modifying the AutoShape anchors. The Rounded button tool uses the same two AutoShape anchors as those of the Beveled button tool. Click and drag the uppermost AutoShape anchor in any direction to simulate the light source's direction. Drag the innermost AutoShape anchor toward the center to increase the depth of the bevel, drag it upward to decrease the depth of the bevel, and drag it right or left to increase or decrease the roundness of the button's shape.

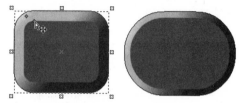

Figure 5-15: You can adjust shadow and depth of the Rounded button AutoShape.

Drawing Free-form shapes

The SWiSHmax Toolbox includes two tools for drawing free-form shapes. Use the Pencil tool to construct flowing shapes and the Bézier tool to draw precise shapes on a point-by-point basis.

Pencil tool

Use the Pencil tool to draw a freehand line object. The line may be an open shape with unconnected endpoints. You can also draw a closed shape, where the starting and ending points are at the same location.

In Figure 5-16, all the shapes were created with the pencil tool. The single jagged line at the bottom is an example of an open shape. The cloud and sun shapes are each closed shapes. When drawing with a free-form tool, SWiSHmax helps you to close a shape. If you look at the figure, you can see the circle at the center of the sun displays a rounded, target-like cursor. When your mouse is over the starting point of a shape, release the mouse when the cursor appears to close the shape. Follow these steps to draw a freeform line using the Pencil tool:

Figure 5-16: You can create open or closed shapes using the Pencil tool.

1. **Click the Pencil tool on the Toolbox to select it.**

2. **Click the tool on the stage at the location where you want the shape to begin and drag the mouse over the stage to construct the rest of the shape.**

3. **Release the mouse again to complete the shape.** If you are drawing a closed shape, click when the endpoint cursor appears over your starting location. The tool is deselected in the Toolbox.

4. **In the Shape panel, click in the Name field to make it active, and type a name to identify the shape.** SWiSHmax names pencil drawings **Shape** by default. The name changes in both the Outline panel and the Timeline.

Bézier tool

If you want to draw a precise shape where you can control the points, use the Bézier tool. As shown in Figure 5-17, the paths you construct using the Bézier tool can be complex.

Figure 5-17: Create more precise shapes using the Bézier tool.

Unlike the Pencil tool, which uses a single click and drag of the mouse to draw the entire object, you draw each segment of a shape using the Bézier tool one click at a time, clicking the mouse each time you want to add a point to the shape. A shape drawn with the Bézier tool is called a *path;* it may be open or closed. Follow these steps to draw a precise shape with angled segments:

1. **Click the Bézier tool on the Toolbox to select it.**

2. **Click the tool on the stage at the location where you want the shape to begin.**

3. **Drag the mouse over the stage to the location where you want to place the first point.** A straight line is drawn along the stage as you move the mouse.

4. **Click to add a point to the shape.** The first segment of the shape is complete; the shape has two endpoints and a line segment.

5. **Move the mouse to where you want the next line segment to end.** Again, a line segment is drawn as you move the mouse.

6. **Continue adding points to the shape.**

7. **To complete the shape, choose one of these options.** When the shape is complete, the tool is deselected in the Toolbox.

    • If you are constructing an open shape, double-click the mouse to end the drawing

    • If you are constructing a closed shape, click the starting point

8. **In the Shape panel, click in the Name field to make it active, and type a name to identify the shape.** Bézier drawings are named **Shape** by default. The name changes in both the Outline panel and the Timeline.

The Bézier tool can also be used to create a path with curved segments; you can adjust the point and the curvature of the path as you draw. Click to place an anchor point, and then drag before releasing the mouse to display *adjustment handles* that let you adjust the curves coming into and out of an anchor after the drawing is completed. After you place a point, the Bézier tool shows a preview of how the path will appear when you click to place the next point.

Follow these steps to draw a curved path:

1. **Click the Bézier tool in the Toolbox.** Move the tool over the Layout panel to the position where you want the curve to start.

2. **Click and hold the mouse button to place the first anchor point.**

3. **Drag the mouse in the direction of the curve you want to place**. You see the angle of the rubber band segments change as you move the mouse, and the adjustment handles swivel as you move the mouse in different directions.

4. **Release the mouse button to add the anchor point.**

5. **Move the tool to the location on the Layout panel where you want to add the next anchor point.** Click and drag to place the anchor point and add handles.

6. **Repeat Step 5 until you have finished placing anchor points.** Figure 5-18 shows several curve segments and anchor points.

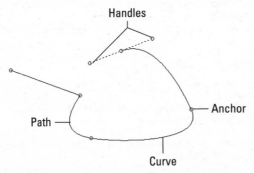

Figure 5-18: You can create a curved path using the Bézier tool.

7. **Double-click the mouse to end the drawing.** If you want to create a closed path (a shape) double-click over the first anchor point you set. When you move the mouse over the first anchor point you see a circle and cross hairs indicating you are in the correct location.

8. **In the Shape panel, click in the Name field to make it active, and type a name to identify the shape.** SWiSHmax names Bézier drawings **Shape** by default. The name changes in both the Outline panel and the Timeline.

Cross-Reference

You can adjust the handles on the path, including changing their shapes, adding, and deleting them using the Reshape tool, described in Chapter 6.

All aspects of a Bézier curve can be modified, including the points, number of points, line segments, and adjustment handles. Read about configuring Bézier curves in Chapter 6.

Changing how you View a Drawing on the Stage

The Toolbox contains a number of tools used to view your work more clearly. The basic tools include the Pan tool, which is used to drag the stage view, and the Zoom tool, which is used to magnify the stage manually. In addition, there are a number of Viewing tools you use to change the view in specific increments.

Pan tool

The Pan tool lets you view, or *pan*, different areas of the Layout panel. Click the Pan tool in the Toolbox to select it. When you position the mouse over the Layout panel, the cursor looks like an open hand similar to that shown in the Toolbox icon. Click the Layout panel and drag in any direction to move the stage around displaying different areas. When you release the mouse, the tool is deselected; to pan the Layout panel again, you must click the Pan tool in the Toolbox again.

Zoom tool

The Zoom tool is like a free-form tool in that you decide how and what you would like to see on the Layout panel. The tool can be used in a number of ways to display specific areas of the screen. For example, you can zoom in incrementally to view an area of interest and then zoom out again. You can also *fence*, or define an area to be magnified. The center of the magnified area is the location on the Layout panel where you click the tool. The Zoom tool remains active until you select another tool in the Toolbox.

Click the Zoom tool on the Toolbox to select it and then position it over the Layout panel. A magnifying glass icon with a plus sign (+) appears. You can use the tool in these ways:

✦ Click the tool on the Layout panel to increase the magnification by approximately 66 percent. Each time you click the tool, the magnification increases by the same percentage.

✦ Press the Shift key and click to decrease the magnification of the Layout panel. When you press Shift, a minus sign (-) appears in the magnifying glass icon, indicating that a mouse click decreases the magnification.

✦ Click the tool on the Layout panel and drag to fence a specific area of the Layout panel, as shown in Figure 5-19. The fenced area magnifies to fill the visible space in the Layout panel. The amount of magnification varies depending on the size and shape of the fenced area and the size of the Layout panel.

Note

You can bypass the Zoom tool altogether using shortcut key combinations. Press Ctrl+Num+ (the plus key on the numeric keyboard) or press Ctrl+Shift++ (the plus key on the keyboard) to increase magnification; press Ctrl+- (the minus key on the numeric keyboard or the minus key on the keyboard) to decrease magnification. Press the keystroke combinations repeatedly to continue to increase or decrease magnification.

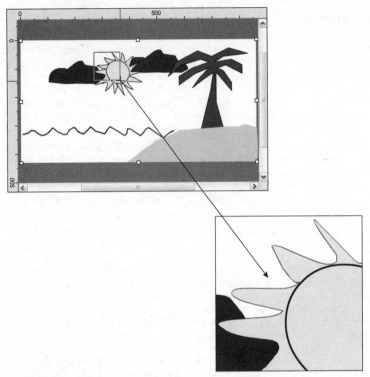

Figure 5-19: Magnify a specific region on the Layout panel.

View tools

The Toolbox contains a collection of tools called View tools. These are used to view the Layout panel in specific ways or show specific magnification values. These tools are not used on the Layout panel as you use the drawing tools. They are clicked in their position on the Toolbox; clicking a tool produces the effect of the tool. You can also select the tools from the View menu. The set of viewing tools is shown in Figure 5-20.

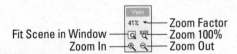

Fit Scene in Window —— Zoom Factor
Zoom In —— Zoom 100%
—— Zoom Out

Figure 5-20: Use the View tools for specific viewing options.

Tip If you can't see the set of tools in the Toolbox, increase the size of the program window, and/or increase the height of the Layout panel.

Zoom Factor

Click the Zoom Factor's drop-down arrow and choose a standard magnification. You can choose a magnification ranging from 25% to 500%. If you use the Zoom tool or shortcut keys, the actual magnification value is shown on the Zoom Factor menu. In Figure 5-20, the Layout panel displays a magnification of 41%.

Fit Scene in Window

This is a very handy tool. Sometimes you can be working on a portion of the Layout panel using a very high magnification. Rather than having to click a tool repeatedly to decrease magnification, simply click Fit Scene in Window. The magnification displayed varies depending on the size of the stage and the size of the Layout panel on your screen. The magnification used by the tool displays as the label on the Zoom Factor tool.

Zoom 100%

The Zoom 100% tool is another very handy viewing tool. Click the tool to see the stage at its actual size. Depending on the size of the movie and the size of the Layout panel, you may or may not see the entire stage. The magnification label on the Zoom Factor menu shows 100% when you use this tool.

Tip   Use the Zoom 100% or Fit in Window tools if you are adding images to your movie to automatically have the image placed at the exact center of the movie.

Zoom In and Zoom Out

The final viewing tools are the Zoom In and Zoom Out tools. You don't select either of these tools. Instead, click the tool on the Toolbox to increase or decrease magnification of the Layout panel's contents. The zoom value is shown as the Zoom Factor menu's label.

Using Guides and Grids

How do you determine where objects should be placed on the stage? The answer depends on the characteristics of the objects and what they are used for. If you have a set of buttons, for example, unless you are designing a free-flowing interface, the buttons are generally lined up in a consistent way, such as with even edges. In your layout, you often have different objects placed in specific locations that correspond with other objects to balance the content of the movie.

Cross-Reference   Learn to organize a number of objects on the stage in Chapter 6.

SWiSHmax provides two types of visual layout assistance shown in Figure 5-21. You can use the *grid*, which is a network of horizontal and vertical lines overlaying the Layout panel at predetermined intervals. You can also used *guides*, which are lines you add in specific areas of the Layout panel to assist in placing objects horizontally or vertically. In addition, to make it easier to use the grid lines and guides, you can use Snap settings to make the content move to the guide or grid lines according to a specified tolerance.

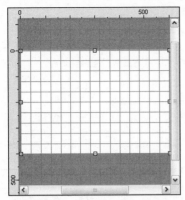

Figure 5-21: The default SWiSHmax grid shows a crosshatch of gray lines overlaying the Layout panel

The Guides panel is one of the panels docked in the panel group at the right side of the SWiSHmax program window. If the panel is not visible, click Panels ⇨ Guides to open the panel with the rest of the grouped panels. Click the panels' tab to move it to the front of the panel group. There are no tools or actions you perform on the Layout panel that activate the Guides panel and move it to the front of the group of panels automatically.

You configure three types of placement assistance tools in the Guides panel: guides, grids, and snap.

Displaying guides

You use guides on the Layout panel and configure their settings in the Guides panel. Guides are used to identify locations on the stage where you want to place objects. You can use the page rulers to set guides where you want them. You can add, modify, and delete guides as needed. You can also lock guides in place. Guides only exist in the Layout panel; they are not exported in a finished movie. You can add and remove guides on the Layout panel in a variety of ways.

✦ **Displaying rulers.** To display the rulers, you can click View ⇨ Show Rulers from the main program menu, click the Show Rulers button on the Guides panel, or right-click the Layout panel and choose Guides ⇨ Show Rulers as shown in Figure 5-22. Once you make your selection, the horizontal and vertical rulers on the left and top edges of the Layout window appear. To remove the rulers again, choose one of the three methods described and deselect the Show Rulers option.

Tip

If you right-click the Layout panel and don't see the shortcut menu commands, try again. You are probably clicking over an object, and instead of showing the Layout panel's shortcut commands you see the object's shortcut menu.

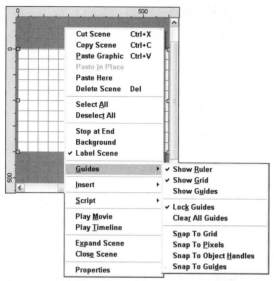

Figure 5-22: Right-click the Layout panel and choose Guide commands from the shortcut menu.

✦ **Adding guide lines.** You use your mouse to add guide lines. You can position the mouse over the top ruler, and then click and drag downward to add a horizontal guide. You can move the mouse over the left ruler and then click and drag to the right to add a vertical guide. A final option is to position the mouse over a ruler and click the ruler. A guide originating at the location you clicked appears.

Tip If you want the guide to align with a marker on the ruler, press Shift as you click the mouse. The guide is placed starting at the closest ruler marker.

✦ **Removing guide lines.** You can remove a single horizontal guide by clicking and dragging it up to the horizontal ruler. To remove a single vertical guide, click and drag it to the left vertical ruler. If you want to clear all guides, click View ➪ Clear All Guides from the main program menu. You can also click the Clear button on the Guides panel or right-click the Layout panel and choose Guides ➪ Clear All Guides.

Tip Don't try to drag the guide lines down or to the right to remove them; that merely repositions them on the Layout panel.

Modifying guides

There are several ways you can customize the guides and make them work for your particular situation. These actions correspond with the tools in the Guides panel, shown in Figure 5-23. You can also choose the same commands using these methods: Right-click the Layout panel and choose Guides and then one of the commands, or choose View from the main program menu and then select one of the commands from the menu.

Figure 5-23: Choose and customize guide settings in the Guides panel.

✦ **Show.** You may need a number of guides for placement as you are assembling a scene, but you may not need to see the guides at all times. Instead of removing the guides, click the Show icon to toggle the guides you have placed on and off.

✦ **Snap.** When the Snap feature is active, editing or moving an object aligns it with the guides on the Layout panel. Click the Snap icon to toggle the feature on and off. You lean more about how to use the Snap features later in the chapter.

✦ **Color.** Click the color swatch to open the Color Chooser and click a new color for the guides. The default color is medium blue, which is a good color if the scene's background is white but is difficult to see if your scene's background is also blue. This command is not available from the shortcut or main program menu, only from the Guides panel.

✦ **Ruler.** Toggle the Layout panels' rulers on or off by clicking the Ruler icon. You click and drag guides from the rulers.

✦ **Lock.** The guides can be moved on the Layout panel at any time. This movement is convenient when you are placing the guides, but isn't very convenient if you are trying to work with the scene and accidentally select and move the guide instead of your scene's objects. Click the Lock icon to lock the guides in their current locations.

✦ **Clear.** When you are finished working with a set of guides you can remove them individually from the Layout panel, or you can remove them all automatically by clicking the Clear button.

Working with grid lines

As explained earlier, the *grid* is an overlay of horizontal and vertical lines. You can use the grid to align objects precisely, and you can force objects to snap to the grid intersections. You can activate the grid from either the Toolbox or the Guides panel. You don't see the grid on an exported movie or while you are testing a movie.

Tip   Like many other viewing tools, you can also choose some of the settings by right-clicking the Layout panel and choosing Guides and one of the commands, or choosing View and one of the commands from the main program menu.

Click the Grid tool at the bottom of the Toolbox in the Layout panel to turn the grid lines on. If you can't see the tools, resize the program window or the Layout panel to display the tools. Alternatively, you can select the tools in the Guides panel.

The grid is either visible or invisible. If the grid lines are visible, clicking the tool toggles them off; if the grid lines are not visible, clicking the tool toggles them to visible. Unlike guide lines, the lines of the grid are static and can't be moved to alternate locations. The controls for adjusting the grid are on the Guides panel, shown in Figure 5-24.

Figure 5-24: Configure the grid lines in the Guides panel.

You can easily change both the color and the configuration of the grid to accommodate the project you are working with. For example, if the background color is similar to the default pale gray color you can change it; you can also adjust the dimensions of the grid:

1. **Click Show Grid on the Toolbox or click the Show Grid icon on the Guides panel.** The default grids appear on the Layout panel.

Note

You can also select the command by right-clicking the Layout panel to open the shortcut menu and then choosing Guides ⇨ Show Grid, or clicking View ⇨ Show Grid from the main program menu.

2. **Click the color swatch to open the Color Chooser.** Click an alternate color to use for the grid lines. Choose a color that contrasts with the background color of the movie or the background color of a particular scene.

3. **Click the H (horizontal) field in the Spacing option to make the field active.** Type an alternate horizontal spacing value for the grid in pixels.

4. **Click the V (vertical) field in the Spacing option to make the field active.** Type an alternate vertical spacing value for the grid in pixels.

Note

You don't have to use the same values for both height and width of the grid spacing.

Adjusting snap options

Snap options are the third type of layout assistance. Snapping automatically moves objects to the nearest defined snap location such as a guide, grid line, or even pixel. Snapping is a useful feature for drawing, editing, and arranging objects on the Layout panel. You can drag an object close to its desired location and when you release the mouse the object snaps to the layout feature according to the level of sensitivity you choose. By default, the snap setting is turned off. You can access the Snap tools in several locations:

✦ On the Toolbox (for Snap to Grid)

✦ In the Guides panel

✦ By right-clicking the Layout panel and choosing Guides, and then a Snap option

✦ By clicking View from the main program menu and choosing an option.

You modify the Snap features in the Guides panel. The Snap tools are shown in Figure 5-25.

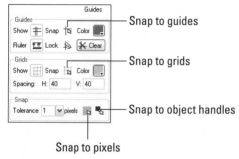

Figure 5-25: Configure the Snap options in the Guides panel.

There are several snap options:

- **Snap to grid.** This option snaps the selected object to the nearest grid lines.

- **Snap to guide.** This option snaps the selected object to the nearest guide line.

- **Snap to object handles.** This option snaps the selected object's handles to those of the nearest object.

- **Snap to pixels.** This option forces the selected object to snap to individual pixels as it is moved or edited.

 Caution You can toggle any or all of the Snap features on at the same time. If your objects don't seem to be snapping as you think they should, check to see which Snap options are active.

Each of the snap options produces a different way to work on the Layout panel. For grids, guides, and object handles, setting the sensitivity of the Snap feature is the same. The higher the sensitivity value, the farther from the active layout feature the object can be in order to snap into position. For example, if you choose a tolerance of 1 pixel, that means the object you draw or move must be within 1 pixel of the grid, guide line, or object handle in order to snap into place. On the other hand, if you choose a tolerance of 12 pixels, you have only to move the object within 12 pixels of the layout feature for it to snap into place. Click the down arrow to open the Tolerance menu and choose an option:

- Very Close — 1 pixel

- Close — 3 pixels

- Normal — 6 pixels

- Distant — 12 pixels

- Very Distant — 24 pixels

If you prefer, click the Tolerance field to make it active and type a pixel value.

Caution You can hide both the grid and guides, and still have snapping active. If your objects seem to move erratically, check to see if the snap features are toggled on. In the Guides panel, the Snap icons look like depressed buttons (they have a border) when they are active. The Snap to Grid button on the Toolbox also looks like a depressed button when it is active.

Summary

This chapter introduced you to drawing in SWiSHmax. You discovered how to use the drawing tools and how to view your drawing on the Layout panel in different ways using a number of tools. You found out about different layout assistance tools designed to make drawing easier and more accurate. You learned how to:

- Describe the different types of shapes you can draw in SWiSHmax.

- Draw basic shapes, such as lines, rectangles, and ellipses.

- Draw using different AutoShapes.

✦ Modify the characteristics of the AutoShapes to change their appearance.

✦ Use free-form drawing tools, including creating angular and curved Bézier shapes.

✦ View the contents of the Layout panel using a number of different tools and settings.

✦ Add guides to the Layout window, as well as how to configure and remove them.

✦ Display and adjust the grid overlaying the Layout panel.

✦ Set different snap features to help you place objects on the stage.

✦   ✦   ✦

Modifying Basic Shapes

In this chapter, you look at ways to manipulate and transform drawn objects in SWiSHmax. Any shape that you construct in SWiSHmax, such as a drawing, text, or a sprite, can be modified; you can modify some of the characteristics of imported images as well.

SWiSHmax includes a variety of tools that you can use to modify the properties of a shape, or of the lines that make up the shape, and you learn how to work with the tools in this chapter. In addition to working with tools, you can also modify shapes numerically in the Transform panel, which you also learn to do in this chapter.

Using a number of objects on the Layout panel's stage at the same time is very common. In SWiSHmax you can use a variety of methods to arrange objects based on their relationships to each other and to the stage.

Manipulating a Shape's Path

After you draw a curve using the Bézier tool, or draw a shape using one of the other drawing tools in the Toolbox, you are not committed to the drawing's shape, nor are you committed to the type of points added to the shape. You can add and remove vertices, and you can redefine each vertex as well as how the curve segments behave.

You can manipulate any drawing you create in SWiSHmax. However, an AutoShape must be ungrouped first before you can modify it with the SWiSHmax drawing tools.

Cross-Reference   Refer to Chapter 5 for information on drawing shapes using SWiSHmax's tools.

Modifying a shape using the adjustment handles

Use the Reshape tool to select different elements of a shape, including vertices, adjustment handles, and the lines between the vertices, or *line segments*. When you click the Reshape tool in the Toolbox and then click an object on the stage, the object's vertices and adjustment handles are active. In addition, selecting the Reshape tool activates the set of four Options tools in the Toolbox.

Freeform shapes, such as those you draw with the Pencil or Bézier tools, display vertices and line segments, as do objects created with the Line, Rectangle, and Ellipse tools. If you want to modify the vertices and line segments of an AutoShape, you have to ungroup the shape first in one of these ways:

✦ Right-click the AutoShape and choose Grouping ➪ Ungroup

✦ Select the AutoShape with the Select tool and choose Modify ➪ Grouping ➪ Ungroup from the main menu

✦ Select the AutoShape with the Select tool and press Ctrl+U

Make any changes to the AutoShape using the AutoShape anchors before you ungroup it. Once it is ungrouped, the AutoShape anchors used to control its characteristics are removed. For example, if you draw a star, you can use the center AutoShape anchor to change the number of points; ungrouping the star AutoShape removes the center AutoShape anchor and you can't change the number of points further.

When you click an object with the Reshape tool, .the vertices display as white anchors along the shape (or around the shape if it is closed); the ends of the adjustment handles display as light blue anchors. Figure 6-1 shows the same AutoShape before and after ungrouping as they appear when selected with the Reshape tool. In the heart shape at the left of the figure you can see the anchor point used to control the shape of the heart AutoShape. The right of the figure shows the same heart AutoShape after it is ungrouped. The green anchor point used to shape the heart is removed, and the vertices and handles display around the shape.

If you are working with a movie background color that is similar to the adjustment handles' color, SWiSHmax automatically inverts the color so you can see what you are working with. The inverted colors are also used when a selected object overlays a dark-colored shape.

Figure 6-1: When you ungroup an AutoShape, its individual segments become active.

The adjustment handles control the shape of the line both coming into and leaving the vertex they are attached to. For example, in Figure 6-2, dragging the left adjustment handle for the vertex labeled A changes the curve between the vertices labeled A and B. Adjusting the right handle for the vertex labeled A changes the curve between the vertices labeled A and C.

To work with the adjustment handles, click one of the blue anchors at the end of each adjustment handle, and move the handle in different directions to see how it affects your shape. You can move the handle up and down, lengthen it, and shorten it. In each case, the angles of the line segments are modified. Figure 6-3 uses the same drawing as that shown in Figure 6-2 and shows the effect of moving the various adjustment handles.

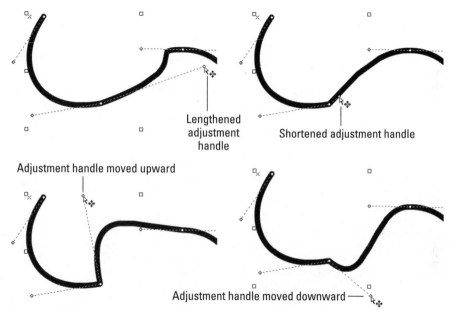

Figure 6-2: Modifying the adjustment handles affects two segments of your drawing.

Lengthened adjustment handle

Shortened adjustment handle

Adjustment handle moved upward

Adjustment handle moved downward

Figure 6-3: Moving an adjustment handle produces different effects.

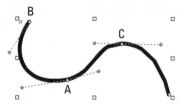

Note When you move adjustment handles, press the Shift key as you drag the handle to constrain the direction from the original position to 15-degree increments.

The closer you move an adjustment handle to a vertex, the more acute the angle between the line segment and the vertex becomes. You can shorten an adjustment handle to a vertex, or extend it beyond a vertex. In Figure 6-4, the adjustment handles of the vertex labeled A have been moved to the opposite sides of the vertex, creating a loop. The line in the figure is the same as that used in Figures 6-2 and 6-3.

These examples show you the types of changes you can make to a shape by moving the adjustment handles, but by far the best way to understand how to work with vertices and adjustment handles is to experiment.

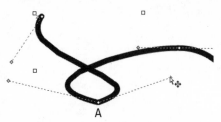

A

Figure 6-4: Pulling an adjustment handle to the opposite side of a vertex creates a loop.

You can modify the color SWiSHmax uses to identify the dashed adjustment handles' line color. The default color is blue. To modify the color of the adjustment handles, follow these steps:

1. **Choose Edit ➪ Preferences or Tools ➪ Preferences to display the Preferences dialog box.**

2. **Click the Appearance tab.** In the Color Options section of the tab, display the Color Chooser by clicking the color swatch located to the left of the Highlight color for bounding boxes, outlines, and motion paths option.

3. **Click to select a color.** The Color Chooser closes.

4. **Click OK to close the Preferences dialog box; the color is now changed.**

Understanding vertex types

A shape may contain several types of vertices. When you draw using the Bézier tool, you can click and drag to add a vertex that has curved line segments coming into and out of the vertex. Drawing with the Pencil tool automatically adds vertices and adjustment handles at the curves in the drawing. If you use the Rectangle or Ellipse tools to draw a basic shape, vertices (and adjustment handles, in the case of the Ellipse) are added automatically.

There are three vertex types that produce curved segments and one that produces sharp corners. They include:

✦ **Cusp.** A cusp vertex has two adjustment handles, which can extend at different angles from the vertex. The line segments coming into and out of the vertex are curved, although the corner created at the vertex's location is not rounded.

✦ **Smooth.** A smooth vertex has two adjustment handles extending at the same angle from the vertex. As a result, the corner at the vertex's location is smooth, although the segments coming into and out of the vertex don't automatically use the same degree of curve.

✦ **Symmetrical.** A symmetrical vertex has a pair of adjustment handles extending at the same angle and for the same length from the vertex. As a result, the corner at the vertex's location is smooth, and the line segments coming into and out of the vertex have the same degree of curve. The three vertices producing curved line segments are shown in Figure 6-5.

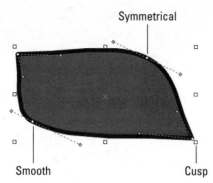

Figure 6-5: Three types of vertices are used for curved line segments.

✦ **Sharpen.** You produce a sharp corner using the sharpen vertex type. This type of vertex controls the corner; as a result, the two vertices to either side of the sharpen vertex have only one adjustment handle for the segment going out of the vertex (Figure 6-6).

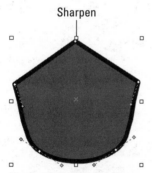

Figure 6-6: Use the Sharpen vertex type for sharp corners.

Follow these steps to change the vertex type:

1. **Move the mouse over the vertex you want to modify.** You see the reshaping cursor display when your mouse is in the correct location. The cursor is a small square surrounded by four arrows. If the center of the cursor shows a blue rectangle instead of a white one, your mouse is over an adjustment handle, not the vertex.

2. **Right-click the vertex to display the shortcut menu, shown in Figure 6-7.** The anchor types are listed in the shortcut menu.

3. **Click to select the vertex type you want to use.** The shortcut menu closes, and the vertex is changed.

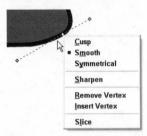

Figure 6-7: Choose a vertex type from the shortcut menu.

Changing the number and locations of vertices

When you draw a square or rectangle, you expect four vertices; for a triangle you expect three vertices. A triangle drawn with the Pencil tool, such as the triangle on the left in Figure 6-8, has more than three vertices if you have an unsteady hand and wiggle the mouse as you draw.

Removing vertices changes the relationships among the remaining vertices; that is, the vertex you remove controlled the line segment going in and coming out of the vertex. Control of the curve of the line segment is transferred to the two vertices that were on either side of the removed vertex. Follow these steps to remove extra vertices:

1. **Move the mouse over the vertex you want to remove.**

2. **Right-click to open the shortcut menu.**

3. **Choose Remove Vertex from the menu.**

4. **The shortcut menu closes and the extra vertex is removed.** The line segments before and after the removed vertexes are adjusted in the shape.

The image on the right in Figure 6-8 shows a triangle shape after several extra vertices are removed.

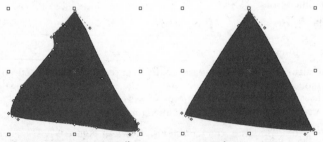

Figure 6-8: You can easily remove extra vertices.

You can also add a vertex anywhere along the path of a shape. Follow these steps to add a vertex to a shape:

1. **Select the Reshape tool in the Toolbox, and click the object to activate the vertices and adjustment handles.**

2. **Move the mouse over a line segment on your shape.** The cursor changes to an arrow and an arc, as shown in Figure 6-9.

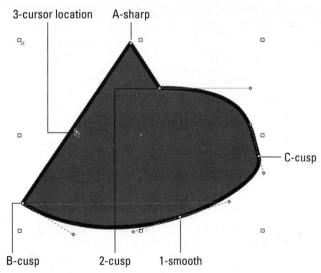

Figure 6-9: New vertices take on the characteristics of surrounding vertices.

3. **Right-click the line segment where you want to place the vertex.** The shortcut menu displays.

4. **Select Add Vertex from the shortcut menu.** The shortcut menu closes and the vertex is added to the line.

If you add a vertex incorrectly, click it with the Reshape tool and drag it right or left to adjust the lengths of the line segments on both sides of the vertex; or you can right-click the vertex and choose Remove Vertex from the shortcut menu and start again.

Caution   The vertex doesn't move along the line segment; you may have to use the adjustment handles to modify the line segments coming into and going out of the vertex.

The added vertex takes on the characteristics of the vertices on either side. To understand this idea more clearly, look at Figure 6-9.

The figure began as a triangle. A, B, and C identify the three original vertices and their types. The vertex labeled 1, added between B and C, is a smooth vertex (it has adjustment handles for modifying the line segments coming into and going out of the vertex). The vertex labeled 2 was added between A and C. Because A is a sharp vertex, 2 is a cusp vertex taking on the characteristic of the vertices on either side, with only the segment going out of the vertex having an adjustment handle. A vertex added at the cursor's location (3 in the figure) would have a sharp vertex because the segment on which it would be added is a sharp line segment.

Changing the characteristics of a line segment

The vertices on a shape determine the characteristics of the line segments coming into and going out of the vertices. You can also control a shape by changing the line segments themselves, which then affects the vertices on either side of the line segment. Follow these steps to modify a line segment:

1. **Select the Reshape tool in the Toolbox, and click the object to activate the vertices and adjustment handles.**

2. **Move the mouse over the line segment you want to modify.** You see the cursor change to an arrow and an arc.

3. **Right-click the line segment to display the shortcut menu.**

4. **Choose a type of line from the shortcut menu.** The menu closes and the line and the vertices on either end are modified.

You can choose three line options, all of which are shown in Figure 6-10:

✦ **Linear.** A linear line segment is straight. There are no vertices on either end.

✦ **Quadratic.** A quadratic line segment can be shaped. It has one control point that slides along a single adjustment handle extending between the vertices on either side of the line segment.

✦ **Cubic.** A cubic line segment can be curved. Separate adjustment handles are added to the vertices on either side of the line segment.

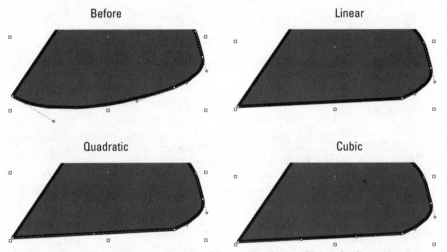

Figure 6-10: You can change a shape and its vertices by modifying the line segments.

Slicing an object

You can change the shape of a drawn object by selecting one vertex at a time and deleting it, or you can use the slice command and delete a segment of the shape. The slice command is only available from the shortcut menu, and can be used with drawn shapes as well as imported images. Follow these steps to slice a shape object:

1. **Click the object with the Reshape tool to activate the shape's vertices.**

2. **Right-click the location on the shape's curve where you want to start the slice.** You can choose an existing vertex, or anywhere along the line segments. The shortcut menu displays.

3. **Choose Slice from the shortcut menu.** The menu closes, and a vertex is added to the shape.

4. **Drag the mouse away from the new vertex.** You see a line extending from the vertex to the cursor; the line changes length and direction as you move the mouse (Figure 6-11).

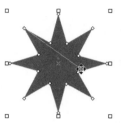

Figure 6-11: The direction of the slice depends on the cursor's location.

5. **Move the cursor over the shape's edge where you want to end the slice and right-click the mouse to display the shortcut menu again.**

6. **Choose Slice from the shortcut menu.** The menu closes, another vertex is added to the shape, and a segment of the shape is removed.

Tip

If you change your mind, or want to start the slice from a different location, click the mouse on the stage. The original slice vertex is removed, and the cursor reverts to the default.

Understanding the slicing process

When you experiment with the slicing process, you see that the segment of the shape that is removed is different depending on which side of the object you place the first slicing vertex.

A drawn shape runs in either a clockwise or a counterclockwise direction. The Rectangle, Ellipse, and ungrouped AutoShapes run in a clockwise direction. A shape drawn with the Line tool, the Pencil tool, or the Bézier tool runs in either direction depending on the direction in which you draw or place vertices. The direction of the vertices is identified for an ellipse in Figure 6-12. The number assignment is arbitrary; I have added numbers to serve as an illustration. You see the vertices run in a clockwise direction, which is the default for the ellipse shape.

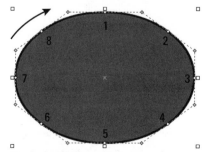

Figure 6-12: Every shape runs in one direction.

The segment removed using the slice command depends on the direction of the shape. Figure 6-13 uses the same ellipse as that seen in Figure 6-12. The left image shows the remaining segments of the shape after starting the slice at vertex 3 and ending at vertex 8 (everything clockwise between the 3 and 8 is sliced away). The right image shows the remaining segment of the shape after starting a slice at vertex 8 and ending at vertex 3 (moving clockwise from the 8 toward the 3 determines what is sliced away).

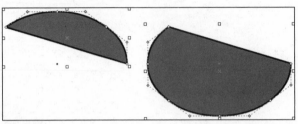

Figure 6-13: The shape segment removed depends on the direction of the slice.

When you start the slice at vertex 3 and end at vertex 8, you are defining all the space between those two vertices as the area you want to remove; the same applies when you start the slice at vertex 8 and end it at vertex 3.

Tip   If you are trying to slice a shape and it doesn't seem to be working, consider the direction of the object. If it is drawn using the SWiSHmax tools, it runs clockwise; if you drew it yourself, the direction may be counterclockwise, therefore causing the problem.

Slicing a shape into two pieces

Using the Slice command removes a segment of the shape. If you want to have a shape broken in two pieces, you need a copy. The key to successfully breaking an object into two pieces that combine visually to create the original object is defining the slice locations precisely. When you move the cursor on the stage, you can see its precise X- and Y-coordinate locations in the status bar at the bottom of the program window. Follow these steps to create two matching parts of a shape using guide lines:

1. **Draw the shape you want to split.**

2. **Select the shape with the Select tool.** Choose Edit ⇨ Copy to copy the shape to the Clipboard.

3. **Choose Edit ⇨ Paste in Place to place a duplicate copy in the same location on the stage as the original.**

4. **Click the Reshape tool to display the shape's vertices.**

5. **Drag guide lines from the rulers and place them at the locations on the shape's edge where you want to slice the object.**

6. **Move the cursor to the starting slice location.** Right-click and choose Slice from the shortcut menu.

7. **Move the cursor to the ending slice location.** Right-click again and choose Slice from the shortcut menu. The first object is sliced, and the segment removed, revealing the underlying complete shape.

8. **Repeat Steps 6 and 7 using the underlying shape, except reverse the direction of the slice.** When you are finished, you have a shape divided into two segments.

You can use this technique to divide a shape into numerous sections. However, if you are planning to split a shape into many segments to use for animation, use the Break command instead. Choose Modify ➪ Break ➪ Break into Pieces and choose options from the Break into Pieces dialog box.

Cross-Reference Learn more about breaking text objects in different ways in Chapter 10 and breaking shape objects in Chapter 12.

Controlling the Position of Objects

Chapter 5 described how to use layout assistance tools like the grid and guide lines to help you position objects. You can move objects on the Layout panel manually, or control their positions precisely using the Transform panel. Figure 6-14 shows a beveled button object selected on the stage. The figure also shows an overlying grid and the Transform panel.

In the figure, the stage is sized at 280 x 240 pixels. The object's size is 200 x 200 pixels, and the grid is set at 20 x 20 pixels. The object is placed 40 pixels from the left edge and 20 pixels from the top edge of the stage.

In the Transform panel, you see the W (width) and H (height) values are both 200 pixels. If you look at the locations listed in the Transform panel, however, you see the X (X-coordinate or horizontal position on the stage) is shown as 140 pixels, and the Y (Y-coordinate or vertical position on the stage) is set at 120 pixels.

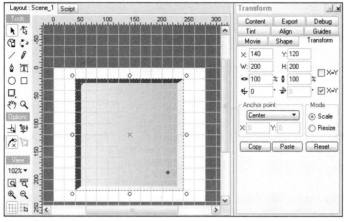

Figure 6-14: A selected object displays location and size values in the Transform panel.

Redefining anchor points

The X- and Y-coordinates are based on the *anchor point* for the object. If you look at any selected object on the Layout panel, you see a small "x" at the center of the object. This is the anchor point. An anchor point serves as a frame of reference when describing an object in relation to other objects, and to the stage. Anchor points are also used with some transformations, such as rotation.

The default location of an anchor point is at the center of the object. If you refer to the Transform panel shown in Figure 6-14, the Center option is shown for the Anchor point location. You can reset an object's anchor point. Follow these steps:

1. **Click either the Select tool or the Reshape tool in the Toolbox.**

2. **Click the object on the Layout panel to make it active.**

3. **Click the Transform panel to display the object's settings.**

4. **Click the Anchor point drop-down arrow to open the menu shown in Figure 6-15.**

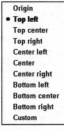

Figure 6-15: Choose an alternate location for the anchor point from this menu.

 Tip

The Anchor point menu options are also available from the Main menu. Choose Modify ⇨ Anchor and select an anchor point location.

5. **Choose an alternate anchor point position from the menu.** The menu closes, and the chosen location displays. The anchor point shifts on the object on the Layout panel.

 Note

If you want to restore the anchor point to its original location, click the Reset button on the Transform panel.

Figure 6-16 shows the same object as that shown in Figure 6-14, this time with its anchor point at the top left. If you look at the object on the stage, you see the anchor point is at the upper left of the object. In the Transform panel, the values for the X- and Y-coordinates now display the coordinates you would expect to see based on the object's location: 40 pixels from the left (X-coordinate) and 20 pixels from the top (Y-coordinate) of the stage.

Most anchor point positions are self-explanatory. The Center location is the default. In general, if you choose the Origin anchor point position from the menu, you don't see a difference in the anchor point's location from that of the Center position.

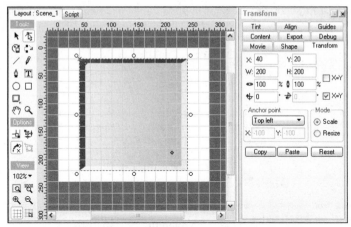

Figure 6-16: Choosing an alternate anchor point location moves the visual anchor on the object and changes the coordinates on the Transform panel.

The Origin anchor point is different from the Center position in an object modified from the original. In Figure 6-17, three copies of the same object are shown. The first displays the default Center anchor point position. The middle shape is a copy of the object after a segment is sliced away. The object still displays the anchor at the Center position, although the center is now that of the sliced object. The shape at the right shows where the anchor point moves when Origin is selected: the center of the original object before slicing occurred.

Figure 6-17: The center and origin anchor points are different if an object is modified from the original.

Caution

If you draw a shape (or use an AutoShape) and then rotate it, be careful when adjusting the anchor point. You can't use the location of the shape on the stage as reference for choosing the anchor point; you must choose an anchor point location in reference to the original orientation of the drawing. For example, if you draw a shape, rotate it 90 degrees clockwise and then choose the Top Left anchor point setting, the anchor point is placed at the top right of the shape as it appears on the stage.

You can also choose a custom location for the anchor point. Follow these steps:

1. **Click the object on the Layout panel with the Select or Reshape tool.**

2. **Click the Transform panel to display the object's settings.**

3. **Click the Anchor point drop-down arrow to open the drop-down menu and choose Custom.** The menu closes, and the two coordinate fields below the Anchor point position are active.

4. **Click the Anchor point X-coordinate field to make it active and type a value; repeat with the Anchor point Y-coordinate field.** The anchor point moves to the custom location.

Tip

You can also move an anchor point visually on the Layout panel. Press the Alt key, and click and drag the anchor point on the object. The new anchor point is labeled as a custom anchor point location.

Moving an object numerically

If you reset an object's anchor point to its top-left corner, you can easily position an object precisely on the Layout panel's stage using the Transform panel — no arithmetic required! Follow these steps:

1. **Select the object on the Layout panel with the Select or Reshape tool.**

2. **Click the Transform panel, bringing it to the top of the grouped panels.**

3. **Click the displayed anchor point value to open the menu and choose Top Left.** The menu closes and the anchor point moves to the upper left of the object.

4. **On the Transform panel, click the X-coordinate field to make it active and type a value; repeat with the Y-coordinate field.** The object moves to the specified location on the stage.

You can set an object's location on the stage in the Transform panel regardless of the anchor point's location on the object. However, unless the anchor point is at the top left, there is a difference between the physical location of the object's edge and the coordinates displayed in the Transform panel.

Here's an example. The coordinates of the upper left edge of the Layout panel's stage are X-axis=0 and Y-axis=0. If you have a square that is 100x100 pixels in size, the anchor point at the center, and you want the square to be placed at the upper left edge of the Layout panel's stage, actual coordinates shown in the Transform panel are X-axis=50 and Y-axis=50 as they are based on the anchor point. If the anchor point is set to the upper left corner, placing the square at the top left of the Layout panel's stage shows the square's coordinates at X-axis=0 and Y-axis=0, equivalent to the stage coordinates.

The Transformation Tools

Depending both on the characteristics of an object and whether the Select or Reshape tool is selected, a number of other tools called Options are active. There are four basic Options tools:

Scale. The Scale tool is used for enlarging or reducing the size of a selected object horizontally, vertically, or both. The widths of line or text elements in the object are resized proportionally as the object is resized.

Resize. The Resize tool is also used for enlarging or reducing the size of a selected object horizontally, vertically, or both. Unlike the Scale tool, the widths of line or text elements in the object don't change as the object is scaled.

Cross-Reference Learn how to work with lines in Chapter 7 and how to use text in Chapter 10.

Rotate/Skew. As the name suggests, the Rotate/Skew tool has two purposes: When the tool is used over the corner handles of an object, the object rotates based on its anchor point position. When the tool is used over the side handles surrounding an object, the object rotates along a specified axis.

Distort. The Distort tool is used to alter an entire object or a selected vertex or line segment in an object by dragging in different directions.

A fifth Options tool, called the Speed tool, shows the frame rate per second when drawing a Motion Path.

Cross-Reference Motion Paths are discussed in Chapter 12.

Using the Scale and Resize tools

The Scale and Resize tools seem similar, but depending on the characteristics of the object to which you are applying the tool, the tools' effects are different. For example, Figure 6-18 shows three shapes. The shape at the left is the original rounded rectangle, the middle shape is 50 percent smaller than the original, and the right shape is also 50 percent smaller than the original. You can clearly see a difference in the shapes: The central shape was resized using the Scale tool. Not only is the rectangle 50 percent smaller than the original, but the width of the line surrounding the shape is scaled to 50 percent as well. Contrast that with the shape at the right of the figure; the Resize tool was applied to this shape. Overall the rectangle is 50 percent smaller than the original, but the line remains the same width as the original. To use the Scale or Resize tools, follow these steps:

Caution If you have a line width set to 0 (zero) it will never scale although it is visible as a one pixel wide line.

1. **Click the Select or Reshape tool in the Toolbox and click the object to select it.** The selected object displays resize handles around its bounding box. The Options tools are activated in the Toolbox.

2. **Click either the Scale or Resize tool and move it over the object.** Click and drag using one of these options:

   • Place the cursor over one of the side handles and drag up/down or left/right to change the size of the object

   • Place the cursor over one of the corner handles and drag toward the center of the object to decrease the object's size; drag away from the center of the object to increase the object's size.

Figure 6-18: Objects may look quite different depending on the tool used.

Maintaining proportion

The relationship of the height to the width of an object is called the object's *aspect ratio*. In order for an object to change size proportionally, its aspect ratio must be 1:1. For every unit of change vertically (increase or decrease), the same unit of change occurs horizontally.

You can control the proportions of the shape as you change the size or scale on the Layout panel. Place the cursor over one of the corner handles and press the Shift key as you drag the mouse to constrain the increase or decrease equally.

Using the Transform panel to control scaling or resizing

You can control the amount of resizing or scaling and also whether to use resizing or scaling using settings in the Transform panel. Follow these steps to resize a shape numerically:

1. **Select the shape on the Layout panel using either the Select or Reshape tool.**

2. **Click the Transform panel's tab in the panel group.**

3. **Click either the Scale or Resize radio buttons to choose the Mode.** Notice in the Toolbox that the corresponding button is active.

4. **Do one of the following:**

   - Click in the W field and type a value for the desired width of the object in pixels; click in the H field and type a value for the desired height of the object in pixels.

   - Click in the Stretch in x direction field (indicated by a square with two horizontal arrows, below the W field) and type a percentage; click in the Stretch in y (indicated by a square with two vertical arrows, below the H field) direction field and type a percentage.

   - Click the Uniform scale check box (the upper X=Y) to make it active. The H and Stretch in y direction fields are grayed out, as shown in Figure 6-19. Enter one value in either the W field or the Stretch in x direction field to set the scale values proportionally.

Tip

If you change the scale or resize an object and want to revert to the original, click the Reset button on the Transform panel.

Caution

With the Resize mode selected, you can change the width and height of an object in the Transform panel without changing the scale of the object. If you manually change the scale on the Transform panel while in Resize mode, the scale also changes. That is, when you are in Scale mode, you can only scale objects; while in Resize mode, you can both scale and resize.

The percentage values displayed in the Transform panel's Stretch in x direction and Stretch in y direction fields may or may not change when you change the size of the shape numerically in the Transform panel, or when you use the Resize tool in the Toolbox.

The Scale tool resizes an object and its component parts proportionally. Resizing the object smaller or larger creates a truly scaled version of the original. Using the Scale tool to decrease an object by a scale factor of 50 percent makes the content and any lines or text decrease in size by 50 percent as well.

The Resize tool doesn't scale the object; it merely makes the amount of space used by the object increase or decrease by the chosen value.

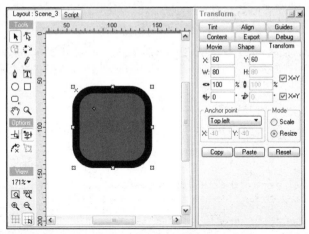

Figure 6-19: Use the Transform panel for precise control of the object's size.

Using the Rotate/Skew tool

The Rotate/Skew tool affects the way an object displays along the X-axis, the Y-axis, or both axes. Use the Rotate/Skew tool to revolve an object equally along both axes; in other words, to *rotate* the object. You can also use the Rotate/Skew tool to revolve an object along one axis or the other, which is called *skewing*. Figure 6-20 shows examples of using each tool. The image at the left is the original image. The central image is rotated 45 degrees, and the image at the right is skewed 45 degrees along the Y-axis. To use the Rotate tool, follow these steps:

Figure 6-20: You can use the Rotate/Skew tool to change the appearance of an object along one axis or both axes.

1. **Select the object on the Layout panel.** The Options tools become active.

2. **Click the Rotate/Skew tool.** A set of eight circular handles displays around the object. The handles are at each corner, and at the center of each side of the object.

3. **Move the mouse over one of the circular corner handles.** You see the cursor change to a circular arrow.

4. **Click the corner handle and drag in a clockwise or counterclockwise direction.** The object rotates around the anchor point.

Unlike the Rotate tool which works on any corner handle of the object in the same way, the Skew tool works differently depending on which handle is used.

Note   You can access several rotation options from the Main menu. Choose Modify ➪ Transform and choose one of the rotation or flip options. You can also reset the transformation using the Reset command in the same submenu.

Follow these steps to use the Skew tool:

1. **Select the object on the Layout panel.** The Options tools become active.

2. **Click the Rotate/Skew tool.** A set of eight circular handles displays around the object. The handles are at each corner, and at the center of each side of the object.

3. **Move the mouse over one of the circular handles along the sides of the object.** You see the cursor change to a double-ended arrow and a parallelogram.

4. **Click the center handle and drag in any direction.** You can flip the object horizontally by dragging left or right, or flip vertically by dragging up or down. Skew in degrees by dragging in any direction.

Caution   Be careful which handle you skew from. The handle at the left center of the object shows a vertical double-ended arrow. If you drag from this handle, the object is skewed along the X-axis. The other three handles on the sides of the object skew along the Y-axis.

You can control both rotation and skew either by pressing the Shift key as you rotate (which constrains the angle to multiples of 15 degrees), or by pressing the Ctrl key as you rotate (which constrains the angle to full rather than partial degrees of rotation).

Using the Transform panel to control rotation and skew

You can control the amount of rotation or skew numerically in the Transform panel. You can set the rotation values and also specify if the object is rotated or skewed. Follow these steps to rotate or skew an object numerically:

1. **Select the object on the Layout panel using either the Select or Reshape tool.**

2. **Click the Transform panel's tab in the panel group.**

3. **Select the type of transformation:**

   - To use rotation, click the lower X=Y check box to select uniform rotation. The angle of Y-axis field is grayed out. Type the desired degree of rotation in the angle of X-axis value field.

   - To use skew, deselect the lower X=Y check box to turn off uniform rotation. Both the angle of X-axis and angle of Y-axis fields are active. Type the desired degree of rotation in either or both of the angle of X-axis and angle of Y-axis value fields. In Figure 6-21, the object's Y-axis is skewed 120 degrees.

On The Web Site   If you would like to experiment with the object used in the examples in this chapter, use the file named ch06_sample01.swi, which is on the book's Web site in the chapter06 folder. The file contains two scenes; the **rotate object** scene is used in these examples.

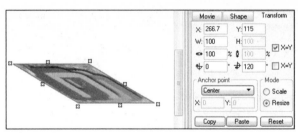

Figure 6-21: Use the Transform panel to set rotation and skew values numerically.

Reusing transformation settings

You can apply settings configured for one object to other objects. The settings that can be reused include: anchor point, scale, size, rotation, and skew. Follow these steps to reuse transformation settings:

1. **Make the Scale, Resize, Rotate/Skew changes to an object as required.**

2. **Click the Copy button on the Transform panel.**

3. **Select the object on the Layout panel that you want to receive the copied settings.**

4. **Click the Paste button on the Transform panel.** The transformation settings are copied to the object.

Note You cannot copy and paste settings created using the Distort tool because the Distort tool's actions are specific to a single object or vertex.

Rotating an object based on the anchor point

An object is rotated or skewed based on the anchor point location. The default position for an anchor point is the center of the object. If you move the anchor point to other locations, you can create composite objects quite quickly, such as a flower. An example of an object containing 14 shapes is shown in Figure 6-22. Follow these steps to create an object using multiple copies:

Figure 6-22: You can create a composite drawing using simple shapes and a well-placed anchor point.

Cross-Reference The petal and center of the flower are colored. You learn about strokes and fills in Chapter 7.

1. **Draw the initial objects.** In the example, the center of the flower is a circle. The petal was created using the Bézier tool.

2. **Click the anchor point location button in the Transform panel and choose Custom from the menu.** You move the anchor point to a custom location around which you want to rotate the object.

3. **Type X- and Y-coordinates in the X- and Y-coordinate fields.** The sample uses values of X=22.5 and Y=82. Alternately, you can select the object, press the Alt key, and drag the anchor point to the center of the circle.

Tip

Using the second option is much faster; calculating the location of the circle's center in relation to the object is difficult to do.

4. **Choose Edit ⇨ Copy, or press Ctrl+C to copy the object to the clipboard.**

5. **Choose Edit ⇨ Paste in Place.** Paste additional copies depending on the size of each object and the diameter of the composite object you are constructing. The sample uses an additional 12 copies of the petal. After the object is copied, you can also press Shift+Ctrl+V to paste the copies into the Layout panel.

Note

Don't use the simple Paste command because that places the copies at the center of the movie. You want the set of objects stacked on top of one another.

6. **Click the Rotate/Skew tool.** The round rotate/skew handles display around the object.

7. **Press the Shift key and drag from a corner handle to rotate the top copy of the object.** The sample object's rotation is 15 degrees, as shown in Figure 6-23. Release the mouse.

Note

Depending on the dimensions of the finished composite image, the number of segments you are creating, and the amount of space you want to leave blank in the center of the composite image, you have to calculate the rotation for each segment in degrees.

Figure 6-23: Use a custom anchor point to assist in placing multiple components of a radially symmetrical object.

8. **Repeat with the remaining objects, evenly distributing them around the composite shape.**

Tip

Holding down the Shift key as you drag the anchor point constrains the rotation to 15-degree increments.

On The Web Site

The flower file is on the Web site in the chapter06 folder if you want to experiment further. The file is named ch06_sample01.swi and contains two scenes; the **flower** scene is used in this example.

Using the Distort tool

The Distort tool is different from the other Option tools in that it has no specific values that can be set in the Transform panel. As you work with the tool, changes made to the object's size and location are listed in the Transform panel, but modifying a specific value or clicking the Reset button in the Transform panel doesn't return the object to its original shape.

The Distort tool works on either the entire shape or an individual vertex depending on what you select. Here's how to use the Distort tool:

1. **Click the Reshape tool, and then click the object you want to modify.** The corner object handles display, as do the object's vertices and adjustment handles.

Note

If you want to distort the shape of the entire object, you can select the object using the Select tool.

2. **Click the element you want to modify:**

   • Click a vertex if you want to distort the shape based on the vertex's position

   • Click a line segment if you want to distort the shape of the line

   • Click an outer handle if you want to distort the entire shape

3. **Drag the element in any direction to modify the shape.**

If you click and drag a vertex, you are restricted by the type of vertices that are on either side of the selected vertex. If you click and drag a line segment, you are restricted by the type of vertices on either side of the line segment. The amount, type, and direction of distortion are not restricted if you click and drag a corner handle of the object. As you move any element of the object, adjustment handles shift to reflect the changes made with the Distort tool. Figure 6-24 began as a square, but has been distorted using vertices, line segments, and the shape's handles.

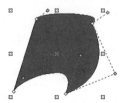

Figure 6-24: Use the Distort tool to quickly reshape an object.

Organizing Objects on the Layout Panel

SWiSHmax provides tools you can use to organize a number of selected objects on the stage. Each object, when selected, is surrounded by eight handles. These handles identify the corners, such as lower left, as well as the center locations on each side of the object, such as left center. You can organize objects on the Layout panel based on the positions of the handles around an object. You can also organize objects based on the anchor point positions, whether or not they are at the center of the objects.

The commands used for arranging a number of selected objects are available from the Main menu by choosing Modify ➪ Align, and then choosing one of the submenus (Top, Distribute, Relative To All Selected, and so on).

Alternatively, you can work with the Align panel. The panel contains the same commands organized in the same way as the Main menu: each command from the Main menu has a corresponding button or menu choice in the Align panel. To apply one of the Align commands, follow these steps:

1. **Click the Select tool in the Toolbox to make it active.**

Tip   You can also select objects using the Reshape tool; the object's selection handles as well as its vertices and adjustment handles display.

2. **Click the first object to which you want to apply the command.** The selected object displays its selection handles.

3. **Press Ctrl and click to select the other objects to which you want to apply the command.** You can also click and drag the Select tool around a number of contiguous objects to select them with one operation. You must select at least two objects.

Note   Although you need to select only two objects to use the Align commands, you must select three objects to use the Distribution commands.

4. **Click the Align panel's tab to display it in the panel group.**

5. **Click an Align option to apply the command.** When the button is clicked, it displays a gold frame—a handy feature if you forget which command was applied.

6. **If required, select a Size by option or choose an Align Relative to option.** The Size by option is used only with the Make Same commands; the Align Relative to options are used by the sets of Align and Distribute options.

Align tools

SWiSHmax divides the tools on the Align panel into categories. Many of the commands are familiar if you have experience with graphic or image design programs.

Horizontal Alignment. The four horizontal alignment options, used to organize a number of selected objects vertically, include commands for aligning objects left, horizontal center, and right. The fourth option, the Align Horizontal Anchor command, aligns the objects according to the location of their anchor point on the X-axis. When the selected objects' anchor points are in different locations, the alignment doesn't look correct until you evaluate the anchor points' positions. In Figure 6-25, the three ellipses are aligned vertically based on their anchor points' positions. The upper ellipse has a bottom-center anchor point location; the central ellipse uses a central anchor point location; and the lower ellipse uses a top-left anchor point position.

Figure 6-25: You can align objects based on their anchor point locations; in this figure the three ellipses are aligned vertically.

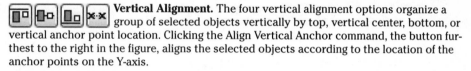

Vertical Alignment. The four vertical alignment options organize a group of selected objects vertically by top, vertical center, bottom, or vertical anchor point location. Clicking the Align Vertical Anchor command, the button furthest to the right in the figure, aligns the selected objects according to the location of the anchor points on the Y-axis.

Horizontal Distribution. Distributing selected objects requires that you have a minimum of three objects selected. The distribution is based on the X-axis locations. You can distribute a number of selected objects left, center, right, or according to their anchor point position.

Vertical Distribution. Choose a Vertical Distribution option to distribute selected objects based on their Y-axis values. You can choose from top, center, bottom, or anchor point locations.

Spacing. You can choose from three different spacing commands. The first two, Space Evenly Horizontally and Space Even Vertically, are quite common commands. The third, Space Evenly Both, saves you one mouse click when you want to space selected objects both vertically and horizontally.

Choosing relativity

Whether you are aligning, distributing, or spacing objects, you can choose from a number of ways that define the objects' relationships among other objects and with other elements of a movie. Click the Align Relative to button on the Align panel and choose an option from the menu, which includes:

✦ **All Selected.** This option makes the alignment options relative to the selected objects.

✦ **Last Selected.** This option makes the alignment options relative to the location of the object you selected last.

✦ **Parent.** Choose the Relative to Parent alignment option when working with a sprite containing a number of objects you want to align. In the case of several objects in a single scene, choosing the Relative to Parent option makes the selected objects relative to the stage (the parent object of the selected objects).

✦ **Stage.** The Relative to Stage option is useful when you want to organize a collection of objects, such as buttons on a scene. The command makes the alignment options relative to the stage.

Caution

Within a sprite, the Relative to Stage option places the object relative to the sprite's coordinates, not that of the movie stage.

To change the relativity option for alignment, follow these steps:

1. **Select the objects on the stage.** The Align panel buttons activate.

2. **Click the Align Relative drop-down arrow to open the menu shown in Figure 6-26.**

3. **Click an option to select it.** The menu closes.

4. **Click to select an Align, Distribution, or Spacing option.**

Figure 6-26: Define how selected objects behave by selecting a relativity option from the menu.

The relativity option you choose makes a difference in many of the alignment options. For example, Figure 6-27 shows three groups of objects on the stage. On the left is the set of three original objects. In the central image, the objects were selected and aligned at the vertical center using the Align Relative to All Selected option. The objects align according to the middle ellipse's location. In the right image, the objects are again aligned at the vertical center, but this time using the Align Relative to the Last Selected option. The lower ellipse was the last one selected, and the upper two move to the right to align with it.

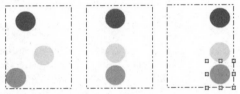

Figure 6-27: The same alignment command can produce very different results based on relativity.

Here's another example using a distribution command. In the left image shown in Figure 6-28, the three ellipses are distributed according to their horizontal centers, and the alignment relates to all the selected objects. Guide lines showing you the even distribution of the objects are added at the locations of each ellipse's center point. In the right image of the figure, the same distribution command is used, but this time the objects are distributed relative to the stage. In this image, you can see that, although the three objects are still distributed evenly, they are now distributed across the entire stage.

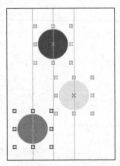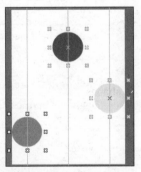

Figure 6-28: This figure compares the difference between distributing a number of objects relative to themselves with distributing them relative to the stage.

Sizing objects using Align commands

The Align panel contains tools for quickly sizing selected objects.

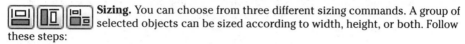 **Sizing.** You can choose from three different sizing commands. A group of selected objects can be sized according to width, height, or both. Follow these steps:

1. **Select the objects on the stage.**

2. **Click the sizing drop-down arrow and choose an option from the menu, as shown in Figure 6-29.** You can choose either Scaling or Resizing. The menu closes.

3. **Click to select a Sizing option.** The selected objects are resized.

Figure 6-29: Choose a sizing method from the menu.

Grouping Shapes

SWiSHmax includes four options for grouping objects, or combining them into one object. These four types of grouping are:

✦ Group as Group

✦ Group as Button

✦ Group as Sprite

✦ Group as Shape

 You can read more about grouping as a group, used for complex effects, in Chapter 12. Learn about grouping objects as a sprite in Chapter 15. See Chapter 16 for information on grouping objects as a button.

As part of the discussion of shapes, only the Group as Shape function is discussed in this chapter. The Group as Shape command creates a single merged shape that can contain punched-out, overlapped, or combined shapes. You can create intricate shapes and cutouts using the command.

 If you try to group objects that contain effects or events as a single shape, the effects or events are removed.

Follow these steps to group objects as a single shape:

1. **Select the objects on the stage.** The stacking order of the objects doesn't make a difference in the outcome of the grouping.

2. **Align or distribute the objects as required.**

3. **Choose Modify ⇨ Grouping ⇨ Group as Shape from the Main menu.** You can also right-click the group and choose Grouping ⇨ Group as Shape from the shortcut menu.

Caution   Don't use the Ctrl+G accelerator key combination to group a number of objects as a shape. The accelerator key groups the objects as a group, which works in a different fashion from a shape group.

4. **A dialog box opens asking if you want to make the overlapped regions of objects with the same fill empty.** Click Yes to close the dialog box and complete the grouping.

Note   If you want to fill the overlapped areas at a later time, you can click the Solid shape with overlap filled check box, located below the Fill preview area on the Shape panel.

Figure 6-30 shows three objects before grouping on the left and after grouping on the right.

To restore a group to its component objects, choose Modify ⇨ Grouping ⇨ Ungroup, or use the Ctrl+U accelerator key combination.

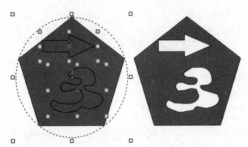

Figure 6-30: You can punch out overlapping areas using the Group as Shape command.

Summary

This chapter explained how to modify the vertices and line segments that make up a drawn shape. You learned about many tools and methods you can use to modify a shape after it is drawn, and how a number of selected objects can be arranged in different ways on the Layout panel. In this chapter, you also learned:

✦ Ways to modify the vertices of a shape, use adjustment handles, and change the characteristics of a shape's line segments

✦ Ways to slice an object

✦ Ways to modify the anchor point of an object for different uses

✦ Methods for using the transform tools, including the scale, resize, rotate/skew, and distort tools

✦ How to align and distribute objects in different ways

✦ How to create a composite shape from a number of shapes

✦   ✦   ✦

Choosing and
Using Color

Most movies produced in SWiSHmax are destined for either Web or computer monitor use. Computer monitors vary in resolution, but all monitors produced in the last few years have the capability to display millions of colors. In this chapter, you learn about working with color on computer monitors.

In the earlier days of the Internet, using only Web-safe colors was necessary to produce predictable results. Although there are fewer restrictions now with regard to choosing color, it's important that you understand how to work with color to ensure accurate and predictable results in your movies.

SWiSHmax uses a tidy system for managing color. You work with the Color Selector, a pop-up window that gives you multiple options for selecting color as well as storing a number of colors for reuse.

Understanding Color

A monitor's display is composed of thousands of pixels arranged in a grid. The color systems you work with in SWiSHmax and other visual design programs are based on color projected or generated by the monitor's pixels. If you understand the basics of color, you can be sure that what you design and see on your monitor is the same as that your viewers see when they look at your work.

RGB color

You view color on a computer monitor using a color system called *RGB color* (Red/Green/Blue) with each pixel containing one red, green, and blue dot. The color you see on a screen is made up of varying amounts of each color displayed by the color dots. When working with color images on your computer, the color dots are referred to as color *channels*.

Each pixel is capable of displaying 256 values or levels of intensity for each of red, blue, and green from 0 to 255. With a value of 0, the pixel's color dot is off; when the color's value is 255 the pixel's color dot is fully on. At any value in between, the pixel's color dot is partially on and displays varying intensity of color.

The RGB color model is an *additive* color model, which means that the greater the amount of each color used in a pixel, the closer the color is to pure white. It also means the less the amount of a color used in a pixel, the closer the color projected is to pure black.

Figure 7-1 is a color bar showing shades of gray. For an RGB value of 255/255/255 (Red=255, Green=255, Blue=255) the pixel displays each color at full intensity, which appears as pure white, shown at the left of the figure. When the RGB value is 0/0/0 (Red=0, Green=0, Blue=0), the pixel doesn't display the colors at all, resulting in pure black, which is shown at the right of the figure. When the RGB values are equal, the color displayed by a pixel is neutral gray and varies in depth or intensity. The higher the number, the closer the shade of gray is to black.

Figure 7-1: Color displays in a range of intensity from 100 percent to 0 percent.

RGBA color

RGBA is similar to RGB color except that it includes one more channel to indicate how transparent a color is. RGBA is an acronym for Red/Green/Blue/Alpha. RGBA is 32-bit color and it is what you work with in SWiSHmax.

Just as with RGB, each of the four channels has a value between 0 and 255. 32-bit color provides more than 4.2 billion color possibilities. This is due to the nature of transparency. A semitransparent pixel displays as a combination of the semitransparent color and the background color. Figure 7-2 shows a semitransparent oval overlaying a pattern; the oval shape's pixels use color values that are combinations of the oval's green color and the background pattern's color.

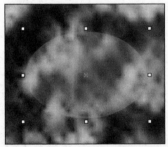

Figure 7-2: Pixels can display a combination of a semitransparent color combined with a background pixel color.

Note   Digital color displayed on a computer monitor is the opposite of using physical color pigments, such as what an inkjet printer uses. With pigments, the less of any color used, the closer the color is to white. This use of physical pigments to form color is referred to as *subtractive* color. The model used for printing is called CMYK (Cyan/Magenta/Yellow/Black) and combines the three colors of ink with black to produce a broad range of printable color.

Monitors display color based on their *bit depth*. Bit depth is also called pixel depth or color depth and measures how much color information is available for each pixel to display on a monitor. Higher bit depths provide more color information to the monitor's pixels and result in more accurate color displays.

A pixel with a bit depth of 1, for example, has two color values — black and white. A monitor with a bit depth of 16 can display 65,536 colors; a monitor with a bit depth of 24 can display 16,777,216 colors. Bit depths range from 1 to 64 bits per pixel. Modern color display systems use a 32-bit color mode that allows them to support RGBA color.

You can check and change the bit depth of your computer. Follow these steps:

1. **Right-click the desktop to display the shortcut menu.**

2. **Click Properties on the shortcut menu to open the Display Properties dialog box.** You can also click Start ⇨ Settings ⇨ Control Panel ⇨ Display on the desktop to open the dialog box. Right-clicking the desktop saves steps.

3. **Click the Settings tab, shown in Figure 7-3.** The tab includes information about the type of monitor you are using, as well as screen resolution and color quality options.

Figure 7-3: Change your monitor's color quality in the Display Properties dialog box.

4. **Click the Color quality drop-down arrow to open the menu.** Click a Color quality setting. The available options depend on your monitor.

5. **Click Apply to apply the settings.** Depending on your computer display's configuration, the screen may flicker, reset itself, and ask you to confirm the change. If you experience this, click Yes to close the message box and return to the Display Properties dialog box.

6. **Click OK to close the Display Properties dialog box.**

Note   Until recent years, a big design concern was using Web-safe colors to ensure consistency across computer platforms. The Web-safe colors were a set of 216 colors that displayed the same on all monitors regardless of browser or computer platform.

Using hexadecimal color values

The *hexadecimal color system* represents colors the same way as the RBG color system, but uses different notation. The term hexadecimal refers to colors using base-16 number values (RGB uses base-10 integer values). Hexadecimal color is referred to as *hex color* or a *hex value*. Hex values compare to integer values like this:

Integer values	0	1	2	3	4	5	6	7	8	9	10	11	12	13	14	15	16
Hex values		0	1	2	3	4	5	6	7	8	9	10	A	B	C	D	E	F

Each hex color contains six numbers — two values for Red, two values for Green, and two values for Blue. The hex color system uses the values 00, 33, 66, 99, CC, or FF for each color (Red, Green, or Blue). Here's how the most basic colors are written and why:

000000. Black contains no Red, Green, or Blue colors.

FFFFFF. White has the most depth of color and is composed of the maximum amounts of each of Red/Green/Blue.

FF0000. Pure Red consists of the most intense red value, FF, and no Green or Blue, each expressed as 00.

00FF00. Pure Green consists of no Red, 00, the darkest value of green, FF, and no Blue, 00.

0000FF. Pure Blue consists of no Red, 00, no Green, 00, and the darkest value of Blue, FF.

Using the SWiSHmax Color Selector

Regardless of whether you are choosing a color for a line you have drawn or want to use a custom color for the guide lines on the Layout panel, you work with the same pop-up window called the Color Selector.

There are numerous methods of choosing and defining colors in the Color Selector. The options include:

✦ Selecting a color from the standard color palette

✦ Selecting a color from the most recently used custom color palette

✦ Typing an RGB value for a color

✦ Typing a hex value for a color

✦ Forcing a color using the Web Safe color palette

✦ Sampling a color from objects on the Layout panel

✦ Defining a custom color in the Windows Color dialog box

✦ Changing a color's opacity

Cross-Reference

This chapter discusses using color with drawn objects and elements such as the movie background or guide lines. Color and transparency can also be applied to images, discussed in Chapter 8.

Using the program's color samples

The Color Selector contains a color palette shown in Figure 7-4. The top row of the palette shows 14 shades of gray, plus white in the upper-left color sample and black in the upper-right two color samples. The left column of the palette displays primary and basic hex colors. In the remainder of the standard color palette, the 216 Web Safe colors are arranged in six blocks of 36 color samples, each arranged in six rows of six color samples. Each block corresponds with one side of a color cube.

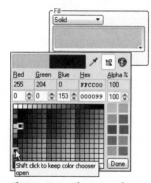

Figure 7-4: Choose colors for some program preferences and your project's objects from the Color Selector.

Each color in the cube uses RGB or hex values based on combinations of these values:

RGB. 0, 51, 102,153, 204, and 255

Hex. 00, 33, 66, 99, CC, and FF

Table 7-1 lists the colors shown in the samples making up the left column of the Color Selector's standard color palette as well as their hexadecimal and RGB values.

Table 7-1: Basic Colors and Values

Color	Hexadecimal value	RGB value
Red	#FF0000	255/0/0
Green	#00FF00	0/255/0
Blue	#0000FF	0/0/255
Yellow	#FFFF00	255/255/0
Cyan	#00FFFF	0/255/255
Magenta	#FF00FF	255/0/255
Dark red	#990000	153/0/0
Medium green	#009900	0/153/153
Medium blue	#000099	0/0/153
Olive green	#999900	153/153/0
Aqua	#009999	0/153/153
Purple	#990099	153/0/153

When you open the Color Selector and click a color sample to select it, the Color Selector closes automatically. To continue to display the Color Selector, press Shift and click one of the colors in the palette. As you move your mouse over the colors in the Color Selector, you notice:

✦ Color samples in the left column of the standard color palette (identified in Table 7-1) are also in the 216-color cube. As your mouse moves over a color sample in the left column, another color sample is highlighted in the palette as well.

✦ RGB and hex values appear in the fields at the top of the Color Selector when you move your mouse over color samples in the standard color palette.

✦ Moving your mouse over the 10 custom color samples in the custom color palette at the right side of the Color Selector does not reveal any color values.

The most basic method of choosing color in SWiSHmax is to use one of the supplied colors, or choose from a number of colors you previously selected. Follow these steps to choose a color from the Color Selector palette:

1. **Where applicable, select the object to which you want to apply color.** Objects on the Layout panel, for example, must be selected while no object selection is required to change the color of the movie's background.

2. **Click the color swatch associated with the item for which you want to pick a color.** The Color Selector opens.

3. **Click a color sample in the standard color palette to select a color, or click a color sample in the custom color palette to select a color from previously used colors.** The Color Selector closes automatically if you click a color from the standard color palette or from the custom color palette.

Creating a custom color

You can create custom colors numerically or by choosing them from different program locations. The Color Selector allows you to type values for colors using either RGB or hex values.

Follow these steps to create a custom color by entering numeric values:

1. **Select the object on the Layout panel for which you want to create the custom color.**

2. **Click the color swatch to open the Color Selector.**

3. **Click one of the Red, Blue, or Green color input fields to make it active.** As soon as you click a field the Color Selector is locked open.

4. **Type the color values using either RGB or hex input.** For RGB color, type values for the color in the Red, Blue, and Green fields. You can also click the arrows to increase or decrease the values of each number as shown in Figure 7-5. For hex color, type the color number in the Hex field.

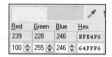

Figure 7-5: Reset the RGB or hex values numerically in the Color Selector.

Note

If you type RGB values, the hex color changes to show the equivalent number; if you type a hex value, the RGB values change to show the equivalent numbers.

5. **Watch the color change in the color preview area.** The left color sample shows the last color selected in the Color Selector, the right sample shows the color change as you modify the settings. In addition, the RGB and hex values of the last color chosen in the Color Selector are shown immediately below the Red, Green, Blue, and Hex labels.

6. **Click Done to close the Color Selector and apply the color to the selected object.** The next time you open the Color Selector the custom color you created is displayed in the custom color palette and is the left sample color in the color preview area at the top of the Color Selector.

Forcing Web-safe color

Regardless of the method you use to select color in SWiSHmax, you can make sure the colors are always from the Web-safe color palette. If you type color values and the color changes before it is applied to your selected object, check that the Web-safe color is toggled off. When the command is active, irrespective of the numbers you type in the fields, the selected color jumps to the closest Web-safe color.

The Web-safe color button is one of the options at the top of the Color Selector. Its default state is toggled off, meaning you can choose any color. The button's background is white when the Web-safe color feature is active. If you click the button to make it active, colors you choose using any method are changed to the closest Web-safe color.

The appearance may change subtly, or you may see a significant difference. In Figure 7-6, the original color's values (a lavender shade) are displayed on the Color Selector below the Red,

Green, Blue, and Hex field labels. Clicking the Web-safe color button forces the color to its closest Web-safe color. The color preview shows the original color in the left sample and the forced Web-safe color in the right sample. In the RGB and Hex fields, the values are changed to reflect the Web-safe color's values. That is, the RGB values change to 255/204/255, and the hex value changes to FFCCFF. The forced color is also lavender, although it is a bolder shade.

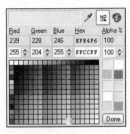

Figure 7-6: You can ensure your movie only uses Web-safe color by forcing color changes in the Color Selector.

Sampling color from your scene

Sometimes you need to use a specific color in a movie that matches color in an image. Instead of trying to guess or experimenting with color until you get the exact shade, you can sample a color from the image.

 The Color Selector includes an eyedropper tool used for sampling color anywhere in the SWiSHmax program window. You can't sample color from a file opened in another program or from anywhere else on your desktop. Follow these steps to sample a color from your movie:

1. **Select the object you want to recolor on the stage.**

2. **Click the Shape tab in the grouped panels to display the Shape panel.**

3. **Click the color swatch to open the Color Selector.**

Caution　Make sure the Web-safe color button is toggled to off. Otherwise, when you try to select a color the sample is forced to the closest Web-safe color.

4. **Click the eyedropper tool to select it.** The cursor becomes an eyedropper shape.

5. **Move the eyedropper tool anywhere over the SWiSHmax program window.** As the colors are sampled with the eyedropper, you see the right sample in the preview area change as well as the RGB and hex values.

6. **When you have the tool over the desired color, click the mouse to capture a sample of the color.** Its RGB and hex values appear in the Color Selector, as well as a sample displayed in the right preview sample area. The Color Selector closes automatically and the color is saved.

Tip　If you are using the eyedropper and change your mind about selecting a color from the Layout panel, click the tool again in the Color Selector to deselect it. The Color Selector remains open until you click Done to close it.

Saving color for a project

SWiSHmax stores the last 10 colors you selected in the Color Selector's custom color palette; if you create more than 10 colors, the first color is replaced. What if you are working on a project that uses a set of specific colors, but there are more than 10? You can scribble the color values on a piece of paper and stick it under your keyboard for future reference and then type the numbers into the Color Selector whenever you need to use a color, or you can make an image to store the color information. You can create and reuse solid colors only; this process doesn't work for color transparency. Here's how to do it:

1. **Start a new file in any image editing or illustration program.**

2. **Type the colors' RGB and Hex values in a list.** You can also add descriptions such as "logo background."

3. **Select each text label and color it the custom color.**

4. **Save the file as an image file.**

5. **Import the file into your SWiSHmax file and put it into its own scene.** When you need to use a custom color, display the image and sample the color with the eyedropper.

Cross-Reference

Learn about importing images in Chapter 8.

Choosing system colors for your movie

Instead of changing color in the Color Selector and typing different numbers in the value fields to attain a shade you want for your movie, you can use the Windows Color dialog box.

The More Colors button on the Color Selector opens the Windows Color dialog box. This is the system's color dialog box used for setting system colors for items like desktop themes and backgrounds. When you launch the Color dialog box an additional control is added to the dialog box to allow you to choose a transparency level as well as other color values depending on the object to which you are trying to apply color. For example, if you are choosing a color for the movie background or guide lines, you can't choose transparency; if you are choosing a color for a line, you can select an Alpha value.

You select a color in the Color dialog box from either the Basic or Custom color palettes.

Follow these steps to use the Windows Color dialog box to choose a color:

1. **Select the object you want to color on the stage.**

2. **Click the Shape panel's tab in the panel group to display the panel.**

3. **Click the color swatch to open the Color Selector.**

4. **Click the More Colors button to open the Windows Color dialog box shown in Figure 7-7.**

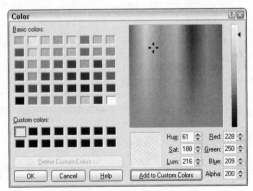

Figure 7-7: Choose additional colors from the Windows Color dialog box.

5. **Choose a color from the Basic or Custom colors palettes.**

6. **Click OK to close the Color dialog box.** The Color Selector closes, and the custom color is applied to the selected shape.

Tip   If you change your mind, you can click Cancel on the Color dialog box to close it and return to the Color Selector. If you want more information, click Help to open the SWiSHmax Help files.

In the Color dialog box you select either a basic color or a custom color. There are a number of ways to define a custom color in the Color dialog box. In each case, you define the color and then add it to the Custom color palette for use in your movie. Follow these steps to define a custom color sample:

1. **From the Color Selector, click More Colors to open the Windows Color dialog box.**

2. **Click the upper-left color sample in the Custom color palette at the left of the Color dialog box to make it active.**

Tip   You can define several custom colors in the Color dialog box. Click the sample box where you want to place the custom color; otherwise the colors are added to the Custom color palette in a sequence from left to right, top row to bottom row.

3. **Define a new color by typing values or clicking the fields' arrows to change the numbers in the RGB fields, including an Alpha channel transparency value.** You can also Type values or click the fields' arrows to change the numbers to create a custom HSL (hue/saturation/luminance) color or click the color display to select a custom color.

Tip   When you select a color using one of these methods, the range of intensities for the chosen color display in the vertical bar at the right side of the Color dialog box. You can choose a specific color intensity by clicking the color bar, dragging the slider upward for a lighter shade, or downward for a darker shade.

About HSL color

You can't choose HSL (hue/saturation/luminance) color directly in SWiSHmax, but you can choose color based on this color model using the Color dialog box. HSL color is also known as HSB (hue/saturation/brightness), HSI (hue/saturation/ intensity), or HSV (hue/saturation/value) color. There are several ways to categorize and measure the component values. The method used in the Color dialog box is described here.

The *hue* describes the position on the spectrum where the color is located ranging from red at the low end of the spectrum, with a value of 0, to violet at the high end of the spectrum with a value of 239.

The *saturation* describes how bright the color is, between gray at the low end and very bright at the high end. The value ranges from 0 to 240.

The *luminance* (or intensity or brightness) describes where on the scale between black and white the color falls. Luminance of a color ranges from black, with a value of 0, to white, with a value of 240.

4. **Click Add to Custom Colors.** The color appears in the upper-left sample position on the Custom colors palette at the lower-left of the Color dialog box.

5. **Click the custom color sample you want to use, and click OK to close the Color dialog box.** The Color Selector also closes, and the custom color is applied to the selected object in your movie.

The next time you open the Color Selector, the custom color samples you used are listed in the Custom color palette. When you open the Color dialog box through the Color Selector, the colors you defined remain in the Color dialog box.

Assigning transparency to a color

Earlier in this chapter, RGBA color was described. The RGBA color model includes Red, Blue, Green, and Alpha channels. In SWiSHmax, you can define Alpha transparency for a number of purposes. Lines and fills can be either solid colors or use a color having varied levels of transparency.

The Alpha channel refers to relative levels of transparency or opacity used in a pixel. *Transparency* and *opacity* are two terms used to describe the same concept in opposite terms. Transparency options range from 1 percent to 99 percent. At 0 percent there is no color, and 100 percent is the default solid color's alpha value. A default color has 0 percent transparency and 100 percent opacity. On the other hand, a color that is 80 percent transparent, for example, has an opacity value of 20 percent. The terms *alpha* and *transparency* are interchangeable.

You can use transparency for a wide number of SWiSHmax effects and also with images.

Cross-Reference   Transparency settings used for images are covered in Chapter 8.

Follow these steps to define transparency for an object:

1. **Select the object on your scene to which you want to apply a transparent color.**

2. **Click the Shape panel's tab in the panel group to display it, and then click the color swatch to open the Color Selector.**

Note   When the Color Selector opens, if you don't see the Alpha settings, you haven't selected the correct type of object. You can't use transparency with guide line colors or the movie's background color, for example. The selected object may be a drawn shape or an image.

3. **Shift+Click the color you want to start from in the standard color palette; this keeps the Color Selector window open.** You can also click one of the Red, Blue, Green, or Hex value fields to make it active, and type the color values or click the arrow keys to increase or decrease the values to reach the desired starting color.

4. **Click the Alpha field and type a value, or click the arrows to increase or decrease the percentage displayed.**

5. **Continue to adjust the percentage value until the color shows the desired amount of transparency.** Each time you adjust the alpha value, you see the samples change in the color preview area on the Color Selector as shown in Figure 7-8.

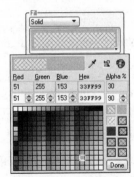

Figure 7-8: Set an alpha level to make chosen colors transparent.

6. **Click Done to close the Color Selector and apply the color to the selected object.** The chosen semitransparent color is also added to the custom color palette in the Color Selector and appears as a color sample with hatched lines.

Caution   When you reopen the Color Selector to work with other colors, the Alpha value remains at the transparency percentage you set for the last custom color.

Transparency settings in the Color dialog box

When you are working in the Color Selector and want to create a custom color, you can click the More Colors button to open the system's Color dialog box. As described earlier, you can set an Alpha value for a color from the Color dialog box. When you do, it is added to the

Custom colors palette in the Color dialog box and you can choose it and apply it in your movie. The color at the chosen transparency level is added to the custom palette in the Color Selector.

There is a significant difference between setting transparency in the Color Selector and choosing it in the Color dialog box. In the Color Selector, you choose transparency based on a range of values expressed as percentages, with 0 percent being a completely transparent color and 100 percent being a completely opaque color. In the Color dialog box, Alpha settings are based on a range of values like those of the RGB values; that is, you choose an Alpha value in a range from 0 to 255. The default Alpha value of 255 results in an opaque color.

To choose an Alpha value in the Color dialog box you have to convert the values to percentages. That is, if you want a color that is 50 percent transparent, type 127 or 128 in the Alpha field, for example. You can also select a color in the Color dialog box, and then adjust the transparency in the Color Selector.

Adding Strokes to Objects

A stroke is a line added to the margin of an object. You can add strokes to drawn lines created with the Line, Bézier, or Pencil tools. You can also add a stroke to a closed drawing or to an image. The processes for modifying strokes on line objects or adding strokes to closed shapes or images is slightly different.

Lines default to display a line; otherwise, the shape is invisible! To modify the stroke displayed by open shapes drawn with the Line, Bézier, or Pencil tool, follow these steps:

1. **On the Layout panel, click the object to be modified.**

2. **Click the Shape tab in the panel group to display the panel.** The Line options appear on the Shape panel as shown in Figure 7-9. The left shape shows the default stroke settings, and the right shape shows a stroke using custom line type, size, and color.

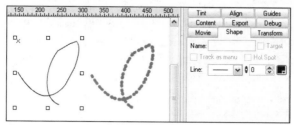

Figure 7-9: Strokes are applied to open shapes by default.

3. **Click the Line drop-down arrow, and choose a line type from the list shown in Figure 7-10.** The stroke is applied to the selected object. In the figure, an example of each included line type is shown on the stage.

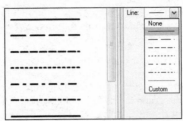

Figure 7-10: Choose a stroke option from the drop-down menu in the Shape panel.

4. **Click in the Size field and type a value, or click the up and down arrows to set the stroke depth.** The depth of the stroke is modified on the selected object.

5. **Click the color swatch to open the Color Selector and choose a color for the line.** The Color Selector closes and the stroke is colored.

Tip   You can use both opaque and transparent color for the stroke.

The next time you draw an open shape or use a tool that creates a line, the default settings appear. Custom settings are not maintained in the program for line strokes. You can modify multiple strokes at the same time. Click the Select tool in the Toolbox to make it active, and then Shift+Click the lines you want to modify. You can also click and drag with the Select tool on the Layout panel to fence the lines for selection. Once you have specified custom line settings, they remain until you change them again.

Closed shapes or images have no default line option. You can add a stroke to a closed shape or image and customize it. Follow these steps to add a stroke to closed shape or image:

1. **On the Layout panel, click the object to which you want to apply the stroke.**

2. **Click the Shape tab in the panel group to display the panel.**

3. **Click the Line drop-down arrow and choose a line type from the list.** The stroke is applied to the selected object.

4. **Click in the Size field and type a value, or click the up and down arrows to set the stroke depth.** The depth of the stroke is modified on the selected object.

5. **Click the color swatch to open the Color Selector and choose a color for the line.** The Color Selector closes and the stroke is colored as shown in Figure 7-11.

Tip   When you have set custom stroke settings for a closed shape or an image, the next time you select a closed shape or image object to apply a stroke, the same custom settings appear.

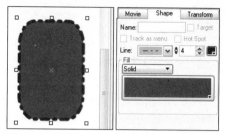

Figure 7-11: Custom strokes can be added to drawn closed shapes or images.

When you draw a shape it has a hairline stroke with a width of 0, and is visually the same as a line width of 1. If you scale the drawing, that is, resize it proportionally, a line width of 0 stays as a hairline stroke, while a line width that is greater than 0 resizes with the shape's size.

As with line shapes, you can select several objects and/or images and apply the same stroke to them at the same time.

SWiSHmax provides a number of line types, or you can create your own custom lines. Follow these steps to create a custom line:

1. **Select the shape or image to which you want to apply the custom line.**

2. **Click the Shape panel's tab in the panel group to display the panel.**

3. **Click the Line drop-down arrow to display the list of options.**

4. **Click Custom to open the Custom Line Style dialog box, as shown in Figure 7-12.**

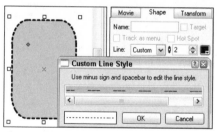

Figure 7-12: You can design your own line types.

5. **Use the spacebar and the minus sign (-) on the keyboard or number keypad to create a pattern.**

6. **Click OK to close the dialog box and apply your custom line.**

The next time you open the Custom Line Style dialog box during your working session, the settings you defined appear again, allowing you to reuse the custom line style. The custom settings aren't stored in the program permanently, however.

Filling Objects

Closed shapes drawn in SWiSHmax are filled with a pure red color by default. You can use several methods for filling objects drawn or added to your movie. These options are available on the Shape panel, and include:

✦ **None.** This option removes all color from an object, leaving it transparent.

✦ **Solid.** The object is filled with one color, which may be opaque or transparent.

✦ **Linear gradient.** A linear gradient fills an object using bands of color.

✦ **Radial gradient.** A radial gradient uses concentric bands of color to fill an object.

✦ **Tiled image.** Multiple copies of a bitmap image are arranged geometrically to fill an object.

✦ **Clipped image.** A single copy of a bitmap image is used to fill an object; it may be resized to fill the entire object.

Adding and transforming image fills and modifying the characteristics of images are discussed in Chapter 8.

In each option, you start the process the same way. Once the shape is drawn or imported into your scene, follow these steps to choose a fill method:

1. **Select the object on the scene.**

2. **Click the Shape panel's tab in the panel group to display the panel.**

3. **Click the Fill button to display the drop-down menu shown in Figure 7-13.** The default fill option, or a previously selected fill option, is named on the Fill button. In the figure, the default Solid label shows on the Fill button.

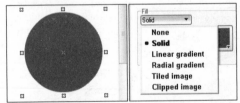

Figure 7-13: You can choose from a number of options to fill objects in your movie.

4. **Click a fill option from the list.** The drop-down menu closes, and you can configure your fill choice.

Using a solid color or no fill for an object

The default fill option for a closed shape is a solid color. Once you have chosen the Solid fill option from the Fill drop-down menu, click the color swatch and choose a color using any of the methods described earlier in the chapter.

To remove a fill entirely, select the object, and then choose None from the Fill drop-down menu.

Applying gradient fills

You can use linear or radial gradients as fills in SWiSHmax. Figure 7-14 shows two rectangles filled with gradients using the program's default settings. The upper rectangle uses a linear gradient and the lower uses a radial gradient.

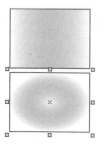

Figure 7-14: You can use either radial or linear gradients as fill types.

Configuring a gradient's color

For each type of gradient you can choose from a list of provided gradients or modify the arrangement and numbers of colors used in the gradient.

Figure 7-15 shows the Fill section of the Shape panel displaying the default color and layout of the colors for a linear gradient. Click the drop-down arrow at the right margin of the gradient sample to open a drop-down menu of preconfigured gradients. Scroll down the list to find a gradient you want to use, and then click the sample to select it and apply it to your selected object. When you configure a custom gradient it is added to the drop-down list of available gradients. Scroll down the list to see what you have used in previous gradients.

Caution Custom gradients are not stored permanently, only during the current work session. When you open the program at a later time, the gradient options default to the original list of options. If you need to reuse a gradient on different occasions, create an image filled with the gradient in an image-editing program and then use the image as a fill for your project. That way, you are always sure to have the correct configuration for the gradient.

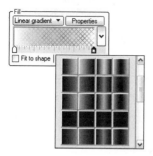

Figure 7-15: SWiSHmax contains a collection of sample gradients you can use.

The default gradient, as well as any gradient you choose from the drop-down menu, displays a number of color tabs along a small ruler in the Fill preview area on the Shape panel. You can add, remove, and adjust the color tabs. Changes you make to the color tabs in the Fill preview area are made to the filled shape on your scene automatically. When you make adjustments to the gradient, the color tabs along the ruler in the Fill preview area change color, the gradient preview shows the modified color scheme, and the filled object on the scene changes as well.

You can modify a gradient's color in several ways:

✦ **Add a color tab.** Click the Fill preview area's ruler to add another color tab. Press Shift+click the ruler to snap the color tabs to the ruler's marks. When you click the ruler, the Color Selector opens, as shown in Figure 7-16. You can choose any combination of opaque and transparent colors that you want.

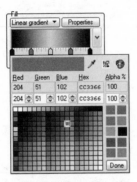

Figure 7-16: Click the Fill preview area's ruler to add a color tab and choose a color for the gradient band.

✦ **Change the color of a gradient band.** Click a color tab on the Fill preview area's ruler. The Color Selector opens. Select an alternate color using any of the methods described earlier in the chapter. The Color Selector closes and the gradient's color changes.

✦ **Adjust the position of the color bands.** Click and drag the color tabs on the Fill preview area's ruler to move the gradient's color bands left or right. You can also remove a color band from the gradient by dragging the color tab past the left or right edge of the Fill preview area's ruler. In the same way, you can modify the sequence of color bands in a gradient by clicking and dragging any color band to a different location along the preview area's ruler.

Note The distance between the color tabs affects the smoothness of the color transition between the bands. The closer the color tabs are to one another, the more intense the color and the sharper the transition from one color to another.

Adjusting a gradient fill's properties numerically

Every gradient can be modified in ways other than its color bands and their relative locations. For example, you can choose which part of a gradient appears in a shape or alter the angle of the gradient.

Follow these steps to modify a gradient fill's properties:

1. **Click the Properties button above the Fill preview area on the Shape panel.** The Gradient Properties dialog box opens.

Note If the Gradient Properties dialog box is inactive (all the settings are grayed out), you have the Fit to Shape command active for the gradient. Click the Fit to Shape checkbox to deselect the command and activate the fields on the dialog box.

2. **Change the gradient's properties as desired by toggling the Uniform check boxes off and on as necessary and typing new values in the fields.**

Tip

If you make changes but aren't sure they are correct, click the Reset Transform button to restore the original values for the properties.

3. **Click OK to close the Gradient Properties dialog box and apply the changes.** You can also click Cancel to close the dialog box without applying the changes.

A gradient's geometric properties are much like those for any object or shape and include:

✦ **X and Y.** The X and Y positions are the coordinates where the gradient is placed in relation to the center point of the object it is filling. By default, a gradient is placed at the object's center and has an X-value (its position on the X-axis of the object) of 0 and a Y-value (its position on the Y-axis of the object) of 0. Figure 7-17 shows copies of the same object using the same gradient with different X and Y coordinates. The object at the left shows the default position, while the gradient at the right shows the gradient using X and Y coordinates of 100, which shifts the visible portion of the gradient down and to the right.

Figure 7-17: You can modify the X and Y coordinates of a gradient.

✦ **Uniform size.** The Uniform scale and size checkbox, shown as the upper Uniform checkbox on the Gradient Properties dialog box, is selected by default making the width and height of a gradient and its X-axis and Y-axis scale option proportional.

✦ **W and H.** The W (width) and H (height) are the gradient's dimensions in pixels. By default, the dimensions of a gradient are 256 x 256 pixels. When you add a new gradient to an object, the dimensions shown in the Gradient Properties dialog box vary according to the object's size as the gradient resizes itself to fill the object. The Uniform checkbox constraining the dimensions is selected.

✦ **X and Y stretch.** The X and Y stretch refers to the scale of the gradient. If the upper Uniform checkbox is selected, then only the X stretch field is active and any value typed in the field applies to both X and Y axes. To stretch the gradient along one axis, deselect the upper Uniform checkbox and then type different values for the X stretch and Y stretch fields. In Figure 7-18, for example, the object's gradient was changed from a circular to an oval by changing the Y stretch. As you can see in the figure, the X and Y stretch values are different; the Y-axis value was increased to 22 percent. As a result, the gradient appears elongated along the Y-axis.

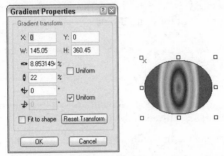

Figure 7-18: Change the shape of a gradient by modifying one of its stretch values.

✦ **Uniform angle.** The second Uniform checkbox on the Gradient Properties dialog box sets the angle of a gradient. By default, the Uniform checkbox is checked and you can change only the X-axis angle to rotate the gradient. Clicking to uncheck the Uniform angle checkbox allows you to skew the angle of the gradient.

✦ **Angle of X-axis.** When the Uniform angle checkbox is selected, as it is in Figure 7-19, the X- and Y-axis values are the same; changing the angle from its default of 0 degrees rotates the gradient. In the figure, the gradient shows the stripes at a 33-degree angle.

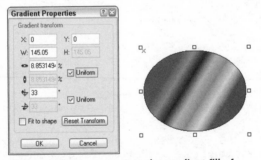

Figure 7-19: You can rotate the gradient fill of an object.

✦ **Angle of Y-axis.** If the Uniform angle checkbox is deselected, you can type a value in the angle of the Y-axis field that differs from that of the angle of the X-axis value to skew the gradient.

Cross-Reference For more information on working with an object's transformation properties, refer to Chapter 6.

Resetting a gradient

On the Shape panel below the Fill preview area you find two commands for controlling how much of a gradient is seen. When you add a new gradient fill to an object, the entire range of the gradient is shown within the boundaries of the object by default, but the gradient isn't locked in that view. To change what is seen within the object's boundaries, choose any of these options:

✦ **Reset Transform.** Click this button to resize the gradient and remove any modifications you have made.

✦ **Fit to Shape.** Click this button to lock the gradient's size and properties to fit within the dimensions of the object.

Figure 7-20 shows the same gradient applied to two identical shapes. In the left shape, you see the entire range of the gradient, as displayed in the gradient preview area on the Shape panel (shown at the far right of the figure). The right shape on the stage shows the gradient after the Reset Transform button has been clicked. You see only the central portion of the gradient as the gradient's default size is much larger than the object to which is it applied.

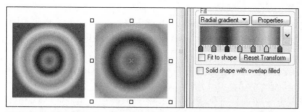

Figure 7-20: This image shows two copies of an object using the same gradient with different fill settings.

Transforming Fills Visually

Gradient fills can be modified visually. The size of the fill in relation to the object's size and its location and rotation can be changed. In many ways, working with a gradient fill's transformation properties is similar to those of a shape, which is discussed in Chapter 6.

The Toolbox on the Layout panel contains a tool called the Fill Transform tool. Click the tool to activate the fill of an object. When the tool is active, some of the Transformation tools in the Options section of the Toolbox become active as well as a number of anchors and handles overlaying the fill on the Layout panel. Both gradient and image fills behave in the same way.

To modify an object's fill using the Fill Transform tool follow these steps:

1. **Click the Fill Transform tool in the Layout panel's Toolbox to make it active.** The Scale and Rotate/Skew tools are activated in the Options section of the Toolbox.

2. **Click one of the Transformation tools in the Toolbox to make it active:**

   • Click the Scale tool. The fill displays a set of eight square-shaped blue handles around the edges of the fill.

   • Click the Rotate/Skew tool. The fill displays a set of eight blue diamond-shaped handles around the edge of the fill.

3. **Adjust the fill as desired by clicking and dragging the handles.**

4. **Adjust the position as desired by clicking and dragging over the fill (not over a handle).**

5. **If you want to modify any changes numerically, click the Properties button on the Fill preview area of the Shape panel to display the fill's properties dialog box.** Make changes and click OK to apply the changes.

6. **Click another tool on the Toolbox to deselect the Fill Transform tool and hide the handles.**

Tip   You can reverse the changes you make to a fill by clicking the Reset Transform button on the Fill preview area of the Shape panel.

Transforming a gradient fill

Both radial and linear gradients behave in the same way when you modify their properties using the Fill Transform tool, although their selection handles look different on the Layout panel.

Figure 7-21 shows a free-form shape with a linear gradient fill at its default size. The Fill Transform tool is selected, and you see the square blue Scale handles around the sides of the gradient fill. You also see dashed horizontal and vertical lines identifying the edges of the gradient fill as well as its horizontal midline. When you compare the appearance of the object's fill to the gradient shown in the Fill preview area on the Shape panel, you see that several bands of color are not fully displayed.

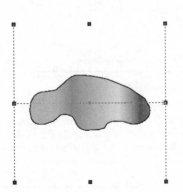

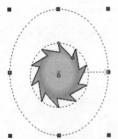

Figure 7-21: At its default size, a gradient may not display all its color bands within the object.

A radial gradient fill displays handles differently. In Figure 7-23, a shape using a radial gradient at its default size is shown at the right of the figure. You can see that there are two concentric rings identifying the gradient, both the outer edges of the default gradient's size as well as an inner ring drawn around the margins of the shape.

Resizing a fill

A gradient can be resized to fit an object or made smaller than the object. Click and drag the corner handles to resize a gradient in both directions; click the upper or lower middle handle to resize vertically, and click the left or right middle handle to resize horizontally. Shift+drag a corner handle to resize the gradient fill proportionally.

When the gradient is the same size as the object you see all the colored bands, as shown in Figure 7-22. In the figure, notice that the Fit to shape option is selected on the Fill preview area of the Shape panel. Clicking the Fill to shape option automatically resizes the gradient to the dimensions of the object. The resize works the same for radial and linear gradients.

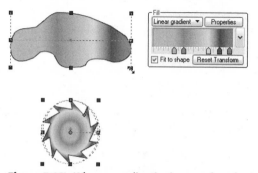

Figure 7-22: When a gradient's size matches that of the object it fills, you see all the color bands.

You can also make a gradient fill smaller than the size of the object. In Figure 7-23, the gradients' resize handles show that the gradient is narrower than the object it is filling. The gradient still fills the object. Click and drag a corner or side anchor to resize the gradient. The smaller you size the gradient, the closer the gradient's color bands move together. On any edge narrower than the object's size, the color band is stretched to fill the shape. Figure 7-23 shows the gradients before being resized.

Figure 7-23: You can resize a gradient smaller that the size of its object.

Moving a gradient fill

The center of a gradient fill is aligned with the center of the object. You can move a gradient fill to create a different effect. When the Fill Transform tool is selected in the Toolbox and you move the cursor over the fill, it changes to a four-angled arrow as shown over both the linear and radial gradients in Figure 7-24. Click and drag to move the fill to another location in relation to the object it is filling. In the figure, the gradient is moved left and downward from both objects' centers. As you move the gradient, you see a dotted line project from the object's center to the gradient's center.

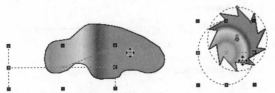

Figure 7-24: Move a gradient to another location in relation to the object's center.

Rotating or skewing a gradient fill

A gradient is applied to an object without any rotation or skew; you can adjust the fill's orientation using the Fill Transform tool. Click the tool in the Toolbox, and then click the Rotate/Skew tool in the Options section of the Toolbox. The diamond-shaped Rotate/Skew handles appear over the fill as shown in the left object in Figure 7-25. Click and drag a corner Rotation handle to rotate the gradient, shown in the central object in the figure. Drag a Skew handle on any side of the gradient to skew it along the X- or Y-axis. The radial gradient fill in the right object in the figure shows a skew of 45 degrees along the X-axis.

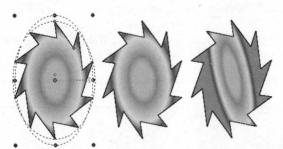

Figure 7-25: Rotate or skew a gradient fill for another effect.

Summary

This chapter was all about color and different ways to use color and images for filling objects and adding strokes to them. You learned about color models, how to work with SWiSHmax color tools, and how to apply and modify object lines and fills. You also learned how to:

✦ Understand different color models, such as RGB and Hexadecimal notation

✦ Use the SWiSHmax Color Selector

✦ Create custom colors in the Color Selector

✦ Work with transparency

✦ Add standard and custom strokes to objects and free-form lines

✦ Apply linear and gradient fills to objects

✦ Customize the appearance of gradient fills

✦　　✦　　✦

Working with Images

Although you can draw many types of shapes and objects in SWiSHmax, you certainly aren't limited to objects you create inside the program. You can import a variety of image formats including raster graphics and vector graphics. The static image file formats you can use in SWiSHmax are described in this chapter. Other formats, such as animations, are discussed in Chapter 9.

It is important to understand the differences between file types, not just file formats. Knowing what you want to work with can save frustration during your movie construction phase, as well as file size and download time when you distribute your finished movie. SWiSHmax uses the image file types commonly used on the Internet as well as a number of other formats.

Preplanning is important to success with images. In addition to choosing a file type, you should understand other characteristics of images and how they impact your project. In this chapter, you learn about resolution, file formats, and image size.

Once you import images into SWiSHmax they can be modified in a number of ways, and in this chapter you learn how to alter many image characteristics. You can even use images as fills for other objects.

Choosing Image Types for a Project

Drawings you create in SWiSHmax are *vector* graphics. Some images you import into the program are vector graphics and others are *raster* graphics.

There is a fundamental difference between a vector graphic and a raster graphic. Raster image formats, such as GIF (Graphic Interchange Format) and JPEG (Joint Photographic Experts Group), store image information on a pixel-by-pixel basis. A raster graphic is also referred to as a *bitmap* because the information is directly mapped to a grid. The image file defines what coordinates on the grid display what color.

Note A bitmap type of image is not the same thing as a Windows bitmap (BMP) file. The BMP file format is one type of raster graphics file format that describes an image on a mapped grid, as are GIF and JPEG file formats.

When choosing a type of image to use, consider the color range and rescale requirements.

Color range. An image can show discrete areas of color, like a cartoon, or *continuous color* like a photograph, which shows many gradations of color. In Figure 8-1, a raster image in a PNG (Portable Network Graphic) file format is shown on the left. You can see the variations in color that make up the photograph. The same image converted to a vector image appears on the right. You can see that the color changes are much sharper and the characteristics of the image are different overall. Instead of pixels, the vector image is made up of a large number of filled shapes and lines.

Figure 8-1: Raster and vector images present the same information in different ways.

On The Web Site If you would like to look at the two images, you can find copies of them on the book's Web site in the chapter08 folder. The files are named island dog.png and island dog.wmf, and are located in the art subfolder.

Rescaling. Vector images are often the right choice for images that need rescaling. Figure 8-2 shows portions of two images on the stage. The left image is a vector image of a balloon drawn in SWiSHmax, the right image is the same balloon, but drawn in an illustration program, saved as a PNG file, and imported into SWiSHmax. The drawn balloons and the imported raster image are quite similar at 100 percent magnification, although the balloon strings on the imported image aren't as clear as they are drawn on a pixel-by-pixel basis.

When you zoom into the image the difference is dramatic. In Figure 8-3, you see the stage zoomed 300 percent; the drawn balloon on the left, its shading, and its string still appear clear and crisp; the imported image of the balloon on the right shows a considerable amount of blurriness.

On The Web Site You can use copies of these files from the Web site if you want to experiment. Open the ch08_sample01.swi file from the ch08_sample01 subfolder in the chapter08 folder on the Web site. The file contains the vector balloons drawn in SWiSHmax. Also in the folder is the source image file named balloons.png.

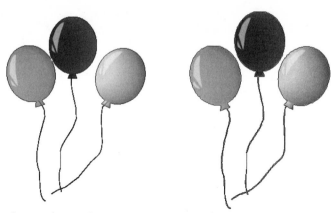

Figure 8-2: At a lower magnification, drawn objects can look very similar to raster images.

Figure 8-3: At a higher magnification, the difference between image types is clear.

Image Formats

Match your choice of file format to the design and use of your graphic. If you are building a small static logo using simple shapes for example, there isn't any need for high-quality JPEG images if a simpler, more compact GIF file could work as well. You can use a range of raster and vector image formats for your SWiSHmax projects as listed in Table 8-1.

Table 8-1: Image File Formats Supported by SWiSHmax

File Type	Extension	Description
Raster Graphics		
Windows bitmaps	.bmp	Uses variable bit depths, alpha channels, lossless compression.
GIF (Graphic Interchange Format)	.gif	Can use only 256 or fewer colors. Ideal for line art, images with areas of transparency, cartoons. Maintains sharpness and resolution even when compressed.
JPEG (Joint Photographic Experts Group)	.jpg	Can use up to 16 million colors; ideal for photographs and artwork. JPEG uses lossy compression.
PNG (Portable Network Graphics)	.png	Compact and versatile format. It supports different bit depths, compression settings, and alpha channels. PNG uses lossless compression.
Vector Graphics		
Windows Metafile	.wmf	Windows format that supports vectors and bitmaps.
Enhanced Metafile	.emf	Windows format that supports vectors and bitmaps.
Flash Graphics	.swf	An exported Flash movie frame. The movie is flattened into a single layer.

Choose the correct size for your project. A logo for a Web site or a SWF Web site's interface isn't a large object. You don't need to use image elements that are scaled for a trade-show poster. Keep the size of your movie in mind when you are assembling material for the project. Where possible, resize images you are intending to use for a SWiSHmax movie project before bringing them into the program. The closer the images are to the size you actually need in your movie the simpler they are to work with. Not only that, but accurately sized images are processed more quickly by SWiSHmax.

On the other hand, don't try to increase the size of an image dramatically to use in a project, either. If you increase a low resolution image significantly, you can end up with a very poor quality image.

Choose the right image resolution. You need high-resolution graphics for printing full-color magazines. You don't need high-resolution images for use in SWiSHmax. Computer monitors can't display a resolution used for printing; the extra image information merely adds to the file's size unnecessarily.

The *image resolution* is the number of pixels of information in a specific area; the most common measurement is ppi (pixels per inch).

Tip

If you are working on an image and aren't sure how it is going to be used, save it with a high resolution. If you need a lower-resolution copy for a SWiSHmax movie, for example, open the file and save a copy at a lower resolution. Don't modify your original.

Optimizing Raster Graphics

The goal of working with images in any program is to use the best size image, with the best quality, and the sharpest resolution, and the smallest file size. The effort — and sometimes it requires considerable effort — is called *optimizing*.

You can increase or decrease the scale of a vector drawing at will without having any negative effect on the way the image appears. When you work with raster images, on the other hand, downsampling to decrease a file's size, also known as *compressing*, causes some formats, such as JPG images, to lose information when the file is compressed. The goal is to balance the image's file size with its quality.

JPEG images use *lossy* compression, which means that some image data is discarded when it is compressed thereby reducing the quality of the final file. Each time you resave a JPG image, you lose some image information. Image data can sometimes be discarded with little or no noticeable difference in quality. In Figure 8-4, the image at the left is the original JPG image. It's almost difficult to identify the subject in the low-quality version at the right.

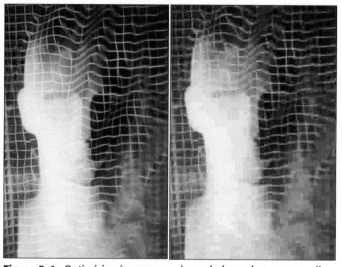

Figure 8-4: Optimizing images requires a balance between quality and file size.

However, not all images loose quality as they are compressed. For example, GIF images use *lossless* compression. This means the compression doesn't remove any information from the image. The compressed image contains all the information, so restoring it to its original dimensions doesn't affect the quality. GIF files are optimized by modifying their color palettes (changing the number of colors used in the image).

Other raster formats you use in SWiSHmax, such as BMP and PNG, also use lossless compression. In the case of both BMP and PNG images, compression is based on bit depth. For example, Figure 8-5 shows the same BMP image at different bit depths. The image at the left uses 8-bit color (Web-safe color), while that on the right uses 24-bit color.

Figure 8-5: Compress BMP files based on their bit depth.

Cross-Reference   Read more about bit depth in Chapter 7.

Preparing Vector Graphics

You consider many of the same factors when preparing vector graphics for use in a movie as you do raster graphics. Coordinate the files' image size and resolution with your movie's size and the type of animation you are planning to use.

Vector illustrations are created from vector lines and fills, not from an arrangement of pixels as raster images are. Efficient vector files are created when the number of lines and fills is reduced as much as possible without corrupting the integrity of the image.

Illustrations can be drawn in any illustration program and exported in a SWiSHmax-native file format. The version of an image you use in a project can look quite different depending on the format. For example, Figure 8-6 shows three versions of the same image; the left is a JPEG version, the center image is an EMF drawing, and the right image is a WMF drawing. Each looks different from the other, although all three could be used in the same way in a project.

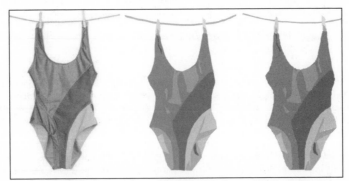

Figure 8-6: The same image can be used in a variety of raster and vector formats.

On The Web Site

The chapter08 folder on the book's Web site contains a subfolder named ch08_sample02. The folder contains an original JPG image, as well as four vector images—three WMF versions and an EMF version. The original illustration is also in the folder, created in Freehand MX 2004, named bathing suit sketch.FH11. A version named bathing suit sketch.FH9 is also in the folder.

Importing Raster Images

Vector images and raster images have different SWiSHmax import processes. You can use a variety of image file types in SWiSHmax, and they can be imported in several ways.

Follow these steps to import raster images into your movie project:

1. **Choose File ⇨ Import.** You can also use several other commands to open the Open dialog box:

   - Choose Insert ⇨ Image

   - Click the Insert image button on the Insert toolbar

   - Choose Insert ⇨ Image from the Outline panel's menu

   - Click the Import button on the Content panel

2. **When the Open dialog box appears, browse to the folder where you are storing image files.**

3. **Click the file name to select it.** To choose multiple contiguous files, click the first image in the list to select it, and then press Shift+click the last image you want to use. The set of images is selected. To choose multiple noncontiguous files, click the first image to select it, and then press Ctrl+click the other images you want to use.

4. **Click Open.** The Open dialog box closes, and the files are imported into the program. Images are placed at the center of the stage automatically.

Tip

You can click and drag images into the program directly from Windows Explorer. Click a file in Windows Explorer to select it and then drag it to the SWiSHmax stage. Images you drag into the program aren't automatically centered on the stage.

Images that you import aren't automatically centered on the stage either. To make sure an image is placed at the exact center of the screen, click either the 100% Zoom or Fit to Scene buttons on the Toolbar before importing the image.

Caution

An imported raster image appears in the Shape panel as a clipped image fill. You can adjust the dimensions and orientation of an image just as you can with a drawn shape. Creating a shape and filling it with an image is a separate process. Image fills are discussed later in the chapter.

Importing Vector Images

Vector images are imported much the same way as raster images, but require an additional step. Once you select the image you want to import, a message dialog box opens asking if you want to merge the objects. Unless you plan to modify individual elements of the drawing, click Yes. The dialog box closes, and the vector image is imported as a single object.

On The Web Site

The chapter08 folder on the book's Web site contains a subfolder named ch08_sample02. In that folder you find the illustration and SWI files used in this example.

A vector image is a group of shapes; it behaves differently than a raster image and the differences are reflected in SWiSHmax:

✦ When you import the object and click Yes in the merging message dialog box, the image is imported as a single shape. If you click No in the merging message dialog box, the image is imported as a group of shapes. In Figure 8-7, the first two images listed in the Outline panel are imported as single objects, while the wmf sketch image is imported as a group of objects. You can see the listing of individual shapes in the Outline panel, and a shape selected on the Layout panel.

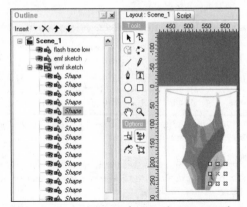

Figure 8-7: An imported vector image contains shapes as listed in the Outline panel.

Tip

You can ungroup the single vector image shape by selecting the image and choosing Modify ➪ Group ➪ Ungroup from the main program menu, by right-clicking and choosing Grouping ➪ Ungroup, or using the Ctrl+U accelerator key combination.

✦ When you import a vector image as a single object, it isn't listed as a clipped image in the Shape panel the way raster images are listed, nor can you use a vector image as a fill for a shape.

✦ Vector images are not listed in the Content panel, while raster images are listed in the Content panel's Images folder.

Reshaping Images

You can modify the physical properties of an image in your movie using the Reshape tools. The processes for reshaping a raster image are the same as those for a vector image or shape. For a vector image, you can select any of the component shapes if it is not a merged graphic, or ungroup the vector image and select individual shapes.

Cross-Reference

Chapter 6 describes in depth how to use the Reshape tool and the Transform tools.

Use any of these methods to reshape an image visually in the Layout panel:

✦ Click the Select tool in the Toolbox to make it active, and then click the image to select it. Resize the image by dragging the corner handles.

✦ Click the Reshape tool in the Toolbox to make it active, and then click the image to display the corner vertices. Modify the image's structure in any of these ways:

  • Click a vertex and adjust the corners of the image

  • Right-click a vertex and change the type of vertex, then move the adjustment handles as desired

  • Right-click a line segment and add a vertex, or change the line segment type

  • Slice the shape

  • Click the Transform tool in the Options area of the Toolbox, and click a vertex or line segment to reshape the vertices and line segments

✦ Modify the image's size or orientation in any of these ways:

  • Rescale or stretch the image in any direction using the Scale tool

  • Resize the image using the Resize tool

  • Rotate or skew the image using the Rotate/Skew tool

Using an Image as a Background

Movies use solid-color backgrounds. You can modify the background color in the Movie panel or use the default white background. You can also use an image as the background of a movie. Follow these steps to use an image for the background of a scene:

1. **Choose Insert ⇨ Scene from the Outline panel's menu.** A new blank scene is added to the project.

2. **Move the scene to the top of the Outline panel's hierarchy.** When you set a scene as the background the content of the scene shows through subsequent scenes added to the movie.

3. **Click the scene's default name and rename it.** Naming the scene "background" or something similar helps to keep track of your movie's contents.

Tip You can also rename the scene in the Scene panel.

4. **With the scene's label selected in the Outline panel, choose File ➪ Import to open the Open dialog box.**

5. **Locate and select the image you want to use for the background and click Open to import the image into the scene.**

6. **Resize the image to fit the size of your movie.** You can use any of the methods mentioned earlier including:

   - Select the image on the stage with the Select tool and drag the corner or side handles until the image is the same size as the movie.

   - Select the image on the stage and then click the Transform tab in the panel group to display the Transform panel. Type new height and width or stretch values for the image.

   - Select the image on the stage, and then click Properties in the Shape panel to open the Image Properties dialog box; modify the height and width or scale values in the dialog box.

Tip If you prefer, you can resize the background image to a smaller size than the movie and use a color for the scene that serves as a border around the image.

7. **On the Scene panel, click the Use this scene as a background option.** In the Outline panel, the icon for the scene changes to display a stack of clapboards as shown in Figure 8-8.

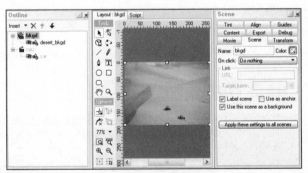

Figure 8-8: A scene used as a background displays a different icon than other scenes in the Outline panel.

When you add additional scenes to the project, the background scene continues to appear behind the other content in your project.

On The Web Site

The book's Web site contains the SWI file and images used in the image background discussion. If you want to experiment with the files, open the ch08_sample03.swi file from the chapter08 folder on the Web site. The chapter's file also contains the car images used — car.jpg and desert.jpg.

Working with Raster Image Properties

Instead of modifying a raster image's physical size and orientation using tools in the Toolbox you can make changes numerically.

Sometimes you import an image into a movie project and then realize that you should have made it darker. Or perhaps you are using an image in combination with other images and need to change the color to match. You can modify several aspects of a vector image's appearance in SWiSHmax by following these steps:

1. **Select the image on the stage.**

2. **Click the Shape tab in the panel group to display the Shape panel.**

3. **Click Properties to open the Image Properties dialog box.**

4. **Make adjustments to the image in these ways:**

   - Transform the image's physical size and orientation in the Image Transform section of the dialog box

   - Choose export settings in the Export Options section of the dialog box

   - Modify the image's appearance in the Adjust appearance section of the dialog box

Cross-Reference

The Export settings are discussed in Chapter 20.

5. **Click OK to close the Image Properties dialog box and apply the changes.**

Note

Vector images do not use the Image Properties dialog box as they are considered drawn shapes or groups of shapes.

Modifying an image's physical size and orientation

A raster image's properties can be altered numerically in the Image Properties dialog box. The Image Transform section of the Image Properties dialog box is shown in Figure 8-9.

Cross-Reference

Vector images are treated as drawn shapes; you modify their physical attributes in the Transform panel. See Chapter 6 for information on working with the Transform panel.

Figure 8-9: You can adjust an image's size and orientation numerically.

Adjust size and orientation properties of an image using the following options:

✦ **X and Y.** The X and Y positions are the coordinates where an image is placed in relation to the stage.

✦ **W and H.** The W (width) and H (height) are the image's dimensions in pixels. When you add an image fill to an object the width and height are adjusted automatically depending on the type of image fill.

✦ **X and Y stretch.** The X and Y stretch refers to the scale of the image.

✦ **Uniform size.** The Uniform scale and size option is selected by default to maintain the image's proportions. Deselect the option if you want to change the width, height, horizontal scale, or vertical scale independently.

✦ **Uniform angle.** The second Uniform option in the Image Transform section of the Image Properties dialog box sets the angle of the image. By default, the Uniform option is selected and the rotation is set at 0 degrees. When the Uniform option is selected, you can change only the X-axis angle to rotate the image. Clicking to deselect the Uniform angle option allows you to skew the angle of the image.

✦ **Angle of X-axis.** When the Uniform angle option is selected, the X- and Y-axis values are the same; changing the angle from its default of 0 degrees rotates the image.

✦ **Angle of Y-axis.** Deselecting the Uniform angle option lets you skew the image's appearance. Type a value in the Angle of Y-axis field that is different than the value typed in the Angle of X-axis field to define the skew.

✦ **Fit to Shape.** Click the Fit to Shape checkbox to have the image's size adjusted to fit the shape of an object if it is used as a fill.

✦ **Reset Transform.** Click Reset Transform to return the settings you modified to their original values.

Modifying a raster image's appearance

Visual properties of a raster image can be modified in the Image Properties dialog box. The original appearance serves as a baseline for the property values. As you can see in Figure 8-10, the initial values for the image are all set at 0, and the resolution is set at 100 percent by default.

Figure 8-10: A raster image's initial appearance is used to create baseline settings.

On The Web Site

The book's Web site contains the SWI file and images used in the appearance modification discussion. If you want to experiment with the files, open the ch08_sample03.swi file from the ch08_sample03 subfolder in the chapter08 folder on the Web site. The folder also contains the two images used in this discussion — car.jpg and desert.jpg.

The Adjust appearance section of the Image Properties dialog box contains several options you can adjust to modify an image. Click and drag a slider left or right to increase or decrease a property's value, click a value's ruler, or click in the property's field and type a number. A preview is shown at the left of the Image Properties dialog box as you make changes. You can also define transparency for the image.

Caution

When you adjust one of the sliders, don't press Enter on the keyboard to apply the changed property value as that closes the Image Properties dialog box. Instead, click in another field on the Image Properties dialog box to apply the changed value.

You can modify these image properties:

✦ **Contrast.** Changing an image's contrast adjusts the light and dark tones of the image. Moving the slider to the far left sets the value to -100 and the image is pure gray; moving the slider to the far right sets the value to 100 and the image displays a limited number of harsh light or dark colors. In the top row of Figure 8-15, the left image shows a decrease in contrast, while the right image shows an increase in contrast.

✦ **Brightness.** Adjusting the brightness of an image modifies the bright and dull tones in the image. Moving the slider to the far left sets the value to -100 and the image is black; moving the slider to the far right sets the value to 100 and the image is white. The bottom row of Figure 8-11 shows decreased brightness in the lower-left image and increased brightness in the lower-right image.

Figure 8-11: Adjust the tonal range of your images using contrast/brightness controls.

✦ **Saturation.** Saturation refers to the amount of color in the image. Moving the slider to the far left sets the value to -100, and the image is desaturated or grayscale. Moving the slider to the far right sets the value to 100, and the image is oversaturated, displaying very intense color.

✦ **Hue.** Adjust the Hue slider to change the overall color in the image. The slider's values range from –180 to 180 and represent degrees on a color wheel. Blue colors are at both ends of the slider. Drag the slider left to change the color through shades of red and purple to blue; drag the slider right to change the color through shades of green and yellow to blue.

✦ **Resolution.** An image shows a resolution value of 100 percent by default. Drag the slider left to decrease the image's resolution without changing the dimensions of the image on your movie.

✦ **Transparency.** You can specify a color or range of color in an image to be transparent. The colors specified as transparent are invisible, and the background displays through the areas on the image; the greater the range, the greater the amount of the image that is transparent.

Follow these steps to select a transparent color:

1. **In the Image Properties dialog box, click the Transparency option to make it active.** A Transparent color button and a Tolerance field appear in the dialog box as shown in Figure 8-12.

Figure 8-12: You can specify a range of transparent colors in the image by adjusting the Tolerance value.

2. **Click the color swatch on the Transparent color dropdown field to open the Color Selector.**

3. **Choose a transparency color by clicking a color on the standard color palette.** You can also choose a color by using one of these methods:

   • Click a color from the custom color palette

   • Type RGB or Hex values for a color in their respective fields

   • Click the Eyedropper tool to select it, and then sample a color on the image in the Preview area of the Image Properties dialog box

   • Click the Windows Color button to open the Color dialog box and choose a color

   The Color Selector closes automatically unless you typed RGB or Hex values for the color. If you used either of those methods, click Done to close the Color Selector and return to the Image Properties dialog box. The chosen color displays in the color swatch next to the Transparent color label.

   Tip   At any time you can force the color selections to Web-safe color by clicking the Use Web-safe button.

4. **Click the Tolerance field and type a value, or click either the up or down arrow to increase or decrease the specified tolerance.** Tolerance refers to the color range affected by the transparency option. The higher the tolerance you set, the greater the range of color selected, and the more extensive the amount of transparency in the image.

5. **Preview the transparency range on the Preview area of the Image Properties dialog box.** As shown in Figure 8-12, the transparent areas on the image show a checked background.

6. **Click OK or press Enter to close the Image Properties dialog box and apply the changes.**

   Note   If you are adjusting color settings and change your mind, click the Reset button to restore the original appearance of the image.

In Figure 8-13 you can see the effect of setting transparent areas. The sample image is a colored car overlaying a bright green background layer; the bright green shows through the areas defined by choosing the transparent color and setting the tolerance, or range of values to include in the transparency.

Figure 8-13: The transparent areas assigned to an image display content on lower layers of the movie.

Use any or all of the settings in combination. To reset the appearance property, drag the sliders back to their original locations or type the original values in the properties' fields. Remove transparency by clicking the Transparency option to deselect it.

Note

Once you close the Image Properties dialog box, you must reopen it to reset the values; the Reset Transform button on the Fill area of the Shape panel doesn't apply to appearance changes.

Working with Image Fills

Images can be used alone as objects in your movie, or you can use them as an object fill for a vector drawing you create in SWiSHmax. SWiSHmax uses two types of image fill — tiled or clipped.

✦ **Tiled image.** A tiled image fill uses multiple copies of a bitmap image arranged geometrically to fill an object.

✦ **Clipped image.** A clipped image fill uses a single copy of a bitmap image that may be resized in different ways to fill an object. When you import an image for use in your project, it is automatically defined as a clipped image although it uses its original shape and dimensions.

A sample of each type of image fill is shown in Figure 8-14.

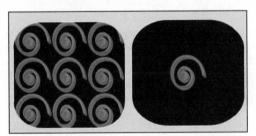

Figure 8-14: You can use images as tiled fills like that shown on the left, or as clipped image fills like that shown on the right.

On The Web Site

The book's Web site contains the SWI file and images used in the image fill steps that follow. If you want to experiment with the files, open the ch08_sample04.swi file from the ch08_sample04 subfolder in the chapter08 folder on the Web site. The chapter's file also contains the images used, named paint1.jpg and paint2.jpg.

You must have a drawn object on the Layout panel to use for the fill. Follow these steps to choose an image fill option:

1. **Select the object on the scene.** The star object in Figure 8-15 is used as an example. The shape is named **star** in the Outline panel.

2. **Click the Shape panel's tab in the panel group to display the panel.**

3. **Click the Fill button to display the drop-down menu shown in Figure 8-15.** The default fill option, or a previously selected fill option, appears on the Fill button.

4. **Choose either the tiled image or clipped image fill option from the list.** The drop-down menu closes and you can configure your fill choice.

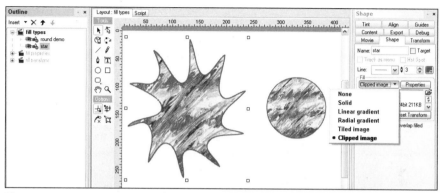

Figure 8-15: You can use one of two image fill options for your movie's objects.

5. **Click the Select New Image button to open the Open dialog box, browse to the location where you have stored the image you want to use, select it, and click Open.** The Open dialog box closes and the object is filled with the image. You can also click the dropdown arrow at the right side of the fill properties preview area on the Shape panel and choose an image from the drop-down menu.

Tip

If you have used an image during your current work session it is listed at the end of the drop-down menu.

Naming objects that use image fills

Be careful when working with objects you intend to fill with images. If you draw a shape and leave its default name, when the file is saved the name of the object changes. In the previous example, the original shape used the default shape name **star**. When the file was saved, the object's name changed to that of the image fill, **paint1.jpg**, and was manually changed back to **star**. A second shape used in the example is named **round demo**. After saving, as you can see in Figure 8-15, the named object's name remains unchanged.

When you have filled a shape, you can adjust size and orientation properties of the image fill using the following options:

✦ **X and Y.** The X and Y positions are the coordinates where an image is placed in relation to the object's center. The location of the image is based both on the type of fill and the sizes of the fill image and the object. For example, a tile fill automatically resizes itself and distributes several copies within the object's shape while a clipped fill resizes itself to fill the object's shape.

✦ **Uniform size.** The Uniform scale and size option is deselected by default for both types of image fill. This allows the program to adjust the image's size and location according to the type of fill you choose. For example, a tiled image won't tile if the size of the image is the same or greater than the size of the object it is filling.

✦ **W and H.** The W (width) and H (height) are the image's dimensions in pixels. When you add an image fill to an object the width and height are adjusted automatically depending on the type of image fill.

✦ **X and Y stretch.** The X and Y stretch refers to the scale of the image. The image fill automatically adjusts the X and Y stretch depending on the type of fill, the object's size, and the fill image size.

✦ **Uniform angle.** The second Uniform option on the Image Transform section of the Image Properties dialog box sets the angle of the fill. By default, the Uniform option is selected and the rotation is set at 0 degrees. When the Uniform option is selected you can change only the X-axis angle to rotate the image. Clicking to deselect the Uniform angle option allows you to skew the angle of the image.

✦ **Angle of X-axis.** When the Uniform angle option is selected, the X- and Y-axis values are the same; changing the angle from its default of 0 degrees rotates the image.

✦ **Angle of Y-axis.** Deselecting the Uniform angle option lets you skew the image's appearance. Type a value in the Angle of Y-axis field that is different than the value typed in the Angle of X-axis field to define the skew.

✦ **Fit to Shape.** Click the Fit to Shape checkbox to have the image's size adjusted to fit the shape of an object.

✦ **Reset Transform.** Click Reset Transform to return the settings you modified to their original values.

Changing an image fill's properties

When an image fill is added to an object it automatically sizes itself according to the type of fill. For example, a tiled fill automatically sets itself into a geometric arrangement of multiples of the image within the object. A clipped image fill automatically resizes the image to fill the shape. Both types of image fill use many of the same properties. For either type of image fill, follow these steps to modify the fill's properties:

1. **Select the object on the Layout panel.**

2. **Click the Shape tab in the panel group to display the Shape panel.**

3. **Click the Properties button on the Fill preview area of the Shape panel.** The Image Properties dialog box opens as shown in Figure 8-16. The example shows the properties for a clipped image fill.

4. **Modify the properties as desired in the Image transform section of the dialog box.** At any time you can click Reset Transform in the Image transform section to restore the default settings.

5. **Click OK to close the Image Properties dialog box and apply the changes to the object's fill.** If you change your mind, click Cancel to close the Image Properties dialog box without applying the changes.

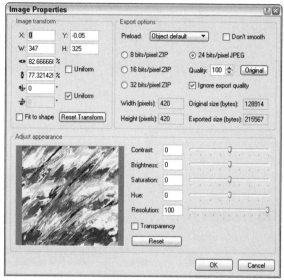

Figure 8-16: You can change a fill's properties in the Image Properties dialog box.

Resetting an Image Fill

When you add an image fill to an object it displays default arrangements. A tiled image fill usually resizes the image to display a number of tiles within the object, and a clipped image fill may resize the image to fit within the object. For both types of image fill you can reset the way the image is used as a fill, although the two types of fill behave differently.

Resetting a tiled image fill

You change the way a tile fill appears in an object from the Shape panel. Resetting the image fill restores the image fill to its original size and orientation. In Figure 8-17, the original image fill is shown at the bottom left for reference. The upper left arrow shape shows its fill using custom settings, while the lower-right arrow shape shows the fill image at actual size within the shape. Select the shape, and then click Reset Transform in the Fill preview area of the Shape panel to restore the original shape, stretch, and other properties of the image fill.

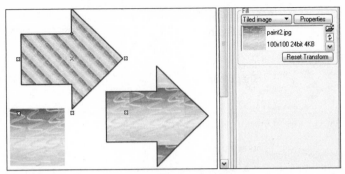

Figure 8-17: You can reset the fill of a tiled image.

Resetting a clipped image fill

You can also reset modifications made to an image used as a clipped fill. Unlike a tiled image fill, which has only one option for resetting, a clipped image fill can use one of two options. When an image is smaller than the object it fills, the default placement of an image is to fit it to the shape. Click Reset Transform on the Shape panel to restore the image used as the fill to its original size.

Figure 8-18 shows a clipped image fill. The original image is shown at the lower left of the figure for reference. When the clipped image fill is applied to the shape it is stretched as shown in the upper left circle shape. Clicking the Reset Transform button in the Fill preview area of the Shape panel restores the shape, stretch, and other properties of the fill to that of the original fill image, as seen in the lower right circle shape. SWiSHmax indicates that the image fill is smaller than the object being filled by showing horizontal and vertical stripes running from the sides of the image at its original size to the edges of the object. To revert to the stretched image fill like that shown in the upper left circle shape, click the Fit to Shape option in the Fill preview area of the Shape panel.

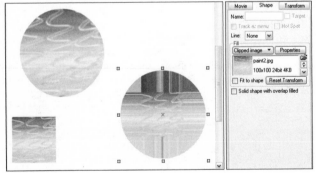

Figure 8-18: Reset and restore sizes of a clipped image fill in the Shapes panel.

Reload the image used for either type of fill in the same way. Click the Reload button in the Fill preview area of the Shape panel shown in Figure 8-19. The fill image is reloaded in the project.

Figure 8-19: Reload an image using a fill from the Shape panel.

 Cross-Reference

You can also reload an image you are using as a fill from the Content panel. Read more about the Content panel and image replacement in Chapter 4.

Transforming an Image Fill

You can modify tiled image fills using the Fill Transform tool. With the tool selected in the Toolbox, click the image fill as shown in Figure 8-20. When you click an object using a fill with the Fill Transform tool, the selection looks different based on the type of fill you select.

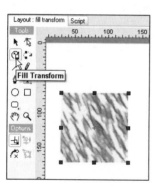

Figure 8-20: Use the Fill Transform tool to modify the appearance of an image fill in a shape.

 On The Web Site

The book's Web site contains the SWI file and image used in the fill transform examples. If you want to experiment with the files, open the ch08_sample04.swi file from the ch08_sample04 subfolder in the chapter08 folder on the Web site. The chapter's file also contains the example's image named paint3.jpg.

Figure 8-21 shows two shapes filled with the same image. The left shape uses a tiled image fill and the right uses a clipped image fill. When the Fill Adjust tool is selected in the Toolbox, the set of blue handles appears around one copy or tile of the image in the tiled image fill, whereas activating the Fill Adjust tool for an object having a clipped image fill shows handles around the edges of the entire shape.

Cross-Reference   Refer to Chapter 6 for more information on using the Fill Transform tool.

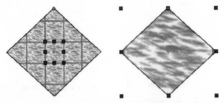

Figure 8-21: The Fill Transform tool selects different items of an object depending on whether it is a clipped or a tiled fill.

Moving an image fill makes a clipped image fill appear quite different but has no effect on a tiled image. In Figure 8-22, both the objects' fills were moved downward and left. In the tiled image fill shown in the left diamond shape, you can't see a difference; the tiling pattern is continuous. On the other hand, the right diamond shape in the figure uses a clipped image fill and shows that when moved, the fill image's border color adjusts (in this case, expands) to fill in the space where the fill image was removed from.

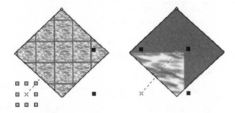

Figure 8-22: Moving a tiled image fill has no effect on the appearance of the fill, unlike the clipped image fill.

You can use the Rotate/Skew tools on both tiled image and clipped image fills. In Figure 8-23, the top pair of images shows objects filled with a tiled image fill and a clipped image fill, respectively, and with the Rotate/Skew handles active. The central pair of images shows both fills using a 40-degree clockwise rotation. The bottom pair of images shows the fills using a 33-degree skew along the Y-axis.

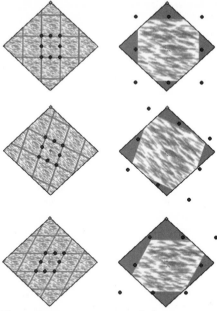

Figure 8-23: Use Rotate and Skew options with both types of image fill.

Summary

This chapter was all about images. You learned how to prepare different types of images for use in a SWiSHmax movie project. Vector and raster images are quite different, and are used and manipulated in different ways, as you saw in this chapter. You also learned:

✦ What types of images you can use in SWiSHmax

✦ What you should consider when preparing images for use in a movie, including format, size, and resolution

✦ How to prepare images for use in a movie

✦ Different methods for importing images into SWiSHmax

✦ How to reshape images

✦ That an image can be used as a scene's background

✦ About the different types of image fills

✦ How to modify and transform image fills

✦ To configure image fills using properties as well as Fill Transform tools

✦   ✦   ✦

Using Animations and Flash Movies in SWiSHmax

You can draw shapes in SWiSHmax, and you can import a range of different raster and vector image formats. You can also import animations in a variety of formats. In this chapter, you see how different types of animated content can be imported into SWiSHmax for use in your projects.

SWiSHmax allows you to reuse animated GIF files created in other programs. In addition, you can use SWF files created and exported from SWiSHmax or from Flash, use stand-alone Projector files created in SWiSHmax, or use one SWI file within another project. You can reuse specific frames from an animation or use the entire file.

There are different reasons why you may want to work with external files in your SWiSHmax movie project. You may have created an animated GIF in another program, for example, and instead of having to re-create the animation you can simply import it. You may have an animation created in another program that contains some content you wish to reuse, or a SWiSHmax file you want to work with in another project.

In SWiSHmax, you can import all these types of material.

Importing Animated GIF Files

One of the most common types of material used on the Internet is the animated GIF file, formally called a GIF89a file. The appearance of motion is produced by displaying a sequence of images, and color can be transparent allowing the page's background to display. In SWiSHmax, you can use animated GIF files and control many features of the animation.

Use one of the Insert ⇨ Content commands or choose File ⇨ Import to display the Open dialog box and browse to the location of the file you want to use. Select the animated GIF file you want to import and then click Open; the Open dialog box closes and the Import dialog box opens as shown in Figure 9-1.

Figure 9-1: You can choose several ways to import an animated GIF file into a movie.

Choosing an importing option

You import an animated GIF in one of three ways:

✦ As one object per frame in a group

✦ As an animated sprite

✦ As a new scene

All three options allow you to import a background as well. The background is imported as a single object named Background and is placed at the bottom of the stack of frames. In Figure 9-2, the Outline panel for three copies of the same animation is shown.

On The Web Site

The animation used for this discussion is named boots.gif. It is available in the chapter09 folder on the book's Web site.

In the Outline panel, the imported frames are listed as separate elements of a group when the One object per frame in a group option is selected.

When you create one object per frame in a group, each frame in the movie contains the objects visible in that frame in a group as shown in Figure 9-3. All the groups are placed into one parent group that functions as a single entity. The result isn't animated, but you can apply effects to play the frames in sequence.

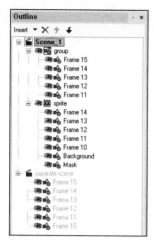

Figure 9-2: You can choose from three ways to import a GIF animation.

Figure 9-3: A group of frames is added to one frame in the Timeline.

 Caution
When you ungroup the imported animation, each frame becomes a child object of the entire scene.

It's easy to ungroup the imported object. Simply right-click the object's name in the Outline panel to display the shortcut menu. Then choose Grouping ⇨ Ungroup to separate the group into individual clipped image objects.

You may want to use this option if you are importing all or a portion of an animation and plan to make a change to the entire animation, such as rotating it.

The most common use of a GIF animation is as a sprite. Use this option if the animation is a single entity in your movie. You also have the option of importing a mask object when creating a sprite from an animated GIF, which serves as a window for displaying other content in the animation.

As shown in Figure 9-4, each frame of the animation has its own row on the sprite's Timeline and each frame is placed at a specific frame of the Timeline following its sequence in the animation. The sprite is part of a movie's default **Scene_1**, and each imported frame is part of the sprite object.

Caution
If you ungroup the sprite, its frames become child objects of the scene.

Figure 9-4: Each animated GIF frame imported as part of a sprite has its own row on the sprite's Timeline.

Cross-Reference

Learn about sprites in Chapter 15.

The third type of animated GIF import creates a new scene. As you can see in Figure 9-5, each animated frame is placed on its own row in the new scene's Timeline, and each object is placed at a specific frame of the Timeline following its sequence in the animation. Each frame of the imported animation is a completely separate object. That is, you can select a frame and transform it as you want without affecting any of the other imported frames.

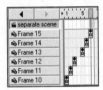

Figure 9-5: You can import animated GIF frames into a new scene.

Understanding frame information and settings

In addition to defining how you want the frames to behave once they are imported into your movie project, you can determine other features as well. Choose options for importing based on how you plan to use the content of the file and the information required:

✦ **Frames.** When you choose an animation to import, its sequence of frames is listed in the Frames area of the Import dialog box. The default option is to import the entire range of frames; you can choose one or several frames as required. Click the sequence of frames you want to import; if you change your mind and decide to import the entire animation, click Select All to reselect the entire sequence.

✦ **Show File Information.** Click Show File Information in the Import dialog box to open the Report dialog box. The report lists common types of information such as duration, frame size, and color.

✦ **Frame Content.** You can modify the image's frame size and transparency properties. The default option is to keep the frames as is. When you choose the default, the imported animation is the same as your original animation. You can also choose to change the frame size to the full size of your movie or to fill transparent pixels. Filling transparent pixels means the color chosen as transparent when you created and saved the original animation is filled with your movie's background color.

Once you import the desired frames into your project, they are defined as separate images. In the Content panel, shown in Figure 9-6, you see that each frame is listed as an image. The individual images use the file's name—in this case boots.gif—followed by the frame number in brackets. When you import a GIF animation as a sprite, it is also listed as a sprite in the Content panel, again shown in Figure 9-7.

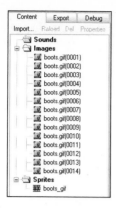

Figure 9-6: Imported GIF animation frames are listed as individual images.

Importing SWF Animations

Sometimes you create a SWF movie from a SWiSHmax project, and then want to duplicate or reuse the movie in another movie project. You may also have SWF movies created in other programs, such as Flash MX 2004. Rather than recreating the movie in your project file, you can simply import an existing SWF movie into a SWiSHmax movie project.

Like animated GIF files, you can import all of an animation, selected frames, or a single frame. You import a Flash movie in one of three ways:

✦ As one object per frame in a group

✦ As an animated sprite

✦ As a new scene

All three of the import options allow you to import a background. SWF files can contain scripting, and you have the option to import decompiled scripts as well. The background is imported as a single object named **Background**; a mask layer is available only when importing an animated sprite. Mask and Background layers are placed at the bottom of the stack of frames. Finally, you can also choose to import text as shapes if the font used in the SWF movie isn't available on your computer. If you convert the text to shapes it can't be edited as letters in your SWiSHmax project, but the letters will look the same as those in the original SWF movie.

Note

Importing an animation as a group of objects isn't commonly used unless you plan to change the frames' content using transform tools. Importing animations as a group of objects can produce a very large file.

On The Web Site

The animation used for this discussion is named eyes.swf. It is available in the chapter09 folder on the book's Web site.

Importing a movie as an animated sprite

Flash movies are commonly used as sprites in a SWiSHmax movie project. To import a SWF movie for use as a sprite in a SWiSHmax project, follow these steps:

1. **On the Outline panel, choose Insert ⇨ Content to open the Open dialog box.**

Note   There are other program locations for importing content under the File and Insert program menus, as well as by clicking Insert Content on the Insert toolbar.

2. **Browse to the location of the SWF file you want to use and select it.**

3. **Click Open in the Open dialog box.** The Open dialog box closes, and the Import dialog box opens, as seen in Figure 9-7.

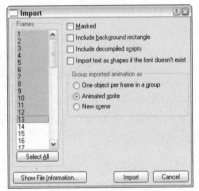

Figure 9-7: You can choose a variety of options for importing SWF files.

4. **Press Ctrl+Click the frames you want to import to select them.** By default all frames are selected.

5. **Click Animated sprite in the Group imported animation as section of the Import dialog box.**

6. **Choose specific sprite options.** You can choose Masked, Include background rectangle, Include decompiled scripts, and .import text as shapes if the font doesn't exist.

7. **Click Import to close the Import dialog box.** The SWF content is imported as a sprite using the SWF file's name.

Imported SWF content displays in the Outline panel and on the Layout panel. Each shape that is used in the animation is listed as a separate shape in the Outline panel, as shown in Figure 9-8. Each shape is placed on its own layer and can be transformed using the SWiSHmax tools as desired.

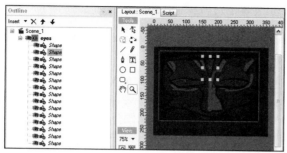

Figure 9-8: A SWF animation imported as a sprite defines each element as a separate shape.

Unlike imported GIF animations, you cannot redefine each shape as a clipped image when you import as a sprite. In the Content panel an SWF animation imported as a sprite shows one listing in the Sprites folder.

 Learn how to work with sprites in Chapter 15.

SWF animations imported as a sprite create a frame in SWiSHmax for each frame of the original animation. The sample animation, eyes.swf, is shown imported into a SWiSHmax movie project in Figure 9-9. The original animation ran for 30 frames; in the SWiSHmax Timeline you see the imported content also runs for 30 frames.

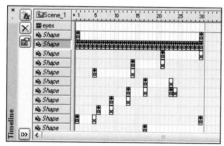

Figure 9-9: An imported SWF animation displays each frame of the animation as separate frames on the Timeline.

Importing a movie as a scene

A movie imported as a sprite is added to an existing or selected scene in the Outline panel, whereas choosing the New scene option creates a separate scene. Follow these steps to import an SWF file as a new scene:

1. **On the Outline panel, choose Insert ➪ Content to open the Open dialog box.**

Note   There are other program locations for importing content under the File and Insert program menus, as well as by clicking Insert Content on the Insert toolbar.

2. **Browse to the location of the SWF file you want to use and select it.**

3. **Click Open in the Open dialog box.** The Open dialog box closes, and the Import dialog box opens.

4. **Click the frames you want to import to select them.** By default all frames are selected.

5. **Click New scene in the Group imported animation as section of the Import dialog box.**

6. **Choose other import settings including background, and include decompiled scripts options.**

7. **Click Import to close the Import dialog box.** The SWF content is imported as a separate scene named using the SWF file's name as shown in Figure 9-10.

Figure 9-10: You can import a SWF movie as a separate scene.

Importing a single frame

You can also import single frames from an SWF movie directly into SWiSHmax instead of exporting single frames from Flash as still images. Follow the steps for importing a movie, choosing only the frame you want to import in Step 4. Figure 9-11 shows three versions of the same frame of a movie all imported differently.

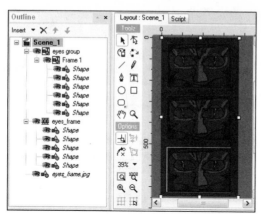

Figure 9-11: You can import a single frame from a Flash movie into your project.

On The Web Site
The single-frame files used for this discussion are named eyes_frame.swf and eyes_frame.jpg. They are available in the chapter09 folder on the book's Web site. Where the discussion refers to an imported frame, Frame 5 of the eyes.swf movie was imported.

The first copy of the frame is imported as a single image from the eyes.swf movie and added as a group of objects. The imported frame uses the file's original name. The name of the group in the figure is changed to **eyes group** to show you the different import formats more clearly.

The central image in the Layout panel in the figure is imported as a single-frame SWF movie. The eyes_frame.swf file was selected and imported as a sprite. The frame appears in the Outline panel as a single sprite containing five shapes.

Note
Interestingly, importing the frame from the entire animation results in a set of six shapes; importing a single frame exported from Flash as a single-frame SWF file results in a set of five shapes. The eyes and eyelids are defined as one object in the single-frame SWF file and as separate objects in the frame imported from the full animation.

For reference, the third imported example is a JPEG image. You can see it is one object. The JPEG image will be listed in the Content panel as an image; the sprite imported from the single-frame SWF file will be listed under the Sprites in the Content panel; the imported **eyes group** version isn't listed, as it is a collection of shapes.

Cross-Reference
Read about working with the Content panel in Chapter 4.

Is There a Difference in Import Methods?

In terms of managing your files and movies, there isn't much difference between using one method of importing or another method. For example, if each of the methods described in this discussion was used alone, the SWI files are virtually the same size (89–90KB) whether the frame is imported from a movie or is imported as a single-frame SWF file exported from Flash. Using an image, for example a JPEG image, produces a considerably smaller SWI file at only approximately 50KB.

The important size issue relates to the exported movie. Using the same settings, a SWF movie exported from SWiSHmax using either of the single-frame import options produces a tidy 9KB file. That contrasts significantly when compared with the SWF created from the version using a JPEG image, which was 49KB.

Converting SWF Information

Not everything you view in a Flash-generated SWF movie appears the same when you import the movie into SWiSHmax due to the characteristics of the SWF format. The file is rendered when exported as a SWF movie; that is, the information in the movie is processed on a frame-by-frame basis. In some cases, you need to choose additional options when importing in order to use the SWF file's information.

Importing movies with color changes

If you look at the selected shape back in Figure 9-9, you see in the Timeline that each frame of the animation includes a separate keyframe and effect. The effect used is the Place effect, which defines when the frame is shown during the course of the animation. The shape (the V at the top of the forehead) is seen for the entire animation. Rather than simply placing the shape in Frame 1, it is placed for each frame in the animation. If you play the movie or the SWF file, you see that the V-shape gradually fades to lighter gray as the movie progresses.

On The Web Site

This discussion refers to the ch09_sample01.swi file. You can download the file from the book's Web site; it is in the chapter09 folder in the ch09_sample01 subfolder. The source file, eyes.swf is in the chapter09 folder.

The SWF format doesn't contain information about gradual color changes. Instead, it must place a separate keyframe for each frame. For example, in Figure 9-12, the V-shape on the forehead is shown as it appears on Frame 1 of the animation. In the Tint panel, the Custom Color appears as dark gray, which is black with a 55 percent alpha level.

Cross-Reference   Refer to Chapter 7 for information on alpha levels.

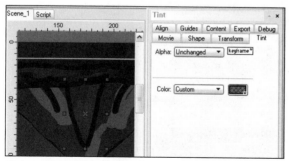

Figure 9-12: Color change is controlled on a frame-by-frame basis.

Note

The gradual change in an object over time, be it color, size, or location, is called *tweening*. Tweening comes from the term *in-betweening*, which originally was used in conventional animation to describe the process of creating intermediate frames to gradually modify the image appearance between significant changes in an animation.

Contrast that with the same area of the forehead in Figure 9-13, shown as it appears on Frame 30. Now the Tint panel appears a barely visible shade of gray, which is black with a 4 percent alpha level.

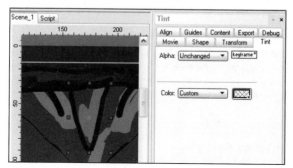

Figure 9-13: The shape's color fades over time.

Importing movies containing scenes

Scenes can't be imported as they exist in a SWF movie. Figure 9-14 shows two frames of a SWF movie in its original form. The image at the left shows the first frame of the first scene; the image at the right shows a frame part way through the second scene. The second scene is launched by clicking CLICK, which is shown in the left frame's image.

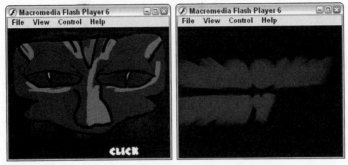

Figure 9-14: The original animation contains two scenes.

On The Web Site

If you would like to experiment with the file used in this discussion it is on the book's Web site. The SWiSHmax file, ch09_sample02.swi, is in the ch09_sample02 subfolder in the chapter09 folder. The source file used in the SWiSHmax project is groovy.swf, which is available in the chapter09 folder. The original Flash file is also available on the book's Web site in the chapter09 folder. The file is a Flash MX 2004 file named groovy.fla.

The first scene contains 27 frames, the second 29 frames. When imported as a sprite without scripts, the frames are listed in sequence regardless of which frame they represented in the original animation, so the sprite lists 56 frames in total. The result of importing the animation as a sprite is that it plays according to the original movie's sequence—the CLICK button's actions aren't functional, and the two scenes play through from the start of Scene_1 to the end of Scene_2.

Note

If you are importing a SWF movie that contains more than one scene and you want to separate them in your SWiSHmax project, import them as a series. That is, choose File ➪ Import and select the frames that make up the first scene, importing them as a sprite. Then repeat as necessary to convert all the scenes from the original movie into separate sprites in your SWiSHmax project.

Importing movies using scripts

Depending on the characteristics of your movie you can transfer actions successfully from an imported SWF movie into your SWiSHmax movie project. When you select an SWF file for import, click Include decompiled scripts in the Import dialog box. The scripts are imported into SWiSHmax along with the other frame information.

Not all actions you added to a Flash movie that was actually created in Flash are included in an SWF animation imported into SWiSHmax. Table 9-1 lists the actions that can be imported with an animation generated in Flash MX 2004.

Table 9-1: Actions imported from Flash MX 2004

Action or Function	Used For...
play()	This function moves the play head forward in the Timeline, commonly used with buttons to control movie clips.
stop()	This function stops the SWF file that is currently playing, commonly used with buttons to control movie clips.
gotoAndPlay()	This function sends the play head to the specified frame in a scene and plays from that frame, or plays from a specified frame in the current scene.
gotoAndStop()	This function sends the play head to the specified frame in a scene and stops it, or stops at a specified frame in the current scene.
stopAllSounds	This function stops all sounds currently playing in a SWF movie without stopping the play head.
setLabel()	This method lets the user set a label for a component.
nextFrame()	This function sends the play head to the next frame and stops it.
prevFrame()	This function sends the play head to the previous frame and stops it. When the current frame is Frame 1, the play head doesn't move.
getURL()	This global function is used to open a Web page in a browser window or to pass data to another application at a specified URL.
fscommand()	These actions let the SWF file communicate with either the Flash Player or the program hosting the Flash Player, such as a Web browser. The command can also be used with other programs.
javascript()	Use JavaScript statements along with fscommand() actions or GetURL() actions to communicate with Web browsers or HTML documents.
mailto()	Use this function to create a link to an e-mail address' URL.
loadMovie()	This function loads a SWF or JPEG file into Flash Player while the original SWF file is playing.
ifFrameLoaded()	This action checks whether the contents of a specific frame are available locally; commonly used for preloaders.*
var = expression	A class is a type of object; characteristics of the class are variables. These statements are used to declare local (within a function) or Timeline variables.
_property = expression	A class is a type of object composed of characteristics and behaviors. The characteristics are called properties of the class, which are represented as variables. For example, Button is a type of class. It has numerous properties, such as _alpha, _height, _name, and so on.

* This action is deprecated in Flash MX 2004; Macromedia recommends using the MovieClip._framesloaded property.

On The Web Site

This discussion refers to the ch09_sample03a.swi and ch09_sample03b.swi files. Download the files from the book's Web site. They are in the chapter09 folder in the ch09_sample03 subfolder. The source file, groovy.swf, is in the chapter09 folder.

You can view the contents of the file including scripts. When you select a SWF file to import, click Show File Information in the Import dialog box to open the Report dialog box, as shown in Figure 9-15.

The Report dialog box shows that the sample movie, groovy.swf, contains both button and frame events. In the original Flash file, the first scene is programmed to loop—the frame event occurs when the playback head reaches the final frame of the scene. Clicking the button moves the playback to the first frame of the second scene—the button event occurs when the button is clicked and the mouse is released.

Cross-Reference

Read about events and actions in Chapters 18 and 19.

```
Report                                                          _ □ ✕
Filename: \\DONNA-BAKER\ebooks\groovy.swf
Version: SWF6
File length: 25005 bytes (18384 bytes filesize)
Frame size: 309 x 240 pixels
Frame rate: 12.00 frames/sec
Total number of frames: 56 frames

- Entire Movie ----Tags---------------|

The following were read:
+      Header:                  20 bytes
+      Shapes:       16      16415 bytes
+       Fonts:        1       2274 bytes
+       Texts:        5        246 bytes
+     Buttons:        1         53 bytes
+  ButtonEvent:       1          0 bytes
+ ButtonScript:       2          0 bytes
+    PlaceTags:     320       5825 bytes
+   RemoveTags:      10         40 bytes
+   ShowFrames:      56        112 bytes
+   FrameEvent:       1          0 bytes
+  FrameAction:       2          0 bytes
+      BgColor:       1          5 bytes
```

Figure 9-15: The Report dialog box shows information about the file you are importing.

Frame scripts

In both the original Flash file and the SWiSHmax version the animation of the creature loops, although the script is written differently in the two programs. The script for the loop is written in the Flash file as

```
gotoAndPlay(1);
```

and attached to Frame 27, meaning that when the playback head reaches Frame 27 it returns to Frame 1 and starts playing again.

After importing the SWF file into SWiSHmax, shown in the sample file, ch09_sample03a.swi, the script is converted to

```
onFrame (27) {
    gotoAndStop(0);
    play();
}
```

Button scripts

The scripts for the button also change from the original Flash file to the SWiSHmax file. In the original Flash file, the script for the button is written as

```
on(release) {
gotoAndPlay("Scene 2", 1);
}
```

When the SWF file is imported into SWiSHmax, the same script converts to

```
on (release) {
    gotoSceneAndStop("<current scene>",27);
    play();
}
```

The "`<current scene>`" replaces the "`Scene 2`" target described in the Flash file because there is only one scene in the SWiSHmax file. The converted action does not play correctly and needs two adjustments. The frame number assigned to the button's action is the same as that assigned to the frame for looping. As a result, the button doesn't work. You must modify the script by deleting the reference to the scene and changing the frame number to comply with the new Timeline. Your script should now look like this:

```
on (release) {
    gotoAndPlay(28);
}
```

The playback head now moves to the start of the text on the Timeline and the movie plays correctly.

On The Web Site

You can test this modified script yourself. The sample file ch09_sample03b.swi in the chapter09 file on the Web site contains the modified script as described in this discussion.

Importing complex frames

Shape morphing is a special kind of tweening where one shape is gradually changed to another shape. Not all shape morphing can successfully be imported into SWiSHmax from a SWF file. The example used in this discussion shows two shapes gradually changing from rectangles to a circle and an octagon.

On The Web Site

A copy of the SWiSHmax file named ch09_sample04.swi is on the book's Web site in the ch09_sample04 subfolder within the chapter09 folder. The file contains the two scenes described in this discussion as well as the two source files used in the discussion named shapes.swf and shapes.gif. The original Flash file, shapes.fla, is also in the folder if you want to experiment with it.

When you attempt to import a complex animation into a SWiSHmax project file, you may see a warning dialog box like that shown in Figure 9-16.

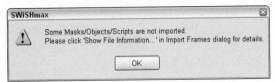

Figure 9-16: Some content can't be imported into a
SWiSHmax movie project.

When you click OK to dismiss the warning dialog box, the Import dialog box opens. To see
what the warning is referring to, click Show File Information in the Import dialog box to display the Report dialog box where the shape information that can't be imported is described.

In the example, the Report dialog box states that two **MorphShapes** were unable to be
imported, that one shape will be imported, and that the animation is 27 frames in length.
Interpreting the report, this means the animation contains two shapes in a form unrecognized
by SWiSHmax, one shape that is recognized, and a total of 27 frames. The unrecognized
shapes, **MorphShapes**, are the content for the first 26 frames; the report also says that one
shape will be imported, and this is the content for the final frame. Whether you import the
file as an animated sprite or a new scene, you have a similar problem with regards to the content on the stage.

If you attempt to import the SWF file as a group of objects, you have one shape displayed on
the final frame of the animation, Frame 27 as seen in Figure 9-17. The previous 26 frames are
blank as they contain the **MorphShape**, which is not recognized by SWiSHmax. If you attempt
to import a selected number of frames, with the exception of the last frame, in this example,
Frame 27, nothing is imported into the project

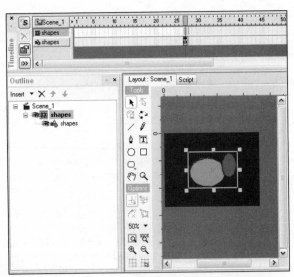

Figure 9-17: The imported SWF file displays only the
last frame.

A similar event occurs if you import the SWF file as a group of objects. In Figure 9-18, the
shapes.swf file is imported as a group of objects. You can see the parent object named **shapes**

contains a sequence of objects representing each frame. With the exception of Frame 27, which has a child shape shown on the Layout panel, each frame's object is blank.

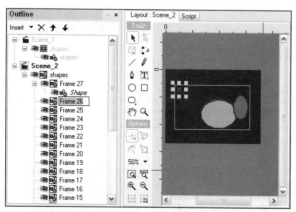

Figure 9-18: Importing the SWF file as a group of objects displays the final frame as well.

If you need to modify the content of the individual frames, you can do one of two things if you have access to the original program file used to create the movie: change the design of the original Flash file to prevent ShapeMorph errors or export the movie from Flash MX 2004 in an alternate fashion. For example, using an animated GIF version of the file produces the full animation, as seen in Figure 9-19.

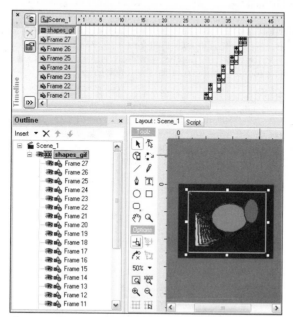

Figure 9-19: Import a complex animation as an animated GIF to prevent import errors.

On The Web Site

You can experiment with an animated GIF version of the shapes movie. It is in the chapter09 folder on the book's Web site in the ch09_sample04 subfolder. The file is named shapes.gif.

Importing masked animations

One method of animating is to use masks. A mask is a shape used as a window or frame for other content. Masks can be imported as part of an animation; depending on how the masking is used, you may or may not have the results you expect. A mask that has motion won't import as constructed. In Figure 9-20, three frames (from the sample mask.swf file) are shown. The animation occurs as the masked image is slowly increased in size during the course of the animation, revealing the underlying image of trees.

Figure 9-20: Imported animations containing masks may not display correctly.

On The Web Site

All the files referenced in this discussion are available on the Web site in the chapter09 folder. In the ch09_sample05.swi file, you will find Place and Remove effects on the Timeline for each sprite. These were added to allow you to see the content of the two sprites separately.

When the file is imported, an error message appears stating that some masks, objects, and scripts are not imported. The error message was shown in Figure 9-16. The Report dialog box for the mask.swf import process describes the problem as related to the masks, as well as a MorphShape error, which occurs as a result of constructing the mask to gradually increase in size over time.

When the file is imported, it appears as a single-frame sprite. In Figure 9-21, you can see the imported content on the sample ch09_sample05.swi file. A single frame of the background image is imported. The other element that is imported is the named **Shape**, which is selected in the Layout panel. This shape was that of the original mask in the source **mask.swf** animation.

Note   If you check the Content panel, the single frame is listed as an image in the Images folder.

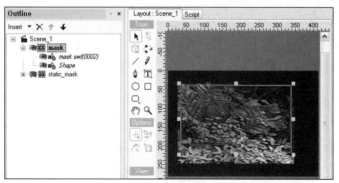

Figure 9-21: An imported masked animation displays only the component elements of the movie.

A similar problem can occur whether the mask is static or animated. In an animated mask, like that of the previous example, the conversion issue arose from the **MorphShape**. A static mask may also produce unexpected results. Rather than producing a mask such as that shown in the left of Figure 9-22, importing into SWiSHmax produces layers like that shown in the right image of the figure.

Figure 9-22: An oval mask to display portions of a layer is translated into separate layers after importing.

The same error message regarding mask/object/script import problems appears when the animation is imported into the SWiSHmax project file. In the Report dialog box, one error is reported, which is the mask used in the animation. One object is added for the text; one frame of the background appears as a named image, and an object named **Shape** using the same oval shape of the original movie's mask is also listed.

Note In Figure 9-22, the contents of the sprite in the right image are moved on the Layout panel so you can see the separate elements.

Importing SWiSHmax Project Files

You can integrate one SWiSHmax project file within another project file. Sometimes you have material that you want to reuse in another project, or you may decide to combine the content of several movies into one master file. Follow these steps to combine project files:

On The Web Site

You can experiment with the files used in this discussion. On the book's Web site, the chapter09 folder contains a subfolder named ch09_sample06. In the subfolder, you will find the ch09_sample06a.swi file used as the original project file, the ch09_sample06b.swi file used as the imported file, and the completed file named ch09_sample06.swi.

1. **Open SWiSHmax and open the file to which you want to insert another SWI project file.** The sample file used is ch09_sample06a.swi.

2. **Choose Insert ➪ Content from the Outline panel's menu to display the Open dialog box.** You can choose an optional Insert ➪ Content program command.

3. **Browse to the location of the file you want to insert into the open project file and select it.** The sample file used is ch09_sample06b.swi.

4. **Click Open to close the Open dialog box.** The Import dialog box opens as seen in Figure 9-23.

Tip

Depending on the type of file you are importing, you may or may not see a listing of frames. In the example, the file selected for import contains one sprite; as a result, there is no listing of frames.

Figure 9-23: Choose several options for importing a movie project file into another movie project file.

5. **Choose an import option for the structure of the SWI file.** Choose from One object per scene in a group, Animated sprite, or New scene. The sample file selection is the Animated sprite option.

6. **Choose other elements if desired.** You can choose a background rectangle for any option, and you can include the masked option for an animated sprite import.

7. **Click Show File Information to display the Report dialog box.** The report includes the file name, size, frame rate, and contents. Click OK to close the Report dialog box and return to the Import dialog box.

8. **Click Import to close the Import dialog box.** The selected project file is imported into the open project file and appears as a sprite in the Outline panel, as seen in Figure 9-24.

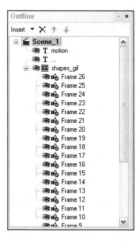

Figure 9-24: The imported project file is added to the open project file according to your chosen options.

Once a project file is imported into another project file you can make any changes to it you require. A frame from the completed sample project file, ch09_sample06.swi, appears in Figure 9-25. The two combined project files produce a movie containing animated shapes as well as text.

Figure 9-25: You can combine two or more movie project files into one project file.

Using Flash Projector (*.exe) files

The final animated file format you can work with in SWiSHmax is the Flash Projector file. A projector file uses the EXE extension, as it is a standalone file that uses a built-in projector. EXE files can be useful for distributing to users who don't have a Flash player available. Follow these steps to use a projector file in your SWiSHmax project:

1. **On the Outline panel, choose Insert ➪ Content to open the Open dialog box.**

Note   There are other program locations for importing content under the File and Insert program menus, as well as by clicking Insert Content on the Insert toolbar.

2. **Browse to the location of the EXE file you want to use and select it.**

3. **Click Open in the Open dialog box.** The Open dialog box closes, and the Import dialog box opens as shown in Figure 9-26.

4. **Click the frames you want to import to select them.** By default all frames are selected.

5. **Choose the features you wish to import.** As with SWF files, you can include mask options, background rectangles, scripts, and importing text as shapes.

6. **Choose a grouping option.** You can select either one object per frame in a group, an animated sprite, or a new scene.

7. **Click Import to close the Import dialog box and import the EXE file's content.**

Figure 9-26: The import dialog box

On The Web Site

If you would like to experiment with importing a projector EXE file, you can use the ch09_sample07.swi file in the ch09_sample07 subfolder located in the chapter09 folder. The folder includes the EXE and source FLA files as well.

Summary

In this chapter, you learned about working with external files. You learned how to use animated GIF and SWF files. You learned about some of the different ways you can import the files into your SWiSHmax project, and also some of the pitfalls and issues to consider along the way. You also learned how to combine SWiSHmax project files. You also learned about:

✦ General ways to insert media files into a SWiSHmax project file

✦ Importing animated GIF files

✦ Importing a SWF animation in different ways

✦ How importing a SWF animation containing scripts can be changed in SWiSHmax

✦ The effects of shape morphing and masking

✦ Importing one SWiSHmax project file into another project file in different ways

✦ Importing EXE files for use in a SWiSHmax project

✦   ✦   ✦

Working with Text

A key component in many movies is text. Building a SWiSHmax movie gives you the freedom to display text on the Web using the fonts of your choice without worrying about the limitations of either HTML or cascading style sheets.

Many SWiSHmax projects contain text; many are text-only. In this chapter, you learn about the different types of text used in a SWiSHmax movie project. You learn how and why to choose font settings and how to control your movie's text. You learn how to configure not only individual letters and words, but blocks of text as well.

SWiSHmax treats text in different ways depending on how it is defined. For example, text that is broken into shapes is handled differently and allows you to apply different commands to it than text that is broken into letters. You learn about the different ways to define text objects, and how they can be transformed.

Adding Text

You work with three kinds of text objects in SWiSHmax. All three types of text share some characteristics; the three types of text have different options as well. These types are:

+ **Static text.** This is the basic text used for displaying your movie's message. Static text is controlled by the design of the movie.

+ **Input text.** This is a text object that can be altered by your viewers. Input text is commonly used for forms where text fields are provided for the viewer to type information.

+ **Dynamic text.** This is a text object that can be altered by a script while the movie is running. A dynamic text object displays data stored in other locations such as other fields or on a Web server.

Regardless of the type of text you use in a movie you start with the same process. Follow these steps to add text to your movie:

1. **Click the Text tool on the Layout panel's Toolbox to make it active.** The cursor changes to crosshairs and the letter T.

2. **Move the cursor to the location on the stage where you want to add the text.**

A Little about Typography

The art and technique of using text is called *typography*. While a full discussion of the subject is far beyond the limits of this book, there are many things to consider when choosing text for a movie.

Some basic considerations include matching the font's characteristics to that of the content and message of the movie, using appropriate font sizes and layouts, and using animation carefully.

3. **Click the stage in the Layout panel to place a text box.** The default text *Text* appears in the text box. The Text panel appears at the front of the panel group.

Note   If you've added text previously, the new text uses the same set of options and characteristics you applied to the previous text.

4. **Click the default text in the Text panel to activate it.** You see a vertical cursor blinking in the text area on the Text panel.

5. **Click and drag to select the existing text and replace it with your text.**

Figure 10-1 shows some text added to a movie project. You see the text box on the stage, as well as the text in the Text tab of the Text panel. In the Text panel, the piece of text has been named **sample_1**. If you name a piece of text, the name appears in the Outline panel. If you don't name the text, the actual text you type is used as the text object's name.

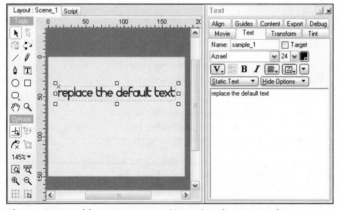

Figure 10-1: Add text to your project using the Text tool.

If you plan to use a large amount of text in your movie, you don't have to retype it. Instead, you can import a text file that is automatically added to the stage as a text object. This feature is especially useful if you are creating a Web interface using SWiSHmax and you have several screens of text you want to add to the movie's scenes.

Tip   You don't have to select the Text tool before importing text files. SWiSHmax recognizes the file format and defines the object automatically. To import a text file into your movie, choose File ➪ Import and browse to the location of the text file you want to use. Select the file and click open.

Caution   You can only import text in a .txt file format.

The text is automatically imported into your movie project and placed on the stage. As you can see in Figure 10-2, the text is on the stage on the Layout panel and the Text panel is active. The text is added to **Scene_1**.

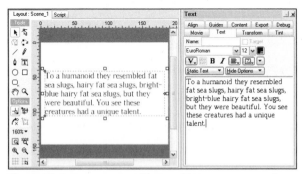

Figure 10-2: Import a text file to add text to your movie automatically.

On The Web Site   If you want to experiment with the text file, story.txt shown in Figure 10-2, it is available on the book's Web site in the chapter10 folder. There is no accompanying SWI file. Feel free to write the rest of the story.

Choosing Basic Text Settings

When you add text to a movie, the Text panel displays a group of default settings you can use to configure the text, as shown in Figure 10-3.

✦ **Name.** The name of the text object can be entered in this field. By default, a new text object is unnamed. When you specify a name for the text object the name appears in the Outline panel and allows the text to be used in scripting.

✦ **Target.** If the text object is going to be used with scripting in your movie it must be identified as a target. Click the target option to make it active. The target option isn't active unless the text object is named.

✦ **Font name.** The currently used font is listed in the font name field. Click the down arrow to open a list of the fonts installed on your computer. Scroll down the list to find the font you want to use. As you move your cursor over a font's name, a sample appears next to the list.

✦ **Font size.** The current size of the font is shown in the field. Click the down arrow to choose from a list of standard sizes, or select the text in the field and type a custom font size. The font sizes are defined in points.

✦ **Font color.** The current text color is shown in the swatch. Click the down arrow to open the Color Chooser and select an alternate font color.

You can choose different types of fonts and define their characteristics as shown in Figure 10-3.

✦ **Font type.** The default font type in SWiSHmax is a vector font. Click the down arrow and choose from different font types, including device and pixel font types.

Caution   You can only specify a single font style and color for a single text object.

✦ **Character options.** This button is active only for dynamic or input text and displays options for embedding font characters in a movie.

✦ **Bold face.** Click to toggle the Bold font face on and off. The default is to use nonbold text.

✦ **Italic face.** Click to toggle the Italic font face on and off. The default is to use non-italicized text.

✦ **Text justification.** Click the dropdown arrow to display a list of options for justifying a block of text. The default setting is left justified.

✦ **Text flow.** Click the dropdown arrow to display a list of options for flowing a block of text. The default setting flows text from left to right, top to bottom.

✦ **Insert character.** Click the arrow button to display a window showing the special characters you can use in a text block. The options vary depending on the font selected.

✦ **Hide Options.** This default setting for text objects hides text configuration options. Click the button to open a list of options.

Figure 10-3: Choose from a number of default text settings in the Text panel.

Selecting a font type

Because your exported SWF movies are vector-based, the default font type in SWiSHmax is a vector font. You can choose from a number of optional font types. Click the Font Type button on the Text panel to display the list of options shown in Figure 10-4, and then click a button to choose a font type. The options include:

Tip
You can also choose any of the font types from the main program menu. Choose Modify ⇨ Font Type ⇨ and choose an option.

✦ **Vector font.** This is the default font used in your SWiSHmax movie. It is good for most purposes; it scales well, but can be blurry if the font is a very small size.

✦ **Device font.** This option tells the Flash Player to use fonts from your viewer's computer rather than using embedded fonts. If the font you choose isn't available on the viewer's computer, the closest match is used. Using Device fonts decreases the size of your exported movie. It is also good for displaying text under 10 points clearly and legibly.

✦ **Pixel-aligned vector.** This vector font type option forces text to be top-left aligned to exact pixels. Use this option when working with a pixel font to make sure the text is aligned automatically.

✦ **Pixel font (sharp).** This is the font type to use if you want your text to appear very crisp even when using small font sizes. Each character of the font is aligned to exact pixels.

✦ **Pixel font (smooth).** Use the smooth pixel font type when you want crisp text characters at small sizes, but with smoothed edges. The Pixel font (smooth) option anti-aliases the corners and diagonal strokes of letters to smooth them.

Note
Choosing either of the Pixel font options converts any font into a pixel font.

Tips for Using Pixel Fonts

Pixel fonts are available from many locations on the Internet. Designed for on-screen use, the fonts maintain a 1:1 ratio between the font characters and your monitor that results in a sharp font, particularly at a small size. Pixel fonts usually include a font size, which is the optimal size at which you should use the font. Here are some tips for working with pixel fonts:

✦ Left justify the text object.

✦ To change the size, use multiples of the original font size. For example, a 9-point pixel font can be resized to 18 or 27 points.

✦ Don't use bold, italics, or other font decorations

✦ Use X- and Y-coordinates that are set at integers when defining a text box's coordinates.

✦ Don't rescale or resize the text.

Alternatively, you can use the Pixel font (smooth) settings in SWiSHmax to convert any font into a Pixel font. Your text will be clear regardless of the font size.

Figure 10-4: Choose from several different font types for your movie.

Using system fonts

Your movie's text can appear slightly different depending on the fonts you choose for your project and whether or not you specify Device font types. There are three fonts, called *system fonts*, which can be used predictably regardless of the viewer's computer. The three system fonts and their common Windows-based counterparts are sans (Arial), serif (Times), and typewriter (Courier).

 Caution   When you choose a system font, you are unable to select any of the vector or pixel font types.

The three system fonts are shown at the top of the Text panel's Fonts drop-down menu as shown in Figure 10-5; samples of each of the system fonts are also shown in the figure on the movie's stage. When you are working in SWiSHmax, the fonts chosen are listed above a horizontal bar at the top of the fonts menu. When you close and reopen the program, the font list is cleared.

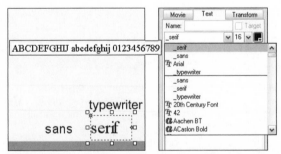

Figure 10-5: The system fonts are shown at the top of the fonts menu along with any fonts selected during the current working session.

Using special characters

In addition to typing text into your text object you can also insert special characters. The characters available depend on the font you are using. For example, a font such as Arial displays a set of special characters very different from the characters available when using a symbol font such as Wingdings.

Follow these steps to insert special characters into your movie's text:

1. **Click the location in the text where you want to insert the character.** The vertical cursor appears in the text.

2. **Click the Insert Character button to display the available characters for the currently active font.**

3. **Move the cursor over the characters to view an enlarged image of the characters.**

4. **Click a character to select it and place it in your text object.**

Viewing text formatting in SWiSHmax

If you have a project that contains several pieces of text, such as animations or information, it can be confusing to keep track of the text as you are working. You can set a preference that shows the formatted text in the Outline and Text panels.

Follow these steps to display text formatting:

1. **Choose Edit ⇨ Preferences or Tools ⇨ Preferences.** The Preferences dialog box opens.

2. **Click the Appearance tab.**

3. **Click the Show Formatting option.**

4. **Click OK to close the Preferences dialog box.**

Thumbnails and text fonts and colors are shown on the Outline, Text, and Timeline panels. As you can see in Figure 10-6, the text used for the title shows the font in the Outline and the Timeline panels in the program.

Figure 10-6: You can display the appearance of text in your project.

Modifying a Text Object's Dimensions

When you add a text object to your project, you can define how the content appears within a *text box,* which is the bounding box surrounding the text on the stage. Using the settings in the Text panel or those available from the main program menu you can define margins for a text box as well as indenting and text justification.

Configuring a text box is done through the Dimensions options. You can also configure the text box's margins and indent directly on the stage in the Layout panel. Margins and indent changes apply to all types of text; justification options vary according to the type of text you are using; text flow options are available only for static text.

Add paragraphs to a text block by pressing Enter on the keyboard as you type in the text area of the Text panel. In the Layout panel, the text is shown on the stage as you type, and lines aren't wrapped by default. Figure 10-7 shows three paragraphs of text in a text object.

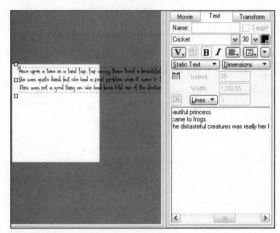

Figure 10-7: Default text is added in a continuous string in a text object.

Once you have added text to your project, follow these steps to modify the dimensions of the object:

1. **Click the Hide Options button to open a list of optional groups of settings that can be applied to text.**

2. **Click Dimensions to select it.** The menu closes and the Dimensions options appear in the Text panel.

3. **Click the Enable Margins and Indent button.** The Indent and Width fields are activated; the Indent field displays the last setting you entered in the field (or 0), and the Margin field displays the width of the text object in pixels. The text you typed in the text area on the Text panel wraps so you can read the lines without scrolling horizontally.

Tip   If you have typed enough text, you have to scroll vertically to read the content in the text area.

4. **Type a value in the Indent field.** The value determines how far the first line of a paragraph is indented in pixels.

5. **Type a value in the Width field.** The text on the stage wraps according to the width of the margin.

Figure 10-18 shows the same text as that shown in Figure 10-7 after indent and width are set.

Note   The Auto-size height and Height/Line button and field are available only for input and dynamic text.

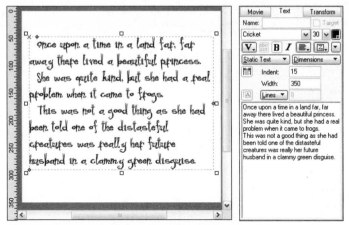

Figure 10-8: Set margins to determine the width of the text object and use an indent for paragraphs if desired.

If you prefer, you can modify the margins of an object visually on the stage in the Layout panel. Follow these steps:

1. **Type a text object.**

2. **On the Text panel, click Hide Options to open the drop-down list and choose Dimensions.** The Dimensions options appear on the Text panel.

3. **Click the Enable Margins and Indent button on the Text panel.** The button is located to the left of the Indent field's label. The Indent and Margin fields in the Text panel become active. On the Layout panel, a set of green diamond anchors appears on the bounding box surrounding the text, as seen in Figure 10-9.

4. **Drag the anchors to change the dimensions of the text box and its contents:**

   • Click and drag the upper-left anchor to the right to increase the indent of the first line of the paragraph.

   • Click and drag the lower-left anchor to the left or right to increase or decrease the indent of the lines in the paragraph other than the first line.

   • Click and drag the handle on the right margin of the text box to the left or right to decrease or increase the width of the text box.

Note

If you click and drag the lower-left anchor farther to the right than the upper-left anchor, you create a hanging indent, which means the body of the paragraph is indented more than the first line of the paragraph. In the Text panel, a hanging indent is shown as a negative value in the Indent field.

The values shown in the Indent and Margin fields in the Text panel change as you move the anchors.

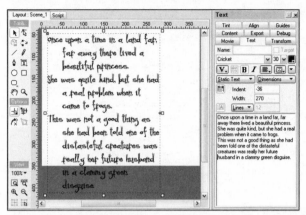

Figure 10-9: Set a text object's dimensions visually on the Layout panel.

Justifying text

Text can be justified in a number of ways. *Justification* refers to the arrangement of the text in relation to the margins of the text box. Click the Text Justification button on the Text panel to display the options, and click a button to apply the option. You can also choose Modify ⇨ Justification ⇨ and choose an option from the main program menu. SWiSHmax has six justification options:

 Left Justify. This is the default option. Text starts at the left margin and has a ragged-right margin. That is, the text appears as it does on this page with some lines narrower than others. All types of text can use the left justification option.

 Center Justify. Text extends to the left and right of the center point of the text box. All types of text can use this option.

 Right Justify. Text is even with the right margin, and has a ragged-left margin. All types of text can use this option.

Left, right, and center justification is available for all types of fonts. The following three justifications are not available for Device fonts:

 Full Justify. This option is available for static text only. The text is stretched or condensed so the left and right margins of all lines except the last line are even. If an indent is used, the first line of the paragraph maintains the indent, and the right margin is justified.

 Full Justify all lines. This option is available for static text only. The text is stretched or condensed so the left and right margins are even for the body of paragraphs. The first line is not justified at the left margin if it is indented; the last line is not affected.

 Full Justify all but the last line. This method of justification is available only for static text. All lines of text are aligned except the last line of the text block. The first line isn't justified at the left margin if an indent is used.

Choosing a text direction

You can change the direction text flows in a text object if you are creating static text. Click the Text Flow button to display the list of options, and click a button to change the direction of the text. You can also choose the options from the main program menu. Select the text, and then choose Modify ➪ Appearance ➪ and choose one of four options.

LR-TB. Choose this option to flow the text from left to right and top to bottom in the text box. This is the default setting.

TB-RL. Choose this option to flow text from top to bottom and right to left in the text box.

RL-TB. Choose this option to flow text from right to left and top to bottom in the text box.

TB-RL. Choose this option to flow text from top to bottom and left to right in the text box.

When you choose an alternate text flow, you can also apply justifications to it. The text is justified according to the text flow direction, not how the text appears in relation to the text box. Changing the text flow doesn't change the justification of the text.

Formatting Text

You can apply formatting to static, dynamic, or input text, but the options vary according to the type of text. Click the Hide Options button on the Text panel to display the drop-down list, and click Formatting to display the formatting options in the Text panel.

Formatting options include kerning and leading, as well as word wrapping and rendering (for dynamic and input text only). *Kerning* refers to the horizontal distance between characters on a line, and *leading* is the vertical distance between lines of text. Static text uses kerning and leading; input and dynamic text types use leading only.

Caution   When you apply kerning and leading to a line of text, it can be applied only once and affects an entire block of text. That is, you can't kern text on one line using one percentage and text on another line using another percentage.

Adjusting kerning

You can adjust kerning in three different ways. Click Auto Kerning to use the font's kerning settings; click the Kerning field on the Text panel and type a value as a percentage; or click the up or down arrows to the right of the Kerning field to increase or decrease the kerning value as a percentage.

You can use both negative and positive numbers — a negative value moves the characters closer together, and a positive value moves the characters farther apart. The default is 0. Figure 10-10 shows three lines of text using the same font and font size. As identified in the figure, the text shows different kerning values.

This is JasmineUPC font

JasmineUPC font kerning at −5

JasmineUPC font kerning at +5

Figure 10-10: You can change the distance between letters using kerning.

Note   If you choose a system font — _sans, _serif, or _typewriter — you can't use the Auto Kern command.

Adjusting leading

Leading can be used by any of the types of text you work with in SWiSHmax. Changing the leading value changes the width of the spacing between lines of text in a text object; obviously, the feature is useful only if your text object contains more than one line.

There are two ways to modify the leading of a text object. You can either click in the Leading field on the Text panel and type a value as a percentage or click the up or down arrows to the right of the Leading field to increase or decrease the leading value as a percentage.

Enter a negative number to move the lines of text closer together; enter a positive number to move the lines of text farther apart. The default setting is 0. Figure 10-11 shows three blocks of text using the same font and font size. As identified in the figure, the text shows the leading values named in the text.

**If the Enterprise was on a five year
mission, why did we see the first 3
years only? (No leading)**

**If the Enterprise was on a five year
mission, why did we see the first 3
years only ? (Leading=-30%)**

**If the Enterprise was on a five year
mission, why did we see the first 3
years only ? (Leading=30%)**

Figure 10-11: You can change the distance between rows of text by adjusting the leading.

Getting the Lead In

By the way, leading is a term that originated in the early days of typesetting where the text for a printed page was laid out using actual letter slugs. If lines were to be moved farther apart, the typesetter added strips of lead between the rows of letters — in other words, leading.

Choosing Advanced Options

The three types of text you create in SWiSHmax—static, dynamic, and input—use many of the same options, but there are also options specific to the text type.

Click the Hide Options button (or the option button that is displayed) on the Text panel to open the list of options, and click Advanced to display the Advanced settings on the Text panel. The Text panel contains several optional groups of configuration settings.

Use parent name as text. This option is specific to static text. Click this option to create a text object from the parent object's name. In Figure 10-12, the command has been selected and uses the parent object's name, in this case, the name of the scene, **Scene_2**. You can see that several things happen in the program window:

✦ The text entry area on the Text panel is disabled.

✦ The text can be configured as desired; in the figure, the text uses a different font and size from the other text boxes.

✦ The text can be named; in the figure the text is named **parent name demo**.

> **Tip**
>
> This naming feature could be very useful in a complex movie. For example, if you have a number of animated scenes, each having an introductory text animation, and have named the scenes, selecting the Use parent name as text option can quickly create your text objects.
>
> The same convenience applies to creating buttons. If you are building a number of buttons using text names, choosing this option quickly adds the text to your buttons' states.

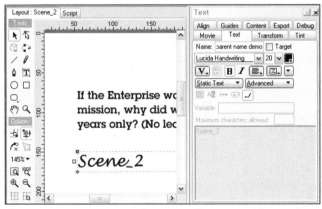

Figure 10-12: You can use the name of a parent object as the text for a text object.

Setting Button Options

Click Hide Options (or the option button that is displayed) to open a list and choose Button to activate options you can use to apply to a text object when creating a button. The two options available for static text are shown in Figure 10-13.

Cross-Reference These items are mentioned briefly here to complete the discussion of the Text panel; for in-depth information about creating buttons, see Chapter 16.

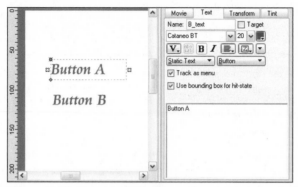

Figure 10-13: You can add button options to static text in the Text panel.

✦ **Track as menu.** Button tracking refers to the behavior of a button in relation to mouse movements. When you create a button object, it tracks the mouse as either a push-button or as a menu. As a pushbutton, the object *captures* the mouse, meaning that all activity is focused on the button until you release the mouse outside the button object's area even if you drag the mouse off the button's defined area. When Track as menu is active the object is responsive to mouse clicks, but if you click outside the object's area the cursor reverts to the default cursor.

Tip You can apply the Track as menu option to dynamic and input text as well as static text.

✦ **Use bounding box for hit-state.** One of the requirements of building a button is defin-ing the space on the movie that can be clicked to activate the button. The bounding box, shown surrounding the text, can be defined as the area used for the button hit-state. If this option is unchecked, the text's letters define the active area.

Additional Options for Dynamic or Input Text

The Text panel contains several optional sets of configuration settings. The three types of text you create in SWiSHmax use many of the same options, but there are also options spe-cific to dynamic and/or input text.

Input and dynamic text are somewhat different than static text. To make it easier to under-stand, a project has been created that shows one block of each type of text and how they work. As the project is described, Text panel options specific to dynamic and input text are also described.

Cross-Reference The scripting necessary to make the text blocks function is mentioned briefly in this chapter; see Chapters 17, 18, and 19 for an in-depth discussion of scripting.

On The Web Site
The project ch10_sample01.swi containing the text objects used in this discussion is available from the book's Web site. The file is in the chapter10 folder in the ch10_sample01 subfolder.

Follow these steps to create an input text object:

1. **Click the Text tool on the Toolbox in the Layout panel to make it active.**

2. **Click and drag on an area on the stage to create a text area.** The Text panel appears at the front of the panel group.

3. **On the Text panel, type a name for the text.**

4. **Click the Static text button to open the list of options, and click Input text.** The list closes, and the button displays the Input text label.

You can now configure the text using the text options described in earlier sections of this chapter.

Embedding text characters

One alternative that becomes active when you choose Input or Dynamic text is the Character Options button. Click the Character Options button to open the Character Options dialog box, as seen in Figure 10-14. The default setting is to embed all font characters. That means the Century Gothic font, which was chosen for the sample project, will have its information embedded in the exported SWF movie. By embedding the characters, you know your viewers will see the text as you intended.

Figure 10-14: You can choose a specific set of characters to embed in dynamic or input text objects.

Caution
Embedding a font in an exported movie is not the same as using a font in a SWiSHmax movie project file. If you use the sample project file and don't have Century Gothic font on your computer, a font will be substituted when you open the file.

You can choose to embed only a specific set of characters. Click Character Options to activate the choices, and then click Only These Characters to activate the options to embed character subsets. You can choose from these options:

✦ **Upper case letters (A..Z).** All capital letters are embedded.

✦ **Lower case letters (a..z).** Only lowercase letters are embedded.

✦ **Digits (0..9).** Numbers are embedded.

✦ **Punctuation.** Punctuation marks are embedded.

✦ **These characters.** You can choose a custom set of characters for embedding. Type the characters you wish to embed in the These Characters field; you don't need spaces or commas between the characters.

Setting height and lines

You can apply some Dimensions options specific to input (and dynamic) text as follows:

✦ Click the Auto-size height button to toggle it on and adjust the text box to a size that fits the font style and size chosen for the text.

✦ Click the Height/Line button and choose Height. Type a value for the height of the text box in the field.

✦ Click the Height/Line button and choose Line. Type a number of lines in the field.

Caution If the Auto-size height option is active you can't adjust the Height or Line values. If the fields are grayed out, click the Auto-size height button to toggle it off.

Tip When you choose either Height or Line values, the other value changes to match according to the characteristics of the font you selected. For example, when using the font in the sample project, changing the Line value to 3 changes the Height to 44; the sample project uses a Line value of 4, which is equivalent to a Height of 57.

In the sample project, the number of lines allowed is set at 4 as shown in Figure 10-15.

Auto-size height button

Figure 10-15: You can set the height of the text box using settings in the Dimensions options.

Formatting dynamic and input text

You can choose two settings in the Formatting options specific to input and dynamic text.

Wrap text at word breaks. This option lets the user enter text that automatically wraps. If this option isn't selected, text only wraps to another line when you press Enter. The sample project's input text field uses text wrapping.

Render text as HTML. This setting preserves HTML 4.01 text formatting for both input and dynamic text fields. You can only see the effects of formatting in a Flash Player or Web browser. Text that is rendered as HTML is automatically set to Device font; normal fonts can't use the Render text as HTML option.

The HTML tags supported are: `<a>` anchor; `<b>` bold; `<font color>`; `<font face>`; `<font size>`; `<i>` italics; `<p>` paragraph; and `<u>` underline. Supported attributes include `align`, `indent`, `leading`, `leftmargin`, and `rightmargin`.

Advanced dynamic and input text options

There are several options specific to dynamic and input text available from the Advanced options. Click the Hide Options button (or whichever button is displayed) to open the list and click Advanced. The Advanced settings appear on the Text panel. All options except the password text option and the maximum character restriction are used in the sample project.

Black Border with White Background. The text field is surrounded by a black border, and the field's background is white. You can use this option for both dynamic and input text.

Text is Selectable. You can click and drag to select the text in the text field when this option is active. The option applies to dynamic text only.

Password Text. The asterisk (*) appears for each text character you type. You often see this option when typing passwords. Use Password text for input text only.

Multiline Text. The user can type several lines of text and press Enter to add new lines. The option is available for input text.

Maximum characters allowed. Type a number in the field to restrict the entry of text to a specified number of characters. This type of restriction is good for fields such as telephone numbers, where you have a definite number of characters required. The option is available only for input text.

Variable. A variable is a named "container" for a quantity that can change within a script in response to user input or executing the script. Variables can hold a variety of objects having many values.

In the sample project, the input text box contains the typed text that creates the content for the variable in the dynamic text box. Executing the script (clicking the button) sends the text to the targeted object; in the sample project, the dynamic text box is the target of the script's action. The sample doesn't use a separate name for the variable — it uses the text box name. Figure 10-16 shows the finished sample project in action.

On The Web Site

For the files used in the sample projects in this chapter, look in the chapter10 folder on the book's Web site.

Figure 10-16: You can send the text from an input text box to a dynamic text box using SWiSHscript.

Transforming Text

Once you have created the text and configured the font and the layout of the text block, you can use the Toolbox tools or the Transform panel to adjust the text block. The options available are:

✦ **Scale.** Click the Scale tool and drag one of the side or corner handles to rescale the text. As you move the anchor points, the text increases or decreases in size.

✦ **Resize.** Click the Resize tool and drag one of the side handles to resize the text box. Resizing has no effect on the sizes of the letters in the text box.

✦ **Rotate/Skew.** Click the Rotate/Skew tool and drag one of the corner handles to rotate the text and the text box; drag one of the handles on the sides of the text box to skew the text and the text box.

Note   See the section "Modifying a Text Object's Dimensions" earlier in the chapter for information on how to adjust margins and indents using the Toolbox tools.

Figure 10-17 shows several copies of the same piece of text. The text farthest to the left on the stage is adjusted using the Scale tool. The upper-center copy is the text before any changes are made; the text at the right shows the effect of using the Resize tool. The lower text block shows several changes made to the same text using the Transform panel settings. As you can see, the text is skewed on both axes, and its scale is also changed.

Figure 10-17: You can modify a text box and its contents using the Toolbox tools or Transform panel settings.

Cross-Reference   See Chapter 6 for discussions on using Transform settings and tools.

Modifying a Text Object

A text object, whether it is static text, dynamic text, or input text, is a complex object. That means the object is a collection of shapes. However, you can only apply one color or font or other type of configuration option to the contents of one text block. If you want to do more exciting things with a block of text than use one color or size or fill, you can break it into shapes or letters, or group it in different ways, which is discussed later in the chapter.

Caution The exception to the "text is a complex object rule" is text that has been defined as a target. In that case, the text is defined as a scripting object, which is a simple object. The sample project's dynamic text block is an example of a scripted object.

There are a number of ways you can modify a block of text. You can group text as a group, break it into letters, and convert it into shapes. When you convert text into shapes, you can group them as a shape or break them into shapes.

Cross-Reference Text can also be grouped as a sprite or converted to a sprite, which is discussed in Chapter 15; or it can be grouped as a button or converted to a button, which is discussed in Chapter 16.

Grouping text

A string of text is a complex object. For some effects and animations you need the text to be grouped. Follow these steps to convert text into a single group:

1. **Select the text on the Layout panel's stage.**

2. **Right-click the text on the Layout panel and choose Grouping ⇨ Group as Group.** You can also choose Modify ⇨ Grouping ⇨ Group as Group from the main program menu, press the Ctrl+G keyboard accelerator keys, or click the Group as Group button on the Grouping toolbar.

When text is grouped as a group, you can no longer modify any of the characteristics of the letters.

Breaking text into letters

You can't combine different fonts, colors, sizes, and other characteristics in the same block of text. However, you can break the text into individual letters and change the characteristics of individual letters if you want. Breaking text applies to static, dynamic, and input text.

Follow these steps to break text into letters:

1. **Select the text on the Layout panel's stage.**

2. **Right-click the text on the Layout panel and choose Break ⇨ Break into Letters.** You can also choose Modify ⇨ Break ⇨ Break into Letters from the main program menu, or click the Break into Letters button on the Grouping toolbar.

When a text block is broken into letters, a single group is listed in the Outline panel as shown in Figure 10-18. The group contains one text object for each letter. You can modify each letter using the Transform tools in the Toolbox or by changing settings in the Transform panel. You can also continue to change the letters in the Text panel because each letter is recognized by SWiSHmax as a text object.

Once the text is broken apart, you can configure each letter using settings in the Text panel as you desire. You can't make adjustments to indenting, margins, or justification for the text block because the text no longer functions as a single text block, but you can adjust margins for the individual letter objects. You can modify the entire block of text using the Scale or Rotate/Skew tools or by changing settings in the Transform panel.

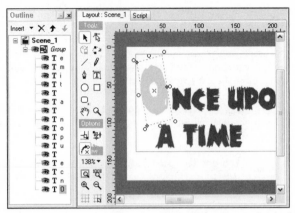

Figure 10-18: You can break a block of text into individual letters.

Changing text into a shape

There are two ways you can change text into a shape — by grouping it as a single shape or by breaking the text into individual shapes. In either case, once you change the text into shapes, it can no longer be edited as text. If you convert the text to a single shape it becomes one simple object.

Follow these steps to change text into a single shape:

1. **Select the text on the Layout panel.**

2. **Right-click the text on the Layout panel and choose Grouping ⇨ Group as Shape.** The dialog box shown in Figure 10-19 appears. You can also choose Modify ⇨ Grouping ⇨ Group as Shape from the main program menu, or click the Group as Shape button on the Grouping toolbar.

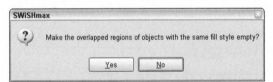

Figure 10-19: When converting text to a shape, you must specify how the shape should handle overlapping areas.

3. **Click Yes or No to dismiss the dialog box.** The text is converted to a single shape. Since letters don't overlap, whether you choose Yes or No won't change the appearance of the group.

The shape is listed in the Outline panel as one object. You can modify the object just as with other drawn shapes. You can apply various fills and strokes and use the Transform tools to alter the shape's appearance, including the Distort tool, as shown in Figure 10-20.

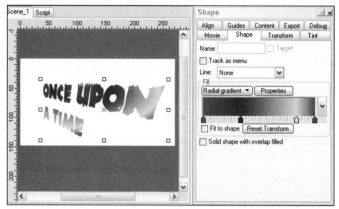

Figure 10-20: You can apply most Transform and Shape settings to a shape converted from a block of text.

See Chapter 7 for information on using color and Chapter 8 for information on using image fills.

Breaking text into multiple shapes

If you break a block of text into shapes it becomes one shape for each letter in the selected text. As with the text converted to a single shape, once you convert each letter into a shape, SWiSHmax no longer recognizes it as a letter. However, you can modify all of its shape properties as you would with any drawn shape.

Follow these steps to change text into separate shapes for each letter:

1. **Select the text on the Layout panel.**

2. **Right-click the text on the Layout panel and choose Break ⇨ Break into Shapes.** You can also choose Modify ⇨ Break ⇨ Break into Shapes from the main program menu, or click the Break into Shapes button on the Grouping toolbar. The text is converted to one shape for each letter. Each letter shape can be modified, filled, and transformed.

The shapes are listed in the Outline panel as a group. If you open the group listing (see Figure 10-21), you see a shape object for each letter; the shapes' names include both the font name and the letter. For example, in the figure the letter O is converted to a shape named **Zombie_O**.

Text may be converted to a group of shapes when importing a Flash file into SWiSHmax. See Chapter 9 for information on importing Flash files. Text and other objects can also be broken into pieces used for animating. See Chapter 14 for information on working with complex effects.

Using Characters as Drawings

Here's a handy trick. If you look through the fonts on your computer you will likely find a number of fonts that are already images instead of letters, such as Wingdings or Dingbats. If you need a drawing of an object look through your fonts. Create a text object using the characters from the font, and then convert the text object into a shape object — instant drawings.

Figure 10-21: A text block broken into individual shapes lists each letter as part of a group.

Summary

In this chapter, you learned how to work with the three types of text you can create in SWiSHmax — static, dynamic, and input text. You learned how to create text and how to configure its appearance. You learned about settings particular to the different types of text. You also saw how blocks of text can be configured and how they can be modified and transformed. In this chapter, you learned:

✦ How to create or import text for your movie

✦ How to modify the characteristics of text such as font, size, and color, kerning, and leading

✦ How to modify the characteristics of a text block including dimensions, justification, and text flow

✦ How to work with dynamic and input text

✦ How text can be used as a scripting object

✦ How to transform text using Transform tools or settings in the Transform panel

✦ About text as an object and how to convert it to different types of objects

✦ That text can be converted to a shape or to multiple shapes

✦   ✦   ✦

Adding Sound

If you are sitting in a theater watching a movie and you hear the sound of an old door slowly creaking open, you expect something negative to happen. While it isn't often that you might need the sound of a creaky old door in a SWiSHmax movie file, there are many times when you can use music or some other sound effect to enhance your projects.

When you move your mouse over an object on a Web page interface and its appearance changes, you know that something will happen if you click that object. As humans, we also respond to auditory cues, and sometimes accompanying a mouse action with a sound such as a click is a finishing touch. When the Internet was new and sound first became available, it seemed every choice was accompanied by clicks and gongs, and many minutes were wasted downloading pieces of (often) horrible music that served as a background score for your site visit.

Fortunately, as both technology and experience advanced, the sound used on Web page interfaces and in SWF movies in general has become much more sophisticated—and generally more appropriate. SWF and scripting allow for much more advanced application of sound, both in how it is served to the user and how it is used on a page.

In this chapter, you learn about sound and the formats you can use in SWiSHmax. You see how to work with sound files and how to manage them. You also learn how sound is used in SWiSHmax and different ways it is controlled.

Understanding Audio Characteristics

There are several pieces of information stored in audio files. Each characteristic contributes to the quality of the sound, as well as the size of the file. Choosing sound for a project is often a balancing act, just as it is with using images in a project. Your goal is to achieve the best compromise between quality and file size.

+ **Sample rate.** *Sample rate*, or *rate*, is expressed in *hertz* (Hz). Each hertz is a unit of frequency in a sound wave of one cycle per second. Our ears generally hear a frequency of up to 20 kHz (20000 Hz or 20,000 cycles per second). WAV files use a rate range of 5000-48000 Hz. Better sound quality comes from higher rates; higher rates also require more processing time and produce larger files.

Note Audio can be resampled to higher or lower rates; that is, a different rate can be defined. Audio can also be upsampled (the rate is increased) or downsampled (the rate is decreased).

Caution MP3 sounds in exported movies must use sample rates of 11025Hz, 22050Hz, or 44100Hz because of a Flash Player limitation.

✦ **Format.** Audio file formats include *mono* and *stereo*. Music sounds best in stereo, while voice and sound effects work well in mono sound. Sound is recorded in two channels — left and right. Monaural (mono) sound processes each of the left and right channels separately. Stereo sound processes both left and right channels at the same time.

Note Sound can also be formatted in Surround or 5.1 sound; SWiSHmax doesn't support Surround Sound.

✦ **Bit depth.** Audio files are generally 8-bit or 16-bit. *Bit depth* describes the number of bits used to represent a single audio sample. Voices have good quality with 8-bit sound; music usually sounds better at 16-bit depth.

Sound Formats

You can use two different sound formats in SWiSHmax — WAV files and MP3 files.

Using WAV audio files

The WAV (waveform) file format stores digital audio data. A WAV file is an audio file format created by Microsoft. Support for WAV files was included with Windows 95 and in all subsequent versions of Windows. The WAV format is used for everything from system and game sounds to music.

The WAV format stores digital audio (waveform) data. It supports a variety of bit resolutions, sample rates, and channels of audio. In addition to the uncompressed raw audio data, the WAV file format stores information about the file's format (mono or stereo), sample rate, and bit depth.

About MP3 encoding

MP3 refers to the MPEG (Motion Picture Experts Group) audio layer 3. An MPEG file can use one of three coding schemes — layer 1, layer 2, or layer 3 — for compressing audio signals. Compressing the sound shrinks the size of the sound file, which is very important for using sound on the Web. You can both import MP3 sounds into a movie and export a movie using MP3 sound. SWiSHmax doesn't process the sound as it is imported. This means if you modify the sound in an external audio editing program and then import it into SWiSHmax, no changes are made to the sound file.

Note You can read more about the MP3 format and how it works at www.mp3-tech.org/.

Using Compressed versus Uncompressed Sound

The impact of compressing sound files can be dramatic. Here's an example: A simple movie is created in SWiSHmax that uses the file called jungle_hi.wav as a soundtrack. The movie also uses another sound file, drum.wav, that plays when the user clicks a red shape. The SWI file is 890KB in size, and the exported SWF movie is 81KB.

When the compressed file, called jungle_low.wav, is used instead of jungle_high.wav, the finished movie file size changes significantly. The SWI movie file size drops to a 214KB, and the exported SWF movie becomes 23KB.

Using the LAME encoder

SWiSHmax uses the LAME encoder for producing MP3 music and sound output. The recursive acronym means "LAME Ain't an Mp3 Encoder." The LAME technology was originally developed as an open source project designed to learn about MP3 encoding, how to make it faster, and produce better sound. In 2000, LAME officially became an encoder.

Note
You can read more about LAME, its history, and how it works at `http://lame. sourceforge.net/`.

On The Web Site
If you want to experiment with some audio files using different sound quality, use the files from the ch11_sample01 folder in the chapter11 folder on the book's Web site. The file named ch11_sample01a uses high-quality sound, and ch11_sample01b, uses lower-quality compressed sound. The folder contains a second sound and SWF movies.

Importing Sound into SWiSHmax

You can import sound files into SWiSHmax for two purposes — as a soundtrack for the movie or scene or as a sound attached to an action. When you import a WAV or MP3 file, as a sound action, it is added automatically to the first frame of the active scene; when you import the file as a soundtrack, it is added automatically to the active scene.

Importing a sound file as an action

One of the default import processes attaches a `playSound()` action to the first frame of the selected scene when you import the file. Once the file is in the program you can change its action.

Follow these steps to import sound into a SWiSHmax movie project as an action:

1. **Choose Insert ⇨ Content from the main program menu.** You can also use one of these methods:

   • Click Insert on the Outline panel to open the list, and click Content

   • Choose File ⇨ Import to open the Open dialog box

   • Click the Insert Content button on the Insert toolbar

2. **Browse to the location on your hard drive where the file is located.** Click the file's name to select it

3. **Click Open to close the Open dialog box.** The dialog box shown in Figure 11-1 appears.

4. **Click No to close the dialog box and import the sound file into your project.** The sound is added to the project, and a `playSound()` action is added to Frame 1 of your movie.

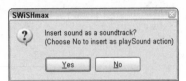

Figure 11-1: You can define a sound as a soundtrack when importing it into your movie project.

 Note   You can remove a sound attached as a `playSound()` action to your movie. Click the Script tab to display the Script panel. Click the first line of the script, for example, `onFrame(1){`, and click the Delete Script button at the top of the Script panel or press Delete on the keyboard. The audio file remains as part of the movie and you can use it elsewhere.

Importing a soundtrack file

You can also import a file directly into SWiSHmax to use as a soundtrack file. The file is placed in its entirety on the selected Scene's Timeline.

Follow these steps to import a soundtrack into your project:

1. **Choose Insert ➪ Soundtrack from the main program menu to display the Open dialog box.** You can also click Insert on the Outline panel and click Soundtrack.

 Tip   If you attempt to choose either menu location again when your movie already contains a soundtrack the option is grayed out.

2. **Browse to the location on your hard drive where the file is located.** Click the file's name to select it.

3. **Click Open to close the Open dialog box.** The sound file is added to the scene automatically. It is listed in the Scene's hierarchy in the Outline panel as well as on the scene's Timeline, as seen in Figure 11-2.

Pausing Music using a Sprite

Stephan Lyon suggests that to pause music, instead of just stopping and restarting it, insert your mp3/wav file as a soundtrack in a sprite by choosing Insert ➪ Soundtrack and place a `music-sprite.gotoAndPlay(1)` action at the end of the soundtrack. You can then pause and resume the music with simple `musicsprite.play()` and `musicsprite.stop()` actions assigned to a couple of buttons. Note however that the sound file may not loop as seamlessly as when you're using the common `playSound()` action.

Note   If you import a sound as a soundtrack, and then change your mind, click the file's name in the Outline panel, and then click Delete to remove it from the scene. The audio file still remains as part of the movie file, and you can use it elsewhere if you want.

Figure 11-2: A soundtrack can be added to your movie automatically.

Importing a sound file for later use

The only program location that allows you to import sound directly into the program without any interaction with the movie's structure is through the Content panel. Follow these steps to add a sound file to the movie's contents:

1. **Click Import on the Content panel to open the Open dialog box.**

2. **Browse to the location on your hard drive where the file is located.** Click the file's name to select it.

3. **Click Open.** The Open dialog box closes and the file is added to your movie. Regardless of the method you use to import sound, it is listed in the Content panel, as seen in Figure 11-3.

Figure 11-3: Add sound to your movie project through the Content panel.

Selecting an encoder

You can set a preference for the LAME encoder in SWiSHmax. You may find that some files you import into the program display a warning like that shown in Figure 11-4.

Figure 11-4: The LAME encoder processes specific sound file characteristics.

Your files are processed using the LAME encoder or the Microsoft Windows system encoder. Whether the option to use the LAME encoder for the file's compression is available in the Properties dialog box depends on whether the preference is toggled on or off.

You can change the program preference. Choose Edit ⇨ Preferences or Tools ⇨ Preferences to open the Preferences dialog box. The General Preferences tab appears by default. Deselect the Always use LAME encoder to encode MP3 sounds in the Export options and click OK to close the dialog box.

Listening to Sound Files

You can listen to your sound files after they are imported into your movie project. The command path you choose to access the play controls varies slightly according to how the sound is used in the movie.

Follow these steps to listen to your imported sound files:

1. **Click the sound file's name to select it from one of these locations depending on its form:**

   - On the Outline panel or the Timeline if the sound is a soundtrack

   - On the Script panel if the sound is attached to an action and the name of the file is selected in the Script panel

   - On the Contents panel's Sounds listing regardless of the form the sound file takes in the movie

2. **Click the Properties button on the Sound panel (for a soundtrack) or on the Script panel (for a sound attached to an action) or on the Content panel (for all types of sound use).** The Properties for Sound dialog box opens, as seen in Figure 11-5. The music file's name is shown in the dialog box.

3. **Click Properties on the Sound panel.** The dialog box also includes the name of your sound file in quotations, such as **"Steppenwolf - Foggy Mental Breakdown.MP3"**, as seen in Figure 11-5.

4. **Click Play.** When you are done listening to the music, click **Stop.**

5. **Click OK to close the Properties for Sound dialog box.**

Properties for Sound: "Steppenwolf - Foggy M...

Documents\My Music\Steppenwolf - Foggy Mental Breakdown.MP3

Imported sound properties

44.1kHz 16bit stereo 234.1s 2340.8 frames

Preload sound: Object or scene default ▼   OK

Export settings   Cancel

Compression: MP3

Channels: Stereo   ▶ Play

Sample rate: 44khz   ■ Stop

4665885

Figure 11-5: You can play the sounds you import into your movie project.

Cross-Reference   You manage sound files in your movie just as you do other types of media. See Chapter 4 for a full discussion of the Content panel.

Working with Sound Files

The two default import options for sound either add a sound as a soundtrack or alternatively add a `playSound()` action to the first frame of the movie. In both cases the sound starts when you play the movie. There are differences between the two options.

A soundtrack added to a movie plays automatically when the exported SWF movie is played. The soundtrack is *synchronized* to the Scene's Timeline, which means that it plays along with the scene's action regardless of the computer's speed. On the other hand, a `playSound()` action is not synchronized with the Timeline and playback results may differ among computers.

Here are some features of both soundtracks and the `playSound()` action to consider when planning your movie:

✦ The root Timeline of your movie can have only one soundtrack.

✦ Soundtracks use an MP3 codec for exporting from SWiSHmax.

✦ Soundtracks don't accept sound effects.

✦ If you are planning an AVI movie export you won't hear the soundtrack because the AVI format doesn't support streaming sound.

✦ Soundtracks can synchronize the audio with your movie's animation while the `playSound()` action can't.

✦ Since soundtracks are streaming audio, they can start playing as the movie loads; the `playSound()` action has to load completely and then it starts to play.

✦ A soundtrack can be stopped and started; a `playSound()` action can only be stopped and restarted from the beginning.

Modifying a sound file

You can modify some of the sound file's characteristics in SWiSHmax including the file's settings as well as when it is preloaded for movie playback. From the listing in the Sound panel (shown in Figure 11-6), on the Content panel, or on the Script panel, you can select several options for managing the sound file. They include the following:

Figure 11-6: Modify sound files using several options.

✦ **Import.** Click Import to open the Import Sound dialog box and locate another sound file you want to use in your movie project.

✦ **Reload.** Click a file name to select it and then click Reload to exchange the version of the file in the movie project with the latest version of the file.

Caution   If the original sound file has been moved to another location on your computer the file isn't reloaded.

✦ **Delete.** You can remove sound files directly from the Sound panel. Select the file you want to remove and click Delete.

✦ **Use.** You can swap the file used as a soundtrack in your movie. Click the file you want to substitute in the Imported Sound Content list in the Sound panel and then click Use. The file is exchanged for the original in the scene.

✦ **Properties.** You can view the properties of a selected sound file. Select the file in the panel, and click Properties to open the Properties dialog box.

Choosing sound file properties

The Properties dialog box includes the name of the file at the top of the dialog box. In addition, the attributes of the file as they exist when you import the file into SWiSHmax are listed under the Imported sound properties heading, including sample rate, format, bit depth, length of file in seconds, and length of file in frames.

Also from the Properties dialog box, there are a number of changes you can make to a sound file including choosing a preload setting and several export settings.

Preloading the sound file

The Preload sound option is used to define when the sound object is written to a SWF file. Based on the type of file and the overall content in the movie, changing the preload order can affect the smoothness of the movie's playback.

The Preload options don't apply to soundtracks, as they are streaming media and can't be preloaded. There are a number of Preload sound content options from which you can choose.

✦ **Disabled.** The sound object definitions are written to the SWF file at the frame where the sound first occurs.

✦ **Before Scene.** The sound object definitions are written at the start of the scene. Depending on the size of the sound object and other objects in the scene this choice may produce a short delay before the scene starts playing.

✦ **Before Movie.** The sound object definitions are written before the movie starts, which can result in a delay before the movie starts playing.

✦ **At Preload Action.** When you use a Preload action, you define the sound objects at the location of the action on the Timeline. Sound (and other format) objects that are in the scene before the Preload action occurs play the same as if the Preload content was disabled.

✦ **Scene default.** The Scene default is the preload option used unless you change scene or movie settings and is based on the preload option assigned for the entire scene.

Cross-Reference   Learn more about preload settings in Chapter 20.

Choosing export settings

You can select a number of export options from the Properties dialog box including compression, channels, sample rate, and bit rate; however, bit rate is not available for MP3 compression. The options change based on which compression setting is chosen. The compression options you can use are None, ADPCM, and MP3.

Choosing None means no compression is applied to the sound file resulting in a larger file for export. The ADPCM (Adaptive Delta Pulse Code Modulation) codec provides high-quality 4:1 compression. MP3 compression uses the LAME encoder if selected; otherwise, the file is compressed using the operating system's MP3 encoder.

If you choose None as the codec type, you can select:

✦ Either Mono or Stereo channels

✦ One of four sample rates, including 5.5 kHz, 11 kHz, 22 kHz, or 44 kHz

Importing Formats

Stephen Lyons suggests that if your sound doesn't loop properly and there's a short pause before it restarts, you've most likely imported an mp3 file. Import the same file in *.wav format, and let SWiSHmax do the compression. Provided the loop was edited correctly, it should now loop seamlessly.

✦ Either 8-bit or 16-bit sample bit sizes

Tip

Sample bit options are available only for uncompressed sound. The 16-bit option creates better quality sound but a larger file size.

Note

The file size in bytes is shown at the bottom right of the Properties dialog box as you make your selections.

When you select the ADPCM codec, you can choose:

✦ Either Mono or Stereo channels

✦ One of four sample rates, including 5.5 kHz, 11 kHz, 22 kHz, or 44 kHz

✦ One of four ADPCM bit sizes, including 2-bit, 3-bit, 4-bit, or 5-bit

Note

The lower the ADPCM bit size chosen, the smaller the file size; the higher the ADPCM bit size, the better the sound quality but the larger the file size.

When you select the MP3 codec you can choose from these options:

✦ Either Mono or Stereo channels

✦ One of four sample rates, including 5.5 kHz, 11 kHz, 22 kHz, or 44kHz

Cross-Reference

Learn more about exporting movies in Chapter 21.

Using Sound Effects

SWiSHmax includes a number of sound effects that you can apply to any type of `playSound()` event. The sound effects can't be used with a soundtrack. The sound effects are accessed through the Script panel.

Follow these steps to apply sound effects to a sound file:

1. Click Script on the program window to display the Script panel.

2. Click Guided to display the guided scripting panes.

Tip

The Guided option is the default; you can choose either Guided or Expert modes.

3. Click the `playSound()` action in the script as shown in Figure 11-7. The sound options become active at the bottom of the Script panel, also shown in the figure.

4. Click the Sound Effect button at the lower left of the Script panel. The Sound Effect dialog box opens. The Sound Effect dialog box includes the name of the sound file as well as the action. For example, the dialog box shown in Figure 11-8 is named `Sound Effect for playSound ("drum.wav")`.

5. Change the sound effect settings as desired.

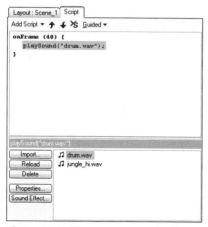

Figure 11-7: You access sound effects through the Script panel.

Figure 11-8: There are a number of effects and settings you can apply to a sound file.

6. Click OK to accept the changes to the sound file and close the Sound Effect dialog box. If you decide not to use sound effects, click Cancel to close the dialog box without making changes to the sound file.

There are a number of settings you can apply to the sound file in the Sound Effects dialog box.

✦ **Don't play sound if it is already playing.** If you have a sound playing in response to an action such as a mouse click, clicking this option prevents the sound from playing again if the user clicks the mouse button again.

✦ **Sound effect.** Click the dropdown arrow and choose a sound effect from the list, as seen in Figure 11-9.

   • **Fade in.** The clip *fades in* or gradually increases in volume as it plays.

   • **Fade out.** As a clip plays and reaches the end it *fades out* or gradually decreases in volume as it plays.

Caution For both the Fade in and Fade out effects, the number of loops you specify determines when the sound reaches 100 percent volume. That is, until the specified number of loops are finished, the sound increases or decreases in volume progressively. If you specify two loops, it takes two loops for the music to increase or decrease; if you specify ten loops, each loop increases or decreases the sound in 10 percent increments or decrements.

- **Pan left to right.** The sound in a mono clip changes from the left channel (which you hear in your left ear) to the right channel (which you hear in your right ear).

- **Pan right to left.** The sound swaps channels in the opposite fashion to the pan left to right effect. That is, the sound gradually moves from playing on the right channel to the left channel.

- **Left channel only.** Stereo sound plays in both right and left channels; this effect confines the sound to the left channel only.

- **Right channel only.** This effect confines the stereo sound to the right channel only.

Note You can't configure each of the sound effects in terms of rate of change, volume settings, and so on. The effects are applied using default settings.

Figure 11-9: You can choose from several sound effects to apply to a sound file.

✦ **Loop sound.** You can specify how many times the sound plays, or *loops*. If you want the sound to loop indefinitely, type a large number in the Loop sound field. The Flash Player doesn't recognize an infinite loop option. The default setting is **1**, which plays the sound once with no looping. If you type **0** in the Loop sound field, it also plays the sound once.

Note Changing the number of times a sound loops has no effect on the size of the exported SWF movie file.

✦ **Volume.** Type a sound volume for playback. The volume is set as a percentage of the original clip's volume.

✦ **Fade in first loop.** Click this option to select it if you are planning to have a sound loop several times during the course of your movie and want the clip to fade in, or gradually increase in volume the first time it is played.

✦ **Fade out last loop.** Click this option to select it if you are planning to have a sound loop several times during the course of your movie and want the clip to fade out, or gradually decrease in volume the last time it is played.

Custom Audio Loops

For your SWiSHmax movie designing pleasure, SWiSHmax expert Peter Thijs has provided two audio loops. The loops are on the book's Web site in the chapter11 folder. Loop1.wav is an easy listening soothing background sound. Loop2.wav is an upbeat loop for the livelier among us.

Summary

Sound effects and music can greatly enhance a movie project. Sound can set the tone for your movie or act as cues for your visitors. In this chapter, you learned about working with sound in SWiSHmax. You learned about the types of files that you can import into the program. You saw the ways sound is attached to a movie and how it can be modified. You also learned:

✦ About the sound formats that can be used in SWiSHmax

✦ What WAV audio files are

✦ About MP3 encoding and the LAME encoder

✦ That sound files have a number of characteristics

✦ Different ways to import sound into SWiSHmax

✦ The impact of using compressed vs. uncompressed audio files

✦ How sound can be an action or a soundtrack

✦ How to listen to and modify sound files

✦ About the different options for preloading a sound file

✦ How to apply sound effects to audio files

✦   ✦   ✦

Animating
Your Movie

Introducing Movie Effects

One of the neatest features of SWF movies is the ability to display animation. If you can think of it and draw it, you can likely animate it. You can create some dazzling effects and animations in SWiSHmax. In addition to the hundreds of pre-configured animations, nearly all of which can be customized, you can create and save your own effects as well. You can also plot the motion of an object on the stage adding another way to create animation.

Using the animation tools and options is relatively straightforward. Perhaps the biggest problem is figuring out which effect to use! To help you, one of the book's appendixes contains tables identifying how the categories of animations work.

As with other aspects of design, you should let the overall message of your movie guide you in choosing the effects for a particular object or scene. For example, a Web site interface for a company selling high-tech surveillance equipment would likely have a much different tone than one selling baby monitors. You might want to use angular, fast animations for the high-tech company, but you would be more likely to use soft, flowing animations for the baby monitor site. Make sure your choice of animation matches the rest of your movie.

Understanding Effects

An animation causes the appearance of an object to change location, size, and/or shape over a specified number of frames in your movie. When you add objects to your movie, such as images or drawings, they occupy space — you can see them on the stage or wherever you have placed them in the Layout panel's workspace, but they aren't seen over time. Until you specify an effect for an object it has no reference on the movie's Timeline.

SWiSHmax characterizes an effect based on several criteria, including:

✦ The complexity of the object to which it is applied

✦ The characteristics of the effects file

✦ Configuration options

Simple effects animate an entire object, while complex effects animate components of an object independently. Although you can apply an effect designed for a complex object to a simple object, you don't see the impact of the effect's action.

Only objects either grouped or broken into pieces can use complex effects as they are intended. The complex objects you can use with complex effects are:

✦ Any group object with one exception: If a group is defined as a Target in the Group panel it becomes a scripting object, which is a simple object.

Note   If you try to group objects where one or more objects contain effects, you can't create a group—instead you create a sprite to incorporate the object's Timeline into the object.

✦ Any text object that is broken into letters.

✦ Any text or graphic object that is broken into pieces.

Cross-Reference   See Chapter 10 for information on grouping and breaking apart text objects. The following discussion describes ways to create complex objects.

Figure 12-1 shows a frame from a sample movie that contains both complex and simple objects. Two copies of the same star are animated using the same effect; one is broken up and produces a much different appearance than the single object. The text title is broken into individual letters and uses a different explosion effect to animate the letters.

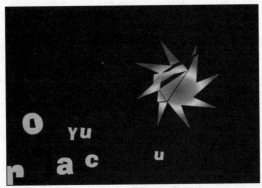

Figure 12-1: You can use either complex or simple effects.

On The Web Site   If you want to experiment with the movie shown in Figure 12-1, it is on the book's Web site in the chapter12 folder. The file is ch12_sample01.swi; it is in the ch12_sample01 subfolder.

SWiSHmax's more than 300 effects are organized into groups based on their general function or purpose. The categories of effects are:

✦ **Place.** These effects are used to show an object in the movie, remove an object from the movie, or move an object over time. The three effects are named Place, Remove, and Move.

✦ **Basic.** These effects are commonly used. They are listed on the main Effects menu and include such effects as fading, blurring, and sliding.

✦ **Core.** These effects include primary types that you can use to create new effects that you can save and reuse. Although you can reuse and save existing effects, there are fewer settings to modify if you start from a Core effect.

✦ **Authored.** Customized effects, or those you create from scratch, are called *Authored* effects. The many special types of Authored effects are listed in five categories, which include the Appear into position, Disappear from position, Loop continuously, One off, and Return to start effects.

Cross-Reference In this chapter you work with the Place effects. For an in depth look at Basic and Authored effects, see Chapter 13. For details on Core effects, see Chapter 14.

All effects can be configured to some degree regardless of how they are applied to an object with the exception of the Remove effect. Some effects have very few configuration options while others are quite complex. The configuration options are listed on tabs in the Effects Settings dialog box.

Cross-Reference Learn how to work with the various configuration tabs in Chapters 13 and 14.

Creating Complex Objects

As you learn throughout this chapter, combining a collection of objects into one group to create a complex object allows you to apply cascading, or sequential, effects to the elements in the group.

Other chapters have described working with groups of shapes, as well as creating a group of letters from a piece of text. Another way to create a complex object is to group a collection of different objects. You can also create a complex object from any type of drawing or image by breaking it into segments. Many of the SWiSHmax effects can be applied to both simple and complex objects with different outcomes.

Grouping as a group

One of the simplest ways to create a complex object is to combine several simple objects. The sample projects used throughout most of this chapter use simple objects grouped together as the content that is animated. To combine a collection of objects as a single group, select the objects and then choose one of these options:

✦ Right-click the selected objects on the Layout panel or the Outline panel to display the shortcut menu. Choose Grouping ➪ Group as Group

✦ Use the Ctrl+G Accelerator keys to create the group.

✦ Choose Modify ➪ Grouping ➪ Group as Group from the main program menu.

Cross-Reference See Chapter 10 for information on how to work with text as objects and groups of objects. See Chapter 6 for information on creating a single object from a number of shapes.

Breaking into pieces

SWiSHmax contains a neat feature that allows you to convert any type of image or drawing from a simple shape to a complex shape. Using a complex shape can create some very interesting effect animations. To break an object into pieces, follow these steps:

1. **Select the object on the Outline panel or the Layout panel.**

2. **Right-click the object and choose Break ➪ Break into Pieces.** You can also choose Modify ➪ Break ➪ Break into Pieces. The Break into Pieces dialog box, shown in Figure 12-2, appears.

Figure 12-2: Break an object into pieces for animation using the Break into Pieces feature.

3. **Click the Break with down arrow to open a drop-down list and choose one of the four types of break:**

   • **Regular Grid.** Breaks the object into pieces according to a grid pattern.

   • **Triangular Mesh.** Breaks the object into pieces according to a triangular-shape pattern.

   • **Random Triangles.** The object is broken into a sequence of randomly sized and oriented triangle shapes.

   • **Random Polygons.** The object is broken into a sequence of randomly sized, and oriented shapes.

4. **Select specific configuration options depending on your choice of break in Step 3.**

   • If you choose either the Regular Grid or Triangular Mesh options, two fields appear for the Column and Row options. Click in the Column field and type the number of columns you want the object broken into; click in the Row field and type the number of rows you want the object broken into.

   • If you choose either the Random Triangles or Random Polygons, you can choose from three options. Click the Ensure all pieces are triangular option to make sure that each broken segment has a triangular shape. Click in the Number field and type how many pieces you want the shape broken into. Click in the Random Seed field and type a value to define how the random shapes are arranged.

5. **Set an inflation value.** The inflation setting is checked by default, and the inflation amount is set at 0.5 pixels by default. This setting increases the size of each piece slightly, which prevents the appearance of lines showing where the object is broken.

6. **Click a Cascade Order option to define the pattern the object uses to animate when a cascading effect is applied.**

7. **Click OK to close the dialog box.** The Break into Shapes command is applied, and the simple shape is converted to a group of shapes.

Figure 12-3 shows an example of each of the four break options. Each example starts with the same oval shape, and all have the same Explode effect applied using the same settings.

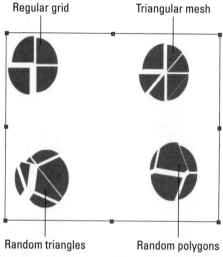

Regular grid   Triangular mesh

Random triangles   Random polygons

Figure 12-3: The Break into Pieces feature produces a range of appearances.

Adding an Effect to Your Movie

Effects can be added to visual objects in your movie including images, text, groups, and sprites. Follow these steps to add an effect to an object in your movie:

1. **Click the object on the Outline panel, on the Timeline, or on the Layout panel to select it.**

2. **Click the frame on the object's row on the Timeline at which you want the effect to start, as seen in Figure 12-4.**

3. **Click Add Effect on the Timeline and select options from the menus.** The effect is displayed over its default frame length on the Timeline as shown in Figure 12-5.

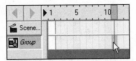

Figure 12-4: Select the frame on the Timeline when the effect is to start.

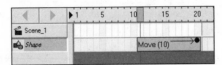

Figure 12-5: The effect is added to the object's row on the Timeline.

4. **Preview the effect.** You can click Play Effect on the Control toolbar or the effect's Settings dialog box as well as from other program locations.

Effects are placed on the Timeline at the frame you selected in Step 2 and are assigned a specified length of time by default. On the Timeline, the effect displays a horizontal bar on the object's row representing the number of frames for which it plays. The bar displays the name of the effect. It also displays the length, or *duration*, of the effect in frames, enclosed in brackets. As you can see in Figure 12-6, if you move the cursor over an effect you see a tooltip that lists the effect's name, its duration, and its start and end frames.

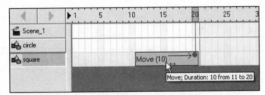

Figure 12-6: The effect's name and duration are shown on the Timeline.

Adjusting Effects

There are a number of functions and adjustments that you routinely use with effects. You might want to change when the object appears in the movie or how long the effect plays. You can copy and paste effects between objects, which is especially handy if you have customized the settings, or you might want to replace or delete an effect. All of these actions can be done from the Timeline.

✦ **Changing an effect's position.** When you are working with effects you often need to change the frame at which the effect starts. Click the effect's rectangle on the Timeline to select it and then click and drag the effect's rectangle left or right on the Timeline to reposition the effect. Dragging the effect rectangle left moves the start frame of the effect earlier in your movie; dragging the effect rectangle right moves the start frame of the effect later in your movie.

✦ **Changing an effect's duration**. Another very common modification made to an effect is changing its duration. Click the effect's rectangle on the Timeline to select it. Move your cursor over either edge of the effect's rectangle. When you see the cursor change to | |, as seen in Figure 12-7, click and drag to shorten or lengthen the effect's duration. When you are working in the effect's Properties dialog box you can also adjust the duration by typing the value in the Duration field.

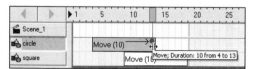

Figure 12-7: Change the duration of the effect by resetting the length of the rectangle on the Timeline.

✦ **Reusing and removing effects.** You can copy and paste effects between objects in SWiSHmax. Click the effect's rectangle that you want to copy on the Timeline to select it. Copy the effect. Click the Timeline at the frame where you want to place the copy of the effect, as well as selecting the object's label to which you want to paste the effect. Paste the effect. If you want to remove an effect from the movie, click its rectangle on the Timeline to select it and then press Delete, or right-click and choose Delete from the shortcut menu, or click Delete on the Standard toolbar.

Note You have to select the object that is to receive the effect, otherwise the effect is pasted to whichever object is the active (selected) object on the Timeline.

✦ **Replacing effects.** You can replace an effect on the Timeline. Click the effect to select it, and then choose the effect you want to use to replace it from the Effects menu. The menu closes and the dialog box shown in Figure 12-8 appears. The dialog box lists the new effect's name as well as the original effect selected on the Timeline and its range of frames. Click Yes to replace the effect and close the dialog box.

Tip If you click No when replacing an effect, the dialog box closes and the effect is pasted to follow the effect you originally selected.

Figure 12-8: You can quickly replace an effect on the Timeline.

Working with the Place Effects

SWiSHmax contains three effects that are referred to as *Place* effects: Place, Remove, and Move. The Place and Remove effects are both one-frame effects. Place defines the frame at which an object first appears in a movie; Remove defines the frame at which an object is removed from a movie. The Move effect is used to plot a motion path for an object over time and can be configured manually on the Layout panel.

On The Web Site

The movie ch12_sample01.swi uses a Remove effect to define the length of time one of the star objects is visible before the movie loops. The project file is in the ch12_sample01 sub-folder in the chapter12 folder.

Cross-Reference

Chapter 4 describes the use of the Place and Remove effects for showing and removing objects in a movie over time.

In addition to using the Place effects for defining the frame at which an object appears, you can also use it to define aspects of the object's appearance. The characteristics you can control include position, scale, rotation, alpha, and color.

In Figure 12-9, one frame from an example movie is selected. The movie consists of two objects. One is a polygon broken into several pieces named **pieces** and the other is a single shape named **weird shape**.

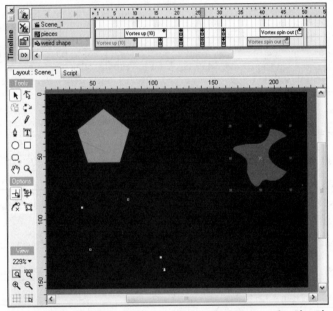

Figure 12-9: You can modify an object's appearance using the Place effect.

Tip   Using descriptive names helps you keep track of the objects in your movie.

On The Web Site

The movie described in this discussion is available from the book's Web site. It is named ch12_sample02 and is in the ch12_sample02 subfolder inside the chapter12 folder.

You can see on the Timeline that each object uses the same effects. However, if you play the movie, you see quite a difference in effects between the two objects. Active effects are used to bring the object on to the stage at the start of the movie and remove it at the end of the movie, and the rest of the animation is done using the Place effect.

The object at the upper part of the stage remains stationary over time and changes color with each new copy of the Place effect. In the object named **weird shape**, several changes occur at each Place effect. In addition to changing color the object also changes location, scale, rotation, and alpha value.

If you look carefully at the Layout panel in Figure 12-9 you see several hollow square dots. These dots represent the location of the **weird shape** object at each occurrence of the Place effect. Also on the Timeline panel, you can see that the Place effect on Frame 26 is selected. On the Layout panel, the selection is represented by the handles surrounding the shape on the stage.

You configure the Place effect in the Place Settings dialog box. Once you apply the effect to an object, double-click it on the Timeline to open its dialog box, as seen in Figure 12-10. Modify the characteristics as desired, and click Close to close the Place Settings dialog box and apply the changes.

Caution   Don't right-click the object on the Layout panel and select Properties because that option displays the object's panel in the panels group and not the effect's properties.

Note   All effects have a Settings dialog box with the exception of the Remove effect.

Using keyframes

A *keyframe* is a frame of an effect that allows you to modify the characteristics of the object. However, each effect you add defines its final frame as a keyframe.

In Figure 12-10, the Transform panel is the active panel and is shown next to the Place Settings dialog box. The settings in both locations are the same. For example, the Scale factor on both the dialog box and the panel are set at 60%.

At the upper-right corner of the Transform panel shown in Figure 12-10 is the notation **keyframe**. When you select an object that contains an effect the only frame you can modify is a keyframe; when you see the values in the fields on the Transform panel in red, you are modifying settings for a keyframe.

Caution   If you modify the characteristics of an object at a keyframe they are changed for the duration of the entire effect.

You can also add a keyframe to an effect already on the Timeline, which effectively breaks the Move effect into segments. To add a keyframe, click the Move effect's frame at which you want to add another keyframe, and then choose Insert ➪ Keyframe. You can also right-click the frame on the object's row of the Timeline to display the shortcut menu and then choose Insert Keyframe.

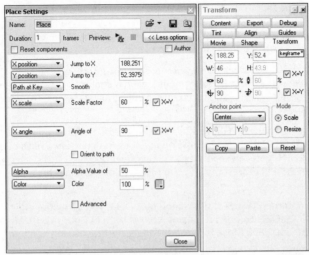

Figure 12-10: You can modify effects in the effect's Properties dialog box; for some effect properties, you can modify them in the panel group.

Using the Move effect

The Move effect can be used to manually position your object over time. Using the Move effect, keyframes, and the Preview Frame mode allow you to control an animation.

On The Web Site

> If you want to experiment with the Move effect you can use the sample described in this discussion. The file is named ch12_sample03a, and is in the ch12_sample03 folder in the chapter12 folder on the book's Web site. The folder includes the project files, SWF movie, other sample files, and the SWF image of the foot used in the animation.

To activate the Preview Frame mode, choose Control ➪ Preview Frame or click the icon on the Control toolbar. The Preview Frame mode shows the content of the Layout panel at a specified frame. The sample movie at Frame 1 is shown in the upper example in Figure 12-11.

The butterfly image is the active object, indicated by the white selection handles surrounding the shape. You can also see another object to the upper left of the Layout panel outside the stage area. In the lower example, also showing Frame 1, the Preview Frame mode has been activated. You see the butterfly's bounding box is now grayed and the object can't be selected. If you look to the left of the butterfly you see a dotted line. This is the motion path.

There are several ways to activate the Preview Frame mode; click again to toggle the mode off:

✦ Click the Preview Frame mode button on the Control toolbar, as seen in Figure 12-11

✦ Click the time ruler on the Timeline

✦ Click the Motion Path tool in the Layout panel's toolbox

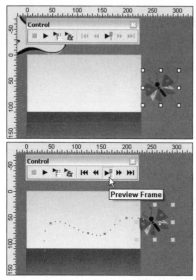

Figure 12-11: Activate the Preview Frame mode to work with the Move effect and keyframes.

Caution If you are working with a Move effect and can't reposition the starting point of an object, check to see the Preview Mode is disabled. When it is enabled, you can't reposition an object on the stage; you can reposition only the end point of the effect.

Using a motion path

Building an animation requires coordinating changes in several locations at the same time including the position of the object on the stage, the transform characteristics of the object on the stage, the placing of the Move effect on the object's row of the Timeline, and the length of the Move effect rectangle (its duration) on the Timeline. There are several ways to add a motion path for an object.

The Motion Path tool is designed to let you add motion path segments to the movie as well as control the speed of the animation.

Follow these steps to add a motion path for an object using the Motion Path tool:

1. **Click the object you want to animate and drag it to the position from which you want to start the animation.** Make other adjustments to the object such as size, scale, rotation, and so on.

2. **Click the Motion Path tool on the Layout panel's Toolbox to select it.** The Speed option appears on the Toolbox. Speed is expressed as pixels per frame.

3. **Click the value shown in the Speed option field to select it and type another speed as required.** The higher the value in pixels typed in the Speed option field, the faster the animation and the fewer frames used for the Move effect, as seen in Figure 12-12.

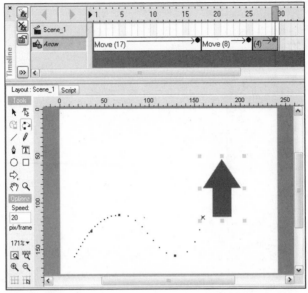

Figure 12-12: The speed of the motion path relates to the length of the effect.

4. **Click the Layout panel's stage with the Motion Path tool.** The object is immediately moved to the tool's location.

5. **Click and drag to add a motion path segment and release the mouse.** The motion path appears as a dotted line with each dot representing one frame of the animation. The final dot of the animation segment is larger and represents a keyframe.

A copy of the Move effect is added to the Timeline representing the amount of space you moved the object in relation to the Speed setting. If you want to change direction for the animation, click and drag to create another segment, which places another Move effect on the object's Timeline. Continue until you have completed the path for the animation.

Correlating speed and space

It can be difficult to imagine how controlling speed affects an animation unless you experiment with it. In Figure 12-12, a motion path is shown for an arrow. You see there are three copies of the Move effect on the Timeline; each is a different length.

If you look at the Layout panel you see three sections to the motion path each containing different numbers of dots that represent the frames used for the animation. The first segment used a speed of 5 pixels/frame, and the Move effect is 17 frames in length. The second segment used a speed of 10 pixels/frame, and the Move effect is 8 frames in length. The third and final segment of the motion path is created at 25 pixels/frame and is a 4-frame Move effect. When played, the speed of the arrow gradually decreases over the course of the animation.

In addition to using the Motion Path tool and drawing on the Layout panel, you can create a motion path in these other ways:

✦ Double-click the stage on the Layout panel with the Motion Path tool in the spot where you want to place a motion path segment and keyframe

✦ Add the Move effect to the Timeline, and then adjust the object at the keyframe

✦ Double-click a frame on the object's row of the Timeline to automatically add a Move effect, and then adjust the keyframe settings on the Layout panel

Adjusting a Move effect's animation

Your project is in Preview Frame mode when you work with animation and the Move effect. While you are in the Preview Frame mode you can make many of the same changes to an object that you would in regular editing mode. However, the changes you make are applied only to the keyframe of a Move effect. There are a number of adjustments you can make to the object during the animation.

✦ **Changing the speed of an animation segment.** On the Timeline, click and drag an end of a Move effect's rectangle to increase its length or decrease its length. The locations you specified for the keyframe of the Move effect preceding the one you are adjusting as well as the one you are adjusting don't change; only the time it takes the object to move from keyframe to keyframe will change.

✦ **Changing an animation segment's length.** Sometimes you have too many short effects or should have added an additional effect segment. Right-click and drag to select the frames you want to change. The shortcut menu appears, as seen in Figure 12-13. Choose one of the options to add or delete frames from the object. Only the selected object's Timeline is affected; objects on other rows are unchanged.

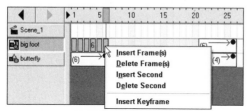

Figure 12-13: Change the length of the effect using the shortcut menu options.

Orienting an animation

If you look at the ch12_sample03a.swf movie you see the butterfly move from right to left across the stage before the big foot appears. Notice how the butterfly is moving in a perpendicular fashion to the motion path. As shown in Figure 12-14, it appears to slide along the motion path.

Figure 12-14: An object maintains the same relationship to a path regardless of the path's direction.

On The Web Site

The two files named ch12_sample03a and ch12_sample03b show the same animation using different orientations; you can see the animations in the SWF movies ch12_sample03a.swf and ch12_sample03b.swf. The files are in the ch12_sample03 folder in the chapter12 folder on the book's Web site.

Orientation may be applied in one of two ways — the object is oriented to a path alone or it is oriented to a path and overrides angle settings.

✦ **Orient to path.** Each keyframe of a Move effect animation has a pair of X- and Y-angle values assigned to the object. The frames of the animation that play in between the keyframes are based on these values. The orientation of the frames between keyframes is a combination of the object's original orientation, X- and Y-angle values, and the direction of the motion path.

✦ **Override angle settings.** If you select to override the angle settings the final frame of an effect shows the object continuing in the direction of the motion path as shown in Figure 12-15, and the precise X- and Y-angle values of the keyframe are ignored. Using this option produces a smooth animation. In the figure, the Transform settings are shown for the keyframe. The Override setting points the butterfly in the direction of the motion path.

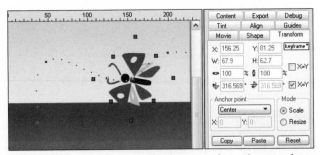

Figure 12-15: Overriding the keyframe angle settings produces a smooth animation.

To apply either setting, double-click the Move effect's rectangle on the Timeline to open the Move Settings dialog box. Click the Orient to path checkbox; click the Override angle settings option if you want the animation to be smoothed. In order to use the Override angle settings, the Orient to path checkbox must be checked first in the dialog box.

Summary

This chapter introduced you to SWiSHmax effects. There are hundreds of effects you can use for your movie projects. Some effects serve specific functions such as defining when an object is seen or removed from the movie, while others are used for animating objects in a variety of ways. In this chapter you learned:

- About the different classifications and categories of effects
- How simple and complex effects work and how to create them
- How effects can be added to an object and then adjusted, replaced, and removed
- How to customize the Place effect
- How to apply the Move effect
- How to work with the Motion Path tool, keyframes, and the Preview Frames mode
- Ways to modify a motion path in your movie
- About orienting an object to a motion path

✦   ✦   ✦

Using Basic and Authored Effects

O ften, you want an object in your movie to appear or disappear in a dramatic way. You can spend a great deal of time working with a sequence of Move and Place effects to achieve your masterpiece, or you can experiment with the hundreds of other animation effects included with SWiSHmax. In this chapter, you learn how to work with two more of the effects categories: Basic and Authored.

Regardless of the type of effect, you can nearly always configure some of the same options such as motion, color, and alpha transformations that are part of so many effects. You can also control how fast the transformations are applied to an effect. As you begin to customize effects you learn there are a collection of other tabs available as well. In this chapter, you look at several tabs used for configuring how the viewer sees an effect.

You often use a number of effects for the same object in the same movie. In this chapter, you also look at coordinating effects.

Common Effect Settings

You can select from a number of common settings regardless of whether you are using Place, Basic, Authored, or Core effects in your movie project. The exception is the Remove effect, which has no configuration options.

To apply any of the Basic effects, right-click the frame on the object's row of the Timeline to which you want to apply the effect to open the shortcut menu. Click Effects and choose the Basic effect from the list.

Once you have added an effect to an object on the Timeline, double-click the effect's rectangle on the Timeline row to open the Settings dialog box. The name of the Settings dialog box also includes the name of the effect. For example, if you have added a Fade In effect to the object, the dialog box is labeled Fade In Settings as shown in Figure 13-1.

Cross-Reference Read Chapter 12 for information on how to add an effect to an object.

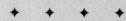

The common settings for SWiSHmax effects include:

✦ **Name.** The name of the selected effect is shown in the Name field. If you want to save the modified effect you can click in the field to activate the text and type a new name.

Load effects settings

Stop | Save settings

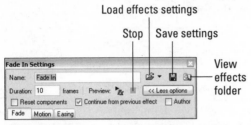

View
effects
folder

Figure 13-1: The Settings dialog box contains common settings.

✦ **Load effect settings.** Click the folder icon to display the Effect menus. You can choose an effect from this menu and substitute its settings for those currently appearing in the Settings dialog box.

✦ **Save settings.** Click the Save icon to open a dialog box to name and save a collection of custom effect settings.

✦ **View effects folder.** Click the folder icon to open the set of folders on your hard drive where the authored effects are stored.

✦ **Duration.** Click in the Duration field and type a number of frames for the effect. When you click out of the Duration field or close the dialog box the effect's duration is changed on the object's Timeline row.

✦ **Preview.** Click the preview icon to play the effect on the Layout panel. When the Preview is running the icon is grayed out.

✦ **Stop.** Click the black square to stop the playback. When the Preview icon is clicked, it is grayed out and the square is active.

✦ **Less options.** Click the Less options button to close some of the tabs in the effect's Settings dialog box. For example, clicking the Less options button for the Fade In Settings closes the Motion and Easing tabs, leaving only the Fade tab. When you click the Less options button, the button displays the More options label.

✦ **More options.** Click the More options button to display some of the effect's settings tabs. For example, clicking the More options button for the Fade In Settings displays the Motion and Easing tabs along with the Fade tab. When you click the More options button, the button displays the Less options label.

Note   Either the Less options or More options button is displayed; the buttons toggle the visibility of the other tabs.

✦ **Reset components.** Use the Reset components option when working with complex effects. If you apply a complex effect such as an explosion, selecting the Reset components option moves the object's elements back to their original positions before the next effect starts.

✦ **Continue from previous effect.** This option is selected by default. When the Continue from previous effect option is active the effect you are configuring starts using the settings with which the previous effect ended. If you deselect this option the StartAt tab appears, and you can configure how the effect should begin on the Timeline.

✦ **Author.** Click the Author option to display the Author and Custom tabs in the effect's dialog box as well as the Reset and Continue options. The Author and Custom tabs are used for configuring new effects. The Author option is available only if the preference for Authoring is selected.

Effects Preferences

SWiSHmax has two preferences related to effects as well as an option to define an effects file storage location. Choose Edit ➪ Preferences or Tools ➪ Preferences to open the Preferences dialog box; click the Effects tab to display the preferences shown in Figure 13-2.

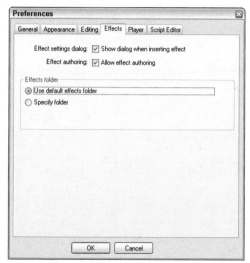

Figure 13-2: Modify effects preferences in the Preferences dialog box.

Change the preferences as desired:

✦ **Click the Show dialog when inserting effect option to automatically display the effect's Settings dialog box when you add the effect to your movie.** This option is very handy if you are working with complicated effects that you plan to modify and is also handy when you are learning to work with effects. Deselect the option if you are working with simple effects such as fades that you merely adjust on the Timeline. The default setting is unselected.

✦ **Click the Allow effect authoring option to display the Author checkbox in the effect's Settings dialog box.** The default choice is selected, allowing you to author any effect.

✦ **Click an option in the Effects folder section to select a location to store effects.** The Use default effects folder option is the default option. You can also click the Specify folder option to choose another location.

Starting with the Basics

SWiSHmax defines several effects and lists them under the main Effects menu. The Basic effects are included with the program, but they don't have a separate effects settings file stored on your hard drive. Basic effects include fades, zooms, slides, and blurs, as well as an effect that repeats previous effects, and another that reverses the previous effect.

To apply any of the Basic effects, right-click the frame on the object's row of the Timeline to which you want to apply the effect to open the shortcut menu. Click Effects and choose the Basic effect from the list.

Cross-Reference   Chapter 12 discusses the basic method for adding effects to the Timeline as well as adjusting the effects' rectangles on the Timeline.

Using Fade effects

The Fade effects gradually change the alpha value of the object to which they are applied. A Fade In effect increases the alpha value of the effect over time; the Fade Out effect decreases the alpha value of the effect over time from 100 percent to 0 percent. The default duration of the Fade effects is 10 frames.

You can change the Fade In effect to the Fade Out effect in the Fade Settings dialog box. For a directional effect like the Fade effects, you can change them in the dialog box rather than reapplying the effect. Double-click the Fade effect on the Timeline to open the Fade In Settings dialog box, as seen in Figure 13-3.

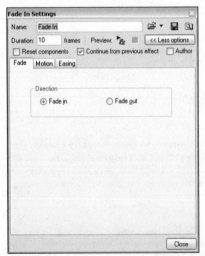

Figure 13-3: Reverse the direction of a directional effect in the Settings dialog box.

To reverse the direction of the Fade In effect, click the Fade Out option on the Fade tab of the Fade In dialog box. You see the name of the dialog box changes. Click Close to close the dialog box. The effect runs in the opposite direction; the Fade Out label appears on the effect's rectangle on the Timeline.

Tip   You can work while the Effects Settings dialog box is open. When you change settings for a selected effect in the dialog box they are shown on the Timeline as soon as you click an alternate tab or field. You can modify, add, and change any effect without having to close and reopen the Settings dialog box.

Using Zoom effects

The Zoom In and Zoom Out effects gradually increase or decrease the size of the object to which they are applied. Their default duration is 10 frames. A Zoom In effect increases the size of the object from 10% at the first frame to 100% at the final frame. To reverse the direction of the Zoom effect, click the Zoom Out option on the Fade tab. You see the name of the dialog box changes. Click Close to close the dialog box. The effect runs in the opposite direction; the Zoom Out label appears on the effect's rectangle on the Timeline.

Using Slide effects

You can place or move an object on the stage to the coordinates where you want it to appear at the end of the effect. This position is called the object's *reference position*. The Slide effects gradually move the selected object from a location offstage to the stage ending at the reference position, or they move the object from the reference position to a location offstage. The default length of the effect is 10 frames.

To select a Slide effect, click the Effects button on the Timeline, and then choose Slide and a direction from the list. The Slide effects are directional effects. As you can see in Figure 13-4, there are eight different Slide In From effects. Click a radio button in the Slide In From section of the dialog box to define the starting location for the effect. Click the Slide out button in the Direction section of the dialog box to change to a selection of options called Slide Out From; choosing one of the sets of eight directions defines the location to which the object moves offstage when the effect is played.

When you apply a Slide effect a motion path is added to the object. As you can see in Figure 13-5, the motion path is a straight path starting from the reference position of the object, and ending offstage in the direction specified by the effect. The figure shows a Slide Out to Right effect.

Cross-Reference   Read about working with motion paths in Chapter 12.

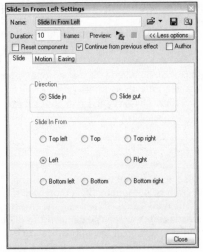

Figure 13-4: You can define a reference position for a Slide effect.

Figure 13-5: The Slide effects automatically add a motion path to the object.

Blurring an object

The Blur effect is a directional effect that occurs over 20 frames by default. You can configure several options to customize the blur used in your movie. Add the effect to the selected object's Timeline and double-click the effect rectangle to display the Blur Settings dialog box, as seen in Figure 13-6.

Click the Blur mode button and choose from three main types of Blur effect:

✦ **Zoom blur.** This is based on the scale of the object. Blurred frames of the object are either stretched outward or squeezed inward depending on the direction of the blur.

✦ **Mirror blur.** This effect displays two sets of duplicate images of the object moving in opposite directions away from the reference position or toward the reference position depending on the blur's direction.

✦ **Slide blur.** The Slide blur displays duplicates of the image moving from the off-screen location you select to the reference position. Although you choose a direction for the blur you don't create a motion path for the object; the direction is confined to the application of the effect only and can't be adjusted.

Figure 13-6: You can choose several options to customize a Blur effect.

Follow these steps to apply a custom Blur effect:

1. **Click the Blur Mode button and select an option.** The available blur mode options include Zoom, Mirror, and Slide.

2. **Click in the Blur amount field and type a value.** The Blur amount is the number of duplicates of the image made to create the effect. At the default value of 5, there are five copies of the object that make up the effect.

3. **Click in the Direction field to select a directions for your effect.** The available options depend on the blur mode you select in Step 1:

   • Zoom blur options include Horizontal, Vertical, and Both directions

   • Mirror blur options include Horizontal, Vertical, FDiagonal, and BDiagonal

   • Slide blur options include eight directions — from each side and from each corner

4. **Click in the Blur scale factor field and type a value.** The percentage value determines how much larger the blurred area is in relation to the actual object's size. At the default 20 percent scale factor, for example, when the effect starts the blurred object is 20 percent larger in size than the actual object. Depending on the direction chosen, the scale factor is applied to the object's X-value, the Y-value, or both.

5. **Choose a fade option.** The default option is Fade when blurred, which fades the object as the blur progresses. Deselecting the option applies the Blur effect without any alpha value change.

6. **Define how the object will initially appear.** In the Begin with components section of the dialog box, click either the Blurred or Clear option. The default is Blurred, which means the object gradually becomes less blurry as the effect is played.

7. **Choose an Acceleration option, if desired, to control the speed of the blur at the start and end of the effect.** Click the At start option to set the blur to gradually increase in speed as the effect plays; click the At end option if you want the effect's speed to gradually decrease as the effect plays. When you click an option, an Amount field appears; click in the field and type a value for the amount of Acceleration. Type **0** for no acceleration; a positive value accelerates at the start or decelerates at the end of the effect while a negative value decelerates the rate of the blur at the start of the effect and accelerates it at the end of the effect.

Tip

For very interesting effects, try using negative numbers for some of the settings, such as the easing options and scale factors.

Figure 13-7 shows three sample Blur effects at the same frame of the animation using default settings. From left to right, the blurs are the Zoom in both directions, Mirror with BDiagonal direction, and Slide from top direction blurs.

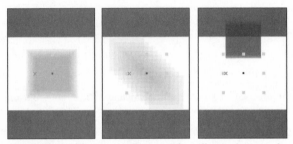

Figure 13-7: You can configure a Blur effect using a variety of options.

Repeating frames

Sometimes you create a fairly complex sequence of effects for a particular object in your movie. If you want to repeat the effects' actions you can either copy and paste each effect or use the Repeat Frames effect. This effect lets you define a portion of the Timeline as a source and then repeats the effects that are on the defining portion of the Timeline. You can also specify the number of repetitions.

Cross-Reference

Another way to work with repeating frames is to construct sprites. Learn how to use sprites in Chapter 15.

Here are some things to keep in mind when using the Repeat Frames effect:

✦ You can't see at a glance what the effects are that make up the Repeat Frames effect's frames on the Timeline.

✦ You can't adjust any of the component effects included in the Repeat Frames effect.

✦ Any changes made to the frames referenced in the effect also appear in the effect. That is, if you include a Fade effect in the sequence you are repeating and change its values, the changes are also applied to the object during the Repeat Frames effect's play on the Timeline.

Caution

Be careful when using the Repeat Frames effect. Looping an entire scene doubles the export size of the file. If you want to create a looping sequence, use a sprite instead.

On The Web Site

If you want to follow along with these steps, the file described is on the book's Web site. It is named ch13_sample01.swi, located in the ch13_sample01 subfolder in the chapter13 folder.

Follow these steps to use the Repeat Frames effect:

1. **Add and configure the initial set of effects on the object's Timeline.**

2. **Click the time ruler to move the play head to the frame at which you want to start the repeating frames.**

3. **Choose Effects ⇨ Repeat Frames.** A single frame effect is added to the Timeline at the play head location.

4. **Double-click the Repeat Frames effect rectangle on the object's row of the Timeline to display the Repeat Frames Settings dialog box.**

5. **Click in the fields and type values for the following settings shown in Figure 13-8:**

   • **Start frame.** Type the frame number at which you want the effect to start repeating; you can also type (-) and a number to count backward.

   • **Number of frames.** This defines how many frames of the Timeline are to be repeated in the effect.

   • **Repeat.** This defines how many times you want the effect to repeat the specified frames.

Tip

In the sample project the Start Frame is entered as 15. Typing **-10** defines the same location, as it is 10 frames prior to the frame at which the Repeat Frames effect is placed.

Caution

You can't specify a number of frames that include only a portion of the current effect on the Timeline. The Repeat Frames effect's settings adjust automatically to either include the full effect or remove the frames of the effect.

6. **Click Close to close the Repeat Frames Settings dialog box.**

Note

Unlike most other effects, you can't resize the length of the Repeat Frames effect on the Timeline; you must open the Repeat Frames Settings dialog box and type a value for the effect's length in frames.

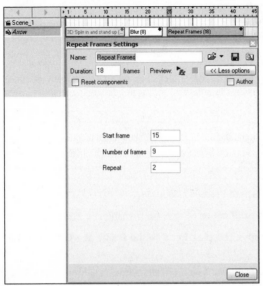

Figure 13-8: Define the portion of the Timeline you want to repeat for the effect.

Reverting the action

You add the Revert effect to an object's Timeline. The effect reverses the position of the effect preceding it on the Timeline, returning the object to its original reference position on the Layout panel's stage. The Revert effect must directly follow the effect you want to revert. Right-click the frame at which you want the effect to start to open the shortcut menu. Choose Effects ➪ Revert. The effect appears on the object's Timeline at its default duration of 20 frames.

On The Web Site

If you want to experiment with this effect, you can use the file from the book's Web site. The file, ch13_sample02.swi, is in the ch13_sample02 subfolder in the chapter13 folder. It contains two examples of the Revert effect — the first one uses the default settings and the second uses a cascade order. The sample ch13_sample04.swi, in the ch13_sample04 subfolder also uses the Revert effect.

How the effect appears in your movie depends on the option you choose in the Cascade tab of the Revert Settings dialog box shown in Figure 13-9. The default option has both the Whole object and Enable cascade options deselected. Click Enable cascade to display a number of options that configure how the effect appears as it runs. The Whole object option applies the Cascade setting to the entire object as opposed to its component elements.

Figure 13-10 shows two frames from the sample movie shown on the Layout panel. The movie, ch13_sample03.swi, includes two copies of the same 25-frame explosion effect in addition to two 20-frame copies of the Revert effect. The upper frame is the 10th frame of the first Revert effect using the default settings. The lower frame is the 10th frame of the second Revert effect with the default Enable cascade option selected. The animation is considerably different in each example.

Figure 13-9: Use the Revert effect to restore positions of objects in your movie.

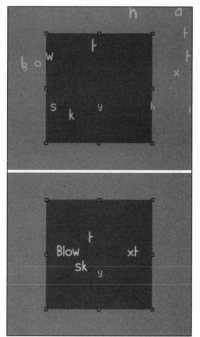

Figure 13-10: The Revert effect works differently depending on whether you enable the cascade function.

Organizing Authored Effects

Most of the effects in SWiSHmax are considered *Authored* effects because they are stored on your hard drive as named effects files using the SFX file extension. The Authored effects are installed with the rest of the SWiSHmax program and stored in a set of folders with the SWiSHmax application files. The program's default installation stores the files at C:\Program Files\SWiSHmax\effects on your hard drive. As shown in Figure 13-11, there are five effects storage folders. These five folders correspond to the five Authored effects menu headings in the Effects menu.

Caution   You must maintain the same path on your hard drive in order for SWiSHmax to locate the effects files; any effects files or folders outside the designated folder aren't available when you are working in the program.

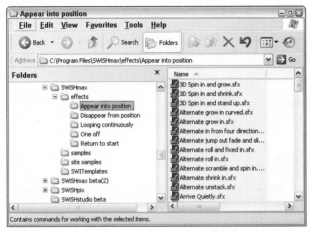

Figure 13-11: Authored effects are stored in five folders on your hard drive.

You can easily save the effects files you modify for use in future projects. You can also store your customized effects in your own effects folder and move existing effects into other folders.

The default effects folders contain dozens of effects. You can use an effect in a project and then save it for reuse at a later time.

Saving an effects file

All of the authored effects can be saved as effects files on your hard drive. Save an existing effect with a new name, or save one you have customized.

To save an effects file, follow these steps:

1. **Double-click the effect's rectangle on the Timeline.** This opens its Settings dialog box.

2. **Click the effect's name field and type the name for your Authored effect.** The Explode effect is used in the example shown in Figure 13-12 and is named Exploding arrows.

3. **Click the Save icon on the Settings dialog box, and browse to the location where you want to store the file.**

4. **Click Save to save the file and close the dialog box.** When you are saving an effect, the only file format option available is the SWiSHmax effects format SFX.

Figure 13-12: Rename an effect that you customize before saving it.

Creating a custom effects folder

You can create a custom effects folder on your hard drive to help organize your work. Use the folder to store effects you save with custom settings as well as original effects and favorite effects. You create a custom folder on your hard drive as you would any other type of folder on your computer. When you create a new folder and store it in the same location as the other effects folders, the next time you open the program your folder is listed under the Effects menu.

Apply an effect to an object on the Timeline and then double-click the effect's rectangle to open the Settings dialog box. If you are working in SWiSHmax and want to create a custom file and folder while you are working with an effect, follow these steps:

1. **Click the Save icon on the Effect Settings dialog box.** This opens the Save dialog box.

2. **Click the New Folder icon at the top of the Save dialog box.** This adds a New Folder within the currently displayed folder.

3. **Type a name for the folder.**

4. **Double-click the folder's name in the dialog box to open the folder.**

5. **Save your effects file in the folder.** When you create a new folder and store it in the same location as the other effects folders, the next time you open the program your folder is listed under the Effects menu. Figure 13-13 shows a new folder named my custom fx, for SWiSHmax effects storage; the folder contains a custom effect named Exploding arrows.sfx.

If you come across an effect you find especially useful or interesting, move the effect into your storage folder. Either open the SWiSHmax effects folders through the effect's Settings dialog box and resave it in your custom folder, or open Windows Explorer and move the SFX file to your custom folder.

On The Web Site You can reuse, export, share, and email SFX files just as you would any other type of file. The custom SFX file created in this discussion is available for you to use from the book's Web site. The file is named Exploding arrows.sfx and is located in the chapter13 folder.

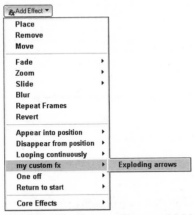

Figure 13-13: Custom effects and folders are included in the program's menu.

Using Authored Effects

SWiSHmax contains five folders of Authored effects that you can apply to your movie's objects. Each menu heading listed in the Effects menu corresponds with a folder of SFX files installed with the SWiSHmax program. The best way to understand how the effects work is to experiment with them.

✦ **Appear into position.** This group of effects animates an object from an offstage location to the reference position at which you placed it on the stage.

✦ **Disappear from position.** This group of effects animates an object away from the reference position at which you placed it on the stage. By the end of the animation the object has disappeared from view.

✦ **Loop continuously.** The looping effects animate an object repeatedly but the animation doesn't necessarily finish at its starting location.

✦ **One off.** The One off effects animate an object in different ways but don't use specific start or end points, nor do they bring an object onstage or move it offstage.

✦ **Return to start.** These effects work much the same way as the Loop effects but function as a real loop. That is, the end of the animation places the object at the same location as the start of the animation.

The folders are named according to the way the effects within each folder behave. For example, the folder (and Effects menu heading) named Appear into position contains an assortment of effects, each of which moves the object in a specified way from offstage or invisible to the object's reference position on the stage.

Setting Authored Effect Options

When you open Settings dialog boxes for most Authored effects you see a number of tabs that contain the settings for the effect. Use the options in the dialog box to customize the effect or for creating your own effects.

Not all tabs are available for all effects; different effects use different combinations of tabs. The tabs available for the Squeeze small jump effect, one of the Disappear from position groups of effects is shown in Figure 13-14. To view the additional tabs in the effect's settings dialog box, click the Author checkbox at the top of the dialog box. For some effects, such as that shown in the figure, there are more tabs available than there is room to display on the dialog box. In that case, click the left and right arrows, also shown in the figure, to display the tabs.

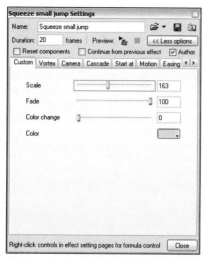

Figure 13-14: Display the authoring tabs to configure the Authored effects.

✦ **Motion.** Set Position, Scale, and Angles for the object you are animating. You can also modify the Alpha and Color of the object on this tab.

✦ **Easing.** Configure the speed at which the characteristics listed in the Motion tab are applied. You can specify how fast the effect's elements accelerate and decelerate.

✦ **Transforms.** Define how characteristics of a complex animation are modified over time, including Position, Spacing, Scale, Angle, Alpha and Color. You can define settings at the start, middle, and end of the animation.

✦ **Cascade.** Cascade options define how the components of a complex object are animated. Depending on the animation, you can modify settings such as the order, overlap, and duration of the components' animation.

✦ **StartAt.** The settings on the StartAt tab are the same as those on the Motion tab. The StartAt options are available only if the effect isn't continuing from a previous effect.

✦ **Camera.** The settings on the Camera tab are used to modify 3D settings. You can modify the camera's position, focus, rotation, and zoom at different times in the animation.

When you choose options to author an effect, SWiSHmax adds two additional tabs in the Effect Settings dialog box:

✦ **Author.** This tab is available only if you select the option in the Effect Settings tab to author the effect. The Author tab includes fields for adding prompts, variables, and other information for designing the effect.

✦ **Custom.** This tab is used with authoring effects and lists default values for custom effect variables.

Modifying an Effect's Motion

Most effects include the Motion tab, which has settings for defining various transform settings that apply to the object's position, color, and alpha value over the course of an effect. The Remove, Place, and Repeat Frames effects don't use the Motion tab.

Modifications are applied to the last frame of the effect, known as its *keyframe*. When you make changes in the Motion tab the settings also display on the program's Transform panel. Changing rotation values on the Motion tab, for example, also changes the values shown in the Rotate fields on the Transform panel.

Cross-Reference   Learn about using the Transform panel in Chapter 6.

The Motion tab for an effect is shown in Figure 13-15, and contains the following options:

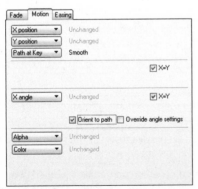

Figure 13-15: Modify an effect's motion in the Motion tab.

✦ **X position.** You can configure the X-axis position for the object over the course of the effect's animation. The default option is Unchanged. Click the X position button to open a list of options. These include:

• **Move to X.** Move the X-axis position for the end of the effect. When you choose this option a field appears. Type a value in pixels in the field.

- **Move Right by** and **Move Left by.** Click one of these options to move the animation right or left over time. When you choose an option a field displays for you to type the value in pixels.

✦ **Y position.** The Y-axis position for the object over the course of the animation can be customized. The default setting is Unchanged. Click the Y position button to open a list of options, which include:

- **Move to Y.** Move the Y-axis position for the end of the effect. When you choose this option a field appears. Type a value in pixels in the field.

- **Move Up by** and **Move Down by.** Click one of these options to move the animation up or down over time. When you click an option a field appears in which you can type the value in pixels.

Note The Slide effects don't include X and Y position settings.

✦ **Path at Key.** Click the Path at Key button and choose either Smooth or Sharp. The Path at Key options affect how the path appears as it enters a keyframe. A Sharp path creates an angle in the motion of the effect at a keyframe; the Smooth path option creates a smooth curve at a keyframe.

✦ **X-axis and Y-axis scale.** The X-axis and Y-axis scales for an object during an effect are equal by default. To configure each axis's scale individually, click the X=Y option to deselect the option and display separate X scale and Y scale buttons. Click either the X scale or Y scale button and choose an option from the list that appears:

- **Resize to 100%.** The object resizes to 100% of its original size as the effect progresses.

- **Resize to scale.** Click the option to display a field. Type a value in the field as a percentage.

- **Increase by.** Click the option to display a field and type a percentage value to increase the scale of the object over time.

- **Decrease by.** Click the option to display a field and type a value in the field as a percentage to decrease the scale of the object over the course of the animation.

Note Zoom effects don't include the X-axis and Y-axis scale option.

✦ **X-axis and Y-axis angle.** Like the scale values, the X-axis and Y-axis angles for an object during an effect are equal by default. To configure each axis's angle individually, click the X=Y option to deselect the option. Separate buttons for X angle and Y angle appear on the tab. Click either the X angle or Y angle button and choose an option from the list that appears:

- **Rotate to zero.** The object rotates to a neutral position through the course of the effect.

- **Rotate to angle.** Click this option to display a field and type a rotation value for the effect to use. The value is expressed in degrees.

- **Rotate CW by.** Click this option to display a field. Type a value in degrees for the object to rotate in a clockwise direction during the course of the effect.

• **Rotate CCW by.** Click this option to display a field and type a value in degrees for the object to rotate during the animation in a counterclockwise direction.

✦ **Orient to path.** Click this option to determine the direction of an object on a path.

✦ **Override angle settings.** Clicking this option forces the object to continue on a smooth path during its animation regardless of keyframe angle values.

 Cross-Reference   The two orientation settings are described in Chapter 12.

Changing Color and Transparency of an Effect

The Motion tab also includes options for transforming the object's color and transparency over time. Both the Alpha and Color changes are applied to the final frame of the effect, which is its keyframe. When you make changes to color or transparency for a keyframe in an effect dialog box, if you click the Tint panel's tab in the program's panel group to display the Tint panel you will see corresponding changes. In addition to modifying the settings on the effect's Motion tab you can also see the values on the program's Tint panel. Figure 13-16 shows Alpha and Color adjustments made to an effect on the Motion tab, as well as on the Tint panel. The Alpha and Color adjustments do the following:

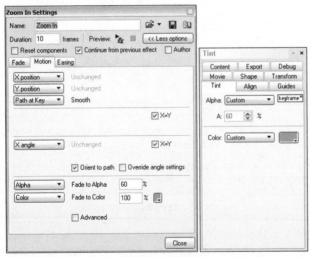

Figure 13-16: Color and Alpha transforms are also shown on the Tint panel.

 Tip   If you don't have the Effects Settings dialog box open and want to adjust the Color or Alpha value, select the effect's keyframe in the Timeline and use the settings in the Tint panel.

✦ **Alpha.** Adjust the Alpha value to modify an object's opacity during the course of the animation. The default Alpha value is Unchanged. Fade effects don't contain an Alpha setting adjustment on the Motion tab. Click the Alpha button to display the list of options shown in Figure 13-17. The Alpha options include:

- **To Transparent.** The object is invisible; its alpha value is 0% by the end of the effect.

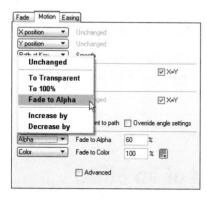

Figure 13-17: You can customize the Alpha value of an object's color during the course of an effect.

- **To 100%.** The object has full color with an alpha value of 100% by the end of the effect.

- **Fade to Alpha.** Click this option to display a field. Type a percentage in the field to specify the final alpha value for the object at the end of the effect.

- **Increase by.** Click this option to display a field and type a percentage value to define how much the alpha value of an object should increase over the course of the effect.

- **Decrease by.** A field also appears when you click this option. Type a percentage in the field to define how much the object's alpha value should decrease over the course of the effect.

✦ **Color.** The final Motion value relates to color. You can choose to animate the color of an effect over time in several ways. The default is Unchanged. Click the Color button and choose an option from the list that appears:

- **Fade to Black.** The object gradually turns black over the course of the animation.

- **Fade to White.** The object gradually turns white during the animation.

- **Fade to Color.** A Color Swatch and a field appear when you click this option. Click the Color Swatch to open the Color Chooser and select a color to use for the effect. Type a percentage in the field to define how much color tint occurs in the effect. Over the course of the effect the object changes from its original colors to the one selected. When you select the Fade to Color option an Advanced setting becomes available. When you click the Advanced option, a set of additional fields appears, as seen in Figure 13-18. In the first column, you can specify a value representing how much each of the red, green, and blue (RGB) color channels' values change during the course of an effect. The second column lists the current RGB color values of the object.

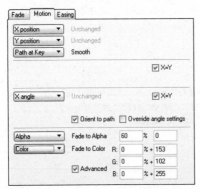

Figure 13-18: You can precisely control color change in each of the RGB channels over the course of an effect.

Using Easing to Modify Speed of an Effect

Most effects include the Easing tab as well as the Motion tab. Double-click the effect's rectangle on an object's row on the Timeline to open the Settings dialog box for the effect. You can specify Easing values for the transform settings modified in the Motion tab. For example, you can specify how fast an effect changes color by using an Easing value.

Note   The Remove, Place, and Repeat Frames effects don't use the Easing tab.

Although you can specify value changes for any of the options, unless you make changes to the transform values or the value is part of the effect's function, easing isn't applied. For example, if you use a Fade effect, you can specify the rate at which the Alpha value changes on the Easing tab even if you don't specify the Alpha value rate in the Motion tab.

To apply Easing, click the check box for the value you want to modify. Click the Start or End check boxes to define whether the change occurs at the start or the end of the effect. When you click a check box, a field appears, as seen in Figure 13-19, and displays the default value of 0.

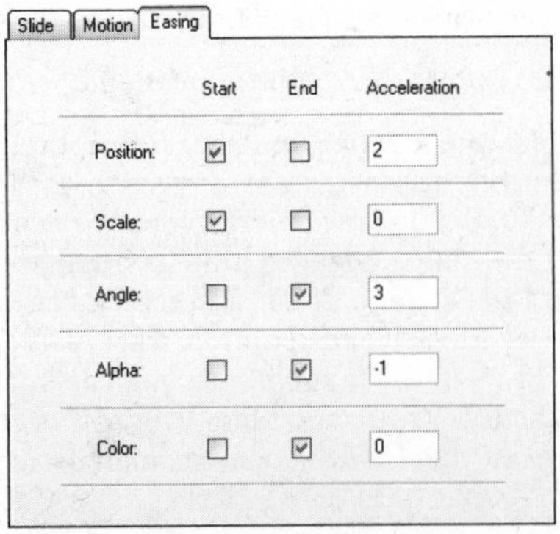

Figure 13-19: Specify the speed of transformations in the Easing tab.

Type a value for the easing in the field. A positive number accelerates the effect at the start or decelerates the effect at the end, depending on which is selected. A negative number decelerates the effect at the start or accelerates it at the end, again depending on which is selected.

Tip

You can choose both the Start and End options for the same transform setting. The value you type in the field applies to both the Start and End equally; you can't apply different amounts of acceleration and deceleration to the same setting.

Transform Parameters used in Effects

The Transforms tab is one of the tabs seen when the Author option is active on the Settings dialog boxes of some effects. Double-click the effect's rectangle on an object's row on the Timeline to open the Settings dialog box for the effect, click the Author checkbox to display the tabs. As you can see in Figure 13-20, the contents of the Transforms tabs are similar to that of the Motion tab used in other effects as well as the Transform panel in the program. To be more precise, the Transforms tab includes three duplicate sets of the options you can set on the Motion tab or the Transform panel.

Cross-Reference

Refer to the earlier section in this chapter for information on using the effects settings' Motion tab; refer to Chapter 6 for information on working with the Transform panel.

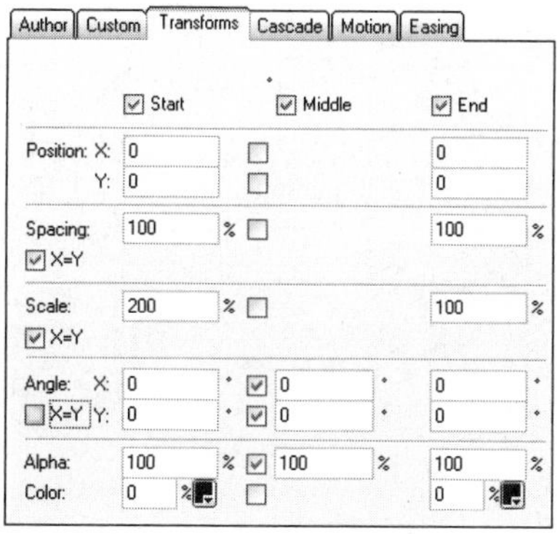

Figure 13-20: The Transforms tab contains basic transformation settings.

Working in the Transforms panel enables you to define parameters for an effect's action at the start and end of the effect. The default selection is the set of parameters for the Start. In the Transforms panel you can set values for Position, Spacing, Scale, Angle, Alpha, and Color.

Here are some tips for working with the Transforms tab:

✦ The Spacing, Scale, and Angle use X=Y values by default. Click the X=Y option to deselect it and specify different values for each axis.

✦ Click the End option to enable a duplicate group of options to control the end of the effect.

✦ You can add a third set of reference values by clicking the Middle option; you can specify any of the settings you want for mid-effect values.

✦ To enable a Middle value, click the check boxes for the individual settings that appear after you click the Middle option.

✦ The End settings use the same values as those used for the Start settings by default.

Controlling How Objects Cascade

You can use the same effect for complex objects as for simple objects by enabling the Cascade options. An effect applied to a single object is predictable; if you have a complex object composed of a number of shapes or letters, cascading defines how the component objects are treated.

Double-click the effect's rectangle on an object's row on the Timeline to open the Settings dialog box for the effect, click the Author checkbox to display the tabs. Not all effects use the Cascade options. The Cascade tab includes a number of options starting with a definition of how the object is treated, as shown in Figure 13-21.

Cross-Reference   Two of the Core effects, Wave and Typewriter, are based on specific motion sequences and don't need any Cascade controls. For more on Core effects, see Chapter 14.

Figure 13-21: The Cascade tab gives you options for defining how an effect is applied to segments of a complex object.

✦ **Whole Object** and **Enable Cascade.** If you click Whole Object, the content of the tab is hidden as you have identified the entire object as a unit. As a result, you don't need to define how the individual elements will appear and animate. When you click Enable Cascade, the remainder of the tab's options are available for configuration.

✦ **Cascade Direction.** Click a button to define the direction of the cascade sequence. From left to right the options are: forward, backward, from two sides to center, from the center to two sides, in both directions interleaving, forward and backward.

✦ **At start.** Specify how the components should appear at the start of the effect. The options are:

  • **Add.** Each component is invisible until it is animated.

  • **Freeze.** The components are visible and are animated according to the cascade direction setting.

  • **Continuous.** The components are visible and animate in sequence from the start of the effect.

  • **Repeating.** The cascade pattern loops.

✦ **At end.** Specify how the components should appear at the end of the effect. Choose from:

  • **Remove.** As each component is animated it is removed from view.

  • **Freeze.** As each component is animated it remains visible.

  • **Continuous.** Each component continues to animate until the end of the effect.

  • **Repeating.** The effect loops.

✦ **Include and order.** The effect is applied to the object following the order you specify. The options available include:

  • **Visible only.** Only visible components are animated. If the animation is a text animation, the spaces and line breaks are not included in the cascade. This is the default setting.

  • **All chars.** All components of the object are animated; for text, this includes space and line breaks.

  • **By X position.** The components are ordered according to their X-axis positions; components having the same X-axis position are animated simultaneously.

  • **By Y position.** The components are ordered according to their Y-axis positions; components having the same Y-axis position are animated simultaneously.

The three values at the bottom of the Cascade tab define when each component is animated. You can activate and define only one of the three values; the other two values are calculated based on the effect's duration and the number of elements in the animation:

✦ **Delay.** The delay is the amount of time between each component's animation expressed as a percentage of the entire effect's duration.

✦ **Overlap.** Type an overlap value to define the amount of overlap between each element in an animation expressed as a percentage of the entire effect's duration.

✦ **Duration.** This is a value that identifies the duration of a component as a percentage of the entire effect's duration. If the Repeating options are selected for either the Start or End option, the Duration setting is unavailable.

Simulating Camera Movement

A number of effects use the Camera tab and its settings rather than the Transforms tab. Double-click the effect's rectangle on an object's row on the Timeline to open the Settings dialog box for the effect; click the Author checkbox to display the additional tabs for the effect.

Any effect that simulates a 3D appearance uses the Camera settings as they provide options for X-, Y-, and Z-axis settings, giving the viewer a sense of perspective as the animation proceeds. Adjusting the camera settings creates a three-dimensional view of the object from different angles or positions. The Camera tab for the 3D Spin Core effect appears in Figure 13-22. The individual settings on the Camera tab are discussed in detail in the following subsections.

Note   The parameters and values used for establishing motion in three dimensions can be difficult to understand. This discussion covers the options in some depth. Apply the descriptions of working in 3D space to any of the 3D Core effects or for modifying existing Authored effects that use 3D space.

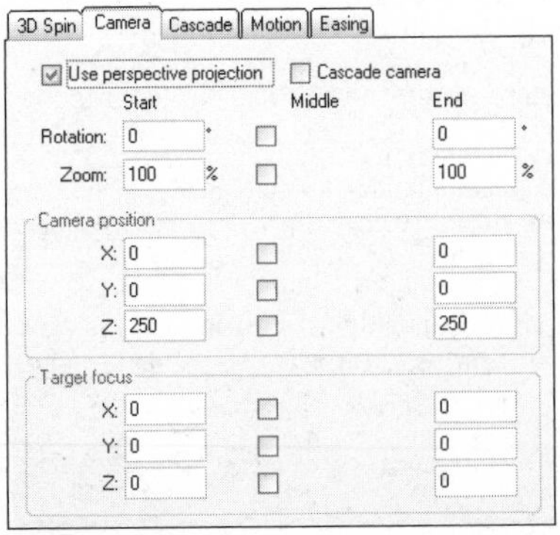

Figure 13-22: You can simulate camera motion in the Camera tab.

Camera type

Perspective is the appearance of objects relative to one another as determined by their distance from the viewer defined along a Z-axis. The X-axis is horizontal and the Y-axis is vertical. You can't go into or come out of your computer's monitor, but using a Z-axis value simulates that movement. Figure 13-23 shows the structure of axes you use to work with perspective values.

The point at which the three axes intersect is called the *Point of Origin*. The values you set for the axes are in relation to the Point of Origin and each unit is equal to one pixel on the animation.

The Camera tab of the effect Settings dialog box provides two basic types of camera. Projection shows the object in relation to the Layout panel; click Use perspective projection to activate the set of default projection options. The cascade view animates each of a complex object's components along the X-, and Y-axes; click Cascade camera to activate the view's options. When you open an effect's settings, the Cascade camera is active by default.

The results of using the two cameras can look similar or appreciably different.

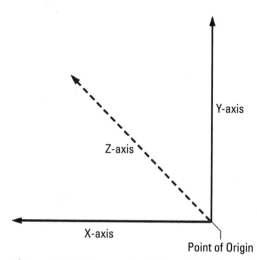

Figure 13-23: You can simulate motion along a Z-axis.

On The Web Site

If you would like to experiment with the movie used in this discussion, you can download it from the book's Web site. It is named ch13_sample03.swi and is in the ch13_sample03 folder within the chapter13 folder.

To illustrate the differences in camera perspective, two sets of grouped objects are used in the ch13_sample03.swi sample project. The top group uses the default Cascade camera setting and is named **default**. The lower group uses the Use perspective projection with default settings and is named **perspective**. Both sets of shapes use the same 3D Spin settings over their default 20 frames. You can see both groups of objects in Figure 13-24 as they appear on the Layout panel's stage at the same frame of the animation. In the figure, the difference between the two camera views is subtle.

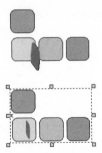

Figure 13-24: You can use one of two camera types for a 3D effect.

Both images show the same group of rectangles during an animation. If you look closely at the top group, you can see that one of the diamond-shaped objects, a rectangle in motion, is wider than that shown in the lower group. The lower group, which uses the perspective camera, displays the object along the Z-axis as well as the X- and Y-axes as shown in the upper group. The diamond-shape looks smaller as the camera is simulating this rectangle as being further away from your view.

Camera rotation and zoom

You can apply camera rotation to the effect regardless of camera type; it will always be an available option from the Camera tab. In Figure 13-25 you can see the outcome of applying a 180-degree camera rotation to the lower group of objects at the end of the animation. The group's original bounding box is shown to the right of the shapes as the objects are rotated 180 degrees away from their point of origin.

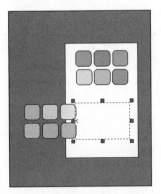

Figure 13-25: Rotate the camera for a different effect.

Note   The rotation shown in Figure 13-25 shows the 3D Spin effect applied to the perspective group in the sample project. The effect runs from Frames 25-44.

You can use a Zoom factor when you choose the Use perspective projection option. Figure 13-26 shows the active Zoom options; the Zoom factor isn't available for the Cascade camera option because you aren't working with perspective in that mode. The Zoom factor can be specified for the start, middle, and end of the effect's animation. The figure also shows a frame from the sample project. A third copy of the 3D Spin effect has been added to the

Timeline and the Zoom factor used. The frame in the figure clearly shows a difference in the size of the object.

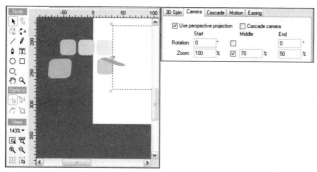

Figure 13-26: Use Zoom settings to simulate the camera moving closer or farther away from an object.

Camera position

The default positions for the camera set the X-axis at 0, the Y-axis at 0, and the Z-axis at 250. Specify where the camera moves during the course of the effect by typing values in the End fields for the X-, Y-, and Z-axis coordinates. In the sample project, a second copy of the 3D Spin effect has been added to the **camera position** group in Frames 70-89. With the Use perspective projection option selected, redefining the three axes' coordinates at 100 produces an interesting effect. Figure 13-27 shows the final frame of the effect. In relation to the group's bounding box, you can see the group is moved to the right (the X-axis is set at 100 pixels) upward (the Y-axis is set at 100 pixels) and closer to the viewer (the Z-axis is set at 100 pixels.)

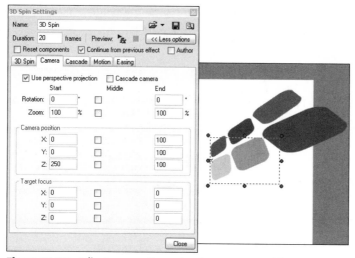

Figure 13-27: Adjust perspective using the camera position.

Target Focus

The *Target Focus* describes the point in 3D space where the camera is aimed. You can set values for the start, middle, and end of each axis' target focus on the Camera tab. The default values are at coordinates 0, 0, 0, which makes the camera's point of origin and focus the same. The final example in the sample project is shown in Figure 13-28. It is a 3D Spin effect applied in Frames 91-110 to a fourth group of objects named **target focus**. The values used for the focus are an X-value of 100, a Y-value of 50, and a Z-value of 200.

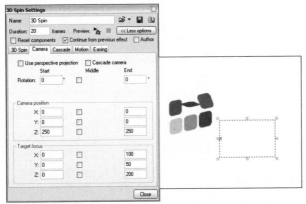

Figure 13-28: Adjust the point in space at which the camera is aimed.

You can see in the figure that the object appears to be above and to the left of the group's bounding box. These changes represent the X-axis and Y-axis coordinates. The group also slants, representing the change in the Z-axis value.

Tip   Working with 3D settings, camera, and their options can be very confusing. The key to understanding how to apply them to your movies is experimenting.

Coordinating Multiple Effects

SWiSHmax does a very good job of coordinating most features of effects integration with a single setting. In the effect's Settings dialog box, the option Continue from previous effect is selected by default. This option starts the current effect using the settings that were put in place by the object at the end of the preceding effect. Using the Continue from previous effect feature generally smoothes the animation. Although the first effect on an object's Timeline has the default option to Continue from previous effect you don't have to toggle the option on or off — it makes no difference in how the effect appears.

There are situations where you have two effects following one another on the Timeline that should be modified manually rather than using the automatic feature. For example:

✦ When one effect starts at a location different than that used by the preceding effect

✦ When you want to prevent smooth transitions between effects and start each effect using the original object's appearance

On The Web Site

The sample project referenced throughout this section has an example of each of these situations. You can experiment with the ch13_sample04.swi file described in this discussion. It is available from the book's Web site and is located in the ch13_sample04 in the chapter13 folder. The sample project contains the StartAt modifications described. The finished SWF movie is also in the folder.

The sample project ch13_sample04.swi contains three animated objects. The group object named **Bars** is a set of four rectangles. There is also a text object and a sprite. The sprite is added to the project to make the animation more interesting, but isn't included in this discussion.

To change how an effect starts:

1. **Click the Continue from previous effect option to deselect it**. The StartAt tab is added to the effect's Settings dialog box.

2. **Click the StartAt tab to display it**. The tab contains the same options as those found on the Motion tab.

3. **Adjust the settings as required to define how the effect starts.**

In the sample project, ch13_sample04.swi, the text uses the Come In-Blur effect, which ends with the text at the reference position shown in Figure 13-29. In the figure, guides are shown at the levels of the **Bars** object's animation; the text is centered between the guides.

Figure 13-29: The sample project uses a blur effect, placing the text in the center of the movie.

The initial effect is followed by the Surfin-Surfin USA effect, which produces a waving motion through the text. As a result, the effect pulls the text down, and it no longer sits within the two guides.

Deselecting the Continue from previous effect option for the Surfin effect adds the StartAt tab to the effect's Settings dialog box. To make the text start at the correct position, the X-position option Jump Up by was selected, and **5** pixels was typed as the value. In Figure 13-30, the first frame of the Surfin effect is shown; now you see that the text is within the guides on the stage.

The sample project also contains a group of rectangles that change their size and configuration over time based on the Unsqueeze in from lines effect. There are three copies of the effect used in the sample, two of which have the effect restart rather than continuing from the previous effect.

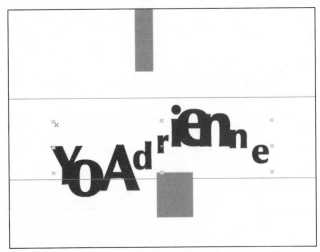

Figure 13-30: Adjust an effect's starting values manually to coordinate with the previous effect.

Summary

Some effects are used on a regular basis, while others are used for special types of animation. In this chapter, you learned about the Basic effects offered in SWiSHmax as well as how to use and store the Authored effects. There are a number of common settings used for effects; most effects can have transform, color, and transparency options customized. You can control the rate at which an effect applies different transformations and how the effect is viewed by controlling transformations and cameras. You learned how to modify how an effect starts.

In this chapter, you learned:

✦ About the common effect settings used by most effects

✦ Ways to use common Basic effects such as Fade, Zoom, Slide, and Blur effects

✦ How to change content on the Timeline using the Repeat frames or Revert effects

✦ How to set Effect Preferences, organize, and save Authored effects on your computer

✦ Methods for modifying and customizing the transform properties of an effect and the speed at which the property changes are applied

✦ That Transforms, Cascade, and Camera settings can determine how the elements of an object appear

✦ About coordinating effects for an object

✦   ✦   ✦

Customizing Core Effects

Sometimes hundreds of effects simply aren't enough! In SWiSHmax, you can choose from the dozens of effects provided with the program — either Basic or Authored effects — or create your own based on the Core effects.

Spend some time experimenting with the SWiSHmax effects. As you experiment, pay attention both to how the effect looks as well as how it is constructed. You find most effects are generated from a collection of primary effects, referred to as the Core effects.

You can customize and save any SWiSHmax effect. Some of the customization tabs are specific to certain sets of options such as Snake or Alternate options. Others, such as Transform options, are available for most of the different Core effects.

Several effect design components are based on 3D settings such as cameras and 3D effects. In this chapter the 3D settings are described in depth using the Camera tab; the principles apply to any 3D values you work with in SWiSHmax.

You work with the Custom and Author tabs in an effect's Settings dialog box to build your own effects. In the Author tab, you define variables for the effects that are displayed in the Custom tab. In this chapter, you learn how to create custom settings in the Author tab as well as how to configure settings on other effect Settings dialog box tabs based on defined variables.

Introducing the Core Effects

SWiSHmax contains a set of 10 Core effects. The effects Settings dialog box for each of the Core effects includes one self-named tab.

Table 14-1 lists the 10 Core effects as well as the settings tabs that are available for each effect. As you can see in Table 14-1 a number of the tabs are used in several of the Core effects. The Cascade tab defines how component parts of an object move during the course of the effect. Because both the Wave and Typewriter effects are based on a particular motion sequence, they don't need any Cascade settings.

The two-dimensional Core effects—Transform, Squeeze, Alternate, and Snake—contain the Transforms tab to configure the effect using X- and Y-axis values. Those effects that create a 3D effect, including the Explode, 3D Spin, 3D Wave, and Vortex Core, use the Camera tab instead of the Transforms tab to accommodate working with X-, Y-, and Z-axis values.

Cross-Reference   Chapter 13 describes the Motion, Easing, Transforms, Cascade, and Camera tab settings.

Table 14-1: Core Effect Settings Options

Core Effect	Settings can be Configured in These Tabs: *
Transform	Transforms, Cascade, Motion, Easing
Squeeze	Squeeze, Transforms, Cascade, Motion, Easing
Alternate	Alternate, Transforms, Cascade, Motion, Easing
Snake	Snake, Transforms, Cascade, Motion, Easing
Explode	Explode, Camera, Cascade, Motion, Easing
3D spin	3D Spin, Camera, Cascade, Motion, Easing
3D wave	3D Wave, Camera, Cascade, Motion, Easing
Vortex	Vortex, Camera, Cascade, Motion, Easing
Wave	Wave, Motion, Easing
Typewriter	Typewriter, Motion, Easing

* Each Core effect also includes the Author and Custom tabs, not included in the table listing.

Squeeze Effects

The Squeeze tab of the Squeeze core effect's dialog box appears in Figure 14-1. As you can see in the figure, the options define animation based on unidirectional motion. You can define the squeeze toward the center, which is the default option, or to the left or right. When you select a Squeeze option you can configure the effect further by using the settings on the other tabs included with the effect.

Cross-Reference   Information on the Transforms, Motion, Cascade, and Easing tabs is available in Chapter 13.

Figure 14-1: Define the direction of the effect in the Squeeze tab.

Alternate Effects

The default options for the Alternate Core effect's Alternate tab appear in Figure 14-2. You use the Alternate core effect to define a pattern for the elements of an object to appear. You can define proportions and directions for the elements as well as the repetition frequency.

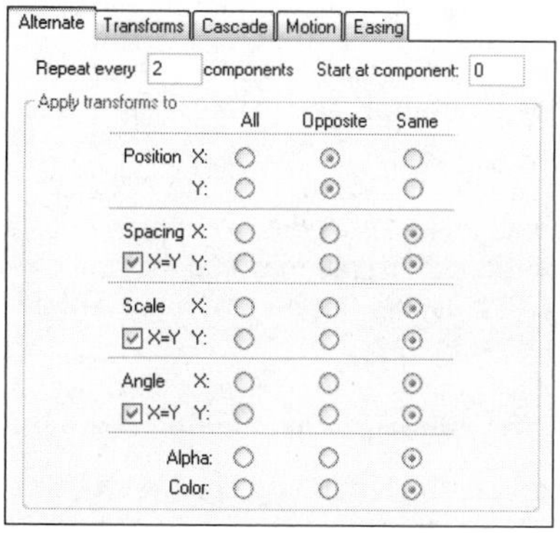

Figure 14-2: Alternate effects are used to display an object's components in a specified patterned sequence.

You can see in Figure 14-2 that the Alternate tab contains the basic transform options seen throughout the program, in the Transform panel or in the Transforms tab of the Effect Settings dialog box, for example. The difference is that there are three columns of settings you can apply to alternating elements or to the entire group.

To use the Alternate effect, configure any changes you want to display over the course of the effect in the Transforms tab, including Position, Spacing, Scale, Angle, Alpha, and Color. On the Alternate tab you can then apply the transformations to the components of the group as the effect progresses in one of three ways:

✦ **All.** The full transform setting changes apply to the components of the group and don't alternate.

✦ **Opposite.** The transform setting is applied to alternate elements of the group as it animates.

✦ **Same.** The transform is applied to all the components in one direction.

The sample project uses examples of each of these three applications.

On The Web Site

If you want to experiment with the Alternate effect and follow along with the steps, you can use the sample project from the book's Web site. This discussion uses ch14_sample01.swi, which is located in the ch14_sample01 folder within the chapter14 folder. The sample effect, Alternating stars.sfx is also in the folder.

To define a sequence for the Alternate effect after applying it to an object on the Timeline, follow these steps:

1. **Click the Transforms tab and make changes you want to appear in the Alternate effect during the course of the animation.**

2. **Click the Alternate tab to display the effect settings.**

3. **Click in the Repeat every xx components field and type the frequency of repetition.** The default value is 2.

4. **Click in the Start at component field and type a number.** The value 0 represents the first component in the group.

Tip

If you use a different value for the Start at component field and it doesn't appear to be animating correctly, check the sequence of objects in the group. You may find that the objects aren't listed in the Outline panel in the same pattern as they appear on the Layout panel. Adjust their positions and your animation should cycle evenly.

5. **Define the transformation characteristics of the animation by clicking radio buttons.**

Figure 14-3 shows two frames from the sample project. In the left image, the first frame of the animation appears; the last frame appears in the right image. You can see how the elements of the group change over time.

Figure 14-3: The custom Alternate effect produces color and alpha changes as well as position and scale changes over time.

Working with Snake Effects

Snake effects can be very dramatic. The Snake Core effect is a 2D effect and uses the Transforms tab for defining transform settings you can use to customize the effect. Snake effects are based on waveforms. For each of the settings available on the Snake tab, you can choose from the same collection of waveform settings as well as a Fixed setting, which uses no waveform. The waveforms and a sample of their appearance are listed in Table 14-2.

Table 14-2: Waveform Variations

Waveform	Type	Characteristics
	Sine	Moves in equal positive and negative curves between start and end values in a smooth curve.
	Triangle	Moves in equal positive and negative curves between start and end values in a sharp curve.
	Square	No curve formation; abruptly changes from start to end values.
	Saw Up	No curve; linear motion from start to end in upward direction and returns to start.
	Saw Dn	No curve; linear motion from start to end in downward direction and returns to start.
	Sqr + Tri	Moves in equal positive and negative curves between start and end values; extreme positions maintained over specified frames.
	Bounce	Moves from start to end in single parabolic curve and back again. (A parabola is a kind of curve; one of the conic sections formed by the intersection of the surface of a cone with a plane parallel to one of its sides.)
	Gravity	Also a parabolic curve, but it continues past the start point rather than bouncing back as in the bounce wave option
	Pulse	Jumps from the start to end value and returns to the start at the beginning of the animation cycle.

The Snake tab of the core Snake effect is shown in Figure 14-4. You see many common transform settings ranging from Position to Alpha and Color.

On The Web Site

The book's Web site contains a sample file you can use for experimenting with the Snake effect. The file is named ch14_sample02.swi and is in the ch14_sample02 subfolder within the chapter14 folder. The values shown in Figure 14-4 are those used for the Snake effect for the chevron object. The values shown in Figure 14-5 are those used for the chevron2 object.

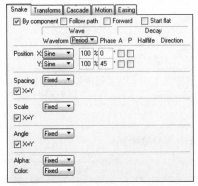

Figure 14-4: Snake effects are based on waveform behavior.

To customize the Snake effect after applying it to an object on the Timeline follow these steps:

1. **Click the Snake tab, and select effect application characteristics from the check boxes at the top of the tab:**

   - **By component.** Click this option to apply the effect to each component of a complex object. Deselect it to apply it to all components at once.

   - **Follow path.** Click this option to have the components rotate to follow the object's path. Deselect it to maintain the object's orientation.

   - **Forward.** Click this option to have the effect flow in a forward direction; deselect it to move the effect in reverse. You can only select this option if you have also selected By component.

   - **Start flat.** Click this option to have the object's elements start from their initial positions and gradually apply the effect; deselect it to have the effect start immediately.

Note   The Follow Path option refers to a path you add within the Snake effect, not another Move effect on the Timeline. Click and drag the object on the Layout panel's stage to add an internal motion path.

2. **Click the Waveform button and choose from two options:**

   - **Period.** Use this option to define the number of frames per cycle. The higher the number, the slower the waves move and the fewer wave cycles appear.

   - **Cycle.** Use this option to define the number of cycles during the effect. If you use this option, changing the duration of the effect changes the speed of the effect and maintains the frequency of the cycles.

3. **Choose a waveform setting for each of the transform characteristics.** The settings include Position, Spacing, Scale, Angle, Alpha, and Color.

4. **Choose characteristics for the waveform:**

   - **Cycles or period.** If you are using cycles, type a number representing how many cycles occur during the effect; if you are using period, type a number representing the percentage of the entire effect's duration used for one wave.

   - **Phase.** Type a value in degrees in the field to identify the location in the wave's cycle where the effect starts. In Figure 14-5, the wave's Y-axis position starts at 90 degrees, which is one-fourth through the wave's cycle.

5. **Choose decay characteristics (shown in Figure 14-5), which describe how the waveform changes over time:**

   - **A.** Click the Amplitude option to restrict the amplitude (range) of the wave for the full range of the wave. If deselected, the amplitude fluctuates during the effect.

   - **P.** Click the Period option to allow the wavelength to fluctuate. If deselected, the period remains static during the effect.

   - **Halflife.** Type a value in the Halflife field to define how long it takes for the wave to halve its value. The higher the value, the slower the rate of decay.

   - **Direction.** When you type a Halflife value, choose a direction for the decay to follow. Figure 14-5 shows the list of options available.

Figure 14-5: Define how the waves behave for each transformation characteristic.

Creating Explosions

You can use the Explode effect to create a wide range of explosive effects. You can assign one or more bombs to the same object and define the power of the bomb as well as its direction. The Explode tab from the Explode Settings dialog box appears in Figure 14-6. The settings used are those applied to the first exploding balloon in the sample file.

On The Web Site

Experiment with the Explode effect using the sample project, ch14_sample03, which is described in this discussion. The file is in the ch14_sample03 subfolder in the chapter14 folder; the folder also contains the two images used in the project, and the exported SWF movie.

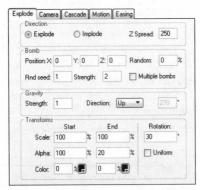

Figure 14-6: These are the explode settings used to create a gentle upward explosion.

Follow these steps to customize an Explode effect after the effect is added to an object's Timeline:

1. **Click the Explode tab in the Explode Settings dialog box.**

2. **Click a direction option for the effect:**

   - **Explode.** This is the default setting. It moves components away from the source.

   - **Implode.** This setting moves components toward the source; the opposite of an explosion.

   - **Z Spread.** This is the amount of Z-axis depth used to distribute exploded components.

3. **Choose settings for the bomb:**

   - **Position.** Define the center of the explosion relative to the center of the object along three axes. The default uses a Y-axis value of 30 pixels, which is below the center of the object making the default explosion appear to go upward.

Tip — You can randomize the bomb's location by typing a value in the Random field to the right of the Position fields. The percentage value is the random amount of offset applied.

   - **Rnd Seed.** The number typed in this field is used to randomize the results of the explosion. The default is a value of 1.

   - **Strength.** The higher the value, the faster the components of the object will explode. The sample project uses a strength of 2 for both objects' bombs.

   - **Multiple bombs.** Click the Multiple bombs option to use more than one bomb. Multiple bombs are positioned relative to each component of the object.

4. **Choose Gravity options:**

   - **Strength.** Define the gravitational pull by typing a value in this field. The default is 1, which approximates Earth's gravity. A higher gravity value can shorten the explosion effect by dragging the elements offstage too quickly.

Experiment with Negative Numbers

Many effect settings can use negative values that create very different effects. For example, using a negative number for the Strength option causes an implosion rather than an explosion. That is, the explosion is sucked inward and upward.

Tip

To approximate the moon's gravity, enter a decimal value of **.17**; type **2.54** to approximate Jupiter's gravity.

- **Direction.** Click this button and choose a direction for the explosion to travel, or click Other and type a value in the field next to the Direction button.

5. **Select any transforms you want to apply during the explosion and type the values in the fields.** You can specify Scale, Rotation, Alpha, and Color. In the sample project, the balloons use 30-degree Rotation and an Alpha fade from 100% to 30%.

Spinning Objects in Three Dimensions

The 3D Spin Core effect is used to rotate the components of a complex object around the three axes over time. Apply the 3D Spin effect to an object on the Timeline. Choose settings from the 3D Spin tab.

Choose a Spin direction. You can choose either Spin forward (the default,) Spin backwards, which animates from the end to the start of the effect, or click the Common axis option, as seen in Figure 14-7. The sample project uses the Common axis option, which makes each element spin according to the center of the object rather than the centers of each component.

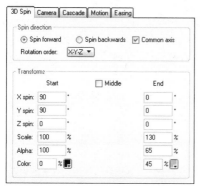

Figure 14-7: Define 3D Spin direction and transforms in the 3D Spin tab.

Choose a rotation order. Click the Rotation order button and choose an axis order. The default is X-Y-Z; the dropdown list contains six order combinations.

The ch14_sample04.swi movie file in the ch14_sample04 subfolder of the chapter14 folder contains an example of the 3D Spin effect applied both to a group of objects as well as some text.

Choose the Transforms and the times at which to apply the changes. The default uses transforms at the start and the end of the effect's animation. Click Middle to add a third column of options.

Using a 3D Wave Effect

The 3D Wave Core effect produces a waving motion through a complex object's components. You can define the pattern as passing through all elements, or fix a direction. Set the effect's characteristics in the 3D Wave tab.

The ch14_sample04.swi movie file in the ch14_sample04 subfolder of the chapter14 folder contains an example of the 3D Wave effect applied both to a group of objects as well as some text. The 3D wave effect is shown in the group named 3d wave and the text 3D Wave from Frames 31-60. The 3D wave effect created in the sample project is also in the chapter14 folder; it is named seagrass.sfx.

Define the wave characteristics for the X-, Y-, and Z-axes as well as color and alpha. The three axes' wave settings are visible by default. Click the Color or Alpha options to display additional columns for configuration, shown in Figure 14-8.

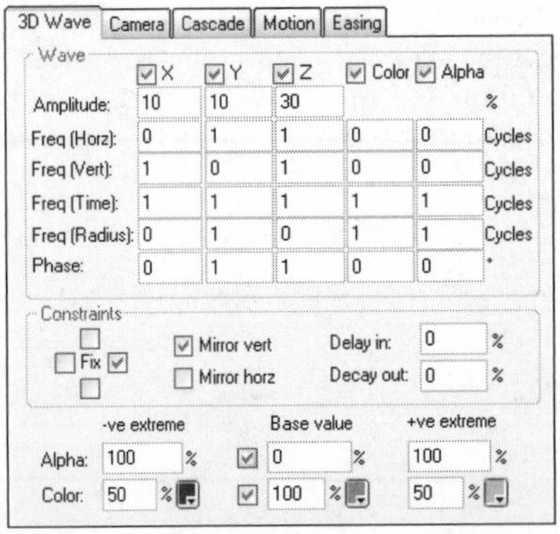

	☑ X	☑ Y	☑ Z	☑ Color	☑ Alpha	
Amplitude:	10	10	30			%
Freq (Horz):	0	1	1	0	0	Cycles
Freq (Vert):	1	0	1	0	0	Cycles
Freq (Time):	1	1	1	1	1	Cycles
Freq (Radius):	0	1	0	1	1	Cycles
Phase:	0	1	1	0	0	°

Constraints

☐ Fix ☑ ☑ Mirror vert ☐ Mirror horz   Delay in: 0 %   Decay out: 0 %

	-ve extreme		Base value		+ve extreme	
Alpha:	100	%	☑ 0	%	100	%
Color:	50	%	☑ 100	%	50	%

Figure 14-8: Define the characteristics for the 3D wave effect.

Set Amplitude, Frequency, and Phase options for each axis. Set cycle values for Color or Alpha configuration if you selected either option.

Choose any constraint options you want to restrict the uniformity of the wave

✦ **Fix.** Click a direction to fix the effect, which means that the selected direction is locked and the effect appears to come from the fixed direction.

✦ **Mirror.** You can specify a horizontal or vertical mirror effect. The sample project uses a horizontal mirror that reflects the wave horizontally around the object's center.

✦ **Delay in.** This decreases the wave height to 0 at the start of the effect. Type a percentage value to define the point at which the delay is finished.

✦ **Decay out.** This decreases the wave height to 0 at the end of the effect. Type a percentage value to define the point at which the decay should start.

Alpha settings. Modify the component's Alpha value according to the height of the wave. Type a value for the wave peak (+ve extreme Alpha), wave trough (-ve extreme Alpha), and for the Base value if desired.

Color cycles. Modify the component's Color according to the height of the wave. Type a value and select a color from the Color Chooser for the wave peak (+ve extreme Alpha), wave trough (-ve extreme Alpha), and for the Base value if desired.

Creating a Vortex

The Vortex Core effect spins the elements of a complex object in three dimensions and then moves the elements out of the swirl depending on the gravitational settings you choose; you can also run the effect inward, as used in the sample project.

On The Web Site

The ch14_sample04.swi movie file in the ch14_sample04 subfolder of the chapter14 folder contains an example of the Vortex effect shown in the group named vortex and the text Vortex from Frames 61-90.

You can configure the Vortex Core effect using directional, gravitational, and transform options, as seen in Figure 14-9.

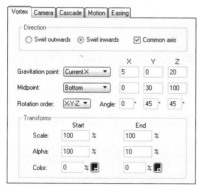

Figure 14-9: Define how an effect swirls in the Vortex Settings dialog box.

Directional options. The default direction for a Vortex effect is an outward swirl. You can also use an inward swirl similar to that used in the sample project. For either direction you can also elect to use a Common axis. The sample project uses the common axis option, which makes each element spin according to the center of the object rather than the centers of each component.

Gravitational options. The Gravitation point is the location to which the components swirl. Click the down arrow on the Gravitation point button and choose one of the 12 options. The options use different directions or different axis settings, or you can create a custom setting. Type values in the X-, Y-, and Z-axis fields to adjust the gravity source. The origin of the object is its center; 1 unit is equal to 1 pixel.

Midpoint options. To set the Midpoint of the swirl, click the Midpoint button and choose from 22 locations. The options use different directions or different axis settings, or you can create a custom setting. Type values in the X-, Y-, and Z-axis fields to adjust the midpoint.

Rotation order. Click the Rotation order button and choose from six variations of the three axes' sequence. The order you select defines the order the elements move through the three axes as they are animated. You can specify an angle in degrees for each axis' rotation. The sample project uses 0-, 45-, and 45-degree rotation along the default sequence, which is the X-Y-Z axis option.

Transforms. Choose the usual transforms that can be applied to most effects. You can choose from Scale, Alpha, and Color settings that can be applied to either the start or end of the effect.

The sample available on the Web site uses two copies of the Vortex effect; one applied to a group of stars and the other to a string of text. The effect used for the group of stars is configured so the stars swirl around and over the text as they gradually appear on the stage.

Using the Wave Core Effect

In addition to the 3D Wave effect, SWiSHmax also includes a basic or 2D Wave Core effect. When you apply the Wave Effect, a rolling wave moves through the text or group of objects. Wave effects are often used for waving banners, such as the one shown in Figure 14-10.

Figure 14-10: Use the Wave effect for creating banners.

You can configure all aspects of the wave, including its direction, rotation, scale of the letters, and the alpha setting for the wave.

On The Web Site

If you want to experiment with the file shown in Figure 14-14 you can download it from the book's Web site. It is named ch14_05.swi and is in the ch14_05 subfolder in the chapter14 folder. The exported SWF file, which is named ch14_sample05.swf, is also in the folder, named ch14_sample05.swf. The sample project contains two duplicate copies of the text and the effect.

Configure the Wave effect in the Wave tab of the effect's Settings dialog box.

✦ **Wave Characteristics.** Choose from a number of different options for configuring the basic characteristics of the wave:

- **Whole Object.** Click this option to apply the effect to the composite object, not to the individual elements.

- **Rotate to follow wave.** Click this option to have the elements rotate to follow the direction of the wave.

- **Decay amplitude of wave.** Click this option to gradually decrease the amplitude of the wave to 0 over the duration of the effect.

- **Start flat.** Click this option to have all elements start from a flat position; otherwise, the elements appear to be moving when the effect starts.

- **End flat.** Click this option to have all elements end in a flat position at the end of the effect; if deselected, the elements appear to be moving at the end of the effect.

✦ **Cycles.** Type a value in the Cycles field to define the number of cycles during the effect. If you use this option, changes made to the duration of the effect will change the speed of the effect.

✦ **Length.** Click in the Length field to specify the distance in pixels from the start of the wave to the end of the wave. The sample project uses the default length of 300 pixels.

✦ **Direction.** Click one of the buttons to choose a direction for the wave. From left to right, as seen in Figure 14-11, the wave's direction options are left to right, right to left, moves from both ends to the middle, and moves from the middle to both ends.

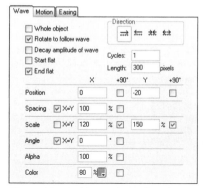

Figure 14-11: Use various directions and transform settings to configure the wave.

Set options for a number of transforms that can be applied to the wave.

✦ **Position.** Set values to define how far each component moves from its original position. You can use negative numbers to represent a shift left on the X-axis or up on the Y-axis; a value of 0 means there is no change in position. You can shift the phase of the wave in addition to defining a position. Click the +90º option to shift the phase of the wave by 90 degrees based on the value you set for either the X-axis or Y-axis positions.

✦ **Spacing.** Type a value to space the wave throughout the effect. When the option X=Y is selected, the values for both axes are the same. The default value of 100% means there is no spacing change over the time of the effect. Click the check box to deselect the X=Y option if you want to set separate values.

✦ **Scale.** Type a value to change the scale of the effect over time. The default is 100%, which is no change in scale. Click the X=Y option to deselect it if you want to change scale values on each axis. In the sample project, the scale is set at X=120% and Y=150%, which means the letters in the object increase in both axes as the wave passes the components.

✦ **Angle.** Type a value to define how each component's axes are rotated as the wave passes through. Click the X=Y option to deselect it if you want to change the angles individually. The default value is 0º, which means there is no change in the angle.

✦ **Alpha.** You can define how much each element of an object fades as the wave passes through. The default is 100%, which means there is no alpha change; at 0%, the element is invisible.

✦ **Color.** You can use the Color setting to define color changes during the wave's passage through a component. Type a value in the color field and click the Color Swatch to open the Color Selector and choose a color. The sample project uses the default value of 0%, representing no change in color for one of the text elements, and a value of 80% using a bright green color for the second text element.

Typing Text Effects

SWiSHmax includes a Typewriter effect as a Core effect. The effect produces interesting results. The sample movie, ch14_sample05.swf, includes the Typewriter effect following the Wave effect. The Typewriter effect is complete with a cursor, although the cursor appears only when the effect is applied to a text object.

On The Web Site

If you want to experiment with the file described in this discussion you can download it from the book's Web site. It is named ch14_05.swi and is in the ch14_05 subfolder in the chapter14 folder. The exported SWF file, which is named ch14_sample05.swf, is also in the folder, named ch14_sample05.swf. The Typewriter effect is used on Frames 21-86 of the text_hilite object.

You can configure a number of settings for the Typewriter effect, as seen in Figure 14-12.

Unlike with most other effects, you don't type a duration in the Duration field at the top of the dialog box, nor is there a default value. The duration depends on the number of character elements as well as the Show Character value you use.

✦ **Show character rate.** Type a value to define how fast the characters are typed on the screen. The value determines the effect's duration. You can use decimal values. The rate of .75 that appears in the sample means that one character is displayed every three-quarter seconds.

✦ **Show cursor while typing.** Click this option to display the cursor. If the object to which you are applying the effect isn't a text object the cursor is hidden.

✦ **Flash cursor rate.** Type a value to control the speed of the cursor flash. The sample uses a value of 4; a value of 1 is the fastest flash speed possible.

Figure 14-12: Set options for a typewriter effect in the Settings dialog box.

Note   You can set the Flash cursor rate to 0; the At start of line flash number and at end of line flash number are then removed from the options.

✦ **At start of line flash number.** Type a value to set how many times the cursor flashes at the start of the line; the sample project flashes the cursor twice before starting the animation.

✦ **At end of line flash number.** Type a value to set how many times the cursor flashes at the end of the line. The sample project uses three cursor flashes at the end of the animation.

✦ **Cursor Character.** Click the character button to open a list of characters available for the cursor. The character set is the same as that used for the text when you use a text object. In the sample project in Figure 14-13, the text uses the irrep font.

Figure 14-13: A typewriter effect is simple and effective.

Authoring Effects

If none of the more than 300 effects and their myriad configurations is right for your project, you can try your hand at programming your own. The simplest way is to start from a Core effect.

When you choose different settings in the existing effects, code in the program produces an outcome based on those settings. For example, if you choose a color in an effect, the color value is entered into the formula for the setting, producing the effect.

There are several elements involved in an authored setting. These include:

Prompt. The name of the custom setting; a prompt is a label such as **Color** or **X-value**.

Variable. The value used in the setting's formula written using alphanumeric characters. A variable is a placeholder in a formula that is changeable, or variable. By changing the value, such as **100** for a Red color value or **-20** for an axis value, you change the content of the formula and produce different effects. SWiSHmax uses some consistent variable names in the effects' programming, such as **a** for alpha settings, or **rgb** for color.

Type. There are several ways you choose a setting for an effect. SWiSHmax offers you a variety of options including checkboxes and sliders.

Values. Parameters you use for effects often have a range of values. For example, you can't logically use a negative number for a color value, or a letter of the alphabet for an axis location.

The Author tab is used to write variables for use in the effect. You construct the variable, assign a name to it, and define its parameters. The effect settings created in the Author tab appear in the Custom tab, where you can set the default values for your custom effect settings. In addition to writing effect variables, you can also set the value of any programmable item in the effect to use one of your effect variables; you can also write a formula containing your variables for use in the effect.

Figure 14-14 shows the sample project used in this discussion. The circle at the left is broken into shapes and uses the custom effect; the central circle is also broken into shapes and uses the Core effect; the circle at the right also uses the custom effect. The custom effect includes three variables. It also contains custom formulas in fields in the Transforms tab.

Figure 14-14: Your custom effects are based on existing Core effects.

On The Web Site

The project described in the discussion is available from the book's Web site. The project file is named ch14_sample06.swi and is in the ch14_sample06 folder within the chapter14 folder. You will find the effect created in this discussion in the folder named alternate_sequence.sfx, as well as an SWF movie of the effect in action named ch14_sample06.swf.

Follow these steps to write a custom variable for an effect:

1. **Select an object on the Layout panel to which you want to apply the effect.** You need to select an object in order to access the Effects menus.

2. **Click the Effects button on the Timeline and choose an effect.** The sample project uses the Alternate effect, which is available by choosing Add Effect ⇨ Core Effects ⇨ Alternate. The effect is applied to the object.

3. **Double-click the effect's rectangle on the Timeline to open its Settings dialog box.**

4. **Click the Author check box.** The Author and Custom tabs are added to the group of tabs.

5. **Click the Author tab to display it.** It has no content by default, but contains a sequence of fields and buttons to author your effect's variables.

6. **Type the name for the first variable in the Prompt field.** Each variable you write is named by typing a name in the Prompt field.

7. **Type a variable in the variable field.** The first variable in the sample project is used for color change; it is named **color change** and its variable is named **cc**.

8. **Click the Type button labeled Edit, and choose an option from the list, as shown in Figure 14-15 (Edit appears by default).** Choices include a Checkbox, Slider, or Color Selector. Depending on the option you choose, additional fields appear to the right of the button. If you choose a slider type of input option, you can specify the minimum and maximum values allowed.

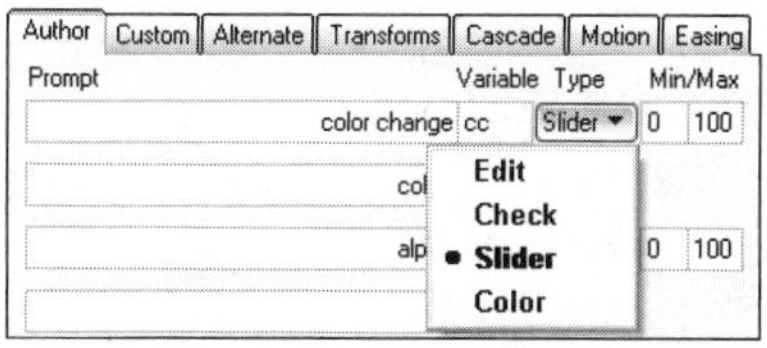

Figure 14-15: Write the first variable for the effect in the Author tab.

9. **Type values in the fields or leave the default range of Min=0, Max=100.**

Add other variables as required, and make sure to save the effect. Two other variables were also created in the sample project. Their structure is listed in Table 14-3. The table also includes the variable constructed in the preceding steps for reference.

Table 14-3: Custom Variables in the Sample Project

Prompt	Variable	Type	Values
color change	cc	Slider	Min=0, Max=100
color	rgb	Color	nil
alpha	a	Slider	Min=0, Max=100

Setting values for custom variables

Once you have defined variables, you can set the values you want to use as default values for the effect. You define the variables' values in the Custom tab. Figure 14-16 shows the Custom tab of the sample project. As you can see, the three variables created are included on the tab as well as the format selected for input. That is, the **color change** and **alpha** variables use a slider, and the **color** variable uses a Color Swatch.

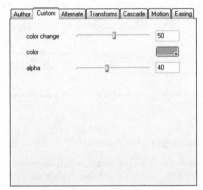

Figure 14-16: The custom variables written in the Author tab are displayed on the Custom tab.

Set values for each of the custom variables as you would for any settings in the effect Settings dialog box. The variables set in the sample project affect settings on the Transforms tab. In Figure 14-17, you can see the Transforms tab of the custom effect.

Figure 14-17: Your custom values are shown elsewhere in the Settings dialog box.

The Color Swatch shows the bright green set in the Custom tab. If you look closely at the figure, you see that the values for the Color and Alpha settings are grayed out, meaning they can't be selected and altered. The user won't be able to change the settings in the tab; they can be changed only through the Custom tab.

Also in Figure 14-17, note that the Alpha and Color both show a value of 60%, although in the Custom tab the **alpha** variable was set at 40. The difference is due to a formula added to the Alpha field in the Transforms tab.

> **Note**   If you are trying to replicate the effect discussed here, you must also make changes on the Alternate tab. Deselect X=Y for Spacing, click the Opposite radio button, and deselect X=Y for Scale and click the Opposite radio button.

Adding formulas to fields

Any field in any effect that shows a grayed-out value means that there is a variable or a formula attached to the field. Right-click the field to activate it. The contents appear in the field in blue text.

Tip

When you are building a formula the text is red; as soon as you have completed a valid expression it changes to blue.

Follow these steps to write a formula for a field:

1. **Right-click the field you want to modify to display the current formula or variable.** The field for the Alpha setting for the sample project is shown in Figure 14-18.

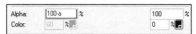

Figure 14-18: Right-click a field to use a custom variable or formula.

2. **Type the variable or formula you want to use in the custom effect.** The sample project uses the formula 100-a for the Alpha setting, which is 100% minus the alpha value specified on the Custom tab.

Note

The example shows the use of a formula rather than typing a simple value. If you test the effect using the formula, the Alpha setting is opposite to that you would expect. That is, if you type **10** in the field, you would expect the object to have 10 percent opacity. However, when you use the formula, the effect shows 90-percent opacity, as the equation is written as 100 percent minus the value typed in the field.

In practical terms, using a formula for defining opacity might be confusing to anyone using the custom effect settings. However, because opacity/transparency is a simple concept to understand, it is a good exercise in learning how to work with a formula.

3. **Click off the field or click another tab to set the value.**

Modifying existing formulas

In addition to writing your own formulas and adding your own custom settings, you can also modify the formulas already existing in an effect. The sample project uses both the custom color change variable as well as modifications to two existing formulas in the effect.

To replicate the sample effect, you need to make changes on the Transforms tab. Right-click the Color field and type **cc** to use the custom **color change** variable; right-click the Position X end field and type **x+3**; and right-click the Position Y end field and type **y-2**.

The effect is designed to have a slight change in both X- and Y-axis positions at the end of each component's animation. To maintain this 5-pixel difference, add a formula rather than a whole number (although you can type a number in the fields, it has a different effect). Using a formula maintains the ratio of motion between the two axes regardless of the values that are entered in the X- and Y-axis position fields for the start of the effect.

You can see the impact of the formulas in the sample project. The project includes a third copy of the circle named **single object** that is a simple shape. It uses the custom effect; if you play the animation, you see the circle shift its position over the course of the animation in the same amount as the pixels defined in the X- and Y-axes end positions in the Transforms tab.

Summary

This chapter was all about the Core SWiSHmax effects. From the set of 10 Core effects you can create innumerable custom effects. You learned the types of configurations for each Core effect, as well as the tabs of options that make up each effect's Settings dialog box. Using a sample project, you saw how a custom effect is authored and configured. You learned:

✦ What makes up the different Core effects provided in SWiSHmax

✦ How to create Squeeze and Alternate effects

✦ How to work with the Snake effect

✦ How to customize Explode effects

✦ How to use different 3D effects

✦ How to use Vortex and Wave effects

✦ How to simulate typing with the Typewriter effect

✦ How to author custom effects based on Core effects

✦   ✦   ✦

Exploring SWiSHmax Objects

◆　◆　◆　◆

◆　◆　◆　◆

Creating Sprite and Instance Objects

When you design a project, you sometimes need to nest animations within one another. For example, on a Web site interface you may want one object animating in a loop that is different from other animations on the page. Perhaps you want to add background animations that loop in different sequences and additional animations that occur when your visitor interacts with the Web page in some way. You may have a group of objects that you want to add a single effect to in addition to the objects' individual effects. In all these instances, often the solution is to use a sprite.

You have likely seen animations where a shape or text acts as a window through which you see the action. This process is called masking. In SWiSHmax, you can create masked animations using sprites.

Sprites are scripting objects. SWiSHmax uses its own language named SWiSHscript, which is an object-oriented scripting language. A part of working with SWiSHscript is addressing an object; in this chapter you are introduced to object naming methods.

What is a Sprite?

The simple explanation: A sprite is a movie within a movie. But, a sprite isn't confined to a single collection of objects. You can add sprites within sprites, within sprites, and so on. The restriction on how many sprite child objects you can place within a parent sprite is based on organizing and keeping track of the action.

You can use more than one occurrence of a sprite in a movie. These occurrences are clones of the original sprite known as instances. Using instances allows you to quickly add more action without having to reconstruct and reconfigure any elements in your movie. Not only is reusing a sprite a good way to save time and assure uniformity, but instances of sprites add very little to a file's size. When you need to change some of a sprite's characteristics, you can also work with a copy of the sprite that allows you to make changes independently of the original sprite.

Creating a Sprite

You can add sprites to your movie in a number of ways, from reassigning content already in the movie as a sprite object to importing some types of animation that are automatically defined as sprites.

There are several ways to add sprites to your movie. These include:

✦ Grouping existing content as a sprite

✦ Converting existing content to a sprite

✦ Importing animated GIF or SWF files

✦ Inserting an empty sprite object

When you create a sprite the selected elements are combined into one unit. On the Timeline, the rows for the individual elements that are part of the sprite are removed, and a single element named Sprite replaces them. When you are working with numerous objects in a scene, not only is using sprites a good idea from a design standpoint but they make working with the Timeline easier.

Reverting sprite status

Regardless of the method you use for creating a sprite, you can restore the individual objects. Select the sprite and then choose one of these methods:

✦ Right-click and choose Grouping ➪ Ungroup from the shortcut menu

✦ Choose Modify ➪ Grouping ➪ Ungroup

✦ Click the Ungroup button on the Grouping toolbar

✦ Press the Ctrl+U Accelerator key combination

Grouping content as a sprite

Perhaps the simplest way to construct a sprite is to group objects. For example, you may have two geometric shapes you want to animate for the background of your Web site interface. Construct each object, add the animation, and then group the objects.

Follow these steps to group objects as a sprite:

1. **Select the objects you want to include in the sprite.** The objects can vary from text to sounds and can also include animation, as in the example seen in Figure 15-1.

2. **Right-click the selected objects in the Outline panel and choose Grouping ➪ Group as Sprite.** You can also choose Modify ➪ Grouping ➪ Group as Sprite or click the Group as Sprite button on the Grouping toolbar. The elements are grouped under a sprite heading in the Outline panel and named **Sprite** by default. The selected elements become child elements of the sprite object.

Caution   Don't select the objects and then use the Ctrl+G Accelerator keys. This creates a group which works differently than a sprite.

3. **Click the Sprite's default name in the Outline panel to activate the text or click in the Name field in the Sprite panel.**

4. **Name the sprite.** Identify the sprite by typing a unique name to use for scripting, modifying blank sprites, or swapping instances.

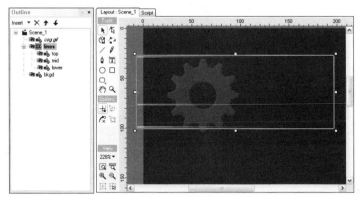

Figure 15-1: Group a number of objects as a sprite.

The sample project used in this discussion is available from the book's Web site. It is named ch15_sample01.swi, and is located in the ch15_sample01 subfolder within the chapter15 folder. The finished movie, ch15_sample01.swf, and the source image are also in the folder.

Grouping as a group

One other grouping option can be used with objects intended for use as sprites. You can group a number of objects together as a group. However, if any of the objects contain effects, they are converted to sprites first and then added to the group.

Select the objects you want to group and choose a Group as Group command from one of the menu paths. If any objects contain effects, the dialog box seen in Figure 15-2 appears. Click Yes to convert any objects with effects into sprites first and then into a group. If you click No, the effects are stripped from the objects with effects and then grouped.

Figure 15-2: To combine several objects as a group and maintain effects, you first convert any objects containing effects into sprites.

Tip

Sprites are scripting objects and are defined as a Target by default. If you create a group you can define it as a target in the Group panel.

When you group objects as a group, the group has no independent status on the movie's Timeline; instead, it appears as a single object. If the group contains sprites, and you want to modify the content of any of the sprites contained in the group, open the group and then double-click the sprite's name to open its Timeline.

Converting content to a sprite

Converting content to a sprite is slightly different from grouping objects as a sprite. Where a number of objects can be grouped as one sprite and each element becomes a child object of one parent sprite object, converting content to a sprite converts each element separately.

Figure 15-3 shows an example. In the Outline panel, you can see one sprite named **lines** that contains elements that were grouped as a sprite. A second copy of each of the elements — named **top**, **mid**, and **lower** — was selected and converted; each becoming its own sprite. The sprite object is named according to each element's name; when the sprite is opened on the Outline panel, you see that each contains the original object as a child object.

Figure 15-3: Converting an object to a sprite makes the original object a child of the sprite parent object.

After selecting the object on the Outline panel, Timeline, or Layout panel, you can use these methods to convert the object to a sprite:

✦ Right-click and choose Convert ⇨ Convert to Sprite from the shortcut menu

✦ Click Convert to Sprite on the Grouping toolbar

✦ Choose Modify ⇨ Convert ⇨ Convert to Sprite

Unlike converting a group to a sprite, converting an object to a sprite doesn't remove it from the scene's Timeline. Each object is redefined as a sprite object containing the original object as a child object and stays on the main Timeline.

Importing sprite content

When you import animated GIF or SWF files they are imported as a sequence of frames. On the Import Frames dialog box you can specify that the animation is imported as a sprite.

Choose File ⇨ Import to open the Open dialog box. Browse for the location of the GIF or SWF file you want to use, select the file, and click Open. The Open dialog box closes, and the Import dialog box opens. Figure 15-4 shows the Import dialog box for an animated GIF file. To import the frames as a sprite, click the Animated sprite option. Click Import and the selected frames are imported as a single sprite named using the imported file's name.

Cross-Reference Learn about importing animations in Chapter 9.

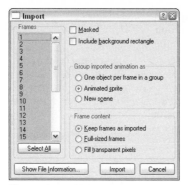

Figure 15-4: You can convert an imported animation into a sprite.

Creating a blank sprite

You can create a blank sprite in SWiSHmax and use it as an instance of another object at a later time or add child objects to it on the Layout panel or the sprite's layout.

To create a blank sprite, choose one of these methods:

✦ Click the Insert button on the Outline panel and choose Sprite

✦ Choose Insert ➪ Sprite from the program menu

✦ Right-click the scene's name in the Outline panel, or select the scene object on the Layout panel and choose Insert ➪ Sprite from the shortcut menu

✦ Click the Insert Sprite button on the Grouping toolbar

A blank sprite is shown on the Layout panel's stage as an icon like that seen in Figure 15-5.

Figure 15-5: A blank sprite displays an icon on the stage.

Tip

Organize sprites as you do single objects of other types. List the objects in the Outline panel according to how you want them to stack in the movie.

Choosing Sprite Characteristics

Sprites are simple objects and are also, by default, scripting objects. When you add a sprite to your project the Sprite panel is activated in SWiSHmax and appears at the front of the panel group. For objects such as shapes, the Target option becomes available as soon as you type a name for the object in the Name field of its panel. The Target option at the top of the Sprite panel is automatically selected, and can't be selected or deselected. However, if you intend to use the sprite as a target in a script, it must be named.

The Sprite panel for the **lines** sprite used in the sample project is shown in Figure 15-6.

Figure 15-6: Choose settings and options for a sprite in the Sprite panel.

There are several settings and options you can select in the Sprite panel. These include:

✦ **Name.** Type a name in the Name field to use for scripting. The name appears in the Outline panel, the object's label in the Timeline, and in the Content panel.

✦ **Target.** This option is unavailable and selected; a sprite is defined as a target by default.

✦ **Track as menu.** For a sprite, this option is disabled.

✦ **Use bottom object as mask.** The object in a sprite placed at the bottom of the stacking order in the Outline panel can be defined as a mask, which is used to constrict view of the remainder of the sprite to specific shapes.

✦ **Stop playing at end of sprite.** Toggle this option to control how the sprite plays. This option is deselected by default, meaning the sprite will loop. Click the check box to play the sprite's Timeline once and stop.

Tip

Use the Stop playing option when you use an animated sprite in response to a user interaction such as a mouse click.

✦ **Display options.** There are three ways to show a sprite in the Layout panel — as a Static Sprite, as an Icon, or showing the first frame. The Static Sprite option is the default.

✦ **Expand (edit in place).** This option is for viewing the contents of a sprite. This is the default option for viewing and is grayed out when you add or create a new sprite. After opening a sprite for editing, the button becomes active.

✦ **Open in Layout.** This option opens the sprite in its own layout view for editing.

✦ **Close.** This option closes an open layout view in the Layout panel, and collapses the sprite in the Outline panel and on the Timeline.

The default option for a sprite is to show the entire sprite on the stage. If your project is very complex, or your sprites contain a lot of objects, choose one of the other options on the Sprite panel. Choosing either of these options may speed up processing when you are working on your movie project.

✦ **Sprite Icon.** This option displays the sprite icon on the Layout panel instead of the sprite's contents. The icon resizes itself to the size of your sprite, as seen in Figure 15-7.

Figure 15-7: Display the sprite's icon on the Layout panel to save processing time.

✦ **First frame.** If you choose this option, only the child objects of the sprite that display in the first frame are seen on the Layout panel.

Tip   You see the entire content of the sprite if you play it or expand the sprite's hierarchy.

Editing a Sprite

You can edit both the content of a sprite as well as the sprite object as a whole. Editing the content of a sprite is similar to editing other types of objects in a SWiSHmax movie project. You can edit a sprite either on the SWiSHmax Layout panel or in a special sprite layout view.

Editing on the Layout panel

Open a sprite in one of these ways:

✦ Click the plus sign (+) to the left of the sprite's name in the Outline panel to display its child objects

✦ Double-click the sprite's label in the Timeline to display its Timeline

✦ Double-click one of the sprite's child objects on the stage to open the sprite

✦ Click Expand (edit in place) on the Sprite panel

When you open a sprite its appearance on the Layout panel changes as shown in Figure 15-8. The image on the left shows a selected sprite in its closed state. It has a dashed box surrounding it and resize handles on the edges of the box. In the Outline panel, the sprite's name is selected, but its hierarchy isn't displayed. The image on the right shows an open sprite. The sprite's bounding box is a solid line, and there are resize handles on the edges of the box.

Caution   If you want to move an entire sprite on the stage, make sure the sprite is closed and you have selected its name. If the sprite is open, when you click and drag, you only move one of the sprite's objects.

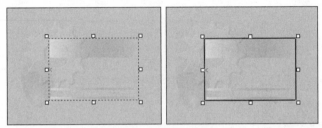

Figure 15-8: A sprite is identified differently on the Layout panel depending on whether it is closed or open.

Once the sprite is open, you can add or remove objects. You can modify existing objects by applying transformations or applying/removing effects. If you are adding objects to a sprite, make sure the sprite's name is selected in the Outline panel. Otherwise, a drawn or imported object is listed as a child of whatever element is selected in the Outline panel.

Tip   If you add a drawing or text to your project, for example, and place it in the root of the scene or within another object by mistake, you don't have to delete and redo your work. Select the object in the Outline panel, and press Ctrl+X to cut the object and place it on the clipboard. Then click the name of the sprite, and press Ctrl+V to paste the object to the sprite. Your object and any settings or effects you previously applied are pasted to its new location.

Editing in a sprite layout view

It's often easier to concentrate on a task when you remove distractions such as other objects in a scene. You can hide the other objects in the Layout panel by toggling their visibility to hidden, or you can open a sprite in its own layout view. Follow these steps to edit a sprite in a sprite layout view:

1. **Click the sprite's name in the Outline panel to select it.** You can also click its label in the Timeline or select it on the Layout panel.

2. **Click Open in Layout on the Sprite panel.** The Layout panel changes to the sprite layout view, as seen in Figure 15-9. The sprite's name is shown on the Layout panel's tab. The default view shows a checkerboard pattern as seen in the figure.

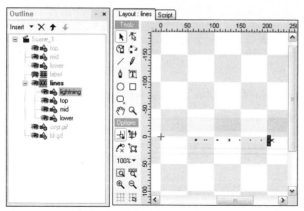

Figure 15-9: You can work with a sprite in isolation in the sprite layout view.

3. **In the Sprite panel, click the Single color radio button, and then click the Color Swatch to open the Color Selector.** Sometimes it is difficult to see the objects clearly against the checkerboard background.

Note

If you can see your sprite's object clearly using the default checkerboard background, omit Steps 3 and 4.

4. **Select a solid color to use for the background.** The Color Selector closes and the background color is changed, as seen in Figure 15-10.

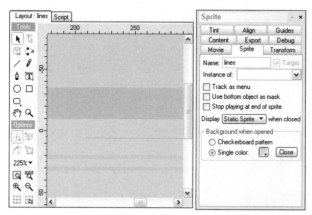

Figure 15-10: Choose a solid color background for working in the sprite's layout if it helps you to see the content more clearly.

5. **Click the object within the sprite that you want to work with to select it and modify it as desired.** You can also import content into the sprite while it is open.

Tip

If you like working in the expanded sprite's layout view, take a minute and open all the sprites you need to work with in your project. You can switch from one sprite to another or to the entire scene by clicking the names in the Outline panel. If you close SWiSHmax and then reopen it, the sprites that were opened remain open, so you can even work through a number of sessions.

6. **Click the sprite's name in the Outline panel to activate the Sprite panel.**

7. **Click Close to close the Sprite layout view and return to the project's Layout panel.**

Note

You can also click the plus (+) button to the left of the sprite in the Outline panel to close its hierarchy or click the Scene's name in the Timeline to close the sprite's layout view.

Tip

You can toggle views between the sprite's layout view and the scene's layout view. When the sprite's layout view is open, click anywhere on the Outline panel aside from the sprite's name or any of its child objects to toggle the regular Layout panel visibility. To return to the sprite's layout view, click the sprite's name again. The sprite's layout view isn't closed until you close it using one of the methods described in the steps.

Understanding the sprite's layout view

While you are in the sprite's layout view take a look at the rulers on the Layout panel's margins. The regular Layout panel uses values on the rulers to define the scene's coordinates. When you open a sprite in the sprite's layout view you see the content using the sprite's coordinates. Here's an example.

In the sample project, the entire movie is shown in the Layout panel. The numbering on the rulers shows the X- and Y-axis positions starting at the upper left of the scene's stage with coordinates of 0,0. The sprite's location is shown at coordinates -10, 58 in the Transform panel.

When the sprite in the sample project is opened, it seems to have moved. That isn't the case—the rulers show the coordinates in relation to the sprite when you use the sprite's layout view. The coordinates are defined based on the sprite's anchor point. In the sample project its anchor point is the center left, as seen in Figure 15-11.

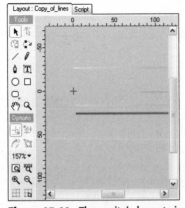

Figure 15-11: The sprite's layout view is based on the coordinates of the sprite.

Often when you open a sprite in its layout view it is difficult to see what you are working with. Choose View ➪ Fit Objects in Window to adjust the contents of the sprite in the Layout panel.

Tip   The Fit Objects in Window command applies to sprites only; it works the same way as the Fit Scene in Window command works for the entire scene's contents.

Editing a sprite object

Often, you build a sprite because you want to have one object contain a number of other animated objects that you may or may not want to use more than once in a project. Here are some tips for editing a sprite object:

✦ **A sprite is a simple object with specific physical characteristics, some of which can be modified like other simple objects.** You can modify:

- Scale

- Rotation/Skew

- Location on the movie's stage; that is, the X- and Y-coordinates

- Anchor Point

- Color

- Alpha value

✦ **A sprite is originally sized according to the size of its contents.** If a sprite contains an image having dimensions of 200 x 200 pixels, then the sprite is sized at 200 x 200 pixels; if it has numerous objects, the size of the sprite is the distance between the left side of the object furthest to the left and the right side of the object furthest to the right. If objects in a sprite are not overlapping, the size of the sprite is based on the size of the objects plus the distance in pixels between the objects.

✦ **If you resize a sprite, resize its contents proportionally.**

✦ **You apply effects to the sprite as a single object.** The content of the sprite will continue to do its thing according to the effects you applied to each of its child objects, and the entire sprite is then animated further.

✦ **You aren't restricted to a specific Timeline length for a sprite.** The component sprites in your scene can have their own timelines of differing lengths. In the sample project, for example, one sprite has a length of 50 frames, another 20 frames, and the scene's Timeline is 60 frames in length.

Playing Sprites

The main Timeline of your movie plays regardless of the animation inside a sprite. When the main Timeline reaches its end, and advances automatically to the next scene, any frames of sprites within that Timeline that haven't played are dropped. For example, on a Timeline of 60 frames, if one sprite's animation is 50 frames, starting from Frame 1, and a second sprite's animation is 20 frames, starting at Frame 51, the final 10 frames of the second sprite won't play before the scene changes.

On the other hand, if the main Timeline is 60 frames, and contains a sprite that is 20 frames long, the sprite's Timeline can play through three times before the scene changes.

Working with a blank sprite

Working with a blank sprite is the same as working with other sprites. You can open the sprite in the Layout panel or in the sprite's layout view. As with other sprites, a blank sprite also has its own Timeline. To add content to a blank sprite in the sprite's layout view, follow these steps:

1. **Click the sprite's name in the Outline panel or click the icon on the Layout panel to select it.** A solid bounding box and resize handles appear around the edges of the sprite.

2. **Click Open in Layout on the Sprite panel to display the sprite's layout view in the Layout panel.** Of course, the view is blank as there is no content.

3. **Choose Insert on the Outline panel and choose an option to add content to the sprite's layout view.** You can also choose one of these options to add content:

   • Right-click the sprite's layout view and choose Insert and an option

   • Click the appropriate button on the Insert toolbar

   • Use the drawing tools and draw a shape

   • Click the Instance of dropdown arrow on the Sprite panel and choose a sprite from the list

Tip   Once you add a sprite to your movie project, the next time you open an Insert menu in the program the Instance option appears on the list of objects.

4. **Make any transform adjustments and add effects to the imported content as required.**

5. **Click Close to close the sprite's layout view.**

In the sample project, the sprites named **cog** and **label** were each added to the project initially as blank sprites.

On The Web Site   The sample project used in this discussion is available from the book's Web site. It is named ch15_sample01.swi, and is located in the ch15_sample01 subfolder within the chapter15 folder. The finished movie, ch15_sample01.swf, and the source image are also in the folder.

Using an Instance of a Sprite

An *instance* is a clone of a sprite. Some of the features of the original sprite, called a *reference sprite* when cloned, can be modified in an instance while others can't. You can adjust transform properties such as scale or the instance's location on the stage without affecting the sprite or object from which the instance was cloned.

Caution   An instance is not the same as a copy. A copy is a separate sprite altogether and isn't tied in any way to the reference sprite. A copy is an object similar to the original but you can change it internally such as changing color of the sprite's Timeline without affecting the reference sprite.

Follow these steps to add an instance to your movie:

1. **Click the scene name or the name of the sprite to which you want to add the instance to select it.**

2. **Choose Insert ⇨ Instance to open the Insert Instance dialog box.** You can also choose from these methods to open the dialog box:

   - Choose Edit ⇨ Make Instance

   - On the outline panel, click Insert ⇨ Instance

   - Right-click the stage on the Layout panel, the label column on the Timeline, or the scene's name in the Outline panel and select Insert ⇨ Instance from the shortcut menu

3. **Click the Instance of down arrow to display a list of objects you can use to generate an instance, as seen in Figure 15-12.**

Figure 15-12: Choose the sprite or object from which you want to generate an instance.

> **Tip**
>
> The object selected when you choose an Insert ⇨ Instance command is not included on the list of possible instance objects.

4. **Click the object you want to use for the instance to select it.**

5. **Click OK to close the Insert Instance dialog box and add the instance to your movie.**

> **Note**
>
> In Figure 15-12, the OK and Cancel buttons are hidden by the drop-down list.

The instance is added to the scene. In the Outline view and Timeline it is named **Instance of xx** (the name of the selected sprite or object); instances display their own type of icon on the Outline panel, as seen in Figure 15-13.

Figure 15-13: An instance is identified by its own icon and label in the Outline panel.

6. **In the Sprite panel, click the name field and rename the instance.** It saves space if you name an instance and even if you remove the word "Instance," you can still distinguish an instance from other types of objects based on its icon.

Adding an instance from the Content panel

The Content panel contains several folders listing some types of objects used in your movie project including a folder for sprites. In addition to adding instances through a menu, you can also add an instance from the Content panel.

Follow these steps to add an instance from the Content panel:

1. **Click the Content panel's tab to bring it to the front of the panel group.**

2. **Click the name of the sprite you want to use as the reference for your instance as shown in Figure 15-14.**

3. **Click Add to Scene, or drag the sprite's name from the Content panel to the Layout panel.** An instance is added to the project.

Note   Instances are not defined as separate sprites in the Content panel, nor are they included in the Sprites folder in the Content panel.

Figure 15-14: You can add an instance to your movie from the Content panel.

Swapping instances

You may add an instance to your movie and then discover that an alternate reference sprite would have been a better choice. You can easily swap instances in SWiSHmax. Follow these steps to change an instance of one sprite to an instance of another sprite:

1. **Click the instance you want to change in the Outline panel to select it.**

2. **On the Sprite panel, click the Instance of drop-down arrow.** The list of existing objects you can use as reference sprites appears.

3. **Click to choose the replacement from the list.** The Instance of list closes, and the instance is swapped.

In the Outline panel, the name is replaced with that of the replacement object as well.

Modifying an instance

Instances have advantages and drawbacks. As you learn to work with them, you begin to understand their characteristics and behavior. Here are some tips to help you understand some of their characteristics.

✦ **Using instances saves you editing time.** If you want to change some feature of a sprite and replicate it through all its instances you can do that in one process. Select the reference sprite and make the changes as required, such as changing effects, color, or actions. All instances are changed, and any instances you add in the future logically have the amended properties as well.

✦ **Opening an instance opens the reference sprite.** Be careful when working with an instance. If you select an instance and then click Open in Layout on the Sprite panel, the parent sprite is opened instead of the instance.

✦ **Safely change "external" properties of an instance.** You can change the characteristics of an instance such as its physical dimensions, orientation, alpha, and color — in other words, the external properties of the instance. You can't change the internal properties; those must be changed on the parent sprite's Timeline.

Note

In the sample project, you can see examples of modified instances. The movie uses a sprite named **cog**, and one instance named **little_cog**, which is 15 percent of the size of the original object; it has another instance named **big_cog**, which is the size of the original object and has an Alpha value of 20 percent.

Using sprite copies

Instead of using an instance of a sprite, use a copy if you want to have an object that is similar to the original but changed internally in some way such as changing characteristics of the component objects or modifying the sprite's Timeline. For example, the sample movie has one sprite named lines, which is the set of horizontal animated lines. It also has a copy of the sprite named **Copy_of_lines**.

Select the sprite you want to use and press Ctrl+C. Then click the scene's name in the Outline panel and press Ctrl+V to add a copy. The copy is a separate object and not tied to the original sprite; as a result it can be edited completely independently. In the finished movie, the copy of the sprite has changes made to its Timeline, which don't affect the reference sprite or other instances.

Note

Also in the finished movie, the sprite is rotated 180 degrees which could be accomplished using either an instance or a copy.

As you can see in Figure 15-15, the copy shows a sprite icon in the Outline panel and is listed as a separate sprite in the Content panel.

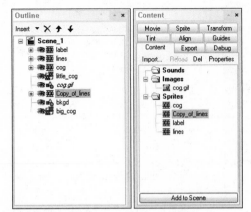

Figure 15-15: Use a copy instead of an instance if you want to change options on the sprite's Timeline or change its components.

Masking Objects Using Sprites

Masking is a very effective technique for creating interesting animations. In order to use masking in SWiSHmax you need to work with a sprite. The object you are using for the mask must be a simple object or a text object. A *mask* is an image with defined areas of transparency that are used to control the visibility of other elements in the sprite; the edges of the mask are defined by the border of the image file.

On The Web Site

The sample project used in this discussion is available from the book's Web site. It is named ch15_sample02.swi, and is located in the ch15_sample02 subfolder within the chapter15 folder. The finished SWF movie, ch15_sample02.swf, is also in the folder.

Follow these steps to create a masked sprite object:

1. **Assemble the components for the sprite.** You need one object that has defined filled areas through which the animation appears. You can configure each object for the sprite as you like using color, effects, and so on.

2. **Arrange the objects on the Outline panel or Timeline.** The sample project uses three elements as shown in Figure 15-16. The lowest element is the rounded rectangle, which you can see on the Layout panel. The grouped object, created from a square broken into pieces, is hidden in Figure 15-16 so you can see the shape used for the mask on the Layout panel's stage.

3. **Select the objects on the Outline panel, the Layout panel, or the Timeline.**

4. **Using a Grouping ➪ Group as Sprite command, combine the objects into a sprite.**

5. **On the Sprite panel, click the Use bottom object as mask option.**

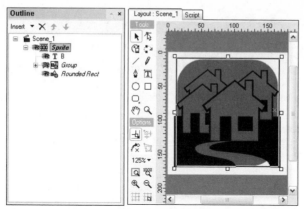

Figure 15-16: The bottom object in the sprite is used as a mask.

6. **Test the movie.** The animation appears through the rounded rectangle-shaped "window" as seen in Figure 15-17.

Figure 15-17: The masking object creates a window effect in the animation.

While you are working, the mask layer is visible in the Layout panel and its effects aren't applied. However, the mask layer is hidden when you are previewing or exporting the movie or playing the Timeline. Whether the mask layer itself is toggled to visible or hidden in the Outline panel has no effect on the exported movie.

Tip

In the sample masking project, the image of the houses is represented in the Outline panel by a Text symbol and the letter B. The image is not really an image at all, but the letter B symbol from the Wingdings font. When you are looking for simple shapes and images, look through the symbol fonts on your system.

Cross-Reference

More on working with text and characters can be found in Chapter 10. See Chapter 8 to learn how to define transparency.

Masked Sprites

Guest author Ian Hinckley points out that when you select Use bottom layer as mask in the Sprite panel, the sprite boundary will retract to the size of the bottom layer and thus all the other content of the sprite will have strange co-ordinates as does the sprite itself, which will report its size equal to the bottom layer even if it contains a number of other objects.

If you find this a strange feature, the simple way around it is to build your sprite as normal and then only when you have completed the design set Use bottom layer as mask. If you need to make further amendments to the sprite, just deselect the mask checkbox before you make your changes, then reset afterwards. This will prevent you from tearing your hair out while building reproducible tutorials.

Using a Sprite as a Targeted Object

Sprites are defined as scripting objects by default, meaning they can be the target of actions generated in other areas of your movie. For example, clicking a button can cause a sprite object to play.

When you create a sprite, the Target option in the Sprite panel is selected by default and the option is grayed out, meaning you can't change its status as a scripting object. Unless you name a sprite, however, it is impossible to use it as a target object.

In the example shown in Figure 15-18, the scene in the Outline panel contains three sprites as well as a button. One of the sprites is named and the other two use the default **Sprite** name.

The example shows the construction of a very simple script for a button. When the user clicks the button, the sprite plays. To write a script for an object, you need to define the target upon which the action occurs.

Look at the drop-down list of Targets in the Script panel shown in the figure. As you can see, the only object that can be selected is the one called **named_sprite**; the other two unnamed sprites are not included in the list.

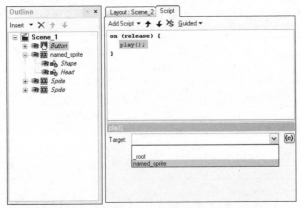

Figure 15-18: Name sprites to use them as targets for scripted actions.

You can also refer to a sprite nested within another sprite to use as a target. The sprite is referenced based on its location in the movie's hierarchy. In the example in Figure 15-19, the same scene structure as that seen in Figure 15-18 appears with one addition: nested within the **named_sprite** sprite is another sprite named **nested_sprite**. In the Script window, the Target drop-down list includes the nested sprite, identified as **named_sprite.nested_sprite**. The levels are identified by inserting a period (.) between each object's level.

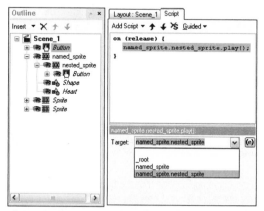

Figure 15-19: A nested sprite is named according to the movie's hierarchy when defining it as a target.

Understanding Hierarchical Names

If you have built any SWiSHmax projects using sprites, you have been working with object orienting programming (OOP) concepts. OOP is based on hierarchical relationships, including *referencing*, or naming of objects. Referencing uses standard rules for writing an object's name.

These rules are called *syntax* and include combinations of words, spacing, and punctuation that a program will understand.

Cross-Reference
Starting in Chapter 17, read about scripting and how to write and work with scripts in SWiSHmax.

Object referencing is based on a hierarchical relationship to either the root of the movie or to an object's parent. You have seen how objects behave within a sprite, and how sprites can be nested within more sprites. There are three levels of referencing:

_root

This term refers to the top-most object in a description. In SWiSHscript, **_root** refers to the main movie you are working in.

_parent

This term refers to an object that contains child objects. The main Timeline of a movie is both a root and a parent. A group named GroupX that is a child of the parent movie is written as **_root.GroupX**. You can also write the object's reference as **_parent.GroupX** as the main movie is the parent of the group object.

You can use multiple levels of parent/child relationships to reference objects that are identified in a string separated by a period (.). For example, an object is named **ShapeZ** and is four levels down in the hierarchy from the main Timeline. The scene contains a group named **GroupX** containing a sprite named **SpriteY** that contains an object **ShapeZ**. The fully referenced name for **ShapeZ** is **_root.GroupX.SpriteY.ShapeZ**.

The complete string identifying the relationship of levels of objects in a movie isn't always necessary; instead, it is based upon where the reference originates. Using the example, if you want to refer to the shape named **ShapeZ** that is part of the sprite named **SpriteY**, you can refer to it as **.ShapeZ**.

this

The term **this.** is used by an object to refer to itself. For example, the horizontal scale of an object can be written as **this._xscale**; the coordinates of an object on the X-axis can be written as **this._x**.

Cross-Reference   Referencing is not limited to names of objects. Chapters 17 through 19 describe scripting processes that include hierarchical references.

Caution   SWiSHscript recognizes *slash notation,* although it has been deprecated and dot notation is preferred. Slash *notation* is a system of defining hierarchies based on using the slash (/) character; the slash notation is converted to a hierarchy as described here. For example, the reference **_root.GroupX.SpriteY.ShapeZ** has a slash notation name equivalent of **/GroupX/ SpriteY/ShapeZ**.

Summary

Sprites are very handy objects, as you have seen in this chapter. They can control their own animation independently and then be added to a larger movie. You can nest Timelines within Timelines; you are restricted only by how difficult it is to organize a movie using a large number of nested levels.

Sprites can be created in a number of ways. All sprites share some characteristics, and you can reuse a sprite at will in your movie by creating instances of it. You learned that an instance is directly associated with the referencing object — the original sprite — and changing an instance can change the original sprite and any other instances in your movie.

You saw that you could use copies of a sprite if you want to make slight changes internally, and that instances can be changed independently with regard to basic object transformations such as location on the Layout panel or rotation. You saw how one object in a sprite can be used as a mask through which the rest of the sprite's objects play. You also discovered how sprites work as targets and how important their naming is with regard to programming your movie projects. In this chapter, you also learned:

✦ Different ways to create a sprite, including importing animations and creating blank sprites

✦ That you can modify a sprite on its own Timeline

✦ To edit a sprite in the Layout panel or by using the sprite's layout view

✦ That clones of a sprite are called instances and can have modified transformation properties

✦ How to use a copy of a sprite if you want to change some of the characteristics of the sprite's elements

✦ That a sprite can designate one layer as a mask through which the rest of the sprite's content appears

✦ How to name sprites and how objects are related to other objects in a movie

✦   ✦   ✦

Building Buttons

Buttons are a fundamental means by which you make your way through a SWiSHmax movie. You can use buttons for navigation, running scripts, submitting data — virtually anything termed *interactive* usually has some sort of button object associated with it.

A button is a simple object. Buttons include four states that correspond with four interactive conditions. You are accustomed to having cues that help identify when an object is a button. Sometimes it is easy to tell an object is a button: for example, text on a page that reads "Click Me" is rather self-evident.

When you position your mouse over a button, the regular mouse cursor changes to a pointing finger. The cursor change indicates that the object is active; clicking it or interacting with it in some fashion is going to produce some outcome.

You can provide more cues to your viewer than a change of cursor appearance. In this chapter, you learn about the button states and the different methods you can use to distinguish one from another for your viewer. You also learn how to create interactivity in your movie by attaching actions to buttons.

Understanding Button Objects

Buttons come in all varieties. In SWiSHmax, you can create a button from most any other type of object. A button can contain animations created in sprites. You can use images, text, sound, or a combination of objects including groups for the Up, Over, and Down states. You can't use a button object within another button object in any state.

Buttons are simple objects even though they can have complicated content and scripting. Buttons are similar to a group although you can't ungroup them.

In SWiSHmax, buttons have four states:

+ **Up state.** This is the default state for a button. The Up state is the way the button appears on the movie prior to any viewer interaction and whenever the mouse is outside the button's area.

+ **Over state.** This is the button's appearance as your viewer moves the mouse over the button. Generally, the Over state is different from the Up state to cue your viewers to the fact that it is an active element that they can interact with.

✦ **Down state.** This state also provides cues to your viewer. Use the Down state to represent a button that has been clicked.

✦ **Hit state.** This state is invisible and defines the active area of the button. Only shapes or text can be used as Hit state content.

Adding a Button to Your Project

As with other objects in SWiSHmax, you can create buttons in a number of ways. To create a button, you can:

✦ Insert a blank button

✦ Convert existing content to a button

✦ Group existing content as a button

Inserting a blank button adds a button object to the movie but it contains no content. Converting and grouping objects as a button are similar. In fact, the process is identical if you have only one object that you are changing to a button object. Grouping and converting processes work differently if you are changing two or more objects.

Inserting a blank button

Sometimes when you are getting a project started you know what you want the movie to contain, but you don't have the material ready. Other times you may want to experiment with your movie's layout or function. Rather than taking the time to import or draw objects, you can insert a blank button into your movie and then add content to the blank button whenever you want. Follow these steps to add a blank button to your movie:

1. **Click the Scene name in the Outline panel or the stage in the Layout panel to select it.** You define the location where the button is to be placed.

2. **Choose Insert ➪ Button from the Outline panel menu.** You can also choose Insert ➪ Button from the Insert menu or click the Insert Button icon on the Insert toolbar. A button shape is added to the Layout panel's stage, the button is listed in the Outline panel, and the Button panel is active in the program's panel group, as seen in Figure 16-1. When the button is deselected, it displays a button shape on the Layout panel as you can also see in the figure.

3. **In the Button panel, click in the Name field and type a name for the button.** Your button is now ready to add content to.

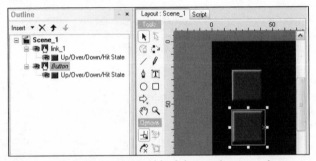

Figure 16-1: You can insert a blank button into a project.

Grouping objects as a button

If you have one object you plan to change to a button, the outcome is the same whether you use grouping or converting options. Grouping one or more objects as a button produces one button that uses the default name **Button**.

Select the object or objects you want to use for a button in your movie's scene. Then choose one of these program locations to group the object or objects as a button:

✦ Right-click the object on the Outline panel, the Layout panel, or the Timeline and choose Grouping ⇨ Group as Button

✦ Choose Modify ⇨ Grouping ⇨ Group as Button from the program menu

✦ Click the Group as Button button on the Grouping toolbar

Converting objects to buttons

The Convert commands work on each object separately. So, if you have selected one object to convert to a button, the result is one button; if you select five objects to convert, the result is five buttons.

Select the object or objects you want to use for a button in your movie's scene. Then choose one of these command options to convert the object or objects to a button:

✦ Right-click the object on the Outline panel, the Layout panel, or the Timeline, and choose Convert ⇨ Convert to Button

✦ Choose Modify ⇨ Convert ⇨ Convert to Button from the program menu

✦ Click the Convert to Button button on the Grouping toolbar

In Figure 16-2, you can see an example of three buttons, each produced by one of the button-creation processes discussed. The example started with four objects — two of which are grouped as a button and two of which are converted to buttons.

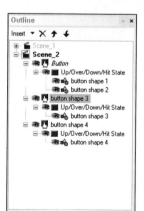

Figure 16-2: Grouping and converting commands can result in different button structures.

The button named **Button** was created using the Group as Button command. The four button states are a child of the button object, and the two original objects are child objects of the of the button states.

Contrast that with the buttons named **button shape 3** and **button shape 4**. These two objects were selected and a Convert to Button command used. You see each becomes its own button, and its name is that of the object it contains. The original objects are each children of their button states.

Editing button content

There is no command you can use to change a button back into its component parts once you have grouped content in your movie as a button or converted an object to a button. This behavior is different than that seen when grouping objects as sprites or groups, which you can then ungroup using the Ungroup command. You can, however, reverse the process manually. Follow these steps to restore the status of button objects to individual objects:

Cross-Reference   Chapter 15 discusses working with sprites.

1. **Delete any button states or objects you don't plan to revert to individual objects.**

2. **Select the content of the button.** You can select one or more objects in the same button state.

3. **Press Ctrl+X, or choose Edit ⇨ Cut to place the content on the clipboard.**

4. **Click the scene's name on the Outline panel and press Ctrl+V, or choose Edit ⇨ Paste to paste the elements into the scene as individual objects.**

5. **Click the button object in the Outline panel to select it.** Delete the button object.

Defining Button States

The default button combines all four states into one unit. However, you can identify separate button states in the Button panel. To separate button states from the single unit, you have to select the states you want to separate in the Button panel as shown in Figure 16-3. You can also right-click the button on the Outline panel, Layout panel, or Timeline, and toggle the separate states on and off.

Figure 16-3: Define the states you want to use in the Button panel.

When you add a button object to your project the Button panel is active and contains these options:

✦ **Name.** Click in the Name field to make it active and then type a name for your button. As soon as you type a name the Target option is active.

✦ **Target.** Click this option to define the button as a target. You more commonly use the button's states to generate action rather than have a button as a target of an action.

✦ **Track as menu.** Click this option to define how the button behaves when the mouse is clicked. The default is to track as a pushbutton; that is, the Track as menu option is not selected. When tracking as a menu, you can click a button and move the cursor to revert to the Up state of the button, unlike the pushbutton mode where the mouse's actions are restricted to the button until you release the mouse. If you click a button and drag away from the button, the button remains active until you release the mouse.

✦ **Has separate over state.** Click this option to add a separate Over state to the button. You can customize the content of the state that is seen when the viewer positions the mouse over the button, which is called a *rollover*.

✦ **Has separate down state.** Click this option to add a separate Down state to the button. You can customize the content of the state that is seen when the viewer clicks the button, which is called a *press*.

✦ **Has separate hit state.** Click this option to add a separate Hit state for the button. You can resize the amount of space that is used to define the button's perimeter. If you choose this option, the Use bounding box for hit-state option is removed from the Button panel.

✦ **Use bounding box for hit-state.** This is the default option for buttons. You can leave the option to use the bounding box surrounding the button's content as the perimeter of the button's activation area. If you click the check box to deselect the option, the shape or letters used in the button define the perimeter of the active area.

When you define different states for your button, they are added to the Outline panel as shown in Figure 16-4. Each object that was part of the initial button is copied to each button state. The relationship between the objects doesn't change in that each state is still a child object of the button object, and each shape is a child object of the state.

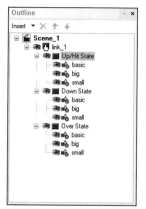

Figure 16-4: Separating states for a button creates duplicate objects on the Outline panel.

In the example shown in the figure, the original button had three objects; defining separate states in the Button panel by clicking the states' options replicates the content in each state. The option to create a separate hit state wasn't selected—note that the Up/Hit state is combined in the button's structure. Toggle the different button states on and off by clicking the options in the Button panel.

Caution   You can't select a button state in the Outline panel and delete it; to remove a button state you have to deselect the option in the Button panel or from the shortcut menu.

Building Buttons

How you construct button state objects is a matter of preference and how you like to work. For example, Figure 16-4 shows three button states, each having a set of three shapes. The three shapes used for the button were created before the button object was defined. The button needs one shape for each state, and two of the three shapes have to be deleted from each button state.

Alternatively, one shape could have been used as the button object's content and then either the Convert to Button or Group as Button commands could be used to create the button. When the button states were defined, the single object would be copied to each state and then each state's shape would be customized.

Either approach produces the same outcome as that shown in Figure 16-5. In the figure, each button state that is defined separately in the Button panel now has one object used for the button state's appearance.

Figure 16-5: You can use different methods of creating content for button states.

Working with button states

Be careful when working with buttons in your movie. It can be difficult to work with the content unless you pay attention to what is selected. Here are some tips:

✦ Click the button's name in the Outline panel to select the entire button and activate the Button panel. Do this if you want to change the states, the name, or delete the button.

✦ If you click a state in the Outline panel, the Group panel appears in the program's panel group although you can't change any group options.

✦ If you click an object that is part of a button state its appropriate panel appears in the program's panel group. For example, clicking a shape or image object displays the Shape panel; clicking a sprite used in a button state displays the Sprite panel.

✦ Click the minus sign (-) to the left of the button's name on the Outline panel to close the button and hide the states and their content. Do this if you want to move the button on the stage, or change characteristics of the content of all the button states such as size or rotation.

✦ When you use multiple states in a button, the Up state is shown in the Layout panel by default. To see the content of another state, click its state in the Outline panel. You can't select another state's content from the Layout panel's stage.

✦ If your button's state has one object, click either the state's name in the Outline panel or the object's name to select it. If you click the state's name, the object is selected as soon as you click the stage.

✦ If the button's states have more than one object and you want to change one of the objects in the state, click the object's name in the Outline panel. The selected object and other objects in the same state are shown on the Layout panel.

✦ You can set button states using the shortcut menu. Right-click a closed button to open the shortcut menu as shown in Figure 16-6. The button states can be toggled as separate or not, and you can also define what states are shown on the stage.

Figure 16-6: You can set button options using the shortcut menu.

✦ If the button's state contains more than one object and you want to move the entire state's contents, click within the state's bounding box but not directly over one of the objects. You will notice different selection arrows appear depending on what you have selected on the Layout panel. A selected object shows a smaller arrow and you see its individual resize handles, as seen in the left image in Figure 16-7; if you click and select the entire state, the selection arrow is larger and no individual element is selected, as seen in the right image in Figure 16-7.

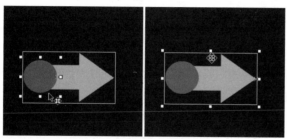

Figure 16-7: You see different selection arrows on the Layout panel depending on what is chosen.

✦ The bounding box looks different based on what you select. If a button is closed, when you select it the bounding box is a dashed line, as seen in the left image in Figure 16-8. If the button is open or you select a state, its bounding box is a solid line, as seen in the right image in Figure 16-8.

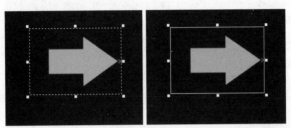

Figure 16-8: The entire button uses a different bounding box style than individual states.

✦ The different states' bounding boxes may be of different sizes depending on the size, arrangement, and location of the content. The left image in Figure 16-9 shows the bounding box for one state; the button's bounding box includes the entire states' margins is shown in the right image in Figure 16-9.

Caution

If you modify the content of the up, down, or over states the hit rectangle isn't automatically adjusted. You have to resize it manually. For example, if you create a button from a text object using the word **Click**, the hit rectangle is the size of the text. If you then change the text object to read **Please Click Here**, the hit rectangle stays at the original size, and won't cover the new text.

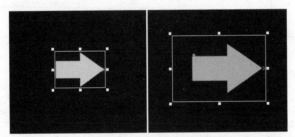

Figure 16-9: The button may show a different bounding box size and location than an individual state.

✦ When you want to add an object to a button state such as a text label or another shape, make sure to select the correct item in the Outline panel. In Figure 16-10, the button's name was selected in the Outline panel and the Layout panel clicked with the Text tool. Although it appears as though the text should become part of the button due to the appearance of the bounding box, when the text is added it isn't a part of the button but a separate object in the scene. You have to select a button state in the Outline panel in order for an object to be added to a state.

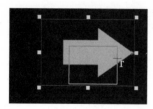

Figure 16-10: Make sure to select the correct listing in the Outline panel before adding objects to buttons.

On The Web Site

If you want to experiment with the button used in this discussion, you can find it on the book's Web site. The button is in the project ch16_sample01.swi that is in the ch16_sample01 folder within the chapter16 folder. Also in the folder, you will find the exported movie named ch16_sample01.swf.

Transforming button content

You can transform the content of a button's state at any time. Take care to select the object to which you want to apply changes either on the Outline panel or the Layout panel.

It is easier to create objects for a button before actually creating the button. Because you don't have to account for parent button states it is easier to configure the content. A simpler structure allows you to make changes to the content either singly or as a group, such as changing size, location, and so on. Another advantage is that you can align the content for the button states using the Align panel. When you are working with objects that are child objects of button states, you can't select them and use the Align panel commands.

Many buttons use the same size objects and locations for all states. It is easy to move the content of your buttons out of alignment. The simplest way to restore alignment uses the Transform panel. Select the object in one of the button states that is in the correct position. Click the Transform tab to display the Transform panel, and click Copy at the bottom of the panel. Select the object that is misaligned in one the states; again click the Transform tab to open the Transform panel, and click Paste. The pasted object includes the X and Y-axis coordinates as well as the horizontal and vertical scale, placing the pasted copy at the desired location.

Tip

You can also manually restore the alignment on the Layout panel by moving objects.

To display and work with all button states visible, follow these steps:

1. **In the Outline panel, click the minus sign (-) to the left of the button's name to close it.**

2. **Choose Edit ⇨ Show All States.** You can also right-click the button in the Outline panel or the Timeline, and click Show All States from the shortcut menu or click the button's eye icon on the Outline panel to cycle to the Show All States option.

Note

When you choose the Show All States command the button's eye icon changes to a stack of eyes rather than the single eye that the default visible icon displays.

3. **Click the plus sign (+) to the left of the button's name to open the button and display the button states.**

4. **Click the state you want to work with.** On the Layout panel the button's states are shown as semitransparent objects; the state you select in the Outline panel is more opaque than the other states' contents and is framed with a bounding box.

Note   The lower button shown in the figure uses the default settings, and the upper button uses the Show All States command.

5. **Make adjustments or transformations to the selected state's objects as desired.** In the sample seen in Figure 16-11 the Over state of the button is the active state, indicated by the solid line surrounding the object on the Layout panel, and the child text object is active, indicated by the dashed line surrounding the letters.

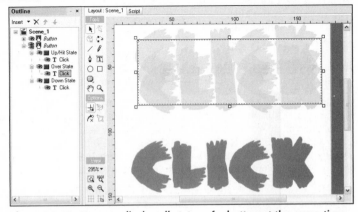

Figure 16-11: You can display all states of a button at the same time.

6. **Click other objects and other states to make changes as required.**

7. **Choose Edit ⇨ Show Up State only.** Alternately, you can right-click the button in the Outline panel or the Timeline and click Show Up State only from the shortcut menu or click the button's eye icon on the Outline panel to cycle to the Show Up State (default) option.

Tip   The menu command toggles between Show Up State only and Show All States.

Testing buttons

Buttons are interactive objects. Unless the movie is running, you can't see the button in action. Activate the button using one of these options:

✦ Click the Play button on the Control toolbar

✦ Click the Play Timeline button on the Control toolbar

✦ Choose Control ⇨ Play Movie

✦ Choose Control ⇨ Play Timeline

✦ Choose File ⇨ Test ⇨ In Player

When the movie is running, you see the Up state by default because that is the appearance of the button when there is no mouse interaction. Position your mouse over the button to see the rollover content in the Over state; click the mouse to see the content in the Down state.

Be sure to click the Stop button on the Control toolbar, or choose Control ⇨ Stop, before attempting to work further with the objects. If you test a button and then try to make changes but the program seems to falter check that the movie is stopped. When it is still running, it attempts to incorporate any changes you make into the preview display and restarts the movie playback.

Working with text buttons

It is simple to configure text for use as buttons in SWiSHmax. In the Text panel, shown in Figure 16-12, you can specify the button characteristics of text even before you convert the text to a button. The Text panel's Button settings include the option to use the bounding box to define the Hit state.

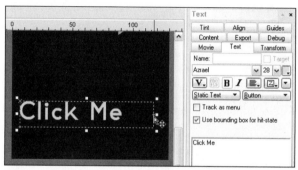

Figure 16-12: You can define the bounding box for a text button in the Text panel.

As you can see in the figure, clicking and dragging the right anchor point on the text box resizes the bounding box's dimensions. If the Use bounding box for hit-state option is selected in the Text panel, the entire space defined by the bounding box is active and responds to your viewer's mouse actions.

Cross-Reference Refer to Chapter 10 for information on working with text in SWiSHmax.

You can use a Group as Button or Convert to Button command to change the text to a button as you would for converting shapes or other objects. Figure 16-13 shows the text seen in Figure 16-12 after converting it to a button. The bounding box is the same size as that selected in the Text panel when the button was a text object.

Figure 16-13: After conversion, the bounding box size remains as defined in the Text object.

Note The bounding box shown in the figures is not seen in the sample movie. The sample movie uses the actual size of the text as the bounding box margins.

Each copy of a text object used in a button state can be modified. Click the text object in the Outline panel to select it. The Text panel is activated in the program's panel group. Modify the text characteristics as desired such as changing to Bold or Italic, change color, change font, and so on.

If you have made a set of text buttons by copying and pasting one button, check the individual buttons' hit areas. Changing a long string of text to a shorter string won't change the size of the hit area automatically.

Using sprites in buttons

Static buttons are fine and cue the viewer to action based on color, size, text, or other simple changes. You can add sprites to buttons for some real visual impact. The sprites are added to a button state in the same ways as you add other types of content. Sprites are commonly used to animate the Up state, the way the button appears on the movie when the viewer isn't interacting with it; they are also often used for the Over state, creating an animated rollover when viewers move the mouse over the button.

To use a sprite in a movie you can either construct it prior to building the basic buttons or convert an object you have inserted in a button state to a sprite and animate it. In addition to defining which state(s) of the button includes animation, you also have to decide whether the animation is going to repeat or run one time only. Select the sprite in the Outline panel and click the Stop playing at end of sprite option on the Sprite panel to deselect it if you want the sprite to loop during the button's play.

 Caution If you add an effect to an object and plan to convert it to a sprite within a button, you can't test the effect from the Settings dialog box. You must interact with the button while the movie is running in order to see the effect.

If you attach the sprite to the Up button state, the effect is visible as soon as the movie begins to play. If you attach the sprite to the Over or Down states, you have to use the mouse to interact with the button to see the sprite in action.

The sample movie contains copies of both the text and arrow buttons each having a sprite animating one or more button states as you can see in Figure 16-14. The text button copy is named **click_me2** and the arrow button copy is named **link_2**. The text button's Over state text is a sprite and uses a transform effect. The **link_2** button's Up state arrow is a sprite and uses two blur effects.

Figure 16-14: Test your sprite's effects while the movie is running.

The length of a sprite's Timeline doesn't have an impact on how your movie works. How your viewer sees the animation is a combination of the length of the sprite's Timeline and how long the viewer is interacting with the button state.

On The Web Site
The SWF movie exported from the sample project described in this discussion is available from the book's Web site. The movie is named ch16_sample01.swf and is in the ch16_sample01 folder within the chapter16 folder.

Tracking settings

The behavior of buttons as you drag the mouse away from the hit area depends on the Track setting you choose for the button. You can choose the Track as menu option from a variety of objects' panels.

The default setting for a button is to Track as a button. In that state, the button *captures* the mouse. When the Track as menu option is selected, the mouse isn't captured. The difference is subtle. Figure 16-15 shows two images of two shapes that are converted to buttons.

The image at the left of Figure 16-15 shows the Track as button setting. The mouse is shown after clicking the button and then dragging off the button to another area of the movie stage without releasing the mouse button. The color of the button reverts to its Up state but the mouse is still active. As you can see in the image, the hand cursor appears although the mouse is moved away from the button. The mouse remains in the captured state until the button is released.

The image on the right side of Figure 16-15 shows the Track as menu setting. When the bottom button is clicked its Over state is seen. However, dragging the mouse off the button to another area of the movie stage returns the button to its default Up state and the mouse to its default cursor even if the button is still depressed (meaning the user has not yet released the mouse button).

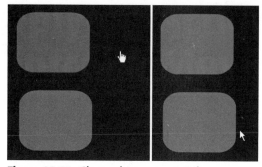

Figure 16-15: Choose how you want the mouse to respond to your buttons.

Creating Button Menus

Sometimes you have one button that performs a single action; more often, you have a set of buttons that are used as a menu for your movie. Plan ahead to save yourself construction time. In the sample movie ch16_sample02.swi, three similar buttons are constructed. Each button contains content for all button states.

On The Web Site

The sample movie described in this discussion is available from the book's Web site. It is named ch16_sample02.swi and is in the ch16_sample02 subfolder within the chapter16 folder. The exported SWF movie, ch16_sample02.swf is also in the folder along with the sound file used for a button action.

Here are some tips to consider when constructing a menu containing several buttons:

✦ Consider the content of each button carefully and determine what elements are constant throughout the set of buttons. Construct these elements for the first button, and then copy the button and paste the rest of the set of buttons to your movie project.

✦ If your buttons are complex in terms of their content, such as those using several sprites, complete one button to your satisfaction first before creating the other buttons. It is simpler to experiment with one button and then copy the button than to try to remember settings to duplicate from one button to another.

✦ If your buttons use content for each state, when possible construct all the content for the first button in all states before creating the other buttons. This way, not only are the buttons copied and pasted; all the content in the various states is copied and pasted as well.

✦ Establish a methodical approach when customizing a set of buttons. For example, you may want to use the same technique for one button state throughout your set of buttons. Open that button state for all buttons and collapse the remaining button states. Not only will you save space on the Outline panel, as seen in Figure 16-16, but also you see only those button states you are working with.

Figure 16-16: Develop a method of keeping track of the button states you are working with in your project.

✦ Lock content in your movie that you don't want to disturb while you are constructing your buttons. In the sample project, both the text heading for the page and the line used as a "clothesline" from which the buttons "hang" are locked to prevent them moving during the button construction process.

✦ Organize the buttons in the Outline panel and Timeline in the same order as they appear on the movie. In the sample movie, the three buttons are listed from top to bottom in the Outline panel and Timeline and from left to right on the stage in the Layout panel.

✦ Consider how many buttons you have in the movie when deciding on button names. In the sample project, there are only three buttons so it is simple to use descriptive names. It is convenient to name text-based buttons using their text as the name. For complex menus you might use both a number (to represent the location on the movie) and a text name for identification.

✦ If you are using behaviors or sounds for your buttons that are similar, consider adding them to the first button before copying and pasting.

Using Disjointed Rollovers

A rollover can be associated with the button object showing another color, text, or a sprite; it can also show content elsewhere on the movie. You create a disjointed rollover when the content seen during a mouse event is located in another part of the stage.

In the sample movie, each button has a disjointed rollover in the Over state. When the viewer's mouse rolls over a swimsuit button, a text message and a background for the message appear on the movie, as seen in Figure 16-17.

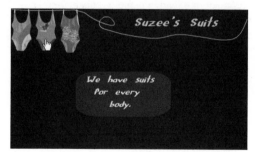

Figure 16-17: Use disjointed rollovers to display content elsewhere on the stage in response to button actions.

In a set of buttons and disjointed rollovers like that used in the sample project, it is important that the text messages and their background shapes be aligned on the stage. You can't see the content of more than one button at a time on the stage. Where each button's text block is of a different size, make note of the location of the first object and then align the remaining buttons' objects using the same X- and Y-axis locations. The sample project's objects use a lower-right anchor point position. When you test the button, be sure to note the alignment of the objects. You can use the guides and gridlines to assist in placement of disjointed objects as well.

If you use disjointed rollovers in your movie, make sure to use a separate hit state for the buttons. The default hit state area for one button may overlap that of another button.

Creating Button Events

A button has four states: Up, Over, and Down, as well as an invisible Hit state that defines the area of response to mouse actions. When you construct a button you can assign different appearances and characteristics to how the button appears during its different states or you can use the same appearance for all states.

A button is a type, or *class*, of object; each class of object has its own characteristics and events associated with it. Although there are only three visual states for a button, there are a number of *button events* that you can use. An event is an activity that is associated with an object class.

If you have experimented with building SWiSHmax buttons and assigning different appearances to the button states, when you test the button you see it responds to your mouse moving over the button or clicking the button. There are other mouse actions or keystrokes you can use to cause the same responses.

The mouse or key activity is called a *trigger*. Activating the trigger causes a *button event*. For example, moving the mouse over a button is the trigger that causes the on(rollOver) button event; clicking the mouse over a button is the trigger that causes the on(press) button event.

Note   Different types of objects have different events associated with them. Sprites, for example, have different events than buttons, which have different events than sounds.

You can use more than one button event at the same time. For example, pressing a specified key and clicking a mouse either over the button or outside the button's area can all make a Timeline play.

When the trigger interacts with the button object, it causes the named event, and an action results. A diagram of the button event process is shown in Figure 16-18.

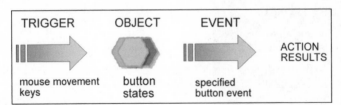

Figure 16-18: Button events occur as part of a sequence used to create interactivity.

In SWiSHmax you can choose these button events and triggers:

  ✦ on(press). Move the cursor over the button and click the left mouse button.

  ✦ on(release). Move the cursor over the button; click and release the left mouse button.

  ✦ on(rollOver). Move the cursor over the button from outside the button's hit area to within the button's hit area; no mouse click involved.

  ✦ on(rollOut). Move the cursor from a location within a button's hit area to outside the hit area; no mouse click involved.

✦ on(dragOut). Move the cursor from a location within the button's hit area to outside the button's hit area with the left mouse button pressed.

✦ on(dragOver). The on(DragOver) event can't occur without the on(dragOut) event occurring first. After moving the cursor from a location within the button's hit area to outside the button's hit area with the left button pressed, move the cursor back over the button's hit area again.

✦ on(releaseOutside). Press the left mouse button and move the cursor from a location within the button's hit area to outside the button's hit area and release the left mouse button.

✦ on (keyPress). Define the key; the event occurs when the key is pressed on the keyboard. Keys and mouse events can be used in combination.

Adding scripts to buttons

Unless your movie is designed strictly as a visual feast, when you click a button you want something to occur. The point of interactive movies is to provide interaction, and buttons are commonly used.

On The Web Site
The sample project ch16_sample02.swi contains scripts created using the processes in this discussion. The project and the ch16_sample02.swf files are in the ch16_sample02 folder within the chapter16 folder on the book's Web site.

Choosing event triggers

The process of writing a script for a button in SWiSHmax is similar regardless of what you want the button to do. The first part of the process is defining what button event to trigger. Follow these steps to define a trigger for a button script:

1. **Click the button name in the Outline panel to select it.** Make sure the button is closed.

2. **Click the Script panel's tab to display the panel.** The Script panel is tabbed with the Layout panel and uses the Guided mode as its default scripting mode.

3. **Click the Add Script drop-down arrow and then choose Events ⇨ Button ⇨ on(release), as seen in Figure 16-19.** The button event is added to the Script panel's text area.

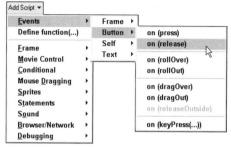

Figure 16-19: Start the script using a selection from the Add Script menus.

Using the menu path described in Step 3 you choose a button event option and then choose an event from the list. The text area of the Script panel shows the beginning of your button's script. When you select a button event, the Script panel displays the options you can use with button events, as seen in Figure 16-20. Click triggers' checkboxes to add or remove other triggers you want the script to use. Your choices include Press, Release, Roll over, Roll out, Drag over, and Drag out. You can also choose a key by clicking the arrow to the right of the Key field and choosing an option from the list.

Figure 16-20: The Script panel displays button event options.

The appearance of the Script panel depends on the type of event you are working with; learn more about the Script panel and scripting in Chapters 17-19.

Choosing a key trigger

You can choose keystroke options to use as triggers for button events from the same Script panel options. In the sample project, **Scene_2** contains both an `on(release)` button event as well as a keystroke option to create the action associated with the button named **back**. Follow these steps to add a keyPress button event to a script:

1. **Choose a button event; the sample project uses the** `on(release)` **event.**

You don't have to use both mouse and key triggers; you can use only keys. Deselect the chosen trigger from the list at the bottom of the Script panel.

2. **On the Script panel, click the Key drop-down arrow to display the menu.**

3. **Click a key option from the menu.** The menu closes and the key is added to the script in the text area and listed in the Key field at the bottom of the Script panel, as seen in Figure 16-21. The sample project uses the Enter key.

Figure 16-21 shows both the key menu as well as how the chosen key is written in the Script panel.

Figure 16-21: Choose a key trigger from the menu in the Script panel.

In the Script panel text area, you see:

```
on(release,keyPress("<Enter>")) {
    }
```

The script says that in addition to using the `on(release)` button event — clicking and releasing the mouse on the button — the action is also triggered by pressing the Enter key on the keyboard.

Defining Button Actions

After you have defined button events, you can give the movie something to do when you trigger the button event by clicking and releasing the mouse over the button. One common action that occurs when you click a button is that a sound plays. Another common action that occurs when you click a button is that your movie plays another scene or area of the Timeline. This discussion shows you how to use both of these types of action.

Using a sound action is a simple way to add a cue to a button for your user. You can use either MP3 or WAV sounds.

Cross-Reference   Chapter 11 has information about working with sound files in SWiSHmax.

Follow these steps to attach a sound action to a button after you have defined a trigger or triggers:

1. **On the Script panel click the Add Script button to open the menu and choose Sound ➪ Play Sound(...).** The menu closes and the Script panel changes to a panel used for working with sound objects. The beginning of the playSound action is added to the upper text area in the Script window, as seen in Figure 16-22.

Figure 16-22: You can add a sound action to the button in the Script panel.

Note

In Guided mode, the text is shown in red in the Script panel when the script is incomplete; text in a complete script is shown in blue.

2. **Click the sound file you want to use from the list at the bottom of the Script panel to select it.**

Note

If you haven't imported any sounds to use in your movie, there won't be any listed in the playSound area of the Script panel. Click Import to open an Open dialog box and locate the sound you want to use.

3. **Check the script in the upper area of the Script panel.** You see the script is completed and the text is blue. You can test the sound action in the movie or wait until you have finished the scripting.

Cross-Reference

The playSound and stopSound actions can't be triggered by the on(releaseOutside), on(dragOver), or on(dragOut) button events because of Flash Player limitations. You can put the sound in a sprite to use the button events. Using Sound events is described in Chapter 18.

The second script that is attached to the buttons produces a change in what the viewer sees when they click the button. That is, when the on(release) event occurs, the second scene in the movie plays.

Follow these steps to add a movie control action to a button after you have defined a trigger or triggers:

1. **On the Script panel click the Add Script button to open the menu and choose Movie Control ⇨ goToAndPlay(...) ⇨ goToAndPlay(FRAME).** The menu closes and the Script panel changes to that used for working with scenes and movies. The beginning of the action is added to the upper text area in the Script window. The script reads:

```
gotoSceneAndPlay("<current scene>",1);
```

The current scene is identified as the scene that will play; you want viewers to go to the next scene when they click and release the mouse button.

2. **Click the drop-down arrow for the Target field to display a list of the target objects in the movie, as shown in Figure 16-23.**

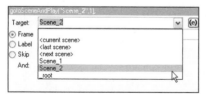

Figure 16-23: Choose a scene for viewers to see when they click and release the button.

3. **Choose the scene you want the movie to display as a result of the action.** In the sample project, Scene_2 is selected from the Target drop-down list. The list closes and the scene's name appears in the Target field as well as in the script at the top of the Script panel.

Tip

You can specify the frame number in the dialog box and also whether the scene plays or stops. The sample movie uses the default options.

4. **Reorder the actions if necessary.** As seen in Figure 16-24 the actions have been reordered. Click the playSound action and then click the up arrow at the top of the Script window to move the action to the top of the list. You want the sound to play before the scenes change.

5. **Click the Layout panel to display the movie's contents.**

6. **Play the movie and test the buttons and their actions.**

Figure 16-24: Change the order of the actions in the Script window.

In the sample movie, all three swimsuit buttons on the first scene use the same two `on(release)` actions. On Scene_2 of the movie the arrow button uses two button events — `on(KeyPress)` using the Enter key, as well as the `on(release)` button event.

Summary

Buttons are an integral part of a project when you want your viewer to interact with your movie. In this chapter, you discovered how buttons are constructed, used, and scripted in SWiSHmax. You learned different ways to add buttons to your movie and how to convert content to buttons. You saw how to work with button states and how to use other objects, such as text and sprites, in your buttons. You learned about button events and how to add two common types of actions to a button — a sound effect and an action to show another scene in the movie. You also learned how to:

✦ Add a blank button to your project and convert existing content in your movie into buttons

✦ Work with the different button states and modify the objects in the states

✦ Use sprites and text in buttons

✦ Define the way the mouse interacts with buttons

✦ Identify button events and triggers, and write scripts for buttons including actions to play sounds and display another scene

✦ ✦ ✦

Adding Interactivity to a Movie

✦   ✦   ✦   ✦

✦   ✦   ✦   ✦

Writing Scripts in the Script Panel

You use interactivity in one form or another for a broad range of events and actions ranging from clicking buttons to typing text to choosing which music plays in the background of your movie.

Although you can program quite complex interactions and activities, you don't have to be a computer programmer to work with SWiSHscript. SWiSHmax provides a guided scripting method that allows you to systematically build and use scripts in your movies. You identify an object you want to apply a script to, and in the Script panel you use the menu items, guides, and prompts to construct SWiSHscript for your movie.

In this chapter, you learn about SWiSHscript as you learn to work with the Script panel. You also learn how to use the Debug panel to test your finished scripts.

Understanding SWiSHscript

You use SWiSHscript to program your movie as well as objects in your movie. You can define a range of actions from events that occur when the Timeline plays a specific frame to when another movie plays to calculating equations to controlling a mouse.

To understand how to write scripts in SWiSHmax you need to remember a few key terms about objects and Object-Oriented languages.

✦ **Actions.** An action instructs a SWF movie to do something. The terms action and statement are interchangeable. This is an example of an action:

```
onSelfEvent (press) {
stop();
}
```

✦ **Argument.** An argument is not a disagreement. In SWiSHscript terms, an argument refers to extra information supplied to a command such as a frame number or sprite name. Arguments are included as part of statements and are enclosed in parentheses. Some statements or actions have no arguments because they haven't anything to point to. For example:

```
stop()
```

stops the play of the Timeline; there is no need for further information. You can use more than one argument in a script; arguments are separated from one another by commas.

✦ **Class.** This is a group of similar objects such as buttons or sprites. Different classes of objects have different characteristics such as properties, methods, and events.

✦ **Constants.** A constant is a property having a value that doesn't change. For example, TAB is a constant of the Key object; it refers to the Tab key and doesn't change. TRUE and FALSE are constants and refer to Boolean objects.

✦ **Event.** Events are actions that occur while a SWF file plays. You can script events that cause actions to occur when a scene loads, when the viewer clicks a button, and so on. Different objects have different events.

✦ **Event handler.** An event handler is an attribute that associates an object with an event. For example, you can associate a button with a mouse click using the `on(click)` event handler.

✦ **Expressions.** An expression is any valid combination of operators and operands that represent a value. For example, in the expression x+2, x and 2 are operands and + is an operator; the expression refers to two more units than x units.

✦ **Function.** A function is a set of statements interpreted all at once by calling the function name. Functions are written in the root of a movie or sprite and can be reused in your movie project.

✦ **Method.** A method is an action that a particular object can perform or defines how an object is manipulated. Methods are always associated with a particular object; they are like verbs in "human" language.

✦ **Object.** Any item that contains data and behaves in a defined way. In "human" language terms, an object is like a noun.

✦ **Operators.** Operators are processes used to operate on values; they may be arithmetic, or strings of text or letters. The statement x+2 is an example of an arithmetic operator, 8 < 80 is an example of a comparison operator.

✦ **Property.** Properties are attributes that define an object. For example, `_visible` is a property of all shape objects that defines whether the shape object is visible or hidden. An object's properties are written as:

```
objectname.propertyname
```

and can contain other objects as well.

✦ **Statement.** A statement is a piece of code or set of commands that accomplishes a single task; a statement and an action are synonymous. A simple statement is normally a single command, such as:

```
a = b + c;
```

✦ **Variable.** A variable is a "container" for storing information. You use variables to store the results of intermediate calculations and data.

The SWiSHscript Language

SWiSHmax uses a language called SWiSHscript that is an ECMA-compliant scripting language. The ECMA (European Computer Manufacturers Association) is a nonprofit international industry association founded in 1961. Its mandate is to standardize information and communication systems.

The core JavaScript programming language is based on the ECMA-262 document that defines the syntax and semantics for a general-purpose, vendor-neutral scripting language called ECMAScript. SWiSHscript, as well as Macromedia Flash MX 2004's ActionScript are both based on the ECMA-262 specification.

Syntax Requirements

All languages — whether computer or human — use specific rules known as *syntax*. SWiSHscript contains a number of rules. Although you don't need to worry about correct syntax when you work with the Guided mode in the Script panel, it's important to understand what the contents of your scripts mean — especially if there are errors. Syntax also includes rules about naming variables, functions, and so on. Although you can label most items as you want, there are some words called keywords that are reserved for use by the SWiSHscript language itself.

SWiSHscript rules

There are a few rules to keep in mind when working with SWiSHscript.

Case Sensitivity. SWiSHscript isn't case sensitive. That means names of objects, variables, and so on do not require consistent capitalization. For example, the three variables written below refer to the same thing:

```
unit=50;
Unit=50;
UNIT=50;
```

Dot syntax. A period (.) is used to indicate properties or methods related to an object or sprite. The period (.) shows relationships between different objects, between objects and actions, and to show relationships between an object and its properties.

Cross-
Reference

In Chapter 15, the discussion "Understanding Hierarchical Names" describes the use of dot syntax in naming objects in your movie.

An expression using dot syntax begins with the name of the object or sprite followed by a period, followed by the next object or property followed by a period, and so on until it finally ends with the element you are specifying. For example:

```
_root.MySprite.rectangle._visible=true;
```

refers to the visible property of a rectangle that is part of a sprite named **MySprite** that is located in the root of a movie.

Cross-Reference   The content to the right of the equals (=) sign is the value of the property; in the example, the rectangle described is visible. The value is called a Boolean value; read about Boolean and other types of values in Chapter 18.

Dot syntax uses aliases to refer to relationships among objects in your movie. Using the alias _root refers to the main Timeline of a movie and creates an absolute path.

The alias _parent refers to the parent object of an object you are describing. You can use a parent object to create a relative target path.

Curly braces. Event handlers, class definitions, and functions are grouped together into blocks with curly braces {}. As you assemble scripts in the Script panel, SWiSHmax places the expressions you write within curly braces. Curly braces group together a bunch of related statements. The opening brace ({) is placed after the event name; when the content is complete, the script is closed with the closing brace (}). You must always use an opening and closing brace.

If you write your code yourself, develop a systematic way to write it. For example, some people like to use the opening and closing curly braces on separate lines while others prefer to end expressions using the curly brace anywhere on the line following the other content.

Semicolons. Each statement you write in SWiSHscript ends with a semicolon. A semicolon works the same as a period at the end of a sentence in that it tells the program it has reached the end of a statement.

Bracket. Arguments that are part of a condition and parameters that are part of a function are enclosed in brackets ( ). For example:

```
gotoSceneAndPlay("Scene_2",6);
```

In this example, the event is a goto event, specifically gotoSceneAndPlay. The argument, or the extra information within the parentheses, provides more information about the command. In the example, the extra information tells the player to go to Scene_2 and start playing at Frame 6. You must always use both opening and closing parentheses.

Comments. Comments are notations you use to keep track of what you are writing. They are also used for sharing information with other SWiSHmax users. Use // to start a single line comment, or enclose a multiline comment with /* and */ to identify the comments. These characters are called *comment delimiters*. For example:

```
on(release) {
gotoSceneAndPlay("<current scene>",15); // single line comment
}
```

or

```
/* sometimes you write very long
comments that continue over several
lines */
```

Comments are not exported with your SWF movie, but they are saved in the SWI project file.

Keywords

There are a number of words that you can't use in your scripts for identifying things such as variables, functions, or label names. The words reserved for specific purposes within the language are listed in Table 17-1.

Table 17-1: SWiSHscript Keywords

Math	String	Timer	Date	Key	Length
text	htmltext	scroll	maxscroll	_root	_parent
this	do	else	for	if	Not
playSound	preloadContent	return	setLabel	setLabelAnchor	StopSound
tellTarget	trace	var	while	with	Return
true	false	PI	E	LN10	LN2
LOG2E	LOG10E	SQRT2	SQRT1_2	newline	Tab
NULL					

Setting Script Panel Preferences

There are several preferences you can set to customize the Script panel. Two of the preferences are selected and used for the figures and sample project files in this and subsequent chapters.

Follow these steps to set Script preferences:

1. **Choose Edit ⇨ Preferences, or Tools ⇨ Preferences.** The Preferences dialog box appears and displays the contents of the General tab.

2. **Click the Script Editor tab to display options you can set for the Script panel, as seen in Figure 17-1.**

Figure 17-1: Choose options for customizing the Script panel.

3. **Change the text options as desired:**

   - Click in the Tab size field and type a value in characters for the amount of indenting used in the Script panel. The default value is 4 characters.

   - Click the Font size down arrow and choose a font size from the list; you can also click the value in the field and type a new value. The default is 9-point text.

4. **Change the display options that you want to use.** The options are unselected by default:

   - Click the Show all objects with script in Guided mode option to display the scene's name as well as the objects in the scene in the Script panel rather than selecting objects from a list.

   - Click the Show all objects with script in Expert mode (on the event outline panel) to provide a similar object list as that in the Guide mode.

Note   Both of the Show all objects with script options are shown as selected in the figures in this and subsequent chapters.

5. **Click OK to close the dialog box and make the changes.**

Saving a Debugging Log

There is one additional preference that you can use for writing scripts. You can simultaneously create a Debugging log file as you work on a movie project. It is very easy to make errors when you are writing scripts for a movie; using a log file is one way in which you can troubleshoot your code. When you are working on large or complex projects, a Debugging log is a good tool to use to troubleshoot errors. This preference is used on a file-by-file basis. The log file is maintained for the project file to which you attach the preference.

Follow these steps to activate a Debugging log:

1. **Choose Edit ➪ Preferences, or Tools ➪ Preferences.** The Preferences dialog box appears and displays the General tab.

2. **Click the Log changes into [AppPath]/log.swi option at the bottom of the dialog box, as seen in Figure 17-2.**

3. **A message appears, also seen in the figure, that explains using the log file can affect program performance.** Click OK to close the message box.

4. **Click OK to close the Preferences dialog box.**

As you work on a project, the content is also written to the log.swi file that is stored in the same folder on your hard drive as the SWiSHmax program.

When you close SWiSHmax and then reopen it for another work session, the information dialog box seen in Figure 17-3 appears. Click OK to close the dialog box. Deselect the preference if you don't intend to log your project file.

Figure 17-2: You can set a preference to store a debugging copy of your project file.

Figure 17-3: SWiSHmax tells you if the debugging log option is active.

Using the Script Panel

The Script panel is designed to write scripted actions for your movie using a sequence of items you choose from menus. As you add items, the Script panel changes its appearance and provides prompts for you to define what you want the movie to do. When you complete your script, you can test the movie and also follow along as the scripts are executed by watching them in the Debug window.

Click the Script tab, tabbed with the Layout panel, to display the Script panel. There are several options that you use to select and order the content of the Script panel.

✦ **Add Script.** Click the Add Script button to open the script menus and choose content for your project's coding.

Note You can also click the Add Script button from the Timeline when you select the scene's label.

✦ **Delete Script.** You can delete events and actions from the Script panel. Select the item you want to remove, and then click the Delete Script button.

Note

You can also click the Delete Script button from the Timeline; the button may also contain the text "Delete Script" depending on your Timeline display settings.

✦ **Up/Down.** Click the Up or Down buttons to move a selected event or action up or down in the script.

✦ **Guided Mode.** Click the Guided mode button to display a prompted Script panel. Using the Guided mode you construct the scripts for your movie using a sequence of menu selections. The Guided mode button toggles to the Expert mode button. The Guided mode is the default for the program.

✦ **Expert Mode.** Click the Guided mode button to display a Script window for text entry at the bottom of the Script panel. You type your own scripts, but you can choose menu items from the Add Script menus. The Expert Mode button toggles to the Guided Mode button.

✦ **Panel Displays.** Click one of the panel display options to reconfigure how the Script panel is shown. You can use the default, which shows the Script window at the bottom of the Script panel and the event outline pane at the top of the Script panel. You can also choose to show the Script window at the side of the panel or remove the event outline pane altogether.

✦ **Evaluate as Expression.** Click this button to activate another Script panel option to assist in writing arguments for your commands.

Guided mode scripting

The simplest way to write scripts for your movie is using the Guided mode in the Script panel. Click the Script tab, which is tabbed with the Layout panel, to display the Script panel

Follow these steps to add a script to your movie:

1. **Select the item for which you want to write the script in the Layout panel, the Outline panel, or the Timeline.** If you don't select an object, the script is applied to the active scene.

2. **Click the Script tab to display the Script panel.** The Script panel is tabbed with the Layout panel by default.

3. **Click the Add Script button to display a menu tree.** The main listing in the menu includes event handlers, actions, and functions.

4. **Click an event handler or action to display a submenu; for some submenus there is a third submenu level.** For example, choose Movie Control ⇨ gotoAndPlay ⇨ gotoAndPlay(FRAME) to select an action that applies to a specific frame in the movie.

Tip

When you choose a menu item it is shown as a label on the bar separating the event outline pane and the Script window.

5. **Type content or select content from the drop-down lists, check boxes, and radio buttons that appear in the Script window at the bottom of the Script panel to complete the statements, as seen in Figure 17-4.**

Figure 17-4: Write scripts using menu items and lists in the Script panel.

Tip

Click and drag the bar separating the Script window from the event outline pane from the Script window to resize each segment of the Script panel.

6. **Click the event outline pane to add the selected content from the Script window.** The text in the event outline pane at the top of the Script panel is red when the statements are incomplete.

Tip

When the statement is complete and required arguments are included, the text is blue. The finished script in the event outline pane is black.

Note

If you want to delete a line from your script, click it to highlight it in the event outline pane and press Delete.

7. **Click the Layout panel tab to display the content of your movie.**

8. **Use one of these methods to test the movie:**

   - Click the Play button on the Control toolbar
   - Click the Play Timeline button on the Control toolbar
   - Choose Control ➪ Play Movie
   - Choose Control ➪ Play Timeline
   - Choose File ➪ Test ➪ In Player

Expert mode scripting

If you are familiar with writing code, you may prefer to write it independently rather than going through a sequence of menu and option selections such as those provided by the Guided mode. In Expert mode, you type scripts directly into the Script window. Click the Script tab, tabbed with the Layout panel, to display the Script panel.

Follow these steps to add a script to your movie using the Expert mode:

1. **Select the item for which you want to write the script in the Layout panel, the Outline panel, or the Timeline.** If you don't select an object, the script is applied to the active scene.

2. **Click the Script tab to display the Script panel.**

3. **Click the Guided mode button to open the list, and choose Expert.** The list closes, and the Script panel's configuration changes.

4. **Click Add Script and select menu items to add actions and events to the script, or type them manually.**

5. **Type properties for the actions and events added from the menu items.** If an expression is incorrect or incomplete, the text in the Script panel is red; when the statement is correct, the text in the Script window at the bottom of the Script panel is blue. Figure 17-5 shows the Script panel as it appears when the expression is incomplete.

Figure 17-5: Write scripts manually in the Script panel's Expert mode.

 Chapters 18 and 19 explain in more detail how to use expressions.

Testing Your Movie's Scripts

The Debug panel is ideal for observing what you script does as your movie runs. When you write scripts it is convenient to read the contents of the Debug panel as the scripts are executed to watch how the script is executed and pick up any errors as they occur in real-time. You can also use a command to execute your scripts and display their results in the Debug panel. The level of debugging you use depends on the complexity of the movie and whether you have added any complex equations or variables that are easier to troubleshoot if you can see the code as it executes.

In this section, you learn about different debugging methods using the Debug panel and its options and how to use Trace actions and comments to evaluate your scripts and prevent errors.

The Debug panel shows the script as it is executed as well as values of any variables you might have in the script.

To use the Debug panel for testing your SWiSHscript after it is written, follow these steps:

1. **Click the Debug panel's tab in the panel group to display it.**

2. **Click Start Output to activate the Debug panel's function.** The button toggles to Stop Output.

3. **Choose an echo option:**

   • Click the Echo script option to activate the output.

   • Click the Echo bytecodes option to display two bytecode options, and then click either the Summary or Detailed radio button, as seen in Figure 17-6.

Figure 17-6: Watch your code execute in the Debug panel.

4. **Click the Layout panel tab to display the movie stage.**

5. **Play the movie.** The initial information about the scene is written to the Debug panel.

6. **Interact with the objects in your movie.** The code is written to the Debug panel.

7. **Stop the movie when you have tested the code.**

8. **On the Debug panel, click Clear to remove the text contents from the panel.**

9. **Click Stop Output when you are finished.** The button toggles to the Restart Output button.

On The Web Site

The project used in the Debug panel discussion is available from the book's Web site. It is called ch17_sample02.swi, and is in the ch17_sample02 folder within the chapter17 folder.

Debug panel information

Choose from three options for displaying the content of your movie as it runs, shown in the Debug panel in Figure 17-6. The options are:

✦ Echo script

✦ Echo bytecode - Summary

✦ Echo bytecode - Detailed

You can also use the Echo script option along with one of the Echo bytecode options. The option you choose depends on the amount of information you want to see about your movie.

Note Bytecode refers to code processed through a virtual machine rather than the computer's processor.

Echo script. The Echo script option does as its name implies — it reproduces the script you have written for your movie as it runs and as you interact with it. If your movie has errors in the order of execution, for example, using the Echo script option can show you how the movie actually executes the code you have written. Listing 17-1 shows the results displayed in the Debug panel when a sample movie is run with the Echo script option. The script includes two actions that occur in response to mouse action. When the mouse rolls over the shape named **oval** it changes its alpha value; the values change again when the mouse is rolled off the shape.

Listing 17-1: **Echo Script Output**

```
Scene_1::onFrame (1,afterPlacedObjectEvents)
}
Scene_1.oval::onSelfEvent (rollOver)
  _alpha=100
}
Scene_1.oval::onSelfEvent (rollOut)
  _alpha=30
}
```

Echo bytecodes - Summary. Use the Summary view to display the processing done in your movie, which is handy for general testing of a movie's function. Listing 17-2 shows the same project's output in the Debug panel when the movie is tested. You see in the output that rather than reproducing the code that is used in the movie, as is done with the Echo script output option, the content includes information about the variables used in the movie and names the targets.

Listing 17-2: **Echo Bytecodes (Summary) Output**

```
::TARGET="/"
::TARGET="/oval"
::setVariable "_alpha","100"
::TARGET="/fade"
::setVariable "_alpha","30"
```

Echo bytecodes - Detailed. Use the Detailed view when you want to display bytecodes for calculations, writing variables, getting variable values, and so on. Listing 17-3 shows the output from the sample movie using the Detailed option. As with the Summary option you see the targets and variables listed. You also see information about the processing required to comply with the variables' values. For example, the project includes a shape object that changes its alpha value when the mouse moves over it. The shape object starts with an alpha value of 50 percent. When the mouse is rolled over the shape object, the alpha value increases to 100 percent; when the mouse is rolled out of the shape object's area, the alpha value decreases to 30 percent. You see separate lines included for each operation that is required to change the appearance of the object to execute the command.

Listing 17-3: **Echo Bytecodes (Detailed) Output**

```
::TARGET="/"
::TARGET="/oval"
::push("_alpha") -> "_alpha"
::push(100) -> 100, "_alpha"
::setVariable "_alpha","100"
::TARGET="/oval"
::push("_alpha") -> "_alpha"
::push(30) -> 30, "_alpha"
::setVariable "_alpha","30"
```

Debugging using the Trace action

SWiSHmax includes an action you can use for debugging called the Trace action. You use the action to display the results of an expression in the Debug Panel when playing your Movie. Use the Trace action when you want to test calculations in your scripts, or make sure that other scripts such as dates are written correctly. In the example below, the full date appears in the Debug Panel when the scene is loaded. The sample movie ch17_sample02 shows an example of the Trace action.

On The Web Site

The project used in the Trace action discussion is available from the book's Web site. It is called ch17_sample02.swi, and is in the ch17_sample02 folder within the chapter17 folder.

The script using the Trace action is written as:

```
onFrame (1) {
    theYear = new Date();
    trace(theYear.getFullYear());
}
```

This script means that on Frame 1 a variable named theYear is declared and its value is new Date(), which is the Date object.

The trace action is added in the next line. Its argument uses the variable named in the previous line and defines its method as getFullYear(), which is a method included in the Date object.

How the Trace action appears in the Debug panel depends on the option you choose. If you use the Trace action without any trace options selected in the Debug panel, when you play the movie you see **2004** written in the Debug panel. The result of running the script is a display of the year, so you know the script is accurate.

Click the Echo script option to display the script from the Script panel as well as the result as shown in Figure 17-7. In the figure, you see the Trace action highlighted in the Script panel; in the Debug panel, you see the script echoed and the output year number on the line following the script.

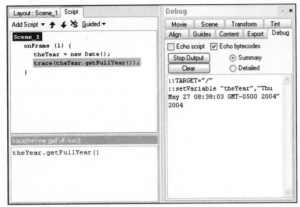

Figure 17-7: You can see the results of your scripts using the Trace action.

Writing a Trace action

The sample project ch17_sample02.swi attaches the Trace action to a scene. Follow these steps to write a Trace action for your movie using the Guided mode in the Script panel:

1. **Click the Add Script button to open the menu, and choose Events ⇨ Frame ⇨ OnFrame(...).** The first line of the script is added to the project and reads:

```
onFrame (1){
}
```

2. **Click the Add Script button to open the menu, and choose Statements ⇨ name=expr; to add the beginning of the variable to the Script panel.** On the Script panel, the text turns red as the expression is incomplete. Several fields appear in the Script window area of the Script panel.

3. **Click in the Name field to make it active and type** theYear. This is the name of the variable.

4. **Click in the field below the Operator button and type** new Date(), **as seen in Figure 17-8.** This completes the variable's expression by defining the Date object as the variable's value.

5. **Click off the Script window area of the Script panel to move the expression to the event outline pane at the top of the Script panel.** The text turns blue. The script now reads:

```
onFrame (1) {
    theYear = new Date();
}
```

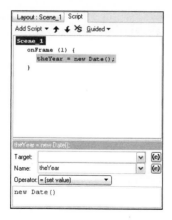

Figure 17-8: Write a statement using the fields that appear after choosing the command.

6. **Click the Add Script button to open the menu, and choose Debugging ⇨ Trace(...).** A blank Script window area opens at the bottom of the Script panel. A new line is added to the text at the top of the Script panel in red and reads:

```
trace ()
```

7. **In the Script window area type** theYear.getFullYear() **and click off the Script window area.** The text is added to the script at the top of the Script panel, and the text turns blue.

Caution When using variables it is very important that the line declaring the variable precede that of the expression using the variable. Otherwise, you receive an error and your script won't run.

8. **Test the script.** Choose different Debug panel output options and see the difference in the displayed output:

   • The four-digit year appears when Echo options are deselected

   • The three lines of script appear, followed by the four-digit year, when the Echo script option is selected

   • The output shows three lines listing the target, variable, and trace output when the Echo bytecodes - Summary options are selected

   • The output shows 13 lines, including the variable and the call method information, when the Echo bytecodes - Detailed options are selected

Handling errors

How you deal with errors, of course, depends on the error involved. The advantage of using the Debug panel is that you can see an explanation of the error, which can help you pinpoint the source of the problem. The sample project, ch17_sample02.swi, can be altered to create a simple error.

Follow these steps to create and resolve a script error:

1. **In the ch17_sample02.swi Script panel, click the variable statement to select it.** The variable is written as:

```
theYear = new Date()
```

2. **Click the down arrow at the top of the Script panel to move the variable to follow the Trace action.**

3. **On the Debug panel, click the Echo script option.** You want the script to be processed in the Debug panel as you test it.

4. **Play the movie.** The dialog box seen in Figure 17-9 appears.

Figure 17-9: SWiSHmax may display a dialog box stating your script has errors when you are testing.

5. **Click Yes to close the dialog box and continue with the script.** In the Debug panel, the error message explains that the Trace action is applied although the program can't find the variable. In Figure 17-10, the output from the Trace action is shown as 0.

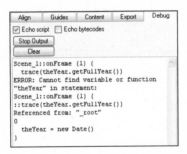

Figure 17-10: Running the script when the variable is in the wrong location results in an incorrect trace result.

6. **In the Script panel, click the variable's line again and click the up arrow to return it to its original location before the Trace action's line.**

If you test the script again, it runs correctly.

Adding a comment

You use comments to make notes as you write scripts. Although it seems extreme when you have only a very short script like that used in the sample project, it is a good habit to develop. Whenever you want to add a comment to your script, click the Add Script button and choose Debugging ➪ // comments. The comment delimiter — the slashes — is added to the script in

SWiSHmax is not Flash

SWiSHmax is a well-developed product. Although it produces SWF output, as does Flash, it is an entirely separate product. If you have experience working with Flash you notice similarities as well as differences. Some of the differences are:

✦ SWiSHmax doesn't support tweening, or frame-by-frame animation. Applying a SWiSHmax effect automatically tweens the content for the duration of the effect.

✦ SWiSHmax doesn't include sound editing. You have to work with sound effects and music prior to importing them into SWiSHmax.

✦ SWiSHmax doesn't include an elaborate interface, nor is it part of an integrated suite of products.

✦ ActionScript 2.0, found in Macromedia Flash MX 2004, is different than SWiSHscript in a number of ways although both are ECMA-compliant languages. As a result, there are differences in how one program handles output from the other program.

✦ Most functions, methods, properties, and classes included in ActionScript 2.0 can be used in SWiSHmax; testing a movie using ActionScript requires you to use the Test in Browser, Test in Player, or Export to SWF options in order to run some scripts as they aren't supported in SWiSHmax's internal player.

✦ Flash and SWiSHmax use different names for similar concepts. For example, SWiSHmax uses sprites; Flash uses movie clips. Flash houses material in the Library; in SWiSHmax, you can see the elements of a project in the Outline panel, and they are listed by type in the Content panel. Not only are the elements listed in the Outline panel, but you also see their relationships to other elements of a project.

✦ SWiSHmax doesn't have the same degree of support for building Web applications as that found in Flash.

✦ Flash doesn't have the same ease of application for using effects that SWiSHmax does.

the event outline pane. Type your comment in the Script window at the bottom of the Script panel. Click off the Script panel to move the comment to the event outline pane. If the comment is in the wrong location, use the up or down arrows to move it.

Note   You have to write multiline comments in Expert mode to use the /* and */ delimiters.

Summary

In this chapter, you were introduced both to the SWiSHscript language and the SWiSHmax Script panel. You learned about the components of the language, and some rules for working with the script language. You saw how scripts can be written in both Guided and Expert Mode in the Script panel. You gained an understanding of expressions and variables. You learned:

✦ Some key terms used in describing and working with SWiSHscript

✦ The syntax required to write SWiSHscript successfully and keywords you can't use in scripts

✦ How to set preferences for the Debug panel

✦ How to create and use a debugging log file

✦ About the Script panel and the two scripting modes you can use in SWiSHmax

✦ The ways you see the output from running your scripts in the Debug panel

✦ How to work with the Debug panel options

✦ That you can use a Trace action to test the results of your scripts

✦ How to handle errors in your scripts

✦ How to add comments to your scripts

✦   ✦   ✦

Understanding Events

You follow the same process in SWiSHmax whether you are building an elaborate testing tool interface or a simple movie with a couple of buttons to control the playback in some way. In each case, the key questions are: What happens, and what makes it happen? The behavior or *action* is caused by some occurrence called an *event*.

Events can be based on a number of different processes. For example, a script attached to a frame on the movie's Timeline that instructs the play head to stop when that frame is reached is an example of a time-based event. Other types of events are based on user input such as clicking a mouse or typing text, or they can even be based on data in the case of scripts that are loaded from external sources.

Events don't happen randomly. The process of controlling events and their actions in many cases is the job of *event handlers*. In this chapter, you learn to work with different event handlers.

Different objects can have different types of events, event handlers, and actions. In SWiSHmax you work with these objects:

  ◆ Frame

  ◆ Button

  ◆ Self

  ◆ Text

  ◆ Sprite and instance

Variables are intermediate storage devices used to hold calculations or data that you write to customize your movie's script. Variables have a number of rules to follow when writing and come in a number of different forms.

Defining Script Objects

As you work in SWiSHmax, you notice that some objects' panels include a check box named Target that becomes active when you type a name for the object. If you have experimented with the Script panel you have seen a field named Target in the lower part of the Script panel like that shown in Figure 18-1; objects you have named and targeted in your movie are included in the list.

Figure 18-1: Named objects that are defined as targets are listed in the Script panel.

The targeted objects—whether images, drawings, or text—are called *script* objects. SWiSHmax defines scenes and sprites as targeted objects as well, but you don't have to designate a scene or sprite as a target because the process is automatic. Sprites inherit the script object properties, and are similar to Flash MovieClip objects. Not all properties or methods used by MovieClip objects are supported by the internal player in SWiSHmax. MovieClip objects work correctly in the Test in Browser and Test in Player options, or in exported SWF movies, offering you extensive programming capabilities in SWiSHmax.

Cross-Reference   Sprites also have a number of specific actions you can apply; these actions are discussed in Chapter 19.

MovieClip properties

SWiSHmax sprites and Flash MX 2004 MovieClip objects are very similar. There are differences in the way SWiSHmax supports the use of some MovieClip properties and methods.

Not all properties or methods used by MovieClip objects are supported by the internal player in SWiSHmax. If you test MovieClip objects in the Test in Browser and Test in Player options, you see the properties and methods perform as intended; they also work as intended in an exported SWF movie you.

Table 18-1 lists the MovieClip methods. It also lists the SWF version that supports the method. Finally, it lists whether you can test the method successfully in the internal SWiSHmax player.

Table 18-1: Sprite/MovieClip Methods and Properties

Method	SWF Version Supported	Internal / External Player Support
MovieClip._alpha	SWF4+	Internal and External
MovieClip.attachMovie	SWF5+	External Only
MovieClip.beginFill	SWF6+	External Only
MovieClip.beginGradientFill	SWF6+	External Only

Method	SWF Version Supported	Internal / External Player Support
MovieClip.clear	SWF6+	External Only
MovieClip.createEmptyMovieClip	SWF6+	Internal and External
MovieClip.createTextField	SWF6+	External Only
MovieClip._currentframe	SWF4+	Internal and External
MovieClip.curveTo	SWF6+	External Only
MovieClip._droptarget	SWF4+	Internal and External
MovieClip.duplicateMovieClip	SWF4+	Internal and External (duplicateSprite)
MovieClip.enabled	SWF6+	External Only
MovieClip.endFill	SWF6+	External Only
MovieClip.focusEnabled	SWF6+	External Only
MovieClip._focusrect	SWF6+	Internal and External
MovieClip._framesloaded	SWF4+	Internal and External
MovieClip.getBounds	SWF5+	Internal and External
MovieClip.getBytesLoaded	SWF6+	Internal and External
MovieClip.getBytesTotal	SWF5+	Internal and External
MovieClip.getDepth	SWF6+	Internal and External
MovieClip.getURL	SWF4+	Internal and External (support getURL() function)
MovieClip.globalToLocal	SWF5+	Internal and External
MovieClip.gotoAndPlay	SWF4+	Internal and External
MovieClip.gotoAndStop	SWF4+	Internal and External
MovieClip._height	SWF4+	Internal and External
MovieClip._highquality	SWF4+	Internal and External
MovieClip.hitArea	SWF6+	External Only
MovieClip.hitTest	SWF5+	Internal and External
MovieClip.lineStyle	SWF6+	External Only
MovieClip.lineTo	SWF6+	External Only
MovieClip.loadMovie	SWF4+	Internal and External
MovieClip.loadVariables	SWF4+	Internal and External
MovieClip.localToGlobal	SWF5+	Internal and External
MovieClip.moveTo	SWF6+	External Only
MovieClip._name	SWF4+	Internal and External

Continued

Table 18-1 *(continued)*

Method	SWF Version Supported	Internal / External Player Support
MovieClip.nextFrame	SWF4+	Internal and External
MovieClip._parent	SWF4+	Internal and External
MovieClip.play	SWF4+	Internal and External
MovieClip.prevFrame	SWF4+	Internal and External
MovieClip._quality	SWF5+	Internal and External
MovieClip.removeMovieClip	SWF4+	Internal and External (removeSprite)
MovieClip._rotation	SWF4+	Internal and External
MovieClip.setMask	SWF6+	External Only
MovieClip._soundbuftime	SWF4+	Internal and External
MovieClip.startDrag	SWF4+	Internal and External (startDragLocked and startDragUnlocked)
MovieClip.stop	SWF4+	Internal and External
MovieClip.stopDrag	SWF4+	Internal and External
MovieClip.swapDepths	SWF5+	Internal and External
MovieClip.tabChildren	SWF6+	External Only
MovieClip.tabEnabled	SWF6+	External Only
MovieClip.tabIndex	SWF6+	External Only
MovieClip._target	SWF4+	Internal and External
MovieClip._totalframes	SWF4+	Internal and External
MovieClip.trackAsMenu	SWF6+	External Only
MovieClip.unloadMovie	SWF4+	Internal and External
MovieClip._url	SWF4+	Internal and External
MovieClip.useHandCursor	SWF6+	External Only
MovieClip._visible	SWF4+	Internal and External
MovieClip._width	SWF4+	Internal and External
MovieClip._x	SWF4+	Internal and External
MovieClip._xmouse	SWF6+	Internal and External
MovieClip._xscale	SWF4+	Internal and External
MovieClip._y	SWF4+	Internal and External
MovieClip._ymouse	SWF6+	Internal and External
MovieClip._yscale	SWF4+	Internal and External

Cross-Reference Appendix H on the book's Web site contains a table listing all the MovieClip properties and methods as well as the SWF Player version supported.

Object properties

All script objects have the same collection of properties, or attributes, that you use to define the object or manipulate to create your movie. The properties available for use by SWiSHmax's script objects, whether they are visible or read only, and a short description are included in Table 18-2. The properties are listed in alphabetical order.

Table 18-2: Script Object Properties

Property	Read Only	Description
_age	Yes	Age in seconds since the object was placed
_alpha	No	Transparency in percentage; 0% is transparent; 100% is opaque
_createEmptyMovieClip*	No	Creates a new empty movie clip which becomes the child of the exsting sprite or movie clip
_currentframe*	Yes	Returns the number of the frame currently playing
_delta	Yes	Time in seconds since the last form was displayed
_droptarget*	Yes	The sprite to which a draggable instance has been dragged over
_focusrect*	No	Highlight displayed around a button that has keyboard focus; the default is true. That is, the highlight is visible.
_framesloaded*	Yes	Number of frames that have been loaded
_getBounds*	No	Properties indicating the bounds of a specified sprite
_getDepth*	No	Depth of a specified sprite
_globalToLocal*	No	Converts the point object from the stage coordinates, which are global, to the sprite's coordinates, which are local
_height*	Yes	The current height of the object or sprite
_highquality*	No	The level of anti-aliasing applied to the movie
_hitTest*	Yes	Whether or not a specified sprite comes in contact with the hit area of a specified target or X- and Y-axis coordinates
_localToGlobal*	No	Converts the point object from a sprite's coordinates, which are local, to the stage coordinates, which are global
_name*	No	Name of the sprite or object

Continued

Table 18-2 *(continued)*

Property	Read Only	Description
_parent*	No	The sprite or object that contains the object being referenced as a child object
_quality*	No	Used to set or retrieve the export quality for a movie
_rotation*	No	Sets or returns the rotation of the sprite or object in degrees
_soundbuftime*	No	The amount of streaming sound to prebuffer in seconds
_swapDepths*	No	Swaps the depth level of a specified sprite with either another move or another depth
_target*	Yes	The target path of the sprite or object
_time	Yes	The time since the movie started in seconds
_totalframes*	No	The total number of frames in a sprite or movie
_url*	Yes	The URL of the .swf from which the sprite was downloaded
_visible*	No	Sets or returns the visibility status of the sprite or object
_width	Yes	The current width of the sprite or object in pixels
_x*	No	Sets or returns the current X-axis coordinate of the sprite or object in pixels
__xmouse*	Yes	Returns the X-axis coordinate of the mouse's current location
_xscale*	No	Sets or returns the scale of the sprite or object on the X-axis as a percentage
_y*	No	Sets or returns the current Y-axis coordinate of the sprite or object in pixels
__ymouse*	Yes	Returns the Y-axis coordinate of the mouse's current location
_yscale*	No	Sets or returns the scale of the sprite or object on the Y-axis as a percentage

* These properties are also supported by the Flash MovieClip object.

Cross-Reference

There are a number of keywords you are not allowed to use when writing your scripts because they are reserved by SWiSHscript. The keywords are listed in Chapter 17.

Text Field Properties

Text fields defined as script objects have three additional properties in addition to those outlined in the Script object properties list.

TextField.maxscroll This read-only property indicates the line number in a text field. The maxscroll value is the line number of the uppermost visible line of text when the bottom-most line in the field is also visible.

TextField.scroll This read-only property controls scrolling in a text field when it is associated with a variable.

TextField.text This property allows access to the text used or placed in the text object.

The maxscroll and scroll properties can both control the display of text in a text field. Using dynamic text and script objects that act as controllers for scrolling the text are commonly used.

On The Web Site

A project using the text field properties is available from the book's Web site in the chapter18 folder. The project uses scrolling text and is described in the discussion about movie control actions. The project is named ch18_sample01.swi and is in the ch18_sample01 folder. The finished SWF movie is also in the subfolder.

Understanding Methods

Methods are actions associated with an object. You don't have to write a method from scratch because it is part of the object's class information. When you are writing SWiSHscript, you assign methods or actions to events. If a mouse click and release over a button plays a sprite, you are using a sprite's method. If the button is clicked and it stops the movie's playback it is an example of invoking a frame's method. Not every method can be applied to every type of object. For example, you can't associate a duplicateSprite method with a button because that method is specific to sprites; and you can't use a gotoAndPlay method for a text object.

Table 18-3 shows a list of common methods used by sprites and movies and what happens if you include the method in your script. The table also makes reference to the Flash MovieClip object.

Cross-Reference

More information on elements of OOP (Object Oriented Programming) and syntax are in Chapter 17.

Table 18-3: Object Methods

Method	Does This...
duplicateSprite	An instance of a sprite is created while the movie is playing. The movie clip equivalent is MovieClip.duplicateMovieClip.
getURL	A document from a defined URL is loaded into a specified browser window. Also applies to the MovieClip object.
gotoandplay	The play head is moved to a specified frame from which the movie plays. Also applies to the MovieClip object.
gotoAndStop	The play head is moved to a specified frame on which the movie stops. Also applies to the MovieClip object.

Continued

Table 18-3 *(continued)*

Method	Does This...
loadMovie	A SWF or JPEG file is loaded into the Flash Player as the original movie plays. Also applies to the MovieClip object.
loadVariables	Reads data from an external file and sets variable values in a Flash Player level or target movie clip. Also applies to the MovieClip object.
nextFrameAndPlay	The play head is moved to the next frame in a scene from which the movie plays.
nextFrameAndStop	The play head is moved to the next frame in a scene on which the movie stops.
play	Plays the movie. Also applies to the MovieClip object.
prevFrameAndPlay	The play head is moved to the previous frame in a scene from which the movie plays.
prevFrameAndStop	The play head is moved to the previous frame in a scene on which the movie stops.
removeSprite	When a sprite has been created using the duplicateSprite() method, the removeSprite method removes the sprite from the movie. MovieClip.removeMovieClip is equivalent.
skipFrameAndPlay	Moves the play head forward a specified number of frames and plays from that frame forward.
skipFrameAndStop	Moves the play head forward a specified number of frames and stops the movie at the specified frame.
startDragLocked	The target sprite or object is draggable while the movie plays; the sprite or object is locked to the center of the mouse position.
startDragUnlocked	The target sprite or object is draggable while the movie plays; the sprite or object is locked to the mouse position where the user clicked on the movie to initiate the command.
Stop	Stops the movie. Also applies to the MovieClip object.
unloadMovie	A loaded movie or movie clip is removed from the Flash Player.

Working with Pseudocode

Plan ahead. Events occur in response to mouse or keyboard actions or in response to the play head reaching a frame in the movie. You can use more than one action in response to an event. You can use different objects to create the same outcome in your movie. Part of the planning process should include defining your movie's function using *pseudocode*.

Pseudocode relies on human language instead of programming language. Sometimes a movie is very simple and pseudocode isn't a requirement. When your movie has some degree of complexity, writing pseudocode makes it simpler for you to keep track of what you are doing, when you are doing it, and what happens as a result.

Here's an example: The sample movie project ch18_sample01.swi contains three musical note images. Each of the three objects behaves in a similar fashion. Pseudocode for one of the objects in this sample movie could be written as shown in Listing 18-1.

Listing 18-1: Pseudocode for an animated movie project

```
The movie loads and stops.
The angled line is animated.
When the mouse is over the musical note it increases in size and
decreases in opacity.
When the mouse is moved away from the musical note it returns to its
original size and opacity.
Click and release the mouse over the note image to play music.
Click and release the mouse over the note image to display some
animated text.
Each time the mouse is clicked and released over an image the text
replays.
```

On The Web Site

The project described in this discussion is available on the book's Web site. The project is named ch18_sample01.swi and is in the ch18_sample01 folder within the chapter18 folder. The finished SWF movie, as well as the three source music files, is also in the subfolder.

The pseudocode isn't in any structured format as you can see; it doesn't even define the specific object it is applied to. Rather, it is designed to outline what happens and when. By way of illustration, if you look in the sample movie you see that there are three musical note images, and each is in fact a different type of object. One note is a button, one a sprite, and one is a simple shape object defined as a target. By the way, the WAV files attached to each object are sounds made by a marimbola (hence the name **mar** given to the sound files).

How Event Handlers Work

An object in your movie that has been named and designated as a target becomes a script object. Once you construct a sprite or add an instance of a sprite you have created a script object, the scene itself is a script object. The next part of the process is deciding how the events and actions are to occur.

There are four types of event handler you can use in SWiSHscript. The three most common types are:

✦ Frame

✦ Button

✦ Self

In addition, when you work with an input text object you can also use one event handler called onChanged().

Using Frame Events in Your Movie

Frame events occur when the movie reaches a frame specified in the script. In the sample movie ch18_sample01, frame events are added both to the main movie's Timeline as well as the Timeline of one of the sprites. The main Timeline has two frame events; the sprite named **or** has one frame event.

There are three frame event handlers you can apply to your movie. These three event handlers are triggered before the specified frame displays in the movie.

onFrame—The event you define is triggered just before the specified frame is displayed in the movie.

onLoad—The event you define is triggered by the loading of the scene or sprite.

onEnterFrame—The event you define is triggered as the frame is entered.

You can use more than one frame event in the same SWiSHscript. The events are applied in a specific sequence. The onLoad event is applied first, followed by the onEnterFrame event, and then the onFrame event. Logically, you want the events that occur when the entire scene loads to be triggered before those that apply to a specific frame.

If you want to add an action using an event handler to the scene you can work through the Script panel. Follow these steps to add an event handler and action to your project:

1. **In the Outline panel, click the sprite to which you want to add the frame event.** If you don't select a specific object the frame event is added to the scene's Timeline.

2. **Click the Script panel's tab to display it in the program.**

3. **Click Add Script and choose Events ➪ Frame ➪ and an event handler.** The sample movie uses the onFrame(...) option as shown in Figure 18-2. The event handler is added to the event outline pane of the Script panel, and the onFrame field is active in the Script window area of the panel. The field displays 1 by default.

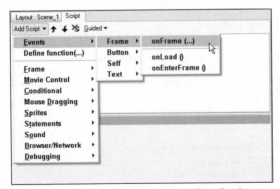

Figure 18-2: Choose the frame event handler from the menu.

4. **Click the number in the onFrame field to select it and type the number of the frame to which you want to apply the command.**

Tip

A script icon is added to the Timeline when you choose the frame.

5. **Click Add Script again and choose an action.** The sample movie uses the `stop()` Movie Control action as seen in Figure 18-3.

Note

The figures in this chapter show the objects that can include scripts in the Script panel. This option is one of the program's Script Editor preferences. Choose Edit ➪ Preferences or Tools ➪ Preferences and click the Script Editor tab. Click the check box to Show all objects with script in Guided mode; the option to Show all objects with script in Expert mode is also selected.

Cross-Reference

Read about setting Script panel preferences in Chapter 17.

Figure 18-3: The selected command is added to the object's script in the Script panel.

You can also attach an event handler from the Timeline. The menu options available vary depending on the object type. Follow these steps to add an `onFrame` event handler from the Timeline:

1. **Click the time ruler to move the play head to the frame at which you want to add the event.** The sample movie's sprite has an action attached to the first frame.

2. **Right-click the Timeline's script row at the specified frame and choose Add Script ➪ Events ➪ Frame and then select an event handler; or choose Insert ➪ Script ➪ Events ➪ Frame and select an event handler.** The sample project uses the `onFrame(...)` event handler as shown in Figure 18-2.

Caution

You can't access the event handler options from the Add Script button on the Timeline. The Add Script menu includes actions only. You can access the event handlers using the Insert ➪ Script command from the main program menu.

3. **Type a number for the frame in the onFrame field displayed in the Script panel.**
When you select the command from the Timeline's menu the Script panel automatically appears and the command is added to the event outline pane.

4. **Click the Add Script button in the Timeline to display the menu and choose an action to add to the script.** The sample movie uses the Movie Control ⇨ stop() action. You can also right-click the script indicator icon on the Timeline and choose the command from the shortcut menu, cclick the Add Script button in the Script panel to display the menu and choose the command, or click the Insert ⇨ Script command and select a menu item.

5. **Test the script.** You can see the script contents added to the Timeline by moving your mouse over the script icon to display a tooltip as shown in Figure 18-4.

Figure 18-4: The script appears in a tooltip when you move your mouse over the script icon on the Timeline.

Frame Actions

In addition to the frame event handlers, there are two frame actions you can use in SWiSHscript. These are the `SetLabel(...)` and `PreloadContent()` actions. The actions can be used with either scenes or sprites.

`SetLabel(...)` — Rather than using a frame number as a reference, you can label a frame using a descriptive name. For example, it may be simpler to keep track of your movie's activity using a name such as **anim_2** to define a frame where an animation starts, rather than using **Frame 27**. When you use a label on the Timeline, you can then choose either the frame or label references when using movie control actions.

Cross-Reference Read about movie control actions in Chapter 19.

To use the `SetLabel` action, follow these steps:

1. **Click the frame on the Timeline's time ruler to move the play head to the frame on which you want to add the action.**

2. **Right-click the frame on the Timeline and click Frame ⇨ SetLabel(...) to access the script SetLabel action.** You can also choose from one of these methods:

   • Right-click the Layout panel and click Frame ⇨ SetLabel(...)

   • Click the Add Script button on the Timeline and choose Frame ⇨ SetLabel(...)

   • Click the Add Script button in the Script window and choose Frame ⇨ SetLabel(...)

   • From the main program menu, click Insert ⇨ Script ⇨ Frame ⇨ SetLabel(...)

3. **In the Script panel, type the name for the frame in the Label field as shown in Figure 18-5.** The example uses anim_2 as the label.

4. **Press Enter or click off the Script panel to add the action to the frame.**

As shown in the figure, when you add a label to a frame it is displayed over the frame on the Timeline.

`Preload Content` — Preloading refers to a method of regulating a SWF movie's playback. Use the `PreloadContent` action to download objects in your movie before they are used. Common uses of preload actions are for sound or sprites that start at the beginning of the movie. Preloading may cause a hesitation before the movie starts, but the resulting action and sound is generally more fluid and uninterrupted.

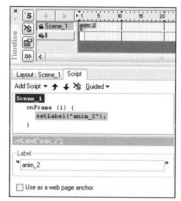

Figure 18-5: Add a label to a frame using an action.

Generic preloading options are handled in the Export panel, where you can define preload requirements for your movie by choosing the before movie, scene default, or at preload action options.

Cross-Reference

See Chapter 21 for information on working with the Export panel and preparing movies for export.

Note

Using the `PreloadContent` action also requires that objects to be preloaded, such as images and sounds, have their corresponding preload options chosen as well. Refer to Chapter 21 for information on specific objects.

To attach a `PreloadContent()` action to a sprite or scene's Timeline, follow the steps outlined for attaching the `SetLabel(...)` action. Choose the command from one of several program locations. The action has no arguments; you don't specify any content for the action within the brackets.

You can use more than one `PreloadContent()` action in one movie. When you have specified an object to preload, it is preloaded when the Timeline reaches the first `PreloadContent()` action before the appearance of the object. In the case of multiple actions, the object specified as being preloaded is loaded before its first use at the closest `PreloadContent()` action that precedes it on the Timeline. For example, an image that is seen at Frame 10 in a movie having `PreloadContent()` actions applied to Frames 1 and 11 is loaded at Frame 1.

Using Self Events in Your Movie

You can define many objects as targets. Once you do, you can access a collection of event handlers and apply many actions to these objects. The actions are called *self events* as they are applied to the object itself. A self event is similar to a button event in that the actions can occur in response to a number of event handlers. The difference is that the self event applies only to the object. For example, if you have a sprite playing, you can stop it using a self event handler and a `stop()` action. If you want to stop the entire movie's playback, use a button instead.

There are a number of self event handlers you can choose in SWiSHscript.

`onSelfEvent (press)` — This event handler triggers an action when the mouse is clicked over the object.

`onSelfEvent (release)` — This event handler triggers an action when the mouse has been clicked and is released over the object.

`onSelfEvent (rollOver)` — This event handler triggers an action when the cursor is moved over the object.

`onSelfEvent (rollOut)` — This event handler triggers an action when the mouse cursor is moved from a position over the object to outside the object's location on the movie.

`onSelfEvent (dragOver)` — This event handler triggers an action when the mouse is clicked on an object, dragged outside the object's boundaries, then dragged back over the object again without releasing the mouse button.

`onSelfEvent (dragOut)` — This event handler triggers an action when the mouse is clicked and dragged over the object and then moved away from the object with the mouse still clicked.

`onSelfEvent (releaseOutside)` — This event handler triggers an action when the mouse is clicked and dragged over the object and then moved out of the object's area on the movie stage and where the mouse button is released.

`onSelfEvent (keyPress(...))` — The event handler is based on a defined key. Pressing the key triggers the action.

The sample project ch18_sample01.swi contains one script object that uses `onSelfEvent` event handlers. The object's script includes one each of `rollOver`, `release`, and `rollOut` event handlers.

Follow these steps to add a self event to an object:

1. **Click the object on the Layout panel's stage, the Outline panel, or the Timeline.**

2. **Click the Script panel's tab to display it.**

3. **Click the Add Script button and choose Events ⇨ Self and one of the options from the SelfEvent submenu.** The event handler is added to the object's script on the event outline pane of the Script panel and the set of SelfEvent options appear in the Script window as shown in Figure 18-6. The selected option is written at the top of the Script window area above the check boxes.

Figure 18-6: The SelfEvent event handlers are listed at the bottom of the Script panel.

4. **Click other check boxes to add or change additional events; click the Key down arrow and choose a key from the list to use as a SelfEvent event handler.**

You can use more than one event handler to trigger the same action.

5. **Click the Add Script button and choose an action.** Depending on the selected action, different options ranging from check boxes to drop-down lists to a blank text input area appear at the bottom of the Script panel.

6. **If desired, click the Add Script button and choose another action.** You can use more than one action in response to triggering an event handler.

7. **Test the script.**

Read about actions in Chapter 19.

The selfEvent event handlers added to the targeted shape object in the sample project use a number of actions. For example, the `onSelfEvent (release)` event handler triggers `TellTarget`, `gotoAndPlay`, and `playSound` actions.

Using Button Events in Your Movie

Buttons are a common type of object used to initiate actions in your movies. Commonly, you define button states in the Button panel and then customize the appearance of the different button states. You assign actions to buttons in the Script panel using the methods described in Chapter 16, which is the same as that described earlier for the `onSelfEvent` event handlers.

In Chapter 16, read about button events, triggers, and event handlers.

As with the other event handlers you can use more than one action for a specified button event handler. For example, the sample project ch18_sample01.swi includes one button named **mar02**. The button's appearance is modified for each state using the Transform panel. In the Script panel, the button includes an `on(release)` event handler that triggers three actions:

✦ The sound mar02.wav is played

✦ The sprite named **or** is called

✦ The sprite named **or** is instructed to go to its second frame (Frame 2) and play

The script for the button reads:

```
on (release) {
    playSound("mar02.wav");
or.gotoAndPlay(2);
}
```

Using Input Text Events in Your Movie

The final type of event handler is specific to one type of object. The `onChanged()` event handler is used only by input text objects. You use the event handler to generate an action when the user modifies text in the input text object. The input text object, as well as other text objects, can also use the events and event handlers common to other script objects.

On The Web Site

The sample movie project ch18_sample02.swi contains an input text object used in this discussion. The file is located in the ch18_sample02 subfolder within the chapter18 folder. The folder also includes the exported SWF movie named ch18_sample02.swf.

To use the `onChanged()` event handler in your movie, follow these steps:

1. **Add the input text object to the movie and name it.** The text object is defined as a target by default. In the sample movie the text object is named **name**.

2. **Click the Script panel tab to display the panel in the program window.**

3. **With the input text object selected, click Add Script to open the menu.** Choose Events ➪ Text ➪ onChanged(). The event handler is added to the text object's script.

4. **Click the Add Script button and choose an action or actions to associate with the event handler.** The sample movie uses five property changes as shown in Figure 18-7.

Note   The sample movie also includes a button with an `on(press)` event handler to move the play head on the Timeline.

```
Layout : Scene_1   Script
Add Script ▾  ↑  ↓  ✕⑤  Guided ▾
   onFrame (15) {
        stop();
       _alpha = 100   ;
   }
 name
     onChanged() {
        _y  -= 3;
        _x  -= 3;
        _yscale += 3;
        _xscale += 3;
        _alpha = 50;
        gotoSceneAndPlay("<current scene>",2);
     }

 _y -= 3;
Target:                              ▾  (e)
Name:   _y                           ▾  (e)
Operator: -= (subtract)      ▾
3
```

Figure 18-7: The input text `onChanged()` event handler triggers action when the text changes.

5. **Test the movie in the player.** When the text is changed in the sample movie, the contents become semitransparent; as each letter is typed, the scale of the letters increases horizontally and vertically by 3 pixels. To compensate for the increase in size, the _x and _y properties are also modified to maintain the location of the object on the stage.

Working with Variables

Variables are intermediate storage for calculations or data. A variable is *declared* or written into the SWiSHscript so the program understands what it is you are talking about. The onLoad() event handler is used to declare variables and set up initial values.

For example, to declare the variable named **a** and assign a value of **100**, you write:

```
a=100;
```

Then you can reuse that value in any way you like, such as:

```
b=a*10
```

In this example the value of **b** is 1000: The variable **a** is equal to 100, and 10 times the value of **a** is 1000.

Here are some tips to consider as you are learning to write variables for using in SWiSHscript:

✦ A variable's name can be alphanumeric, and can also include a period, underscore, and square brackets.

✦ A variable name can't start with a number.

✦ Upper- and lowercase characters aren't recognized as different characters. For example, BIGEFFORT, BigEffort, and bigeffort are all considered the same variable.

✦ A variable can start with an underscore, but this can be confusing as SWiSHmax uses the underscore to represent sprites.

✦ Spaces are not allowed in variable names.

✦ Use multiword names for good descriptive names and easy recognition.

✦ Get in the habit of using the same naming structure. For example, use lowercase for the first word and uppercase letters for the first letter of subsequent words or underscores between words. For example, bigEffort or big_effort.

Data types describe the kind of information a variable can hold. You can use a number of different types of data in variables you write in SWiSHscript.

Numbers. You can use either integers or floating-point numbers. An integer is a whole number, while a floating-point number uses decimal places.

Strings. A string includes characters that aren't used mathematically, such as messages. Use the same type of quotation marks at the beginning and end of a string.

Boolean. A Boolean value is always true or false. You use text in the assignment statement without quotation marks surrounding the words true or false.

Arrays. An array is made up of one or more characters or related values surrounded by quotation marks. An array can be complete words such as:

```
"Monday, Tuesday, Wednesday, Thursday, Friday, Saturday, Sunday"
```

Learn how to write and work with SWiSHscript variables in Chapter 19.

Summary

Events or actions can occur in a number of ways. For certain types of objects, special structures called event handlers are provided that are used as triggers for actions applied in your movie. Events are most commonly triggered in response to user input or when the play head reaches a specified frame on the Timeline. In this chapter, you learned about script object properties as well as methods for sprites and other objects. You saw how to use different event handlers in SWiSHscript. You learned how to:

✦ Define script objects and their properties

✦ Choose and use object methods

✦ Organize your scripting using pseudocode

✦ Work with event handlers

✦ Use frame events and actions

✦ Use self and button events

✦ Use a special input text event handler

✦ Write variables

✦ Differentiate among types of variables

✦   ✦   ✦

Applying Actions to Control a Movie

Actions are operations triggered by events. Events may be initiated by event handlers, as in the case of buttons or self-events, or by Timeline or other specified conditions occurring in the movie. Actions can do everything from play sounds to load other movies to open Web pages or e-mail programs. In SWiSHscript, you can create complex actions based on variables or functions or perform calculations.

Although an in-depth discussion of programming is beyond the scope of this book, the actions you use in SWiSHscript are described in this chapter. And, some of the more common actions you work with are covered in detail, such as controlling how and when a movie starts or stops playing, how a mouse behaves, how to send an email from a movie, and so on.

Categorizing Actions

In addition to working with objects, including event handlers, you can work with a variety of different types and categories of actions.

- ✦ **Frame actions.** These actions are attached to specified frames in the movie and are described in Chapter 18.

- ✦ **Movie control actions.** Use these actions to control the stop and play processes in your sprite or movie.

- ✦ **Conditional actions.** These define how your movie behaves based on defined conditions such as if or else.

- ✦ **Mouse Dragging actions.** These define how an object is dragged on the movie.

- ✦ **Sprite actions.** Choose actions that are specific to sprites such as targeting, duplicating, or removing a duplicate of a sprite from your movie.

- ✦ **Statements.** Write statements to expand other actions or define parameters such as properties or variables that are used in other actions.

- ✦ **Sound actions.** Use these to start or stop sound in your movie.

✦ **Browser and network actions.** Use actions that interact with Web pages such as loading Web pages, launching e-mail, or using full-screen options to play your movie.

✦ **Debugging actions.** Test and monitor the action in your movie. Debugging actions are covered in Chapter 17.

✦ **Define function.** Use this action to construct functions for your movies, which are then executed on a call from a script in your movie.

Writing Expressions

You can use written parameters for many events and actions. In many cases, you must specify a parameter in order to complete the statement. Expressions can be written for many processes in SWiSHmax. You access the expressions options through the Script panel.

Follow these steps to write an expression for an action or event:

1. **In the Script panel, choose the event or action for the object for which you want to write the expression.**

2. **Click the Expressions button to activate the expressions option.** A pair of brackets ( ) surround the Target field on the Script window at the bottom of the Script panel as shown in Figure 19-1.

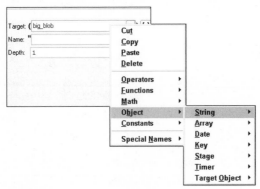

Figure 19-1: Write expressions using the Script Syntax menu.

3. **Right-click the Target field to display the Script Syntax menu shown in the figure.**

4. **Create your expression by using the choices from the menu and submenus by and typing values in the fields on the Script window.** As the components are selected, they are displayed in blue in the Target field.

5. **Press Enter or click off the Script panel to add the content you have written in the Script window at the bottom of the Script panel to the event outline pane at the top of the Script panel.**

Accessing the Script Syntax Menu

The Script Syntax menu is available by right-clicking a field when you have clicked the Expression button on the Script window area of the Script panel. The menu is also available by right-clicking whenever a Script window is available at the bottom of the Script panel for typing content directly, such as when constructing a statement.

In the Script Syntax menu, in addition to the Cut, Copy, Paste, and Delete commands, you find listings for a wide variety of content you can use to construct your scripts. The menu includes operators, functions, classes, and methods. You can select items from the menu instead of typing them manually. The menu includes:

✦ **Operators.** Includes arithmetic, logical, comparison, and equality operators for creating expressions. Operators are described in Table 19-1.

✦ **Functions.** Includes a list of built-in functions ranging from `eval(string)` to `isNearThis()`.

✦ **Math.** A listing of Math object and methods such as `Math.round ({number})`.

✦ **Object.** Includes object types such as **string**, **array**, **date**, **timer**. Choose from a set of cascading submenus that include properties for different types of objects.

✦ **Constants.** Select Constant values such as true and false.

✦ **Special names.** Choose generic object names including _root, _parent, and this.

Selecting Operators

An expression consists of operators and operands. *Operators* are terms that calculate a new value from one or more *operands*. For example, the addition (+) operator adds two or more operands, together to produce a new value. Table 19-1 describes common types of operators you can work with in SWiSHmax.

Table 19-1: Operators

Arithmetic Operators:	Refers to...	Arithmetic Operators:	Refers to...
+	addition	%	Modulus - returns the remainder in a division question
-	subtraction	++	Increments a value
*	multiplication	--	Decrements a value
/	division	add	Used to add (concatenate) two strings together instead of the plus sign (+) *

Number Comparison Operators:	Refers to...	Number Comparison Operators:	Refers to...
==	equal to	<=	Less than or equal to
!=	not equal to	>	Greater than
<	less than	>=	Greater than or equal to

String Comparison Operators:	Refers to...	String Comparison Operators:	Refers to...
Eq	equal to	Le	Less than or equal to
Ne	not equal to	Gt	Greater than
Lt	less than	Ge	Greater than or equal to

Logical Operators:	Refers to...	Logical Operators:	Refers to...
&&	and	!	Not
||	or	?:	{condition}?{then}:{else}

*You can't use the plus sign (+) to add strings because strings aren't numbers; using the (+) yields a value of 0.

Note   String comparison operators are not uppercase or lowercase dependent.

Order of Operations

SWiSHscript uses a specific order to calculate values in your scripts. This order is:

✦ Parentheses

✦ Exponents

✦ Multiplication and division

✦ Addition and subtraction

For example:

```
Equation01=((2+4)/2+6-2)*3
Equation01=21
```

The calculations are done in this order:

✦ The value of the operation in the inner parentheses: **(2+4)=6**

✦ The value of the operations inside the outer parentheses in order with multiplication and division preceding addition and subtraction. That is, **6/2=3**, and then **3+6-2=7**

✦ Calculations outside the parentheses: **7*3=21**

Movie Control Actions

SWiSHscript includes a number of actions you use to control how your movie plays. Many of the commands are very straightforward; a few are more complex. Most commands require an argument to define the affected frame, label, or scene.

Play and stop commands

`play()` **and** `stop()` — These two commands are fundamental. A script placed on the Timeline using the `play()` command plays the Timeline; similarly, a script using the `stop()` command stops the playback.

`gotoAndPlay()` **and** `gotoAndStop()` — Click Add Script ➪ Movie Control and then choose an action; these two actions include several subcommands. The options for the `gotoAndPlay()` command are shown in Figure 19-2 and described here. The `gotoAndStop()` commands are equivalent; that is, stopping the playback based on defined locations rather than playing from a defined location as the `gotoAndPlay()` commands. For each command the script is placed on a specified frame, and a target frame and Timeline are specified in the script.

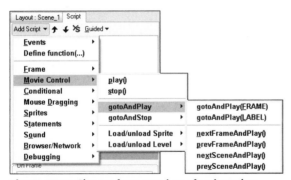

Figure 19-2: Choose from a variety of actions that control the play of your movie.

`gotoAndPlay(FRAME)` **and** `gotoAndPlay(LABEL)` — For these two commands, define the frame at which the movie starts playing, or name the label at which the movie starts playing.

Tip   To use the Label option, you must have a label attached to the Timeline. See Chapter 18 for information on using the `SetLabel` action.

`gotoAndPlay` ➪ `nextFrameandPlay()` **and** `gotoAndPlay` ➪ `prevFrameandPlay()` — For these two commands, the play head is instructed to move one frame in the specified direction from the frame on which the script is defined.

`gotoAndPlay` ➪ `nextSceneandPlay()` **and** `gotoAndPlay` ➪ `prevSceneandPlay()` — For these two commands the play head is instructed to move to either the preceding or following scenes from the one containing the script; a frame can also be specified in the target scene. If unspecified, the play head starts at Frame 1 of the designated scene.

`loadMovie()` — You can use the `loadMovie()` command to load another SWF movie into a SWF movie that is already running.

`loadVariables()` — You can use the `loadVariables()` command to load content from another file based on defined variables.

`unloadMovie()` — Use this command to remove a movie that you previously loaded into a SWF movie.

On The Web Site

The folder ch19_sample01 within the chapter19 folder on the book's Web site contains several sample files. The folder includes two project files and exported SWF movies. The sample project ch19_sample01a.swi uses Load/Unload Sprite control for loading and unloading two movies.

To use the Load/Unload Sprite category of movie control actions in your movie, follow these steps:

1. **Select the sprite to which you are going to attach the action.** In the sample movie, ch19_sample01a.swi, the sprite is named **loader**.

2. **Click the Add Script button, and choose Movie Control ⇨ Load/unload Sprite ⇨ loadMovie().** The menu closes and the action is added to your movie and attached to an `onLoad` event automatically added to Frame 1.

3. **Click in the URL field and type the path for the movie you want to load.** In the sample movie, both the current movie and the one being loaded into the frame are in the same folder, so only the movie's name is typed in the field, as shown in Figure 19-3.

Figure 19-3: Type the location for the file you want to load into the movie.

4. **Leave the Load into Sprite option as is; click the Sprite down arrow and click** loader **to select the sprite.** The first action is complete, and is written as:

```
loader.loadMovie("ch19_sample01x.swf");
```

Note

The figures in this chapter show the objects that can include scripts in the Script panel. This option is one of the program's Script Editor preferences. Choose Edit ⇨ Preferences or Tools ⇨ Preferences, and click the Script Editor tab. Click the Show all objects with script in Guided mode option; the option to Show all objects with script in Expert mode is also selected.

Cross-Reference

Read about setting Script panel preferences in Chapter 17.

Once the movie has been loaded and played, you can remove it again. You can use any object in the movie as the trigger to initiate an `unloadMovie()` action. In the sample movie, a script object is used to both unload one movie and load another movie.

Follow these steps to unload a movie using the `unloadMovie()` action:

1. **Select the object to which you are going to attach the action, and apply an event handler if necessary.** In the sample movie, ch19_sample01a.swi, the action is attached to a text object named **sprite_show**, which has an `onSelfEvent (release)` event handler.

2. **Click the Add Script button, and choose Movie Control ⇨ Load/unload Sprite ⇨ unloadMovie().** The menu closes, and the Unload Movie options appear at the bottom of the Script panel, as shown in Figure 19-4.

Figure 19-4: Select the sprite to be unloaded from the list.

3. **Click the Sprite down arrow and choose the sprite to be unloaded from the list.** In the sample movie, the script reads:

```
_parent.loader.unloadMovie();
```

4. **Choose File ⇨ Test ⇨ In Player to test the movie.** When you test the movie internally you won't be able to see the external movie load although you can follow the action in the Debug panel.

Note The sample movie ch19_sample01.swi contains a second movie that is loaded into the same text object described in the steps, and then removed using another `unloadMovie()` command attached to another text object.

An important detail to keep in mind is the location of your files as you are working with load and unload events. When you use a Movie Control action that requires a file external to the one you are working in, during testing you may see an error in the Debug panel like that shown in Figure 19-5.

Figure 19-5: Specify the correct folder location to avoid errors.

Fortunately, the error message is quite descriptive and the problem is easily solved. Follow these steps:

1. **Choose Edit ➪ Preferences or Tools ➪ Preferences to open the Preferences dialog box.** Click the Player tab.

2. **Click the Test/Load Movie Folder radio button that corresponds to the location where you plan to store the files.**

3. **If you choose the Specify Folder option, click Browse and locate the folder on your hard drive.**

4. **Click OK to close the Preferences dialog box.**

5. **Test the movie again.**

Using load/unload level commands

SWiSHscript contains a set of three options for controlling movies using movie level actions. The concept is the same as that used to define stacking order of objects in your movie. Just as objects in higher levels appear in front of those at lower levels in the movie's object stacking order, the same applies to the movie level.

The bottom level of the movie is level 0. This movie sets the frame rate, frame size, and background color for other movies that you may load. To choose one of the commands, select the object to which you want to apply the command and attach an event handler if required. Then click the Add Script button and choose Movie Control ➪ Load/Unload Level, and choose one of these options:

`loadMovieNum()` — You can use the `loadMovie()` command to load another SWF movie into a SWF movie that is already running.

`loadVariablesNum()` — You can use the `loadVariables()` command to load content from another file based on defined variables.

`unloadMovieNum()` — Use this command to remove a movie that you previously loaded into a SWF movie.

On The Web Site

> The folder ch19_sample01 within the chapter19 folder on the book's Web site contains a project file called ch19_sample01b.swi. This project includes Load/Unload level commands and an example of the `loadVariables()` command. A JPG image is used as the imported movie for the sample project.

Follow these steps to load a movie into another movie based on levels:

1. **Select the object to which you want to attach the command.**

2. **Click the Add Script button and choose Movie Control ➪ Load/Unload Level ➪ LoadMovieNum().** In the sample project, the `loadMovieNum()` action is attached to a text object named **show** and uses an `onSelfEvent (release)` trigger.

3. **In the Script window area of the Script panel, click in the URL field and type the path to the file you want to load.**

4. **Click in the Level field and type a number representing the level at which the movie is to be loaded.** As you can see in Figure 19-6, the sample movie loads into the default Level 1 location.

Figure 19-6: Specify the movie and level in the Script panel.

Note Experiment with the level. In the sample movie, using the default Level 1 location shows the image movie overlying the original movie. If you change to Level 0, the movie takes on the size of the image; the text in the original movie is removed.

5. **Choose File ⇨ Test ⇨ In Player to test the movie.**

Caution Refer to the steps on choosing a movie folder storage location from the previous section if you have a location error.

Note The sample movie also contains a command to unload the movie.

Working with a variable as a Movie Control option

The sample movie ch19_sample01b.swi also contains a `loadVariablesNum()` command attached to one of the text objects. Clicking the text object removes the image movie placed earlier in the script and also loads a variable from a text file into a dynamic text field placed on the page. To use this process, you must have:

✦ An object used to trigger the action; the sample project uses a text object that is targeted and named **hide**

✦ An object used to hold the results of calling the variable; the sample project uses a dynamic text field that has been targeted, named **final words**, and has a variable named **message**

✦ An external file that contains the variable and its value; the sample project references an external file named ch19_sample01.txt

Note If you are using text in a file, you must use & (ampersand characters) before and after the text. The characters tell the Flash Player that the content between the characters is text. You can't use an ampersand in the text itself.

Follow these steps to use a variable to control content loading in a movie:

1. **Select the object to which you want to apply the action.**

2. **Click the Add Script button and choose Movie Control ⇨ Load/Unload Level ⇨ loadVariablesNum.**

3. **On the Script window at the bottom of the Script panel, click in the URL field and type the name of the file whose variable is to be loaded.** The sample project uses the file named ch19_sample01.txt.

4. **Click in the Level field to activate it and type the number corresponding to the level at which you want to place the imported content.** The sample movie uses the default 0 level.

Note   The text import is different than the movie import described earlier in this chapter. In that process, loading an external movie into Level 0 replaces the existing content; in this case, because the receiving object is a dynamic text object placed on the existing movie, setting the movie level to 0 has no effect on the appearance of the movie.

5. **Click Load Variables Only at the bottom of the Script window.**

6. **Choose File ⇨ Test ⇨ In Player to test the loading of the external image movie.** When the **that's enough** text is clicked, the first movie (the JPG image) is removed. The Flash Player reads the text file specified in Step 3 and loads the value of the variable named **message**, added to the dynamic text field as shown in Figure 19-7.

Figure 19-7: The movie loads the value of the variable from the external file.

Controlling How a Movie Behaves

You can specify how your movie behaves under certain conditions using SWiSHscript. Scripts are executed from top to bottom. You can modify the order in which scripts are applied in three general ways:

✦ By repeating code until a condition becomes false, at which time the regular script order resumes

✦ By executing code if a certain condition is true or false

✦ By using a named function that is called and executed; the script may then return to the default order

SWiSHscript includes a number of conditional expressions that you can create using the Script menu options. For each option, select the object to which you want it to apply, click the Add Script button, and then choose Conditional and one of the options.

Code that is executed based on a true or false value uses one of several conditional `if` statements:

`if(frameLoaded())`—This action is useful for preloading content. First, define a specific frame, and then once the frame's content is loaded into the Player, you can initiate other actions such as playing the Timeline. Specify the frame either by number or by label.

`if(isNearThis())`—This action is used to control sprites. You can perform actions on one sprite based on its location with reference to another sprite. Specify what "near" means by choosing one of three options. You can define the value based on the bounding boxes of the two sprites, select a value in pixels for the X-axis coordinates of the sprites, or specify X- and Y-axis distances between the sprites.

`if(droptarget==)`—Use this condition if you are working with sprites and also using `startDrag` and `stopDrag` actions. Specify an action that occurs if the condition is met. For example, if a sprite is dropped on another named sprite, some event occurs such as playing the Timeline.

`if(chance()){`—You can randomize the response of objects in your movies. Use the Random chance value to define the probability that a specified action will result from an event. For example, if you have a button with an `onRelease()` event that plays from a specific frame on the Timeline, if you include a Random chance condition, the event may or may not occur. You specify the probability as a percentage. You can use this action for some types of games, such as horoscopes or other similar types of games that return a text answer that is randomized.

`if(){`—Once the condition of a controlling `if` statement is met, that is, one of the previous conditions on this list, use the `if()` statement to start another set of actions to perform. For example:

```
Var01=3;
Var02=5;
    Trace(Var01);
    Trace(Var02);
    If (Var01>Var02) {trace ("You Lose Baby");
}
```

In this example, "You Lose Baby" will be displayed in the Debug panel when `Var01>Var02`. If the condition is not met, nothing is displayed in the Debug panel.

`} else {`—When the condition of the controlling `if()` statement is not met, you can use an `else` statement to define an alternate set of actions to perform.

`} else if() {`—When the condition of the controlling `if()` statement is not met, you can use an `else if` statement to add an additional `if()` action for evaluation.

Tip   The else and else `if()` commands aren't available unless there is an `if()` statement in the script and it is selected when you open the Add Script ➪ Conditional menu.

Use an action to create a branching structure in your code, and control its execution using cases, with or without an optional default action:

`switch(){`—When you want to create a branching structure in your statements, use the `switch` action. You can write multiple cases; the `switch` action evaluates the first expression and compares it to each expression in the `case` actions. When a match is found, the statements of the `switch` action execute; if there are no matches, and a `default` action is used, statements are executed from the `default` action.

`case...:`—When you use a `switch` action, define a statement or statements that are executed if the case is the same as the `switch` action's argument. Using a single `case` action is the same as using a single `if` statement; using multiple `case` actions is the same as using `else...if()` actions.

`default:`—Use a `default` action to define a statement or statements that are executed if a `switch` action's arguments don't match any defined `case` arguments. The `default` action is the same as using an `else()` action with an `if()` action.Code that is repeated until a condition becomes false uses one of several looping commands. These include:

`while()`—Use the `while()` statement to generate a loop of actions to perform during the time the condition of a controlling `if()` statement is met.

`do {...} while()`—Use this action to generate a loop of actions and evaluate the condition while the condition of a controlling `if()` statement is met.

`for()`—Similar to a while loop, the `for()` statement generates a loop of actions to perform during the time the condition of a controlling `if()` statement is met for a specified number of times.

`for...in()`—Use this action to cycle through properties of an object or through the elements of an array and execute statement or statements for each property or element.

Two additional actions can be used with other actions to control execution of the code:

`break`—The `break` action is used within conditional loops or within a case's statements in a `switch` action. In a `loop` action, the `break` action stops the loop and the statement following the loop is executed. In a `switch` action, the `break` action tells the script to skip the remaining statements in that case and jump to the next statement.

`continue`—The `continue` action is used in conditional loops. The way it behaves depends on the type of loop used. It can be used with `while()`, `do...while()`, `for()`, or a `for...in()` loop.

Working with Functions

Function commands cause the script's execution flow to move to the named function, execute code within that function and then return to the script's original flow of operations in response to a return command. Unlike conditional statements, functions don't ask any questions, such as `if()?`

SWiSHscript includes a number of functions; you can also write your own. A custom function can hold up to four arguments and can return a value.

Functions typically contain several components:

✦ Declaration of the procedure (name)

✦ Code

✦ Return process

✦ Termination

Arguments or parameters are placeholders that let you pass values to a function. In the following example, the function named intro uses two values it receives for the parameters name and city.

```
function intro (name,city) {
introText= "Hi " + name + "! How's the weather in " + city + "?";
}
```

Functions often have a return value. When the function is called, the return could be, for example, **Hi Joe! How's the weather in Omaha?**

> **Note** Spaces are not added in the script automatically. You have to add them within the string in order to have the returned value written correctly.

You can also use built-in functions such as call() to call a function. SWiSHscript includes many built-in functions. To access the built-in functions, click the Expressions button to the right of the fields on the Script panel, and then right-click the field to open the menu.

eval(string)—This function uses the name of a variable in the expression, and is used to reference a variable name. In the example, the eval(string) function is used to determine the value of the expression "time" + x which results in a variable named time2. The eval(string) function returns the value of the variable and assigns it to y:

```
time2="now";
    x=2;
    y=eval("time" add x);
trace(y); //Output:now
```

> **Note** The SWiSHscript eval() function returns references to variables; the Flash MX eval() function returns references to objects, properties, and movie clips as well. The JavaScript eval() function evaluates statements.

variable(string)—This function uses the name of the variable in the string. It can contain any valid expression and be written as variable(string)=expression. The function returns the value of the variable defined by the string. In the following example, the variable(string) function is used to determine the value of the new variable rightnow.

```
time2="now";
    x=2;
    y=variable("time" add x);
trace(y);
    variable(time2)="rightnow"
trace(now); //output is the new variable "rightnow"
```

getProperty() — This function is used to return a specified property value of a sprite instance. In this example, the function returns the height for the object named blob and assigns the value to the variable blobSize.

```
{
blobSize=getProperty (_root.blob,_height);
blobSize=getProperty (blobSize, _height);
blobSize=_root.blob.getProperty(_height);
}
```

Tip The getProperty function isn't always necessary, but shows the code more clearly. As your skill develops you can use dot notation instead. That is, blobSize = _root.blob._height; means the same as the code example with less writing.

Number(expression) — Use this function to convert an expression to a floating-point number. The return is based on the characteristics of the expression:

✦ In a numeric expression, the return is the result, such as (Number (2+2)) which returns 4.

✦ In a Boolean expression, the return is 1 if true and 0 if false, such as (Number (4!=4)), which returns 0 or false because 4 is in fact equal to **4**.

✦ In a string, the function behaves like a parseFloat() function that is returning 0 if the contents can't be evaluated as a numeric expression. For example, (Number ("data")) displays 0 as the word data isn't numeric.

String(expression) — Use this function to convert an expression to a string. The return is based on the characteristics of the expression:

✦ In a Boolean expression the return is either 0 or 1 such as (String (4!=4)), which returns 0 or false.

✦ A number returns the number as characters. For example, (String (4.0)) returns "4.0".

✦ A string returns an expression. For example, (String(_root.a1.)) returns /a1.

Int(value) — This function converts a floating-point number to an integer, but doesn't round up the number. The function's value is the number to be converted. For example, Int(4.4) and Int(4.8) both return a value of 4.

parseInt(string) — Use this function to convert a string to an integer. The function returns the integer except when the string can't be converted to a number, in which case the return is **0**. The value is the string to be converted. For example, both parseInt("99.9") and parseInt("99redballoons") return 99; while parseInt("balloon") returns 0.

parseFloat(string) — Use this function to convert a string to a floating-point number. The function reads the numbers in the string until it reaches a character that isn't part of a number. For example, (parseFloat("balloons")) returns 0. The examples (parseFloat("99balloons")) and (parseFloat("99")) both return a value of 99; (parseFloat("-2aa")) and (parseFloat("-2a2a")) both return the number -2.

isNearTarget() — This function is used to describe a location of one sprite or object in relation to another. The function returns a Boolean true if the two objects are "near"; otherwise, it returns a Boolean false.

The measure of "near" can be defined and is calculated on the basis of the center of the objects, or the objects are considered near by default if their bounding boxes overlap. The arguments include the name of the sprite, X-axis value near the boundary, or Y-axis value near the boundary. The value of "near" is defined based on the distance on center between the objects; when the value is less than the radius of the X-axis parameter, the objects are defined as "near." You can use pixel values, such as 10 used in this example, or overall distance in pixels to define the values.

```
onFrame(1) {
    if (_root.purple.isNearTarget(10,10)) {
        this._alpha=50;
    } else {
        this._alpha=100;
    }
}
```

isNearThis() — This function is very similar to the isNearTarget() function. In the sample project a sprite named **orange,** the left ellipse shown in Figure 19-8, uses the bounding box of a sprite named **purple,** the right ellipse shown in the figure, to define "near." The function goes on to describe what happens. That is, if the orange sprite is clicked when the sprite is within the purple sprite's bounding box its opacity decreases to 50 percent.

```
onSelfEvent (press) {
    if (_parent.purple.isNearThis()) {
        _parent.orange._alpha=50;
    }
}
```

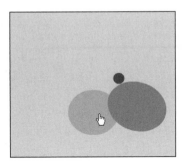

Figure 19-8: By stating a definition for "near," you can influence the relationship between sprites.

On The Web Site

The folder ch19_sample02 within the chapter19 folder on the book's Web site contains a project file called ch19_sample02.swi. This project includes sprites using the isNearThis() function as well as mouse drag functions. A copy of the exported SWF movie is also in the folder.

Mouse Dragging Actions

You can define how a sprite or other object is dragged on your movie using mouse dragging actions. For example, define how scrollbars move on a block of text or how game pieces are moved on the stage.

Note   The sample project ch19_sample02.swi contains three sprites, one of which uses a drag action.

SWiSHscript uses two actions named startDragLocked() and startDragUnlocked() in comparison to Flash MX, which uses the single startDrag() action.

startDragLocked()—Use this command to start a dragging action. You can define the target object or use **this** as the default. You can define a bounding region for the sprite using coordinates defined as left, right, top, bottom; the values are defined in relation to the sprite's parent.

One sprite can be dragged at a time, and the drag motion is locked to the center of the mouse location on the screen. Dragging continues until a stopDrag() action occurs or the drag actions are applied to another sprite.

startDragUnlocked()—Like the startDragLocked() action you can define the coordinates of the sprite's bounding box for purposes of defining an active area on the screen that responds to a mouse click. Unlike the locked action, this action locks the mouse position to the location where you first clicked the mouse button, which may or may not be in the sprite's area of the screen. Dragging continues until a stopDrag() action occurs or the drag actions are applied to another sprite.

The sample project ch19_sample02.swi uses the following code for the sprite named **orange**:

```
onSelfEvent (press) {
    this.startDragUnlocked();
}
onSelfEvent (release) {
    stopDrag();
}
```

stopDrag()—Use the stopDrag() action to stop a previously defined startDrag() action, either locked or unlocked. You don't have to define any arguments for the action nor do you have to identify the name of the sprite to which the action is applied. The sample project uses the stopDrag() action.

Sprite Actions

In addition to many other actions applicable to the sprite object, you can use three actions designed specifically for sprites. You can use a tell action, as well as duplicating and removing sprites.

tellTarget()—You can use this action to direct actions to a named sprite or movie rather than the sprite or movie currently running. You define the target sprite for the action and then define the applicable actions.

Caution   You can't us a sprite inside a button as a target; if a sprite is within an unnamed sprite or group it can only be referenced from one of the objects inside the sprite.

You can nest targets inside other targets, which requires specifying the target by using a path. In the sample project ch19_sample02.swi, the **orange** sprite (the upper left ellipse in Figure 19-9 identified with the hand cursor) has a `tellTarget()` action that is applied to the **little_blob** sprite, the small ellipse at the right of the movie stage shown in the figure that resizes the sprite.

```
onSelfEvent (press) {
    tellTarget (_parent.purple.little_blob) {
        _yscale=50;
        _xscale=50;
    }
}
```

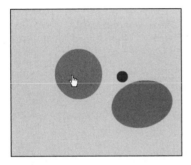

Figure 19-9: Use a `tellTarget()` action to specify a sprite for an event to influence.

There is a second `tellTarget()` action applied to a different trigger that instructs the **little_blob** sprite to reset itself to its original size. The action is used by the **orange** sprite.

```
onSelfEvent (release) {
    tellTarget (_parent.purple.little_blob) {
        _yscale=100;
        _xscale=100;
    }
}
```

Note   The `tellTarget()` action affects the original sprite only. The project also includes commands to create a duplicate that is unaffected when the orange sprite is clicked.

`duplicateSprite()` — This action duplicates a named sprite in your movie. You can specify a depth for the sprite. The original uses level 0, so use a value of 1 or higher to overlay the sprite. Duplicate sprites appear in front of all static objects.

In the sample project, the sprite at the lower right named **purple** contains a `duplicateSprite()` action. It duplicates the **little_blob** sprite (shown as a small ellipse) when it is pressed as shown in Figure 19-10. The script is written as:

```
onSelfEvent (press) {
    little_blob.duplicateSprite("little_blob1",2);
    _y -= 5;
}
```

Figure 19-10: An event attached to an object can trigger the duplication of a sprite.

In the script, you see the event is a mouse click applied to the **purple** sprite. The sprite to be duplicated is named in the second line along with the function. The name of the duplicate, as well as its levels, is shown in brackets. When the duplicate is created, it is offset from the original by 5 pixels on the Y-axis.

removeSprite() — This action is used to remove a sprite you created using the duplicateSprite() action. You don't have to use the same trigger or the same object. In the sample project ch19_sample02.swi the duplicate sprite is removed at a specific frame. The frame event handler is attached to the **little_blob** sprite's Timeline.

```
onFrame (30) {
    removeSprite();
}
```

Be careful when using press and release events on sprites in your movies. If you attach an on(press) or on(release) event handler and action, the sprite is exported from SWiSHmax as a button and no longer works as a sprite. In the sample project, ch19_sample02.swi, if the tellTarget() action is attached to the sprite named **orange**, it doesn't animate after export. Attach mouse events to a button or other object: in the sample project the duplicateSprite() action is added to the object **blob1** in the sprite **purple** and acts upon the **little_blob** sprite.

Statements as Actions

SWiSHscript includes several options you access from the Add Script button's menus to use for creating statements in your movie's scripts. Select the object to which you want to apply the action; then click the Add Script button on the Script panel to open the menus. Choose Statement and one of the following options:

evaluate — Use the evaluate command to evaluate an expression. You can also use the command to enter script into the Script panel in Guided mode without having to use a menu sequence and selection process.

name=expression — This is a multipurpose action that you can use to change properties of an object, sprite, or movie.

Follow these steps to use the name=expression statement:

1. **Choose the target from the Target drop-down list in the Script window area of the Script panel.**

2. **Select a variable or property from the Name drop-down list.** You can choose from a list of operators as shown in Figure 19-11.

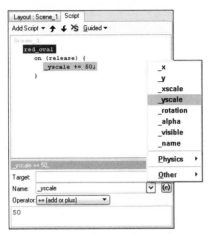

Figure 19-11: Select a property from the Name menu.

3. **Click the Operator down arrow and choose an operator.** The default value, which is =(set value), appears.

4. **Type the value in the Script window area of the Script panel.**

5. **Press Enter or click off the Script panel to move the content to the object's script.** In the figure, when the object named **red_oval** is clicked and released, its Y-axis scale value is increased by 50 pixels.

`function();` — Choose this command to call a function you defined. Select the sprite or movie that contains the function.

`call();` — Use this menu option to call the actions in a labeled frame. Name the target movie or sprite to call, and then select the label of the frame you want to call.

`return...;` — The return action is used to return a value from a function. Select the command, and then type the string or expression for the value you want to be returned. For example, if you are using a function used to return the sum of two numbers, include the return action and write the script as:

```
function sum(a,b) {
    return a + b;
}
```

Logically you should have something for a returned value to do. A common use of the `return` action is creation of a variable that results from a call to the function and is based on the returned value. The preceding code, using sample values for a and b, would continue as:

```
New_value = sum (8,10)
trace (new_value);
```

The output from the function using the example's values is 18.

Sound Actions

You can use three different sound actions. In addition, you can apply an imported sound to the movie as a sound track.

Cross-Reference   See Chapter 11 for information on working with and applying sound in your movies.

playSound() — Choose the playSound() action to attach a sound action to an event handler or action. Choose the file you want to play and its characteristics in the Script panel.

stopSound() — Stop the play of a specified sound using this action.

stopAllSounds() — Use this action to stop play of all sound in the movie.

Caution   Sounds can only be played in response to a frame event or the press, release, rollOver, or rollOut mouse events. You can't use the dragOver, dragOut or releaseOutside events due to a limitation in the Flash Player. In addition, you can't initiate a sound action from a Conditional statement.

Browser/Network Actions

SWiSHscript includes four actions in the Script panel that you use to interact with a browser or network program. Because the browser and network commands work externally to SWiSHmax, test the projects as you develop the script in a player or export to SWF and HTML.

getURL() — Use this action to load a Web page into a target frame of a browser or program playing the movie.

fscommand() — Use this command to send commands to your browser or to the Flash Player.

javascript() — You can add scripts directly to a movie in the Script panel using the javascript() command.

mailto() — Use this command to send e-mail.

Load a Web page

You can use the getURL() action to load a Web page into a target frame of the browser or program playing the movie. The SWiSHscript uses references to standard browser window options.

Follow these steps to use the getURL() action in a movie:

1. **In the Script panel, select the object and an event handler if required.**

2. **Click the Add Script button and choose Browser/Network ➪ getURL().**

3. **In the script window area of the Script panel click in the URL field and type the address for the page you want to load.** You can specify an absolute or relative path for the file.

Tip

If you don't specify an absolute path the Flash Player looks for the URL based on the location of the SWF file.

4. Click the Window down arrow and choose a frame into which the content is to be loaded, as shown in Figure 19-12. You can use the standard target frame options including _self, _blank, _parent, and _top.

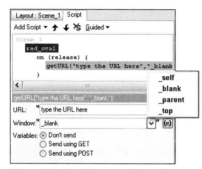

Figure 19-12: Choose a frame for the content.

Tip

You have to include the protocol. For example, add "http://" when addressing an external URL.

5. Choose a Send Variables method. The default is Don't send, which prevents the `getURL()` action from sending variable information to the link defined in Step 3. Other choices include Send using `GET`, which adds variable information to the end of the URL, or Send using `POST`, which sends variable data using a separate HTTP header.

6. Press Enter or click off the Script panel to move the content to the object's script.

Player and browser commands

The `fscommand()` is used to send commands to your browser or to the Flash Player. You can choose from a variety of options that define how the browser or Flash Player uses your movie. As the operation of the command is external, you can't test it within SWiSHmax.

Follow these steps to choose and use an `fscommand()` in your movie:

1. In the Script panel, select the object and an event handler if required.

2. Click the Add Script button and choose Browser/Network ➪ fscommand().

3. Click the down arrow and choose a command from the Command field, as shown in Figure 19-13.

4. Type the argument for the chosen command in the Argument field. The list of available command options follows these steps.

5. Press Enter or click off the Script panel to move the content to the object's script.

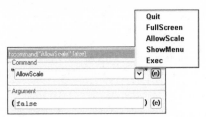

Figure 19-13: You can choose from several fscommand options.

If you are working with a SWF movie, you can choose a number of fscommand() options for the same movie. If you are using the movie with a stand-alone Projector (you are exporting the movie in the EXE format), you can use only the Exec commands.

Cross-Reference   Read about exporting to a stand-alone Projector in Chapter 21.

There are several commands from which you can choose, or you can write your own:

Allow Scale—This command displays the exported movie in the Flash Player at a scaled value if the command's value=true. If its value=false, the movie always plays at 100 percent.

Show Menu—Use this command to specify whether the viewer can use a menu or not. If the value of the command is true, the Flash Menu displays on a right-click or Ctrl+click (Mac). If the value=false, a right-click action displays About Shockwave Flash only on Windows; on a Mac, Ctrl+click displays a grayed-out menu.

FullScreen—This command specifies the use of the computer screen. The SWF movie is shown at full-screen size if the value=true; the movie is shown at its original size if the value=false.

Exec—This command executes a specified program and is used for Projectors only.

Quit—The Quit command closes the SWF file and doesn't require an argument.

If you use an fscommand() within an HTML page there are no predefined commands; instead, the fscommand() triggers JavaScript on the page. The command can also trigger VBScript. When you are exporting a movie and an HTML page that includes fscommand information, SWiSHmax adds the script to the HTML page.

Cross-Reference   See Chapters 21 and 22 for more information on using HTML pages.

Adding JavaScript

You can add JavaScript directly to a movie using the Script panel using the javascript() command. Type the JavaScript in the Script panel's Script window. SWiSHmax formats the script using JavaScript tags in the HTML page. You can't test a JavaScript command from within SWiSHmax or in a stand-alone Flash Player.

Sending e-mail

The final browser/network action is used to send e-mail. When you use this command, the Flash Player launches the client's default e-mail program and can include content you specify in SWiSHmax.

Follow these steps to use the `mailto()` command:

1. **In the Script panel, select the object and an event handler if required.**

2. **Click the Add Script button, and choose Browser/Network ⇨ mailto( ).**

3. **Click in the To field and type the e-mail address for the recipient.** Add a CC address if desired.

4. **Click in the Subject field and type a subject line for the e-mail.**

5. **Type text for the message.**

6. **Press Enter or click off the Script panel to move the content to the object's script.**

The `mailto()` command is added as a single string in the Script panel. You can test the script from within SWiSHmax. Play the movie and trigger the action. An e-mail window opens containing the content you specified in the script, as shown in Figure 19-14. You can change any of the content automatically added to the e-mail message.

Figure 19-14: Include a `mailto()` command to launch an e-mail editor from your SWF movie.

Understanding Physics Properties

SWiSHmax can be used for designing games. Many games use conditions that define how objects interact with one another. In order to make this interaction more realistic you can apply physics properties to your objects to control properties such as an object's velocity, acceleration, or friction. For example, if you design a game that can drag one object to strike another object, you can control the velocity of the stricken object.

Cross-Reference

In order to use physics properties you have to enable the physics properties for both the movie and objects that use the properties on the Export panel. These items are described in Chapter 21.

Some properties of objects include physics extensions. You can use a range of different physics properties for common properties such as alpha and rotation. Table 19-2 lists the common object properties that include physics extensions.

Each property includes the formula for the property extensions as well as their values. For example, _xscale includes acceleration, friction, and velocity physics property options. The acceleration property is written as _axscale (acceleration of _xscale) and is expressed as pixels per second or a specified number of seconds. Similarly, the friction property is written as _fxscale and is expressed as a percentage; the velocity property is written as _vxscale and is expressed as a percentage per second.

Table 19-2: Physics Components of Common Properties

Property	Acceleration	Friction	Velocity
_X	_aX (pixels/sec/sec)	_fX (%)	_vX (pixels/sec)
_Y	_aY (pixels/sec/sec)	_fY (%)	_vY (pixels/sec)
_xscale	_axscale (%/sec/sec)	_fxscale (%)	_vxscale (%/sec)
_yscale	_ayscale (%/sec/sec)	_fyscale (%)	_vyscale (%/sec)
_alpha	_aalpha (%/sec/sec)	_falpha (%)	_valpha (%/sec)
_rotation	_arotation (deg/sec/sec)	_frotation (%)	_vrotation (deg/sec)

acceleration—The rate at which the speed of the object changes is its acceleration. The default acceleration of an object is 0, which means the speed is constant and the object neither accelerates nor decelerates. If an object has a speed of 5 pixels per second, for example, and has a rate of acceleration of 10 pixels per second, after one second its velocity is 15 pixels per second; after two seconds its velocity is 25 pixels per second, and so on.

friction—The rate at which the speed of an object decreases. Friction is expressed as a specified percentage per second rather than a fixed value as used for expressing acceleration. For example, an object may have a friction value of 5 percent applied to its _frotation value.

velocity—The rate of speed at which an object moves is its velocity. Velocity is expressed as pixels per second. For example, an object may have a velocity of 20 pixels per second.

Objects commonly use values in combination. For example, using both velocity and a friction rate, the values may be written as:

    _frotation=5, _vrotation=45.

After one second, the object has rotated (45-5 percent)=42.75 degrees due to the friction drag; after two seconds, the object rotates an additional (42.75-5 percent)=40.6 degrees. SWiSHscript includes three additional read-only physics properties that are specific to SWiSHscript:

age — Use the _age property to return the age of an object in seconds.

delta — The _delta property is used to define the time in seconds since the last frame was displayed.

time — Use the _time property to return the amount of time in seconds since the movie started.

Summary

Actions are the key to interactivity in SWiSHmax. You can write scripts manually in the Script panel using the Guided mode or use the Expert mode and write your own scripts. In this chapter you learned about the categories of actions you work with in SWiSHscript. You saw how actions are categorized and applied. You learned about the different types of actions and how they are used. Using several sample movies, you learned how some of the more common actions are used in SWiSHmax movie projects. You also learned how to:

✦ Categorize actions

✦ Write expressions, use operators, and choose script syntax options to assist in writing scripts

✦ Modify the order of operations using conditional expressions

✦ Use functions

✦ Apply mouse-dragging actions to sprites

✦ Use different types of statements

✦ Work with browser and network actions

✦ Understand physics properties

✦   ✦   ✦

Distributing SWiSHmax Movies

Testing Movies and Preparing for Export

Once your masterpiece is created and scripted and your experimentation is finished, it's time to export the finished movie and dazzle the world. Or is it? Exporting in different media, such as a SWF movie or a stand-alone Projector have different requirements, but all forms of export benefit from a systematic evaluation and testing of your product.

Testing a movie on your own computer is substantially different from loading a movie on a Web page that is accessible to everyone. One of the biggest factors to consider is file size. The majority of people using the Internet still use dial-up connections. Waiting a long time, or even an undefined length of time, is not a good way to entice visitors to your site, nor is it likely to compel them to return if they have to wait for a long time to see your page. "A long time" is defined by the individual visitor and can vary from a few seconds to minutes.

File size is also important if you are outputting your movie to a CD or creating a stand-alone Projector. Bloated movie files often produce stuttering playback.

Preparing for export requires several stages, which you learn about in this chapter. The first step is general troubleshooting. Unless your movie plays correctly and you can interact with it as planned, it isn't ready for export.

Each component of a movie project — from text to images to effects — has an impact on the movie you are exporting. You see how to approach each component with the idea of optimizing the content while minimizing the component's size. You'll learn some tips that will help you make a more compact movie.

The requirements for export differ based on the intended use. Although discussions about specific export formats are included in Chapter 21, you'll see how to evaluate a movie using a group of common settings within the context of exporting a SWF movie, as well as those that apply to the entire movie, a specified scene, or a selected object.

Testing Your Movie

Hopefully you are testing a movie project periodically as you are developing it. It's important to see if an effect looks right, for example, or that a link actually works. SWiSHmax includes a number of ways to test a movie. Each has its purpose, and each is different.

Play Timeline or Movie. From within SWiSHmax, you can use one of several locations to choose the Play Movie or Play Timeline commands. Rather than viewing the entire movie, save time when you have several sprites and/or scenes in a movie by using the Play Timeline command. When you are working with an effect, you can save time by using the Play Effect command to test your settings before viewing an entire scene or Timeline. When you test a movie internally you can't access some external files.

Test in Player. Use the Test in Player option to see your movie in action without having to create a formal export. Choose File ⇨ Test ⇨ In Player, or use the Ctrl+T accelerator keys. A Flash 6 Player opens, and your movie runs. You can test the movie's interactive features in this test mode.

Test in Browser. Use the Test in Browser option to see your movie as it will appear on a Web page using default settings. Choose File ⇨ Test ⇨ In Browser, or use the Ctrl+Shift+T accelerator keys. Temporary SWF and HTML files are created. The page uses the same color as the movie's background color.

Report. The Report file contains a wide range of information about your movie including the frames, content, scripts, and size. As you prepare your movie for export, review the report to see where you have made file size savings.

 Tip The status bar at the bottom of the program window displays the file's size in kilobytes once you have used either Export or Test commands. Prior to testing or exporting, the status bar message located at the bottom right of the program window reads "Unknown Size". The size display lasts only for the current session; when you reopen the file at a later time the "Unknown Size" label is again visible.

 Tip If you have turned off the status bar you can show it again by choosing View ⇨ Status Bar.

Testing Checklist

If you do a lot of work with SWiSHmax, as with other design programs, it pays to be organized. Decide in the early stages of a project what you want to accomplish, and then develop your movie with the intended output in mind. For example, if you are creating a SWF movie that contains animated GIF files, create the animations using the same frame rate as that in the movie; modify or create images that are the correct size and resolution for the movie.

 Cross-Reference See Chapter 3 for discussions on project planning.

There are some basic testing items to consider when you are preparing for export:

✦ **Can you see everything in your movie as intended?** If not, check in the Outline panel to make sure that the objects are visible; you may have an object's visibility toggled to hidden or need to reorder the objects in a scene.

✦ **Is the playback correct?** That is, does the movie stop and start as it should? If not, check the Timelines to make sure the stop() and play() and other similar actions are placed correctly.

✦ **Do your sprites play correctly?** Do they stop when they should stop or loop when they should loop? Check each sprite to make sure its play option is correct (see Figure 20-1).

Figure 20-1: Make sure the sprite's playback option is correct in the Sprite panel.

✦ **Do your scripts run as intended?** If not, here are some things to look for:

- **Check names.** Make sure the names of variables and any objects referenced are correct.

- **Check paths.** When you are referencing objects or variables make sure relative paths are identifying the correct object.

- **Check the Test/Load movie folder.** You can choose a folder location in the program preferences to use for testing and loading movies. Choose Edit ⇨ Preferences or Tools ⇨ Preferences and check that the folder named on the Player tab is the correct folder.

Cross-Reference

For information on choosing a folder preference, see the discussion in Chapter 19.

- **Check URLs.** Check the paths for any URLs written in the movie's script.

- **Check quotation marks in your scripts.** Some commands require double quotes; others single quotes.

Preparing for Archiving

One aspect of creative work that is often overlooked is the importance of archiving. Once you have worked long and hard to create your movie, take a few minutes and organize what you have built.

Check the names of the objects in your movie to see that they are unique, understandable, and follow some method of naming that is useful to you. When you return to a project at a later date, the content in the project file makes more sense if you have followed a standard naming process.

Combine content in a complex project. Where you have numerous objects in a movie, it can sometimes help to keep track of your movie's components if you group similar objects.

On The Web Site

For an example of a movie whose contents are grouped for ease of use, see ch20_sample01a.swi, located in the ch20_sample01 subfolder in the chapter20 folder on the book's Web site. That project file combines numerous similar objects into groups.

Add comments in your scripts. Notes can often help you make your way through some complicated scripting as you are developing your movie. Comments will certainly help when you return to a project after being away from it and can't remember which variable refers to which object.

Notes about the content in the movie itself can be equally valuable for future reference. For example, you may have done a considerable amount of image modification in SWiSHmax that you are repeating for a series of images. Perhaps at a later date you plan to replace images with those that you modified in an external image manipulation program. Whatever the case may be, there are two simple ways you can add notes to yourself in SWiSHmax.

You can add a text block to a project and write a note to yourself. Use static text and default fonts. Hide the text object before exporting the movie. You have a ready-made reference the next time you return to your project. As shown in Figure 20-2, you can also place the note in a separate scene to separate it from your movie's content.

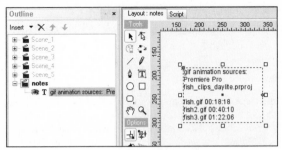

Figure 20-2: Write important information in a note and save it in a blank scene.

Alternatively, use the Script panel to store information about your movie. In Figure 20-3, you can see that information about the movie's source files is added to a multiline comment in the Script panel. If you write notes as a comment in the Script panel, you don't have to add a text object to the movie, of course.

Note   Either method of storing information has virtually no impact on your movie's size. The example shown in the figures was created using the ch20_sample01.swi sample project. The version containing the note was 4220.4KB in size; both the version containing the comment and the version without any comment were 4220.2KB.

Store your SWiSHmax project file, an exported version of the movie, and the source files in the same location on your hard drive. That way, everything you need is available when you return to the project at a later time. Delete extra material such as images when you complete the project.

Figure 20-3: Store information about your movie in a comment.

Reading Reports

An exported SWF movie file can have a surprisingly large file size. Numerous graphics, intensive effects, and multiple shapes can contribute to making a movie's size unacceptable for your needs.

There are many things you can do to modify the content of your movie to save file size. Some instances require that you make changes or substitutions to the actual content of the movie; in other instances the key is in understanding how to modify movie content to reduce file size. Regardless of the methods you use, the first thing to do is look at the movie's report. An example of a report segment is shown in Figure 20-4.

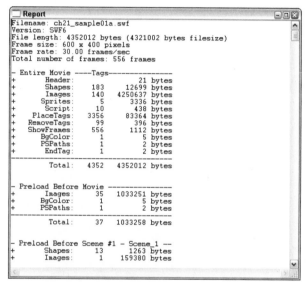

```
Report
Filename: ch21_sample01a.swf
Version: SWF6
File length: 4352012 bytes (4321002 bytes filesize)
Frame size: 600 x 400 pixels
Frame rate: 30.00 frames/sec
Total number of frames: 556 frames

- Entire Movie ----Tags----------------
+       Header:                21 bytes
+       Shapes:      183    12699 bytes
+       Images:      140  4250637 bytes
+      Sprites:        5     3336 bytes
+       Script:       10      438 bytes
+    PlaceTags:     3356    83364 bytes
+   RemoveTags:       99      396 bytes
+   ShowFrames:      556     1112 bytes
+      BgColor:        1        5 bytes
+      PSPaths:        1        2 bytes
+       EndTag:        1        2 bytes
------------------------------------------
        Total:     4352  4352012 bytes

- Preload Before Movie ----------------
+       Images:       35  1033251 bytes
+      BgColor:        1        5 bytes
+      PSPaths:        1        2 bytes
------------------------------------------
        Total:       37  1033258 bytes

- Preload Before Scene #1 - Scene_1 --
+       Shapes:       13     1263 bytes
+       Images:        1   159380 bytes
```

Figure 20-4: A report displays information about the movie on a frame-by-frame basis.

On The Web Site

The report shown in the figure is taken from one of the sample projects available on the book's Web site, ch20_sample01a.swi. The chapter20 folder contains a subfolder, ch20_sample01, which includes three versions of the same movie using different methods for reducing file size.

A report is a very valuable tool. You can see clearly where the resources are used in your movie. You can also see where you might consider making changes to save file size, or where you should increase the amount of information to be preloaded, for example. In a complex project, or one in which you have to be very concerned about the final SWF movie's size, save the report. The report is displayed in a Notepad window in SWiSHmax. Although you can't save it directly, copy the content from the report and paste it into a blank Notepad file, which you can then save and print.

Segments of the report generated by the sample project are described here. In each category of the report, its purpose and an interpretation of the report is given along with probable areas where savings in file size may be found.

Basic structural information. The report starts with a text block giving general information about the movie. This information includes the name of the file, SWF version used, file length, frame size, frame rate, and total number of frames in the movie. If you refer to the report image in Figure 20-4, you see the frame rate is 30 fps; the frame rate may be a likely area to look for file size reduction.

General details about the movie. The next section of the report describes the number of tags and what type of element or process uses them. The general details for the sample movie are shown in Listing 20-1.

Listing 20-1: **Tag Allocation for a Sample Movie**

```
- Entire Movie ----Tags---------------
+       Header:                21 bytes
+       Shapes:     183     12699 bytes
+       Images:     140   4250637 bytes
+      Sprites:       5      3336 bytes
+       Script:      10       438 bytes
+    PlaceTags:    3356     83364 bytes
+   RemoveTags:      99       396 bytes
+   ShowFrames:     556      1112 bytes
+      BgColor:       1         5 bytes
+      PSPaths:       1         2 bytes
+       EndTag:       1         2 bytes
-------------------------------------
        Total:    4352   4352012 bytes
```

As you can see in the code listing, this sample movie contains a lot of shapes, which are letters in the movie, and images, which are frames of animated GIF movies.

Note   Text is not exported as shapes by default. When complex effects are used, the letters are defined as individual objects as they are animated individually.

The movie also has literally thousands of Place tags, which may be a good area to consider with regard to saving file size. The sample movie contains three animated GIF sequences that contribute greatly to the processing required by the Flash Player and are a likely area to be examined to save file size.

Tip   If you look at the listing you see there are five sprites listed. The movie contains three sprites and two groups. The groups are included within the sprite count and identified as a group as their information is described in the report.

The ShowFrames value of 556 is the same as that of the total movie, which is 556 frames in length. The movie uses one background color (BgColor), has one PSPath (a path that is opened for programming commands as they are received by the SWF Player), and uses one EndTag. The Total shown at the end of the Entire Movie report displays the total number of tags to be processed and the total number of bytes in the movie.

Note The PSPath is an undocumented tag that is used simply for importing the SWF into Flash.

 Tip To easily convert the bytes value to kilobytes, divide by 1000. The sample movie is 4325KB in size.

Preload Before Movie. The Preload Before Movie listing identifies the content that is preloaded before the movie starts playing. In the sample shown in Figure 20-4, one background color, one PSPath, and 35 images are preloaded. The segment also lists the tags' size in bytes. If the movie is jerky or stutters during playback, changing the preload before movie settings may be of value.

Information about scenes. The next segment of the report describes the processing requirements for the movies' scenes. The information for the first scene in the sample movie is described in Listing 20-2.

Listing 20-2: **Information Reported About a Scene**

```
- Preload Before Scene #1 - Scene_1 --
+       Shapes:     13      1263 bytes
+       Images:      1    159380 bytes
---------------------------------------
         Total:     14    160643 bytes

- Scene #1 - Scene_1 ----------------
+      Sprites:      1       471 bytes
----- Sprite #1 - [ as effect group] -
+    PlaceTags:     17       457 bytes
+   ShowFrames:      1         2 bytes
+       EndTag:      1         2 bytes
---------------------------------------
+       Script:      2        80 bytes
+    PlaceTags:   1506     37996 bytes
+   RemoveTags:     18        72 bytes
+   ShowFrames:    100       200 bytes
---------------------------------------
         Total:   1627     38819 bytes
```

Perhaps the most telling items in the report are the PlaceTags. The description of the scene from the sample movie shown in Listing 20-2 identifies 13 shapes and 1523 Place tags. In the movie, the first scene includes text that has been broken into shapes and animated. As a result, the complex requirements for defining each shape's location on each frame generate a large number of Place tags.

Frame lengths. The final segment of the report lists the frame lengths on a scene-by-scene basis. Each frame in your movie is numbered; in the report, the frames' sizes in bytes, and the total size of the movie to a specified frame in both bytes and as a percentage of the whole movie are listed. For example:

```
- Scene #1 - Scene_1 -----------------
      -Frame-    -Bytes-    -Total-    -%-
           0    1194379    1194379    27%
           1        434    1194813    27%
```

This segment of the report describes the start of **Scene_1**. You see that the lengths of Frame 0 and Frame 1 are vastly different. When **Scene_1** starts, it preloads 61 images and 62 shapes. When Frame 0 has been loaded, 27% of the movie's content, or almost 1.2MB of data, has been loaded.

Optimizing Movies

Optimizing a movie's components means generating the best output under specified conditions. Optimizing a movie requires skill and patience. The goal is to produce a movie using the right effects and objects, displaying it at the highest quality, and having the smallest file size. Achieving these three goals in one movie requires compromise, and that is where skill and patience enter the picture! A movie running at 30 fps and using very high-quality, resized images and multiple effects is going to be enormous.

The first question is about design. Do you need all the exploding, swirling, whirling imagery, or can you substitute effects that convey your message but without the expenditure of file size? While that decision is beyond the scope of this chapter, it is something to keep in mind as you design your SWiSHmax projects. Designing with certain criteria in mind will result in less work when you optimize the final movie.

As you plan, keep in mind that you can often substitute different techniques that produce similar output and save file size. There can be savings in all aspects of your movie, including:

✦ The movie's basic characteristics

✦ The movie's structure

✦ The fonts you use

✦ How you modify the text

✦ The audio files you select

✦ How you format the audio

✦ The images you select

✦ How you compress images

✦ How you select and apply effects

✦ Your choice of export methods

Choosing efficient movie settings

Consider the speed and size of your movie carefully. Try to correlate these characteristics with your intended product. For example, if you have a movie that is used as a form there is no need for a high frame rate. In fact, you could slow the frame rate down to 1fps (frame per second) without noticeable difference if the form contains only one frame. The change in frame rate won't affect the size of the movie appreciably because only a single frame is processed.

Changing frame rate. If you are building a movie that uses a number of effects or animated GIF movies, you should evaluate the speed of the movie carefully and correlate the speed with your intended use. When the movie is designed for playback on a desktop, frame rate is usually not an issue. Then again, if you are planning on using your movie on the Web there's little value in using a fast frame rate, such as 30fps. Viewers are reluctant to wait a long time for a large number of frames to preload. If you don't preload the frames, the playback is likely to be very jerky, and your goal of a smooth, slick movie playback isn't achieved anyway.

Modifying frame size. If you are using images for backgrounds or to fill much of the movie's space, you should also look at the physical size of the movie. Can you convey your message in a movie that is 400 x 200 pixels in size as well as in one that is 600 x 300 pixels in size? Although the answer to that question may be a design decision, keep it in mind. If you find at the end of a movie construction process that you are using only a portion of the movie's stage, trim the movie's size. If your movie consists only of vector images, such as drawings done in SWiSHmax or text, changing dimensions won't affect the size of the movie in kilobytes.

On The Web Site

The book's Web site contains three versions of a movie project for your experimenting pleasure in the ch20_sample01 subfolder located in the chapter20 folder. The first version of the file, ch20_sample01a.swi uses full-size, animated text, and untrimmed images. The second version, ch20_sample01b.swi is 1MB smaller due to trimmed images, simpler animation and a lower frame rate. The third version, ch20_sample01c.swi, is the same as the second version except that all the content has been placed in one scene rather than several scenes.

Structuring the movie

The way your movie is constructed can have an impact on its size. Consider how you use scenes and sprites.

Changing the number of scenes. Adding or removing extra scenes in your movie has little or no impact on the exported movie's size. For example, the sample project ch20_sample01b.swi file contains five scenes, while the ch20_sample01c.swi movie contains only one scene. When the finished movies are exported as SWF movies, the movie containing one scene is 4KB smaller than that containing several scenes. The time expended on converting the content from several scenes to one scene isn't worth the savings nor is it efficient in terms of working with the movie. Many people find it simpler to organize a complex project using discrete scenes for different purposes; combining everything into one scene could be time-consuming as you try to remember how the components are placed and used.

Applying uniform backgrounds. One area where you can see file size savings is by using a unified scene background. For example, instead of using a separate background image on each scene of a movie, consider whether one background would work for the entire movie and place that one image in a scene specified as a background.

Cross-Reference

Refer to Chapter 8 for information on using an image as a movie background.

Reusing sprites. Where possible, create sprites and use instances rather than constructing multiples of the same object. Not only does using sprites save construction time, it also saves file size as you are using a clone of an object rather than constructing multiple objects.

Removing objects. The SWF export settings for all versions include an option for removing objects automatically when they are not visible. Using this option can save file size as objects aren't processed if they are hidden from view.

Learn about exporting in different SWF formats in Chapter 22.

Making decisions about text

Animated text can add much visual impact to some movies; other movies are entirely text-based and don't use any animation. Regardless of your focus, you can save file size by using fonts and text intelligently.

Choosing fonts. Fonts are embedded in your exported SWF movie. Some fonts are much larger than others. Experiment with different fonts, especially if you have a font-intensive movie. Also, consider using the system fonts for general-purpose text. If your movie contains a sequence of similar scenes, such as one image and one message per scene, use the same font and the same color. Not only does repeating the font and color add a sense of consistency to the movie; it saves file size.

Read about working with text and choosing fonts in Chapter 10.

Exporting options for text. Unless you are planning to reuse a movie in Flash MX 2004, you don't need to use the text object option on the Export panel when exporting a movie in SWF format. Deselect the Allow import of text as text object option as shown in Figure 20-5. The option is available for all SWF versions in the Export panel. You can also experiment with the Text as Shapes and Share Font options on the Movie and Scene Export panel settings. In some cases, depending on the complexity of your text and its animation, you can save file size.

Figure 20-5: Deselect the text object option to save space.

Chapter 21 describes in depth the Export settings for different forms of export.

Breaking up text. Unless you have a need for text to be broken into shapes, such as using an image fill, you can save file size by leaving it as a block of text rather than shapes. Each character is defined as a shape with regard to the SWF export tags, but processing is faster when the text is seen as a sequence of similar shapes rather than discrete objects. The same applies to breaking text into letters. Unless there is a specific need, leave the text as text.

Optimizing effects

One area where you can see considerable savings in file size is in the effects you use. The more complex the effect, the greater the impact it has on the file's export size. Particularly resource-intensive effects are those like explosions or some of the 3D effects where numerous objects or components are moving at the same time. These kinds of effects require a large number of Place tags for each frame of the exported movie. Other "expensive" effects are those that change the color and position of the object or objects to which they are applied as they also require a large number of Place tags per frame.

The effects you choose are primarily a design decision. Sometimes you can substitute an effect that is less intensive in terms of file size and still produce much the same outcome. In the sample project ch20_sample01a.swi, the text uses a custom 3D effect that requires breaking the text into shapes as it also includes an image fill. The second version, ch20_sample01b.swi, uses a much simpler effect and the text remains as a single object. Figure 20-6 shows a frame from each text animation—the left image is from the ch20_sample01a.swi movie. When your intention is to save file size, substituting with a simpler effect can provide much the same overall sense of movement. The image on the right in the figure is a frame from the ch20_sample01b.swi movie that uses a less complex effect applied to solid-color text.

Figure 20-6: Different effects can produce similar results.

Cross-Reference Learn about the different categories and types of effects in Chapters 12, 13, and 14.

Sometimes a movie can be centered on certain complex and multiple effects. In that case, look for other areas to trim file size. You may find savings in frame rate, image compression, or other areas.

Saving file size with audio compression

Audio can enhance a movie tremendously, but it can also significantly increase the movie's file size. Check for several features of the sound files when trying to conserve export file size. Some of the techniques are design-based; most are related to export options.

Importing sound. If possible, process your sound before importing it into SWiSHmax. When using a simple sound, such as a click that accompanies button events or scene changes, the sound doesn't need a high sample rate or bit depth, nor does it have to be stereo sound. You can modify the settings in SWiSHmax prior to export, of course, but you don't have the same precise control of the sound that you have in a dedicated audio manipulation program.

Using loops. Whenever possible use short music loops instead of songs. An audio clip can be looped to play for the duration of a visitor's viewing of your movie and adds very little to the file size in comparison to one full-length piece of music.

Using the LAME Encoder. SWiSHmax uses the LAME encoder and compresses sound for export in the MP3 format. The results are very good and can save a great deal of file size.

Modifying export settings. You can save a considerable amount of file size when exporting audio. You have to carefully balance the quality of the sound against the value it has for your movie. In the earlier example of a button event, the type and quality of the sound isn't as important as the fact that it exists. Your visitors are cued with a click sound on a button event whether it is in stereo or mono, is 8-bit or 16-bit sound, or has a 5.5 or 44kHz sample rate. On the other hand, if your movie is designed to promote your band, limiting the size of your audio files may not be an option, and you have to look elsewhere for savings.

Compressing audio

Modify the audio compression and choose a preloading option in the Sound Properties dialog box. In the Script panel or the Content panel, select the sound file you want to modify and click Properties to open the Properties for Sound: "[filename]" dialog box.

The effect of modifying settings can be extreme. The following example uses a 609KB WAV file with 32kHz, 16-bit stereo options settings:

✦ When the movie is exported using no compression, the SWF movie is 790KB.

✦ Using ADPCM compression, 5-bit ADPCM depth, and retaining the quality settings, the exported SWF movie's size drops to 255KB.

✦ Using MP3 compression drops the SWF movie's size to 77KB.

✦ Decreasing the quality of the audio to the lowest sample rate, using mono sound, and MP3 compression results in a final file size of 10KB.

If the goal of using the clip was to simply have music in the movie, then lower-quality settings are sufficient. In the trial, the 10KB movie's sound was almost unusable. However, using a low sample rate and retaining stereo sound produced an almost satisfactory movie score with a 20KB movie size. The best compromise between output quality and minimal file size used the MP3 compression and a 22kHz sample rate for an exported file size of 39KB.

On The Web Site

The sample movie used in this experiment is available from the book's Web site in the chapter20 folder. The file is named ch20_sample02.swi and is in the ch20_sample02 folder. The original WAV file is also in the folder; none of the exported SWF movie versions is included in the folder. The sound is attached to an `on(release)` event applied to a simple shape in the movie.

Choosing preload options

In SWiSHmax, you can choose preload options in several locations, including the Sound and Image Properties dialog boxes, as well as the Export panel in the Movie, Scene, and Selected Object settings. Preloading files is not the same thing as creating a preloader; a preloader is a separate movie that plays as the content you designate for preloading is loaded into the Flash Player.

Regardless of the area in which you apply the settings preload options work the same. The preload options for an audio file are shown in Figure 20-7.

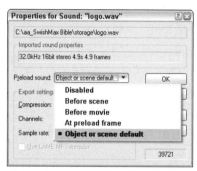

Figure 20-7: Define a preload setting for an audio clip in the Properties for Sound: dialog box.

You can choose from:

✦ **Disabled.** The content isn't preloaded; content appears at the frame on which it is placed. Without preloading, you may experience some hesitancy in the movie's playback.

✦ **Before scene.** The content is loaded into the Frame 0 location of the scene in which it is used in the movie. Depending on the size of the content and the viewer's download speed, using this option can result in a delay before the scene's playback starts.

✦ **Before movie.** The content is loaded into the Frame 0 location for the entire movie; this option can also result in a delay before the movie starts playing.

✦ **At preload frame.** The sound is loaded into a specified frame to which a `preloadContent()` action has been attached. The action applies only to content that displays on or after the frame on which the action has been placed. Content that appears earlier in the movie loads at the frame where it first appears similarly to using the Disabled option.

✦ **Object default or Scene default.** The default location for preloading an image or sound is set in the Export panel as is the scene default. Settings chosen in the Export panel are applied as the default for the movie unless you specify a different preload option for a specific object or scene.

Tip   The Object default option is available only in the Image and Sound Properties dialog boxes; the Scene default is available only on the Export panel.

Content in your movie can be preloaded in different ways. In addition to standardized locations, such as before a scene or before the movie, you can specify a preload frame in the movie.

Follow these steps to add a preload action:

1. **On the Timeline, right-click the frame to which you want to apply the action.** The shortcut menu appears.

2. **Choose Add Script ⇨ Frame ⇨** `preloadContent()`.

3. **To add the action following placement of objects in the frame, click the After events for placed object option at the bottom of the Script panel.** An icon showing an open folder is placed on the frame as shown in Figure 20-8.

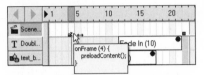

Figure 20-8: Define the frame to use for loading your movie's objects by adding a preload action.

Optimizing project images

Images are one area where you can save a great deal of file size. There are issues to consider prior to importing the images into your movie project as well as when preparing for export.

Image formats. Experiment with different image formats and compare file size and quality. You may find you have a better quality image using a GIF file than a JPG image; the reverse may also be true. Keep in mind that image resolution and compression can be modified in SWiSHmax as well as your image processing program. When possible, experiment with using vector graphics instead of raster graphics with the goal of saving file size.

Cross-Reference Chapter 5 discusses raster and vector graphics; Chapter 8 describes importing images for your movie projects.

Sizing images. One of the simplest things to do before starting a project is resizing your images. Although you can certainly resize any image you import into SWiSHmax, your exported SWF movies are smaller if the images are sized correctly at the start.

The two versions of the movie are the same aside from the image sizes. The sample movie, ch20_sample03a.swi, produces a SWF movie of 55KB; the second sample movie, ch20_sample03b.swi, produces a SWF movie that is 28KB in size. The only difference between the two movies is that in the second sample the images were sized according to the size required in the movie prior to importing them into SWiSHmax.

On The Web Site The two project files described here are available from the book's Web site. They are both in the ch20_sample03 subfolder located in the chapter20 folder. The project ch20_sample03a.swi uses images that require resizing; the file ch20_sample03b.swi uses images sized for the movie. The movies' images are also in the folder on the Web site.

Trimming images. Make sure to trim images as well as resizing them. Remove the extra space around an image. The blank or background-colored pixels are included in the file's dimensions and size, and therefore affect the output whether or not there is visible content.

Something else to consider is using converted video. The sample files in the ch20_sample01 series include animated GIF imports that were converted from digital video clips. As you can see in the sample frame from the ch20_sample01a.swi file shown in Figure 20-9, the converted video resizes itself when the aspect ratio is changed on export and the frames include black edges. Trim the clips before adding them to the SWiSHmax project.

Figure 20-9: Trim images to decrease file size.

Matching frame speeds. Matching frame speeds can have a great deal of impact on your movie when using imported animations. Either match the movie project's frame rate to the animation or vice versa. If you have an image manipulation program that can generate animated GIF files such as Fireworks or a video editing program that can produce animated GIF output such as Premiere Pro, use the programs' power to decrease the size of your files.

Although the imported animated GIF file is a sequence of images, it is based on an animation. If the original animation was built using a 10fps frame rate, for example, there is no visual value in increasing the frame rate of the SWiSHmax movie.

The ch20_sample01 files include the same animated GIF files. However, the ch20_sample01a.swi file uses a 30fps frame rate, while the ch20_sample01b.swi file uses a 10fps frame rate. In the output, the animations in both movies appear to run at the same speed.

Compressing images in SWiSHmax

You can adjust the resolution and compression of an image in SWiSHmax. SWiSHmax offers two ways to adjust image settings — in the Image Properties dialog box or through the Export panel.

Note Shapes can be optimized in the Export panel only.

The option you choose depends on the movie. In the Image Properties panel you adjust each image individually; you can compress image and shape quality and resolution throughout an entire scene or a movie from the Export panel.

Follow these steps to adjust compression and resolution in a single image:

1. **Select the image on the Layout panel or the Outline panel.**

2. **Click the Shape panel's tab to display it at the front of the panels group.**

3. **Click Properties to open the Image Properties dialog box.**

4. **Modify the compression options in the Export Settings area of the dialog box.** The options available vary according to the file format. As you make modifications you can see the size of the image that will be exported displayed in the Export size (bytes) field.

5. **Click the Preload Settings button to open a list of options.** Choose an alternate preload option if desired.

6. **Change the image's resolution by clicking and dragging the Resolution slider or typing a value in the Resolution field.** Preview the image in the preview area as you adjust the settings. The modified file size is shown in the Export Settings area.

7. **Click OK to close the Image Properties dialog box and apply the changes to the image.**

The options available for compression vary according to the type of image you are compressing. For JPEG images you can choose bit depths; for both PNG and GIF images, you can choose only standard ZIP and JPEG compression options. The Image Properties dialog box for a JPEG image is shown in Figure 20-10.

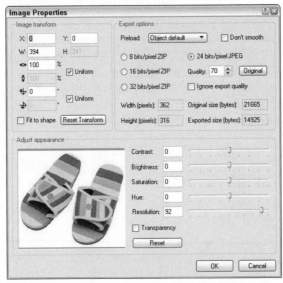

Figure 20-10: Set compression options for individual images in the Image Properties dialog box.

Preload. Click the Preload button and choose an option for loading the image in the exported SWF movie. You can choose from:

✦ **Disabled.** The preload options are not used for the image.

✦ **Before scene.** The image is loaded into the Frame 0 location of the scene in which it is used in the movie.

✦ **Before movie.** The image is loaded into the Frame 0 location for the movie regardless of the scene in which the image appears.

✦ **At preload frame.** The image is loaded into a specified frame to which a preloadContent() action has been attached.

✦ **Object default.** The default location for preloading an image set in the Export panel.

Smoothing. Toggle the Don't Smooth option on and off. When selected, the image is smoothed, or anti-aliased.

Bits/pixel ZIP compression. Choose one of the three options for compressing using the ZIP process. When you choose a ZIP compression option the JPEG compression options are disabled.

JPEG compression. You can use 24-bit/pixel JPEG compression for the image. When you choose this option, quality options become available.

Quality. Click the field and type a value, or use the up and down arrows to adjust the quality of the image. A lower-quality image results in a smaller file, but may be of insufficient clarity.

Tip   Compressing your images is a way you can often save a considerable amount of file size.

Ignore export quality. Click this option to override the settings you use for the overall movie that are chosen in the Export panel.

File size (bytes). The original size of the image in bytes and the exported size of the image in bytes are both displayed at the lower right of the Export options area of the dialog box. As you make modifications they are reflected in the exported size field.

Original. Click the Original button to return to the settings used by the file when it was imported into your movie.

Resolution. Click in the Resolution field and type a value, or click and drag the slider to adjust the resolution of the image. The original resolution is considered to be 100 percent; dragging the slider decreases the resolution, which is shown in the preview area at the left of the Image Properties dialog box. As you adjust the resolution, the change in the exported size of the image is shown in the Exported size field.

Choosing export settings

In addition to choosing compression settings in the Sound Properties and Image Properties dialog boxes for specific items, you can adjust many settings for the overall movie that affect the compression and output quality. The movie settings you select for a project are used as the settings for testing your movie in the Flash Player.

The Export panel includes settings panels for different aspects of your project as well as different file formats. When you choose an option from the Export Options for drop-down list, the corresponding panel is shown in the Export panel. Regardless of the export format, you can use a collection of common settings for the movie, scene, and a selected object.

Caution   When you choose settings for export in one project, they remain in subsequent projects. You have to set the export settings for each project individually.

Movie and scene export options

With few exceptions, the movie and scene export options are the same. You can choose options for text, images, and quality. Because a scene is a child object of a movie, many of the settings categories include an option to use the parent movie's setting when you are using the export settings for a scene.

The Export panel in Figure 20-11 shows typical export options for a movie. For each setting, click the button displayed and choose an option from a drop-down list. For the options that specify a value, click in the field to activate it and type the value you want to apply to the project or object.

Figure 20-11: Choose common settings for the movie or scene in the Export panel.

Export options for. Click the button displaying the current settings and choose an option from the drop-down list. You can choose from Movie or This Scene options. If an object is selected on the Outline panel or Layout panel, the Selected Object option is also available.

The Export options for list also includes defining export formats such as SWF, AVI, HTML, and scripts. These items are discussed in Chapter 22.

Preload content. Choose one of four options available for movie export settings, and one of five options available for export settings applied to a scene. The options include:

✦ **Disabled.** No preload command is used and the content is loaded as it appears.

✦ **Before scene.** Content is loaded into the Frame 0 location for a scene.

✦ **Before movie.** Content is loaded before the movie starts.

✦ **At preload frame.** Content is loaded at a specified preload frame.

✦ **Movie default.** This option is also available when using the Export options for scene and applies the default used for the movie to the selected scene.

Share fonts. You can choose one of three options for font sharing for the Movie export option, and one of four options for font sharing when you are setting options for a scene. Font definitions are written to the SWF file to define the shapes of characters. The definition is a subset of the font; that is, only those characters used in the movie are actually described in the SWF file's code. The options are:

✦ **Disabled.** When the Share fonts option is set to disabled, a separate font definition is written to the SWF file for each text object. Using this setting can add greatly to a file's export size.

✦ **Across scene.** The font definitions for all characters in a scene are written to the SWF file at the start of the scene. This option is useful if you are using several different fonts in your movie and don't want the movie to hesitate before it starts as the font descriptions are loaded in the SWF movie.

✦ **Across movie.** The font definitions are written to the SWF file at the start of the first scene containing text objects and having the Share fonts option set to Across movie. This option can delay the start of a movie, but make scenes load more smoothly.

✦ **Scene default.** This setting is available only when you are using the Export options for This Scene options. The scene default is the same as that set for the Across movie settings.

Note

Using the font option Across movie usually produces the smallest exported movie size but can produce a delay before the movie starts as the font definitions are loaded.

Tip

If you are using a preloader scene, sometimes it is smoother to use the Across scene option for the preloader scene and the Across movie option for the rest of the movie.

Text defined as. The Movie export options have two settings for Text defined as, while the Scene export options have three choices. You can define text either as text or as shapes. Sometimes you can save file size by using text as shapes. You have to experiment with your movie to see if changing formats has any value.

✦ **Text defined as Text.** This option exports text objects using font definitions and can be set both using the Movie and Scene export panels. If you are using modified quality settings for the images in your movie, experiment with the Text defined as options. Sometimes, decreasing the quality of the shapes can wreak havoc on the appearance of the text.

Note

Text defined as Text is also used when exporting the SWF movie to other programs such as Macromedia Flash MX 2004.

✦ **Text defined as Shapes.** The text in the movie or scene is defined as shapes rather than letters. Using this option prevents you from later editing the text in either SWiSHmax or other programs that can import and use a SWF movie such as Flash.

✦ **Scene default.** This setting is available only when you use the Export Options for This Scene panel. The scene default uses the text definition selected for the movie.

✦ **Text effects use.** For the Movie export panel only, you can select to export text effects as either shapes or letters. If your movie uses a lot of text, or uses complex text effects, experiment with the two optional export formats to see if either option can reduce exported movie size.

Defining image characteristics

For both Scene and Movie Export panels, you can choose from three settings to define the quality of the images and shapes in the movie. The settings you select for the entire movie are used as a default unless you specify specific settings for a scene or individual objects. If you have set specific quality and resolution settings for individual images, they are not over-ridden by settings in the Export panel. When the Selected Object panel appears in the Export panel, only the Shape quality setting is available.

✦ **Image quality.** If your images use JPEG compression, you can specify a quality level. Click in the Image quality field to activate it, and then type the value. At 100% value the image uses the settings with which it was imported.

✦ **Image resolution.** Decreasing the resolution of images, although it can reduce the size of your exported movie, can also produce unsatisfactory images because the pixels increase in size as the resolution is decreased.

Cross-Reference

Chapter 5 describes image resolution in detail.

✦ **Shape quality.** Decreasing the quality of a shape decreases the complexity of the image and gradually smooths the image. The 100% value for a shape is the original quality as it existed when the shape was drawn or imported.

Use the settings in the Export panel in combination with the settings for individual images. Sometimes it is more convenient to use an overall image quality setting for the movie, and then evaluate the images as the movie is tested and individually adjust only those images whose quality is unacceptable. Changing image quality level as well as resolution can certainly decrease the size of an exported SWF movie.

Be careful using the quality settings in conjunction with text shapes. In the sample project ch20_sample04.swi, the graphic image is a WMF vector drawing that SWiSHmax defines as a shape. Defining the text as a shape can create significant problems in the output although it can save a great deal of file size.

Figure 20-12 shows three images of the same frame of the movie exported using different settings. All three versions use the Text defined as Shapes option in the Export options for Movie settings in the Export panel. The left image is the final frame of the movie in which the drawing is set to its default quality and resolution. The exported movie, ch20_sample04a.swf, is 114KB in size.

The central image is the final frame of the movie with the Shape Quality set to 80%. It looks very similar to the original movie doesn't it? If you look closely you can see the details on the doors are less distinct, but the text is virtually the same. The settings used for the second sample, ch20_sample04b.swf, would be effective output settings for producing a quality movie with a small file size. The second sample is much smaller than the original; its size dropped to 49KB. The right image shows the same frame with the Shape quality set at 60%. The exported SWF movie, ch20_sample04c.swf, is only 14KB, but it's not of much value as the image is unrecognizable. The text looks interesting, though.

Figure 20-12: Test your output carefully when using image quality changes in combination with text.

On The Web Site

The sample project is available from the book's Web site. The ch20_sample04 subfolder, located in the chapter20 folder, contains the project file as well as the source image used in the sample. The folder also includes three exported SWF movie files that correspond with the images used in this discussion.

Summary

This is the first of two chapters looking at how you prepare a movie for export, how you test the movie, and then how you choose export settings. A testing checklist was described in this chapter that you can use to systematically evaluate your movie when you are getting ready to export it. You saw how to organize the content of a movie for storage. You learned many ways to optimize the content in your movie within the context of exporting a SWF movie, and how to weigh the quality against the file size for different components. You also saw how to work with preload options, as well as choosing export settings for a movie, scene, or object.

In this chapter, you also learned how to:

✦ Test a movie to ensure it runs correctly and its scripts work as designed

✦ Prepare a movie for archiving by grouping content and writing notes

✦ Use the Report command to analyze a movie and read a movie report with a view to saving file size

✦ Plan a movie with the goal of optimizing its size based on design and construction methods

✦ Make compression and optimization choices about text, images, and audio files that are efficient

✦ Select export settings for a movie, scene, or selected object

✦   ✦   ✦

Exporting SWiSHmax Movies

In the early days of Flash and SWF movies, using a movie in a Web page was often a calculated risk. Downloading a movie was a lengthy process for viewers using very slow modems, one for which they sometimes had to download and install a player first. Unless there was a compelling reason to do that, many people simply moved on to another site. The technologically curious would take the time to download and install players and then wait and wait and wait for the files to download. Sometimes the wait was worth it — unfortunately it often wasn't! But the mere fact that the technology existed was incredibly cool, and the dog could always be taken for a walk while a file downloaded.

SWF movies shown in Flash Players have become omnipresent. The Flash Player is preinstalled with both the Windows XP and Apple Macintosh operating systems; Flash Player 7 is also now available for Linux. Macromedia Flash Player is the world's most highly distributed software platform; more than 480 million users are estimated to have the software.

If a movie has been carefully designed and optimized for export, as discussed in Chapter 20, choosing the right export settings make Flash SWF movies relatively painless for your users to download and view. That doesn't mean you don't have to consider how to best use your movie and distribute it to your most likely audience. SWiSHmax provides extensive export settings for three versions of SWF. In this chapter you see how to use each version and how to modify settings according to the content of your movie.

Your SWF movies don't often display by themselves: usually you see a SWF movie embedded within a Web page. In this chapter the issues involved in using a movie in a Web page are covered, and you learn ways to configure both the Web page and the movie to create the output you need.

SWF isn't the only way to export a movie, of course. You can also use your movies in a variety of other formats, such as video and a standalone projector. SWiSHmax offers you many ways of configuring the output to best meet the movie's and your users' requirements.

Choosing a SWF Version

SWiSHmax has three SWF export versions you can choose from: you can export a movie in Versions 4, 5, and 6. All three versions share common settings. For example, you can offset your exported movie regardless of format, and remove or mask objects not appearing on the stage. All three support the "text import as text object" option used if you import a SWF movie into SWiSHmax or Flash MX 2004.

The version you choose depends on your audience and the device for which you are creating the movie. The vast majority of users worldwide can use material formatted in Flash Player 6.

At the time of this writing, cell phones do not support all of the Flash Player 5 functionality, and therefore Version 4 is recommended for developing movies for telephone playback. Pocket PCs, on the other hand, are capable of using Flash Player 6; only the version 6 Player is currently available for download.

Exporting a SWF movie

The process for exporting a SWF movie is the same regardless of the export version you choose. Make sure the Export panel, which is visible by default, is accessible. If you can't see the Export panel in the program's panel group, however, choose File ⇨ Export ⇨ Display Export Panel to make the panel visible. Alternatively, choose Panels ⇨ Default to reset the default panel display, which includes the Export panel.

Follow these steps to export a SWF movie:

1. **Click the Export tab to display the Export panel.**

2. **Click the Export options for: down arrow and choose SWF (Flash) from the drop-down list.** The Export panel displays the SWF panel.

3. **Click the SWF version to export: down arrow and choose a version from the list.** The Export panel displays the option for the SWF version selected.

4. **Choose the options as required for your movie.** As shown in Figure 21-1, the SWF6 Export panel includes five optional settings.

Figure 21-1: You can choose a number of optional settings for exporting SWF.

5. **Test and optimize your movie using the selected settings.**

6. **Choose File ⇨ Export ⇨ SWF.** You can also use the Ctrl+E accelerator keys.

7. **Name the file and choose the storage location in the Save dialog box.** Click OK to export the movie.

SWF export options

The SWF Export panel contains a list of five options if you choose SWF6, and four options if you choose either SWF5 or SWF4:

Compress SWF file. This option is available only for SWF6 exports. Compression is a major advantage of SWF6 over earlier versions of the player.

Offset to suit use as a Movie Clip. Use this option if at some point you intend to use a movie exported from SWiSHmax in Macromedia Flash MX 2004. The default setting is off (unchecked), which places the movie down and to the right on the stage. When you use this option, movies imported into Flash as a Movie Clip are centered.

Cross-Reference   Chapter 22 describes using your exported SWiSHmax movies in Macromedia Flash MX 2004.

Remove off-stage objects. When working with a movie file, you see that the elements are animated regardless of their location with respect to the stage, as shown in Figure 21-2. Use this setting to prevent content outside the margins of the stage from animating. Removing off-stage objects can be useful in decreasing the file size of some animations, such as exploded text or shape animations. The default setting is on (checked).

Caution   If you want to import the SWF movie into Flash MX 2004 or back into SWiSHmax, deselect this option to prevent the animation from stalling when objects reach the margins of the stage.

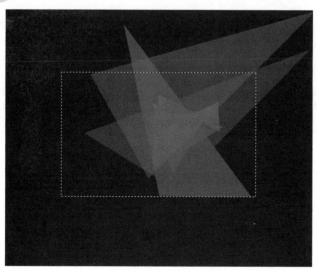

Figure 21-2: Objects or portions of objects that move off-stage can be removed to decrease the size of your exported movie.

Mask off-stage objects. Masking off-stage objects hides the elements when they are outside the margins of the movie, as shown in Figure 21-3. Using the masking option can add to the exported movie's size slightly. The default setting is on (checked). You can use both removing and masking off-stage actions in combination.

Caution Using the masking option hides dynamic or input text that uses device fonts, which is a limit of the Flash Player.

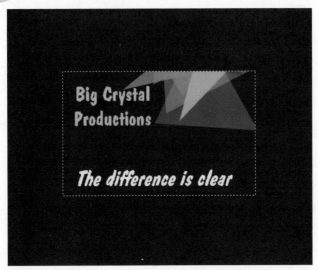

Figure 21-3: Masking hides objects outside of the stage's margins.

Caution If you want to import the SWF movie into Flash MX 2004, you may need to deselect this option. Importing the SWF movie into Flash MX 2004 can cause a program error due to an import bug. The error doesn't occur if the SWF movie is loaded into another movie using a `loadMovie()` action.

Allow import of text as text object. When you want to work with the exported SWF movie in either Flash MX 2004 or SWiSHmax, select this option to preserve the text as text. Maintaining text as text increases the file size slightly; deselecting the option results in smaller SWF movies. The default setting is on (checked).

Caution The allow import of text as text object option must be selected if you want to import the movie into Flash MX 2004 or SWiSHmax and prevent errors.

For the most part, modified settings are required only if you are importing your SWF movie into SWiSHmax and/or Flash MX 2004. If you are preparing content for distribution, you don't have to worry about any cautions. If you do plan to reuse the material and find that using the options increases file size, export one version for Web use, for example, and another for use in projects that are stored locally.

On The Web Site If you would like to experiment with the movie shown in this discussion, you can download it from the chapter21 folder of the book's Web site. The file is named ch21_sample01.swi and is in the ch21_sample01 subfolder. The crystal used in the animation was drawn in SWiSHmax.

Selecting Script Export Options

The three versions of SWF you can choose in SWiSHmax have some differences with regards to the script options available for export. SWF4 has several more options than either version 5 or 6.

To choose script export options, follow these steps:

1. **Click the Export options for: down arrow and choose Script from the drop-down list.** The Export panel displays the Script panel.

2. **Click the SWF version to export: down arrow and choose a version from the list.** The Export panel displays the script options for the SWF version selected.

3. **Choose the options as required for your movie.** Figure 21-4 shows the Script export options available for SWF4.

Figure 21-4: Different SWF versions provide different script options.

Common script options

All three versions of SWF share two common script options: Include tracing in the movie, and support physics properties.

Support physics properties. Unless you are using physics properties in your movie, you don't need to select this option available from the Export options for Script panel, shown in Figure 21-5. For any object in your movie that has physics properties, you must also select the Uses physics properties option for the object. Select the object on the stage and choose the Selected Object option from the Export options for drop-down list.

Tip

If you aren't using any physics properties in your movie, be sure to check the Support physics properties is deselected on the Export options; leaving the option selected adds to the file's size unnecessarily.

Figure 21-5: You can specify that an exported movie and its objects support physics properties.

Include tracing in SWF file. Choose this option to allow SWF debugging if the movie is loaded into another movie.

SWF6 script export settings contain one additional option:

Expose SWF6 properties. If you export a SWF6 movie and have used buttons and/or text as targets, choose this option to use the property native to SWF6 in the movie's script.

Script support for SWF4

If you plan to export a movie in SWF4, you can choose from several additional script settings depending on the content of your movie.

Global mouse properties. When you use cursor tracking and your script uses the `_xmouseglobal` and `_ymouseglobal` properties, click the global mouse properties option. This allows for tracking X-axis and Y-axis cursor coordinates.

Shared advanced math library. Click this option if your movie is using math functions. SWiSHmax creates a small (approximately 9KB) sprite designed to simplify the script calls. The Flash Player then calls the scripts from one single source, which can speed up the processing of your movie. If you don't choose this option, each math method is called as it is used.

Caution
If you load the movie containing a math library into another SWF movie, the receiving movie must also have the math library sprite. If you load the movie containing a math library into a non-SWiSHmax movie, the math functions don't work.

Fix Flash rotate and shrink bug. Click this option only if your movie contains objects that include rotations. SWF4 contains an inherent bug that shrinks objects as they rotate.

Exporting HTML from SWiSHmax

One of the slickest export features in SWiSHmax is the ability to export your movie embedded in a complete Web page. This allows to you to prepare your movie for use on the Internet in one step. You can either create a Web page outright or copy the HTML for your movie to the clipboard for inclusion in an existing Web page.

The HTML generated by SWiSHmax uses HTML 4.0. Follow these steps to export your movie and a Web page:

1. **Click the Export options for: down arrow on the Export panel and choose SWF (Flash) to display the Flash Export panel.**

2. **Click the SWF version to export: down arrow and choose the version you want to export.** Make adjustments to the SWF and Script export options as required.

3. **Click the Export options for: down arrow on the Export panel and choose HTML (Tags) to display the HTML Export panel.**

4. **Click export settings as required.**

5. **Choose File ⇨ Export ⇨ SWF and HTML.** You can also use the Ctrl+P accelerator keys. The files are exported to your storage folder and a dialog box opens (see Figure 21-6).

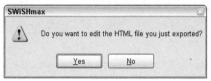

Figure 21-6: You can edit the HTML page you just created.

6. **Click Yes to close the dialog box.**

7. **Edit the HTML page as required and save it.**

The exported HTML page contains two tags, and much of the information is duplicated. The <object> tag is used by Internet Explorer to start the Flash Player and load the movie. The <param> elements name and assign parameter values, such as the movie's quality or background color, that are passed to the player.

The second tag used is the <embed> tag. This tag isn't part of the HTML or XHTML specification, and actually prevents pages from being validated. The <embed> tag is used by Netscape and Netscape-like browsers for displaying Flash movies. Rather than parameters, like those used by the <object> tag, the <embed> tag uses parameters as names with value attributes.

The HTML Export panel contains a number of options, as shown in Figure 21-7. You can configure the HTML to specify size, location, quality, and other aspects of the movie's playback on the Web page.

Figure 21-7: Configure the HTML page's display of your SWF movie.

Size=100%. The default for this option is deselected. The movie's code includes the height and width according to the settings you defined in SWiSHmax. For example, the ch21_sample01.swf movie is 450 pixels wide and 280 pixels high. After exporting the movie, the size reference in the HTML reads:

```
id="ch22_sample01" width="450" height="280">
```

If you use the Size=100% option, your movie is scaled to fill the entire Web page and is written as:

```
id="ch22_sample01" width="100%" height="100%">
```

Device Font. This option is selected by default. If the required fonts are available, the movie playback utilizes the user's device fonts for displaying static text.

Cross-Reference   Refer to Chapter 10 for discussions on font types.

Play. The default option is selected. The movie plays when the Player starts.

Loop. The default option is for the movie to loop or play repeatedly.

Tip   If you have the Loop option selected and your movie isn't looping, check the Movie panel. You may have the Stop playing at end of movie option selected, which overrides the export setting.

Menu. Another default option is for displaying a menu. The menu is available when the user displays the page showing your SWF movie. The default option allows display of the Flash Player's right-click menu (available as Cmd+Click on Macintosh OS) when the viewer interacts with your movie as shown in Figure 21-8. If you deselect this option the viewer will only have the About Flash menu available.

Figure 21-8: You can specify the extent of the menu control for your exported movie.

Base. If you want to define relative path names for your movie, click the Base field to activate it, and then type a URL for the directory in which you are housing the HTML and SWF content. This base URL is most often your Web site's main folder or a subfolder within it. The Base field is blank by default.

The Base URL is most often used when your movie contains getURL() actions. Adding a getURL() action can include writing an absolute path to a referenced file; if not then the Flash Player uses the URL of the HTML file as its presumed location. When you add a Base URL in the HTML Export panel, you override relative paths defined in individual actions.

Quality. You can choose from several levels of quality for your exported movies. Quality is based on the amount of anti-aliasing (smoothing) in the movie. Your computer allocates a specific amount of system resources to processing a movie; the quality level defines whether resources are geared towards performance or appearance. The High quality setting is the SWiSHmax default option.

You can choose from five different quality settings:

✦ **Low.** Playback speed is the priority and anti-aliasing is turned off.

✦ **Autolow.** Playback speed is the initial priority; anti-aliasing is turned on if the Flash Player detects a fast enough processor.

✦ **Autohigh.** Both playback speed and anti-aliasing are given equal priority at the start of the movie. The Flash Player detects the playback rate; if the frame rate of playback is lower than that specified in the movie, anti-aliasing is turned off.

✦ **High.** The movie's appearance is given priority over speed. Anti-aliasing is always used. If animation is used in the movie, bitmaps aren't smoothed; if animation isn't used in the movie, bitmaps are smoothed.

✦ **Best.** The movie's appearance is top priority. All output, whether animated or not, is anti-aliased at all times.

Scale. You can define how the movie size appears in the browser window when using an export option different than the original movie's size, such as showing it at 100% of the browser window's size. Three options are available:

✦ **Show all.** Show all is the default. The movie's appearance is the same as what you see when testing the movie in a player or exporting the SWF only.

✦ **No border.** The movie is scaled to fill the area specified in the movie's settings. There is no distortion as the movie's aspect ratio is maintained, but the movie may be cropped.

✦ **Exact fit.** The movie is fit to a specified area, but it may distort.

Align movie. You can specify the alignment of a SWF movie's content within the movie's window on the HTML page. If your movie is cropped, choosing an alignment option also defines the type of cropping. The Align movie setting is written in the HTML tag as a value for the parameter "salign" within the <object> tag, and as a value in the <embed> tag. The value for a movie aligned at the top right of the window, for example, is written as a parameter of the <object> tag as:

```
<param name="salign" value="tr">
```

and as an attribute of the <embed> tag as:

```
salign="br"
```

The movie alignment options, their cropping settings, and the value displayed in the movie's tags are listed in Table 21-1.

Table 21-1: Movie Alignment Options

Option	Description	Cropping	Tag
Default	Centered in the movie window	All sides	`nil`
Left	Aligned at left side of the movie window	Top, bottom, right sides	`value="l"`
Right	Aligned at the right side of the movie window	Top, bottom, left sides	`value="r"`
Top	Aligned at the top of the movie window	Left, right, bottom sides	`value="t"`
Bottom	Aligned at the bottom of the movie window	Left, right, top sides	`value="b"`
Top-left	Aligned at the upper left of the movie window	Bottom, right sides	`value="tl"`
Top-right	Aligned at the upper right of the movie window	Bottom, left sides	`value="tr"`
Bottom-left	Aligned at the bottom left of the movie window	Top, right sides	`value="bl"`
Bottom-right	Aligned at the bottom right of the movie window	Top, left sides	`value="br"`

Note   When using default settings for `nil`, the `salign` parameter is not included in the movies' code.

Align window. As with other objects placed in an HTML page, you can specify the alignment of a SWF movie's window on the page. The Default option centers the movie in the browser window; cropping can occur on any side as pages are resized.

You can also specify that the window is aligned at the left, right, top, or bottom of the browser window. Cropping will occur on edges not specified by the alignment option. For example, if you choose to align at the right then the top, bottom, and left of the window may be cropped.

Mode. If your work is designed for display using Internet Explorer on a Windows system, you can use window Mode options. The options are used to define the characteristics of the movie's window as a parameter of the `<object>` tag, written as:

```
<param name="wmode" value="opaque">
```

and as an attribute of the `<embed>` tag written as:

```
wmode="opaque"
```

To use these settings, the Flash Active X control is required. Three options are available:

✦ **Window.** The movie is played in its own window in the browser. This is the default option; there are no parameters or attributes written to the HTML page.

✦ **Opaque.** The movie is placed in a window that blocks the content on the page from showing through.

✦ **Transparent.** The background of the HTML page shows through transparent areas of the movie, depending on the browser. For example, transparency is supported only in Internet Explorer 5.0 and newer; and not supported in Netscape browsers.

Figure 21-9 shows an example of the Opaque window mode in action. If the window mode is left at its default, changing the page's color also changes the field color of the SWF movie; changing the wmode parameter/attribute to opaque leaves the field color of the original SWF movie intact.

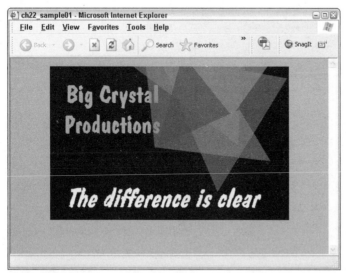

Figure 21-9: You can specify the opacity of the window displaying your SWF movie.

Script Access. Three options are available for allowing script access in the SWF's code. Consider these options if you are using either FSCommand() or getURL() actions in your movie's script. The Script Access options are only available for Flash Player 6 or newer.

Note   The Flash Player 6 version required is v.6.0.40.0.

✦ **Never.** No FSCommand() or getURL() scripts are run.

✦ **Always.** Script access is allowed.

✦ **SameDomain.** If the scripting targets referenced from the SWF movie are located on the same Web domain, the script is run.

Tip   If you are working with loadMovie() and loadVariables() scripts, or using external PHP scripts, check the Script Access settings — incorrect settings prevent the scripts from running.

Copy HTML to Clipboard. Rather than choosing the option to export the HTML to the clipboard through the File menu, you can choose this option directly on the HTML Export panel. The HTML for the movie is automatically placed on the clipboard for you to use in other Web development programs.

Tip   You can also use the Ctrl+H accelerator keys to copy the HTML to the clipboard.

The HTML for a SWF movie is shown in Table 21-2. A description of each line of the code's purpose is included in the table.

Note   On a Web page, the lines aren't broken as shown in the table.

Table 21-2: Sample SWF Movie Tags

Code	Explanation
`<object classid="clsid:D27CDB6E-AE6D-11cf-96B8-444553540000" codebase="http://download.macromedia.com/pub/shockwave/cabs/flash/swflash.cab#version=6,0,79,0"`	The class of object identified along with the opening `<object>` tag
`id="ch22_sample01" width="450" height="280">`	The name of the object, which is the file's name, as well as the height and width in pixels
`<param name="movie" value="ch22_sample01.swf">`	The first parameter that identifies the type of object and the object's value as the movie file
`<param name="bgcolor" value="#000033">`	The background color parameter
`<param name="quality" value="high">`	The quality of the movie parameter
`<param name="devicefont" value="true">`	Parameter defining whether device fonts are used; in this case they are used
`<param name="salign" value="br">`	The alignment of the movie in the window; in this case bottom right is the value of the parameter
`<param name="wmode" value="transparent">`	The window mode parameter, which in this case is transparent
`<param name="allowscriptaccess" value="samedomain">`	Script access is allowed, in this case the same domain option is the value for the parameter
`<embed type="application/x-shockwave-flash"`	The opening embed tag and its attribute, which is a SWF application
`pluginspage="http://www.macromedia.com/go/getflashplayer"`	The location of the Flash Player
`width="450" height="280"`	The width and height of the movie; pixels is the understood value
`name="ch22_sample01" src="ch22_sample01.swf"`	The name of the movie and its source file
`bgcolor="#000033" quality="high"`	The background color and quality of the movie
`salign="br" wmode="transparent"`	The window alignment, in this case bottom right, and its mode, in this case transparent

Code	Explanation
`swLiveConnect="true"` `allowScriptAccess="samedomain">`	The `swLiveConnect` attribute is Netscape-specific and required to run a Flash Player and movie. The script access allowed, in this case the same domain option
`</embed>`	the closing `<embed>` tag
`</object>`	the closing `<object>` tag

Cross-Reference Learn more about working with exported HTML in Chapter 22's discussion on using SWiSHmax with Dreamweaver MX 2004.

Exporting Video

You can export your masterpiece as a video in AVI format instead of SWF. Video exported from SWiSHmax does not include any interactive actions or elements except those for playing sound either as a soundtrack or as a frame action. Video export is useful if you intend to use your movie in other programs such as Adobe Premiere Pro, PowerPoint, Adobe Acrobat, or any other programs that can run video.

Follow these steps to export a video from SWiSHmax:

1. **Click the Export panel in the panel group.**

2. **Click the Export options for: down arrow and choose AVI (Video).** The AVI Export panel displays.

3. **Click the Setup Compression down arrow to open the Setup Compressor for AVI Export dialog box.**

4. **Choose the desired codec from the drop-down list and then choose the codec's configuration options.**

5. **Click OK to close the Setup Compressor for AVI Export dialog box and return to the AVI Export panel.**

6. **Choose options for the movie's dimensions on the AVI Export panel including height, width, aspect ratio, and use movie size.**

7. **Type a value in the Make movie longer by: field if you want to make the movie longer.** The movie's frame rate is adjusted to comply with the new length.

8. **Choose File ➪ Export ➪ AVI.** The Export to AVI dialog box opens. You can also use the Ctrl+M accelerator keys to export the AVI movie.

9. **Choose a name and folder location for the finished movie in the Export to AVI dialog box.**

10. **Click Save to close the Export to AVI dialog box.** The message box shown in Figure 21-10 displays. Click OK to close the dialog box and save the movie.

Figure 21-10: An AVI movie export runs two separate processes.

As outlined in the SWiSHmax dialog box that displays when you choose the export command, exporting video is a two-stage process after the file is initially saved. The audio is captured and then the data is recorded. Depending on the size of the movie, an export may take a considerable length of time. After you finish processing the file, test it to see and hear how it plays. Sometimes you may notice some stuttering in the audio, which, as described in the message dialog box, can result from resources being taken from SWiSHmax to apply to other processes. Shutting down other programs before you export video can provide for better export quality and audio syncing.

If you incorporated a sound loop such as that used in the sample project, you hear a substantial difference between the exported AVI movie and an exported SWF movie. Sound doesn't loop the same way in the exported AVI as it does in the SWF movie; the playback stops at the audio frame corresponding to the last frame of the movie, and then restarts as the movie restarts.

Having the video portion of the movie correlate with the audio improves the playback to some extent. In the sample project, for example, the audio clip is 40.4 frames in length; when the movie is exported at its original length (that used for the earlier sample ch21_sample01.swi project file), the sound stops partway through the sequence. Increasing the length of the movie to twice that of the audio loop (to 81 frames) improves the audio looping—although it still hesitates as the movie is restarted.

The nature of video is different than SWF. If you need looping audio, export the movie as a SWF movie; use video when you need one-time playback.

On The Web Site

The project file used in this discussion is named ch21_sample01a.swf and is located in the ch21_sample01 subfolder within the chapter21 folder on the book's Web site. The file is the same as the one used earlier in the chapter except that it also contains an audio loop, tune.wav. An exported movie named ch21_sample01a.avi is also in the folder.

Setting movie dimensions

The AVI Export panel includes options for sizing the movie, both in terms of frame size and length. The optional settings are shown in Figure 21-11.

Depending on the content in the movie, you may not have good results resizing the movie unless you maintain the *aspect ratio*, or the vertical and horizontal proportions of the movie. The default option uses the movie's original dimensions and locks the aspect ratio, as shown in Figure 21-11. Click the Width field and type a different value if you want to resize the movie proportionally. If you want to change the aspect ratio, click Lock aspect ratio to uncheck the option, and then type values in both the Width and Height fields. If you click the Use movie size option, both Height and Width fields are grayed out.

Figure 21-11: You can modify the length and size of the exported movie.

You can also add frames to the end of the movie. You may want to do this if you are fitting an exported video into another sequence, for example, and intend to use the movie in a program such as Premiere Pro and want extra frames for handles to use for applying effects. Click the Make movie longer by: field to activate it, and then type the value for the additional frames. Adding blank frames to the movie increases the file size.

Compressing video

Video clips are larger files than SWF movies. You can use a compressor/decompressor, or *codec*, to decrease the size of the file while preserving quality. When exporting a video program, choose a codec which compresses the information for storage and transfer, and then decompresses the information so it can be viewed again. Compressing the video program makes it play smoothly on a computer. SWiSHmax provides five codec options. In each case, click Setup Compression on the AVI Export panel to open the codecs' dialog box.

Most of the codec options, with the exception of the Intel IYUV codec, include several configuration options as shown in Figure 21-12. The best way to choose compression options is to experiment. In most cases, you have to weigh file size against movie quality.

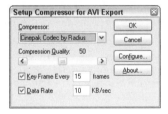

Figure 21-12: Most codecs offer similar optional settings.

Compression Quality. Drag the slider left to decrease quality, and drag the slider right to increase quality. A higher quality, although producing better output, creates a larger file.

Key Frame Every. Compression keyframes are placed during export of the AVI movie at the interval you specify. During compression, keyframes are stored as complete frames. The frames between the keyframes are called *intermediate frames*. Only the differences between a keyframe and each intermediate frame are stored in the file, which significantly reduces the file's size. The fewer the number of keyframes, the smaller the file size, but the lower the image quality and playback. The greater the number of keyframes, the larger the file size, but the better the image quality and playback.

Data Rate. You can specify the *data rate*, expressed as KB of data processed per second, which controls the amount of video information that must be processed each second during playback. Specifying a data rate sets the maximum data rate because the actual rate varies depending on the content of each frame.

Configuration. Some codecs' settings include a second configuration dialog box. If you can set other options, the Configuration button on the Setup Compressor for AVI Export dialog box is active.

About. Click About to open a dialog box identifying the codec, its manufacturer, version, and date of copyright.

Using the Cinepak codec

The Cinepak codec, which has extremely low CPU requirements, was originally designed for playing small movies on single-speed CD-ROM drives. Use a Cinepak codec if you want your movie to play back on the widest range of computers. You should use a data rate setting with the Cinepak codec to prevent flat areas of color from appearing blocky. To configure the Cinepak codec, click the Configuration button and choose Compress to Color or Compress to Black and White. The Compress to Color option is selected by default.

Using the Intel Indeo R3.2 codec

Indeo R3.2, originally knows as "RealTime Video 2.1" (RT21), was developed by Intel in the 1980s. Indeo is very similar to the Cinepak codec, but takes about a third less time to compress video. Indeo is useful for CD-ROM playback and for movies where the background is static. It has fairly high compression times and plays back on a wide variety of machines.

The Indeo R3.2 codec attains higher compression ratios, better image quality, and faster playback than the Microsoft Video 1 codec. When used with a data rate for playback, this codec produces movies that are comparable in quality to those compressed with the Cinepak codec. The recommended keyframe interval for Indeo is 4 regardless of the frame rate. The Indeo R3.2 codec has no advanced configuration options.

Using the Microsoft Video 1 codec

The MS Video 1 codec was originally developed and shipped with Video for Windows (Windows 3.1), and is a general-purpose codec that can be used with virtually any computer.

Select the Microsoft Video 1 compressor from the Setup Compressor for AVI Export dialog box and then click Configuration to display a Temporal Quality slider. Temporal quality lets you adjust the quality of the intermediate frames in the movie. Temporal compression, also referred to as frame differencing, compares a frame with the one before it and eliminates redundant information. SWiSHmax uses a default ratio of .75, which is a common value. Drag the slider left to decrease or right to increase temporal quality.

Using the Indeo video 5.10 codec

The Indeo video 5.10 codec is good to use for video distributed over the Internet. Indeo video 5.10 includes features such as a quick compression option, flexible keyframe control, chroma keying (transparency), playback effects, and on-the-fly cropping that reduces data load. This codec also employs a progressive download feature that adapts to different network bandwidths.

You can customize the export using a number of configuration options as shown in Figure 21-13.

Figure 21-13: You can customize the Indeo video 5.10 codec extensively.

Quick Compress. This option uses the codec's default settings. If you click the Quick Compress check box, the remaining options on the dialog box are grayed out.

Scalability. The content of the movie can be scaled to reduce data load.

Transparency. Set a chroma key value (transparency) based either on the first frame of the movie or an alpha channel if one exists in the movie.

Viewport Size. Click the arrow and choose a size for the viewport in pixels; the default is the full image size. The playback application can tell the codec to decode only a rectangular sub region, called the viewport, from the source video image.

Access Key. Click Enable to activate a progressive download option, and type a value in the field.

Load Default. Click Load Default to restore the default settings for the codec's configuration.

Intel IYUV codec

The Intel IYUV codec is used for exporting video intended for eventual playback on a television. The video is exported using interlaced data, which is the format required for television screens. Choosing the Intel IYUV codec deselects all the other options in the codec configuration dialog box.

Checking a codec

Sometimes you have a movie but aren't sure what codec was used in its creation. Follow these steps to view codec information:

1. **Open Windows Explorer and locate the movie file.**

2. **Right-click the file and choose Properties, or choose File ⇨ Properties from the Windows Explorer menu.** The Properties dialog box opens.

3. **Click the Summary tab and then click Advanced to display the full properties of the clip.** The Advanced properties include information about the sample size, data rate, and the codec used to create the video file, as shown in Figure 21-14.

Figure 21-14: The file's properties include video information.

Exporting a self-playing movie

You can create and distribute a version of your movie called a *projector*, which is similar in many ways to the SWF movie, but runs as an executable file. Its extension is EXE like other executable programs. A projector is a stand-alone Flash Player, meaning users don't have to have the Flash Player installed on their computer in order to view your movie. Projectors you create in SWiSHmax are SWF6 files. As with other SWF movies, you can import a projector file into SWiSHmax as content for other movie projects.

Cross-Reference SWiSHstudio can create a project file automatically. Learn how to use SWiSHstudio in Appendix E, located on the book's companion Web site (`www.wiley.com/go/swishmax`).

Follow these steps to export a projector from SWiSHmax:

1. **Click the Export panel's tab to display the Export panel.**

2. **Click the Export options for: down arrow and choose SWF (Flash) from the drop-down list.** The SWF Export panel displays.

3. **Click the SWF version to export: down arrow and choose SWF6 from the drop-down list.** The SWF6 settings display.

4. **Click the settings and options you want to use in the exported movie.**

5. **Choose File ➪ Export ➪ EXE (projector).** You can also Choose File ➪ Test ➪ In Player, and then choose File ➪ Create Projector from the player's menu. An Export to Project dialog box opens.

6. **Name the file and select a storage location.** Click Save to close the dialog box and export the projector.

You can use FScommand() scripts when creating a projector; however, only available options provided by SWiSHmax can be used, as shown in Figure 21-15.

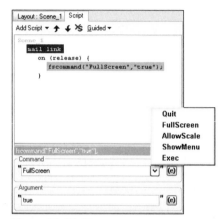

Figure 21-15: You can use some FScommand() options with projectors.

The available Command options (and their arguments) are:

AllowScale. Allows scaling of the projector window. true allows scaling; false maintains the movie's original size.

ShowMenu. Displays the Flash Player menu when using a right click in Windows or Ctrl+click on a Mac. true allows the menu options to display; false displays "About Shockwave Flash" only (Windows), or grays out the menu (Mac).

FullScreen. Displays the movie at full screen size. true allows the screen to resize; false maintains the movie's original size.

Exec. When using a projector, you can specify a program to be opened. The argument is the path to the program.

Quit. Closes the projector; true closes the projector, and false maintains playback.

Supplying information

You should include information about your movie. When you consider that many viruses are transmitted by executable files, your viewers are more likely to open a file if they understand the source.

Follow these steps to add information to an executable projector file:

1. **Open Windows Explorer and locate the file.**

2. **Right-click the file and choose Properties, or choose File ➪ Properties from the Windows Explorer menu.** The Properties dialog box opens.

3. **Click the Summary tab to display the text fields shown in Figure 21-16.**

Figure 21-16: Add information about the movie to the file's properties.

4. **Type information in the fields as required.** When your viewer clicks Advanced properties on the Properties dialog box, the Advanced tab displays the information you added.

Creating an autorun CD

Creating a projector file is useful for adding your movie to a CD because you don't need a browser or a separate Flash Player. You can use the projector file in a number of ways, and the viewer can access it through a variety of methods, such as from an HTML page containing a link, a Flash interface, or a Director interface. You can also create an autorun file, which is a short information setup file you create in Notepad that launches the movie automatically.

An autorun file named ch21_sample01a.exe has been created for the sample movie used in this discussion. Follow these steps to create an autorun movie playable from a CD:

1. **Export the projector movie from SWiSHmax.**

2. **Using Notepad, type the following:**

```
[AutoRun]
open=ch21_sample01a.exe
icon=ch21_sample01a,0
```

Note Substitute the name of your file in both the `open=` and `icon=` lines.

3. **Click Save to open the Save dialog box.**

4. **Click the Save as type drop-down arrow and choose All files.** The default file type for Notepad is .txt.

Tip You can use another text editor if you prefer; just remember to save the file with the correct extension.

5. **Name the file** autorun.inf.

6. **Click Save to save the file.** Close Notepad.

On The Web Site The sample movie and files are available from the book's Web site. Both files described in this discussion, ch21_sample01a.exe and autorun.inf are located in the chapter21 subfolder named ch21_sample01.

After you have saved the instruction file, you can then create the CD. If your movie is intended for cross-platform use, consult the Help files of your CD program or utility to see if any particular restrictions on playback exist. For example, ISO9660 format, which is Windows/Intel-specific, won't produce an autorun CD that plays the projector on a Macintosh computer.

To create the CD, follow these steps:

1. **Place both the autorun.inf and EXE projector files in the same folder.**

2. **Open your CD-burning program or utility.**

3. **Add both the autorun.inf and EXE projector files to the root of the CD.**

4. **Follow the routine of your program or utility for burning the CD.**

Tip If you need to create cross-platform compatible material, you can burn a SWF movie and HTML page onto a CD. The movie will then run regardless of operating system.

Cross-Reference SWiSHstudio can create an autorun CD automatically. Learn how to use SWiSHstudio in Appendix E.

Summary

After your movie is completed and optimized, you can choose from a wide range of different distribution options. You can export in a variety of SWF formats, as well as exporting the HTML used to display the movie in a browser. You can also create an executable stand-alone projector or export a movie in a video format.

In this chapter, you also learned about:

✦ The different SWF versions you can export from SWiSHmax and how to choose the right SWF version for exporting your movie

✦ Circumstances when you should select script options before exporting a movie

✦ Exporting HTML with your SWF movie and copying the HTML for use in other programs

✦ How to choose the correct HTML settings for your movie

✦ Configuring settings for exporting a video, including choosing codecs

✦ How to find codec information from your desktop

✦ Exporting a stand-alone projector movie

✦   ✦   ✦

Using SWiSHmax SWF Movies in Other Programs

Your SWiSHmax creations aren't limited in terms of where you use them. You can reuse your SWF movies created in SWiSHmax in a variety of other applications and with other SWF movies. For example, you can reuse your SWiSHmax-produced SWF movies in Flash MX 2004. You usually export a SWF movie and an HTML page for use on a Web site.

Whether you are a hand coder or use a WYSIWYG editor such as Dreamweaver MX or Front Page, you can reuse the SWF and HTML exports readily. One concern that many Web site builders deal with is compliance with XHTML standards. SWiSHmax and Flash MX 2004 both export Web pages as HTML 4.0, which is not standards-compliant. This chapter shows you a method for creating XHTML-compliant pages.

This chapter also shows you how you can use SWF movies you export from SWiSHmax in PowerPoint presentations, and how to define Adobe Acrobat settings for using SWF movies in PDF files.

 Cross-Reference   Chapter 21 describes choosing SWiSHmax settings for export in detail.

Using SWiSHmax SWF Movies in Flash MX 2004

Considering how you want to use a movie prior to exporting it from SWiSHmax is important. If you plan to use the movie in Flash MX 2004 for another project, there are several issues to keep in mind and several negative outcomes that can occur if you don't take precautions.

If you plan to use a movie both as a standalone SWF movie and also within a Flash MX 2004 project, creating two copies — one for each purpose — sometimes makes sense. You can optimize the standalone movie for playback, and configure the one used in Flash MX 2004 to prevent import errors.

Note   You can't use a SWI project file in Flash. Just as the FLA file format is the proprietary format of the Flash program, SWI is the proprietary format of SWiSHmax.

There are several ways in which you can use your SWF movies created in SWiSHmax in a Flash MX 2004 project. The option you choose depends on what you want to do with the contents of the SWF movie exported from SWiSHmax.

You can import the movie directly into a Flash MX 2004 layer. This option is best if you don't need to make any changes to the movie in Flash MX 2004. If you want to work with the movie's frames in Flash MX 2004, such as moving the movie or resizing it, it is simpler to import the movie into a movie clip. You can also use a `loadMovie()` action to associate the movie with the Flash MX 2004 movie without embedding it in the Flash MX 2004 project when you want to preserve all of the original SWF movie's functions. You can also choose File ➪ Import ➪ Import to Library to import the movie as a movie symbol; working with symbols in Flash MX 2004 is beyond the scope of this book.

Importing a SWF movie into Flash MX 2004

Flash MX 2004 can use a SWF movie created in SWiSHmax or any other program that generates SWF-format files. However, what you see when the file is imported has some limits. The SWF file format is a rendered file format; that is, the information is processed during export. The ability to modify specific settings and content of the file is removed in order to compress the data and produce the small file size and scalable output characteristic to the SWF format.

A SWF movie is imported into Flash MX 2004 using the File ➪ Import ➪ Import to Stage or Import to Library commands. The imported movie has the following characteristics:

✦ Sounds are not imported

✦ Layers are lost

✦ Only the first frame of a sprite is loaded

✦ Buttons are imported displaying the graphics in the Up keyframe converted to graphic symbols; other content is lost

✦ Motion paths are not imported, but the content displayed on each frame is imported as a separate image in an individual keyframe

✦ Bitmaps used in the movie are imported and renamed using a default numeric sequence

Importing a SWF movie into the Flash library

The simplest way to add a SWF movie you created in SWiSHmax is to place the file directly on the stage or on a layer; this method is useful if you don't need to make any changes to the movie. The problem is that each frame of your movie is shown as a separate keyframe in Flash MX 2004, just as importing SWF or animated GIF movies into SWiSHmax produces individual frames for the animation. When you think you may need to change the movie, such as changing its location or dimensions, create an instance and import the movie as a symbol, described in the following section.

Caution   If you choose File ➪ Open to import a SWF movie into Flash MX 2004, the movie opens in Test Movie mode, and can't be edited or changed.

Follow these steps to import a SWF movie into Flash MX 2004:

1. **Open the Flash MX 2004 FLA file into which you want to add the SWF movie.** Alternatively, you can choose File ⇨ New to start a new project.

2. **Click Add Layer on the Timeline to add a new layer.** Double-click the layer's name to activate the field and name the layer.

Caution   If you don't add the new layer, the imported movie is added to the default Timeline.

3. **Choose File ⇨ Import ⇨ Import to Stage.** This opens the Open dialog box.

Locate and select the SWF movie you want to import. Click Open to add the movie to the FLA file. As you can see in Figure 22-1, a SWF movie has been added to the FLA project's Timeline in its own layer. Each frame of the original SWF movie becomes a keyframe in the project file.

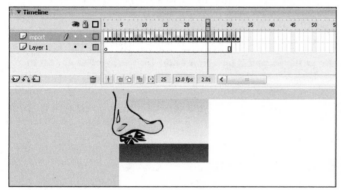

Figure 22-1: Importing a SWF movie places each frame on its own keyframe.

Placing a SWF Movie into a Movie Clip

Rather than placing each frame of a SWF movie into a new Flash MX 2004 project, you can place the entire movie into a movie clip. Using an instance created in Flash MX 2004 to hold the keyframes of the SWF movie is much simpler than importing each keyframe when you need to make changes to the keyframes, such as moving the imported content on the stage. Sounds and actions in your SWF movies are not imported into the Flash MX 2004 file.

Follow these steps to create a movie clip and place a SWiSHmax SWF movie:

1. **Open the Flash MX 2004 project into which you want to place the SWF movie.** Alternatively, you can choose File ⇨ New to start a new project.

2. **Choose Insert ⇨ New Symbol, or press Ctrl+F8 accelerator keys.** The Create New Symbol dialog box shown in Figure 22-2 opens.

3. **Type a name for the symbol in the Name field, and click the Movie clip Behavior radio button.**

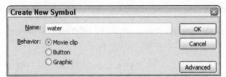

Figure 22-2: Create a new symbol to hold the SWF movie.

4. **Click OK to add the symbol to the Library.**

5. **Choose File ➪ Import to Library.** In the Open dialog box, locate the SWF movie you want to use and click Open. The frames and the movie are added to the Library.

6. **The editing view for the symbol displays on the program window as shown in Figure 22-3.** Click the back arrow or the **Scene1** label to return to the main view.

Figure 22-3: Return to the main project view.

7. **On the Timeline, click New Layer to add a new layer to the project.**

8. **Double-click the layer name, and type a new name for the layer as shown in Figure 22-4.**

Figure 22-4: Name the new layer to avoid confusion.

9. **Make sure the play head is at Frame 1 or the frame at which you want the movie to start playing.**

10. **Select the SWF movie clip in the Library, and drag it to the scene.**

11. **Test and save the movie.**

Using a loadMovie() action to control a SWF movie

Instead of importing a SWiSHmax SWF movie as a movie symbol in Flash MX 2004, you can use the loadMovie() action in an FLA project and play your existing SWF movie complete with sounds and actions.

Follow these steps to use a loadMovie() action in Flash MX 2004:

1. **In Flash MX 2004, open the FLA project file to which you want to add the SWF movie.**

2. **On the Timeline, click Add Layer.** This adds a new layer for the imported movie.

3. **Double-click the default layer name to activate the field and type a new name for the layer.**

Tip

Naming layers is especially useful if you are working with several movies.

4. Move the play head to the frame on the Timeline where you want the new movie to begin.

5. In the Actions panel, click the Add a new item to the script button (+) and choose Global Functions ➪ Browser/Network ➪ loadMovie. The script is added to the Script area on the Actions panel.

Tip

You can also use the Behaviors panel to add the action. Click the Behaviors panel drop-down arrow to display the content. Click Add Behavior, and then choose Movieclip ➪ Load External Movieclip. A dialog box opens in which you select the file and its target.

6. Specify the name of the file as well as its target in the default script as shown in Figure 22-5.

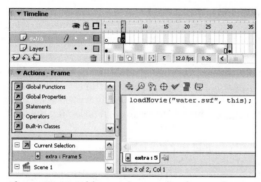

Figure 22-5: Add an action to play the movie at a specified frame.

Note

The `loadMovie()` action is written as `loadMovie("url",target[, method])`. The url is the absolute or relative URL of the SWF movie file; the target is the path to the target movie clip; and the method is an optional parameter used for specifying a method for sending variables, and which must be `GET` or `POST` in format. When there are no variables, omit the parameter.

7. Test and save the movie. Make sure to store the SWiSHmax SWF movie in the same folder as the Flash MX 2004 movie to prevent errors.

Here are some other tips for associating a SWF movie with another SWF movie in Flash MX 2004:

✦ If you want to monitor the download progress, use `MovieClipLoader.loadClip()` instead of `loadMovie()`.

✦ Use `unloadMovie()` to remove SWF files that were loaded with `loadMovie()`. This is especially useful if you are loading more than one movie.

Note

You don't need to add an `unloadMovie()` action when loading a new SWF movie into the same location as a previously defined `loadMovie()` action. When you load a new movie into a level, any movie existing at that level is automatically unloaded.

✦ If you want to load a SWF movie file into a specific level, use `loadMovieNum()` instead of `loadMovie()`.

✦ A SWF movie loaded into a target movie inherits the position, rotation, and scale properties of the targeted movie clip. The upper-left corner of the SWF file aligns with the registration point of the targeted movie clip. When the target is the root Timeline, the upper-left corner of the SWF file aligns with the upper-left corner of the Stage.

Troubleshooting SWiSHmax movies Used in Flash

As previously noted, making two copies of your SWiSHmax SWF movies is sometimes practical—one for general use, and another to import into Flash MX 2004. You may encounter a number of configuration issues if you use your movies in Flash MX 2004. In all cases, you have to experiment with the export settings in SWiSHmax, regenerate the SWF movie, and then re-import the movie into Flash MX 2004. The configuration issues you may encounter include the following:

✦ **Offsetting.** Some movies may shift down and to the right when used in Flash MX 2004, while others may shift up and to the left. The solution is the Offset to suit use as a Movie Clip setting on the SWiSHmax SWF (Flash) Export panel. If the animation shifts down and to the right, click to select the Offset to suit use as a Movie Clip setting. If the animation shifts up and to the left, deselect the option.

✦ **Masking.** If you have created a SWF movie in SWiSHmax using the Mask off-stage objects setting in the SWF (Flash) Export panel, and then import the resulting SWF into Flash MX 2004, you may receive an error when you subsequently try to export the movie from Flash MX 2004. Export the movie from SWiSHmax again, deselecting the Mask off-stage setting.

✦ **Animating off-stage objects.** If you find that the movie you import into Flash MX 2004 produces output that makes the objects pause or stick at the edges of the stage, deselect the Mask off-stage options on the SWF (Flash) Export panel.

✦ **Font info records.** Flash MX 2004 may not always import your SWF movies; the program may crash instead. The culprit is the font information record, which sends the font information that Flash MX 2004 needs to the SWF movie. Two actions in SWiSHmax can cause this error:

• If you select the Solid shape with overlap filled check box on the Shape panel, the shape is exported as a font, which uses a different behavior and information than overlapping shapes.

• If you deselect Allow import of text as text object on the SWF (Flash) export panel, the font information record is omitted from the exported movie for all text.

Using SWF movies in Dreamweaver

One of the most common and popular programs for Web page design is Dreamweaver, now in MX 2004 version. Like other programs, you export the SWF movie from SWiSHmax and then import it into your HTML page in Dreamweaver MX 2004.

On The Web Site   The files used in these discussions are available from the book's Web site. In the chapter22 folder, the ch22_sample01 folder contains SWF, HTML, and XHTML files as well as the source SWiSHmax project file.

The parameters that are passed to Dreamweaver MX 2004 depend on how you add the SWF content. If you export both SWF and HTML from SWiSHmax, you can use the HTML page in Dreamweaver MX 2004 and it will have all the exported HTML parameters you set in SWiSHmax. However, if you place the SWF object on a page from within Dreamweaver MX 2004, there are fewer parameters, although you can add more to the page.

Caution   When exporting a movie to use in Dreamweaver MX 2004, deselect the Offset Movie to suit use as a Movie Clip option on the SWF (Flash) Export panel.

If you export a movie that contains links to Web pages, be sure to specify the target in the SWiSHmax project. For example, if you have a script that reads:

```
on (release) {
    getURL("http://www.google.com/");
}
```

Specify the window in which you want the linked page to open by including a target property such as:

```
on (release) {
    getURL("http://www.google.com/", target="blank");
}
```

Follow these steps to insert a SWF movie into a Dreamweaver MX 2004 document:

1. **Create or open the XHTML or HTML page in which you want to insert the SWF movie.**

2. **Choose Insert ➪ Media ➪ Flash, or click the Flash icon on the Insert Media menu as shown in Figure 22-6.** The Select File dialog box opens.

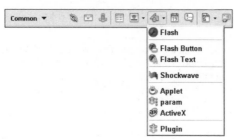

Figure 22-6: Insert a SWF movie directly into a Web page.

3. **Locate and select the SWF movie you want to insert on the page.** Click OK to add the content.

4. **Add other characteristics if desired in the Properties panel as shown in Figure 22-7.** Some of the settings are contained within the SWF movie while others, such as background color, must be set manually in Dreamweaver MX 2004.

5. **Save and test the page.**

Tip   You can also copy the HTML from the movie in SWiSHmax. Choose File ➪ Export ➪ Copy HTML to clipboard. Then open your Web page editing program, open the code view, and click to move the insertion point to the location at which you want to enter the copied code. Choose Edit ➪ Paste or press Ctrl+V to paste the content into the page.

Figure 22-7: Modify the SWF movie's parameters in the Properties panel.

The code written by Dreamweaver MX 2004, as well as that written in SWiSHmax, includes both the `<embed>` and `<object>` tags; the former is required by the Netscape Navigator browser, the latter by Internet Explorer.

Neither product automatically generates standards-compliant code; that is, code that complies with the standards set by the W3C (Worldwide Web Consortium). SWiSHmax generates HTML 4.0 Transitional, and Dreamweaver MX 2004 can generate XHTML 1.0 Transitional. However, in addition to redefining some of the SWF content's parameters, you must define CSS styles in order for the page to duplicate the layout provided with the HTML exported from SWiSHmax.

Once you modify the code, you can test it on the W3C Validation Web site, or using the Dreamweaver Results panel:

1. **Open the Results panel.** This is tabbed with the Properties panel at the bottom of the program window.

2. **Click the Validation tab.**

3. **Click the green arrow to open a drop-down menu and choose Validate Current Document.** The document is evaluated and a report is generated. If the code has been written correctly, the report indicates that the page contains valid XHTML Transitional code. Any errors in the code are listed if they exist; use the description of the errors to correct your page and validate the page again.

On The Web Site

The chapter22 folder on the book's Web site contains a Web page in XHTML 1.0 Transitional that contains valid code. The page is named ch22_sample01A.html. Note that the movie will play in most, but not all, browsers; in addition, converting a page that uses this code to a PDF does not embed the movie correctly in the PDF document.

Using SWF movies in FrontPage

Microsoft FrontPage is another popular Web design program that enables you to easily add your SWiSHmax SWF movies to a Web page.

Follow these steps to add and configure a SWF movie in FrontPage:

1. **Open FrontPage, choose File ➪ Open, and locate the page into which you want to use the SWF movie.**

2. **Choose View ➪ Page to display the Page view, and click the Design option at the bottom left of the program window.**

3. **Choose Insert ➪ Picture ➪ Movie in Flash Format to open the Select File dialog box.**

4. **Locate the file you want to use, and click Insert to close the dialog box.** The content is added to the page in a rectangular box showing the file's name, as shown in Figure 22-8.

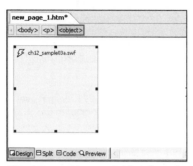

Figure 22-8: You can add and preview imported movies in FrontPage.

5. **Click the object to select it, and then click Preview at the bottom of the program window.** The movie plays on the page.

6. **Right-click the object on the page, and choose Movie in Flash Format Properties to open the Properties dialog box.**

7. **Modify the properties of the SWF movie as desired.** You can change appearance properties, as shown in Figure 22-9, or click the General tab to change general properties such as the playback options and plug-ins information.

8. **Choose File ⇨ Save to save your Web page.** You are also prompted to save the embedded SWF file.

9. **Test the movie in a browser.**

Figure 22-9: Adjust the SWF movie's properties in the Properties dialog box.

Embedding a SWF Movie in PowerPoint

You can use SWF movies in Microsoft Office programs. This discussion describes using SWF movies in PowerPoint, as it is the program in which movies are most commonly used. Although placing a SWF movie takes only a couple of steps, additional configuration options and settings are available to make using SWF in a presentation easier. For example, you can embed the SWF movie in the presentation so you don't have to distribute both the PPT and SWF movies to your viewers.

On The Web Site

The chapter22 folder of the book's Web site contains a sample PPT file that uses an embedded SWF movie. The file is named ch22_sample01.ppt, and is located in the ch22_sample01 subfolder.

The Shockwave Flash Object is an Active X control that Windows programs require to use SWF movies—this object is usually stored in the WINNT/Downloaded Program Files folder on your hard drive. Windows has used the control since Windows 98.

Follow these steps to use a SWF movie in PowerPoint:

1. **Open PowerPoint, and open or start the presentation into which you want to add the content.**

2. **Choose View ⇨ Toolbars ⇨ Control to display the Control toolbar.**

3. **Click More Controls ⇨ Shockwave Flash Object as shown in Figure 22-10.** The drop-down list closes, and the cursor changes to cross hairs.

4. **Click and drag to draw a rectangle on the slide.** The rectangle is displayed as a white box with an X drawn through it.

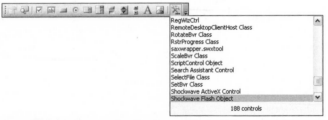

Figure 22-10: Choose the Shockwave Flash Object control from the Control toolbox.

Tip

The Flash object added to a presentation is always shown above any other content on the slide.

5. **Right-click the rectangle on the slide to open the shortcut menu and choose Properties.** The dialog box shown in Figure 22-11 opens.

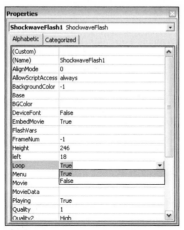

Figure 22-11: Set properties for your movie.

6. **Click the following properties and change their values.** To change the value, click the property to activate it. A drop-down arrow appears in the right column; click the arrow and choose an option from the list.

   • **Embed movie.** Change to True.

   • **Loop.** The default is True, which loops the movie; click to change to False, which plays and then stops the movie.

7. **Click the Custom field at the top of the dialog box to activate it.** A button displaying an ellipsis appears in the right column. Click the button to open the Property Pages dialog box shown in Figure 22-12.

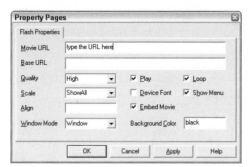

Figure 22-12: Type in the path of your SWF movie to embed it.

8. **Type the URL for the movie in the Movie URL field.** Change other properties of the movie as desired and click OK.

Tip

Some of the settings in Property Pages are the same as those on the Properties table. You can change parameters in either location.

9. **Click the Slide Show from Current Slide button at the bottom left of the program window.** The slide displays at full screen size and the SWF movie plays. Press Esc to close the play back and return to the program.

10. **Save the PPT file.**

If you are testing the presentation and your movie isn't playing correctly, check that the files are stored in the correct folders and that the URL you specified is typed correctly.

Restarting a SWF movie in PowerPoint

When you move from one slide to the next, the action on the previous slide stops; this includes SWF movies, which may or may not have finished playing when the visible slide is changed. If you then return to the slide containing the movie, you see it stopped at whatever frame was playing when the slideshow is advanced, and the movie doesn't restart automatically.

Follow these steps to modify the file to restart a movie automatically:

1. **Double-click the embedded SWF movie on the slide to open the Microsoft Visual Basic program.** The program displays the structure of the presentation in a hierarchy, the code for the selected slide in a code window, and the Property Pages dialog box described earlier.

2. **The code window displays the two headings and the two lines of code for the object (Figure 22-13).**

Caution

The first drop-down field should read ShockwaveFlash1; the second should read OnReadyStateChange. If you see something different, click the drop-down arrows and find the correct terms.

3. **Type this line, shown highlighted in Figure 22-13, between the two existing lines of code:**

```
swf.playing=true
```

Figure 22-13: Type the additional line of code to replay the movie automatically.

4. **Press Return.** The text changes to display the code's formatting and reads:

```
swf.Playing = True
```

5. **Click the X to close the Visual Basic window and return to PowerPoint.**

6. **Save and test the presentation.** Each time you return to the slide containing the SWF movie, the movie should continue playing.

Altering the code to restart the movie doesn't guarantee that the movie restarts at the first frame. You can adjust your SWiSHmax movie file before exporting the SWF to make sure that it restarts correctly. In the project, add a `gotoSceneAndStop()` action to the final frame that returns the play head to the first frame.

Note You can use the same methods described in this discussion to embed SWF movies into other Office programs, such as Microsoft Word and Access.

Viewing SWF Movies in Acrobat

Adobe Acrobat 6 supports the embedding and displaying of SWF movies through the conversion of an HTML page containing the SWF movie. Converting Web pages that contain SWF content to PDF documents is most common, but you can also convert a Word document containing a SWF movie.

On The Web Site The PDF document converted using the method described in this discussion is included in the chapter22 folder in the ch22_sample01 subfolder. The file is named ch22_sample01.pdf.

Within Acrobat you can define how multimedia contents are referenced and used. Follow these steps to open a Web page containing a SWF movie in Acrobat as a PDF document:

1. **Open Acrobat and choose File ⇨ Create PDF ⇨ From Web Page.** The Create PDF from Web Page dialog box opens.

2. **Click Settings to open the Web Page Conversion Settings dialog box.**

3. **Click HTML in the File Type Settings list, and then click Settings to open the HTML Conversion Settings dialog box.**

4. **Click the Multimedia drop-down arrow and choose an option as shown in Figure 22-14.** You can disable multimedia capture, embed it, or link it by URL. Embedding multimedia content when you are distributing a PDF document is best; that way you don't have to distribute any files along with the PDF document.

5. **Click OK twice to close the sequence of dialog boxes and return to the Create PDF from Web Pages dialog box.**

6. **Choose the Web page you want to convert as well as the path, server, and site settings.** Click Create to convert the Web page containing the movie to PDF. The page displays in the Acrobat document pane.

7. **Test the page.** Your animation should play as shown in Figure 22-15, and any links associated with your animation should be active.

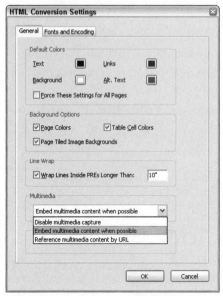

Figure 22-14: Choose a method for using SWF movies in Acrobat in the HTML Conversion Settings dialog box.

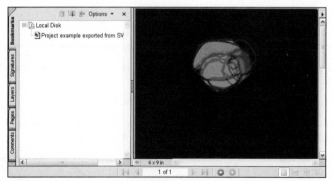

Figure 22-15: Test the functioning of your movie from within the PDF document.

Summary

This chapter provided information on integrating the output from your SWiSHmax projects with other programs. The programs covered included Flash MX 2004, two common WYSIWYG Web page editors, and other software.

In this chapter, you learned:

✦ How to export a movie intended for use in Flash MX 2004

✦ The different methods of importing a SWF movie into Flash MX 2004

✦ How to import a SWF movie directly into a Flash MX 2004 layer

✦ About problems you may encounter when using SWiSHmax SWF movies in Flash MX 2004 and how to solve them

✦ How to add a SWF to a Web page in Dreamweaver MX 2004 and FrontPage 2003

✦ How to embed a SWF movie in PowerPoint, and how to modify the movie's code in PowerPoint to restart or rewind the movie

✦ How to use your movie in Acrobat

✦   ✦   ✦

Sample Projects

Building Menus

*Special thanks to Ian Hinckley
for contributing this chapter.*

♦   ♦   ♦   ♦

In This Chapter

Making a simple
text menu

Using a sprite method
for a dynamic menu

Using effects in response
to mouse actions

Using mouse actions in
a dynamic menu

Adding backgrounds
and fading titles

Programming a menu
follower

Modifying scripts to
run in the internal
Flash Player

♦   ♦   ♦   ♦

You use menus principally to guide users around your site, so your menus should follow some basic rules:

+ Menus must be clear and readable

+ Menus must reflect the content currently on the page

+ Menus must behave as the user reasonably expects

+ Menus must be easy to use

The many different types of menus available can be built in many ways; for the purposes of this discussion, only menus on one level are covered: where the application provides data to the menu. Using various of the Sprite methods, such as `loadVariables`, `loadVars`, and the XML object, you can read data from remote sources and apply that data to your menu. This chapter concentrates on techniques for creating menus as well as some interface methods. The way in which you place the data into the right place at the right time is more a data issue, and mixing the various techniques shown in this book to develop your own data delivery/loading systems is up to you.

Creating a Simple Text Menu

Using blocks of text is the simplest way to create a menu. This first example shows how to construct a simple menu.

**On The Web
Site**

All the project files used in this chapter are available from the book's Web site in the folder named chapter23.

Follow these steps to construct a simple text menu and add an action:

1. **Place six static text boxes on the stage, left align them, and distribute them vertically.** Use 14 point Arial font for the text.

**Cross-
Reference**

Refer to Chapter 6 for information on using alignment and distribution tools.

2. **Modify the text for each text box.** Change the labels to read as follows: **home**, **contact**, **download**, **portfolio**, **links**, and **forum**.

3. **Place one dynamic text box at the bottom of the stage.** Name the text box **mtxt**, and make it a target. Make sure to size the text box wide enough to hold the text; on the Dimensions settings in the Text panel set a width to at least 160 in order to fit the text.

4. **In the Script panel, working in Expert mode, enter the following code for each static text box:**

```
on(release){
    mtxt.text = "you pressed home";
}
```

5. **Modify the word** home **in the action according to the link.** For example, in the links text box, the line should read:

```
mtxt.text = "you pressed links";
```

6. **Choose File ⇨ Test ⇨ In Player, or press the Ctrl+T accelerator keys to test the movie.** Click on one of the text boxes, and in the dynamic text box at the bottom of the stage, read which menu item was clicked.

In this simple example, you placed a piece of descriptive text on the stage to let you know what happened, but you could have launched a Timeline effect, used gotoAndPlay() to move the play head to a particular frame or label inside another sprite, loaded some variables, and so on. In fact, clicking the menu and trapping the click event inside the on(release) event is the starting point for however you want the movie to respond to the mouse click. You could have used the on(press) event to trap the click just as easily, but in most cases you don't want to take action until you release the mouse.

Cross-Reference   Refer to Chapter 19 for information on working with actions.

Now you have the first menu, but it's not very flexible, is it? You can build the same menu using some dynamic techniques.

Creating a Dynamic Menu Using a Sprite Method

The sprite method duplicateSprite() enables you to copy a sprite at run time and create as many copies as you need. In this example, you use duplicateSprite() to create five copies of a dynamic text box, set the text value, and assign an onRelease event all dynamically. You also add some functionality to allow the menu to be vertical or horizontal.

1. **Place one dynamic text box on the stage, name it** menutext, **and make it a target.**

2. **Place another dynamic text box at the bottom of the stage, name it** mtxt, **and make it a target.**

3. **Click the Script tab to display the Script panel, and using the Expert mode type the following code for Scene_1.** Enter the code listed in the left column of Table 22-1. The right column of the table provides explanations for the code you write.

4. **Choose File ⇨ Test ⇨ In Player, or press the Ctrl+T accelerator keys to test the movie.** You'll see almost exactly the same movie as before.

Table 23-1: Dynamic Menu Script

Type This	Comment
`onLoad(){`	The initiating action
`  menudata = ["home","contact", "download","portfolio","links","forum"];`	An array containing your menu data.
`  vertical = false;`	You want the menu to be horizontal, so vertical is false.
`  for(n=0;n<menudata.length;n++){`	A loop to occur six times (as many times as there are menu data elements).
`    temp = (n==0) ? menutext : menutext.duplicateSprite("mt"+n,n);`	If *n* is zero, you don't need to duplicate the sprite. If *n* is more than zero, you use `duplicateSprite` to create a copy of menu text. You assign either the original or the copy to temp, which is a temporary variable.
`  if(vertical)`	Test to check whether you want the menu to go vertically or horizontally.
`      temp._y += n * temp._height;`	If vertical is true, you increase the _y value of the `menutext` object.
`    else temp._x += n * temp._width;`	If vertical is false, you increase the _x value of the `menutext` object.
`    temp.text = menudata[n];`	You set the `menutext` object's text value to the relevant element in the `menudata` array.
`    temp.id = n;`	Set a property in the `menutext` object to identify it.
`    temp.onrelease = function(){`	Set up an `onrelease` event.
`      mtxt.text = "you pressed " + menudata[this.id];`	When the mouse is clicked on this object, you show the same text in our descriptive box as on the menu, just to let you know it all works.
`    };`	Close all statements.
`  }`	
`}`	

You can also customize the script:

✦ To make the menu vertical, change the line `vertical=false` to `vertical=true`.

✦ To change the menu's text, simply change the data in the `menudata` array.

Quite a powerful approach to creating a menu, I think you'll agree.

Using an onRelease Event for Initiating Effects

Just to demonstrate that you can use the `onRelease` event to kick-start some movie effects, in example3.swi, I've added a box to the screen and another array named `menuboxsizes`, which contains six arrays of size pairs (that is, width and height pairs).

When you click on a menu item, you use the `id` property that you added to access the `menuboxsizes` array and resize your box according to the menu item you select, as shown in Figure 23-1.

Figure 23-1: You can use an array that includes size pairs to reshape a shape according to the menu item selected.

I've added some easing code to smooth out the resizing. As the code for this example is basically the same as for example2.swi, I'll leave you to review what's going on and maybe to use this as the basis for your next movie.

Substituting Code

The construct `(condition)?if true: if false;` that was used in the previous example is used in the remaining examples for this chapter. As a comparison, both the code snippets shown here do the same thing. You can write

```
reply = (txt == "hello") ? "hello" : "goodbye";
```

which means the same thing as

```
If(txt == hello){
   reply = "hello";
} else {
   reply = "goodbye";
}
```

Writing the code all in one line just looks neater, I think.

Building Another Dynamic Menu

A short while ago, I came across this next menu effect while browsing and I think it looks great. The code is similar to what has been used previously in this chapter, but with the addition of some rollover effects. As with the previous examples, start with the basics and then work up to a more complex version.

On The Web Site As a reminder, all the files used in this chapter's examples are on the book's Web site in the folder named chapter23.

Follow these steps to construct a dynamic menu with rollover, rollout, and click events:

1. **Place one dynamic text box on the stage, name it** menuinfo, **and make it a target.**

2. **Place one sprite on the stage, name it** menus, **and place inside it a second sprite named** menu0.

3. **Inside the** menu0 **sprite, place a dynamic text box, name it** mtxt, **and make it a target.**

4. **Type the code in Listing 23-1 inside the** menus **sprite.** You should recognize the majority of this code as the basis of the last two examples, but in an expanded form:

Listing 23-1: **Code for the Menus Sprite**

```
onLoad(){
    menuitem = new array();
    selected = -1;
    targetalpha = 100;
    for(n=0;n<5;n++){
        menuitem[n] = (n==0) ? menu0 : menu0.duplicatesprite("menu" +
n,n);
        menuitem[n]._x += n * menuitem[n]._width;
        menuitem[n].mtxt.text = "menu " + n;
        menuitem[n].id = n;
        menuitem[n].onrollover = function(){
            _parent.menuinfo.text = "you're over menu " + this.ID;
            selected = this.ID;
        };
        menuitem[n].onrollout = function(){
            _parent.menuinfo.text = "you're not over a menu";
            selected = -1;
        };
        menuitem[n].onrelease = function(){
            _parent.menuinfo.text = "you clicked menu " + this.ID;
        };
    }
}
```

Continued

Listing 23-1 *(continued)*

```
onEnterFrame(){
    for(n=0;n<menuitem.length;n++){
        targetalpha = (n == selected || selected == -1) ? 100 : 40;
        menuitem[n]._alpha = math.approach(menuitem[n]._alpha,
targetalpha, 0.8);
    }
}
```

---

5. **Choose File ⇨ Test ⇨ In Player, or press the Ctrl+T accelerator keys to test the movie.**
   You'll see alpha changes as you rollover and rollout of the menu, as well as other changes that occur when you click a menu item.

What has been added?

✦ Instead of assigning the object reference of our duplicated sprites to a temporary variable, this time you keep track of the references using an array called menuitem. Just to refresh your memory, this allows you to say menuitem[n] rather than this["menu" + n] to access the particular menuitem you want through the value of *n*; I think this method is more flexible and easier to use.

✦ You're using a variable named selected to let you know which menuitem has been rolled over.

✦ You've also added some easing code on the _alpha value of the menu items.

When you rollover an item, for example menuitem[0], the menuinfo dynamic text box displays "you're over menu 0," and then the variable selected is set to the object's id property, which is also zero.

In the **menus** sprite's Timeline, the onEnterFrame loop looks at each of the elements in the menuitems array once each frame tick. If the selected variable is the same as either the value in the for...next loop or (the || sign), nothing has yet been rolled over (in which case selected is still -1, as set in the onLoad event); the _alpha value is 100, otherwise it's 40. The math.approach method is saying move menuitem[n]._alpha towards targetalpha in 80 percent steps, so it fades out on the menu items not currently rolled over. This is quite powerful and yet easy to script.

Enhancing the Menu

The next few examples build on the previous examples. You see how to add a background, change alpha values, and construct a follower.

Applying a background

The example5.swi version adds a background to each menu item so that the menu looks like a bar but keeps the effect the same. Aside from the scripting for the background, the example5.swi project file is the same as that used in the example4.swi project.

You need a shape within the **menu0** sprite to use as the background. The sample project uses a black rectangle to provide the best contrast. Draw the rectangle and align it with the mtxt object, placing the rectangle at the bottom of the sprite's stack, as shown in Figure 23-2. Draw the rectangle to the same width as the `mtxt` object, and two pixels higher. In the sample project, the shape is 59 x 18 pixels in size.

Test the movie in the Flash Player. You see the background's opacity change as you rollover and rollout, which is a great addition to your menu arsenal for the addition of just one object.

Figure 23-2: The background must be added in the correct order.

You can modify the backgrounds, such as changing the background rectangle's width. Here's an example where you change only one line in the script. Change

```
menuitem[n]._x += n * menuitem[n]._width;
```

to

```
menuitem[n]._x += n * (menuitem[n]._width + 1);
```

Experiment further with the backgrounds and place another background rectangle behind the first. If you do, make the second rectangle wider by the width of your gap. You can see an example of the outcome of adding a second rectangle in the sample project, example5a.swi.

Changing the alpha values

You can modify the alpha values in other ways for a different effect. You could, for example, increase the brightness in the `menuitem` that is rolled over while the others remain dim. To achieve the alpha change, you need one small modification to the existing structure.

Change the line

```
targetalpha = (n == selected || selected == -1) ? 100 : 40;
```

to

```
targetalpha = (n == selected) ? 100 : 40;
```

That's the only change you need to make. Neat, don't you think?

Using a follower

Another enhancement you may want to add is a visual device to follow the mouse selection. You see this on many Web sites and it can be useful, although sometimes the followers are truly dreadful. The approach taken here is minimalist. The sample has a single line that slides along the menu as you move the mouse. Follow these steps to add a follower to the menu:

1. **Open the** menus **sprite in the Outline panel.**

2. **Draw a line inside the** menus **sprite; make sure the line is stacked above the** menu0 **sprite.**

Tip

The line should be below the menu0 sprite on the stage; the sample uses a line 59-pixels wide; its Y-axis location is 0, and its X-axis location is 18.

3. **Name the line** follower **and make it a target.**

4. **In the Script panel, add one line to the** `onLoad` **event.** This line of script initializes the target value and defines it as equal to the initial position of the follower:

```
targetx = follower._x;
```

In the sample project, the line is added as the fourth line of the script following the `targetalpha = 100;` line.

5. **Add two lines of script to the** `onEnterFrame` **loop.** Add the first line of script outside the `for...next` loop to set the follower target as the `_x` property of the rolled-over menu item:

```
targetx = menuitem[selected]._x;
```

Add the second line of script inside the `for...next` loop. This just advances followers' `_x` value towards that of `targetx`.

```
follower._x = math.approach(follower._x, targetx, 0.95);
```

You have seen how to construct two different menu styles, use a similar method of generation, and some techniques for four different effects. These examples should lead you to discover many more techniques for yourself.

Using the Flash Player

You may have found that some of these menu movies don't play inside SWiSHmax unless you export the files as SWF or test them in the player. SWiSHmax's internal player only supports a subset of the available scripting commands; exporting or testing in an external player gives you access to almost the full range of Flash ActionScript, with the exception of `attachmovie` and the Flash `componentware`.

On The Web Site

All the project files used in this chapter are in the chapter23 folder on the book's Web site.

These menu examples don't work in SWiSHmax, due to the dynamic attachment of the `onrollover`, `onrollout`, and `onrelease` events. The sample movie project, example7internal. swi, does work in the SWiSHmax internal player. All I've done is move the three events from being dynamically attached to the objects in the sprite duplication loop to being inside the script tab of the **menu0** sprite. When **menu0** is duplicated, the code is also duplicated. Study the code and see the differences in referencing by using _parent to navigate back up the movie's object layers.

Just to prove that you can build good-looking scripted menus that work well in the internal player, take a look at example8internal.swi.

You need little introduction to the code and concepts used in this movie, so concentrate on the **topbar** sprite and the shape attached to **menubar0** that is offset 1 pixel to the right and below the bar rectangle inside the **topbar** sprite. When you click on the bar, it moves 1 pixel to the right and down, thus giving the effect of a button being pressed. The effect can also be achieved using the built-in button effects, but this just demonstrates that you can script it yourself.

Notice also that I haven't scripted the rollover and rollout effects; instead, I placed some built-in effects on the Timeline that are accessed using frame labels.

Tip Remember to stop the play head after effects to prevent the playback from crashing straight into the next effect.

At the beginning of this chapter, I mentioned that I was focusing on the menu design and generation techniques rather than the data delivery, and I used arrays as my data delivery medium. If you choose to use text files or XML as your data vehicle of choice, as long as you place the data from the external source into arrays such as demonstrated here, the examples can be used as they are once the arrays are populated with the external data.

Cross-Reference The book's Web site contains an appendix that describes working with XML as the basis for building menus for your movies. Please consult Appendix G for more information and tutorials.

Summary

You can build basic menus or basic menus with some flexibility added. Ultimately you have the power to build whatever you like, and use either built-in Timeline effects or script the menus to show off your design skills. Whichever you choose, you can be sure that SWiSHmax has the power to deliver anything you want; the only limit to your achievement is your imagination. In this discussion, you learned how to:

✦ Build a simple menu using text items

✦ Make a menu dynamic using a sprite method

✦ Initiate effects in response to an `onrelease` event

✦ Use rollover effects in a dynamic menu

✦ Enhance a menu using backgrounds

✦ Program alpha value responses to mouse actions

✦ Construct a follower to follow the mouse as the movie plays

✦   ✦   ✦

Welcome to Preloaders

*Special thanks to Ian Hinckley
for contributing this chapter.*

No matter how well you design your movies, it's the preloader, not a blank screen, that keeps the casual browser interested in waiting to see your latest creation.

Preloading is a subject best approached bit by bit, so that's exactly how I'll do it in this chapter.

Movie/Sprite Properties and Methods

In this chapter, I show you a number of preloaders from basic to much more interesting, but before jumping in with both feet, take a little time to consider the movie/sprite methods and properties that form the backbone of the examples in this chapter and on the book's accompanying Web site.

Movies and sprites share two properties. Both have read-only access and return numbers. The `_framesloaded` property returns the number of frames downloaded in the Timeline in which it is used; the `_totalframes` property returns the total number of frames in the Timeline in which it is used.

Movies and sprites also share three methods that are used in this chapter. Each returns a number. The methods under consideration are:

`getBytesLoaded()` — This read-only property returns the number of bytes currently loaded in the specified target.

`getBytesTotal()` — This read-only property returns the total bytes in the specified target. When using this method for a _root path, a level, or a movie loaded into a sprite, the value returned is the total bytes of the SWF file.

`getPercentLoaded()` — This read-only property returns the current percentage of the total bytes loaded for the specified target. The value is the same as multiplying the result of `getBytesLoaded` by 100 and then dividing by the result of `getBytesTotal`. This method is SWiSHscript-specific and is not supported by Flash MX.

Building a Simple Preloader

The first example is very simple and shows that preloaders can easily be accomplished in three lines and do not need to use complex scripts. Follow these steps to create a preloader movie:

On The Web Site   The example described in this tutorial is example1.swi. It is available at the book's Web site in the chapter24 folder. Take a sneak peek before you follow the tutorial and then return to this point.

1. **Start a new SWiSHmax project.** The default project includes one scene named **Scene_1**.

2. **Click the** Scene_1 **name in the Outline panel to activate the scene's name.** Change the name of the scene to **preload**.

3. **On the Outline panel, choose Insert ⇨ Scene to insert another scene.** Name the new scene **movie**. This scene contains the main movie.

4. **Click the preload scene's label to make the scene active.** In the Layout panel, you see the name of the scene listed on the Layout panel's tab as **Layout : preload**.

5. **From the main program menu choose Insert ⇨ Text to place a text field on the movie's stage.**

6. **Click and drag the text field to the top left of the stage.** Make sure your new text field is the selected object by either clicking on it on the stage or selecting it in the Outline Panel.

7. **Click the Text tab in the program's panel group to display the Text panel.**

8. **On the Text panel, click the text type panel and select Static Text.**

9. **In the text area at the bottom of the Text panel type** loading movie, please wait, **as seen in Figure 24-1.**

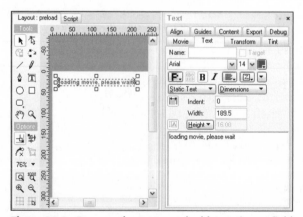

Figure 24-1: Rename the scene and add a static text field.

Adding the SWiSHscript

Once the scene is renamed and you have added the text, you are now ready to add the SWiSHscript to make the preloader work. In this chapter, since you write the majority of code manually, change the display to the Expert mode. Click the Script tab to display the Script panel; click Guided and choose Expert to toggle the Script panel's display to the Expert mode.

Click on the Script tab and type the following code:

```
onFrame(1){
   if(_framesloaded == _totalframes)
   nextSceneAndPlay();
}
onFrame(2){
   prevFrameAndPlay();
}
```

What is this script telling the movie to do? Consider it line by line, as described in Table 24-1.

Table 24-1: Understanding the Preloader Code

Type This Line...	Which Means...
onFrame(1)	This tells the player to execute all the code inside the curly braces { } in Frame 1 of this Timeline.
if(_framesloaded == _totalframes)	This if statement is considering whether the current value of _framesloaded is equal to _totalframes. That is, has the movie completely loaded? If it has completely loaded, then the next line is executed.
nextSceneAndPlay()	This tells the player to go to the next scene and start playing. In our example, this is the scene named **movie.**
onFrame(2)	This tells the player to execute all the code in Frame 2 of the movie scene's Timeline. Execution only occurs when the movie has not yet completely loaded.
prevFrameAndPlay();	Sends the play head back to the previous frame (Frame 1) to start over.

Before your first preloader is ready for testing, you'll need to place some content in the scene named **movie**, otherwise there will be nothing for the preloader to preload. Place an image of approximately 50KB in this scene. To add the image, click the **movie** scene's label on the Outline panel to select it, and then choose Insert ➪ Image from the Insert menu and locate your image through the Open dialog box.

Note The sample movie contains several images of approximately 10KB each.

Congratulations, your first preloader is ready for testing! Choose File ➪ Export ➪ HTML + SWF or use the Ctrl+P accelerator keys to create the movie and Web page. Open your Web browser, and load the HTML page you just created. The image will load after a few seconds; until it loads completely, the text you added in the preloader scene appears on the stage.

Adding a text effect to the preloader

Although the first preloader you built works, and it informs your viewer that something is happening, it isn't very exciting. You can make it more exciting by adding effects to the preloader movie. In this example, you add a text effect to the preloader. Follow these steps to add a text effect; the steps continue from those in the previous discussion:

On The Web Site

The sample project described in this discussion is available from the book's Web site in the chapter24 folder. The sample is called example2.swi.

1. **Choose File ➪ Save As and save your movie as** example2.swi.

2. **In the Outline panel, right-click the** loading movie, please wait **text item in the** preload **scene to display the shortcut menu.**

3. **Choose Grouping ➪ Group as Sprite.**

4. **Click the Sprite tab in the panel group and deselect the Stop playing at end of sprite option if it is selected.**

5. **Open the new Sprite in the Outline panel by clicking on the plus (+) sign to the left of the name.** The sprite appears on the Timeline.

6. **Add an effect to the sprite's text.** I've chosen Pulsing, which you can find by clicking the Effect button and choosing Effect ➪ Looping continuously ➪ Pulsing.

7. **Double-click the effect's rectangle on the Timeline to open the Pulsing Settings dialog box.**

8. **Change the effect's duration to 20 frames.** Click Close to close the Pulse Settings dialog box.

You placed this effect on its own Timeline inside a sprite because it runs independently of the main movie's own Timeline without the need for any scripting to make it loop.

When you test your uploaded SWF movie this time, the text pulses during the preloading, as seen in Figure 24-2.

Figure 24-2: The preload movie's text pulses as the sprite plays.

Using an Event Handler in a Preloader

The first two examples used a simple frame loop; that is, they execute one frame and then in the next frame go back to the first. This type of loop can be an effective solution, but it isn't the most stylish way to achieve your goal. In this example, you amend your script to use the onEnterFrame event handler. The onEnterFrame event handler executes a chunk of code per frame and updates the stage at the end of each frame.

On The Web Site

The sample project using the modified code described here is available from the book's Web site in the chapter24 folder. The sample is called example3.swi; an example named example4.swi shows how to make the preloader more portable.

Continuing from the previous example, follow these steps to use the onEnterFrame event handler instead of a frame loop:

1. **Choose File ➪ Save As and save your movie as** example3.swi.

2. **Click the Script tab to display the Script panel.**

3. **Select all the code in the Script panel and delete it.**

4. **Type this replacement code:**

```
onEnterFrame(){
  if(_framesloaded == __totalframes){
    nextSceneAndPlay();
  }
}
```

5. **Export the movie, or test it in a Web browser.**

The movie appears exactly the same as sample2.swi; the code required is smaller and neater.

Making a Preloader Portable

Your preloader is now quite well advanced, but not quite as portable as it might be. It has two Timelines — one on the _root Timeline and another inside the sprite. You can copy the script and the sprite into your next movie, but you can improve the portability in one easy step.

On The Web Site

The sample project using the modified code described here is available from the book's Web site in the chapter24 folder. The sample is called example4.swi.

Follow these steps to make the preloader portable. The steps continue from the previous example:

1. **Save the SWiSHmax project file as example4.swi.**

2. **Click the** preload **scene's label in the Outline panel to select it.**

3. **Click the Script tab to display the Script panel.**

4. **Select all the code in the Script panel and remove it.** You can choose Edit ➪ Cut, use the Ctrl+X accelerator keys, or right-click the code on the Script panel and choose Cut from the shortcut menu.

5. **Click the Sprite in the Outline panel to select it.**

6. **Click the Script tab to display the Script panel for the Sprite.**

7. **Paste the code you cut in Step 4.** You can choose Edit ➪ Paste, use the Ctrl+V accelerator keys, or right-click the code on the Script panel and choose Paste from the shortcut menu.

Remember from an earlier discussion that _framesloaded and _totalframes relate to the Timeline in which they are invoked, so at the moment they refer to the sprite's Timeline. You want them to refer to the main movie's Timeline, which is the _root timeline. To change the scope of the two properties, you use dot notation, and the code becomes:

```
onEnterFrame(){
  if(_root._framesloaded == _root._totalframes){
    _root.nextSceneAndPlay();
  }
}
```

Cross-Reference

See Chapter 17 for information on syntax, including dot notation.

Using _root as a scoping device can sometimes cause a problem. In this example, _root refers to both _root and the dot notation level one above the sprite. If you copy the sprite into another sprite assuming that it will still refer to one level above you would be wrong. If you want only to refer to the level one above, change _root to _parent, but for purposes here, both are acceptable.

Making Preloaders Accurate

You now have a preloader nicely wrapped up inside a sprite that you can copy and paste into any movie. That's excellent. You've done well coming so far, but you still have a small distance to go before finishing.

Most preloaders on the Web use a visual device to display the progress of the preloading. You can use the framecount for this, but that isn't always accurate. Consider a 20-frame movie that is 100KB and another that is 19 frames totaling 19KB. The framecount preloader will tell us that 5 percent of the movie has loaded after the first frame, when in reality it is 84 percent. SWiSHmax provides the three methods described at the start of the chapter that allow us to build a preloader that more accurately shows the progress of the download.

On The Web Site

The sample project using the modified code described here is available from the book's Web site in the chapter24 folder. The sample is called example5.swi.

Follow these steps to build a more accurate preloader that displays detail. The steps follow from the previous example:

1. **Choose File ➪ Save As and save the SWiSHmax project file as** example5.swi.

2. **In the Outline panel, click the sprite named Sprite to select it.** Change its name to **loader.**

3. **Select the** loader **sprite in the Outline panel, and add two dynamic text fields to the sprite:**

   - Choose Insert ⇨ Text from the Outline panel's menu.
   - Click the Text tab to display the Text panel.
   - Click the text type button and choose Dynamic Text.
   - Click the Target option to make the text a target.
   - Name one text field **percentloaded**; name the other text field **bytesloaded**.
   - Resize the **bytesloaded** text field to be two to three times wider than the **percentloaded** text field.

Note
The sample project's bytesloaded field is 190 pixels wide; the percentloaded text field is 90 pixels wide.

4. **Click the Rectangle tool, and draw a shape within the** loader **sprite:**

   - Name the rectangle **bar** in the Shape tab.
   - Click the Target option in the Shape tab to make the shape a target.
   - Change the color to your own preference.

5. **In the Transform tab, change the size of the bar to 100 pixels wide and 4 pixels high.**

6. **Align all three text fields and the object called** bar, **as seen in Figure 24-3.** I put a border around the dynamic text fields so you can see them, but this is not necessary.

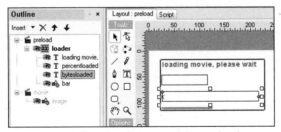

Figure 24-3: Align the elements of the preloader on the stage.

7. **Click the loader sprite's Script tab, and replace all the code in the Script panel with the following:**

```
onEnterFrame(){
  pcl = _root.getPercentLoaded();
  bar._xscale = pcl;
  percentloaded.text = int(pcl) + "%";
  bytesloaded.text = int(_root.getBytesLoaded()/1024) + " kb of " +
_root.getBytesTotal()+ " kb";
  if (pcl >= 100){
    _root.nextSceneAndPlay();
  }
}
```

Once again, consider this code line by line. The lines of code and their explanations appear in Table 24-2.

Table 24-2: Script and Explanation of Code for Preloader

Line of Code...	Means...
`onEnterFrame() {`	An event handler that executes each frame.
`pcl = _root.getPercentLoaded();`	You know that `getPercentLoaded()` returns the percentage of bytes loaded so far. You then assign this value to a variable named `pcl`.
`bar._xscale = pcl;`	`pcl` holds the percentage of bytes loaded so far and you want the bar to expand in line with the download progress; you assign the value of `pcl` to the `_xscale` property of `bar`. The bar will expand to the right as the value of `pcl` increases.
`percentloaded.text = int(pcl) + "%";`	Place the nonfractional value of pcl into the dynamic text field named `percentloaded` and add a % sign to make it look better.
`bytesloaded.text = int(_root.getBytesLoaded()/1024) + " kb of " + int(_root.getBytesTotal(/1024))+ " kb";`	`getBytesLoaded()` returns the number of bytes loaded so far, and if you divide that number by 1024 you get the number of kilobytes (kb) loaded so far. `getBytesTotal()` returns the total number of bytes of the download. This line places the value of these two methods into dynamic text field **bytesloaded**. I added "kb" to the end of each value for formatting purposes.
`if (pcl >= 100) _root.nextSceneAndPlay();`	A slightly shorter condition than in previous examples. You already have the percentage bytes loaded assigned to pcl, so you test whether that value is more than or equal to 100. If it is, you goto the `_root` next scene and start playing.

On The Web Site
You can add all sorts of additional data to this preloader such as speed of download or bytes left to download. I'll leave it to you to add these as an exercise to test your understanding of what you've achieved so far. I've included this version of the preloader as well. The sample project, example5a.swi, is available from the book's Web site in the chapter24 folder.

Circular Preloader

Now that you have built your first preloader and you understand the various properties and methods that provide the backbone of most preloaders, you can mix in some Timeline effects to develop a preloader that many people want to use, but are sometimes confused by its complexity. It needn't be that way.

There are several stages to this preloader. First, construct the objects. Then add effects and create sprites. Finally, add some SWiSHscript. This example starts with a new SWiSHmax project file.

On The Web Site

This version of a preloader is available as example6.swi from the chapter24 folder on the book's Web site.

Constructing the preloader's objects

Start a new SWiSHmax project file and follow these steps to construct the objects used for the circular preloader:

1. **In the Outline panel, choose Insert ⇨ Sprite.** Name the sprite **preloader**.

2. **On the Sprite tab, click the Use bottom object as mask option.**

3. **On the Transform tab, click the Anchor Point button and choose top left from the drop-down list.**

4. **Click the Rectangle tool in the Toolbox, press Shift, and click and drag to draw a square.**

5. **In the Transform panel, resize the square to 50 x 50 pixels.**

6. **Copy the square and paste three more squares on the stage for a total of four squares.**

7. **Configure the four squares.** Name and set anchor points for each of the squares as follows:

   • Name one square **rotator**, and set its anchor point to bottom right. On the Shape panel, click the Target option to make this square a target.

   • Name one square **q1**, and set its anchor point to bottom left.

   • Name one square **q2**, and set its anchor point to top left.

   • Name one square **q3**, and set its anchor point to top right.

   When the anchor points are set, ensure that both the X- and Y-axis coordinates of each square are 50. You will now have the effect of a 100-x–100-pixel square with the rotator square at top left.

8. **Draw one more 100-x-100-pixel square.** In the Shape panel, name the shape **backmask**, and click the Target option to make it a target.

Tip

Change the color of the newest square in the Shape panel for ease of identification

9. **On the Transform panel, click Anchor Point and choose center left from the drop-down list.** Set the shape's X-axis and Y-axis coordinates to 50.

10. **Drag the** backmask **square to the bottom of the stacking order in the Outline panel.** You have a set of four squares that make up a larger square and another square you use as a mask.

Applying effects

Once the objects are drawn, you need to add effects to simulate the sweeping effect in the circle. The appearance is based on the rotation of the **rotator** object and its anchor point location. Because the **rotator** object's anchor point is the bottom right, the square appears to pivot around a point central to the larger backmask square, as seen in Figure 24-4.

Figure 24-4: The effect is based on the motion of the rotator square.

Follow these steps to add the effects to the preloader:

1. **In the Timeline panel, right-click the rotator object to open the shortcut menu and choose Move.** The Move effect is added to the object at its default length of 10 frames.

2. **Double-click the effect's rectangle on the Timeline panel to open the Move Settings dialog box.**

3. **Click the Duration field to activate it and type** 100.

4. **Click X angle to open its drop-down list, and choose Rotate CW by, as seen in Figure 24-5.**

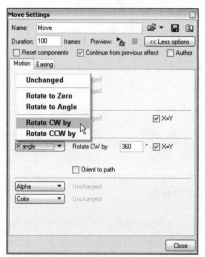

Figure 24-5: Rotate the object clockwise during the Move effect.

5. **Click the Rotate CW by field and type** 360.

6. **Click Close to close the Move Settings dialog box.**

The **rotator** square completes a revolution every 100 frames. You also need to add an effect to each of the other three 50-x-50-pixel squares. For each square, right-click its row on the Timeline and choose Place from the shortcut menu. The effect should be added to the Timeline at these frames:

✦ Square **q1**. Insert the Place effect at Frame 25.

✦ Square **q2**. Insert the Place effect at Frame 50.

✦ Square **q3**. Insert the Place effect at Frame 75.

The larger square, named **backmask** also needs effects. It uses both a Place and a Move effect. Follow these steps to apply effects to the object:

1. **Right-click Frame 1 on the object's row on the Timeline to open the shortcut menu and choose Place.**

2. **Right-click the backmask object's row on the Timeline at Frame 50 and choose Move.**

3. **Double-click the Move effect's rectangle to open the Move Settings dialog box.**

4. **Click the Duration field and type** 1 **to decrease the duration to 1 frame.**

5. **Click X position to open its drop-down list and choose Move Left by.** In the field that appears, type **50,** as seen in Figure 24-6.

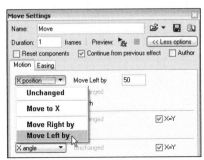

Figure 24-6: Add a Move effect to the backmask object.

Creating and masking a sprite

You combine some of the objects already created into sprites and then construct another sprite to create the rotation effect. You also add two text objects that are scripted in the following section.

Follow these steps to create a sprite and dynamic text objects for your preloader:

1. **Select the five squares you have built in the project. Right-click and choose Grouping ⇨ Group as Sprite to create a sprite.**

2. **Name the sprite** rotmask.

3. **On the Sprite panel, click the Use bottom objects as mask button.** You add several objects to the sprite and one is later designated as a mask.

4. **Add two dynamic text fields to the scene:**

   - Choose Insert ⇨ Text from the Outline panel's menu.

   - Click the Text tab to display the Text panel.

   - Click the text type button and choose Dynamic Text.

   - Copy and paste the dynamic text object to the stage.

   - Name one text field **percentloaded**; name the other text field **bytesloaded**.

5. **Add two circles to the scene:**

   - Click the Ellipse tool in the Toolbox, and draw a circle on the stage with a radius of 50 pixels. Press Shift as you click and drag to constrain the ellipse to a circle.

   - On the Transform panel, set the X-axis position to 50 and the Y-axis position to 0.

   - Copy and paste the circle to the stage.

   - Name one circle **bgcolour**; name the other circle **mask**.

Your completed objects should look like the listing in the Outline panel shown in Figure 24-7.

Figure 24-7: Arrange the objects as shown to create the masking effects.

Please note the order of the objects inside the **preloader** sprite. If your project's order is different, use the up and down arrows to amend the order.

Adding the script

Select the **preloader** sprite in the Outline panel. Click the Script tab to display the sprite's Script panel. Type the code shown in Listing 24-1, which should be very familiar:

Listing 24-1: **Script for the Preloader Sprite**

```
onEnterFrame(){
  pcl = int(_parent.getPercentLoaded());
  rotmask.gotoAndStop(pcl);
  percentloaded.text = int(pcl) + "%";
  bytesloaded.text = int(_parent.getBytesLoaded()/1024) + " kb";
```

```
   if (pcl >= 100){
     _parent.nextSceneAndPlay();
   }
 }
 onFrame (10) {
   stop();
 }
```

The only line that hasn't been seen before is `rotmask.gotoAndStop(pcl);`. Remember, you used a 360-degree rotation in the Move effect on the **rotator** object over 100 frames. Executing the new line of script positions the play head at the frame represented by the percentage of the movie loaded. The effect is to show the **rotmask** sprite one frame at a time as the percentage increases.

Can you see how this works?

✦ As the **rotator** object rotates, each time it completes 25 percent of its rotation one of your squares replaces it, and because you are seeing this through a mask within the **rotmask** sprite, it looks as though the object just rotates smoothly.

✦ Because the whole **preloader** sprite is also masked, the only part of this you see is a circle.

I told you it was easy.

Preloading External Movies

Now that I have covered enough whole movie preloaders for you to build many of your own, I want to turn to the subject that confuses almost everyone — preloading external movies.

Preloading external movies requires a new sprite method, the `loadMovie(url)` and `loadMovie(url,method)`. The method loads the SWF or JPG from a specified URL into the sprite.

Caution If you are going to load a JPG file, it must not be a file saved in progressive format.

The method argument is an optional string to indicate the method used to send variables to an external script and the values available are `GET` and `POST`.

You are going to consider the basic usage of an external preloader. Then you learn how to develop the preloader as a means of controlling the loading of as many movies as you need, one after the other.

Building the external movie loader

The first example is a basic external loader. The basic code you use to build an external movie loader is the same as for a whole movie loader, but you place it inside a sprite and target the sprite into which you want to load the external movie.

The basic external movie loader used in this discussion is available from the book's Web site. It is named example7.swi and is in the chapter24 folder.

Using a new SWiSHmax project, follow these steps to create a basic external movie loader:

1. **Select the scene in the Outline panel and choose Insert ➪ Sprite from the Outline panel's menu.** Name the newly inserted sprite **loader**.

2. **Within the loader sprite insert two more sprites.** Name one sprite **movieholder** and the other sprite **plbits** (for preloader bits).

3. **Within the plbits sprite add a dynamic text field.** Name the field **plp,** and click the Target option on the Text panel to make it a target.

4. **Also within the plbits sprite add three rectangles with these characteristics:**
   - Name **bgbar**; set it as a target; make the fill color black; set the anchor point at top left; set the width at 140 pixels and height 15 pixels; set the X-axis and Y-axis coordinates at 0,0
   - Name **ptr**; set the anchor point to center left; make width 100 pixels and the height 4 pixels; set the X-axis at 0 and Y-axis at 8
   - Name **plbar;** set it as a target; set the anchor point at center left; make the width 100 pixels and the height 4 pixels; set the X-axis at 0 and Y-axis at 8

5. **Select the plbar object in the Outline panel.** On the Transform tab, click the Resize radio button in the Mode section, and set the X scale value to 1.

6. **Check the order of the objects in the scene.** They should be arranged as shown in Figure 24-8.

Figure 24-8: Make sure the objects are arranged in the order shown in the figure.

Scripting the external movie loader

You can add code to the **loader** sprite. Select the loader sprite in the Outline panel, and then click the Script tab to display the Script panel. Type the code shown in Listing 24-2:

Listing 24-2: Script for an External Movie Loader

```
function startloading(mclip){
   cliptoload = mclip;
    gotoAndPlay("preload");
}
```

```
onFrame(10){
    setLabel("finishedloading");
    plbits._visible = false;
}
onFrame(11){
    stop();
}
onFrame(20){
    setLabel("preload");
    plbits._visible = true;
    movieholder.loadMovie(cliptoload);
}
onFrame(25){
    pcl = movieholder.getPercentLoaded();
    plbits.plbar._xscale = pcl;
    plbits.plp.text = int(pcl) + "%";
    if (pcl >= 100){
        gotoAndPlay("finishedloading");
    }
}
onFrame (26) {
    prevFrameAndPlay();
}
onFrame (30) {
    stop();
}
```

The analysis of the script is shown in Table 24-4. For each line of code used in the script, you can read an explanation of its use.

Table 24-4: Understanding the External Movie Loader Script

This Line or Lines...	Means...
`function startloading(mclip){`	This function receives the name of the movie you want to load.
`cliptoload = mclip;`	Sets the `cliptoload` property to the name of the movie you want to load.
`gotoAndPlay("preload");`	Send the sprite play head to the `preload` label.
`}` `onFrame(10){`	The location of the next action.
`setLabel("finishedloading");`	This is where you arrive when the movie has finished loading.
`plbits._visible = false;`	Hide the **plbits** sprite because you no longer need it

Continued

Table 24-4 *(continued)*

This Line or Lines...	Means...

`}`
`onFrame(11){`
`    stop();`
	Stop the sprite at this point.

`}`
`onFrame(20){`
`    setLabel("preload");`
	Start the preloading.

`    plbits._visible = true;`	Show the **plbits** sprite.
`    movieholder.loadMovie(cliptoload);`	Start loading the movie assigned to `cliptoload` into the **movieholder** sprite.
`}` `onFrame(25){`	Frame where next action is located.
`    pcl = movieholder.getPercentLoaded();`	Assign the percentage of the movie downloaded so far to `pcl`.
`    plbits.plbar._xscale = pcl;`	Sets the X scale of `plbar` to the amount loaded; as percentage increases, so does `plbar`.
`    plbits.plp.text = int(pcl) + "%";`	Show the percentage value loaded in `plp`.
`    if (pcl >= 100){`	If `pcl` is 100, that is, if the movie is loaded.
`        gotoAndPlay("finishedloading");`	Send the play head to `finishedloading` label, where this sprite will stop.
`    }` `}`	Frame where next action is located.
`onFrame (26) {`	
`    prevFrameAndPlay();`	You only get here if the movie is not wholly loaded; the play head goes back to the previous frame.

`}`
`onFrame (30) {`
`    stop();`
	Stop.

Most of the code described in the listing or in the table is familiar because it's similar to that used earlier in your whole movie loader. This preloader is called by invoking the `startloading` function. If you want to load movie0.swf, use `loader.startloading("movie0.swf");` where **loader** is the name of the sprite where the function resides.

The anchor point of plbar is set to center left so that the increases in _xscale move away to the right and shows the line growing in length as the percentage of the movie loaded approaches 100 percent.

Using External Loaders with Destination Sprites

Now you've built your first external loader. This basic approach is all well and good, but what if you want to load the movie into a sprite somewhere else?

On The Web Site

The basic external movie loader used in this discussion is available from the book's Web site. It is named example8.swi and is located in the chapter24 folder.

Follow these steps to create an external loader. This time, the loader uses a destination sprite and an eased and hidden preloader bar.

1. **If you have the example7.swi project file open in SWiSHmax, save it as** example8.swi. If you prefer, you can open the example7.swi file from the book's Web site and save it as **example8.swi**.

2. **Delete the** movieholder **sprite nested within the** loader **sprite.**

3. **In the Outline panel, click Scene_1 and then choose Insert ⇨ Sprite from the Outline panel's menu. Name the new sprite dest0.**

4. **Add two dynamic text fields within the** plbits **sprite having the following characteristics:**

   • Name one field **loadingname**; set it as a target in the Text panel, sized at 200 x 15 pixels

   • Name one field **kbs**; set it as a target in the Text panel, sized at 60 x 15 pixels

5. **Position the two text fields to the right of the** plp **text object on the stage as shown in Figure 24-9.**

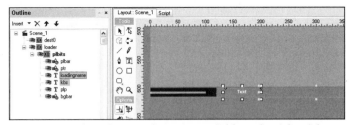

Figure 24-9: Place the new dynamic text fields to the right of the other text block in the sprite.

6. **Replace the code in the** loader **sprite's Script panel with the code shown in Listing 24-3:**

Listing 24-3: **Scripting a Loader Sprite**

```
onLoad(){
    targety = _y = Stage.height;
    plbits.bgbar._width = Stage.width;
}
onEnterFrame(){
    _y = Math.approach(_y, targety, 0.8);
}
function startloading(mclip,holder){
    cliptoload = mclip;
    movieholder = holder;
    targety = Stage.height - _height; //moves the bar up by its own
height
    gotoAndPlay("preload");
}
onframe(10){
    setLabel("finishedloading");
    targety = Stage.height; //moves the loader bar back down again
}
onframe(11){
    stop();
}
onframe(20){
    setLabel("preload");
    plbits.loadingname.text = cliptoload;
    lt = getTimer();
    movieholder.loadMovie(cliptoload);
}
onframe(25){
    pcl = movieholder.getPercentLoaded();
    plbits.plbar._xscale = pcl;
    plbits.plp.text = int(pcl) + "%";
    plbits.kbs.text =
int((movieholder.getBytesLoaded()/1000)/((getTimer()-lt)/1000)) + "
KB/s";
    if (pcl >= 100){
        movieholder.movieloaded = true;
        gotoAndPlay("finishedloading");
    }
}
onFrame (26) {
    prevFrameAndPlay();
}
onFrame (30) {
    stop();
}
```

There are a number of differences between this script and that used for the example7.swi project.

The `startloading` function now has two arguments: the original movie to load and the name of the sprite into which you want to load the movie. You are still using the variable name `movieloader` to avoid changing your code, and you assign the value of `holder` to movieholder.

The loader bar now hides under the stage; it eases in when the loading starts and eases out when the loading is complete. The first line moves the bar up by its own height when loading starts. `Stage.height` returns the movie height. The second line moves the loader bar back down.

The easing is defined in these two lines:

```
targety = Stage.height - _height;
targety = Stage.height;
```

Set the easing values in this line of code; the code eases the _y value toward the `targety` 80 percent at a time:

```
_y = Math.approach(_y, targety, 0.8);
```

Add the approximate speed of the loading using this line of script, which captures the timer value before the loading starts:

```
lt = getTimer();
```

During the loading, the elapsed time is recaptured, the start value is deducted, and the number of bytes loaded in that period of time is displayed in the **kbs** text field in this line of code:

```
plbits.kbs.text = int((movieholder.getBytesLoaded()/1000)/
((getTimer()-lt)/1000)) + " KB/s";
```

The name of the file being loaded shows as a result of using the following line of code; `cliptoload` is a string value, so it can appear in a text field.

```
plbits.loadingname.text = cliptoload;
```

Apart from those few small changes, you now have a very flexible external loader that takes the name of the movie you want loaded and the sprite into which you want it loaded as its arguments. The **loader** bar appears and disappears as necessary.

In Frame 1 of the movie, you learn how to use this loader:

```
loader.startloading("movie0.swf", dest0);
```

This is quite cool and very useful, but what if you need to preload more than one external movie? You learn this in the final section of this chapter.

Preloading a Number of External Movies

The previous example showed you how to load an external movie into a sprite. The final example is similar to example8.swi but includes the ability to load as many movies as necessary while targeting the menus that will call on these loaded movies.

On The Web Site The external movie loader used in this final example is available from the book's Web site. It is named example9.swi and is in the chapter24 folder.

For example, the preloader is called with a function call written like this:

```
loader.startloading(["movie0.swf","Movie 1",dest0,menu0],
["movie1.swf","Movie 1",dest1,menu1]);
```

You pass an array or arrays to the `startloading` function. The array elements are:

✦ **Element 1.** Name of movie to load, either a SWF or JPG movie

✦ **Element 2.** Text to display as movie is loaded

✦ **Element 3.** Sprite you want the movie loaded into

✦ **Element 4.** Name of menu that will ultimately call on this movie once loaded

You can pass as many arrays as you wish. In this example, as shown in the line of code written above, the intention is to load two movies.

The idea behind the menu link is that when a movie starts you may have five or six menu items that show an external movie when clicked. What happens when the movie hasn't actually loaded yet? You can use a movie like the one exported from example7.swi to load as needed, but wouldn't it be great if the menu item didn't work until the movie is loaded?

The approach used in this example is to pass the menu that calls this movie and disable it to begin with. When the movie loads, the menu is switched back on. You can adapt this approach so that before you disable the menu item you set its text value to `"movie loading..."` and then before enabling it, set it to its text. There are many, many options you can use.

I'll leave it to you to view the code used in example9.swi, which is basically the same as example8.swi. However, because you don't know in advance how many movies you'll want to load, count the number of arrays passed in the function call and then split those values into some new arrays that are then used.

Cross-Reference   Arrays are discussed in Chapter 18.

The arguments property is an array itself and, therefore, can be accessed in the same way as an array. You can determine its length and access parts of the array to access the arguments itself.

The only other extra is that the movie doesn't jump to the `finishedloading` label when the first preload is complete. The movie checks whether the correct number has been preloaded based on the number of arguments for the `startloading` function. If there is more to preload, the movie jumps back to the `preload` label, accesses the array data for the next preload, and repeats that process as many times as necessary.

I like example9.swi, so please use the file on the Web site. I have also provided movie0.swf and movie1.swf for you to preload to test the file. See how the two red buttons stay disabled until the movie loads. When you click the newly enabled button, the text in the loaded movie changes, so it shows you how to access variables in loaded movies as well.

There are many extras that you could add, but I'll leave it to your imagination. Let me know how you get on; I'd love to see your own developments.

Summary

You can apply the same logic to `loadVars()` and the XML object to view the progress loading either a text file containing variables or an XML file.

Here are some basic things to remember:

✦ When used in a compressed movie in Flash Player 6, `getBytesLoaded` returns the number of bytes in the uncompressed movie, not the compressed value.

✦ When loading a JPEG, it must have not been saved as progressive.

✦ Use the methods and properties discussed; don't be afraid, and you'll have some beautiful preloaders all of your own before too long.

✦ ✦ ✦

Constructing a Web Site Interface

CHAPTER 25

*Special thanks to Peter Thijs
for contributing this chapter.*

Suppose you have a client who wants a new Web site. How do you approach and construct the project? In this chapter, you learn to build a Web site, step-by-step, complete with buttons, actions, preloaders, externally loaded content, and both beginning and ending animations. For each component of the site, you can read an explanation for why it is done as well as how it is constructed.

In this chapter, the basic interface for the site I build consists of five content pages, including Home, About, Products, Services, and Contact. Each content page uses a separate preloader. The Contact page consists of a form constructed with PHP. A short opening animation is used to introduce the site. All the text content is loaded from an external text file for easy updating in the future.

At the end of the process, the result is several well-structured SWI files, a site that is easy to update through the text files, and one that doesn't require horizontal scrolling at a screen resolution of 800 x 600 or higher or vertical scrolling at a screen resolution of 1024 x 768 or higher.

Before starting a project, do some groundwork to determine the client's needs. The only thing to worry about in this chapter is how to make an interface and site in SWiSHmax.

Cross-Reference   Learn more about project planning Chapter 3.

Starting the Site

First, decide what size the site is going to be. There are two size restrictions: When the site is shown at a resolution of 800 x 600 pixels there should be no horizontal scrolling, and when the site is shown at a resolution of 1024 x 768 pixels there should be no vertical scrolling.

Start a new movie project in SWiSHmax. Click the Movie tab to display the Movie panel. Set the Width to 760, Height to 560, Frame rate to 30 fps, and click Stop playing at end of movie. The Hex color value used for the sample movie is #99A7AE. Choose File ⇨ Save and save the new project file. The sample project is named main.swi.

On The Web Site

The sample files, including all the SWI, SWF, HTML, and other files, are available from the book's Web site in the chapter25 folder.

The site's interface includes six major parts: the header, menu bar, content window, news scroll, a place for special actions or a feature, and a footer. Rather than constructing each component individually, completing its design, and then working on the next component, it is simpler and more efficient to create placeholders, which helps you organize the layout correctly and saves time in the long run. Create six placeholders for the items on the interface.

Header placeholder. Draw a rectangle and size it at 750 x 100 pixels. I chose 750 pixels as the width to allow for a 5-pixel border on each side of the header. Name the rectangle **headerplace.** Click the Transform tab to display the Transform panel. Set the Anchor point to Top left, click the Resize radio button in the Mode section, and set both X- and Y-axis positions to 5.

Tip

Setting the anchor point for the rectangle to the top left makes it easy to define the location of the object on the stage.

Menu bar placeholder. Select the **headerplace** object in the Outline panel and choose Edit ⇨ Copy or press Ctrl+C to copy the object. (I like to use shortcuts when possible). Then choose Edit ⇨ Paste in Place or press Ctrl+Shift+V to paste a copy of the object at the same location on the Layout panel's stage.

In the Outline panel, you will notice that both objects have the same name. Click the top object's name to activate the name and then rename it **menuplace.** With the **menuplace** object in the Outline panel selected, change the Y-axis value to 110 pixels and height to 20 pixels in the Transform panel.

Footer placeholder. Select the **headerplace** object in the Outline panel again, and copy it and then paste it in place. In the Outline panel, you see two objects with the same name again. Click the top object's name to activate the name and then rename it **footerplace.** On the Transform panel, change the Y-axis value to 505 and the height to 50 pixels.

News placeholder. Use a copy of the **headerplace** rectangle, copied and pasted in place. Rename the rectangle **newsplace.** In the Transform panel, change the size to 200 x 180 pixels, and the Y-axis location to 135.

Feature placeholder. Click the **newsplace** object to select it and then copy and paste in place. Rename the shape **featureplace.** In the Transform panel, set the Y-axis value to 320 pixels.

Content window placeholder. Copy the **newsplace** object and paste it in place again. Rename this object **contentplace.** In the Transform panel, change the X-axis location to 210, the Y-axis location to 135, and change the size to 545 x 365 pixels.

You now have the blueprint for the site. The layout looks like the image shown in Figure 25-1.

Now that all the placeholders are created and added to the project, it's time to rearrange the Outline panel in a logical manner. This site is arranged from top to bottom and left to right. Using the up and down arrows in the Outline panel, reorder the objects in this order: **headerplace**, **menuplace**, **newsplace**, **featureplace**, **contentplace**, and **footerplace**. Of course, you can move the objects as you are creating them. Just make sure when you are finished that the objects are arranged logically.

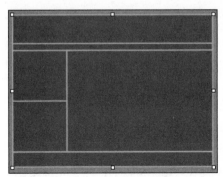

Figure 25-1: The completed blueprint for the site includes six placeholders.

Constructing the Menu Bar and Buttons

In order to more easily control the menu and separate it from the rest of the movie, you can group it as a sprite by right-clicking the **menuplace** object on the Outline panel and choosing Grouping ➪ Group as Sprite from the shortcut menu. Name the sprite **menu**.

The sprite contains the **menuplace** rectangle, which uses the default SWiSHmax red color. Select the **menuplace** object, and then select Linear Gradient in the Shape panel. Change the start color to #666666, with an alpha value of 100; change the end color to #000000, with an alpha value of 100. Click the Properties button on the Shape panel to open the Properties dialog box. Set both width and height of the gradient to 98, and set the rotation to 90 degrees.

Creating the button objects

Select the **menuplace** object, copy it, and paste it in place. Rename this new object **button1,** and then make transform and gradient changes to the new object. In the Transform panel, change the height to 14, the width to 120, the X-axis to 10, and the Y-axis to 3. On the Shape panel, click Properties to open the Properties dialog box for the gradient and change the rotation to -90 degrees. Change the start color for the gradient to #999999 in the Color Selector.

You need copies for another button state and a mask. Copy and paste in place a copy of the **button1** rectangle. Rename the new copy **overstate**. In the Shape panel, change both start and end gradient colors to #FFFFFF (white); change the alpha value for the end color to 0%. In the Transform panel, change the Y-axis value to 17. The two buttons' states overlap, as shown in Figure 25-2.

Figure 25-2: The two button states overlap on the menu bar.

When the user rolls the mouse over the finished button, the bottom object appears to slide up. You use a mask and an effect to create the motion. To create the mask, select **button1** in the Outline panel, copy it, and paste in place another copy; name this copy **mask**.

Make sure the elements in the **menu** sprite are in this order in the Outline panel: **overstate, button1, mask**, and **menuplace**.

Now that you have the objects for the button, you can add some actions on the **menu** sprite's Timeline.

Follow these steps to add effects to the **overstate** button element:

1. **Click the** overstate **object to select it.**

2. **On the Timeline, right-click Frame 1 of the** overstate **object to open the shortcut menu and choose Place.**

3. **Right-click Frame 3 of the** overstate **object's row on the Timeline to open the short-cut menu again.** Choose Move. Leave the Move effect's default length at 10 frames.

4. **Double-click the Move effect's rectangle on the Timeline to open the Move Settings dialog box.**

5. **Click the Motion tab, click the Y position button, and then choose Move to Y from the drop-down list.** Type **3** in the Move to Y field, and click Close to close the Move Settings dialog box.

6. **Right-click the** overstate **object's row on the Timeline at Frame 14 to open the short-cut menu.** Choose Place to add another Place effect.

Creating the button

You use three elements to create a single button. In the Outline panel, press Shift+click to select the **overstate, button1**, and **mask** objects. Right-click and choose Group ⇨ Group as Sprite from the shortcut menu. In the Sprite tab, name the sprite **button1** and click the Use bottom object as mask option.

Double-click the **button1** sprite's name in the Outline panel to open the sprite and display its Timeline. Right-click the **button1** sprite's row on the Timeline at Frame 2 to open the shortcut menu. Choose Movie Control ⇨ stop to add the `stop()` action to the frame. Add additional `stop()` actions at Frames 13 and 15.

Right-click Frame 1 of the **button1** sprite's Timeline to open the shortcut menu. Choose Frame ⇨ setLabel( ). The Script panel appears and the action is added to the script window in red. Click the Label field at the bottom of the Script panel and type **off** as the label for the frame. Follow the same method and add a label named **over** to Frame 3; add a label named **hit** to Frame 14. The Timeline with the actions and labels is shown in Figure 25-3.

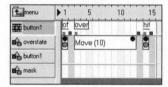

Figure 25-3: The button sprite uses several actions.

Finally, the button needs some text. Make sure the **button1** sprite is open and selected in the Outline panel. Use the Text tool and draw a static text box over the button area. Name the text object **home**. Use Verdana text at 10-point size in white. The width field on the Dimensions settings of the Text panel is set at 120; the text for the button is **HOME**. Center the text on the button.

On The Web Site

Refer to the sample project files in the chapter25 folder on the book's Web site for specific text settings.

Adding the remaining buttons

Now that you have one perfect button, you can add the other button sprites by copying and pasting. Click the **button1** sprite to select it in the Outline panel and copy it. Then select the **menu** sprite in the Outline panel and paste the sprite into it.

Copy and paste four copies of the **button1** sprite into the **menu** sprite. Place and name the button sprites as:

✦ **button2**, text label is **ABOUT**, X-axis position of 175

✦ **button3**, text label is **PRODUCTS**, X-axis position of 315

✦ **button4**, text label is **SERVICES**, X-axis position of 455

✦ **button5**, text label is **CONTACT**, X-axis position of 595

Using Hotspots

You need actions for the five buttons. I always use different shapes with the actions applied to hotspots rather than having actions applied to objects within button sprites as it is easier to control.

To add the first hotspot, open the **menu** sprite in the Outline panel. Draw a rectangle over the HOME button. Name the rectangle **hotspot1** on the Shape panel and make sure it has no line or color fill. On the Transform panel, size the rectangle at 120 pixels wide and 14 pixels high, and drag the hotspot rectangle over the HOME button.

Right-click **hotspot1** in the Outline panel to display the shortcut menu. Choose Grouping ➪ Group as Sprite. Name the sprite **hotspots**.

Earlier in the chapter you added labels to the Timeline. It's time to use those labels and add the actions to the buttons. Follow these steps to add rollover and rollout actions:

1. **Click the** hotspot1 **shape inside the** hotspot **sprite to select it.**

2. **Click the Script tab to display the Script panel; click Add Script and choose Events ➪ Button ➪ on(rollOver).**

3. **Click Add Script again and choose Movie Control ➪ gotoAndPlay ➪ gotoAndPlay (LABEL).**

4. **At the bottom of the Script panel, click the Target down arrow and choose _parent.button1, or you can type the target's name.**

5. Click the Label down arrow and choose over, or you can type the label's name.

6. Click Add Script and choose Events ➪ Button ➪ on(rollOut).

7. Click Add Script again and choose Movie Control ➪ gotoAndPlay ➪ gotoAndPlay (LABEL).

8. At the bottom of the Script panel, click the Target down arrow and choose _parent.button1, or you can type the target's name.

9. Click the Label down arrow and choose off, or you can type the label's name.

Test the movie. As you move the mouse over the hotspot, you see that the mask layer in the button moves; when you rollout the mouse, the mask layer moves back to its original location.

There are five buttons in the movie; logically you need five hotspots. Copy **hotspot1** and paste four more copies into the **hotspot** sprite. For each hotspot, you must also change the location on the movie. Table 25-1 lists the changes you make to the script target for each hotspot.

Table 25-1: Modifying Hotspots

Hotspot Name	X-axis Position	Rollover Script Target	Rollout Script Target
hotspot2	175	_parent.button2	_parent.button2
hotspot3	315	_parent.button3	_parent.button3
hotspot4	455	_parent.button4	_parent.button4
hotspot5	595	_parent.button5	_parent.button5

When you click a button, you want the **over** state to stay and the button to become inactive. Use a sequence of Place and Remove effects to control the button's appearance. Double-click the **hotspots** sprite's name in the Outline panel to display its Timeline and select all the hotspot shapes; that is, **hotspot1** through **hotspot5**. Right-click Frame 1 for any of the objects to display the shortcut menu and choose Place. Each shape has an initial Place effect applied.

For each hotspot, add Remove and Place effects at these frames:

✦ hotspot1: Remove Frame 2, Place Frame 3

✦ hotspot2: Remove Frame 3, Place Frame 4

✦ hotspot3: Remove Frame 4, Place Frame 5

✦ hotspot4: Remove Frame 5, Place Frame 6

✦ hotspot5: Remove Frame 6

Select all five hotspot shapes again. Right-click at Frame 7 of any object to open the shortcut menu and choose Remove to add Remove effects to the set of hotspots.

Next, labels need to be applied to the Timeline of the **hotspots** sprite. You are going to use these shortly to control the action. For each action, right-click the **hotspots** sprite's frame on the Timeline and choose the action from the shortcut menu. Frame 1 uses a stop() action; for the remaining frames, choose Frame ➪ Set Label; the frame's action is added to the movie's script in the Script panel. Type the name for the label in the Label field.

✦ **Frame 1.** Choose Movie Control ⇨ stop from the right-click shortcut menu.

✦ **Frame 2.** Type **home** in the label field.

✦ **Frame 3.** Type **about** in the label field.

✦ **Frame 4.** Type **products** in the label field.

✦ **Frame 5.** Type **services** in the label field.

✦ **Frame 6.** Type **contact** in the label field.

✦ **Frame 7.** Type **inactive** in the label field.

The completed set of labels, as well as the hotspots' effects, is shown on the Timeline in Figure 25-4.

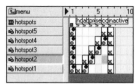

Figure 25-4: Each hotspot has effects and the sprite has labels.

Before leaving the work on the menu, rearrange the sprites and buttons. Make sure the **hotspots** sprites are first, followed by the buttons in sequence from **button1** to **button5**.

Configuring the News Scroll Feature

On the site interface, you built a **newsplace** placeholder, which is used for the news scroll feature. The news scroll needs scroll arrows and uses an external text file for simple updating.

First, right-click the **newsplace** object in the Outline panel and choose Grouping ⇨ Group as Sprite. Name the sprite **news**. All objects used for the news scroll are added to the **news** sprite. Make sure before adding each element that the **news** sprite is selected in the Outline panel.

Select the **newsplace** shape inside the **news** sprite and change its color to white. Copy and paste in place a second shape, and name this shape **background**. Change the **background** shape's color to gray, and change its width to 198 x 178 pixels to make it slightly smaller than the **newsplace** shape. Nudge the **background** shape down and to the right one pixel.

Draw another rectangle; name this rectangle **titlebackground**. Change its color to #343E43 (dark gray). Set the rectangle's dimensions to 180 x 17 pixels, with an X-axis value of 10 and a Y-axis value of 10. Make sure the anchor point is set at top left.

Draw a text block on the Layout panel over the **news** sprite's area. Use white text, center justify the text, set its width to 180, and type **Latest news** in the text entry area in white text. Center the text on the sprite.

You use dynamic text to create the news scroll itself, and then add arrows that will be used to scroll the text in the **news** sprite. Draw a text block on the Layout panel over the **news** sprite's area. In the Text panel, name the text **textscroll**, and click to select the Target option. Choose Dynamic text from the text types, and type **Loading** in the text entry area. In the Dimensions settings, set the width to 180 and the height to 10 lines. In the Advanced settings, click in the variable field and type **newsvar** to name a variable. On the Transform panel, set the text block's X-axis coordinates at 10 pixels and the Y-axis at 35 pixels.

The text field is ready for the dynamic text; now you need to make arrows and a scroller. The arrows are created from Webding characters. Draw a text box on the **news** sprite's area of the Layout panel. Select the Webdings font from the Font drop-down menu. Type the number **5**, which is the up arrow in Webdings. Deselect Enable margins and indents in the Dimensions settings to cause the text object to resize correctly. In the Transform panel, set the X-axis location to 175 and the Y-axis location to 30.

Copy the **5** text object and paste in place a copy of the object within the **news** sprite. In the Text panel, type **6** in the Text entry area; this is the down arrow in Webdings. In the Transform panel, change the Y-axis location to 145.

At this point, the **news** scroller should look like what is shown in Figure 25-5.

Figure 25-5: The **news** scroller uses up and down arrows for moving the content.

Next, you create hotspots for the arrows in the same way as you did for the menu buttons. I like to use invisible rectangles as hotspots to put actions on them; I find it easier to control everything that way. Of course, this is a personal choice, and you can do it differently if you want.

Make sure the two hotspots are within the **news** sprite. The two text objects are named **5** and **6**; change the names to **uphotspot** and **downhotspot**, respectively. Convert both hotspots to sprites, naming them **up** and **down**, respectively. Move each hotspot over the up and down arrow objects on the movie.

Double-click the **up** sprite in the Outline panel to open its Timeline. Right-click the sprite's Timeline and choose Movie Control ➪ stop( ) from the shortcut menu. Click Frame 2 on the Timeline, and then click the Script tab to display the Script panel. Click Add Script and choose Events ➪ Frame ➪ onFrame( ). Frame 2 is identified in the script. Click the Add Script button again, and choose the Statements ➪ evaluate command. In the text entry field at the bottom of the Script panel, type **_parent.textscroll.scroll -=1;** and click off the text entry field to move the text to the script.

Right-click Frame 3 on the Timeline and choose Movie Control ➪ gotoAndPlay( ) ➪ prevFrameAndPlay( ). As you see later, this script causes a loop.

You also need a hotspot for the down arrow. Copy the **up** sprite in the **news** sprite in the Outline panel, and paste a copy into the **news** sprite.

You also have to change one of the lines of script for the sprite. Change to Expert mode in the Script panel and select the line of script that reads:

```
_parent.textscroll.scroll -=1
```

Change the line to read:

```
_parent.textscroll.scroll +=1
```

If you look carefully, you see the only change required is to replace the minus sign (-) with a plus sign (+). You need more actions to make the scrollers work. Follow these steps to add the actions to the hotspots:

1. **In the Outline panel, open the** up **sprite and select the** uphotspot **object.**

2. **In the Script panel, click Add Script and choose Events ⇨ Button ⇨ on(press).**

3. **Click Add Script again and choose Movie Control ⇨ gotoAndPlay ⇨ gotoAndPlay(FRAME)**

4. **Type** 2 **in the Frame field that appears at the bottom of the Script panel.**

5. **Click Add Script again, and choose Events ⇨ Button ⇨ on(release).**

6. **Click the Add Script button, and choose Movie Control ⇨ gotoAndStop ⇨ gotoAndStop(FRAME).** Leave the default value for the Frame field set at **1**.

When you click the hotspot, the Timeline will go to Frame 2 and play; at Frame 3 it will go back to Frame 2 (based on your earlier scripts), execute the script at Frame 2, and thus loop. When you release the mouse you need the scroll to stop, which requires the final scripts. When the mouse is released, the Timeline of the **up** sprite returns to Frame 1 and stops, thus ending the loop and the scroll. Repeat the same process with the **down** sprite, using the **downhotspot** shape.

Tip

Instead of manually selecting all the script elements again, change to Expert mode and copy the scripts from the **uphotspot** shape. Then select the **downhotspot** shape and paste the script into the text entry area on the Script panel.

Creating an opening sequence

The **news** scroller needs an interesting opening sequence; you can construct a sequence showing one layer opening from one corner followed by the next layer opening from the opposite corner. Follow these steps to build the animation for the news scroller:

1. **Double-click the** news **sprite in the Outline panel to open its Timeline.**

2. **Click the** newsplace **shape in the Outline panel or Timeline.** Check that the **newsplace** shape's anchor point is set to the top left in the Transform panel.

3. **Right-click Frame 1 of the** newsplace **shape's row on the Timeline and choose Place to add a Place effect.**

4. **Double-click the Place effect to open the Place Settings dialog box.**

5. **Click X scale and choose the Scale Factor option from the list.** The Scale Factor 0% displays; leave the default settings.

6. **Right-click Frame 2 of the** newsplace **shape's row on the Timeline to open the shortcut menu and choose Move.**

7. **In the Move Settings dialog box, click X scale and choose Resize to 100%.**

Note If your object isn't resizing correctly, you probably drew it using the incorrect Mode. The animation needs the Resize option selected in the Mode area. If you are having resizing problems, replace the object or you can reset it and start again.

8. Click the Easing tab of the Move Settings dialog box. Click the Position Start option, and type **3** in the field.

9. Click Close to close the Move Settings dialog box.

The white background of the news scroll area grows from the top left to its original size. Now, do the same thing for the background, only this time the object grows from bottom right to full size.

Follow the steps for the **newsplace** shape's animation with these changes:

✦ Change the anchor point to Bottom right

✦ Add the Place effect at Frame 11

✦ Add the Move effect at Frame 13

Finally, you need to place the rest of the news scroll objects.

Select all the objects inside the **news** sprite except for the **newsplace** and **background** shapes, and including the **up** and **down** sprites. Right-click on Frame 23 of the **news** sprite's Timeline and choose Place from the shortcut menu to add a Place effect to the objects, as shown in Figure 25-6. When the movie plays, first the white background and then the gray background grow in sequence.

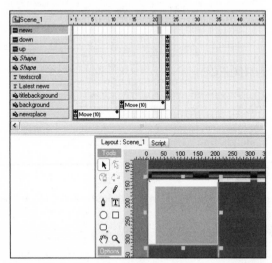

Figure 25-6: The **news** scroller animation displays the background layers first and then the rest of the content.

Scripting to load the text file

The **news** scroller displays the content of an external text file in the **news** sprite. You added Place effects to the sprite's objects to display them at Frame 23; you also need the text file to appear at the same frame. Follow these steps to script the sprite:

1. **Select Frame 23 of the** news **sprite on the Timeline.**

2. **In the Script panel, click Add Script and then choose Events ➪ Frame ➪ onFrame( ).** Frame 23 is added to the script as you selected it in the Timeline.

3. **Click Add Script again, and choose Movie Control ➪ Load/unload Sprite ➪ loadVariables( ).** Several input fields appear at the bottom of the Script panel.

4. **Type** news.txt **in the URL field at the bottom of the Script panel.**

5. **Click Variables and choose Send using 'GET' from the drop-down list.** Leave the Load variables only option selected.

6. **Right-click Frame 24 and choose Movie Control ➪ stop.**

The **news** scroller is almost finished. You added a URL to the script referencing a file named **news.txt**. The text file, available from the book's Web site, contains the news.txt file. The text includes:

```
&newsvar=dd/mm/yyyy
This can be one news item that can be put here.
dd/mm/yyyy
This can be your second item of news, maybe an update of some sort.
dd/mm/yyyy
This can be the third item. Who knows how many items will get to be in
here?
&
```

The Flash player reads everything between the first and last ampersands (&). After the first &, the variable is defined followed by the value of the variable, which is everything after the equal sign (=). The Flash Player stops when it encounters the second &.

To test the **news** scroller, choose File ➪ Export ➪ HTML + SWF. Open the file in your browser; you see it works like a charm. The news scroll is finished!

Constructing the Feature Section

The feature section uses the same animation as the news scroll, except that the animations are done in the opposite directions. (Refer back to the discussion on configuring the news scroll feature.) The two different animations give an interesting effect. The **featureplace** object you use now is one of the original placeholders you created at the start of the project.

The pair of objects used for the feature area is the same as the pair you built for the **news** scroller. Add a title background and text as you did for the **news** scroller. Name the rectangle used for the background **titlebackground**. Add a text label, and type **Featured product** into the text entry area of the Text panel.

The space in the feature area is used to draw your viewers' attention. You can show something about a product or a special offer. Using a placeholder sprite, all you have to do to update the item is create a new image and save it reusing the name of the image in the sprite.

Double-click the **feature** sprite in the Outline panel to open it, and then Choose Insert ⇨ Sprite from the Outline panel to add a new blank sprite within the **feature** sprite. Name the new sprite **image**. Draw a rectangle inside the image sprite and name it **placeholder**. You can leave the default color because the rectangle is replaced by an image. Resize the rectangle to 180 x 125, set the X- and Y-axis values to 0, and choose Resize mode. Select the **image** sprite in the Outline panel, and in the Transform panel, set the X-axis to 10 and the Y-axis to 40.

The **image** sprite is placed in the **feature** sprite, as seen in Figure 25-7. The image used for the sprite is a JPEG. As long as the image uses the same dimensions, 180 x 125 pixels, any image can be used in the sprite.

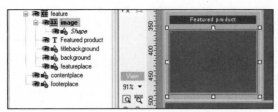

Figure 25-7: The image sprite displays an image that can be easily changed.

Double-click the **image** sprite in the Outline panel to open its Timeline. Right-click Frame 1 of the sprite to open the shortcut menu and choose Movie Control ⇨ Load/unload Sprite ⇨ loadMovie( ). In Guided mode on the Script panel, type **feature.jpg** in the URL field at the bottom of the Script panel. The finished script reads:

```
onFrame (1) {
   loadMovie("feature.jpg");
}
```

Right-click the sprite's Timeline at Frame 5 to open the shortcut menu, and choose Movie Control ⇨ stop.

The final touch for the feature is an opening sequence. Using the same technique as that used for the **news** scroll, add the effects and modify settings for each shape.

✦ **featureplace.** Anchor point bottom left, Place effect Frame 1 (set the X scale to Scale factor 0 %, leaving X = Y checked), Move effect Frame 2 (X scale to Resize to 100%; in the Easing tab click the Start Position option and type **3** as the value in the field).

✦ **background.** Select the **featureplace** shape inside the **feature** sprite and copy and paste in place a second shape, and name this shape **background**. Change the **background** shape's color to gray, and change its width to 198x178 pixels to make it slightly smaller than the **featureplace** shape. Nudge the **background** shape down and to the right one pixel. Set its Anchor point top right; add a Place effect at Frame 12 and a Move effect at Frame 13.

Finally, to finish the section, add more Place effects. Select the **titlebackground**, **title**, and **image** sprites in the Outline panel. On the Timeline, right-click Frame 23 and choose Place. Right-click Frame 24 of the **feature** sprite and choose Movie Control ⇨ stop from the shortcut menu.

Caution   Make sure the JPEG image uses a non-progressive format. In order to load an external image, you must use SWF version 6.

Configuring the Content Window

For the content window you are going to use an animation similar to one that you have built for other areas. Refer to earlier sections of the chapter for full instructions on how to build the second layers used for animation.

Rename the **contentplace** shape as **contentplace1**, and then group it as a sprite named **content**. Then paste in place two copies of the shape; name these **contentplace2** and **background**. The objects use the same effects and the same effect settings as those used previously.

✦ **contentplace1.** color white, #FFFFFF, anchor point top right, Place effect Frame 1, Move effect Frame 2

✦ **contentplace2.** color white, #FFFFFF, anchor point bottom right, Place effect Frame 1, Move effect Frame 2

✦ **background.** Color #99A7AE, size 543 x 363, nudge down and right one pixel, anchor point center left, Place effect Frame 12, Move effect Frame 13

To finish the animation, right-click Frame 25 of the **content** sprite and choose Movie Control ⇨ stop to add a stop action to the sprite's Timeline. The **content** sprite is basically finished. What about the content? That is added separately; the sole purpose of the **content** sprite is to provide animation and serve as a background for the content that is loaded externally into levels.

Finishing the Header and Footer

The **headerplace** and **footerplace** objects were added at the start of the project. It's time to replace them with some finished content. The finished header includes the company logo and name; the footer contains company information such as the address and e-mail address. Both elements are animated later in the chapter.

Header. To finish the header, select the **headerplace** shape and choose a linear gradient fill starting at white and ending at black. The logo I constructed is a simple vector graphic made of three overlapping circles as well as one text object for the company name, as seen in Figure 25-8.

Figure 25-8: Construct a simple graphic and text for the company header.

Create a sprite from the **header** objects. Select the **headerplace**, **text**, and **graphic** objects in the Outline panel. Right-click and choose Grouping ➪ Group as Sprite from the shortcut menu. Name the sprite **header**.

Footer. The footer consists of a gradient background and the company's address and e-mail address. The sample project uses the same gradient for the footer as that used for the header, but reverses the gradient's angle of rotation. Add text for the different address items and then create a sprite. Select the **footerplace** object and the text blocks used for the address in the Outline panel. Right-click and choose Grouping ➪ Group as Sprite from the shortcut menu. Name the sprite **footer**.

Constructing a Preloader

The project uses a preloader movie, which is seen while the main movie's content is being downloaded to your viewer's computer. Select the scene in the Outline panel and draw a rectangle of any size on the stage. Name the rectangle **background**, and color it white. In the Transform panel, set the Mode to Resize, Anchor point to center, size it at 100 x 3 pixels, and center the rectangle on the movie.

Copy the rectangle and paste it in place. Rename the copy **loaderbar**, and click the Target option in the Shape panel. In the Transform panel, set the Mode to Scale, the Anchor Point to center left, deselect X=Y, and set the width percentage to 0.1.

Select the two rectangles and group them as a sprite. Name the sprite **preloader**.

The **preloader** sprite is complete, but it isn't programmed yet. Click Frame 5 in the **preloader** sprite's Timeline. In the Script panel, click Add Script and choose Events ➪ Frame ➪ onFrame() to add the structure of the script to the sprite. In Expert mode, type the script's contents between the curly braces {} added with the Add Script selection. The complete script reads:

```
onFrame (5) {
  Loaded = _parent.getPercentLoaded();
  loaderbar._xscale = Loaded;
  if (Loaded >= 100) {
    _parent.gotoAndPlay(3);
  }
}
```

Right-click Frame 6 of the **preloader** sprite's Timeline to open the shortcut menu. Choose Movie Control ➪ gotoAndPlay ➪ prevFrameAndPlay.

A breakdown of the script is shown in Table 25-2.

Next, add some actions to the scene's Timeline to allow the **preloader** to work correctly. Select **Scene_1** in the Outline panel, and right-click Frame 2 of **Scene_1** to open the shortcut menu. Choose Movie Control ➪ stop.

Table 25-2: Understanding the Preloader Script

Line in Script	Means...
`Loaded = _parent.getPercentLoaded();`	The variable `Loaded` is declared; the value of the `Loaded` variable is equal to `_parent`; this means the main scene, and the only scene for that matter. The `getPercentLoaded()` part of the statement returns the percentage of the movie that is loaded.
`loaderbar._xscale = Loaded;`	The **loaderbar** shape has a width of 0.1%. In the second line of script, the `_xscale` (width) of the **loaderbar** object is equal to the value of the Loaded variable. The width of the **loaderbar** object increases along with the percentage of the movie that is loaded.
`if (Loaded >= 100) {`	The **preloader** sprite checks the loaded percentage one time at Frame 5, but you need it to keep checking to see how much progress has been made. So, as in the up and down scroll of the **news** scroll you built earlier, you need to set up a loop, which is done in Frame 6 of the **preloader** Timeline.
`_parent.gotoAndPlay(3);`	When the movie's play head reaches Frame 6, it returns to Frame 5 and checks the progress of the movie's loading. The loop continues until 100 percent of the scene is loaded, at which time the `if` statement will kick in and send the scene's Timeline to Frame 3.

Add effects to the scene's sprites. For the **preloader** sprite, add a Place effect at Frame 1; add a Remove effect at Frame 3. For the other sprites, add a Remove effect at Frame 1. The **Scene_1** Timeline is shown in Figure 25-9.

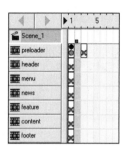

Figure 25-9: Add effects and a stop action to complete the Timeline.

Adding the effects completes the way the **preloader** works. At Frame 1 of the movie, only the **preloader** sprite is placed, so only that sprite is visible. At Frame 2, the stop action stops the main Timeline of the movie. When the **preloader** runs, it loops until 100 percent of the movie is loaded; when the if statement's condition is true, that is, when 100 percent of the movie has loaded, the scene's Timeline jumps to Frame 3, the **preloader** sprite is removed, and the rest of the movie plays.

Animating the Opening of the Movie

Earlier in the chapter you built the news, feature, and content components using their own opening animations. You also need a simple animation for the header, menu, and footer. The animations are simple slide-in effects that you can add to the main Timeline.

Right-click Frame 3 of the **header** sprite and choose Slide ➪ Slide in from top. Leave the default frame length of 10 frames. Repeat for both the **menu** and **footer** sprites.

The sprites that have their own animations — **news**, **feature**, and **content** — need to be placed. For each of these sprites, right-click Frame 13 and choose Place, as seen in Figure 25-10.

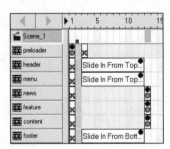

Figure 25-10: Animate the rest of the interface components.

Adding Content and Navigation

All the content pages in the site have the same structure using a preloader, opening sequence, and a stop action. All the pages include a label after the stop where the end sequence begins, and at the very end of the pages' Timelines, there is an if statement that drives the loading of a different page.

I'm not going to explain every page because they work in the same way, but I will, however, explain how to build and configure the home page.

Open the main page of the movie, main.swi, in SWiSHmax. You need one last action to control the navigation among the site's pages. Select **Scene_1** in the Outline panel, and then open the Script panel. Click Add Script and choose Event ➪ Frame ➪ onLoad( ). Add one line as shown below to complete the script:

```
onLoad () {
    navvar = 1;
}
```

You add a variable, **navvar**, to control the navigation of the site's pages. Each page uses an if/else statement that tests the **navvar** variable.

Creating a content page

It's time to make the first content page. You still have main.swi open in the program. Save the file, and then choose File ➪ Save As and save it using another name. The first content page is named home.swi. The page needs to be modified from the original. Delete the sprites, leaving the **preloader** and **content** sprites only. Remove the onLoad script from the scene. Select the **preloader** sprite in the Outline panel, and move its position to an X-axis location of 430 and its Y-axis location to 325.

The home.swi file now contains a **preloader** in the correct position and a content window, which is used as a placeholder. You can add what you like in the **content** sprite and add an opening animation if you like as well, starting at Frame 3 in the Scene's Timeline to follow the **preloader** sprite and the stop actions. You will need a stop action after the opening animation to display the content.

If you look at the home.swi project file available from the book's Web site, you see some elements are added to it; its Timeline is shown in Figure 25-11.

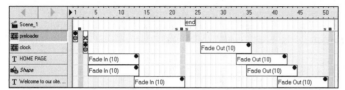

Figure 25-11: Add effects and actions to control the content page.

Rather than describing how each component is made in this example, I'll explain what is used to complete the page:

- ✦ **preloader sprite.** The **preloader** sprite is placed at Frame 1 and removed at Frame 3, just as in the main.swi file.

- ✦ **Fade in effects.** The opening animation I built for the page uses fade in effects starting at Frame 3; the effects also include a sprite with a masking effect placed at Frame 3.

- ✦ **gotoAndStop.** The gotoAndStop() script sends the **hotspot** sprite in the main file to the correct label, making the button inactive.

- ✦ **Stop.** The stop() action allows the content to stay visible and prevents the closing sequence from playing automatically.

- ✦ **end label.** A label named **end** is added to the Timeline following the stop() action. The label is used by all the buttons for navigation. When another button is pressed, the play head moves to the label's frame and then plays the closing sequence.

Scripting the content pages' navigation

If you look at Figure 25-11, you see a script indicator at Frame 50. Earlier you added a navvar variable to an onLoad() event for the main page of the site. Each content page contains an if/else statement using the navvar variable to determine which page is loaded; each page's script is slightly different, of course.

This is the script added to Frame 50 of the home.swi file's Timeline:

```
onFrame (50) {
  if (_level0.navvar==2) {
    loadMovie("about.swf");
  } else if (_level0.navvar==3) {
    loadMovie("products.swf");
  } else if (_level0.navvar==4) {
    loadMovie("services.swf");
  } else {
    loadMovie("contact.swf");
  }
}
```

On The Web Site   All pages for the site are available from the book's Web site in the chapter25 folder.

You can use the services.swi, products.swi, contact.swi, and about.swi files in addition to the home.swi file discussed in this section. If you look at the pages, you see that they are constructed in a similar fashion to the home.swi file.

Constructing the contact page

The site's content pages are similar in how you modify and construct them; the one page that contains different processes is the contact page containing a form. The contact.swi file, available from the book's Web site, uses PHP as a method for transporting information from your site. The structure of the page is the same; it uses a **preloader** sprite, and the content fades in starting at Frame 3. The contact page uses three static text objects, three input fields, two buttons, a dynamic text field, and a **placeholder** sprite.

✦ **Static text.** The three static text objects are the **name**, **email**, and **message** objects. You also need three input text fields. The set of fields and text creates a form, as seen in Figure 25-12.

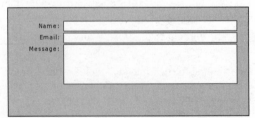

Figure 25-12: Use several static and input text fields to create a form.

✦ **Input text fields.** The three input text fields are used for your viewers to enter information. The names of the input text fields and their variables are:

• nameinput, variable named Name

• emailinput, variable named Email

• messageinput, variable named Message

✦ **Buttons.** The page uses two text buttons for clearing and submitting the form's content. You build the first button and then duplicate and modify it for the second button. Use the text CLEAR for one button and SEND for the other button.

✦ **Dynamic text field.** Draw a text field, and name the text object **stat.** Choose the Dynamic text option, and set the text block's dimension to a width of 250. In the Advanced settings of the Text panel, name a variable **status**.

Now that you have constructed the elements for the contact page, group them as a sprite; name the sprite **contact**.

Next, you need hotspots for the buttons. Select the **contact** sprite in the Outline panel; you want the hotspot to be a part of the sprite. Draw a rectangle the size of the **CLEAR** button, set the fill and line to invisible, and type the following script for the object on the Script panel:

```
on (release) {
    Name = "";
    Email = "";
    Message = "";
    status = "";
}
```

The script tells the variables Name, Email, Message, and status to empty themselves. When the user clicks the **CLEAR** button, the contents are equal to blank, or clear.

Add the following script to the **contact** sprite's Timeline that ensures the input fields are empty when the user opens the contact page. Although not strictly necessary, it is a failsafe. At Frame 1 of the **contact** sprite, add the following script:

```
onFrame (1) {
    Name = "";
    Email = "";
    Message = "";
}
```

At Frame 2, add a Place effect for all objects in the sprite; at Frame 3, add a Stop script to the **contact** sprite's Timeline. Finally, at Frame 4, add Remove effects to the objects in the sprite.

Now the user has a blank form when the contact page is loaded, but you also want the input fields emptied when the **SEND** button is clicked. To do this, use another sprite.

With the **contact** sprite selected in the Outline panel, choose Insert ➪ Sprite from the Outline panel's menu. Name the sprite **empty**. On the Script panel, type the following script for the sprite:

```
onFrame (2) {
    stop();
}
onFrame (20) {
    _parent.name = "";
    _parent.email = "";
    _parent.message = "";
}
```

That's finished. Now for the **SEND** button. Draw another rectangle, this time over the **SEND** button, making sure you have the **contact** sprite selected in the Outline panel. The final content of the sprite is shown in Figure 25-13.

Figure 25-13: The contact sprite contains two buttons and hotspots.

Name the rectangle **send**. In the Script panel, add this script for the object:

```
on (release) {
    if (Name eq "") {
        status = "Please enter your name";
    } else if (Email eq "") {
        status = "Please enter your email address";
    } else if (Message eq "") {
        status = "Please enter your message";
    } else {
        loadVariables("email.php",'POST');
        status = "Thank you for contacting us";
        empty.gotoAndPlay(3);
    }
}
```

First, the if statement checks whether Name (the first variable) is empty or not. If it is empty, "Please enter your name" appears on the status line. If Name isn't empty, the script checks the Email variable. If its value is empty, the message "Please enter your email address" appears in the status variable line. Next, if **Name** and **Message** fields aren't empty, the script checks the Message variable. If that is empty, the script causes the message "Please enter your message" to appear in the status variable line. If all three variables contain content, the else action is run, loading the variable and transmitting the content, displaying the final message, and emptying the fields again.

Working with PHP

You will notice from the script that the final section of the sprite's script calls for a PHP page. The file, email.php, is the motor that drives the form, taking the variables' content and sending it to you. When the form is correctly filled in and submitted, the viewer sees the message "Thank you for contacting us." Construct the PHP page in Notepad as shown in Listing 25-1:

> ### Listing 25:1 **Contents for the email.php File**
>
> ```
> <?php
> $name = $_POST['Name'];
> $email = $_POST['Email'];
> $message = $_POST['Message'];
> $name = stripslashes($name);
> $email = stripslashes($email);
> ```

```
$message = stripslashes($message);

$rec_email = "youremail@yourdomain.com";
$subject = "Standard subject";

$msg_body = "Name:   $name\n\n";
$msg_body .= "E-Mail:  $email\n\n";
$msg_body .= "Comments:  $message\n\n";
mail($rec_email, $subject, $msg_body);
?>
```

Save the document as email.php. Of course, to use the file you have to change the e-mail address in the code to your e-mail address; you can also change the subject line. Make sure to leave the rest of the script intact.

To use the form, upload the file to the same directory as your SWF files. Finally, you must change the file attributes after uploading (the CHMOD) to 755.

Note   By the way, you can't test the form offline on your computer, and your server needs to provide PHP support. You may find that many free hosts do not allow PHP support.

Cross-Reference   Read about PHP scripting in Appendix F, which is available from the book's Web site.

Finishing the Site's Navigation

The main.swi page contains a number of hotspots in the menu section. The page also contains the navvar variable; this variable is redefined by pressing one of the menu buttons' hotspots. The variable for each page is specified using a single digit. That is, the home page is 1, the about page is 2, the products page is 3, the services page is 4, and the contact page is 5.

To finish the site's navigation, add the functions to the buttons' hotspots. Open main.swi in SWiSHmax. Select the **hotspot1** object in the **menu** sprite. In the Script panel, add the following on(release) script to **hotspot1**:

```
on (release) {
  _parent.button2.gotoAndPlay("off");
  _parent.button3.gotoAndPlay("off");
  _parent.button4.gotoAndPlay("off");
  _parent.button5.gotoAndPlay("off");
  _parent.button1.gotoAndPlay("hit");
  _level5.gotoAndPlay("end");
  _root.navvar = 1;
this.gotoAndStop("inactive");
}
```

Here's how the script works. The _parent.buttonx.gotoAndPlay("off") sends all the buttons to their starting state. If there is another button on the hit state, it is now forced to return to its neutral state. However, **button1** will go to the hit state. It needs to stay on the hit state because you want the button to maintain its hit appearance.

You will also see that _level5 is targeted in the script, which when executed goes to the **end** label and plays.

The **home** button is **hotspot1;** defined in the line _root.navvar = 1. When the script runs, from this point on the navvar is equal to 1. The if/else statement in the content.swi file loads home.swf in the end when navvar=1.

You don't want anything to interfere with the actions, and to achieve this, the final line leads to a gotoAndStop action where all the hotspots are removed.

Script the remaining hotspots in the same way. In each case, their respective variables are called in the root.navvar line, and the states of the buttons are modified to return all the buttons except the button you are scripting to their off states. For example, in **hotspot2**, the line _parent.buttonx.gotoAndPlay("off") is set to off for all the buttons except button 2, which is written as _parent.button2.gotoAndPlay("hit");.

On The Web Site

Please refer to the main.swi file in the chapter25 folder on the book's Web site for the full scripts for all buttons.

When the scripting is finished, test the pages. The final site interface is shown in Figure 25-14. To use the site, export each of the pages as a SWF movie. Make sure to store both the SWF movies and the text files you used for the news scroller in the same folder. Enjoy!

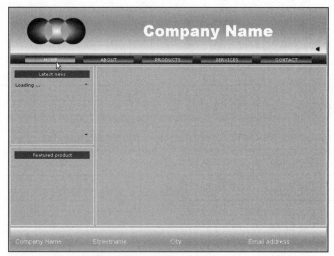

Figure 25-14: The final site interface is complete with several animations and coordinated components.

Summary

This project chapter presented a Web site interface designed by Peter Thijs. This project showed you how to:

+ Plan and start a Web site project
+ Create the basic page and add placeholder objects
+ Design and construct a menu bar complete with animations and hotspots
+ Build a news scroller that uses externally loaded text files
+ Create opening animations for the interface's components
+ Build preloaders for the movie
+ Construct additional pages for the site
+ Design and construct a form complete with a PHP script
+ Design and add navigation scripts for the site

✦   ✦   ✦

Constructing a Shopping Cart Using SWiSHmax and PHP

*Special thanks to Rob Wells
for contributing this chapter.*

Welcome to the tutorial. First let me just reassure you — this is
not as hard as it may seem. Just follow the procedure carefully
and you're flying!

In this shopping cart tutorial, you create a SWiSHmax movie that can
be used for online purchases. The tutorial shows you how to program
two items which can both be added to the cart unlimited times. You
will also include postage and packaging fee calculations, and create a
Submit form.

The tutorial describes how the sample movie is constructed. For
your own use, you can change values such as prices and fees.

Right! Let's get started...

You need the following for this tutorial:

   ✦ **SWiSHmax**

   ✦ **Notepad.** Notepad is needed for the PHP script that submits
     the order to the company. Notepad is installed with your oper-
     ating system accessories. From the desktop, find the program
     by choosing Start ➪ Programs ➪ Accessories ➪ Notepad.

   ✦ **A server that supports PHP.** You need this or the shopping
     cart will not work. If you currently have a Web site, check with
     your ISP to see if it supports PHP. You can sign up for a free
     account at some sites, but you may experience problems with
     your script.

   ✦ **A pen and paper.** Always useful but not essential.

Caution

The shopping cart **will not** work inside SWiSHmax or out of it. You
must upload all files to a server or the order will not be sent.

Constructing the Basic Movie

Open SWiSHmax—you'll not get far otherwise! A new blank movie appears by default.

Click the Movie tab, and choose the basic settings for the movie. The sample uses these movie settings:

- ✦ Set the width to 500 pixels, and the height to 294 pixels
- ✦ Set the frame rate to 60 fps
- ✦ Color white

Choose File ➪ Save to open the Save dialog box. Save the movie in a blank folder as **cart1.swi**, preferably somewhere you won't forget.

On The Web Site   The book's Web site contains all the shopping cart project files in the chapter26 folder.

Creating the Product Sprites

The project contains a main sprite that holds the shopping cart as well as the majority of the script to make the shopping cart work. You start by making a new sprite, and then nest a sprite for the first product. The nested sprite contains a text label for the product's name as well as a dynamic text object and a named variable to use for programming the product's quantity and pricing.

Follow these steps to create the container sprite and the first product sprite:

1. **On the Outline panel, choose Insert ➪ Sprite from the panel's menu.** A blank sprite is added to the Outline panel in Scene_1.

2. **Name the sprite** cart. It is essential you use this name and not make up your own.

3. **Click the sprite's name to select it, and then choose Insert ➪ Sprite again from the Outline panel's menu.** Name this sprite **product1**.

4. **Choose the Text tool in the toolbox and click and drag to create a block of text.** No specific requirements are needed, just the name of your first product. Click the text and type **Animal Shirt**.

5. **Using the Text tool again, draw a small box that is about five numbers wide (00000) more if you want.**

6. **Click the Text panel's tab to display the Text panel.** You are going to change some of the text box settings so your script will know where its information is coming from. The changes you need to make are shown in Figure 26-1.

7. **Name your text.** For this example, call it **_quantity1**. When you type the name, the Target option becomes active.

8. **Make sure to click the Target option.** This is essential as you reference the text object in the shopping cart's scripting.

Figure 26-1: Be sure to choose the right settings for the text box.

9. **Click the Static Text button to display the drop-down list.** Choose Dynamic to display the Dynamic Text settings in the Text panel.

10. **Click the Dynamic Text down arrow to display a drop-down list.** Click Advanced. This displays the Advanced settings on the Text panel.

11. **Click the button directly below the Dynamic Text button that shows a box and lines.** Your text field should now have a black border around it.

Note   Using the black border and white box is not required but it *does* help visually.

12. **Click the Variable input field to activate it.** Type **quantity1** to name the variable.

Tip   You may want to add a block of text above this input field on the movie to remind you that this box is the quantity of your first item.

13. **Delete the default text in the Text input area and type** 0.

Constructing buttons

Once the text field is finished you need a pair of additional objects to use for plus (+) and minus (-) buttons. The buttons are programmed to add or remove the product from the shopping cart. You make them from text objects, and then convert them to shapes. Follow these steps:

1. **Choose the Text tool in the toolbox and draw a new text block.** Type + (plus) in the Text field. The Text panel's settings reset to the default Static text options. Choose _sans font, 14pt size, and leave the default black color.

2. **Right-click the (+) text block and choose Copy Object.**

3. **Move the cursor to another location on the Layout panel's stage, right-click and choose Paste Object.** A copy of the (+) text is added to the stage.

4. **On the Text panel, click the text entry field and change the plus (+) sign to a minus sign (-).**

5. **Right-click the (+) text object in the Outline panel to open the shortcut menu. Choose Grouping ➪ Group as Shape.** Click Yes to close the dialog box that asks if you want to make the overlapped regions of objects with the same fill style empty.

6. **In the Outline panel, the text object is listed as a Shape object.** Click the default name and type **add** to rename the shape.

7. **Repeat Steps 5 and 6 with the (-) text object.** Name the (-) shape **remove**.

Adding additional text

The sprite needs two more blocks of text. The first is a label for the currency, which is a static text object. The second text block is a dynamic text object that will hold the results of the calculations when the user orders a product.

Follow these steps to add the second label text and the dynamic text object:

1. **Click the Text tool in the toolbox and draw a text box to the right of the other objects.** You can arrange the objects precisely later. For now, just draw the text box in the general area of the movie stage.

2. **In the Text panel, select the default text in the text entry area and type a currency symbol.** The sample project uses the UK pound sign (£). The currency symbol is static text and doesn't need any settings; it is merely there to let both you and the customer know that the number is a currency.

3. **Click the Text tool in the toolbox again, and draw one more text block to the right of the other objects.**

4. **On the Text panel, name the text _total1.** The name is the word "total" followed by the number 1.

5. **On the Text panel, click the Target check box.** The text object is going to be used for scripting and has to be defined as a target for the script.

6. **Click the Static Text button to display the drop-down list.** Choose Dynamic to display the Dynamic Text settings in the Text panel.

7. **Click the Dynamic Text down arrow to display a drop-down list.** Click Advanced to display the Advanced settings on the Text panel.

8. **Type** total1 **for the variable name in the Advanced settings.**

9. **Select the default text in the text entry area and delete it.** Leave the text block blank for now.

You may want to add a piece of text above this block saying Total or something similar. The set of text boxes and shapes as well as their listing in the Outline panel are shown in Figure 26-2.

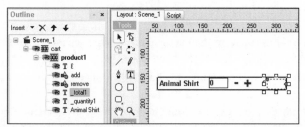

Figure 26-2: The set of text boxes and shapes are used in a specific order.

Scripting the Sprite

The **product1** sprite needs some script. You add a script that executes when the sprite is loaded in the movie and then add a second script that calculates the product price based on the quantity the viewer types in the field.

Writing a variable for the product1 sprite

The first script you write for the sprite loads variables for the product processing fee and product cost into the movie. To make sure the variables are loaded, you attach the script to the onLoad() event for the sprite.

Follow these steps to add scripts to the **product1** sprite:

1. **Click the** product1 **sprite in the Outline panel to select it.**

2. **Click the Script tab to display the Script panel.**

3. **Click the mode button, as seen in Figure 26-3, and choose Expert.** You type most of the script manually.

Figure 26-3: Use the Expert script mode to program the movie's elements.

4. **On the Script panel, click the Add Script button and choose Events ➪ Frame ➪ onLoad().** The structure of the action is added in the Script panel, and reads:

```
onLoad() {
}
```

5. **In the Script input area at the bottom of the Script panel, click after the opening curly brace (()) and press Enter to go to the next line.** Content that you add between the curly braces executes when the sprite loads.

6. **Add the following line to the script on the new line following the opening curly brace.** You are adding a new variable and declaring its value:

```
pandp=2;
```

Don't add any spaces to the variable as you type the content. The variable represents the postage and packaging fee for **product1**. In this case, you use **2**, for £2. Do not enter your currency symbol, just the number. Type a **;** (semicolon) after the number.

7. **Press Enter to go to the next line.** Type another variable, this time representing the price of the product, which is 10. Enter this text:

```
price=10
```

Excellent! The onLoad script is done for now!

Adding a calculation script

The next script the sprite needs is a Frame event used for calculating the product costs. First you add an equation to calculate the total based on price and quantity, and then add a line of script that displays the total when the movie plays the sprite's frame.

Make sure the **product1** sprite is still selected, and then follow these steps to add the next script to the project:

1. **Click the Add Script button on the Script panel to open the menu.** Choose Events ➪ Frame ➪ onEnterFrame() to add the structure of the script to the Script panel.

2. **Click the script after the opening curly brace and press Enter to add a new line to the script.**

3. **Type this line:**

   ```
   total1=(pandp+price)*quantity1;
   ```

   This script calculates the total cost of the first product. Earlier you assigned a variable named **total1** to the text object named **_total1**. You also assigned a variable named **quantity1** to another text object named **_quantity1**. The script used for the onEnterFrame() event uses the values for these variables.

4. **Press Enter to go to the next line.** Type this script as shown in Figure 26-4:

   ```
   _root.quant1=quantity1;
   ```

   When the movie plays and the play head enters the frame, the **_total1** text field displays the calculation you added in the script. That is, the cost of the postage and packaging (**pandp**) and the price are added together, and then multiplied by the **quantity1** value.

Figure 26-4: Add scripts to the sprite to calculate the cost for the item.

Testing the script

It's time to test the script. You have added several text objects and assigned variables. It's time to test that the variables are working correctly and that your scripts are written correctly. Follow these steps:

1. **Click the _quantity1 text object in the Outline panel to select it.**

2. **In the Text panel, click the 0 text you added originally, and replace it with a number larger than 0.** You are testing the script using values, and if you leave the default 0, you can't calculate any prices.

3. **Choose File ➪ Test ➪ In Player.** The Flash player opens, as seen in Figure 26-5. The quantity shows the number you just added, and the total appears following the currency symbol.

4. **Close the Flash Player and change the _quantity1 text back to 0.** You want the default number 0 to display in the finished movie.

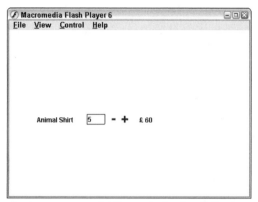

Figure 26-5: Test the first script in the Flash Player.

Adding scripts to buttons

Earlier you created plus and minus symbols from text, to which you now add scripts. The symbols are used as buttons; the scripts allow you to click the button and either add to the quantity of an item in the shopping cart by clicking the + button, or decreasing the quantity of an item in the shopping cart by clicking the - button.

Note If you want, you can use a rollover effect on the buttons; it won't affect the script or the shopping cart.

1. **Select the add object in the Outline panel, and click the Script tab.** This displays the Script panel.

2. **Click the Add Script button and choose Events ➪ Button ➪ on(release).** The script is added to the Script panel.

3. **In the script entry area at the bottom of the Script panel, click following the opening curly brace and press Enter to go to a new line.** Type:

```
quantity1=quantity1 plus 1;
```

The script targets the **quantity** text block, which contains the variable named **quantity1**, and tells it to add 1 to the current number when the button is released.

The **remove** button object is a little more complex because you can't have the number drop below 0; use an if() statement to prevent the problem.

1. **Select the remove object in the Outline panel, and then click the Script tab to display the Script panel.**

2. **Click the Add Script button and choose Events ➪ Button ➪ on(release).**

3. **Type the if() statement script shown here after the opening curly brace ({) in the script.** The complete script for the remove object is:

```
on(release) {
    if (quantity1 == 0) {
        quantity1 -= 0;
    } else {
        quantity1 -= 1;
    }
}
```

The reasoning behind the complete script is:

✦ if (quantity1 == 0) { The script checks to see if the value of **quantity1** (number) is equal to 0 when the object is clicked and released.

✦ quantity1 -= 0; This is the action that occurs if the result is true, that is, if the value of **quantity1** is indeed 0. To prevent the value of **quantity1** from dropping below 0, the script instructs the program to subtract 0, or in other words, nothing. This condition is of no value if the test returns false and you want the number to decrease by 1.

✦ } else { This is where the else statement comes in. It says that if the quantity is not equal to 0, the action within the else statement should be performed. You set the action to decrease the number in **quantity1** by 1.

Test the movie again. Choose File ➪ Test ➪ In Player. Click the **add** and **remove** buttons and watch the numbers change. That's the first product complete! Give yourself a pat on the back and go grab a cup of coffee.

Adding the Second Product

Now that the first product and your cup of coffee are finished, it's time to start on the second product. A shopping cart usually contains more than one product. This section of the tutorial shows you how to add a second product; you can reuse the process as many times as you like to create as many products as you wish. If you are confident, why not give this section a go by yourself? Remember to change the variables in the script and objects.

If you prefer, follow these steps to create and script the product:

1. **In the Outline panel, right-click the** product1 **sprite to open the shortcut menu and choose Copy Object.**

2. **Right-click the** cart **sprite — the main sprite — to open the shortcut menu and choose Paste Object.** You have a second copy of the sprite in the movie.

3. **Click the sprite copy's name and rename it** product2.

4. **On the Layout panel drag the new sprite below the location of the** product1 **sprite on the stage, as seen in Figure 26-6.**

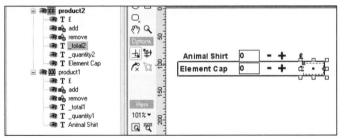

Figure 26-6: Align the products on the Layout panel.

5. **Open the** product2 **sprite.**

6. **Click the product name text object to select it, and then change its name to** Element Cap.

7. **Click the** _total1 **text object in the Outline panel to select it.** In the Text panel, change its name to **_total2** and change its variable's name to **total2**.

8. **Click the** _quantity1 **text object to select it.** In the Text panel change its name to **_quantity2** and change its variable's name to **quantity2**.

9. **Click the Script tab to display the Script panel.** You change the values to those for the second product.

10. **Change the postage and price values for the second product.** Change the variable values in the onLoad( ) script to read:

```
onLoad() {
    pandp=2;
    price=5;
}
```

11. **Change the references in the** onEnterFrame( ) **script to read:**

```
onEnterFrame() {
    total2=(pandp+price)*quantity2;
    _root.quant2=quantity2;
}
```

12. **For the Add button's script, change the two references to quantity1 to quantity2.**

13. **In the Remove button's script, change the three references to quantity1 to quantity2.**

Calculating the Grand Total

Now, go back to the main sprite, **cart**, to add the grand total information and display. Start by creating a couple of new text blocks to inform the customers of the postage and packaging fees and product prices. In this section, you create and script the Grand Total, which calculates the total cost of all the products and quantities ordered.

Follow these steps to finish the product calculations:

1. **Create a new text block.** In the Text panel type this text and place it on the stage, as seen in Figure 26-7:

```
Grand total (inc. postage and packaging):
```

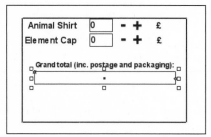

Figure 26-7: Add a text field explaining the values the viewer will see.

2. **Create another text block.** Choose these settings in the Text panel:

   - name the text **_gtotal**
   - click the Target option
   - choose Dynamic text
   - name a variable **gtotal**
   - delete the text from the text entry area

3. **Click the** cart **sprite to select it and then click the Script tab to display the Script panel.**

4. **Click the Add Script button and choose Events ⇨ Frame ⇨ onEnterFrame( ).**

5. **Add the script shown between the curly braces.** The final script reads:

```
onEnterFrame() {
    gtotal="£" add product1.total1 plus product2.total2;
}
```

This script first displays a currency symbol, which you can change to your own currency, and then adds a sum. The sum calls the value from the two totals in the two products' sprites and adds them together, eventually displaying the result in the **gtotal** dynamic text block.

That's the main shopping cart complete!

Writing the PHP Script

Now you need a PHP script that will process the order and forward it to your e-mail address. Work in Notepad or a similar text editor to write the script.

Type the script shown in Listing 26-1:

Listing 26-1: **Script for the PHP File**

```
<?
   if ($send=="yes") {
       $to = "your_email@swish.com";
       $subject = "Product Order";
       mail($to,$subject,$msgVar,$tfrom);
   }
   echo "&report=Your order has been placed!&";
     ?>
```

Save the file as contact.php. Don't save the file using the default .txt extension in Notepad as a text file or it won't work as a PHP script.

Here's how the script works:

✦ First, a variable is checked in the movie for the value **yes.** You create the variable in the next section. If the value of the variable is not **yes**, the order isn't processed; if the value is **yes,** the product order is sent.

✦ **$to** displays the e-mail address of the user; **$subject** is the subject line of the e-mail.

✦ **mail($to,$subject,$msgVar,$tfrom);** is the part of the script that sends the e-mail. You may notice that **$msgVar** is not included in the PHP script — this variable will be created in SWiSHmax in the next section.

✦ **echo "&report=Your order has been placed!&";** sends a message back to the movie when the order has been sent successfully. The variable is named **report**, which is also created in the next section.

Using a Final Sprite and Effects

Now it's time to go back to SWiSHmax and finish the cart. You need one more sprite to call the PHP script and submit the order as well as a button:

✦ **Add a Sprite.** Select the **cart** sprite in the Outline panel and choose Insert ⇨ Sprite from the Outline panel menu. Name the new sprite **Submit**.

✦ **Add a block of text within the Submit sprite.** In the Text panel, type **Continue** in the text entry area. You can leave the default settings or modify the font's characteristics if you want.

✦ **Create a button.** Right-click the **Continue** text object in the Outline panel and choose Convert ⇨ Convert to Button from the shortcut menu. The button will take you to the **Submit** sprite when it is clicked.

Now that the **cart** sprite has these new objects, as seen in Figure 26-8, you need to add some actions to them. The idea is that some objects are placed at a certain frame and then removed at another specified frame so you see only what you need to see as the movie plays.

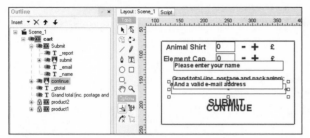

Figure 26-8: Add the final sprite and objects to the cart sprite.

Add labels and actions

First, add two labels to the **cart** sprite's Timeline.

1. **Right-click Frame 1 and choose Frame ⇨ Set Label.** The script appears in the Script panel automatically, and displays in red text as you are working in Expert mode.

2. **Look for the script reading:**

```
onFrame (1) {
    setLabel();
}
```

3. **Type** cart **inside the brackets following setLabel( ).** Be sure to include the quotation marks; the line should read:

```
setLabel("cart");
```

4. **Repeat the process at Frame 6.** The label for Frame 6 is **"submit"**.

5. **Add two stop actions to the Timeline.** Right-click Frame 5 and choose Movie Control ⇨ stop( ) from the shortcut menu. Add another stop action to Frame 10.

Add effects

You also need to add Place and Remove effects to the objects in the **cart** sprite. The effects, as well as their frame numbers, are listed in Table 26-1 and shown in Figure 26-9.

Table 26-1: Place and Remove Effects

Object*	Place Effect at Frame	Remove Effect at Frame
Submit sprite	6	1
continue button	1	6
_gtotal text	1	6
Grand total text	1	6
product2 sprite	1	6
product1 sprite	1	6

*If you have added other items to the movie, make sure to add Place and Remove effects.

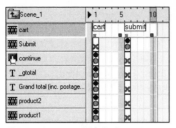

Figure 26-9: Add labels, stop actions, and effects to the Timeline.

Programming the Submit Actions

If you analyze the actions you just added, you see that everything except the **Submit** sprite is on the stage. However, when the **Submit** sprite is placed, everything else is removed. The **continue** button is used to control the **Submit** sprite. The scripts you write in this section produce a popup message if the viewer tries to submit an order without setting the quantity; you also add the final text objects for the form and program the submit process.

Adding actions to the continue button

Follow these steps to program the **continue** button:

1. **Select the** continue **button in the Outline panel, and click the Script tab to display the Script panel.**

2. **Click the Add Script button, and choose Events ➪ Button ➪ on(release).**

3. **Add the script shown between the curly braces. The final script reads:**

```
on(release) {
    if (gtotal == "£0") {
        getURL('javascript:alert("There are no items in your shopping
cart!")');
    } else {
        gotoAndPlay("submit");
    }
```

Consider how this script works. You don't want to go to the **submit** section unless there is something to submit, obviously. The dynamic text block named **gtotal** is used to display the grand total of product selections; you can use this text block's contents to control the action.

First, the script calls **gtotal** and checks if its value is **£0**. If the result is true you don't have an order to submit; instead, a simple JavaScript alert window appears. You can change the text inside if you want.

The **else** statement, as you have seen before, contains the action that is executed if the return of the **gtotal** test is false. In other words, if the **gtotal** value isn't 0, that means the viewer wants to submit an order. In the script, the movie will go forward to the **submit** label you created earlier.

Add more text items

The **submit** sprite needs four more components, all of which are text items:

✦ **_name.** Create a text box, and name it **_name**. Click the Target option on the Text panel and enter a variable named **name**. Set the type to Input Text. If you want, add a border to the text. You want the customers to know that they must type their names here, so type **Please enter your name** in the text entry area.

✦ **_email.** Create another text block, this time named **_email**. Click the Target option on the Text panel, and select Input Text as the text type. Enter a variable named **email**. Again, add a border if you want. Type **And a valid e-mail address** in the text entry area.

✦ **_report.** Click the Target option on the Text panel, and select Dynamic text as the text type. Name the variable for the text block **report**. Remember that PHP script and the message that would be sent to '**report**'? This is it!

✦ **The fourth and final piece of text is used for another button.** Create one last text block using default settings. In the text entry field type **SUBMIT**. You can configure the text however you want or leave the default options.

Configuring the submit button

In the Outline panel, right-click the **SUBMIT** text object in the **submit** sprite to open the shortcut menu. Choose Convert ➪ Convert to Button. Name the button **submit**, as seen in Figure 26-10. Open the Script panel; you are going to add an `on(release)` event to the new button.

Click the Add Script button and choose Events ➪ Button ➪ on(release). Within the curly braces ({}) type the code shown in Listing 26-2. The code includes the opening and closing elements added when you choose the `on(release)` event.

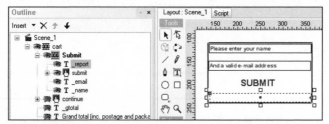

Figure 26-10: Add input and dynamic text and one button to the submit sprite.

Listing 26-2: Code for the Submit Button

```
on(release) {
    if (name == "Please enter your name" || name == "") {
        getURL('javascript:alert("Please enter your name")');
    } else if (email == "And a valid e-mail address" || email == "") {
```

```
        getURL('javascript:alert("Please enter a valid e-mail
address")');
    } else {
        report = "processing, please wait...";
        send = "yes";
        this.loadVariables("contact.php",'POST');
        send = "no";
    }
}
```

Here's what the script is doing:

✦ The `if (name == "Please enter your name" || name == "")` statement checks the name input field. If it has been left blank or deleted, a JavaScript alert is activated. In the script, `||` means "or".

✦ The `else if` statement applies in the same way to the e-mail input field

✦ The `else` statement contains the script to execute when the result is false; the PHP script is called and the order sent. The PHP script included the variable **send**, which must be **yes** or the order will not be placed.

✦ The line `this.loadVariables("contact.php",'POST');` calls the PHP script.

✦ Afterward, the **send** variable is set back to **no** because you don't need it open any longer.

Almost done! You need one last script for the submit button. In the Script panel, add an `onEnterFrame()` script to the button. Use the script shown in Listing 26-3:

Listing 26-3: **The onEnterFrame() script for the submit button**

```
onEnterFrame() {
    msgVar = _root.name add ", " add _root.email add "<p>" add "Product
1  x" add _root.quant1 add "<br>" add "Product 2  x" add _root.quant2;
    _root.name=name;
    _root.email=email;
}
```

Do you remember that variable in the PHP script named **msgVar**? This is the script that gathers the information for it.

You can probably guess what the script does. Basically it shows all the information entered by the customer. The `<p>` and `<br>` are HTML tags that will cause line breaks in the final e-mail to keep things tidy.

Following the **msgVar** script are two new variables, **name** and **email**, which are placed in the root of the movie. They hold the values of the two input fields, **name** and **email**.

Alternate Line Breaks

The HTML tags used in the submit button may not work for all email programs. Instead of using the `<p>` and `<br>` HTML tags, you can also use the PHP script tags `\n` and `\r\n`. See Appendix F on the book's Web site for information on using PHP scripts.

Exporting the Finished Product

That's it! Congratulations on completing this tutorial and making a successful shopping cart.

To export the movie, choose File ➪ Export ➪ HTML+SWF. Save your movie to the same folder as your PHP script; you can name it whatever you want.

Upload the files to your server and test!

Caution   On free servers, you may experience problems that may be as severe as the PHP script not working.

Now that you have created a shopping cart using two products, here are a few possibilities with which you may want to experiment:

✦ **Add items to the basket from other pages.** It is quite simple to add items from other pages; just make sure that you target the quantity box correctly.

✦ **Add more products.** Add as many products as you like, as long as you work carefully and slowly. Make sure you keep raising the numbers at the end of the variables: 3, 4, 5, and so on.

✦ **Add more customer detail field.** Again this shouldn't pose much of a problem. Make sure you include the field variables in the `msgVar` variable.

✦ **Add graphics.** Graphics won't affect your cart at all, so feel free to experiment and play with graphical elements.

Summary

This project chapter presented a shopping cart built in SWiSHmax and powered by PHP scripting prepared by Rob Wells. The project showed you how to:

✦ Construct a basic movie to use for the shopping cart

✦ Create and script the first product sprite

✦ Create and script a second product

✦ Script the movie to apply totals and grand totals

✦ Write a PHP script

✦ Create and program a sprite for submitting values

✦ Export and test the movie

✦   ✦   ✦

Building a SWiSHmax Image Gallery

Special thanks to Stephan Lyon
for contributing this chapter.

In this chapter, you'll create an image gallery that uses a movable thumbnail scroller. Clicking a thumbnail loads the appropriate external image. File size is minimized by storing the images externally. A percentage preloader will inform your visitors of how long they'll have to wait for each image to load.

The main advantage of a thumbnail scroller is that it provides previews of the images, and because only a few are being displayed at the same time, it saves space. The position of the mouse cursor determines the speed and direction of the scroller.

In my opinion, it's always a good idea to create a new directory on your hard drive where you can store all project files. Name it something like **my_gallery**.

Preparing the Images

Begin by preparing the thumbnails in your favorite graphics program. In this example, I have a set of 10 images in the gallery; each is named sequentially from 001 to 010. I used thumbnails from the gallery images that I've slightly downsized. The names are the same as the full-size image but include "thumbnail" in their titles, such as 001thumbnail.jpg.

Caution The gallery images MUST be in non-progressive JPG format; otherwise you won't be able to load them in your movie!

The dimensions of the thumbnails aren't all that important, but try to make all of them the same size. I chose 90 x 90 pixels and turned JPG compression off, resulting in a maximum quality and a rather large file size. For re-creating this example, I recommend you stay with the 90-x-90-pixel format and prepare 10 images. When you're done, you will have a total of 20 images in your project folder.

On The Web
Site

The complete project described in this chapter as well as all the source files are available
from the book's Web site (www.wiley.com/go/swishmax) in the chapter27 folder.

Note

The images used in the project are courtesy of Miriam Lyon.

Starting the Project

Launch SWiSHmax. Open the program and choose the export option first. Click the Export
tab in the panels group to display the Export panel. Click Export options for to open the drop-
down list and choose SWF (Flash). Now click SWF version to export and choose SWF6. The
finished movie is exported in SWF6 format. Size the movie to 600 x 500 pixels with a frame
rate of 25fps.

**Cross-
Reference**

For complete instructions on choosing export settings, see Chapter 21.

Now begin your project.

Importing and arranging thumbnails

The thumbnails are imported into SWiSHmax and arranged in a sequence that is then converted to a sprite. Follow these steps to import and modify the thumbnails used for the
project:

1. **On the Outline panel, click Insert ⇨ Image and browse to the folder where you are
   storing the images.**

2. **Select all of the thumbnails you want to use, and then click Open.** The Open dialog box
   closes and the thumbnail images are imported into your movie project. The images are
   stacked at the center of the Layout panel's stage. You'll only see one of them because
   they're layered on top of each other.

3. **Click the Transform panel's tab to display the Transform panel.** Click the Anchor
   Point button and choose Top left from the drop-down list to reset the anchor points for
   all the thumbnails.

Tip

Provided you haven't clicked anywhere after importing the thumbnails, they should all still
be selected in the Outline panel. Press Shift+click to select them if they aren't selected.

4. **In the Outline panel, click to select the first thumbnail, 001thumbnail.jpg, if you
   are using the files provided on the Web site.** The remaining thumbnail images are
   deselected.

5. **In the Transform panel, click the X-axis field to select it and type 0; click the Y-axis
   field to select it and type** 0. The thumbnail moves to the upper-left corner of the movie
   stage.

6. **In the Outline panel, select the next thumbnail,** 002thumbnail.jpg.

On The Web Site

All of the file names referenced in this set of steps refer to the files available on the Web site. They can be found in the chapter27 folder.

7. **In the Transform panel, click the X-axis field to select it and type** 100; **click the Y-axis field to select it and type** 0. The thumbnail moves to the upper edge of the movie stage and 10 pixels to the right of **001thumbnail.jpg**.

8. **Repeat these steps until all 10 thumbnails are arranged across the top edge of the movie stage with 10-pixel spaces between them, as shown in Figure 27-1.** The anchor point of the final thumbnail is set at 900, 0; the entire set of thumbnails extends for 990 pixels along the upper edge of the movie stage.

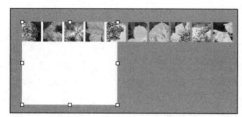

Figure 27-1: The set of thumbnails extends across the stage.

Creating a sprite

Next, create a sprite from the images and configure them as one unit. Follow these steps to build the sprite:

1. **Select the set of 10 thumbnail images.** You can press Shift+click in the Outline panel or use the Selection tool and draw a marquee around the group of images on the movie stage.

2. **Right-click the group of images and choose Grouping ⇨ Group as Sprite from the shortcut menu.**

3. **Click the sprite's name in the Outline panel and name it** thumbnails.

4. **In the Transform panel, click the Anchor Point button and choose Top Left from the anchor point options.**

5. **With all 10 images selected, click the Shape tab to display the Shape panel, and click Properties to open the Image Properties dialog box.**

6. **Click in the JPEG Quality field to select it and type** 70. You can also use the down arrow to decrease the quality of the image.

Note

A quality setting of 60 to 70 decreases the file size significantly and still maintains a good quality image.

7. **Click OK to close the Image Properties dialog box.** The quality of all 10 thumbnail images has now been changed.

Masking the Sprite

Now, on to one of the trickier parts of the project. Depending on how wide you want the scroller to be, you'll have to copy as many thumbnails as can fit inside the scroller area and paste them next to the existing ones. Then you add a mask to hide all but those you want displayed at one time.

Sound complicated? Maybe Figure 27-2 will help clarify things. The top row in the illustration shows the configuration used in this project.

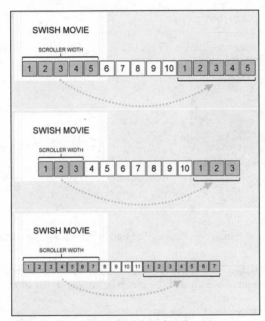

Figure 27-2: Add a set of thumbnail copies depending on the desired width of the scroller.

Double-click the sprite's name in the Outline panel to open it. Select 001thumbnail.jpg to 005thumbnail.jpg inclusive.

Press the Ctrl key and drag the image group to the right on the Layout panel's stage to follow the original set of 10 images. You now have a set of 15 thumbnails.

Note   Check the copied images' locations in the Transform panel. The first copy should have an X-axis value of 1000; the fifth copy should have an X-axis value of 1400. The set of images now stretches from 0 to 1490 pixels across the movie stage.

Next, you have to mask the **thumbnails** sprite. After all, you want only five images to show at the same time; to do that, you make a parent sprite and add a mask shape.

Follow these steps to create and apply a mask:

1. **Right-click the thumbnails sprite and choose Grouping ⇨ Group as Sprite from the shortcut menu.** The original thumbnails sprite is now a child of a new sprite.

2. **Click the new sprite's name in the Outline panel to activate the field.** Name the sprite **navigation**.

3. **With the navigation sprite's name selected in the Outline panel, click the Rectangle tool in the Layout panel's toolbox.** You add a shape that is a child object of the **navigation** sprite.

4. **Draw a rectangle that is 500 x 100 pixels.** Position the rectangle so it covers the first five thumbnails.

5. **In the Outline panel, move the shape to the lowest position within the navigation sprite (just below the thumbnails sprite).** You see the rectangle behind the images on the Layout panel's stage as shown in Figure 27-3.

Figure 27-3: Move the masking rectangle below (behind) the thumbnail sprite.

6. **Click the Sprite tab to display the Sprite panel, and click Use bottom object as mask.**

7. **Click the Transform tab to display the Transform panel.**

Tip

In case the entries in the transform panel are grayed out and can't be edited, you'll have to close the sprite by clicking the little minus sign next to it in the Outline panel.

8. **Click the Anchor Point button to display the drop-down list and choose Center.**

Caution

It is important to reset the anchor point to the center location or the scroller won't work correctly.

9. **In the Layout window, drag the navigation sprite to the bottom of the canvas and position it so the mask is centered horizontally.** Use the Transform panel for exact positioning; for example, if your canvas is 600 pixels wide, the correct X-position would be 300.

Scripting the Scroller

And now for a little scripting — select the navigation sprite in the Outline panel. Click the Script tab and then click Expert mode from the Guided/Expert mode toggle button. Type this script into the text field:

```
onEnterFrame() {
if (_root.imagescroll) {
    thumbnails._x-=_xmouse/50;
```

```
if (thumbnails._x >= -245) {
    thumbnails._x = -1245;
} else if (thumbnails._x <= -1245) {
    thumbnails._x = -245;
  }
 }
}
```

If you're interested in how this script works and are new to scripting, here's a brief explanation:

Depending on the mouse position, the **thumbnails** sprite scrolls slower or faster to the left or to the right. The value for `thumbnails._x-=` represents the sprites' moving distance per frame divided by 50. The movement is based on the **navigation** sprite's center, which is why you earlier set the anchor point of that sprite to center. When the mouse is positioned at the **navigation** sprite's center, the **thumbnails** sprite won't move; if the cursor is placed at another location, the sprite moves accordingly. For example, moving the cursor 30 pixels to the left moves the sprite — (minus minus) 30/50 pixels per frame to the right. In other words, the sprite moves to the right. Modify the value of 50 to change the scroller speed. Higher values result in slower scrolling movement.

Note   In other words, the mouse is moved 30 pixels to the left of center. In the script, the setting is `_xmouse / 50` (`_xmouse` gets the position of the mouse cursor), so it moves 30 divided by 50 (pixels) to the right (based on the "-=" Operator).

The initial position of the **thumbnails** sprite within the **navigation** sprite is at -245 pixels. When it's scrolled to an X-position of -1245, which is 1000 pixels to the left and the width of the 10 thumbnail images, the script tells it to jump back to its initial position. As soon as it leaves its original position to the right, it jumps to X = -1245.

Note   You'll have to tweak the values given for the script when your scroller's size differs from the one in my example.

The `if` statement is a condition that hasn't been set in the script yet. The statement `if(_root.imagescroll)` is a condition that determines when the scroller starts playing. To keep the scroller from playing right away, the `_root.imagescroll` condition has to be true before anything moves. Using `_root.` in front of the `imagescroll` property makes this condition available across the movie and all sprites.

Note   Writing `if(_root.imagescroll)` is the same as writing `if(_root.imagescroll== true)` and writing `if(!_root.imagescroll)` is the same as writing `if(_root. imagescroll==false)`. The shortened version just saves a little time when typing.

You don't want the scroller to play before the mouse cursor has moved on top of the thumbnails, and the set of thumbnails is a convenient place for setting the condition.

Open the **navigation** sprite on the Outline panel and click the **thumbnails** sprite to select it. You attach the next script to the **thumbnails** sprite. Click the Script panel, which should still be in Expert mode. Type this script:

```
onLoad() {
    _root.imagescroll=false;
}
on (rollOver) {
    _root.imagescroll=true;
}
```

Now it is time to test the movie. You can either test the movie within SWiSHmax or test in a player. If you've done everything correctly, the thumbnail images should scroll to the left or right at variable speeds when you move your mouse from side to side on top of the images.

If everything works, great! If not, double-check to see if you've missed some steps.

Constructing the Image Loader

Continue creating the main images loader. Start with a number of sprites added to the scene. Follow these steps to construct an image loader:

1. **Click the** Scene_1 **label in the Outline panel to select the scene.**

2. **Click the Insert button on the Outline panel and select Sprite.** A new blank sprite is added to the project. Name the sprite **images**.

3. **With the** images **sprite selected, click the Anchor Point button in the Transform panel and choose Top left from the drop-down menu.**

4. **In the Outline panel, click the** images **sprite to select it.** Add two more sprites within the **images** sprite. Name these sprites **preloader** and **image (**See Figure 27-4**).**

5. **Click the** preloader **sprite to select it in the Outline panel.**

6. **In the Transform panel, click the Anchor point button and choose Top left from the drop-down menu.**

7. **Click the Script panel's tab to display it.** The **preloader** sprite should be selected, and the Script panel should be in Expert mode.

8. **Type the following script for the** preloader **sprite.** The script is used to define locations for the playback head when the movie runs:

```
onFrame (1,afterPlacedObjectEvents) {
    setLabel("showimage");
    stop();
}
onFrame (3,afterPlacedObjectEvents) {
    setLabel("checkloadingstatus");
}
onFrame (4,afterPlacedObjectEvents) {
    _root.percent_loaded = _root.images.image.getPercentLoaded();
    if (_root.percent_loaded >= 100) {
        gotoAndStop("showimage");
    }

}
onFrame (5,afterPlacedObjectEvents) {
    prevFrameAndPlay();
}
```

Once the basic loader is constructed, you have to add some messages as text objects. You also need some Timeline actions to control the text objects.

Follow these steps to add text messages:

1. **Select the** preloader **sprite.** Add a text object within the sprite.

2. **Select the Text tool in the toolbox and click the stage on the Layout panel.** You need a text message. I've found the text tool in the Layout window is the most convenient way to do this.

3. **In the Text panel, check that the Static text option is active.** Choose a font, size, and color. The sample movie uses Arial Black text, 33pt, and a pale gray color.

4. **Type a message such as** LOADING IMAGE **into the text box.**

5. **With the** preloader **sprite still selected, create a second text box.**

6. **In the Text panel, choose Dynamic text from the text type button options.** This text box has to be dynamic text because its contents will be variable; it tells the viewer what percent of the image has been loaded.

7. **Click in the name field to make it active, and type** percent **to name the text object as shown in Figure 27-4.**

Figure 27-4: Your project has several sprites containing different objects.

8. **With the** percent **text object selected, click the Script tab to display the Script panel.** Type this script:

```
onenterframe() {
    this.text = _root.images.image.getpercentloaded();
}
```

9. **In the Layout panel, click both text objects to select them and align them.** Close the sprite in the Outline panel.

10. **Close the** images **sprite and center it on the movie stage.**

The text objects need some Remove() and Place() actions to control them; otherwise, they'll always show up, even when they're not needed because the image is already loaded.

Set these effects on the **preloader** sprite's Timeline:

✦ **Frame 1.** At Frame 1 of both the **LOADING IMAGE** and **percent** text objects, add a Remove effect.

✦ **Frame 3.** At Frame 3 of both the **LOADING IMAGE** and **percent** text objects, add a Place effect.

Cross-Reference   Place and Remove effects are described in Chapter 4.

Earlier you placed another sprite named **image.** This sprite is used to hold the actual full-sized images in the movie.

Select the **image** sprite on the Outline panel. Then click the Rectangle tool in the toolbox, and draw a rectangle about 500 x 350 pixels on the stage. Make sure it's placed inside the sprite! The project's flower images are sized at 500 x 350 pixels. You can color the shape to make positioning it within the movie a bit easier.

In the Transform panel, click the Anchor Point button and choose Top left. Place the rectangle at 0,0 coordinates within the **image** sprite. Close the sprite, and position the sprite on the movie stage. You can now change the rectangle's color to anything you like. In the project, the rectangle is invisible.

Finishing the Image Scroller Movie

You're just about done. All you have left to do is assign some actions to the thumbnail images; if you don't, nothing will happen when you click them.

On the Outline panel, click the **navigation** sprite to open it, click the **thumbnails** sprite to open it, and then click 001thumbnail.jpg to select it. Click the Script tab to display the Script panel and type this script:

```
onSelfEvent (release) {
    _root.images.image.loadMovie("001.sgl");
    _root.images.preloader.gotoAndPlay("checkloadingstatus");
}
```

Much of this script is probably familiar to you. But what about sgl? What's the *.sgl suffix? Well, it's actually the initials of my name. So, change it to anything you like. While this might seem a little strange to you, there's a good reason for changing the suffix from *.jpg or *.jpeg to *.anything. The preloader may not work properly when loading files with the *.jpg extension, so make sure to change the suffixes of your images before attempting to test your movie.

Tip   If you can't see the folder options, you have to tweak your computer's file display settings. Check the operating system Help files for directions on making extensions visible.

Now what exactly happens when you click a thumbnail? First of all, the **preloader** sprite is being addressed. It's sent to the checkloadingstatus label at Frame 3 where both text objects will appear. At Frame 4, the loading status of the **image** sprite's contents is being checked until it has loaded 100 percent of the content. Now the text objects disappear because the play head is sent back to Frame 1 of the **preloader** sprite. And, of course, the same button click will load the image into the **image** sprite.

Caution   The script requires the images to be in the same folder as the exported SWiSHmax movie, otherwise you'll have to tweak the paths. For example, if you want to keep the images in a subfolder called "images", it'll have to be _root.images.image.loadMovie("images/001.sgl");.

Copy the entire script, and one by one select each thumbnail and paste the script in the Script panel. Remember to change the file names to correspond with the numbers of the thumbnails. For example, change 001.sgl to 008.sgl for 008thumbnail.jpg's script.

That's it! Time to test your movie! Click File ➪ Export ➪ HTML+SWF. Click "No" to dismiss the dialog box asking if you want to edit the HTML. Save the files in the same folder that contains the images.

Double-click the HTML document to open it in your Web browser window. Test it to see that the images appear correctly as you click the thumbnails. If they don't display correctly, check the images' suffixes, the actions' paths, and whether you've set the export options to SWF 6 as mentioned earlier in the chapter. If the images display off-center, check whether the **images** and **image** sprites have their Anchor Points set to Top left and have been placed correctly. You won't see the preloader in action when you view the file offline, because the images will load instantly off your hard drive.

If everything works correctly, launch your FTP program and upload the complete folder to your Web server. View the file in your browser. Now you should see the preloader working. If not, make sure you don't have any errors in your scripts and haven't renamed the **preloader** sprite. Also keep in mind that the preloader will play only once per image; after that the image is being stored in your browser cache. Clear the cache to view the preloader again.

Summary

This project chapter presented an image gallery using a thumbnail scroller prepared by Stephan Lyon. The project showed you how to:

✦ Organize and prepare images

✦ Import the image sequence and organize the content

✦ Create a single sprite from the thumbnails

✦ Build a mask to display the thumbnails correctly in the movie

✦ Script the scroller's response to cursor movement

✦ Prepare an image loader using sprites and text objects

✦ Construct a preloader

✦ Script the thumbnails to load the images correctly

✦　　✦　　✦

Building a Daily Horoscope in SWiSHmax

In This Chapter

Writing variables and messages in a text file

Creating a container sprite

Setting up a dynamic text field

Loading variables

Checking for loaded variables

Creating an array

Retrieving random values from an array

Special thanks to Brian Ayers for contributing this chapter.

This chapter explores methods used to create a daily horoscope for your Web site. Each time this file runs, it loads variables stored in a TXT file and stores their values in an array for later use. Mathematical functions generate a random number that you can use to retrieve one of the elements in the array and display its value in a specified text field.

Using an external text file rather than storing all of the messages directly in your movie reduces the size of the exported SWF file. External files are also generally much easier to update on a regular basis and can be edited by someone who doesn't have Web-design experience.

Writing the Text File

It isn't necessary to have your messages planned and written at this stage, but it helps to create a dummy text file that can be used for testing purposes. There are specific rules when typing variables in a text file, and there are also several tips that you should make into habits.

In external TXT files, variables are defined with an ampersand (&) character in front of them and an equals sign (=) before the variable's corresponding value. It is good practice to include numbers at the end of variables that could be used consecutively or randomly. Below are two sample variables as written in a TXT file:

```
&myMessage1=Hello World!
&myMessage2=Live long and prosper!
```

External variables can act independently, or they can be associated with variables already set in your movie. For example, a dynamic text field can have the variable `myVar` associated with it, and the external text file can use `&myVar=message`, which automatically displays its value in that text field when loaded.

To prepare the text file, open Notepad or your favorite text editor and create several variables as described. Write a different message as the value for each of the variables. Create as many messages as you like. The more there are, the less likely it is that the same message will appear when selected randomly.

When you have finished writing the variables and messages, change the name of the last variable in the file to &theEnd. As an example, if your text file (full of variables and messages) looked like this:

```
&message1=Hello World!
&message2=Goodnight World!
```

Before finishing the file, it should look like this:

```
&message1=Hello World!
&theEnd=Goodnight World!
```

After changing the name of the last variable, save the text file as horoscope.txt.

Creating a Container Sprite

For this project, open a new file in SWiSHmax. Click the Movie panel tab in the panels group to display the Movie panel. On the Movie panel, give the file a width of 400 pixels and a height of 250 pixels.

Start with a blank sprite. You use this sprite as a container to hold the value of each variable in the text file. It is not always necessary to use a container sprite for variables, but there is a good reason for it in this example!

Follow these steps to add the new sprite:

1. **Choose Insert ⇨ Sprite from the Outline panel.** A new, blank sprite is added to your project.

2. **On the Sprite panel, name this sprite** container.

3. **On the Outline panel, click the Eye icon next to the sprite's name to hide it from view, as seen in Figure 28-1.** The container sprite will not have any objects in it, nor will it have any actions attached to it.

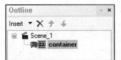

Figure 28-1: Hide the container sprite in the Outline panel.

Setting up the Dynamic Text Field

The random messages you configure are displayed on the movie in a text field. As the messages are random, and use scripting, you need a dynamic text field to display their contents. A dynamic text field changes its content in response to script commands. Follow these steps:

1. **Select the scene from the Outline panel to make sure the text object is not inserted in the container sprite.**

2. **Choose Insert ⇨ Text from the Outline panel's menu to insert a default text object in the center of your movie.**

3. **In the Text panel, type** messages **in the name field.** Select the Target option as well.

4. **In the Text panel, select your desired font character set, font size, font color, font type, and font justification.**

Tip Make sure to leave the font justification set to Left justified if you are using a bitmap font or one of the pixel font options in SWiSHmax.

5. **In the Text panel, make sure to select Dynamic Text, using the drop-down menu under the font type.**

6. **If you have not selected one of the device fonts (_sans, _serif, or _typewriter), open the Character Options dialog box (the ABC I 123 button) on the Text panel.** Click the All Characters option, as shown in Figure 28-2, and close the character options window.

Figure 28-2: Make sure that the All Characters option is selected.

7. **Open the Formatting options on the Text panel and click the Wrap text at word-breaks button, as seen in Figure 28-3.**

Figure 28-3: Choose the text wrap option to display the messages correctly.

8. **Open the Dimensions options on the Text panel and disable Auto-size height mode.** Use the drop-down menu next to the auto-size icon and select Lines. Make sure the text field is large enough to hold the text from any of your custom messages. This means that the text field may need to be set to several lines. In addition to setting the number of lines, you can set the width of the text field in the Dimensions options.

Tip You can type a long, temporary message into the text field to assure that it is tall enough and wide enough to hold the longest message in your external text file. Just be sure to delete it after you have finished sizing the text field.

9. **Delete the default "text" on the Text panel to complete the dynamic text field, as shown in Figure 28-4.**

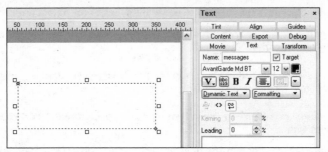

Figure 28-4: Set the dynamic text options and delete the default text.

Loading the Variables

Now that you have created a sprite and added a dynamic text field, you can create variables that will load text into the field when you play the movie. The process of loading the external variables into the container sprite is quite simple. Follow these steps:

1. **Select the scene in the Outline panel.**

2. **Open the Script panel and make sure that Guided mode is selected.** If Expert mode is selected, click the Expert button to open the drop-down menu and select Guided.

3. **Click the Add Script button and choose Events ⇨ Frame ⇨ onFrame() from the menu.**

4. **In the On Frame field at the bottom of the Script panel, type** 2.

5. **Press the Add Script button again and choose Movie Control ⇨ Load/unload Sprite ⇨ loadVariables(...) from the menu.**

6. **In the URL field at the bottom of the Script panel, type** horoscope.txt, **which is the name of the external text file.**

7. **In the Sprite field at the bottom of the Script panel, type** container. If you prefer, click the drop-down arrow next to the field to display the menu and choose the **container** sprite from the list, as seen in Figure 28-5.

The finished script should read:

```
onFrame (2) {
container.loadVariables("horoscope.txt");
}
```

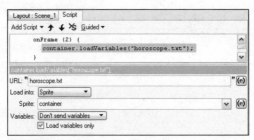

Figure 28-5: Specify the variable to load into the container sprite.

Tip
It is a good idea to always skip Frame 1 unless absolutely necessary. The Flash player has a nasty habit of skipping events on Frame 1; it is best to start your scripts on Frame 2 instead.

Checking for Loaded Variables

Even though the external text files will generally be relatively small, it is important to verify that the variables have loaded before attempting to do anything with that data. That is the reason for adding a specific variable (theEnd) at the end of the text file. If you check to see if the last variable in the file has been fully loaded, you will know the rest have been loaded as well. Follow these steps to add verification:

1. **Click the Add Script button and choose Events ⇨ Frame ⇨ onFrame(...) from the menu.**

2. **In the On Frame field at the bottom of the Script panel, type** 4. Skip Frame 3 because it will be used within the script.

3. **Click the Add Script button again and choose Conditional ⇨ if(...){ from the menu.**

4. **Type** container.theEnd == undefined **in the field at the bottom of the Script panel**

5. **Click the Add Script button again and choose Statements ⇨ name= expr; from the menu.**

6. **At the bottom of the Script panel, click the Target drop-down arrow and select** messages **as the target.**

7. **From the drop-down menu to the right of the Name field, select Text ⇨ text. In the** value field below the Operator, type **Loading ... Please Wait**.

8. **Click the Add Script button again and choose Movie Control ⇨ gotoAndPlay ⇨ prevFrameAndPlay from the menu.**

The completed script for this frame should look like the script that appears in Figure 28-6.

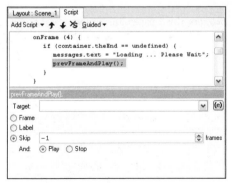

Figure 28-6: Add a script to determine if the content of the variable has loaded.

The finished script reads as:

```
onFrame (4) {
  if (container.theEnd == undefined) {
   messages.text = "Loading ... Please Wait";
   prevFrameAndPlay();
  }
 }
```

The variable named theEnd was placed at the end of the external text file and is the last item loaded. This script creates a loop that checks to see if the variable is still undefined at Frame 4. If it is undefined, and if it is still undefined, it displays the loaded message and jumps back to Frame 3 to repeat the loop, which is why you skipped Frame 3 in the script. When the if condition is no longer true, the loop is broken and the movie continues to play.

Creating and Populating an Array

Just like loading the variables into a container sprite, creating an array to hold their values is also not always necessary. An array is a group of characters or related values surrounded by quotation marks. It can be complete words, such as days of the week, or paragraphs and sentences, as you are constructing in this project. It does, however, make it much easier when dealing with random values and eliminates the need to number your variables externally.

Follow these steps to set up the initial array:

1. **With the Scene selected in the Outline panel and the Script panel open to Guided mode, click the Add Script button and choose Events ➪ Frame ➪ onFrame() from the menu.**

2. **In the On Frame field at the bottom of the Script panel, change the default value to 5.** The onFrame() event will be placed at Frame 5.

3. **Click the Add Script button again and choose Statements ➪ name = expr; from the menu.**

4. **Type daily in the Name field at the bottom of the Script panel; type** new Array() **in the field below the Operator, as shown in Figure 28-7.** The script should appear as follows:

```
onFrame (5) {
daily = new Array();
 }
```

There are several methods you can use to populate the array with the value of each variable. Do you remember at the start of this chapter how I said that there was a good reason for loading the variables into a container sprite? You are about to find out why!

To populate the array, you are going to use a for...in conditional statement to determine the exact content of the loaded variables. The for...in statement will retrieve the name of every object inside a sprite. Because the variables are the only thing loaded into the container sprite you created earlier, using this conditional statement gives you exactly the information you need—the name of each variable. As the conditional statement cycles through each variable, you will tell it to add the value of the variable to the array set up previously.

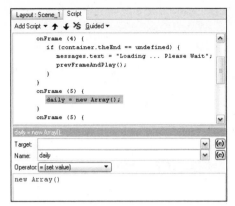

Figure 28-7: Add the script to create a new array for the movie.

Follow these steps to populate the array; continue from the previous set of steps:

1. **Highlight the last statement added in the Script panel for Frame 5, which was the** `daily = new Array()`; **statement.**

2. **Click the Add Script button and choose Conditional ⇨ for(...){ from the menu.**

3. **At the bottom of the Script panel, click the for(.. in ..) option, as seen in Figure 28-8.**

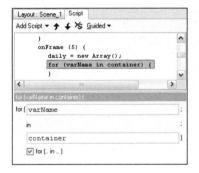

Figure 28-8: Create a variable inside a `for...in` conditional statement to hold the name of each object inside the specified target.

4. **Type varName in the upper field at the bottom of the Script panel.**

5. **Type container in the lower field at the bottom of the Script panel.**

Caution

Do not press Enter after typing **container** because that will add a new line; to finish the script, simply click the mouse elsewhere on the screen.

6. **With the** `for...in` **conditional statement highlighted in the Script panel, click the Add Script button and choose Statements ⇨ name = expr; from the menu.**

7. **Type varValue in the Name field at the bottom of the Script panel.**

8. **Right-click in the field below the Operator field and choose Functions⇨ eval(\{string\}) from the menu.**

9. **Inside the parentheses for the** eval **function, type** "container." add varName, **as shown in Figure 28-9.**

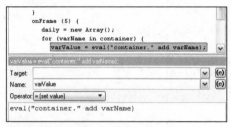

Figure 28-9: Type the values for the evaluation function.

10. **Click the Add Script button again and choose Statements ⇨ Evaluate from the menu.**

11. **Type** daily **in the field at the bottom of the Script panel.**

12. **Right-click the field at the bottom of the Script panel to open the shortcut menu.** Choose Object ⇨ Array ⇨ \{array\}.push(\{value...\}), as shown in Figure 28-10. The method is added to the field's contents.

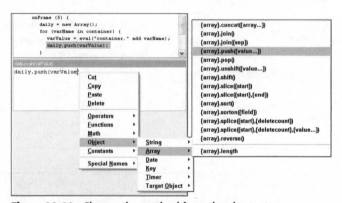

Figure 28-10: Choose the method from the shortcut menus.

13. **Type** varValue **within the parentheses for the** Array.push() **method at the bottom of the Script panel.** The final script for this Frame event should read:

```
onFrame (5) {
 daily = new Array();
 for (varName in container) {
  varValue = eval("container." add varName);
  daily.push(varValue);
 }
}
```

I will try to explain this script in the simplest terms I can. On Frame 5, a new array named `daily` is created. By default, the array is empty. Next, the `for(..in..)` conditional statement cycles through each object inside the **container** sprite and assigns the name of each object to the variable `varName`. The value of each variable is evaluated and assigned to the variable `varValue`. The `Array.push()` method is used to add new elements to the end of an array. The `for(..in..)` conditional statement will repeat this process until it runs out of objects to evaluate. This will assure that each of the externally loaded variables has its value added to the array quickly and efficiently.

Displaying Random Array Entries

The movie will use mathematical functions to generate a random number; which is then used to retrieve one of the array elements and display it in the dynamic text field. The random function needs a maximum value to keep it from selecting a number that doesn't correspond to an index position in the array.

Numerically indexed arrays, such as the one in this example, always begin with 0 (zero) as the first position in the array. The last index position is determined by one less than the total number of elements in the array. You can get the total number of elements by using the `Array.length` function. That value will also be used as the maximum value when generating a random number.

Follow these steps to generate a random number based on the length of the array:

1. **In the Script panel, click the Add Script button and choose Events ⇨ Frame ⇨ onFrame( ) from the menu.** Change the Frame number to **6**.

2. **Click the Add Script button again and choose Statements ⇨ name = expr; from the menu.** Type **total** in the Name field, and type **daily.length** in the text entry field below the Operator.

3. **Click the Add Script button and choose Statements ⇨ name = expr; again.** Type **randNum** in the Name field.

4. **In the text entry field below the Operator, right-click and choose Math ⇨ Math.randomInt({max}) from the shortcut menu.**

5. **Type total within the parentheses for the** `Math.randomInt()` **function.**

6. **Click the Add Script button and choose Statements ⇨ name = expr; again.**

7. **Click the drop-down arrow to the right of the Target field and choose** messages **from the list.**

8. **Click the drop-down arrow to the right of the Name field and choose Text ⇨ text from the menu, as seen in Figure 28-11.** In the text entry field below the Operator, type **daily[randNum]**. The finished script for the onFrame event will read:

```
onFrame (6) {
total = daily.length;
randNum = Math.randomInt(total);
messages.text = daily[randNum];
}
```

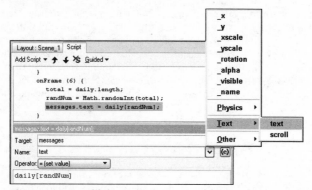

Figure 28-11: Add the script for generating a random number.

9. **To finish the script, click the Add Script button and choose Events ⇨ Frame ⇨ onFrame() from the menu.** Change the frame number to **7.**

10. **Click the Add Script button again and choose Movie Control ⇨ stop() from the menu.** The entire script now reads:

```
onFrame (2) {
 container.loadVariables("horoscope.txt");
}
onFrame (4) {
 if (container.theEnd == undefined) {
  messages.text = "Loading ... Please Wait";
  prevFrameAndPlay();
 }
}
onFrame (5) {
 daily = new Array();
 for (varName in container) {
  varValue = eval("container." add varName);
  daily.push(varValue);
 }
}
onFrame (6) {
 total = daily.length;
 randNum = Math.randomInt(total);
 messages.text = daily[randNum];
}
onFrame (7) {
 stop();
}
```

Setting Load Movie Preferences

For your file to work within SWiSHmax, you need to ensure that you set the appropriate preference options for the internal player.

Follow these steps to set player options.

1. **From the main menu, choose Tools ⇨ Preferences to open the Preferences dialog box.**

2. **Click the Player tab.**

3. **Click the Specify Folder radio button in the Test/Load movie folder section.**

4. **Click the browse button to the right of the input field to open a Browse for Folder dialog box, as seen in Figure 28-12.**

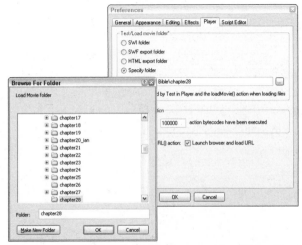

Figure 28-12: Choose the folder you used for storing the text file.

5. **Choose the folder that contains the horoscope.txt file and click OK to close the dialog box.** The folder's name appears in the field to the left of the Browse for Folder button.

6. **Click OK to close the Preferences dialog box.**

7. **Press Play on the Control toolbar to play your movie.**

If you want to plug this random message feature into another movie, simply group all of the objects into a sprite, cut the script attached to the scene, and paste it onto the parent sprite.

Save your project file as daily_horoscope.swi. You can add other components to the movie such as frames and backgrounds for the content, as well as a button for choosing another horoscope, as seen in Figure 28-13. Your file is now ready to be exported and uploaded to your Web site!

Figure 28-13: The finished movie displays a random message when the Replay button is clicked.

Summary

This project chapter prepared by Brian Ayers showed you how to build a horoscope of the day project. You learned how to:

✦ Use a text file to create messages that respond to variables

✦ Create a sprite and a dynamic text field to hold the messages

✦ Load and check variables

✦ Create and use an array

✦ ✦ ✦

Appendixes

✦ ✦ ✦ ✦

✦ ✦ ✦ ✦

About the Contributors

This book contains material contributed by some of the most influential people in the SWiSHmax community. They deserve a little praise and recognition.

Brian Ayers

Brian Ayers started using computers at the tender age of five. His father, a Senior Software Engineer and Brian's idol, guided his development with the aid of a Commodore 64 and taught him to program in Basic and Logo.

Brian's proficiency in HTML, CSS, PHP, and SQL is self-taught. He came into Web design through his activities as a gamer. When his Unreal Tournament gaming team wanted a Web site, he went searching for information. He spent days building variations of the team's Web site, complete with assorted cheesy java applets and animated gifs, and in the process came across SWiSH. The rest, as they say, is history.

He founded the largest online SWiSH community, www.swish-tutorials.com, in 2002. The site currently boasts over 64,000 members. He started working for SWiSHzone in late 2003 as a Technical Writer and has contributed to several of their software packages including SWiSH2, SWiSHmax, SWiSHstudio, and SWiSHvideo.

He has also published tutorials for various Web sites including Sonify.org and FontsForFlash.com. He is a musician and works as a freelance Web designer in his spare time. Brian spends nearly all his time and energy on the SWiSH community, with little time for other portfolio-building efforts. As he states, "Honestly, a lot of my best work usually finds its way into the downloads section at Swish-Tutorials."

Brian has spent most of his life attached to a keyboard.

Stephan Lyon

Stephan Lyon studied classical piano, but too soon found out that it was just one of many areas of interest. He started writing commercial music in the early 1990s, which is when he developed his fascination of working with computers.

Stephan lives close to Munich, Germany, with his wife Miriam and his little son. Stephan currently co-leads a renowned music school. He actually can't tell anymore when his attention was first attracted to SWiSH 1.5, but he remembers it being love at first sight. Stephan is a moderator at swish-tutorials.com as well as flashkit.com.

Ian Hinckley

Born several centuries ago in 1963, Ian was lucky enough to own a Science of Cambridge MK14 computer in 1980 and from there on his interest in computers has never been far behind. At school, Ian wrote a fully functional word processor, long before schools could afford their own and all in 16k of RAM using a Luxor ABC80, Z80 machine code, a Zilog book, a hex converter and a cassette tape recorder for storage. He still has the source code but rarely goes into that part of the garage.

After school and college studies, Ian passed the exams to become a member of the UK's leading accounting body the Institute of Chartered Accountants in England and Wales and later on passed the even more difficult exams to become a member of the Institute of Taxation. Ian would love to hear from anyone who needs a multi-skilled Finance Director/Head of IT as those kind of interesting roles seem all too difficult to find :).

None of this has anything to do with computers or programming, but it is a profession that has provided many opportunities to manage large-scale IT projects and to develop custom applications for clients from accounting packages in the days of DOS through to multi-site stock control packages using MS Windows' server, database and middle-tier technologies. Ian also develops solutions using MS Office and enjoys being one of the very few genuinely IT literate financiers: it's always interesting to hear what the head of IT has to say before asking why it will take three to four hours to add an e-mail address to Exchange Server, and that if they would like, show them how to do it in less than two minutes. Sadly, these meeting happen all too frequently.

Ian discovered Flash programming a couple of years ago when asked to review some code by a friend who was making an unhealthy amount of money developing on-line games, but had no time to follow it up. His interest was rekindled when upgrading to SwishMax; Ian has spent the last year or so reading almost every Actionscript book available and is now happy to take up most scripting challenges as long as it's for a good cause.

Ian has never built a Web site.

Peter Thijs

Peter's voice was first heard in 1971 and was an omen of what was to come. By the age of five he was playing music; reading notes long before he could read the alphabet.

Peter studied the clarinet and from there went on to include bass guitar, acoustic double bass, electric guitar, and keyboards. Instead of a higher education in music, Peter turned to teaching. He holds a degree in teaching English, Geography, and Economic Science for children ages 12-18. However, instead of teaching, he is an executive in a non-profit organization that assists the unemployed in job training, marketing, and workforce reentry.

Peter stumbled into the world of Web design when he was assigned the task of designing and constructing the organization's intranet. Peter used Internet resources as a source for information and is self-taught.

In his quest for information and ways to improve both his understanding and his organization's intranet, he stumbled across SWiSH, and realized it was the program he had been searching for. As his skill and knowledge developed, he came across swish-tutorials.com, where he is now a moderator, which he credits as teaching him "all he knows about SWiSH."

Peter maintains a personal site at www.tisse.com.

Rob Wells

Rob was born and raised in the U.K where he still currently lives. He has always been interested in computers. His other hobbies include skating, BMX'ing, and running around like a madman.

Nothing, however, interested him more than Web sites and how they were designed. He started using free programs such as the Cnet Quicksite Builder and Homestead to make his own Web sites, soon realizing both how shocking his sites were in comparison to those he saw elsewhere on the Internet, and the amount of extra useless code the builder had plonked in for no apparent reason.

Over the last few years, he discovered the glory of programming languages, graphic design, 3D animation, Flash, and, most important, SWiSH.

Rob started with a trial download of v1.5 of SwiSH. He was amazed by the simplicity and quality of output. He began to visit support forums, asking for help and posting his own examples. He slowly gained experience and confidence, which has led to his winning a number of competitions, serving as a moderator on SWiSH sites, and writing a tutorial for *The Official SwishMax Bible*.

✦ ✦ ✦

Web Sites of Interest

There is a wealth of material available on the Internet that you can access to learn more about SWiSHmax. You can exchange ideas with other aficionados, view sample sites, and access many tutorials and tips on working with SWiSHmax.

This appendix contains listings and information on some useful sites. This resource is by no means exhaustive. One thing you may notice as you review the listings here is how interconnected the SWiSHmax community is; be sure to follow links to other sites from the sites listed in this appendix.

SWiSHzone (www.swishzone.com)

One of the best SWiSH sites is the SWiSHzone Web site. You can use it as a launching point for your SWiSHmax adventures. On the main company site you find information about the programs and how to use them. You also find contests, demos, forums, and links to other sites.

SWiSHmax-Centric Web sites

Several outstanding Web sites exist that focus on SWiSHmax and other SWiSHzone products. Check out these sites for information and resources to help you develop your SWiSHmax skills.

Free Academy of Career Training (www.freeacademy.com)

This site offers a range of eBooks, including several related to SWiSH and SWiSHmax.

Frets Files (www.frets-files.com)

One of the foremost SWiSHmax-oriented Web sites. On Frets Files, you'll find everything from forums to tips and tutorials.

Rainbowfly.net (www.rainbowfly.net)

Rainbowfly Forums contain a number of download areas and tutorials, as well as forums on using SWiSHmax.

SwiSH-DB (www.swish-db.com)

This large site includes a SWiSHmax area in addition to a large number of Flash and Photoshop tutorials. You can also find information on commercial plug-ins as well as SWiSHmax eBooks.

Swish It (www.swishit.com)

This site contains a number of interesting tutorials and downloads.

Swish-Tutorials (www.swish-tutorials.com)

Swish-Tutorials bills itself as a premier SWiSH community, and the site is just that. The site includes a number of forums, and you can find animated tutorials, downloads, and plug-ins galore.

SWiSHmax Sites in Other Languages

The SWiSHmax community is global. Here are some sites that are non-English. From the main SWiSHzone site, click a flag below the company's name to view the site in one of several languages.

A list of non-English product and information sites at SWiSHzone is available at `www.swishzone.com/sites.php?do=page&cat_id=4`. You can access forums in different languages from the front page of the swishzone.com site by clicking one of the flag buttons.

SWiSHunion (www.hot.ee/swishportal/Main.htm)

A Russian-language site, it includes information about SWiSHmax and other SWiSHzone products.

SWiSHZone.iT (www.swishzone.it)

This is an Italian site that includes forums and product download areas.

SwiSHZoNE.net (www.swishzone.net)

This large German-language SWiSH site includes forums, newsletters, and other information on SWiSHmax.

Tutoriales-SWiSH (www.maskeamigos.com/tutoriales)

This is a Spanish site that includes a section on SWiSHmax and other SWiSHzone products, including tutorials.

Web-Related Sites

Flashkit (www.flashkit.com)

With almost half a million users, Flashkit is one of the largest Flash and SWF-related communities online.

Actionscript Dictionary (www.macromedia.com/support/flash action_scripts/actionscript_dictionary)

This page is the index for Macromedia's actionscript dictionary in the Flash Support Center Information Sites.

Total-Impact (www.total-impact.com)

The Total Impact site is a Web developer community including information on Flash, CSS, Web site building, and other related topics.

Wow-Factor (http://www.wow-factor.com)

A site showcasing some of the best SWiSH and Flash designed Web sites.

Movie Content

Very often you create content in SWiSHmax using items such as images and sound. Here are some design and content sources you may find useful.

Fonts

The right font can be the perfect finishing touch for your movie. You can also use letters and image fonts for objects in your movies.

eXtremefonts (www.extremefonts.com)

This Web site includes a searchable collection of over 1,800 free and sometimes unusual fonts.

Fonts-For-Flash.com (www.fonts-for-Flash.com)

This site is an excellent source for pre-made pixel and bitmap fonts. Most are not free – but they do have several sets that are free.

Dingbat pages (www.dingbatpages.com)

As you may expect based on the name, you can access from this site many versions of ding-bats that you can use for creating simple shapes in your movies. The fonts include both free and shareware fonts.

ThemeWorld (www.themeworld.com/fonts)

This site has hundreds of fonts available for download. The fonts include extensive previews of the characters as well as font information.

Photos and Images

A picture says a thousand words. Finding the right image can be a very time-consuming effort. Here are some sites that can make your search a little easier.

All Free Original Clipart (www.free-graphics.com)

As the site's name suggests, you can search for and download thousands of images. It also has links to other free clipart sites.

Animations.com (www.animations.com)

You can find thousands of animated GIF files at this site.

Barry's Clipart Server (www.barrysclipart.com)

Barry has collected thousands of free clipart, animation, and photo files.

stock.xchng (www.sxc.hu)

stock.xchng is a photo exchange site launched in February 2001. The more than 120,000 members have access to at least 85,000 photographs. You must be a member in order to access the images.

z-objects (www.z-objects.com)

z-objects.com designs and sells collections of vector graphics objects ranging from gears and grids to circles and stripes. The product line includes sets of EMF images designed specifically for SWiSHmax.

Sound

Many movies benefit from well-chosen sound, either as audio cues or as soundtracks. Here are some commercial and free sites where you can find all kinds of sound for your projects.

EchoVibes (www.echovibes.com)

EchoVibes offers a good collection of sound files free for downloading and using in your movies.

PartnersInRhyme (www.partnersinrhyme.com)

PartnersInRhyme offers free sound loops, sound effects, and music in addition to purchased sounds. You can buy individual loops or collections. The site also includes links to tutorials, tools, and utilities.

Studio Cutz (www.studiocutz.com)

The Studio Cutz Collections are high-quality music CDs designed for all types of media including video, film, web, and multimedia productions. You can buy music in a variety of formats from this commercial site.

Mixed Content

Some sites offer one-stop shopping for a variety of materials and information you can use in your SWiSHmax movies.

3D Café (www.3dcafe.com)

This site offers graphic art and other design resources. The "Free stuff" section of the site includes fonts, models, textures, sound effects, and more.

Clipart.com (www.clipart.com)

Clipart.com is a subscription-based site that offers a range of media for your projects including clipart, fonts, sound, and photos.

FlamingText (www.flamingtext.com)

This large site contains thousands of pieces of clipart, backgrounds, fonts, as well as online design of text effects.

Graphics.com (www.graphics.com)

This general graphics information site houses large numbers of forums, product information, downloads, and so on.

Information and Standards

SWiSHmax movies and sites aren't created in isolation from other technologies. Here is a list of sites where you can find information about Web technology and different standards to consider when building your movies and sites.

PHP.net (www.php.net)

This is the home site of the PHP scripting language.

The W3C CSS Validation Service (http://jigsaw.w3.org/css-validator/)

Validate your Web site's CSS against W3C's CSS Standards.

The W3C Markup Validation Service (http://validator.w3.org/)

Test your Web pages' structure against W3C Web standards including HTML 4 and XHTML.

W3C (www.w3.org)

The World Wide Web Consortium (W3C) develops Web technologies that include specifications, guidelines, software, and tools.

Web Accessibility Initiative (www.w3.org/WAI)

This site is a branch of the W3C that considers accessibility issues and accessible Web design.

W3Schools (www.w3schools.com)

This site is one of the best online resources for learning Web-related technologies and processes.

✦   ✦   ✦

Menus, Toolbars, and Keyboard Accelerators

One of the things that can take the most time when learning a new program is figuring out where the program's designers put the commands. Fortunately, the menu items in SWiSHmax are consistent with those of other Windows applications, so you aren't coming into the program without any knowledge — assuming you have used a computer before!

This appendix describes the contents of the commands listed in the SWiSHmax main menu headings. You'll also find the contents of the default set of toolbars described. This appendix also describes the commands you can activate using accelerator keys.

Table C-1: The File Menu

Command	Description
File ➪ New	This command opens a new blank SWiSHmax movie. If you already have an open movie, you are asked to save the movie before creating a new one.
File ➪ Open	To open an existing SWiSHmax file, choose this command. A dialog box opens that allows you to browse through your computer's files to locate the .swi file you want to open.
File ➪ Save	This command opens a dialog box for saving your SWiSHmax file. If the file has already been saved on your hard drive, any changes you made to the file since the last time you saved it are saved. A new movie is automatically saved with the .swi extension.
File ➪ Save As	The Save As command opens a dialog box for saving your file with another name or in a different location on your hard drive. If you are saving a file for the first time, the dialog box that opens when you choose Save is the Save As dialog box.
File ➪ New from Template	This command starts another movie project using one of the SWiSHmax templates or a custom template you have added to the program's template storage folder.
File ➪ Save as Template	If you have created a new layout for a movie and want to save it to reuse at a later time, choose Save as Template. The Save Template dialog box opens; you name the file and it is added to the program's template list.
File ➪ New Window	This command opens another program window. Use two or more windows if you want to copy objects from one movie to another.
File ➪ Samples	The Samples command opens a listing of sample .swi movies. Choose a sample from the list to open it in the program. There are a number of samples included with the program, and you can download more from the SWiSHzone Web site.
File ➪ Import	This command opens a dialog box for selecting files from your computer to use in a movie project. You can import a single file or multiple files.
File ➪ Export	The Export command opens a menu that contains options for exporting files from SWiSHmax. The options include: **SWF.** Choose this to export a Shockwave Flash movie from SWiSHmax. **HTML + SWF.** Choose this to export both a Flash movie and a Web page from SWiSHmax. **EXE (projector).** Choose this to export a free-standing movie from SWiSHmax. An executable file means the viewer doesn't need a Flash player to watch your movie. Instead, the viewer opens the file and the movie plays itself. **AVI.** Choose this to export a video movie from SWiSHmax.

Command	Description
File ⇨ Copy HTML to Clipboard	Choose this to copy the contents of the movie's Web page to the clipboard. You can then paste the Web page contents into another program such as Dreamweaver for further editing.
File ⇨ Display Export Options	You can toggle these options on and off by clicking the command. When it displays a check mark, the option is selected. When the Display Export Options command is deselected, you can't choose an export option.
File ⇨ Test	When you click Test, a menu opens offering three options for testing your movie:
	In Player. This option allows you to view a temporary .swf file in the Macromedia Flash player.
	In Browser. Choose this option to see your movie play within a Web page. Temporary .htm and .swf files are created, your default browser opens, and the HTML page containing the movie is shown in the browser.
	Report. This option displays a text document describing the contents of your movie. The report contains information about the types of objects, sizes, sounds, and so on.
File ⇨ Close	Choose this command to close the .swi file currently displayed in the program. Clicking Close doesn't close the program; if there is only one window open, a new blank file is displayed in the program.
File ⇨ Exit	Choose this command to close SWiSHmax and all open .swi files.

Table C-2: The Edit Menu

Command	Description
Edit ⇨ Undo	Choose the Undo command to reverse the previous change you made in a movie you are working on. You can continue clicking the Undo command until you have undone all the changes made in the movie since it was last saved.
Edit ⇨ Redo	Choose Redo to reapply the most recent command you have undone. You can continue to click the Redo command until you reach the final command executed in a movie.
Edit ⇨ Cut Object	This command works with either objects or effects. Click an effect on the Timeline or an object in the Outline or Layout panels to select it, and then choose the Cut Object command. The effect or object is removed from the program and copied to the system clipboard.
Edit ⇨ Copy Object	This command works with objects, effects, and scenes. Select an object, effect, or scene on the Timeline, Layout, or Outline panels, and then choose the Copy command to place a copy of the object on the clipboard. The selected object is not removed from the movie.

Continued

Table C-2 *(continued)*

Command	Description
Edit ➪ Paste Image	The Paste Image command is used with graphics. It is also used with effects and scenes, as well as other types of objects such as sound. Choose the Paste Image command to paste an object from the clipboard into the current movie.
Edit ➪ Paste in Place	This command pastes a copied object at the same location as the original based on the X- and Y-coordinates of the original object, unlike the Paste command that places the object at the center of the Layout panel.
Edit ➪ Delete Object	This command deletes a selected object or effect.
Edit ➪ Select All	This command selects all objects in the current scene.
Edit ➪ Deselect All	Choose this command to deselect all objects in the current scene.
Edit ➪ Find	Choose the Find command to open the Find dialog box and type a search term. You can search for text in the movie, as well as text in actions, scripts, sounds, image files, and effect filenames.
Edit ➪ Track as Menu	Track is one of two options for defining how a button behaves in response to mouse movement. A button tracks the mouse as either a pushbutton or as a menu. When a button is used as a pushbutton, clicking the button directs events to the button until you release the mouse. If you click this command, the selected button is tracking as a menu, which means the mouse isn't captured when you click the button.
Edit ➪ Make Instance	This command is used to create an instance, or clone, of a sprite object. A sprite object is a simple object that has its own Timeline and effects and is used within your main movie. For example, you can create one animated button using a Timeline, and convert it to a sprite, and then add instances of the sprite to complete your set of buttons for the main movie.
Edit ➪ Show	The Show command makes a selected object visible in the movie.
Edit ➪ Hide	This command hides a selected object on the stage on the Layout panel from view. Hide an object when you want to work with another object lower in the stacking order. When you play the scene or movie, the hidden object is visible.
Edit ➪ Lock	The Lock command prevents the selected object from being edited. The object is locked until you choose Lock again to toggle the command off and unlock the object.
Edit ➪ Show all States	This command is used for buttons. You see all states of a button stacked above one another to assist in placing and editing the button state objects. The layers are translucent, and the selected state appears darker.
Edit ➪ Hide all Except	This command hides all objects in the scene or movie except for the selected object. Hidden objects are visible if you play the movie.
Edit ➪ Lock all Except	Use this command to lock all the objects in a scene or movie except for the selected object. The objects remain locked until you choose the Lock command again to toggle the lock to Off.
Edit ➪ Open Object	Choose this command to open a selected sprite's Timeline and Layout panel so you can edit its contents.

Command	Description
Edit ⇨ Expand Object	This command expands a selected object on the Outline panel so you can edit its child objects. A child object is a component part of a larger object. For example, the over state shown when a mouse is over a button is a child object of the button.
Edit ⇨ Close Object	Choose this command to close an open or expanded object on the Layout and Outline panels.
Edit ⇨ Properties	Choose the Properties command to display the properties of a selected object in the Object panel.
Edit ⇨ Preferences	Choosing this command opens the dialog boxes for setting SWiSHmax options such as keyboard strokes and custom toolbar contents.

Table C-3: The View Menu

Command	Description
View ⇨ Preview Frame	This command modifies the Layout panel's view to show the frame identified by the play head on the Timeline. Use the Preview Mode to see an object at a particular frame in the animation or to modify a frame if it is a keyframe.
View ⇨ Toolbars	Choose this command to open a submenu. Visible toolbars are indicated by a check mark before the toolbar's name. To close a toolbox, choose the toolbar again from the submenu. The check mark is removed, and the toolbar is toggled to Off. There are five toolbars and a customizing option:
	Standard. The Standard toolbar contains commands from the File menu, such as starting a new file or saving or opening a movie file; commands from the Edit menu, such as Copy and Paste commands and the Undo and Redo commands; the order commands from the Modify toolbar; and two Help commands.
	Insert. The Insert toolbar contains some commands from the Insert menu, such as Insert Text and Insert Image.
	Control. The Control toolbar contains commands for controlling playback of the Timeline.
	Grouping. The Grouping toolbar contains items from the Grouping, Convert, and Break Apart commands from the Modify menu, such as Group as Button, Convert to Button, and Break into Polygons.
	Export. The Export toolbar contains commands from the File menu, such as Export to SWF and Test in Player commands.
	Customize. The Customize command opens a dialog box used to customize commands, toolbars, tools, the keyboard, and menus.

Continued

Table C-3 *(continued)*

Command	Description
View ⇨ Status Bar	This command toggles the Status Bar at the bottom of the program window off and on. The Status Bar displays information about a selected command or tool, the X- and Y- coordinates of the cursor on the Layout panel's stage, and the estimated file size of the movie when exported as a SWF file.
View ⇨ Zoom In	Choose this command to increase the scale of the objects displayed on the Layout panel.
View ⇨ Zoom Out	Choose this command to decrease the scale of the objects displayed on the Layout panel.
View ⇨ View at 100%	This command displays the movie at its actual size in the Layout panel.
View ⇨ Fit Scene in Window	Choose this command to fit the entire stage in the Layout panel's workspace regardless of the panel's size.
View ⇨ Fit Objects in Window	Choose this command to fit all selected objects into the Layout panel regardless of the panel's size. If no object is selected, the command works the same as the Fit Scene in Window command.
View ⇨ Show Rulers	Choose the Show Rulers command to add or hide vertical and horizontal rulers along the top and left sides of the Layout panel's workspace. Toggle the command to show or hide the rulers.
View ⇨ Show Grid	Use this command to show or hide the grid overlying the workspace in the Layout panel. Toggle the command to show or hide the gridlines.
View ⇨ Show Guides	Choosing this command shows or hides guides in the Layout panel. You pull Guides from the rulers along the edges of the Layout panel to use for positioning elements on the stage.
View ⇨ Lock Guides	This command prevents movement of existing guides on the Layout panel with the Select tool, while still allowing you to add new guides.
View ⇨ Clear All Guides	Choose this command to remove guides you have added to the Layout panel.
View ⇨ Snap to Grid	Make objects on the stage align with the Grid lines when they are moved within a specified distance of the Grid lines using the Snap to Grid command. Toggle the command to turn the Snap to Grid feature on and off.
View ⇨ Snap to Pixels	Automatically align (snap) an object's handles and locations to the nearest pixel when the object is moved on the stage using the Snap to Pixels command. Toggle the command to turn the Snap to Pixels feature on and off.
View ⇨ Snap to Object Handles	When this command is active, an object's handles automatically align (snap) to neighboring objects. Toggle the command on and off to activate and deactivate the Snap to Object Handles feature.

Command	Description
View ⇨ Snap to Guides	This command automatically aligns (snaps) an object's location to the nearest Guide when you move or edit the object on the stage. Toggle the command to turn on and turn off the Snap to Guides feature.
View ⇨ Show All Images	This command is selected by default. If you have a very complex or large movie file, toggle the Show All Images command off to display only selected images; the other images display their shape only.
View ⇨ Smooth Edges and Images	This command is selected by default. Toggle the Smooth Edges and Images command on and off. When off, the movie displays faster, but the edges of objects may be jagged or pixilated. When on, the edges of images and text are anti-aliased or smoothed.

Table C-4: The Insert Menu

Command	Description
Insert ⇨ Scene	Choose Scene to insert a new scene into the movie, complete with its own Timeline and Layout panel display.
Insert ⇨ Text	Choose Text to insert a text object into a selected scene, sprite, or group. The command activates the text tool, adds a text object to the listing in the Outline panel, adds the default text block to the stage, and displays the Text panel.
Insert ⇨ Button	Choose Button to insert a button object into a selected scene, sprite, or group. A small square is placed on the stage, the button object is added to the scene, sprite, or group in the Outline panel, and the Button panel is activated.
Insert ⇨ Sprite	Choose Sprite to insert a sprite object into a selected scene, sprite, or group. A small sprite is placed on the stage, the sprite object is added to the scene, sprite, or group in the Outline panel, listed in the Content panel, and the Sprite panel is activated.
Insert ⇨ Image	Choose Image to insert an external image into a selected scene, sprite, or group. A dialog box opens for you to locate and select the image file. The image is placed on the stage, added to the scene, sprite, or group in the Outline panel, listed in the Content panel, and the Shape panel is activated.
Insert ⇨ Content	Choose Content to insert an external file into a selected scene, sprite, or group. A dialog box opens for you to locate and select the file. The object is added to the scene, sprite, or group in the Outline panel, listed in the Content panel, and the Shape panel is activated. The Insert ⇨ Content command is the same as the File ⇨ Import command.

Continued

Table C-4 *(continued)*

Command	Description
Insert ⇨ Soundtrack	Soundtrack inserts an external audio file into a scene or sprite as a soundtrack. The sound object is automatically displayed as a soundtrack on the Timeline. It is listed in the scene or sprite in the Outline panel, listed in the Content panel, and the Sound panel is active. Once you select a file to use as a Soundtrack, the command is inactive.
Insert ⇨ Instance	Instance inserts a copy, or clone, of a specific sprite into the current scene, sprite, or group. When you choose the command, a small dialog box opens with a drop-down list of the available objects in your movie that can be cloned. Select an option from the list.
Insert ⇨ Effect	Choose Effect to insert an effect into an object or selected group of objects. The effect is placed at the frame identified by the play head on the Timeline. There are 16 categories of effects in a number of submenus.
Insert ⇨ Script	Choose Script to add a script to a selected object or the frame identified by the play head on the Timeline. Select from 11 categories of actions, events, or define functions options. Scripts added to frames display an indicator on the Scene's row on the Timeline.
Insert ⇨ Insert Frame(s)	Choose Insert Frame(s) to insert a new frame on the Timeline before the frame indicated by the play head on the Timeline.
Insert ⇨ Delete Frame(s)	Choose Delete Frame(s) to delete the frame indicated by the play head on the Timeline.
Insert ⇨ Insert Second	Choose Insert Second to insert one second's worth of frames (based on the movie's frame rate) into the movie starting at the play head's location on the Timeline. An effect must be selected on the Timeline to activate the command.
Insert ⇨ Delete Second	Choose this command to remove one second's worth of frames (based on the movie's frame rate) from the movie starting at the play head's location on the Timeline. An effect must be selected on the Timeline to activate the command.
Insert ⇨ Keyframe	Choose this command to add a keyframe to a Move effect on an object's row of the Timeline.

Table C-5: The Modify Menu

Command	Description
Modify ⇨ Group	You can group objects in SWiSHmax in a number of ways depending on what you want to do with the group. In this section you also find the command to reverse the other Group commands. **Group as Group.** Use this command with a variety of objects to group them as one. You can combine a variety of objects into one group and then apply effects. **Group as Button.** This command groups the selected objects together as a button, automatically creating the button states.

Command	Description
Modify ➪ Group	**Group as Sprite.** When you use this command, the selected objects are grouped together as a sprite, an object that has its own Timeline and contains effects.
	Group as Shape. Choose this command to group selected objects together as a single shape. You can use the shape as a mask or a layer used to change the appearance of other underlying layers.
	Ungroup. When you want to split a group or a sprite into separate objects, click this command.
Modify ➪ Convert	You can use the Convert commands to change the characteristics of a selected object or objects. You also find the commands for breaking objects into smaller units for adding effects in this group of commands.
	Convert to Button. Choose this command when you want to convert selected objects into individual buttons. A button can be an image, a drawing, text, or a combination.
	Convert to Sprite. Choose this command to convert a selected object into an individual sprite.
	Break into Letters. Apply this command to text. The command converts a text object into a group object containing a separate text object for each letter, which allows you to edit or animate each letter.
	Break into Shapes. Use this command with both shapes and text. With a shape group, the command breaks it into individual shapes; with a text object, the text object is broken.
	Break into Pieces. This command allows you to convert an object into a group object composed of a number of shapes that can be animated with effects like explosions.
Modify ➪ Order	Change the visibility of the layered images in your scene by using these commands.
	Bring to Front. This command moves the selected object in front of all other objects.
	Send to Back. This command moves the selected object behind all other objects.
	Bring Forward. Use this command to move the selected object one layer forward toward the top of the stack of objects.
	Send Backward. Use this command to move the selected object one layer backward toward the bottom of the stack of objects.
Modify ➪ Transform	Apply some simple commands for rotating and flipping objects in this group of commands, as well as a command to undo previously applied Transform settings.
	Rotate 90. This command rotates the object 90 degrees clockwise.
	Rotate 180. Use this command to rotate a selected object 180 degrees, or one-half of a revolution.

Continued

Table C-5 *(continued)*

Command	Description
Modify ➪ Transform	**Rotate 270.** Use this command to rotate a selected object 270 degrees, or three-quarters of a revolution.
	Flip Horizontal. This command flips the selected object laterally.
	Flip Vertical. Use the Flip Vertical command to vertically flip the selected object upside down.
	Reset. If you need to remove Transform settings you applied, use this command. The object returns to its default settings, with the exception of position, which must be modified numerically or by dragging the object on the stage.
Modify ➪ Align	You'll find a collection of commands used to organize the layout of a group of objects on the stage in this selection.
	Left. Align selected objects at their left margins using this command.
	Center (Horizontally). Align selected objects so their centers are at the same level across the stage using this command.
	Right. Choose this command to align selected objects to a consistent right margin.
	Anchor (Horizontally). This command aligns selected objects across the stage based on their anchor points.
	Top. Choose the Top alignment command to align selected objects on the stage with their top edges even.
	Center (Vertically). This command aligns selected objects on the stage with their centers even vertically.
	Bottom. The Bottom alignment command aligns selected objects on the stage with their bottom edges even.
	Anchor (Vertically). This command aligns selected objects vertically based on their anchor point positions.
	Relative to All Selected. Choose this command to apply an alignment option relative to the locations of all the selected objects.
	Relative to Last Selected. Choose this command to apply an alignment option relative to the location of the last object selected.
	Relative to Parent. This command applies an alignment option relative to the selected object's parent.
	Relative to Stage. Choose this command to apply an alignment option relative to the selected objects' relationship to the stage.

Command	Description
Modify ⇨ Align ⇨ Distribute	A number of selected objects can be organized on the stage in consistent ways using these commands.
	Left. Choose this command to distribute selected objects horizontally based on their left sides.
	Center (Horizontally). Choose this command to distribute selected objects horizontally based on their centers.
	Right. This command distributes selected objects horizontally based on their right sides.
	Anchor (Horizontally). Distribute selected objects horizontally across the screen according to their anchor point positions using this command.
	Top. Use this command to distribute selected objects vertically according to their top edges.
	Bottom. Use this command to distribute selected objects vertically according to their bottom edges.
	Anchor (Vertically). This command distributes selected objects vertically according to their anchor point locations.
Modify ⇨ Align ⇨ Space Evenly	Use these commands to space selected objects on the stage.
	Horizontally. This command distributes selected objects by evenly spacing them horizontally on the stage.
	Vertically. This command distributes selected objects by evenly spacing them vertically on the stage.
	Both. Use the Both command to distribute selected objects by evenly spacing them both horizontally and vertically on the stage.
Modify ⇨ Align ⇨ Make Same	This group of commands is used to make the sizes of a number of selected objects equal.
	Width. Apply this command to make selected objects the same width regardless of height.
	Height. This command makes selected objects the same height regardless of width.
	Both. Apply the Both command to make selected objects the same height and width.
	by Scaling. This command scales the selected objects to the same size.
	by Resizing. Apply this command to resize the selected objects to the same size.

Continued

Table C-5 *(continued)*

Command	Description
Modify ⇨ Justification	Use these commands with text to define how a block of text is distributed between its margins.
	Align Left/Top. This command aligns the selected lines of text with the left/top of the text block; the text displays ragged right/bottom edges.
	Center. Choose the Center command to center the selected lines of text with ragged left and right edges.
	Align Right/Bottom. Apply this command to align the selected lines of text to the right/bottom of the text block, with ragged left/top edges.
	Align Full. Align the selected text lines on both sides if the lines extend across the text block using the Align Full command.
	Align Full for all lines. Choose this command to align the lines of selected text on both sides regardless of the length of the lines.
	Align Full for All but Last Line. This command aligns the lines of selected text on both sides with the exception of the last line only, which may use a ragged right/bottom edge.
Modify ⇨ Appearance	These commands are used to change the typeface of selected text and to determine the direction the text flows in a text block.
	Bold. Make the selected text bold by clicking this command.
	Italic. Make the selected text italic using the Italic command.
	LR-TB Flow. Choose this command to display selected text from left to right, top to bottom.
	TB-RL Flow. Display selected text from top to bottom, right to left using this command.
	RL-TB Flow. This command displays selected text from right to left, top to bottom.
	TB-LR- Flow. Choose this command to display selected text from top to bottom, left to right.
Modify ⇨ Font Type	You can choose from several categories of fonts using the options in this group of commands.
	Vector Font. This command is the default option. The edges of the letters are smooth and even regardless of magnification or the size of the font, although they can appear blurry at very small sizes.
	Device Font. When file size of your finished movie is a concern, click the Device Font command. Using a Device Font instructs the Flash Player to use fonts from the computer displaying the movie rather than embedding the fonts in the movie file, thereby decreasing file size.

Command	Description
Modify ➪ Font Type	**Pixel Font (sharp).** Choose this command to convert a vector font to a pixel-based font. The font's pixels are aligned to pixels on the computer monitor, which makes the text appear very crisp, especially when using small font sizes.
	Pixel Font (smooth). For an effect similar to the sharp Pixel Font command choose this command. The smooth Pixel Font command anti-aliases (smoothes) the corners and diagonal lines of letters to make the letters appear less jagged.
	Vector Font (pixel aligned). This command forces text to align to the top-left of a whole pixel; use with pixel fonts for consistent alignment of the letters.

Table C-6: The Control Menu

Command	Description
Play Movie	This command plays the movie starting at the location of the play head on the Timeline.
Play Timeline	This command plays the active scene or sprite.
Play Effect	Click Play Effect to view a selected effect in a scene.
Preview Frame	Click this command to switch the view in the Layout window to Preview Mode. In Preview Mode you see the frame identified by the play head in the Layout window.
Stop	Click Stop to stop the play head and the movie playback.
Step Forward	Move the play head one frame forward by choosing this command.
Step Backward	Move the play head one frame backward by choosing this command.
Cue to End	Click Cue to End to move the play head to the last frame of the scene or movie.
Rewind to Start	Move the play head to the first frame on the Timeline by choosing this command.

Table C-7: The Tools Menu

Command	Description
Preferences	You can open a dialog box used to program options by choosing the Preferences command.
Customize	This command opens a dialog box that allows you to customize the Toolbars and Menus.
Keyboard Map	Open a listing of keyboard shortcuts and descriptions of the functions using the Keyboard Map command.

Table C-8: The Panels Menu

Command	Description
Layout	The Layout panel displays the objects in your movie on a stage surrounded by a larger workspace, with the Toolbox at the left of the panel.
Timeline	The Timeline panel displays the contents of your movie based on time. The Timeline visually represents the frames of your movie.
Outline	The Outline panel shows the hierarchy of your movie. The content of scenes is outlined and its components are listed according to their position in the stacking order.
Movie	The Movie panel shows common properties of your movie, such as the background color, size of the movie and frame rate.
Object	The Object panel shows the properties of a selected object. The Object panel is actually one of seven different panels depending on the type of object selected. It can show the properties of the following: button object, group object, scene object, shape object, sprite object, text object, and sound object.
Script	The Script panel is used to control action for a selected scene or object. You can work with the events and actions for the selected scene or object in the Script panel, writing scripts manually or using a guided method.
Transform	The Transform panel shows a selected object's position, size, angle of rotation, and anchor point locations.
Tint	The Tint panel is used to adjust a selected object's color transform properties including color and alpha (transparency) values.
Align	The Align panel displays the options for aligning, distributing, spacing, and resizing a group of objects.
Guides	The Guides panel includes settings for controlling the placement Guides, Grids, and Rulers on the Layout panel.
Content	The Content panel shows the content available for use in your movie, and is divided into sounds, images, and sprites.
Export	The Export panel shows you options for controlling the SWF and HTML of your movie for export to files or to use in a Flash player.
Debug	The Debug panel is used to evaluate the scripts used in your movie. The Debug panel shows scripts as they are executed, as well as the value of your scripts' variables.
Reset to Defaults	Choose this command to restore the program layout to its default arrangement with the Timeline stretched horizontally across the screen; the Outline panel below the Timeline at the left of the screen, the Layout and Script windows tabbed in the center of the program window; and the remaining panels tabbed together at the right of the program window.

Table C-9: The Help Menu

Command	Description
SWiSHmax Help Topics	This command opens the SWiSHmax Help files. In the Help files you find information on how to use the program organized according to a list of contents, an index, or you perform a search for a specific topic.
SWiSHmax Tutorials	This command opens the SWiSHmax Help files, but also displays a collection of tutorials that help you learn how to use different program features and produce different types of output such as buttons or a Web interface.
Go to SWiSHmax Web site	This command opens your browser and go to the SWiSHzone Web site, the company that created the program.
Go to the SWiSHmax Support Forums	This command also opens your browser and loads the home page for the SWiSHmax support forums. The support forums are a valuable source of information on working with the program.
About Macromedia Flash	This command opens your browser and goes to the Flash Player Web site.
About LAME MP3 Encoder	Read information about the LAME MP3 encoder used in SWiSHmax by choosing this command.
Purchase SWiSHmax	Choose this command to go to the company's Web site to purchase a key if you are using a trial version of the program.
Check for Update	Choosing this command opens a browser window and takes you to the company's Web site to check for an updated version of the program. You either see a message saying the version you are using is current or receive information on how to update your program.
About SWiSHmax	To read about the application, its version number, and copyright information, choose this command.

Table C-10: The Standard Toolbar

Icon	Command	Description
▯	**New**	Click this icon to open a new blank SWiSHmax movie. If you already have an open movie, you are asked to save the movie before creating a new one.
📂	**Open**	Click this icon to open an existing SWiSHmax file. A dialog box opens to allow you to browse through your computer's files to locate the SWI file you want to open.

Continued

Table C-10 *(continued)*

Icon	Command	Description
	Save	Click this icon to save a SWiSHmax file. If the file has already been saved on your hard drive, any changes you made to the file since the last time you saved it are saved.
	Find	Click the Find icon to open the Find dialog box and type a search term to locate text anywhere in the movie, including text objects, actions, scripts, and effect and filenames.
	Cut	Select an effect on the Timeline or an object in the Outline or Layout panels, and then click the Cut icon. The effect or object is removed from the program and a copy of the object is placed on the clipboard.
	Copy	Select an object, effect, or scene on the Timeline, Layout, or Outline panels, and then click the Copy icon to place a copy of the object on the clipboard.
	Paste	Click the Paste icon to paste a copied object from the clipboard into the current movie.
	Delete	Click the icon to delete a selected object or effect.
	Bring to Front	Move the selected object in front of all other objects by clicking Bring to Front.
	Send to Back	Click Send to Back to move the selected object behind all other objects.
	Bring Forward	Click to move the selected object one layer forward toward the top of the stack of objects.
	Send Backward	Click this icon to move the selected object one layer backward toward the bottom of the stack of objects.
	Undo	Click the Undo icon to reverse the last change you made in the movie you are working on. You can continue clicking the Undo command until you have undone all the changes made in the movie since it was last saved.
	Redo	Click the Redo icon to reapply a command you have undone. You can continue to click the Redo command until you reach the final command used in the movie since it was last saved.
	SWiSHmax Help Topics	Click this command to open the SWiSHmax Help files to find information and tutorials on working with SWiSHmax.
	Help	Click this icon to activate an interactive cursor. Move the cursor over an item on the program window, such as a button, and click to display the corresponding information from the main Help files.

Table C-11: The Insert Toolbar

Icon	Command	Description
	Scene	Click the Scene icon to insert a new scene into the movie, complete with its own Timeline and Layout panel display.
	Text	Insert a text object into a selected scene, sprite, or group by clicking the Text icon.
	Image	Click the Image icon to insert an external image into a selected scene, sprite, or group. A dialog box opens for you to browse to the image file's location and select it.
	Content	Click the Content icon to insert an external file into a selected scene, sprite, or group. A dialog box opens for you to locate and select the file.
	Button	Insert a button object into a selected scene, sprite, or group by clicking the Button icon.
	Sprite	Click the Sprite icon to insert a sprite object into a selected scene, sprite, or group.

Table C-12: The Control Toolbar

Icon	Command	Description
	Play Movie	Click this icon to play the movie starting at the location of the play head on the Timeline.
	Play Timeline	Click Play Timeline to play the active scene or sprite.
	Play Effect	Play only a selected effect in a scene by clicking this icon.
	Preview Frame	Click this icon to switch the view in the Layout window to Preview Mode. In Preview Mode you see the frame identified by the play head in the Layout window.
	Stop	Click Stop to stop the play head and the movie playback.
	Step Forward	Move the play head one frame forward by clicking Step Forward when the Preview Frame option is selected.
	Step Backward	Click this icon to move the play head one frame backward when the Preview Frame option is selected.
	to End	Move the play head to the last frame of the scene or movie by clicking Go to End when the Preview Frame option is selected.
	Rewind to Start	Click Rewind to Start to move the play head to the first frame on the Timeline when the Preview Frame option is selected.

Table C-13: The Grouping Toolbar

Icon	Command	Description
	Group as Group	Group a variety of selected objects as one object using Group as Group.
	Group as Button	Click this icon to group the selected objects together as a button, automatically creating the button states.
	Group as Sprite	Group selected objects together as a sprite by clicking the Group as Sprite icon. A sprite is an object that has its own Timeline and contains effects.
	Group as Shape	Click this icon to group selected objects together as a single shape.
	Ungroup	Split a selected group or a sprite into separate objects by clicking this icon.
	Convert to Button	Convert a selected object (or objects) into individual buttons by clicking Convert to Button.
	Convert to Sprite	Convert a selected object into an individual sprite by clicking Convert to Sprite.
	Break into Shapes	Break a shape group into individual shapes or a text object into letter shapes by clicking this icon.
	Break into Letters	Click this icon to convert a selected text object into a group object containing separate text objects for each letter.
	Break into Pieces	Convert a selected object into a group object composed of a number of shapes that can be animated by clicking this icon.

Table C-14: The Export Toolbar

Icon	Command	Description
	Export to SWF	Click this icon to export a Shockwave Flash movie from SWiSHmax.
	Export to HTML + SWF	Export both a Flash movie and a Web page from SWiSHmax by clicking this icon.
	Export to EXE (projector)	Click this icon to export a free-standing movie from SWiSHmax.
	Export to AVI	Export a video movie from SWiSHmax by clicking AVI.
	Export HTML to Clipboard	Click this icon to copy the contents of the movie's Web page to the clipboard.

Icon	Command	Description
	Test In Player	View a temporary SWF file in the Macromedia Flash player by clicking this icon.
	Test In Browser	Watch your movie play within a Web page by clicking Test In Browser.
	Report	Display a text document describing the contents of your movie by clicking Report.

Table C-15: The File Menu Accelerator Keys

Command	Accelerator keys
File ⇨ New	Ctrl+N
File ⇨ Open	Ctrl+O
File ⇨ Save	Ctrl+S
File ⇨ New Window	Ctrl+Shift+N
File ⇨ Export ⇨ HTML+SWF	Ctrl+P
File ⇨ Export ⇨ SWF	Ctrl+E
File ⇨ Copy HTML to Clipboard	Ctrl+H
File ⇨ Export ⇨ AVI	Ctrl+M
File ⇨ Test ⇨ In Player	Ctrl+T
File ⇨ Test ⇨ In Browser	Ctrl+Shift+T
File ⇨ Close	Ctrl+F4

Table C-16: The Edit Menu Accelerator Keys

Command	Accelerator keys
Edit ⇨ Undo	Ctrl+Z
Edit ⇨ Redo	Ctrl+Y
Edit ⇨ Cut Object	Ctrl+X
Edit ⇨ Copy Object	Ctrl+C
Edit ⇨ Paste	Ctrl+V
Edit ⇨ Paste in Place	Ctrl+Shift+V

Continued

Table C-16 *(continued)*

Command	Accelerator keys
Edit ⇨ Delete Object	Delete
Edit ⇨ Select All	Ctrl+A
Edit ⇨ Deselect All	Ctrl+Shift+A
Edit ⇨ Find	Ctrl+F
Edit ⇨ Properties	Alt+Enter

Table C-17: The View Menu Accelerator Keys

Command	Accelerator keys
View ⇨ Zoom In	Ctrl+= or Ctrl+Shift+= or Ctrl+Num+
View ⇨ Zoom Out	Ctrl+- or Ctrl+Shift+- or Ctrl+Num-

Table C-18: The Insert Menu Accelerator Keys

Command	Shortcut Key
Insert ⇨ Insert Frame(s)	F5
Insert ⇨ Delete Frame(s)	Shift+F5
Insert ⇨ Insert Second	Ctrl+F5
Insert ⇨ Delete Second	Ctrl+Shift+F5

Table C-19: The Modify Menu Accelerator Keys

Command	Accelerator keys
Modify ⇨ Group ⇨ As Group	Ctrl+G
Modify ⇨ Group ⇨ Ungroup	Ctrl+U
Modify ⇨ Appearance ⇨ Bold	Ctrl+B
Modify ⇨ Appearance ⇨ Italic	Ctrl+I

Table C-20: The Help Menu Accelerator Keys

Command	Accelerator keys
SWiSHmax Help Topics	F1

✦　　✦　　✦

SWiSHmax Effects

The SWiSHmax program contains literally hundreds of special effects you can use in your movie projects.

This appendix lists the effects available in the program according to the type of effect. There is also a description of how the effect looks, whether it has any restrictions, and its duration in frames.

Some effects work well for complex objects; others work equally well with simple objects. Some effects, such as a 3D Spin effect, produce only minimal animation of simple objects such as slight movement or change in scale because the effect isn't intended for that type of object. When you are working with complex effects, the more segments or letters making up the object, the more complex the effect appears. The best types of objects to which the effect should be applied are specified in the tables. The duration listed is the default applied when the effect is chosen.

This appendix describes the effects' defaults. When you choose an effect it can be customized to perform much differently than the description. Use these descriptions as a starting point.

Note At the time of publication, the descriptions in this appendix are the default names and settings for SWiSHmax effects.

Table D-1: Place Effects

Effect	Description	Default Duration
Place	Displays a selected object on the stage.	1
Remove	Removes a selected object from the stage.	1
Move	Moves a selected object on the stage over time.	10

Table D-2: Fade Effects

Effect	Description	Default Duration
Fade In	Gradually makes the selected object visible.	10
Fade Out	Gradually makes the selected object invisible.	10

Table D-3: Zoom Effects

Effect	Description	Default Duration
Zoom In	Increases scale of the selected object over time based on the anchor point position of the object.	10
Zoom Out	Decreases scale of the selected object over time based on the anchor point position of the object.	10

Table D-4: Other Single Effects

Effect	Description	Default Duration
Blur	Objects gradually become clearer over time; customizes the type and direction of the blur.	20
Repeat Frames	Defines a portion of the Timeline as a source and specifies how it is repeated.	1
Revert	Reverses the position of the effect preceding it on the Timeline by returning the object to its original reference position on the stage.	20

Table D-5: Appear Into Position Effects

Effect	Description	Default Duration
3d	Grow/shrink/stand-up options. Using different approaches the object reaches full size onscreen. Modifies rotations, color, and fade.	20
Alternate	The Alternate effects are designed to be used with a group of shapes; each component is moved to the stage according to an alternating pattern. 9 options — based on object offset, squeeze, and other custom settings.	20
Arrive quietly	Best with group of objects; customizes scale/rotation/fade; object moves to designated stage location from offstage by rising vertically from the start position and then dropping to the final location as it fades in.	20
Arrow-arrowbic background	Strobe-like color changes from default to silver white and back to default; components increase and then decrease in size in accordance with color changes.	20
Blaster-bang	Image or components appear at magnified size and very brightly contrasted color, gradually fade to default color and size.	20

Effect	Description	Default Duration
Bullet	Fly by in/ripple in options – images pulse; the components are assembled in complex object during pulses.	20
Come around from back	Object or components appear to grow in size and rotate around a point.	20
Come in	Four options – objects gradually fade in and decrease in scale from very large number (default 500 on come in-appearance) or increase in scale and fade in.	20
Curl-curl in	Starting from the center of the object, each character increases in visibility and spins in from left to right.	20
Drop from high places	Object changes scale and opacity as it rotates into position from a location above the stage.	20
Drop in and bounce	Drops a specified distance and bounces a specified number of times (default is 200px and 4 bounces).	30
Fade	Three effects – object fades in as with the standard fade effect but also uses color as part of the effect.	20
Flatten-flat in	Object rotates on the Y-axis and appears from flat to standing.	20
Flatten-turn in	Object or component rotates on Y-axis and appears.	20
Flip and shrink in	Object starts at 400% scale and faded; gradually decreases to original size and opacity. In complex objects the components are overlapped and each sized at 400% scale.	20
Fly in, zoom and settle	Object passes from right to left across stage and then returns to the final location, decreasing in size and increasing in opacity. In a complex object the components overlap and appear to chase one another in sequence.	20
Grow in and widen	A simple object merely increases in size and opacity; in a co mplex object the effect is applied to each element and produces an interesting overlap.	20
Implode	Four options – Objects change scale and rotate into position. Complex object effect shows cascading objects with effect applied to each object.	20
Kerning-kern in	Complex objects or text slowly assume their location by moving components closer together in a uniform pattern; a simple object remains stationary and increases in opacity.	20
Move together from random directions	Complex objects and text elements move through color changes and rotate in varying degrees and then move to the final location from various angles. Simple object merely moves through color change and rotates.	20
Out of the blue	Final size is 50% of object's original size. Components of complex objects change scale and opacity and rotate into their final locations from different directions. Simple objects use one change of scale, rotation, and opacity.	20

Continued

Table D-5 (continued)

Effect	Description	Default Duration
Perfect landing 1 and 2	Objects and components move in from the right of the stage and across to the left to the final locations increasing in speed as they move. Version 2 adds a downward motion as the object moves across the stage.	20
Random jump in	Text and complex objects' elements gradually increase in size and opacity and come to their final location; a simple object merely increases in size and opacity and moves slightly down the stage.	20
Roll in-Swiss roll	Complex objects: components making up left half of object rotate and increase in opacity as they move into place followed by the right half of the object. Simple object: left half displays, object rotates -360 degrees on the Y-axis and increases to its final size and opacity.	40
Scale in	Objects decrease in scale from 1000% to original size. In a complex object the component elements appear from both ends and then gradually appear toward the center of the object (depending on cascade order).	20
Scale in and back	In a complex object, components appear at 500% scale and red in color, decrease in size and rotate into their positions; simple objects appear at 500% scale in red and decrease to final position and size.	20
Scale letters	Applies to text objects; when used on complex object produces simple cascade entry of component elements, simple shape merely decreases in scale to size.	20
Shoot in from the hip	Simple object: shape rotates into position and changes color from default blue to object's color. Text and complex objects rotate according to cascading order and change color during rotation to be composed at the final location.	20
Shrink in	Object increases in scale along the X-axis to the original object's size.	20
Shrink stretch and grow in	Objects increase in scale and then bounce back to original size as they change color.	20
Spin	Four options — component parts originate from different directions in different effects; objects spin into position and increase in opacity. Spin in and unspin, spin in from outside, and spin back and in effects also animate color change. In simple objects the effect is minimal, such as partial rotation or spin.	20
Squeeze	Six effects — scale, fade, color, property settings, some use squeeze setting as well. Objects appear on stage from varying directions and then move to final location, may include accelerated motion as well or changes in direction as the object moves into position. The effects work similarly with simple and complex effects, although more dramatic with complex objects.	20

Effect	Description	Default Duration
Stream and turn in from side	Objects move across stage past final location and then return to that location in the effect. Color change and scale change during effect; objects elongated (increase in size along the Y-axis greater than along the X-axis). Works with both complex and simple objects.	20
Stream in	Objects move into the final location from an offstage position directly to the final location in the effect. Color change and scale change during effect; objects elongated (increase in size along the Y-axis greater than along the X-axis). Works with both complex and simple objects.	
Swirl in	Effect uses axis-offsets and color, opacity, and scale changes. Objects start at 600% scale and rotate into position as they decrease in scale.	20
Tall and thin and back	Objects start and end with designated color, passing through a color change and 700% increase in scale midpoint in the effect.	20
Twister-twist again	Partial rotation and opacity change in simple object. Complex object components spin counterclockwise and assemble in their final locations.	20
Typewriter*	Four text effects — length varies according to the amount of text in the object; modifies length based on Show character setting. Optional effects based on speed and cursor visibility. Complex object displays one segment at a time on the stage in its final location with this effect; simple object appears at the final frame of the effect.	Varies
Unsquash in	Object or component stretched 800% along X-axis, decreases to original dimension and changes color during the effect. Simple object starts at 800% of X-axis size, returns to 100% X-axis and then decreases to approx. 5% of Y-axis size and finally returns to object's original size.	20
Unsqueeze	Object or component starts at 1500% of Y-axis scale and gradually decreases to final size in the Unsqueeze in from lines effect; the Unsqueeze from jump effect moves the components onstage higher than their final locations and they accelerate to the final location during the latter frames of the effect.	20
Vortex drop down and apart	For all vortex effects, objects drop into position around the center of the object in a complex object; simple object uses overall motion of the effect, such as rotation, to move into position. Color changes from black and slight changes in scale.	20
Vortex in and stand up	Color changes from black and objects fly in.	20
Vortex spin back	Objects decrease in scale from 2000% and color changes.	20
Vortex up	Color changes from black and increases in opacity; object moves from below final location and loops into final location.	20

Continued

Table D-5 *(continued)*

Effect	Description	Default Duration
Vortex up and slide forward	Objects increase in scale and fly upward accelerating into final location as the composite object increases in scale to its final size.	20
Weave into center	Objects increase in size and alternate combining into final object (complex object). Simple objects show opacity change and bounce once.	20
Whirlpool in	Objects rotate around an axis as they rotate into their positions, changing size and opacity during effect. This effect is useful for both complex and simple objects.	20
Wild-alternate -alternate 3	Components move into place in an alternating sequence.	20
Wild-fade in	Fades in components of a complex object in a sequence.	20
Wild-fall down	Drops and rotates objects into position.	20
Wild-flow in.	Moves objects into a group and changes scale and opacity as the composition moves to its final location.	20
Wild-low scale	Changes the color and scale from 800% to the final size with components at their final locations.	20
Wild-revert	Builds the complex object by rotating the elements into their location without changing opacity or color.	20
Wild-rotate	Changes opacity and rotates the objects at their final locations.	20
Wild-flow	Moves objects across the stage increasing opacity and decreasing size to land directly at their final locations.	20
Wild-slide up	Moves components and increases their size at their final locations.	20
Wild-slip in	Rotates objects, increases in opacity, and decreases in scale from 800% to final size at their final locations.	20
Wild-spring	Moves objects from above and to the left of the final location, increasing opacity slightly.	20
Wild-squeeze	Changes components from 150% scale and size and decreased opacity to final size and 100% at the final location.	20
Wild-to infinity	Rotates components 45 degrees, decreases scale from 1000%, and increases opacity at their final locations.	20
Wild-turn and turn in	Decreases scale from 200% and increases opacity as components move from offset position to final location or rotate into position.	20
Wild-typewrite*	Text displays from left to right; component objects appear according to cascading order.	20
Wild-uncompress	Objects decrease from 400% stretch on X-axis to final size and increase opacity at their final locations.	20

Effect	Description	Default Duration
Wild-warp in	Components are offset, decreased in scale, faded, and rotated at a 45-degree angle; gradually come together and compose final object at final location.	20
Wild-web	Objects move in a flat loop and then in a second abbreviated loop as they increase in opacity, and decrease in scale to assemble in order at the final location.	40
Wild-zoom in	Components decrease in size and increase in opacity at their final locations in sequence.	20
Wild-zzzip	Objects rotate into their final positions in sequence from an offset position, changing opacity and scale.	20
Wind	Three effects — breeze, storm, and vaporize. The effects are similar but vary in the strength, speed, and direction of the effect as the object appears.	20

* Text effects have limited or little effect on shapes or complex objects.

Table D-6: Disappear from Position Effects

Effect	Description	Default Duration
3d spin	Object or component spins clockwise by default and fades. Use with both complex and simple shapes.	20
3d spin out	Specifies rotations for each element/shape as it spins and fades. Default is one rotation. Use with both complex and simple shapes.	20
3d spin out and grow	Specifies a size for the spinning elements at the end of the effect; the default is 800%. Use with both complex and simple shapes.	20
3d spin out from center	The elements spin away from the center of the object, change color, and fade. Use with both complex and simple shapes, but most effective with complex objects.	20
Bubble burst	Components or objects drift upward, change color, and then fade.	20
Come in-blur out -disappear -mystery -bye bye	Four effects — Fades and increases/decreases size of element or shape. Variations are based on the increase in size of the elements as the effect plays with the exception of the bye bye effect, which decreases the size of the elements and fades them out as the effect plays. Works with both complex and simple shapes.	20
Curl-curl out	Object or element dramatically stretches along one axis as it rotates and fades along a motion path added from the object's original location across the stage.	20
Drop away	Object rotates 90 degrees and moves downward from the original location as it fades out.	20

Continued

Table D-6 *(continued)*

Effect	Description	Default Duration
Explode-down -down slowly -toward	Three effects—Explode down looks similar to the Drop away effect when used with simple object. These explode effects move components downward.	20
Fade-burn out -standard -wipe out	Three effects—Object fades out as with the standard fade effect, but also uses color as part of the effect. Burn out changes color to red as it fades out.	20
Feather falling	Objects float and drift. Specifies drift characteristics and wavelengths. Works with complex and simple objects.	30
Flatten-flat out	Rotates the object or components on the X-axis as they move downstage until they disappear. Works with both complex and simple objects.	20
Flatten-turn off	Components or objects decrease in X-axis scale until they disappear. Works with both complex and simple objects.	20
Kerning-kern out*	Effect moves complex object components or text letters away from each other in a uniform pattern as they fade; a simple object remains stationary and decreases in opacity.	20
Move apart in random directions	Object or components revolve twice as they rotate in varying directions at various speeds and fade out.	20
Open up the curtain	Simple object increases slightly in size as it fades. The component parts of a complex object move farther apart and fade out.	20
Radiation	Two options—Warm Glow In and Warm Glow Out. Direction of effect can be specified; object or elements increase in size at their original locations and fade out. Simple object fades out as it increases (Warm Glow In) or decreases (Warm Glow Out) in size slightly.	20
Random-jumpback	Objects move up slightly and decrease in scale as they fade. Works with both simple and complex objects.	20
Random-spin and rise	Objects rotate three revolutions as they move apart, fade, and move upward. Works with both complex and simple objects.	20
Rise and inflate	Objects or components increase in size, move upward on stage, and change color to magenta.	20
Scale out	Objects increase in scale to 1000% as they move toward the center of the screen, fade, and color changes to cyan.	20
Scale out and squeeze in	Object components decrease in scale and move away from one another and then move back together as they fade and change color to red.	20

Effect	Description	Default Duration
Spin back and out	Components are separated and move upward and outward off the upper stage in a swirling pattern; two revolutions show each element twice on stage as they slowly decrease to 50% scale. Simple objects revolve and change size.	20
Spin out and unspin	Objects start effect using black, change color to red as they appear to spin clockwise and move down the stage; direction reverses and objects turn blue and decrease in scale as they move upward.	20
Spin out random to side	Components rotate and spin out at different speeds to the default right side. Objects in a complex object move apart and become transparent.	20
Spin out to outside	Components change color to red, fade, increase in size, and move out in sequence from original location to offstage bottom; the default effect uses four rotations.	20
Spin random away	Objects rotate and decrease size to 0% as they fade. By default the components are split from the center and move to either side of the stage.	20
Spin random toward	Objects rotate and increase to 500% as they fade.	20
Squash out	Simple object: Object decreases in width, and then increases to 1000% width as the height decreases. Complex object: Components are flattened at their original locations and increase in X-scale by 1000% as they change to red color.	20
Squeeze	Seven effects — all work with complex objects. Single objects fade and change color but remain stationary. Some effects create rotation in a simple object. All effects use a squeeze function that changes the objects' scale, a color change, and some fade to 50%.	20
Squeeze and cascade out	Default squeeze is 300; color changes to lime green as the objects fade and move offstage.	20
Squeeze and rotate out	Default squeeze is 300. Objects revolve twice as they move offstage; color changes to lime green.	20
Squeeze and swoop away	Objects separate and increase in size as they move to the bottom of the stage, and then reverse direction and continue to increase in size as they move offstage at the top of the stage; color changes to blue.	20
Squeeze out to lines	Components increase in scale to 1500%, rotate -90 degrees, and spin out from their original locations in the complex object as they change color to magenta.	20
Squeeze out with rotate	Objects rotate -360 degrees and move apart as they change color to red. Components move down and to the right from their original locations.	20

Continued

Table D-6 *(continued)*

Effect	Description	Default Duration
Squeeze out with spin	Objects rotate 180 degrees and move apart as they change color to red. Using a 3D appearance, components move down and to the right from their original locations.	20
Squeeze small jump	Components move to the center of the stage—left half moves to the right and right half moves to the left, stacking atop one another as they move downward, increase in scale to 200%, and fade out completely.	20
Stream and turn out to side	Objects appear to move to the same location on the stage and then revolve to move offstage in sequence along an X-axis as the color changes to magenta. Works with both complex and simple objects.	20
Stream out	Objects move from their location offstage in sequence while changing color to magenta and fading. Works with both complex and simple objects.	20
Swirl out	Complex object components move apart from upper left to lower right, move upward and to the right, increase scale and change to green color as they fade and move downward on the stage.	20
Vortex	Components move upward and to the left from the top left of the object, rotating on the Y-axis and Z-axis as they become transparent.	20
Vortex down	The vortex effect is applied, and the components drop down as they rotate and disappear.	20
Vortex down and away to side	Components move as per vortex effect and pass to the right of the object and drop downward as they rotate and disappear.	20
Vortex down and fly away	As with the vortex down effect; the entire object decreases in Y-scale as it rotates on the Z-axis and moves upward as the effect is applied.	20
Vortex spin out	As with the vortex effect; the scale increases to 2000% as the components rotate and fade.	20
Vortex sucked up	Object components move as per the vortex effect; components disappear quickly as they move upward.	20
Vortex together and fly up	The object gradually decreases in scale as it moves upward on stage and fades. For both simple and complex objects.	20
Vortex up and away to side	Components move upward and to the side and then move to the right of the object and disappear across the right stage. The entire object stretches horizontally and moves right as the effect is applied.	20

Effect	Description	Default Duration
Whirlpool out	The object or components move upward and rotate counter-clockwise about a center point twice, gradually fading. A complex object's elements gradually get further apart as the effect progresses.	20
Wild-alternate 2	Alternating components move upward and downward as they increase in scale and fade. A simple object moves upward slowly as it fades.	20
Wild-boring one	Each component increases in scale to 1000% on one axis, rotates; and fades. Also works with simple objects, which rotate as a single unit and fade	20
Wild-compress	Each component is stretched horizontally at its original location and fades in a sequence. Also works with simple objects.	20
Wild-flow out	Complex object components stream upward from the group, fading, and then drop down again at a 45-degree angle to fade out completely. Works with simple objects.	20
Wild-SL-fade up	Elements fade as they stretch 500% horizontally and move upward offstage in sequence. Also works with simple objects.	20
Wild-slide away	Object components gradually increase in width, decrease in height, and disappear. Works with simple objects.	20
Wild-splatter	Components explode gently from the center of the object and fade as they move outward. Simple object appears to rotate on the Y-axis and Z-axis in a counterclockwise direction as it fades.	20
Wild-turn out	Components move downward from the complex object, breaking apart slightly and increasing in scale to 1000% as they fade. Simple object rotates clockwise, increasing in scale and moving downward as it fades.	20
Wild-turnout	Objects move upper left from the object in a number of streams and decrease in scale and rotate three times. Simple object decreases in scale and moves upward and to the left as it disappears.	20
Wild-X-Y-scaleaway	Components sequentially increase in size on Y-scale by 300%, then quickly return to original shape and increase in size on X-scale by 300% and then fade out. Simple object stretches and fades.	20
Wild- Y-fade	Objects or components stretch 800% on their Y-scale and fade out. Works with simple object.	20
Wild- zoom out	Components of a complex object gradually appear and then fade as they increase in scale to 200% disappear. Simple object gets larger and fades.	20
Wind	Three effects based on severity of effect — breeze, storm, and vaporize. The effects are similar but vary in the strength, speed, and direction of the effect as the object disappears.	20

* Text effects have limited or little effect on shapes or complex objects.

Table D-7: Looping Effects

Effect	Description	Default Duration
3d corkscrew	Components of a complex object rotate around the X-axis at different speeds, changing color to red and back to the original color. A simple object rotates around the X-axis and changes color every ½ revolution.	20
3d spin whole object	The entire object (complex and simple) revolves around a center point located at the object's center. The perspective used makes the object appear to be standing on its side and rotating away from the viewer as it revolves around the center point. Complex object components separate and change size as they revolve.	30
3d twist and turn loop	Objects (simple and complex) appear to rotate around all three axes, changing visible dimensions during the rotations as well as changing to red as they rotate around the Y-axis and then back to the original color. Complex object elements tumble from upper to lower area of the composite object as they rotate.	20
All at sea	In a complex object, the components are combined into a number of larger triangles. The effect produces a jointed waving motion throughout the object; colors change through blue to white. The depth of the object is defined in the effect as the eye level. Not useful for a simple object as the object is stationary and merely changes color from blue to white.	20
Boogie	A simple object increases in size dramatically, changes colors, and rotates horizontally on the screen in an erratic pattern. A complex object's components are combined into a number of larger triangles. The effect produces an undulation in the object with varying color changes including yellow, red, blue, orange controlled by the Hallucinations checkbox.	20
Breakout	A complex object's components move around the Z-axis, bouncing at the lower limit of the object and repeating. The scale of the elements is decreased, and groups of elements follow the same paths. A simple object appears to be anchored at the bottom, and it stretches slightly and tilts to the left and right slightly during the effect.	20
Breaststroke	Complex object elements are combined into larger joined triangles. As the effect plays, the object appears to undulate from one side of the effect to the other; colors change to green, red, blue. In a simple object, the object changes to a brown color and decreases its height, and then returns to its original dimensions.	30
Cascade around circle	In a complex object, the components stream in a wide revolution around the object's center point in a clockwise direction. In a simple object, the object revolves clockwise around its center point in a wide revolution.	20

Effect	Description	Default Duration
Cascading rainbow bulges	In a complex object, the components undulate slightly and change color through red, blue, and green. The undulation runs from the left to the right side of the object. In a simple object, it remains stationary and changes color through red, blue, and green.	20
Cascading waves	Similar to All at Sea effect. Rather than a jointed object, a complex object's elements move independently of one another as they undulate, revealing the movie's background. Undulations are accompanied by color changes from blue to white. A simple object is decreased in scale on the Y-axis, remains stationary, and pulses from blue to white.	20
Circle- slow clock	A complex object's components move in three streams clockwise around the center point of the object in a wide revolution; the streams come together at the right and left of the object's center point. A simple object revolves clockwise around a center point.	20
Curtain waving	A complex object's components are combined into larger joined triangles. The effect causes an undulation vertically from the bottom to the top of the object. The object's colors change to bands of yellow, light green, and medium green with yellow at the lower part of the object. A simple object is colored light green and tilts clockwise and then counterclockwise slightly as it stretches on the Y-axis and returns to its original height.	20
Disco	A complex object's components move in a band the same height as the original object and appear to travel in a flat spiral counter-clockwise around the object's center point. As the objects move they change color through bright green, red, orange, and yellow. Simple objects move left and then right, moving slightly downward as they travel left and slightly upward as they travel right. Objects change through bright green, yellow, red, and orange.	20
Flag-waving banner	In a complex object, the components appear to move down and to the right of the object and then up and to the left of the object (within the object's shape boundaries). A simple object appears to rotate around the X-axis as it moves up and left, and then down and right from its original location.	20
Flag-waving flag	A complex object moves in the same way as the waving banner effect except that the motion is more extensive, moving outside the object's boundaries. A simple object moves in the same way as the waving banner as well, and further to the left and right than the waving banner effect.	20
Flag-waving	For complex objects the effect undulates from the left to the right side; the left margin of the image appears stationary, and the effect is greater the further right the effect moves. Complex object's components are combined into larger joined triangles. A simple object rocks back and forth on the X-axis.	20

Continued

Table D-7 (continued)

Effect	Description	Default Duration
Flapping wave	For both simple and complex objects, the object undulates in all directions from the center of the object. A complex object's components are combined into larger joined triangles.	20
Hidden message	Components of a complex object change color from blue to purple to invisible on a repeating basis as the elements change size and move slightly. In a simple object, the object remains at its original size and location and passes through color changes from blue to purple to invisible.	45
Jellyfish	Components of a complex object cycle through shades of blue decreasing and increasing in size on the X-axis and Y-axis in an undulating pattern. A simple object moves up and down on the Y-axis as it cycles through shades of blue.	20
Jump for joy	The elements in a complex object move in a curve. At the start of the effect the left third of the object moves up and beyond the margin of the object, as the effect progresses the left third of the objects move down, and the right third of the objects move up and outside the margin of the object. The components move in a supine S-curve pattern. A simple object moves up and down slightly.	20
Move around circle	Complex object components move in a stream around the object's center point clockwise in a circle. At the top of the circle the original shape is assembled before the components stream downward. A simple object revolves in a large circle around the object's center point clockwise.	20
Move around circle and spell	Complex object components fade and move in a stream counterclockwise around the center point. At the apex of the circle the components increase in size and opacity and turn red for several frames. In a simple object, the object moves counter-clockwise around the center point, increasing in size and turning red at the apex of the circle.	20
Move around circle flat and spell	Both simple and complex objects move around the Y-axis decreasing in size and opacity as they move further away on the Z-axis. At the closest position the complex object's components reassemble the object for several frames, and a composite of the object flashes in red below the object.	30
Move around diamond	Objects move counterclockwise around the object's center in a diamond pattern. Components in a complex object stream in a band around the diamond pattern.	20
Move around rectangle	Objects move counterclockwise around the object's center in a rectangular pattern. In a complex object the components stream in a narrow band, increasing in width at the upper and lower edges.	20

Effect	Description	Default Duration
Orbit circle	Objects appear to rotate around the Y-axis clockwise. At the position farthest from the viewer on the Z-axis the object decreases in scale and turns a purple-blue, returning to the original size and color at the position closest to the viewer on the Z-axis.	20
Orbit circle flat	Similar to the orbit circle effect, the object rotates clockwise around the Y-axis. It doesn't change color, but does decrease in size at the farthest position on the Z-axis.	20
Orbit diamond	Similar to the other orbit effects, this effect rotates the object clockwise around the object's center point changing scale on the Z-axis as the object moves away from the viewer, and also changing the color to red. The orbit is not circular; instead, the object travels in a diamond-shaped pattern.	20
Pistons	In a complex object, the components are moved in thirds. The left third moves upward and starts its downward motion while the middle third moves upward, and starts its downward path, while the right third moves upward. The segments move up and down in the same sequence creating a piston appearance. A simple object moves up and down slightly.	20
Pulsing	Complex object components change in undulating pattern from left to right, changing color to red and bright green, and also changing alpha and size. Simple objects increase and decrease in size in pulse, changing to green and red and returning to their original color.	20
Push over hills	Objects move from left to right, bouncing three times, starting at 50% scale and to the left of their original locations. Complex objects appear to move toward the viewer as they move on the downward path of the bounces. Simple objects rotate and bounce, changing scale on the downward path of the bounces.	40
Quiver-stand still	Complex and simple objects stay at their locations, jiggling up and down and changing angles slightly.	20
Rainbow-slow whirl	Complex object components combined into larger joined triangles. Color pulses from left to right through red, green, and blue. Simple objects blink through the color sequence.	20
Rainbow-bulges	Complex object components combine into larger joined triangles and cycle through red, blue, and green. The components increase and decrease in size in an undulating pattern as the colors change. Simple objects blink through the color sequence.	20
Rippling water	Complex object components combine into larger joined triangles and cycle through shades of blue. The components increase and decrease in size in an undulating pattern as the colors change. Simple objects change color from light blue to dark blue and repeat.	20

Continued

Table D-7 *(continued)*

Effect	Description	Default Duration
Rocking	Components of a complex object rock back and forth from their center points 30 degrees; a simple object rocks back and forth on its Y-axis.	20
Rollercoaster	Complex and simple objects both use the effect similarly. The objects move in a series of rotations around all three axes, appearing to move away from the viewer, as well as climbing up and down hills.	80
Rotate and scale	Components of a complex object rotate around their center points, changing scale to 200% and color to dark blue as they rotate. Simple objects rotate clockwise, increasing in scale and changing color, then decreasing to their original color and size.	20
Rubber trampoline	Components of complex objects increase in size slightly and then return to their original object size; it has no effect on a simple object.	20
Shaking a spring	Simple and complex objects display the effect similarly. The object is bounced on all three axes—twice on the X-axis, three times on the Y-axis, and four times on the Z-axis.	20
Shout-crawler	In a complex object, the components are shown on the stage for several frames, increase in scale, and disappear. In a simple object, the object remains stationary and visible, disappearing for several frames.	20
Shout-shout aloud	No effect on a simple object aside from increasing scale to 900% and blinking at the end of every repetition of the effect. In a complex object, individual components are shown in sequence at 900% scale, shrink and disappear.	20
Snake-flat	An object moves in two circuits. It starts offset to the left of its original location, flows downward, below the original location, and then reassembles to the right of the original location in the first half of the effect; in the second half of the effect, the object flows across the object's original location and downward to the left, looping upward, downward, and to the right across the object's original location, and then back upward and left to the original location. The effect also works with simple objects, although the object doesn't change its dimensions.	20
Snake-rollercoaster	The motion follows the same circuits as the flat snake. The object's components change size and opacity as they move away from the viewer.	40
Snake-rolling banner	The object appears to rotate around the Y-axis, decreasing in size and opacity as it moves away from the viewer on the Z-axis. Works with both complex and simple objects.	20
Spinning coins loop	The object rotates to the left and then to the right; each rotation also decreases and then increases the height as it changes rotation. In a complex object, each component rotates independently. Works with both simple and complex objects.	20

Effect	Description	Default Duration
Squeeze elastic to side	The object is stretched at the start of the effect and extends to the left of its original location. It is squeezed as it moves to the right of its original location changing color to magenta and fading, and then the object moves to the left returning to the effect's starting point and the original color. The effect works with both complex and simple objects. Although simple objects are moved, their dimensions don't change.	20
Surfin-pass the bucket	Components of a complex effect are increased in scale on a random basis, causing an irregular random change in the shape of the object. In a simple object, it increases and then decreases in scale.	20
Surfin-pistons	In a complex object the components are moved in thirds. The left third moves upward and starts its downward motion while the middle third moves upward and starts its downward path while the right third moves upward. The segments move up and down in the same sequence creating a piston appearance. The objects move slightly higher and lower than the margins of the original object's location. A simple object moves up and down slightly, changing scale at the highest and lowest points of its motion.	20
Surfin-surfin USA	This effect is similar to the Surfin-pistons effect except that the scale change is greater.	30
Tigger jumping	The complex and simple objects move similarly using this effect. The object is moved to the right of its original location and components squashed together at the start of the effect, and then the object jumps five times counterclockwise. During the first three jumps the objects decrease size and opacity creating the appearance of moving away from the viewer; the last two jumps increase the size and opacity to simulate motion toward the viewer.	40
Tornado	The components of a complex object or a simple object rotate on their X-axis and Y-axis. In a complex object the motion is random. At the default settings, the components of a complex object stay mainly within the margins of the original object; increasing intensity increases the distance that components are moved.	20
Tube-corkscrew	Objects are rotated on the Y-axis as they appear to move backward and then forward on the Z-axis. At the distance farthest from the viewer the object decreases scale and opacity. In a complex object, the components move independently.	20
Wagging tail	Objects are tilted at a 15-degree angle and then move up and down slightly. A complex object's components move up and down in sections starting from the left and moving to the right.	20
Wiggle-color cycle	Objects rotate left then right on the Y-axis and decrease their height at the end of each rotation. Colors change to red and bright green. In a complex object, the components are each animated and move randomly.	20

Continued

Table D-7 *(continued)*

Effect	Description	Default Duration
Wild-3D rotate	The effect appears to flip around the X-axis as the objects appear to move farther from the viewer and decrease in scale and opacity. The object flips again and the object appears to return to its original scale and opacity.	20
Wild-alpha wave	Objects increase in scale on either the X- or Y-axis and decrease in scale on the Y- or X-axis creating a stretched appearance. At the maximum scale, the object is also faded. Works with both simple and complex objects. In a complex object, components are animated randomly.	20
Wild-big up	Components in a complex object increase in size to 150% and fade to 50% one by one as they drop below the original Y-axis location and then jump back to the Y-axis location and original size and opacity. This effect isn't useful for a simple object as it remains stationary and increases in size and transparency once during the effect.	20
Wild-big wave	Components of a complex effect are faded, offset slightly, and increased in size. The effect moves across a complex effect in a rippling motion from one corner to another. In a simple object, the effect causes the object to increase in scale and transparency, and then return to its original dimensions and opacity.	20
Wild-flimmer	The components of a complex object change in opacity in a rippling manner from one side to another. In a simple object, the color fades and returns to its original opacity.	20
Wild-halfturn	Objects are rotated 45 degrees and then rotate a further distance and return to their original rotated location. As the objects drop they fade slightly. A simple object rocks back and forth on the Y-axis.	20
Wild-planetflow	Objects appear to move in an orbit from a position to the left of their original location to a location farther away from the viewer and to the right of their original location, creating an elliptical orbit. At the point where the object is farthest from the viewer, the object decreases in scale and opacity; at the point closest to the viewer, the object increases in scale. Works with both complex and simple objects.	20
Wild-pop big	As the effect plays, objects increase in size to 400% and fade out. A complex object's components increase individually, and many are visible at the end of the effect's cycle. A simple object increases in scale and disappears at the end of the effect.	20
Wild-pulse	Works with both complex and simple objects. In a complex object, the individual components increase slightly in scale and decrease in opacity. The change in size and opacity pulses across the object.	20
Wild-rainbow	Works with both simple and complex objects. A simple object changes color from red to blue to green and back to its original color. In a complex object, the colors pulse across the object. Different components display the different colors for varying lengths of time.	20

Effect	Description	Default Duration
Wild-silver blob	Works with both simple and complex objects. In a complex effect, the components rotate 30 degrees positively, and negatively in unison in a complex object, changing color from their original color faded 50% to white at the -30-degree point.	20
Wild-stress	For a complex object, the components blink four times during the effect; a simple object flashes four times during the effect.	20
Wild-wave	Components of a complex object and move up and down in a wave pattern. The components fade and rotate 20 degrees at the top of the wave motion. Simple objects rotate slightly to the right as they fade and return to their original opacity and orientation.	20
Zig-zag	Objects start to the left of their original location and then move in a zig-zag fashion to the right of their original location in three zig-zags. Objects are squashed horizontally, increasing their size vertically; the objects change dimension to become slightly wider at the bottom of each zig (or is it zag?)	20

Table D-8: One off Effects

Effect	Description	Default Duration
3d appear then zoom away at angle	Objects spin forward rotating 90 degrees on the X-axis, increasing in scale to 100%, and then disappear as the objects decrease in scale and spin away from the viewer. The complete object in a complex object is never seen assembled on stage.	20
3d spin-perspective	Components appear, rotate 90 degrees, increase in opacity, and assemble at 50% final size; camera perspective is from lower right of the object.	20
3d spin-whole object half turn	The object or components appear to move to create a mirror object of the original object. Simple objects move to mirror position and decrease scale.	30
3d spin-whole object hinged on side	The object starts from a mirrored-object position and moves toward the camera appearing to rotate about the Z-axis as the Y-axis value decreases dramatically. Both complex and simple objects use the effect in the same way.	30
Alternate	Every four components repeat the effect by default; objects move into final location from opposite directions, increasing in opacity. Simple object moves down screen and increases opacity.	20
Alternate stack	Same as the Alternate effect except that components move away from the final location.	20
Cinema-star wars	Regardless of the object complexity or X-axis position on the stage, the object moves from below the stage to above the stage decreasing in width and opacity. Moves along the original object's Y-axis position.	20

Continued

Table D-8 *(continued)*

Effect	Description	Default Duration
Drift past	Objects appear to start from their original location at a decreased scale, explode outward, and then slide downward and off the left or right stage as they decrease in opacity. For both simple and complex objects.	20
Drop down and bounce	Objects drop and bounce four times (default). Use with both simple and complex objects. Complex objects drop and bounce as a unit.	30
Explode	Components increase in scale, decrease in opacity, and move apart from a central point. Explodes upward and then gently cascades down with gravity value of 1 by default. Simple object merely moves upward and decreases opacity.	20
Falling leaves	Objects float, drift, twist, and fall. Works with complex and simple objects.	40
Gravity-drop it	Two effects that apply to both complex and simple objects. Objects or components drop vertically and bounce four times in a wave fashion.	20
Gravity-spider	The Spider effect is the same as the Gravity-drop it effect, but uses less bounciness.	20
Mexican wave	Object leans from left to right as effect plays; changes from default color to chosen object color.	20
Spiral	Inward and Outward — object moves in three concentric spirals disappearing at the center of the object; for both simple and complex shapes, the actions are the same.	20
Squeeze	Only works for complex objects; a simple object remains stationary. Object segments come together as they drift across the stage.	20
Vortex in/out and disappear	Simple object rotates around Y-axis and stretches along Y-axis, fades, and moves upward. Complex object components move outward from a single point, increasing in size and opacity before disappearing at the component's original location.	20
Wild-beat	Simple objects display effect. Complex object elements move sequentially, overlapping from left to right to assemble finished object.	20
Wild-flame jump and jump	Both effects move object components sequentially across the screen, bouncing once. The Flame Jump effect also changes the object's color to red during the bounce portion of the effect. Simple objects display the effect motion and color change.	20

Table D-9: Return to Start Effects

Effect	Description	Default Duration
3d-agitator	Object appears to be hinged at left side; swings away from the viewer and then returns, changing through red as it animates. Works with both complex and simple objects.	20
3d-hinge backward	Object offset to the left; appears to be rotating away from the viewer to a point in the distance and then rotating back to start position, color changes through red and back to original color. Works with all object types.	20
3d-scale and twist	Object appears to be rotating forward about the X-axis, increasing in scale to 200%. Color changes through red and back to original color. For complex and simple objects.	20
3d-twist and turn	Complex object appears to be hinged at upper edge, object swings forward toward viewer on X-axis; changing color to red, individual components appear to rotate away from the viewer on both X- and Y-axis and then return to original size, and object returns to original location. Simple object appears to rotate away from the viewer around both X- and Y-axis and changes color through red and returns to the original color.	20
Accordion	Object or components move upward and to the left slightly as the object is squeezed, squashed, and stretched. Color changes through red and back to original color. Works with both complex and simple objects.	20
Alternate gunslinger	Some components of a complex object move upward and rotate 1¼ revolutions clockwise as they stretch and then return to their original location and orientation. Simple object rotates and stretches.	20
Bullet-fly by	Each component of a complex object pulses twice, one pulse at an increased size. Simple object merely changes size twice during the effect.	20
Bullet-heart beat	Objects pulse twice in unison. The first pulse increases the scale of the components, and they return to less than their original size appearing to move away from one another; during the second pulse the components increase in scale again and then return to their original size. Simple objects pulse twice.	20
Bullet-ripple	Objects pulse twice in cascading fashion. Simple objects pulse twice.	20
Can-can kicks	Components of a complex object are skewed 75 degrees and during the effect rotate a further 15 degrees in groups. The motion is repeated twice during the effect. A simple object appears to be hinged at upper right; the object is skewed and rotates slightly clockwise and returns to its original skewed position.	20
Caterpillar wiggle	Complex object appears to ripple with elements moving upward and downward slightly in a fluid repeating motion. Simple objects rotate slightly to the left and then to the right on the Y-axis.	30

Continued

Table D-9 *(continued)*

Effect	Description	Default Duration
Chaos	Object moves through red and blue in addition to the original color. Components appear to move as though rippling underwater, undulating effect. Components remain in their original location and change shape to maintain the undulation that is triangle-based. Simple object pulses through red and blue and returns to original color.	90
Coming at you wave	Object increases in scale by 800% and fades 90% and then returns to starting size and opacity. Works for both complex and simple objects.	20
Double arch and dive	Objects rotate approximately 45 degrees clockwise and move upward decreasing in scale to 50%, then rotate approximately 45 degrees counterclockwise, increase in scale as they return to their original location. Works with both complex and simple objects. Complex objects' components split into two opposing streams; one stream moves in opposite angles to the other stream.	20
Dragged away by center	Complex object elements move upward as they decrease in scale and opacity; each element moves the same distance. Then the elements return to their original locations, size, and opacity. A simple object decreases in scale and opacity as it moves upward on the stage, increases in scale and opacity as it returns to its original size and location.	20
Executive toy	In a complex object, the components appear to move to the left, swing around toward the viewer, and then swing back into their original locations. Simple object effect rotates the object counterclockwise as it rises in a flat loop that appears to rotate around the Y-axis.	20
Frequency-1000 hertz	Bands of components in a complex object increase in scale to 300% in a set of three sequences. Simple object appears to rotate away from the viewer on the Z-axis, increasing and decreasing in height twice at its farthest point from the viewer.	40
Go around to back	Complex object components move in an orbit-like loop counterclockwise increasing in scale and then decreasing back to the original location. There is a several-frame pause between loops. This effect moves a simple object in an orbit-like loop around a central point; the object decreases in scale appearing to move away from the viewer, and then returns to the original location; the effect repeats in a smooth uninterrupted loop.	20
Jump up out and twist	A simple object appears to bounce as the effect repeats. The object moves upward and increases in scale, moves downward and decreases in scale to its original size and location. In a complex object, the components move away from one another and increase in scale as they move upward and twist, and then return to their origin and pause for several seconds.	20

Effect	Description	Default Duration
Kinetic-skid	Complex object components move away from the entire object in groups as the entire object moves to the right, the objects reassemble in their original location, and then the object moves to the left and components move out from the object, finally reassembling as the object swings back to its original location. Simple object moves back and forth to the left and right.	20
Mexican wave 2	Object, either simple or complex, appears to be anchored at the bottom edge. The object stretches left to right and then bounces back down to original size in a ripple effect. Color changes to orange and back to original color.	20
Pull-down and bounce back	Simple object appears to drop and then bounce back to original location; complex object's components cascade down in groups and bounce back to original location.	20
Pull-forward at ends	Simple or complex object stretches downward from original location and increases in size as it changes color to blue, then bounces back to original location.	30
Rotate-turn	Components appear to rotate and fade in a rippling motion from one corner of the object to the diagonal corner and return to original orientation and opacity. Simple objects appear to rotate counterclockwise around the Y-axis twice, with the first revolution being faster than the second.	20
Scale wave shot	Simple objects appear to rotate around the X-axis in a positive Z-axis direction (toward the viewer). In a complex object, the motion appears in a wave from left to right. As the wave passes it appears as though the objects are shrinking and fading; as the wave passes to the next segment, the previous components return to their original sizes and opacity.	20
Scurry around	A simple object moves in a smooth orbital path clockwise as the effect repeats; a complex object completes one animation and pauses for several seconds before the loop restarts.	20
Shuffle	Very similar to the Go around to back effect except that the path is much wider. A simple object moves in a smooth path as the effect repeats; a complex object completes one animation and pauses for several seconds before the loop restarts.	20
Slow swell	The object appears to be anchored at the bottom edge, the object increases in scale and passes through blue, and then returns to the original color as it decreases to the original scale. For both simple and complex objects.	20
Spin-pancake	Objects move in a clockwise direction, increasing in scale 300% and fading and stretching. In a complex object the individual components are animated and then the entire object sits stationary for the latter frames of the effect. A simple object loops the effect smoothly.	20

Continued

Table D-9 *(continued)*

Effect	Description	Default Duration
Spinning coins	Simple object rotates slightly and appears to spin on the Y-axis like a coin; the effect spins the object twice by default. In a complex object, each component spins individually.	20
Squish rotate and grow in	The objects start the effect colored red and faded. The objects rotate as they move upward and decrease in scale and opacity and then return to their original locations, scale, and opacity. For both simple and complex objects.	20
Stretch down and back	A simple object appears to be anchored at the top edge and stretches down, turning blue before it snaps back to its original size and color. In a complex object, the components drop sequentially, changing color to blue, and then returning to their original size, color, and location.	20
Surfin-hectic	A simple object increases in scale and then decreases to original size twice during the effect; between scale changes it moves upward, and then moves back downward to the original location at the end of the effect. In a complex object, the components increase in scale and change position slightly on an individual basis creating a fibrillating appearance.	20
Tube-bottleneck	A simple object loops in a wide orbit around the X-axis, fading as it appears farthest from the viewer. In a complex object, the components appear to be dropping in a stream through a narrow path and changing opacity, hence the name.	40
Tube-rollin	For both simple and complex objects, the objects appear to revolve around the X-axis in a tight orbit, fading as the object appears to be farthest from the viewer.	20
Twist up and fade	Simple object moves upward and decreases opacity and then returns to original location and opacity. A complex object's components twist to the right, increase in scale, move upward and decrease opacity, and then reverse changes to restore the original configuration.	20
Wave	14 effects—all use similar settings. Using two cycles, the basic Wave produces two bounces, each of which moves the components in groups that shift slightly horizontally in one bounce and then the opposite direction shift in the next bounce. A simple object has slight motion upward and then returns to the original location.	30
Wave-dizzy	Simple object stretches on the X-axis 1000% and fades as it stretches, returning to the original size and opacity. A complex object stretches and fades the individual components in a rippling effect from the bottom of the object to the top of the object.	20
Wave-jump for joy	Complex object components or simple objects move right and increase in size vertically and horizontally (ratio 2:1) and fade, then return to their original locations, size, opacity.	20

Effect	Description	Default Duration
Wave-lighthouse	Similar to the Wave-dizzy effect; as the simple object stretches it turns white and then returns to its original size and color. A complex object stretches the individual components in a rippling effect from the bottom of the object to the top of the object, each turning white when it has reached its maximum stretch.	20
Wave-on diet	For both simple and complex objects, the object stretches vertically and narrows horizontally; at the end of the stretch the objects become yellow; color and size return to the originals during the latter part of the effect.	20
Wave-red sea	For simple objects, the object appears to be anchored at the bottom and stretches upward, turning red, and then returning to its original color and size. Complex objects stretch individual components vertically as they turn red; the components appear to stretch from the bottom-most components first and then upward through the object's components.	20
Wave-std wave	Complex objects throw components upward starting from the bottom-most components and then upward through the object's components. A simple object bounces the object vertically once.	20
Wave-fade	The objects ripple through varying opacities twice during the effect. In a complex effect, groups of components are faded at once.	20
Wave-rotate	Groups of components in a complex object rotate counter-clockwise 45 degrees and then return to the original location. Can't be used with a simple object.	20
Wave-scale	For both simple and complex objects, the elements increase in scale by 200% and then return to their original size.	20
Wave-skew	Components of a complex effect are each skewed by 45 degrees and then return to their original dimensions. In a simple object, the object appears to wobble left and right.	20
Wave-stretch tall	For both complex and simple objects, the elements are stretched vertically without affecting the width of each component and then return to their original sizes; the cycle occurs twice during the default effect.	20
Wave-stretch tall and skinny	Components in a complex object as well as a single object are stretched vertically and narrow in width in this effect; the cycle occurs twice during the default effect.	20
Wave-wide	For both complex and simple objects, the elements are stretched horizontally and then return to their original sizes.	20
Wave-wide and short	Components in a complex object as well as a single object are stretched horizontally and narrow in height.	20
Whirlpool whip	In a simple object this effect makes the object move in a circle on the stage. For complex objects the components follow one another in a circle clockwise using a cascading order that produces a ripple effect	20

Continued

Table D-9 *(continued)*

Effect	Description	Default Duration
Whirlpool whirl	Complex object components move away from their original locations in a wide clockwise circle to the right and then reassemble in their original locations. Simple objects move in a clockwise circle.	40
Wiggle-the wave	In a complex object, each component tilts to the left and changes color to yellow, then tilts to the right and changes to magenta, and then returns to the original orientation and color. A simple object tilts left and right, changing color to yellow, magenta, and then returning to its original color.	20

Table D-10: Core Effects

Effect	Description	Default Duration
Transform	Stationery; object originally displays at twice its size and then scales gradually to its normal size cascading from left to right.	20
Squeeze	Components drift from the left and right side toward the center to combine into single object.*	20
Alternate	Complex object: Upper and lower groups of components combine in even pattern. Simple object: Object drifts downward.	20
Snake	Complex object: Components loop in sequence counterclockwise one cycle. Simple object: Object loops counterclockwise; invisible for portion of loop.	20
Explode	Complex object: Components drift slowly and explode gently upward and to the right and left using the default bomb location. Simple object: Object gradually moves upward and decreases in scale.	20
3D spin	Complex object: Components rotate into view from upper-left element. Simple object: Has little effect.	20
3D wave	Complex object: Wave applied from left to right, top to bottom; motion moves each segment right and left; up and down as the wave moves. Simple object: Produces slight counterclockwise rotation.	20
Vortex	Complex object: Components move up; the left half of the object moves to the right and the right half of the object moves to the left and disappears sequentially as they are pulled to the center of the object. Simple object: Object moves up slightly and disappears.	20

Effect	Description	Default Duration
Wave	Complex object: Groups of components angle up and down, and the wave ripples through the individual components in the group. Simple object: Object bobs up and down, moves slightly left to right and back.	20
Typewriter	Complex object: Individual components are drawn on stage in sequence from left to right; for text, also shows a cursor and spaces #. Simple object: Has little effect; object visible, invisible over duration of effect.	Variable, depends on object content

* applies to complex objects only

best suited for text objects

✦   ✦   ✦

Index

In this index, please note that any page references to letter and number combinations, such as H-2 or E-7, point to material that can found in correspondingly lettered appendixes available on the book's Web site at www.wiley.com/go/swishmax

Continued

V

variables
    arrays for, 582–586
    checking for loaded variables, 581–582
    for custom effects, 316–318
    for daily horoscope project, 580–582
    data types, 403
    defined, 370, 403
    loading content based on, 410, 413–414
    PHP, F-4–F-6, F-8
    for shopping cart sprite, 555
    using in SWiSHscript, 403
vector images. *See also* images
    formats supported by SWiSHmax, 170
    importing, 174
    preparing for movies, 172–173
    raster images versus, 167–169
    ungrouping, 174
vertices
    adding, 120–121
    changing types, 119–120
    line segment characteristics and, 121–122
    removing, 120
    types of, 118–119
video. *See* AVI video
Video 1 codec (Microsoft), 470
View menu
    Accelerator keys, 620
    overview, 28–29, 605–607
    Show Rulers command, 108
    Toolbars command, 41
View tools, 106–107
viewing. *See also* playing; previewing
    effects folder, 270
    guides, 108–109
    movie elements in panels, 37–41

movie report, 70–71
object properties in Content panel, 90–91
SWF movies in Acrobat, 489–490
testing completed movie, 21–22
text formatting, 221
thumbnails in Outline panel, 77–78
tools for changing views, 105–107
Vortex effect, 311–312

W

Watermark option (SWiSHstudio), E-15–E-17
WAV audio files, 238. *See also* sound files
Wave effects
    3D Wave, 310–311
    Wave (2D), 312–314
Web browser
    fscommand() for, 425–426
    loading a Web page, 424–425
    playing movies in, 22
Web pages. *See also* Internet resources
    building in PHP, F-9
    exporting movie with, 22, 460–461
    Flash versus SWiSHmax and, 385
    loading into target frame of browser, 424–425
Web site interface project
    buttons, 529–531
    content pages, 542–547
    content window, 539
    feature section, 537–539
    header and footer, 539–540
    hotspots, 531–533, 534–535, 547–548
    menu bar, 529–533
    navigation, 542, 543–544, 547–548

news scroller, 533–537
opening animation for movie, 542
placeholders, 528
preloader, 540–541
starting the site, 527–529
Web-safe colors, 141, 144, 147–148
Wells, Rob (contributor), 551, 593
window styles (SWiSHstudio), E-9–E-11
Windows Color dialog box
    selecting colors, 149–151
    transparency settings, 152–153

X

XML (eXtensible Markup Language) menus
    action attributes, G-2
    adding a follower, G-12–G-13
    basic document, G-1–G-2
    building the menu structure, G-5–G-6
    expanding the menus, G-11–G-13
    multilevel drop-down menus, G-12
    with revised sprite, G-7–G-11
    using XML data in SWiSHmax movies, G-3–G-5

Z

Zoom effects, 273, 624
Zoom Factor tool, 107
Zoom 100% tool, 107
Zoom tool, 105–106
zooming
    camera for effects, 294–295
    effects for, 273, 624
    tools for, 105–106, 107
    vector versus raster images and, 168–169